Federal Tax Research

EIGHTH EDITION

William A. Raabe, Ph.D., CPA
The Ohio State University

Gerald E. Whittenburg, Ph.D., CPA
San Diego State University

Debra L. Sanders, Ph.D., CPA
Washington State University

SOUTH-WESTERN
CENGAGE Learning™

Australia • Canada • Mexico • Singapore • Spain • United Kingdom • United States

SOUTH-WESTERN
CENGAGE Learning™

Federal Tax Research, 8th edition
William A. Raabe, Gerald E. Whittenburg,
Debra L. Sanders

VP/Editorial Director: Jack W. Calhoun

Editor-in-Chief: Rob Dewey

Acquisitions Editor: Keith Chasse

Senior Developmental Editor: Craig Avery

Marketing Manager: Kristen Hurd

Content Project Manager: Jennifer A. Ziegler

Manager of Technology, Editorial: John Rich

Website Project Manager: Brian Courter

Manufacturing Coordinator: Doug Wilke

Production Service: Newgen, India

Senior Art Director: Michelle Kunkler

Internal Designer: Juli Cook

Cover Designer: Rose Alcorn

Cover Image: © Isabelle Rozenbaum /
PhotoAlto Agency RF Collections

For product information and technology assistance, contact us at
Cengage Learning Academic Resource Center, 1-800-423-0563

For permission to use material from this text or product,
submit all requests online at **www.cengage.com/permissions**
Further permissions questions can be emailed to
permissionrequest@cengage.com

Library of Congress Control Number: 2007943841

ISBN-13: 978-0-324-65965-8

ISBN-10: 0-324-65965-2

South-Western Cengage Learning
5191 Natorp Boulevard
Mason, OH 45040
USA

Cengage Learning products are represented in Canada by
Nelson Education, Ltd.

For your course and learning solutions, visit **academic.cengage.com**

Purchase any of our products at your local college store or at our preferred
online store **www.ichapters.com**

Printed in the United States of America
1 2 3 4 5 6 7 11 10 09 08 07

William A. Raabe, Ph.D., CPA, teaches graduate tax courses at the Fisher College of Business of The Ohio State University, and at the Capital University (OH) Law School. He is a leader among business school tax faculty in incorporating developments in technology into curricula for the educational development of tax professionals.

Dr. Raabe's teaching and research interests focus on multijurisdictional taxation and financial planning, and he is recognized as the leader among business school academics in the fields of state and local income, sales, and property taxation. Dr. Raabe is the author or editor of approximately twenty books, including *South-Western Federal Taxation, Schedule M-3 Compliance,* and the *Multistate Corporate Tax Guide.* He has received university-wide recognition as the winner of the AMOCO Foundation Award for Teaching Excellence, and the Wisconsin Institute of CPAs named him the Educator of the Year.

Gerald E. Whittenburg, Ph.D., CPA, EA, is a professor in the School of Accountancy at San Diego State University. A graduate of the University of Houston, Dr. Whittenburg is interested individual and corporate taxation, pension plans, and tax research methodology.

Dr. Whittenburg is also an author of the textbook *Income Tax Fundamentals.* In addition, he has published articles in journals such as *Advances in Taxation, Practical Tax Strategies,Taxes—The Tax Magazine, Journal of Taxation of Investments, Journal of Taxation of Employee Benefits, Journal of Taxation of Financial Institutions, Valuation Strategies, Journal of Small Business Strategy, The Tax Adviser,* and *Journal of Accounting Education.* He has received numerous awards for teaching, including the Trustee's Outstanding Faculty Award for the entire California State University System. Recently, Dr. Whittenburg was awarded a Fulbright Fellowship to the Ukraine. In this picture, he is shown in front of St. Michael's Church in Kiev.

Debra L. Sanders, Ph.D., CPA, is a professor in the Washington State Unmiversity School of Accounting, Information Systems and Business Law. She has received numerous awards for outstanding teaching, research, and service including the Boeing Distinguished Faculty Research Award, the Shell Corporation Outstanding Teacher Award, and the College of Business and Economics Outstanding Service Award.

Dr. Sanders, a graduate of Arizona State University, publishes in both academic and professional journals. Her work has appeared in the academic journals *Behavioral Research in Accounting, National Tax Journal, The Journal of the American Taxation Association, Advances in Taxation,* and *The International Journal of Accounting.* Professional journals that have published her articles include *Taxation for Accountants, Taxation for Lawyers, The Review of Taxation of Individuals, Taxes, The Tax Adviser,* and *Journal of Financial Planning.*

BRIEF CONTENTS

CONTENTS

The Eighth Edition of *Federal Tax Research* reflects the increasing importance of online research databases in tax research practices, and the changing nature of the tax profession. Now more than ever, our text is *the* essential learning tool for tax research, both online and using standard library materials. From its new complete chapter on international tax research, to its host of new and valuable tax links and illustrative research cases, *Federal Tax Research 8/e* remains justifiably the market leader among tax research texts.

This popular book has been prepared as a comprehensive, stand-alone reference tool for the user who wishes to become proficient in Federal tax research. It is written for readers who are familiar with the fundamentals of the Federal income and transfer tax law, at a level that typically is achieved on the completion of two comprehensive introductory courses in taxation in either (1) the accounting program in a business school or (2) second- or third-year courses in a law school.

Nearly every accounting, tax, and tax law student can benefit from the strategies found in this book. The text is most appropriate for:

- Upper-level accounting students in a business school (i.e., seniors in a four-year program or those in the fifth year of a 150-hour program) who desire additional information concerning the practice of taxation.

- Those who are enrolled in a nontax graduate program in business administration (e.g., an MBA or MS—management program) and would like further practical training in the functions of taxation in today"s business environment.

- Second- or third-year law school students, especially those who desire a more detailed and pragmatic introduction to a specialized tax practice.

- Those who are commencing a graduate degree program in taxation, in either a business school or a law school, and require a varied and sophisticated introduction to the procedures of tax research and to the routine functions and implications of a tax practice.

- Practicing accountants and attorneys who need an introduction, updating, or refresher relative to tax practice and research as an element of their career paths.

STRUCTURE AND PEDAGOGY

Too often, existing textbooks ignore the detailed, pragmatic approach that students require in developing effective and efficient tax research skills.

That is why we have included an unprecedented degree of hands-on tax research analysis throughout the text. This book does not simply discuss tax research procedures or the sources of the Federal tax law; nor does it pro-vide a mere sample of the pertinent tax reference material. Rather, the Eighth Edition reflects our conviction that readers learn best by active learning and real-world experience with the most important elements of the Federal tax law. We have applied this conviction to the many important features of the Eighth Edition.

- **NEW:** A full chapter on international tax research opportunities reflects the importance of this type of tax work in today's practice.

- **NEW:** Exercises, problems, and research cases are included throughout that help students learn using actual online research tools and methods discussed in the text.

- **NEW:** Increased emphasis on ethical constraints and tax penalties as restrictions on taxpayer and tax advisor behavior.

- Spotlight on Taxation boxes in every chapter provide additional research tips, tax information, news, background, and factors to consider in developing a tax research solution.

- An introduction to tax practice continues to provide details on such valuable topics as preparer penalties, statutes of limitation, interest conventions, and return selection for IRS audits.

- The book's continuing focus on tax planning fits perfectly with this growing trend in tax practice.

- The text has been thoroughly updated with developments that affect those who conduct tax research, including revisions to codes of ethics, IRS organizational structure and enforcement functions, and other principles that control tax practice.

- Hundreds of exercises and discussion questions allow the reader to learn by exploring the reference materials in a well-developed tax library in their research strategies.

- Assignments allow students to construct case briefs, file memos, client letters, and other elements of a comprehensive client file—vital skills they will need in practice.

- Hundreds of reproductions and illustrations have been excerpted from the most important tax reference materials and expose students to the real world of tax research.

- Summary charts, diagrams, and other study aids are integrated throughout the text that summarize the elements of primary and secondary sources of Federal tax law and encourage students to develop their own research routines and techniques.

Focus on Online and Computerized Research

The use of online databases and computerized research has become indispensable in tax practice, and the previous edition was at the forefront of coverage of these innovative tools. For the Eighth Edition, however, we focus the majority of our coverage on online and computerized research. Presenting and discussing these new tools, strategies, and research tactics now eclipses our discussions of traditional paper-based resources. We reviewed every internet research tool available, and the text now includes the deepest analysis of the use of computer research tools available for this purpose. Other important features include:

- Expansion of the review of tax ethics, including tax and non-tax sources of guidance for the conduct of today's tax practice.
- More material than ever on the role of tax research on the CPA exam.

- Tax Tutor online tutorials and interactive quizzes under the Student Resources page at the book's web site reinforce the tax research coverage in each chapter.

- The instructor's portion of the web site for the text **http://academic.cengage. com/taxation/raabe** includes suggested solutions for assigned material, a generous test bank, multiple quizzes for each chapter, instructor PowerPoint slides, and lecture notes. The web site also offers templates for commonly used research documents, and sample syllabi so that the instructor can share in the learning approaches used by the text's many adopters.

As a result, we believe that *the Eighth Edition is indispensable to learning and performing real-world online and computerized tax research*.

USING THE TEXT

The text's exercises, cases, and advanced cases offer enough variety in both difficulty and subject matter that they may be assigned to individual readers, or to student groups of two or three, for their optimal use. The instructor also should consider giving each student in the course a different research case to complete, thereby both discouraging joint work and reducing the strain on the pertinent library resources.

Given both the nature of the tax research process and the limited tax library resources that are available to most firms and universities, the instructor must take care (1) to assign discussion materials for which the necessary resources are available and (2) to work through the assignment himself or herself, to as-certain that one's target solution to the assignment reflects the very latest in the development of the Federal tax law.

The instructor may want to defer the assigning of certain research cases until a specific electronic research service is discussed, which will provide additional illustrations. Alternatively, the reader could be encouraged to rework a previous assignment once the computerized tax reference tools have been introduced.

We discussed the instructor's resource page content above.

ACKNOWLEDGMENTS

We are grateful to the reviewers of the Seventh Edition who provided valuable comments and insights, which guided us in the development of the Eighth Edition

Adrian Allen, Shaw University

Rose Bailey, Gardner-Webb University

David R. Connelly, Western Illinois University

Patti Davis, Keystone College

Andrew Lafond, Philadelphia University

Tom Largay, Thomas College

Ernest Larkins, Georgia State University

Margaret Reed, University of Cincinnati

Robert Ricketts, Texas Tech University

Lee A. Sartori, Walsh College

James Trebby, Marquette University

Thomas C. Pearson, University of Hawaii at Manoa

Donald Williamson, American University

We wish to thank all of the book's student and faculty readers who have provided their detailed feedback and suggestions. Without your responses our efforts would have been greatly diminished in scope. Any errors, of course, are the sole responsibility of the authors. We are also grateful to Thomas Pearson for his comments on Chapter 10.

We welcome your comments and suggestions for further improvements to this text. Please feel free to use the following addresses to convey these remarks.

William A. Raabe
Fisher College of Business AMIS
The Ohio State University
Columbus, OH 43210
614.292.4023
raabe@fisher.osu.edu

Gerald E. Whittenburg
School of Accountancy
San Diego State University
San Diego, CA 92182-0221
g.e.whittenburg@sdsu.edu

Debra L. Sanders
Department of Accounting and Business Law
Washington State University
Pullman, WA 99164-4729
dsanders@wsu.edu

William A. Raabe
Gerald E. Wbittenburg
Debra L. Sanders

February 2008

The Tax Research Environment

Introduction to Tax Practice and Ethics

Learning Objectives

- Describe the elements of modern tax practice in the United States.

- Distinguish between open and closed transactions.

- Identify sources of legal and ethical standards that guide those who engage in tax practice.

- Examine in detail the major collections of ethical standards that bear upon tax practitioners today.

- Place tax issues in a broader context of ethics and morality.

- Understand the limitations on tax research by CPAs and other nonattorneys.

Chapter Outline

Chapter Outline (continued)

AT THE START OF the twenty-first century, tax practice and **tax research** are continuing to evolve into an electronic and paperless reporting system. For example, 2007 is the first year that over 50 percent of individual taxpayers e-filed their tax returns. In keeping with this transition to an all-electronic tax system, tax research is almost 100 percent computer based. The Uniform CPA Exam recognizes this transition and includes a set of "simulation" questions that require that the candidate demonstrate accounting and tax research skills by completing short computer research cases online. However, before the tax practitioner can complete a tax research project, he or she must understand the tax research process and all its elements, and how each element relates to solving a specific tax problem. The primary purpose of this book is to inform the user on how effectively to obtain tax research results in a timely and efficient manner.

The practice of taxation is the process of applying the tax law, rules, regulations, and judicial rulings to specific transactions to determine the tax consequences to the taxpayer involved. There are many ways to practice tax. One can practice tax directly through jobs such as a CPA, tax attorney, **Enrolled Agent (EA)**, or commercial income tax return preparer. In addition, tax can be practiced indirectly by such individuals as controllers, accountants, CFOs, and others who do tax work as part of their other duties. An understanding of taxation and the tax practice environment is essential to the individual who wants to have a position in the tax area.

Taxation is the process of collecting revenue from citizens to finance government activities. In a modern technological society such as that of the United States, however, taxation comprises an interaction among several disciplines that is far from simple. The tax system is derived from law, accounting, economics, political science, and sociology (Exhibit 1-1). Principles of economics, sociology, and political science provide the environment, while law and accounting precepts are applied in a typical tax practice.

Tax policy questions concerning the effects that a specified tax law change will have on economic growth, the effects of projected inflation on the implementation of the tax law and vice versa, and the effects of the tax law on the United States' balance of payments are addressed by economists. Political scientists, economists, and sociologists, alternatively, examine issues such as who bears the ultimate burden of a tax, how a tax bill becomes law (including practical effects of the legislative process), the social equity of a tax, and whether a tax is discriminatory. Attorneys interpret (and often create) taxation statutes, and accountants apply the tax laws to current or prospective economic transactions.

Exhibit 1-1: Elements of Taxation

ELEMENTS OF TAX PRACTICE

The tax laws of a democratic country such as the United States are created by a political process. In recent years, the result of this political process has been a law that levies taxes on income, sales, estates, gifts, and other items that usually are reflected by the accounting process. Thus, tax practice can be described as the application of tax legislation to specific accounting situations. The elements of modern tax practice can be separated into three categories: compliance, planning, and litigation, which are all supported by tax research. How these elements of tax practice fit together is illustrated in Exhibit 1-2.

Tax Compliance

In general, **tax compliance** consists of the gathering of pertinent information, evaluation and classification of such information, and the filing of necessary tax returns. Tax compliance also includes other functions necessary to satisfy government requirements, such as representation at a client's Internal Revenue Service (IRS) audit. Commercial tax preparers, EAs, attorneys, and CPAs all perform tax compliance to some extent. Noncomplex individual, partnership, and corporate tax returns often are completed by commercial tax preparers. EAs, attorneys, and CPAs usually are involved in the preparation of more complex tax returns; in addition, they provide tax-planning services and represent their clients before the IRS. The elements of tax compliance and administration are examined in more detail in later chapters.

Tax Planning

Tax planning is the process of arranging one's financial affairs to optimize (i.e., usually to minimize current tax payments, but not always) tax liabilities. However, whereas **tax avoidance** is the legitimate object of much of modern tax practice, **tax evasion** constitutes the illegal nonpayment of a tax and cannot be condoned. Fraudulent acts of this sort are unrelated to the professional practice of tax planning.

Tax planning can be divided into two major categories: **open transactions** and **closed transactions**. In an open transaction, the tax practitioner maintains some degree of control over the attendant tax liability because the transaction is not yet completed; for example, the title to an asset has not yet passed. If desired, some modifications to an incomplete transaction can be made to receive more favorable

Exhibit 1-2: Elements of Tax Practice

tax treatment. In a closed transaction, however, all of the pertinent actions have been completed; therefore, tax planning may be limited to the presentation of the facts to the government in the most favorable, legally acceptable manner possible.

SPOTLIGHT ON TAXATION

Case Quotation

There is nothing inherently illegal or immoral in the avoidance of taxation (i.e., Tax Planning) according to the tax system's rules. The eminent Judge Learned Hand best expressed this doctrine in the dissenting opinion of *Commissioner v. Newman*, 159 F.2d 848 (CA-2, 1947):

Over and over again, courts have said that there is nothing sinister in so arranging one's affairs as to keep taxes as low as possible. Everybody does so, rich or poor, and all do right, for nobody owes any public duty to pay more than the law demands: taxes are enforced extractions, not voluntary contributions.

Tax Litigation

A specialized area within the practice of law is the concentration on **tax litigation**. Litigation is the process of settling a dispute with another party (here, usually the IRS) in a court of law (here, a federal court). Typically, a tax attorney handles tax litigation that progresses beyond the initial appeal of an IRS audit result. Accountants and other financial advisers can also serve in a support capacity. Later chapters of this book contain additional discussions of the various opportunities and strategies available in tax litigation.

Tax Research

Tax research is undertaken to answer taxation questions. The tax research process includes the (1) identification of pertinent issues, (2) determination of proper authorities, (3) evaluation of the appropriateness of these authorities, and (4) application of these authorities to specific facts. Tax research techniques are examined in Chapters 2 through 10 of this text.

RULES AND ETHICS IN TAX PRACTICE

A person who prepares tax returns for monetary or other compensation, or who is licensed to practice in the tax-related professions, is subject to various statutes, rules, and codes of professional conduct. All tax practitioners are regulated by *Circular 230*, Regulations Governing the Practice of Attorneys, CPAs, EAs, Enrolled Actuaries, and Appraisers before the IRS. The ethical conduct of an attorney is also governed by the laws of the state(s) in which he or she is licensed to practice. Most states have adopted, often with some modification, guidelines that are based on the **American Bar Association (ABA)** Model Code of Professional Responsibility or the newer ABA Model Rules of Professional Conduct.

CPAs who are members of the **American Institute of Certified Public Accountants (AICPA)** must follow its Code of Professional Conduct and any other rules generated by the state board(s) of accountancy. The AICPA has also produced a series of Statements on Standards for Tax Services (SSTS), which contain advisory guidelines for CPAs who prepare tax returns.

Although CPAs who are not members of the AICPA are not bound by the Code of Professional Conduct and the SSTS, those rules and standards are a useful source of guidance for all members of the profession. Statutory tax law also specifies certain penalties and other rules of conduct that apply to everyone (e.g., attorneys, CPAs, and EAs) in addition to their respective professional standards, and also to commercial tax preparers who are not attorneys, CPAs, or EAs. Chapter 13 addresses these rules. The basic overlapping sources of rules and ethics for tax practitioners are illustrated in Exhibit 1-3.

Circular 230 (Complete Text in Appendix C)

Circular 230, which constitutes Part 31 of the Treasury Department Regulations, is designed to provide protection to taxpayers and the IRS by requiring tax preparers to be technically competent and to adhere to **ethical standards**. *Circular 230* contains the following definition of **practice before the IRS** in Section 10.2 of Subpart A.

> *...matters connected with presentation to the Internal Revenue Service or any of its officers or employees relating to a client's rights, privileges, or liabilities under laws or regulations administered by the Internal Revenue Service. Such presentations include the preparation and filing of necessary documents, correspondence with and communications to the Internal Revenue Service, and the representation of a client at conferences, hearings and meetings.*

Under this definition, practice before the IRS consists primarily of the representation of clients during audit procedures, such as a meeting with a revenue agent on behalf of a client to establish the correctness of a taxpayer's return. The preparation of tax returns or the furnishing of information to the IRS in response to a request for such information is not considered practice before the IRS. (Tax return preparation rules are addressed by various statutes discussed in Chapter 13.) *Circular 230* also states who may conduct such a practice and sets forth the disciplinary procedures that apply. In addition, CPAs, lawyers, and tax return preparers are (or may be) regulated by the states. As a result, there can be additional statutes, regulations, and requirements that must be met by individuals who practice in certain states.

Who May Practice [*Circular 230* §10.3] Under Section 10.3, Subpart A, of *Circular 230*, the following individuals may practice before the IRS.

1. Attorneys

2. CPAs

Exhibit 1-3: Sources of Rules and Ethics for Tax Practitioners

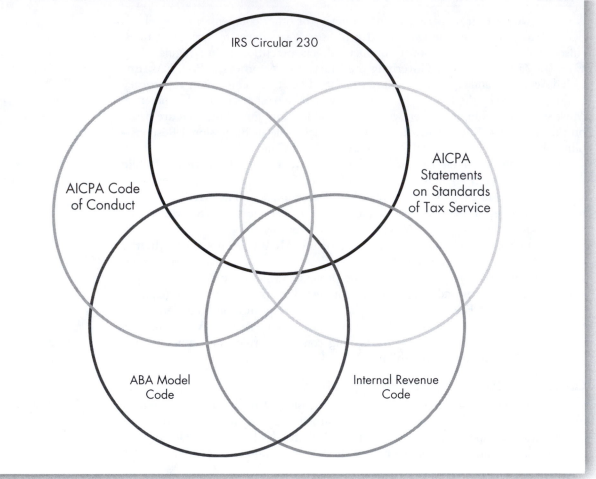

3. Enrolled agents

4. Enrolled actuaries

To qualify under this rule, an attorney must be a member in good standing of the bar of the highest court in any state, possession, territory, commonwealth, or the District of Columbia. Likewise, CPAs and Enrolled actuaries must be qualified to practice in any state, possession, territory, commonwealth, or the District of Columbia. No further substantive examination is required.

Enrolled Agents (EAs) [*Circular 230* §§10.4, 10.5, and 10.6]   Individuals who are not attorneys or CPAs can qualify to practice before the IRS by becoming an EA. An EA is someone who has either passed a special IRS examination (currently given once a year, in October) or worked for the IRS for five years. The procedures for becoming an EA are detailed in *Circular 230*, Subpart A, §§10.4, 10.5, and 10.6. EAs have the same rights as attorneys and CPAs to represent clients before the IRS. Under *Circular 230*, an EA must renew his or her enrollment card on a three-year cycle.

For each enrollment cycle, EAs, like attorneys and CPAs, must meet certain continuing education requirements as defined in Subpart A, §10.6. For an EA's enrollment card to be renewed, he or she must complete seventy-two hours (i.e., an average of twenty-four hours per year) of qualifying continuing education for each three-year enrollment period. In addition, a minimum of sixteen hours of continuing education credit must be completed during each year of an enrollment cycle. Subpart A, §10.6(f) defines what qualifies as continuing education for EAs.

Circular 230 allows an individual to be an attorney or CPA and an EA simultaneously. Being both an EA and an attorney or CPA might be useful to certain tax practitioners who practice across state lines. For example, a CPA in Texas who is also an EA can practice in any state. The EA's card is effectively a national license to practice before the IRS anywhere in the United States (including territories). In addition, most state taxing agencies grant an EA the right to practice before that state agency.

For more information on EAs, see the following two web sites. The first site is EA information on the IRS's web page and the second is the web site of the National Association of Enrolled Agents (NAEA).

http://www.irs.gov/taxpros/agents/
http://www.naea.org/

Limited Practice without Enrollment [*Circular 230* §10.7] In *Circular 230*, the IRS has authorized certain individuals to practice without being an attorney, CPA, or EA. Individuals (with proper identification) can represent themselves under §10.7(a) and participate in IRS rule making as provided for under §10.7(b). In addition, under §10.7(c), individuals (with proper identification and authorization, IRS Form 2848) are allowed to represent taxpayers in the following special situations.

1. An individual may represent a member of his or her immediate family.

2. A regular full-time employee of an individual employer may represent the employer.

3. A general partner or regular full-time employee of a partnership may represent the partnership.

4. A bona fide officer or regular full-time employee of a corporation (including a parent, subsidiary, or other affiliated corporation), an association, or organized group may represent the corporation, association, or organized group.

5. A trustee, receiver, guardian, personal representative, administrator, executor, or regular full-time employee of a trust, receivership, guardianship, or estate may represent the trust, receivership, guardianship, or estate.

6. An officer or regular employee of a governmental unit, agency, or authority may represent the governmental unit, agency, or authority in the course of his or her official duties.

7. An individual may represent any individual or entity before personnel of the IRS who are outside the United States.

Tax Return Preparers [*Circular 230* §10.7] Any person who signs a tax return as having prepared it for a taxpayer is authorized to conduct "limited practice" before the IRS (with proper taxpayer authorization) under §10.7(c)(viii). *Circular 230* requires that such person must not be disbarred or suspended from practice before the IRS or his or her profession. A tax return preparer can make an appearance as the taxpayer's representative only before the Examination Division of the IRS. A tax return preparer may not represent a taxpayer before any other IRS division, including the Appeals and Collection Divisions [IRS Publication 947]. In addition, the following actions are outside the authority of an unenrolled preparer [*Rev. Proc.* 81-38, 1981-1 C.B. 386].

1. Executing a claim for refund for the taxpayer

2. Receiving checks in payment of any refund of taxes, penalties, or interest for the taxpayer

3. Agreeing to later assessment or collection of taxes than is provided for by the applicable statute of limitations

4. Executing closing agreements with respect to tax liability or other specific matters for the taxpayer

5. Executing waivers of restriction on assessment or collection of a tax deficiency

Practice Before the IRS [*Circular 230* Subpart B] Subpart B of *Circular 230* provides a set of rules of conduct for those individuals authorized to practice before the IRS. Attorneys, CPAs, and EAs must observe the following rules of conduct (among others) when practicing before the IRS.

1. A tax practitioner must furnish information, on request, to any authorized agent of the IRS, unless the practitioner has reason to believe that the request is of doubtful legality or the information is privileged [§10.20(a)].

2. A tax practitioner must provide the Director of Practice of the IRS, on request, any information concerning the violation of any regulation pertaining to practice before the IRS. The tax practitioner must testify in a disbarment or suspension proceeding, unless there is reason to doubt the legality of the request or the information is privileged [§10.20(b)].

3. A tax practitioner who knows of client noncompliance, error, or omission with regard to the tax laws must advise the client of that noncompliance, error, or omission [§10.21].

4. Practitioners must not unreasonably delay matters before the IRS [§10.23].

5. Practitioners must not accept assistance from or employ a disbarred or suspended person or a former IRS employee disqualified from practice under another rule or U.S. law [§10.24].

6. Partners of government employees cannot represent anyone for which the government employee-partner has (or has had) official responsibility [§10.25]. For example, a CPA firm with an IRS agent as a partner cannot represent any taxpayer that is (or was in the past) assigned to the IRS agent/partner.

7. No former government employee shall, subsequent to his or her government employment, represent anyone in any matter administered by the IRS if such representation would violate other U.S. laws [§10.25].

8. No tax practitioner may act as a notary public for his or her clients [§10.26].

9. Fees for tax work must not be contingent or unconscionable [§10.27], and a practitioner must not negotiate a taxpayer's refund check [§10.31].

10. No tax practitioner can represent conflicting interests before the IRS unless he or she has the express consent of the directly interested parties [§10.29].

11. In general, a practitioner must, at the request of a client, promptly return any and all records of the client that are necessary for the client to comply with his

or her Federal tax obligations. The practitioner may retain copies of the records returned to a client [§10.28].

Due Diligence [*Circular 230* §10.22]   Section 10.22 of *Circular 230* requires tax practitioners to use due diligence in preparing tax returns and in their practice before the IRS. Due diligence is not defined in *Circular 230*. However, the Second Circuit in *Harary v. Blumenthal*, 555 F.2d 1113 (CA-2, 1977) has held that due diligence requires that the tax practitioner be honest with his or her client in connection with all IRS-related matters. In the view of the IRS, the failure to exercise due diligence involves conduct that is more than a simple error, but less than willful and reckless misconduct (*Coursebook Training 994-102*, IRS, December 1992). In determining if a practitioner has exercised due diligence, the IRS uses several factors, including the nature of the error, the explanation of the error, and other standards that apply (e.g., the AICPA SSTS that are discussed later in this chapter). In essence, due diligence means a tax practitioner should use reasonable effort to comply with the tax laws.

> **Example 1-1** Judy is a CPA who fails to include rental income on a tax return she completed for a client. The omitted rental income was from a new rental property purchased by the client this year and therefore had not been reported on prior years' tax returns. The taxpayer did not mention the new rental property to Judy in any communications with her. Under these circumstances, Judy has exercised due diligence in preparing the tax return. However, if Judy also kept the rental income records for the new rental property and still omitted the income from the tax return, she would not be exercising due diligence.

Contingent and Unconscionable Fees [*Circular 230* §10.27]   Tax practitioners are prohibited from charging **contingent fees** on an original tax return by §10.27(b) of *Circular 230*. Examples of contingent fees include a fee that is based on a percentage of the refund on a tax return or a fee that is a percentage of tax "saved." Although contingent fees are prohibited for the preparation of an original return, a practitioner may charge a contingent fee for an amended return or a claim for refund (other than a claim for refund made on an original return). The tax practitioner must reasonably anticipate, at the time of the fee arrangement, that the amended return will receive a substantive review by the IRS.

> **Example 1-2** Oak Corporation has been audited by the IRS for its tax return filed two years ago. The controller of the company completed the original return. The IRS is asserting that Oak underpaid its taxes by $100,000. Oak contacted Joe, a CPA, and engaged him to handle the appeals process with the IRS. In this situation, Joe can use a contingent fee arrangement. (For instance, Joe's fee could be 30 percent of any amount by which he could get the IRS to reduce the assessment.)

Section 10.27(a) also prohibits a tax practitioner from charging an unconscionable fee. This term is not defined in *Circular 230*. If a tax practitioner charges a fee that is out of line with some measure of the value of the service provided to a client, then the fee would be unconscionable. For example, a CPA could not charge a fee of $10,000 to an unsophisticated taxpayer (such as an elderly person) for simple tax work that most CPAs would complete for less than $500.

Solicitation and Advertising [*Circular 230* §10.30]   An attorney, CPA, or EA may use public communication to obtain clients under §10.30 of Subpart B. Types of public communication allowed by this provision include billboards, telephone books, and advertisements in newspapers, on radio, and on television. However, such public communications must not contain false, fraudulent, unduly influencing, coercive, or unfair statements or claims. If done in a dignified manner, examples of items that a practitioner may communicate to the public include (1) his or her name, address, and telephone number, (2) names of individuals associated with the practitioner, (3) a factual description of services offered, (4) credit cards accepted, (5) foreign language ability, (6) membership in professional organizations, (7) professional licenses held, and (8) a statement of practice limitations. Attorneys, CPAs, and EAs also must observe any applicable standards of ethical conduct adopted by the ABA, the AICPA, and the NAEA.

Best Practices [*Circular 230* §10.33]   Section 10.33 of *Circular 230* states that tax advisors should provide clients with the highest quality representation concerning Federal tax issues by adhering to best practices in providing advice. According to *Circular 230*, the best practices rules are aspirational. Thus, a practitioner who fails to comply with best practices will not be subject to discipline by the IRS. Still, tax professionals are expected to observe them to preserve public confidence in the tax system.

Best practices to be observed by all tax advisors include:

1. Communicating clearly with the client regarding the terms of the engagement. For example, the advisor should determine the client's expected purpose for and use of the advice and should have a clear understanding with the client regarding the form and scope of the advice or assistance to be rendered.

2. Establishing the facts, determining which facts are relevant, evaluating the reasonableness of any assumptions or representations, relating the applicable law (including potentially applicable judicial doctrines) to the relevant facts, and arriving at a conclusion supported by the law and the facts.

3. Advising the client regarding the importance of the conclusions reached, including, for example, whether a taxpayer may avoid accuracy-related penalties under the *Internal Revenue Code* if a taxpayer acts in reliance on the advice.

4. Acting fairly and with integrity in practice before the IRS.

According to *Circular 230*, these procedures are to help to ensure best practices for tax advisors. In addition, tax practitioners with responsibility for overseeing a firm's practice of providing tax advice or of preparing tax returns should take reasonable steps to ensure that the firm's procedures for all members, associates, and employees follow "best practices procedures."

Tax Return Positions [*Circular 230* §10.34]   Tax practitioners under *Circular 230* must meet certain standards with respect to advice given to clients on tax return positions. Under §10.34, a practitioner must not sign a tax return if he or she determines that the return contains a position that does not have a **more-likely-than-not** chance of being sustained on its merits if challenged by the IRS.[1] The more-likely-than-not standard is met if analysis of the tax return position by a reasonable and well-informed person knowledgeable in the tax law(s) would lead such person to conclude that the position has a greater than 50 percent likelihood of being sustained on its merits [§10.34(a)(4)].

---

[1] In May 2007, Congress amended the Code and changed the "realistic possibility" (33%) threshold of Section 6694 to a "more-likely-than–not" (over 50%) standard. We assume that related documents such as *Circular 230* and SSTS No. 1 will adopt this standard after the publication date of this text. The "realistic possibility" standard still applies to all tax returns filed before the enactment date of this change.

A practitioner may recommend a position on a tax return that does not meet the more-likely-than-not standard if the position is not frivolous and the position is disclosed on the tax return. A frivolous position is one that is patently improper under the tax law. When analyzing the merits of a tax return position, the authorities applicable under IRC §6662 and Reg. §1.6662 should be used to decide if the more-likely-than-not standard has been met. See Chapter 14 for further discussion of pertinent restrictions on tax return positions.

Covered Opinions [*Circular 230* **§10.35]** *Circular 230* imposes strict standards on "covered opinions." This term includes written advice (including electronic communications such as e-mail) concerning one or more federal tax issue(s) arising from:

1. A transaction that is the same as or substantially similar to a transaction that, at the time the advice is rendered, the IRS has determined to be a tax avoidance transaction and identified by published guidance as a listed transaction under 26 CFR 1.6011-4(b)(2);

2. Any partnership or other entity, any investment plan or arrangement, or any other plan or arrangement, the principal purpose of which is the avoidance or evasion of any tax imposed by the *Internal Revenue Code*; or

3. Any partnership or other entity, any investment plan or arrangement, or any other plan or arrangement, a significant purpose of which is the avoidance or evasion of any tax imposed by the *Internal Revenue Code*, if the written advice:

   a. *Is a reliance opinion*. A reliance opinion is written advice that concludes at a confidence level of a greater than 50 percent likelihood that one or more significant Federal tax issues would be resolved in the taxpayer's favor;

   b. *Is a marketed opinion*. A marketed opinion is written advice that the practitioner knows or has reason to know will be used or referred to by a person other than the practitioner (or a person who is a member of, associated with, or employed by the practitioner's firm) in promoting, marketing, or recommending a partnership or other entity, investment plan or arrangement to one or more taxpayers;

   c. *Is subject to conditions of confidentiality*; or

   d. *Is subject to contractual protection*.

In addition, §10.36 requires a practitioner who has principal authority and responsibility for overseeing a firm's practice of providing advice concerning Federal tax issues must take reasonable steps to ensure that the firm has adequate procedures in effect to ensure compliance with §10.35. Any such practitioner can be subject to discipline for failing to comply with the requirements of §10.36.

SPOTLIGHT ON TAXATION

E-mail Disclaimer

As a result of *Circular 230* covered opinions rules, most CPAs and other tax advisors include some form of blanket disclaimer in the tag line of all their e-mail sent to clients. An example of such a disclaimer would be:

continued

continued

> I am required by IRS Circular 230 to inform you that, unless otherwise expressly indicated, any Federal tax advice contained in this communication, including attachments and enclosures, is not intended or written to be used, and may not be used, for the purpose of (1) avoiding tax-related penalties under the Internal Revenue Code or (2) promoting, marketing, or recommending to another party any tax-related matters addressed herein.

Other Written Advice [Circular 230 §10.37] A practitioner must not give written advice (including electronic communications) concerning one or more Federal tax issues if the practitioner:

1. bases the written advice on unreasonable factual or legal assumptions (including assumptions as to future events),

2. unreasonably relies upon representations, statements, findings, or agreements of the taxpayer or any other person,

3. does not consider all relevant facts that the practitioner knows or should know, or

4. in evaluating a Federal tax issue, takes into account the possibility that a tax return will not be audited, that an issue will not be raised on audit, or that an issue will be resolved through settlement if raised.

When applying the provision, all facts and circumstances, including the scope of the engagement and the type and specificity of the advice sought by the client, will be considered in determining whether a practitioner has failed to comply with this section.

Circular 230 can be found on the IRS's web site at **http://www.irs.gov/pub/irs-pdf/pcir230.pdf**

AICPA Code of Professional Conduct

Members of the AICPA are subject to the Institute's Code of Professional Conduct. The Code is relevant to all of the professional services performed by CPAs, including those services provided in the practice of public accounting, private industry, government, or education. It was previously referred to as the AICPA Code of Ethics. Changes adopted in 1988 were believed necessary to reflect the significant changes in the profession and the environment in which CPAs practice, although the basic tenets of ethical and professional conduct remained the same. One of the most significant changes was the expansion of the rules to apply to all members in all fields of practice, except where the wording of the rule limits the application to a specified field of practice. Under the prior Code of Ethics, only members engaged in the practice of public accounting were required to observe all of the rules. Other members, such as those in the fields of education, government, and industry, were subject only to the rules requiring integrity and objectivity and the rule prohibiting members from performing acts discreditable to the profession.

In addition, the rule prohibiting a CPA in public practice from engaging in a business or an occupation concurrently with the practice of public accounting, which would create a conflict of interest in rendering professional services, was deleted from the Code of Professional Conduct. The members of the Institute felt that such conflicts of interest are effectively prohibited under new Rule 102, Integrity and Objectivity.

The Code of Professional Conduct was designed to provide its members with the following.

1. A comprehensive code of ethical and professional conduct

2. A guide for all members in answering complex questions

3. Assurance to the public concerning the obligations and responsibilities of the accounting profession.

The AICPA Code of Professional Conduct consists of two integral sections: the principles and the rules. The principles provide a foundation on which the rules are based. The principles suggest that a CPA should strive for behavior above the minimal level of acceptable conduct required by law and regulations. In addition to expressing the basic tenets of ethical and professional conduct, the principles are intended to provide a framework for the CPA's responsibilities to the public, clients, and colleagues. Included are guidelines concerning the member's responsibility to perform professional services with integrity, objectivity, and **independence**.

The rules consist of a set of enforceable ethical standards that have been approved by a majority of the members of the AICPA. These rules are broad in nature and apply to all of the professional services that a CPA performs, whether in the practice of public accounting or in the fields of education, industry, or government. The only exceptions to the rules occur when their wording indicates that their application is limited to a specified field of practice only, or with respect to certain activities of those who are practicing in another country. In the latter case, however, the CPA must adhere to the ethical standards of the foreign country.

Any failure to follow the rules under the Code of Professional Conduct may result in the offender receiving admonishment, suspension, or expulsion from membership in the AICPA. The rules apply not only to the CPA, but also to those employees who are under his or her supervision, partners or shareholders in the practice of the CPA, and any others who act on the CPA's behalf (even if they are not compensated for their activities). As previously discussed, the Code of Professional Conduct is applicable to all of the professional services performed by a CPA, including services rendered in the fields of public accounting, such as tax and management advisory services, education, industry, and government.

In addition to the principles and rules, the Code of Professional Conduct provides for three additional promulgations. These are interpretations of rules, ethics rulings, and "ethics features." Interpretations of Rules are issued by the Division of Professional Ethics of the AICPA. They provide additional detailed guidelines for the scope and application of the rules. These guidelines are enforceable, and the CPA must be prepared to justify any departure from them.

The Division of Professional Ethics of the AICPA also issues ethics rulings to further explain the application and interpretation of the rules of conduct and to provide interpretations of the rules in specific circumstances. A member who, in similar circumstances, departs from the findings of these ethics rulings must be prepared to justify such departure. In addition, the Division of Professional Ethics publishes a column in the *Journal of Accountancy* dealing with issues of professional ethics. These informal articles are intended to address issues raised in questions submitted by members of the AICPA. The questions and answers contained in the articles are not considered formal rulings by the AICPA.

Rule 101: Independence   Under Rule 101, a CPA (or CPA firm) in public practice must be independent of the enterprise for which professional services are being provided. Independence is required not only for opinions on financial statements, but also for certain other reports and services where a body of the AICPA has promulgated standards requiring independence. A CPA is not independent if one or more financial relationships exist with a client during the period of professional engagement or at the issuing of the opinion. Thus, independence is impaired if a CPA:

1. has any direct or material indirect financial interest in the client's enterprise;

2. has any jointly held material investment with the client or with its officers, directors, or principal stockholders;

3. has any loan to or from the client, an officer of the client, or any principal stockholder of the client, except for loans, such as home mortgages, that were obtained under normal lending procedures;

4. is an officer, director, employee, or underwriter of the client during the period that is covered by the financial statements, during the period of the professional engagement, or at the time of expressing an opinion; or,

5. is related as a trustee, executor, or administrator of any estate that holds a direct or material indirect financial interest in the client.

These independence standards also apply to a CPA who is restricted to doing tax work in a partnership with other CPAs who are examining related financial statements. For instance, a tax partner in a CPA firm should not own stock in a client whose financial statements are audited by her partners in the firm, even though she may have nothing to do with the audit of that client's statements.

Rule 102: Integrity and Objectivity   All professional services by a CPA should be rendered with objectivity and integrity, avoiding any conflict of interest. A CPA should not knowingly misrepresent facts or subordinate his or her judgment to that of others in rendering any professional services. For example, in a tax practice, the CPA may be requested to follow blindly the guidelines of a government agency or the demands of an audit client. Rule 102 prohibits such blind obedience. Prior to the most recent revision of Rule 102, a CPA in tax practice could resolve doubt in favor of the client. This phrase was omitted in the revised language because resolving doubt in favor of a client in an advocacy engagement is not considered as impairing integrity or objectivity and thus need not be specifically "allowed."

Rule 201: General Standards   The CPA must comply with the following general standards, as well as any interpretations of such standards, of the AICPA Code of Professional Conduct.

1. The CPA must be able to complete all professional services with professional competence.

2. The CPA must exercise due professional care in the performance of all professional services.

3. The CPA shall adequately plan and supervise the performance of all professional services.

4. The CPA must obtain sufficient relevant data to afford a reasonable basis for any conclusion or recommendation in connection with the performance of any professional services.

The standard requiring "professional competence" recognizes the need for members of the profession to commit to a program of professional development, learning, and improvement. Such a program of professional continuing education is also recognized in the standard of "due professional care."

Rule 202: Compliance with Standards A CPA, whether providing tax, management advisory, audit, review, compilation, or other professional services, must comply with all standards promulgated by bodies designated by the AICPA Council.

Rule 203: Accounting Principles A CPA is prohibited from expressing an opinion that financial data of an entity conform with Generally Accepted Accounting Principles if those statements or other financial data contain any material departure from the profession's technical standards. In some cases where a departure is present but the financial statement or other financial data would have been misleading without that departure, a member may be able to comply with this rule by describing the departure, the effect of the departure, and the justification for it.

Rule 301: Confidential Client Information A CPA in the practice of public accounting must not disclose confidential client data without the specific consent of the client. Rule 301 does not, however, apply:

1. If there is a conflict with Rules 202 (Compliance with Standards) and 203 (Accounting Principles) as set forth by the AICPA Code of Professional Conduct;

2. If the CPA is served with an enforceable subpoena or summons, or must comply with applicable laws and government regulations;

3. If there is a review of a CPA's practice under AICPA or state society authorization; or

4. If the CPA is responding to an inquiry of an investigative or disciplinary body of a recognized society, or where the CPA is initiating a complaint with a disciplinary body.

In connection with this rule, members of the investigative bodies who may be exposed to confidential client information are precluded from disclosing such information.

SPOTLIGHT ON TAXATION

Confidentiality

A Texas District Court held that the identities of taxpayers who hired the accounting firm of KPMG to participate in a tax shelter later identified as potentially abusive by the IRS were not protected from disclosure under the §7525 confidentiality privilege for communications between taxpayers and federally authorized tax practitioners. Disclosing taxpayers' identities to the IRS would only reveal their participation in these shelters, and it would not reveal any confidential communications made regarding these tax shelters. *John Doe 1 and John Doe 2 v. KPMG*, 93 AFTR 2d 2004-1759 (DC N. Tex.).

Rule 302: Contingent Fees A CPA in public practice cannot charge or receive a contingent fee for any professional services from a client for whom the CPA or the CPA's firm performs audit, review, or compilation work. For example, a fee schedule of $5,000 for a qualified audit opinion and $35,000 for an unqualified opinion would not be allowed. Rule 302 also prohibits a CPA from preparing an original or amended tax return, or claim for a tax refund for a contingent fee.

A contingent fee is defined here as a fee established for the performance of any service pursuant to an arrangement in which no fee will be charged unless a specified finding or result is attained, or in which the amount of the fee is otherwise dependent on the finding or result of such service. Solely for purposes of this rule, fees are not regarded as being contingent if fixed by courts or other public authorities, or, in tax matters, if determined based on the results of judicial proceedings or the findings of governmental agencies.

Rule 501: Acts Discreditable A CPA must not commit an act that is discreditable to the profession. This rule is not specific as to what constitutes a discreditable act; however, violations have been found when the CPA committed a felony, failed to return client records after a client requested them, signed a false tax return, or issued a misleading audit opinion.

Rule 502: Advertising and Other Forms of Solicitation A CPA in public practice cannot seek clients through false, misleading, or deceptive advertising or other forms of solicitation. In addition, solicitation by the use of coercion, overreaching, or harassing conduct is not allowed. The Institute has placed no restrictions as to the type, media, or frequency of a CPA's advertisements, or on the artwork that is associated with them. Under Rule 502, an activity would be prohibited:

1. If it created false or unjustified expectations of favorable results;

2. If it implied the ability to influence any court, tribunal, regulatory agency, or similar body or official;

3. If it contains a representation that specific professional services in current or future periods will be performed for a stated fee, estimated fee, or fee range when it was likely, at the time of the representation, that such fees would be substantially increased and the prospective client was not advised of that likelihood; or

4. If it contains any other representations that would be likely to cause a reasonable person to misunderstand or be deceived.

For example, a radio spot that states a CPA firm "can beat the IRS every time" would be in violation of Rule 502.

Rule 503: Commissions and Referral Fees A CPA in public practice cannot charge or receive a commission or referral fee from a client for whom the CPA or the CPA's firm performs audit, review, or compilation work. Thus, under Rule 503, a CPA who does only tax or other nonaudit work for a client may accept or pay a commission. The CPA must, however, disclose the commission to the client or other party in the transaction. In addition, a member who accepts or pays a referral fee for recommending or referring any service of a CPA must disclose that fact.

Rule 505: Form of Organization and Name CPAs may practice public accounting only in the form of organization permitted by state law or regulation whose characteristics conform to resolutions of the AICPA Council. Under Rule 505, a CPA cannot practice under a firm name that is misleading. The names of one or more past owners may be included in the firm name of a successor organization. In addition, all partners or members of a firm must be members of the AICPA if a firm is to designate itself as "Members of the AICPA."

Statements on Standards for Tax Services

To assist CPAs, the AICPA has issued a series of statements as to what constitutes appropriate standards for tax practice. These SSTS delineate a CPA's responsibilities to his or her clients, the public, the government, and the profession. The SSTS is a set of enforceable standards. They are intended to specifically address the problems inherent in the tax practitioner's dual role in serving the client and the public. The statements are intended to supplement, rather than replace, the AICPA Code of Professional Conduct and *Circular 230*. They are designed to address the development of tax practice as an integral part of a CPA's practice and the changing environment in which tax practitioners must operate, including the rapidly changing tax laws.

SSTS No. 1: Tax Return Positions   In providing professional services that involve tax return positions, a member should have a good-faith belief that a recommended position has a more-likely-than-not chance of being sustained if challenged; otherwise, such a position should not be recommended by the member.[2] A member may reach a conclusion that a position is warranted based on existing law and regulations, as well as on other sources such as well-reasoned articles by tax specialists, treatises, IRS General Counsel Memoranda and written determinations, and explanations of revenue acts as prepared by the Joint Committee on Taxation.

In this statement the members of the AICPA have adopted a standard that is similar to the substantial authority standard of IRC §6662; however, the statement specifically states that the member may reach a conclusion based on authority as specified in the statement without regard to whether such sources are treated as "authority" under IRC §6662. Thus, a member who is in compliance with SSTS No. 1 may still lack substantial authority for taking a position under §6662. In cases where a taxpayer insists on a specific position, a member may sign the return even though the position does not meet the above standard, provided that (1) the position is adequately disclosed on the return by the taxpayer, and (2) the position is not "frivolous." Under no circumstances should a member recommend a tax return position that is exploitative or frivolous.

In cases where the member believes that the taxpayer may have some exposure to a penalty, the statement suggests that the member advise the taxpayer of such risk. Where disclosure of a position on the tax return may mitigate the possibility of a taxpayer penalty under the *Internal Revenue Code*, the member should consider recommending that the taxpayer disclose the position on the return.

SSTS No. 2: Answers to Questions on Returns   Before signing a return as the preparer, a member should make a reasonable effort to obtain from the taxpayer appropriate answers to all questions on the taxpayer's tax return. Where the taxpayer

---

[2]As stated previously, in May 2007, Congress amended the Code and changed the "realistic possibility" (33%) threshold of Section 6694 to a "more-likely-than not" (over 50%) standard. We are assuming the related documents such as *Circular 230* and SSTS No. 1 will adapt this new standard after the publication date of this text. The "realistic possibility" standard still applies to all tax returns filed before the enactment date of this change.

leaves a question on the return unanswered and reasonable grounds exist for not answering the question, the member need not provide an explanation for the omission. The possibility that an answer to a question may prove disadvantageous to the taxpayer, however, does not justify omitting the answer.

Reasonable grounds may exist for omitting an answer to a question on a return. For example, such an omission is acceptable where:

1. The pertinent data are not readily available and are not significant to the determination of taxable income (or loss) or the tax liability;

2. The taxpayer and member are genuinely uncertain as to the meaning of the question on the return; or

3. An answer to a question is voluminous (however, assurance should be given on the return that the data can be supplied upon examination). In this regard, a notation on Form 1120 and related schedules that information will be provided on request is not considered acceptable (*IRS Brooklyn District Newsletter* No. 47, 10/89).

SSTS No. 3: Certain Procedural Aspects of Preparing Returns In preparing or signing a return, the member ordinarily may rely without verification on information that the taxpayer or a third party has provided, unless such information appears to be incorrect, incomplete, or inconsistent. A more formal audit-like review of documents or supporting evidence is generally not required for a member to sign the tax return. Where material provided by the taxpayer appears to be incorrect or incomplete, however, the member should obtain additional information from the taxpayer. In situations where the statutes require that specific conditions be met, the member should determine, by inquiry, whether the conditions have been met. For example, the Code and Regulations impose substantiation requirements for the deduction of certain expenditures. In such a case, the member has an obligation to make appropriate inquiries.

Although members are not required to examine supporting documents, they should encourage the taxpayer to provide such documents when deemed appropriate; for example, in the case of deductions or income from a pass-through entity, such as a partnership, the entity's documents might be useful in preparing the owner's tax returns.

The member should make proper use of the prior year's tax return when feasible to gather information about the taxpayer and to help avoid omissions and errors with respect to income, deductions, and credit computations.

SSTS No. 4: Use of Estimates A member may prepare tax returns that involve the use of the taxpayer's estimates if it is impractical to obtain exact data and if the estimated amounts appear reasonable to the member. In all cases, the estimated information must be supplied by the taxpayer; however, the member may provide advice in connection with the estimate. When the taxpayer's estimates are used, they should be presented in such a manner as to avoid the implication of greater accuracy than exists. Situations where the use of estimates may be appropriate include cases where the keeping of precise records for numerous items of small amounts is difficult to achieve, where data are not available at the time of filing the tax return, or when certain records are missing.

The use of estimates in making pertinent accounting judgments where such use is not in conflict with the *Internal Revenue Code* is not prohibited under this statement; such judgments are acceptable and expected. For example, the income tax regulations permit the use of a reasonable estimate for accruals if exact amounts are not known.

Although in most cases the use of estimates does not necessitate that the item be specifically disclosed on the taxpayer's return, disclosure should be made where failure to do so would result in misleading the IRS about the accuracy of the return. For example, disclosure may be necessary where the taxpayer's records have been destroyed in a fire or where the taxpayer has not received a Schedule K-1 from a pass-through entity at the time the return is filed. Tax practitioners should make their taxpayers aware that the tax law does not allow estimates of certain income and expenditure items, and that more restrictive substantiation requirements apply in cases of certain expenditures, such as travel and entertainment expenses.

SSTS No. 5: Departure from a Position Previously Concluded in an Administrative Proceeding or Court Decision   The recommendation by a member as to the treatment of an item on a tax return should be based on the facts and the law as they are evaluated at the time during which the return is prepared or signed by the member. Unless the taxpayer is bound by the IRS to the treatment of an item in later years, such as by a closing agreement, the disposition of an item in a prior year's audit, or as part of a prior year's court decision, the member is not prevented from recommending a different treatment of a similar item in a later year's return. Thus, a member may sign a return that contains a departure from a treatment required by the IRS in a prior year, provided that the member adheres to the standards in SSTS No. 1.

In most cases, a member's recommendation as to the treatment of an item on a tax return will be consistent with the treatment of a similar item consented to in a prior year's **administrative proceeding** or as a result of the prior year's court decision. In deciding whether a recommendation contrary to the prior treatment is warranted, the member should consider the following.

1. Neither the IRS nor the taxpayer is bound to act consistently with respect to the treatment of an item in a prior proceeding; however, the IRS tends to act consistently in similar situations.

2. The standards under SSTS No. 1, Tax Return Positions, must be followed. In determining whether such standards can be met, the member must consider the existence of an unfavorable court decision and the taxpayer's consent in an earlier administrative proceeding.

3. In some cases, the taxpayer's consent to the treatment of an item in a prior administrative or judicial proceeding may have been due to a desire to settle the issue or a lack of supporting data, whereas in the current year these factors no longer exist.

4. The tax climate may have changed for a given issue since the prior court decision was reached or the prior administrative hearing concluded.

SSTS No. 6: Knowledge of Error: Return Preparation   The member must advise the taxpayer promptly, regardless of whether the member prepared or signed the return in question, when he or she learns of an error in a previously filed tax return or becomes aware that a required return was not filed. Such advice should include a recommendation for appropriate measures the taxpayer should take. However, the member is neither obligated to inform the IRS of the situation, nor may he or she do so without the taxpayer's permission, except as provided by law.

If the member is requested to prepare the current year's return, and the taxpayer has not taken action to correct an error in a prior year's return, the member should consider whether to proceed with the preparation of the current year's return. If the current year's return is prepared, the member should take reasonable steps to ensure that the error is not repeated.

A member may advise a taxpayer, either orally or in writing, as to the correction of errors in the prior year's return. In a case where there is a possibility that the taxpayer may be charged with fraud, the taxpayer should be referred to an attorney. If a member discovers the error during an audit or other nontax engagement, he or she should refer the taxpayer to the tax return preparer. If the item in question has an insignificant effect on the taxpayer's tax liability, the item should not be considered an "error" under this statement. In addition, the term "error" does not include a situation where the taxpayer's position satisfied the standards under SSTS No. 1 at the time the return was filed.

SSTS No. 7: Knowledge of Error: Administrative Proceedings When a member represents a taxpayer in an administrative proceeding (such as an audit), and the member is aware of an error other than one that has an insignificant effect on the taxpayer's tax liability, the member should request the taxpayer's agreement to disclose the error to the IRS. Lacking such an agreement with the taxpayer, the member may be under a duty to withdraw from the engagement and may consider terminating the professional relationship with the taxpayer. Disclosure, once agreed on, should be made in a timely manner to avoid misleading the IRS.

SSTS No. 8: Form and Content of Advice to Taxpayers In providing tax advice to taxpayers, the member must use judgment that reflects professional competence and serves the taxpayer's needs. The member must assume that any advice given will be used to determine the manner of reporting items on the taxpayer's tax return; therefore, the member should ensure that the standards under SSTS No. 1 are satisfied. When providing advice that will be relied on by third parties, the member's responsibilities may differ. Neither a standard format nor guidelines have been issued or established that would cover all situations and circumstances involving written or oral advice from a member. When giving such advice to taxpayers, in addition to exercising professional judgment, the member should consider each of the following.

1. The importance of the transaction and the amounts involved

2. The specific or general nature of the taxpayer's inquiry

3. The time available to develop and submit the advice

4. The technical complications that are presented

5. The existence of authority and precedents

6. The tax sophistication of the taxpayer

7. The possibility of seeking legal advice

Written communication is recommended in important, unusual, or complicated transactions, while oral advice is acceptable in more typical situations. In the communication, the member should advise the taxpayer that the advice reflects his or her professional judgment based on the current situation and that subsequent developments may affect previous advice, such as stating that the position of authorities is subject to change (see Chapter 11).

When subsequent developments affect the advice that a member has previously communicated to a taxpayer, the member is under no obligation to initiate

Exhibit 1-4: Summary of AICPA Statements on Standards for Tax Service

Statement	Summary of Contents
1	Specifies the standards for professional services that involve tax positions
2	Explains how a member should handle answering questions on a tax return
3	Describes the procedural aspects of preparing a tax return
4	Defines when a member can use an estimate in preparing a tax return
5	Explains what a member should do about items on a current return when similar items were audited on a prior year's return or were the subject of a judicial hearing
6	States what a member should do upon learning about an error in a prior year's tax return
7	Gives the procedure to follow if an error is discovered during an audit
8	Establishes standards for the giving of tax advice to taxpayers

further communication of such developments to the taxpayer unless a specific agreement has been reached with the taxpayer, or the member is assisting in the application of a procedure or plan relative to such advice.

Exhibit 1-4 summarizes the main topic of each of the AICPA SSTS. The complete text of the SSTS can be found on the AICPA web site at: **http://www.aicpa.org/download/tax/SSTSfinal.pdf**

Sarbanes-Oxley and Taxation

In 2002, Congress passed the Sarbanes-Oxley Act, which addressed the corporate management abuses that took place during the 1990s and early 2000s in publicly traded American corporations. These corporate governance breakdowns culminated in spectacular business failures such as with Enron, WorldCom, Global Crossing, Waste-Management, Sunbeam, and others, and led to the eventual failure of the Big Five CPA firm of Arthur Andersen.

The Sarbanes-Oxley Act made it "unlawful" for an auditor to provide any of the nonaudit services listed in the Act. In addition, the Act provided that a registered public accounting firm "may engage in any nonaudit service, including tax services, that is not described [in the list of nine specifically prohibited services] for an audit client only if the activity is approved in advance by the audit committee of the issuer" in accordance with the Act. The prohibited services are:

1. Bookkeeping or other services related to the accounting records or financial statements of the audit client

2. Financial information systems design and implementation

3. Appraisal or valuation services, fairness opinions, or contribution-in-kind reports

4. Actuarial services

5. Internal audit outsourcing services

6. Management functions or human resources

7. Broker or dealer, investment adviser, or investment banking services

8. Legal services and expert services unrelated to the audit

9. Any other service that the Public Company Accounting Oversight Board determines, by regulation, is impermissible.

It should be noted that tax compliance work is not one of the prohibited services. However, tax work is subject to the preapproval process. The audit committee needs to know about the proposed tax-related services in order to preapprove them. Many corporations now take work to CPA firms other than the auditor, rather than seek approval of the audit committee. As a result, many companies divide their audit and tax work between different firms. This appears to be an unintended result of the Sarbanes-Oxley Act.

Investors, on the other hand, would probably prefer that the audit committee be aware of everything that is going on within a company and actually preapprove the work instead of having the work go elsewhere. Currently, the audit committee may not even be aware if someone other than the auditor is being used for non-audit work. Such decision making remains hidden from audit committee review. Tax practitioners will have to wait to see how this contradiction plays out. Perhaps audit committees will get more comfortable with their Sarbanes-Oxley responsibilities and this division of traditional audit and tax work may decline in future years.

In addition to being a response to corporate governance and accounting transparency failures, the Sarbanes-Oxley Act is a response to the general failure of business ethics. For example, the proliferation of abusive tax shelters and super-aggressive tax avoidance strategies (which are discussed shortly) are examples of other business ethical problems.

ABA Model Code of Professional Responsibility

The ABA Model Code of Professional Responsibility includes nine canons, which may be thought of as statements of principles. Canon 6, for instance, requires an attorney to represent a taxpayer competently. Each canon is followed by a series of ethical considerations (ECs), which in turn are supported by disciplinary rules (DRs). The ECs are aspirational in character, setting forth objectives toward which all attorneys are to strive. The DRs set forth minimum standards of conduct. Any failure to abide by the DRs may subject the attorney to disciplinary procedures and punishment.

In nearly all jurisdictions, the ABA Model Code was adopted by the appropriate policy agency, although sometimes modifications were made. In August 1983, the ABA adopted the Model Rules of Professional Conduct, which, in a majority of the states, have substantially replaced the Model Code as the guide for attorney professional conduct.

The ABA has a Standing Committee on Ethics and Professional Responsibility that answers questions concerning ethics and professional conduct. Requests for opinions from the committee should be directed to the American Bar Association Center for Professional Responsibility in Chicago.

Neither the ABA Model Code nor the Model Rules have the force of law. Each was designed to be adopted by the appropriate agencies that govern the practice of law in the states. In many jurisdictions, the state supreme court is charged with policing the practice of law; in other states, the legislature bears this responsibility. Attorneys should consult their own jurisdiction's ethical guidelines to determine whether the provisions of the ABA Model Code or the Model Rules, or some modification of these doctrines, have been adopted.

The current status of the ABA Model Rules can be found on the ABA web site at: **http://www.abanet.org/cpr/mrpc/mrpc_toc.html**

NONREGULATORY ETHICAL BEHAVIOR MODELS

Since the turn of the twenty-first century, nonregulatory ethical models have become more relevant and applicable to professions such as accountancy and law. Tax practitioners need to be aware there is substantially more to ethical behavior than just following the rules of ethics or conduct of professional organizations such as the AICPA or the ABA. The regulatory rules are generally straightforward. They usually list a defined set of acts that are prohibited by members of the profession. For example, under SSTS No. 6, a CPA cannot disclose an error in a client's tax return to the IRS without the client's permission. On the other hand, nonregulatory ethics involve making choices that are not always clearly spelled out such as disclosure of client tax information.

Ethical Dilemmas

An ethical dilemma occurs when someone is faced with a situation to which there are no clearly defined answers such as, by regulation or law. In other words, there are multiple "right" answers (or put another way, no obviously wrong answers).

> **Example 1-3** Bill, a CPA, has been requested by his CPA firm employer to join "The Macho Men," a private club. Most of the movers and shakers (i.e., clients and potential clients) in town are members of this club. However, the club does not allow female members. *If you were Bill, what would you do? How do you think Bill's female co-workers would feel about him joining a club that discriminates against women?* There is no "right" answer to these questions because they are ethical dilemmas to which there are several right answers.

As is illustrated in this example, making the choice in an ethical dilemma can be complicated. How then, is a person supposed to deal with a situation such as this? The answer can be assessed through several generally recognized forms of ethical reasoning.

SPOTLIGHT ON TAXATION

Quotation

Ethics is knowing the difference between what you have the right to do and what is the right thing to do

Supreme Court Justice Potter Stewart

Ethical Reasoning

There are several approaches to resolving an ethical dilemma. Len Marrella notes that there are three common lines of reasoning to solve an ethical dilemma.[3] These are called End-based reasoning, Rule-based reasoning, and Care-based reasoning.

---

[3] *In Search of Ethics: Conversations with Men and Women of Character*, DC Press, 2001.

Each of these approaches attempts to provide a framework in which to resolve an ethical dilemma.

End-Based Ethical Reasoning End-based ethical reasoning was popular in the 1800s. Its main tenet was that an action was right if it produced at least as much net good as any alternative action could have produced. Hence, an ethical decision was the one that did the most good for the largest number of people. In summary, competing ethical solutions are resolved in terms of the "end-result."

John Stuart Mill was a proponent of this philosophy. He encouraged individuals to examine the consequences of various alternatives and to rely heavily on facts when making ethical choices.[4] The steps in applying End-based reasoning can be summarized as follows.

1. Identify the courses of action available

2. Identify stakeholders who will be impacted by the various choices of action and what benefit or harm may come to them as the result of a given choice.

3. Choose the action with the greatest benefits and the least amount of harm.[5]

To a CPA this type of decision making is similar to cost-benefit analysis. However, applying cost-benefit analysis to an ethical decision is not as easy as applying it to a financial decision. The real problem is that End-based reasoning does not consider justice, fairness, integrity and similar concepts in arriving at a choice. Ethicists consider this to be one of End-based reasoning's major failings.

Rule-Based Ethical Reasoning Rule-based reasoning is based on what is referred to as "Kantian ethics," which were derived from the writing of the German philosopher Immanuel Kant. He held that individual actions should be such that we would accept similar behavior from everyone else. Kant believed rules are made to apply to everyone and there were no exceptions—period. According to Kant, lying and stealing were always unethical, and therefore there is no such thing as a "white lie" to protect someone's feelings or reputation. This thinking today is usually referred to as "Zero Tolerance" and many times leads to unjust results. For example, what if a six-year-old first grader is expelled from school for bringing a plastic picnic knife to school to eat his lunch, in violation of the no-weapons policy at his school. Is this fair or just?

Care-Based Ethical Reasoning Care-based reasoning is found in the moral teachings of almost every culture and religion. In Western culture it is called the "Golden Rule," which states, "Do unto others as you would have them do unto you." From an ethical reasoning point of view it says make decisions that would result in the treatment you yourself would like to receive. Care-based reasoning can be described as doing what is "fair and just."

Ethical Professional Behavior

Professional ethical behavior is the result of the interaction of personal morality, social responsibility, business ethics, and other general ethical standards. Exhibit 1-5 illustrates these ethical standards and shows possible business and accounting areas that could be affected by ethical failures.

---

[4]Velasquez, M., Andre, C., Shanks, S., and Meyer, M., "Thinking Ethically: A Framework for Moral Decision Making," *Issues in Ethics*, Vol. 7, No. 1, Winter 1996.
[5]Ibid.

Exhibit 1-5: Sources of Ethical Behavior and Impacts

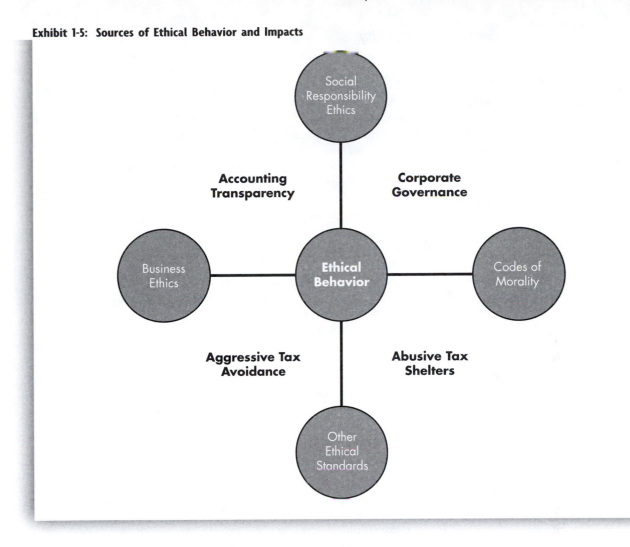

Morality

The subject of morality fills tens of thousands of books. Publications as diverse as the Bible and popular novels examine morality in one way or another. When something is judged to be morally right or wrong (or good or bad), the underlying standards on which such judgments are based are called moral standards.

According to some people's moral standards, cheating "just a little" in computing a tax liability is morally acceptable. Most people in the United States believe that everyone cheats a little on their taxes. Cheating significantly may be viewed differently, but where is the dividing line between morally "OK" tax cheating and morally wrong tax evasion? Under the self-assessed tax system in the United States, different moral standards provide different answers—from complete honesty to various degrees of dishonesty. The tax practitioner must be ready to work with clients holding various systems of morality and to accept the consequences of the moral choices made, including the possibility of losing a client, paying fines and penalties to the IRS, or even going to jail.

Social Responsibility

The tax practitioner must be aware of social responsibility in areas such as environmental protection, equal opportunity, and occupational safety. Since World War II, society has held the business world increasingly responsible for meeting certain noneconomic standards. In 1970, Milton Friedman, the Nobel Prize–winning economist, said that the "social responsibility" of business is merely to increase profits. But the prevailing sentiment today is that business and the professions should return something to society to make it better, not just to make a profit. For the tax practitioner, this could mean going beyond the minimum legal responsibility to provide equal opportunity in the hiring of employees by making special recruitment efforts, or it could mean volunteering time to help charitable organizations with their tax problems.

Business Ethics

In recent years, one of the major topics in the business world has been the question of business ethics. Many people believe that ethics has application only in one's personal life, not in the business or professional arena. Like Milton Friedman, they think that the only business of business is to make a profit. This view is popular because (1) people who work in business or professions must concern themselves with producing goods and services to earn a profit, and (2) it is easier to measure profit than it is to make value judgments. People are more comfortable discussing problems in terms of profits, rather than in terms of the ethical impact of the entity and its actions. Few business and professional people are trained in ethical analysis, and, therefore, they usually are not familiar with how to evaluate a problem in terms of ethics.

> **Example 1-4** Bruce owns a successful small business. The business is operated as a corporation. During the year, Bruce makes numerous personal long-distance phone calls from the office, uses the company credit card to purchase gas for his family's personal automobiles, sends personal items using the company's FedEx account, and is reimbursed by the company for meals and entertainment expenditures that are primarily personal in nature. These items are deducted by the corporation on its tax return. *Would you sign this company's Form 1120 as the tax return preparer? If you also audited this company, what would you do about these transactions?*

That business and professional organizations have ethical responsibilities is readily apparent to anyone who reads the popular press. The lawsuits brought on by the savings and loan failures of the late 1980s and against the large international accounting firms in the last two decades are prime examples of society holding business to a standard of ethical conduct. Most of the big CPA firms have settled lawsuits (both in and out of court) against them for millions of dollars for what was, in part, a business ethics failure.

Tax Planning Ethics

In addition to the previously discussed corporate governance issues addressed in the Sarbanes-Oxley Act, there are many examples of suspect ethics practices in the area of taxation. The following are some "classic" examples of the aggressive tax planning arrangements that have been promoted in recent years by CPAs, lawyers, and others.[6]

---

[6]For an expanded discussion of tax planning abuse during the 1980s and 1990s, see *Tax Shelter Hustlers*, Forbes (December 14, 1998), p. 198.

Example 1-5 Cerveza Corporation is primarily in the beverage supply business. The taxpayer classified itself as a security dealer and then marks down (and claims a tax deduction for) its accounts receivable based on the contention that they are not marketable and some of the accounts will not be paid. This practice was prohibited by Congress in 1998.

Example 1-6 Sneaky Inc., a United States-based corporation, pays $600,000 to buy an expiring foreign copyright that has one royalty payment left. The last payment is for $800,000, less $240,000 of foreign tax credit (30% of $800,000). On this deal the buyer has lost $40,000 ($600,000 payment less $560,000 net final royalty), but has purchased a $240,000 foreign tax credit that can be used to offset $240,000 of tax on Sneaky's other foreign income.

Example 1-7 Cheater Corporation borrowed $300,000 and used the proceeds to purchase a $2,000,000 single premium life insurance policy. The policy is a universal life insurance policy. Like many life insurance policies, this policy pays interest that is tax-free on the cash value of the policy. As a result of this transaction, the corporation receives an interest deduction for the loan and earns tax-free interest on the policy. This type of transaction was stopped by Congress in 1996.

SPOTLIGHT ON TAXATION

Ethics

The taxing authorities of several U.S. states post the names of delinquent taxpayers on their web site. The stated purpose of the postings is to "shame" the taxpayers who have not paid their state taxes into paying them. Although this posting clearly is legal, is it ethical? For example, suppose a family has a child with leukemia and has horrendous medical bills and cannot afford to pay their taxes. Should they be held up to ridicule because they are doing the right thing and taking care of their child, even if it prevents them from paying their taxes?

Other Ethical Standards

The study of nonregulatory ethics could be expanded to cover such other issues as public policy, religious beliefs, and cultural values, issues that are beyond the scope of this text. Most of such topics would be addressed in a university course on ethics or business ethics. A tax practitioner can expand his or her understanding of the application of ethics to accounting and business situations by referring to the books on the following reading list.

- Armstrong, Mary Beth, *Ethics and Professionalism for CPAs* (Cincinnati: South-Western Publishing Co., 1993).

- Brooks, Leonard J., *Business and Professional Ethics for Directors, Executives, and Accountants* (Mason: South Western Business & Professional Publishing, 2004).

- Buchholz, Rogene, *Fundamental Concepts and Problems in Business Ethics* (Englewood Cliffs, NJ: Prentice Hall, 1989).

- Collins, Denis, and Thomas O'Rourke, *Ethical Dilemmas in Accounting* (Cincinnati: South-Western Publishing Co., 1994).

- Donaldson, Thomas, *Corporations and Morality* (Englewood Cliffs, NJ: Prentice Hall, 1983).

- Marrella, Len, *In Search of Ethics: Conversations with Men and Women of Character* (Sanford, FL: DC Press, 2001).

- Velasquez, Manuel, *Business Ethics: Concepts and Cases*, 5th ed. (Englewood Cliffs, NJ: Prentice Hall, 2002).

- Velasquez, M., Andre, C., Shanks, S., and Meyer, M., "Thinking Ethically: A Framework for Moral Decision Making," *Issues in Ethics*, Vol. 7, No. 1 (Winter 1996).

The following are examples of nonregulatory ethics dilemmas that could arise in a business, accounting, or tax setting. As shown in these examples, the application of ethics to tax and business situations is not clear-cut. Many times, doing what is "right" may not be possible. The tax practitioner is faced with challenges on how to apply proper business ethics on a daily basis.

Example 1-8 Hilary is a CPA who is a sole practitioner. This year, one of her clients, Gold Corporation, opened a new division in Europe. Gold is a long-time client of Hilary's, and she is anxious to keep it. However, Hilary has no experience in international tax and would not be able to give Gold the kind of tax advice needed for the new division. The ethical question is whether Hilary should inform the client of her lack of knowledge in this area and risk losing the client, or whether she should remain silent and "wing it" on the international tax issues. What should Hilary do in this situation?

Example 1-9 Patrick is a CPA who is a partner in a successful local CPA practice. The state in which Patrick lives has a forty-hour annual continuing professional education (CPE) requirement. If the CPE requirement is not met, a CPA will have his or her license suspended and will not be able to practice. Patrick is approached by the Flight-by-Night CPE Company about signing up for some of their CPE courses. The company representative tells Patrick that they will report that Patrick attended the courses so that he gets the CPE credit, even if he does not attend. Because Patrick is overloaded with work, he considers this a "low hassle" way to get his CPA license renewed. Would it be ethical for Patrick to obtain his CPE credit this way?

Example 1-10 Devona is an auditor in the Boston office of a large international CPA firm. She is sent on an inventory observation for a new client of the Houston office of the firm. The Houston office gives her a six-hour budget for the job. When she arrives at the client's office, Devona discovers that the Houston office has substantially underestimated the size of inventory to be counted. The client has a $20,000,000 inventory comprised of more than 6,000 different items. The client plans to take twenty hours to complete the count. Devona is up for promotion, and she does not want to have a negative personnel review because she overran the budget on this job. Therefore, she considers spending the budgeted six hours on the observation and signing off in the audit work papers that she completely observed the inventory. Devona thinks this would be OK since she perceives there is only a small risk of a material misstatement of the inventory. Would it be ethical for Devona to do this?

Example 1-11 Last year, one of Andy's clients, Trout Corporation, had a significant tax problem. Andy needed thirty-five hours of research time to arrive at an answer to Trout's problem. This year, another of Andy's clients, Bass Corporation, had the same problem. Because of his experience with Trout, Andy could solve Bass's tax problem in three hours. The ethical question is whether Andy should bill Bass for three hours or thirty-five hours of professional consulting time. There are two ways to look at this situation. Andy only spent three hours on the job, so he should only bill for three hours of time. Yet, there is "value" in Andy already knowing the approach to take on the Bass matter, so perhaps he should bill for that knowledge and not just for the actual time spent working on the problem. What should Andy do in this situation?

Example 1-12 Betty is negotiating a transaction on behalf of one of her clients, John Carp. During the process, Betty becomes aware that the other party to the transaction does not adequately understand the tax consequences of the proposed transaction, which are highly favorable to Carp. In fact, if the transaction were completed as proposed, the other side would suffer significant negative tax consequences. Ethically, should Betty inform the other party of the potential negative tax consequences of the proposed transaction?

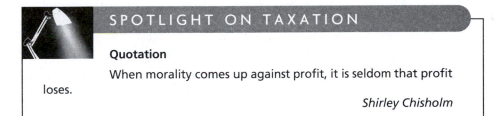

SPOTLIGHT ON TAXATION

Quotation

When morality comes up against profit, it is seldom that profit loses.

Shirley Chisholm

Ethics Training and Education

State Boards of Accountancy are the organizations with the responsibility to license and regulate the practice of public accountancy in each state. Recently, the state boards as a group have increased the ethics training for initial licensing and license renewals in response to highly publicized ethical lapses. A study found that most states had some kind of ethics training requirements for CPA licensing and continuing practice.[7] His findings can be summarized as follows. All states have some form of ethics training to *become* a CPA, but fewer than half (twenty-three states) have an ethics training requirement to *maintain* a CPA license.

Type of Ethics Training Required	Number of States Requiring
Required Course before Taking CPA Exam	32
Ethics Course Must Be Part of a Degree	15
Ethics Exam Taken at Time of CPA Exam	16
Ethics Exam Taken Separately	22
Ethics Required for CPE	23

Some states have multiple ethics training requirements; therefore, the numbers add up to more than fifty.

---

[7]Misiewicz, K., "The Normative Impact of CPA Firms, Professional Organizations, and State Boards on Accounting Ethics Education," *Journal of Business Ethics*, 2006.

TAX RESEARCH BY CERTIFIED PUBLIC ACCOUNTANTS

Over the years, the tax community has addressed the issue of whether the practice of tax law by a CPA or other nonattorney constitutes the **unauthorized practice of law**. The problem stems from the tax law itself, passed in 1913. The provisions of early tax law called for an income tax, but the statute was not specific about the accounting methods to be used in implementing it. In fact, not until 1954 was a formal statutory effort made to address accounting issues in the computation of taxable income. For this reason, many attorneys avoided tax work, allowing CPAs to fill the void and provide taxpayers with most of the professional-quality tax work.

When a CPA resolves an issue in most nonroutine tax situations, he or she is, to some extent, solving a legal problem. The issue is not whether the CPA is rendering legal service but, rather, how much legal service is provided. When does the CPA cross the mythical boundary and begin an unauthorized practice of law? Neither these professions nor the courts have promulgated binding guidelines on this issue. Instead, the Federal agencies seem to have taken the lead in attempting to solve this problem.

Historical Developments

Lowell Bar Association v. Loeb, 315 Mass. 176, S2 N.E.2d 27 (1943), addressed the issue of the unauthorized practice of law by nonattorneys engaged in tax practice. The Lowell Massachusetts Bar Association sued Birdie Loeb, a commercial tax preparer, for her preparation of simple wage-earner tax returns. On appeal, the court held that the preparation of "simple" tax returns did not constitute the unauthorized practice of Massachusetts law because tax return preparation could not be identified as strictly within the legal discipline. Tax practice includes interaction among various disciplines, including law, accounting, economics, political science, and others.

Subsequent courts attempted to adopt the Lowell "wholly within the field of law" test in other jurisdictions, but they found that defining the boundaries of the legal profession was so difficult and the 1943 opinion was so general and vague that the Lowell precedent was of little value in other situations.

Probably the best known case concerning a tax accountant's unauthorized practice of law is *Bercu*, 299 N.Y. 728, 87 N.E.2d 451 (1949). Bercu was an accountant who consulted with a client concerning whether sales taxes that were accrued, but not yet paid, could be deducted on a tax return. The taxpayer who requested this advice was not one of Bercu's regular clients. Bercu advised the client that the sales tax could be deducted when it was paid. Bercu presented a bill to the client and, when it was not paid, sued the client to collect the fees.

Ultimately, the State Court of New York held that it was not proper for Bercu to render services in such a situation. The court indicated that Bercu could have provided this type of service and answered the sales tax question had it been incidental to the tax return work he regularly performed for his clients.

This "incidental to accounting practice" test became the chief issue in several subsequent cases concerning the unauthorized practice of law. In a Minnesota case, *Gardner v. Conway*, 234 Minn. 468, 48 N.W.2d 788 (1951), a person who was neither an attorney nor a CPA attempted to answer difficult and substantial questions of law. The court held that the practitioner improperly gave advice to the client and rejected the "incidental to practice" test as an approach to providing guidelines for the definition of tax practice.

In a California case, *Agran v. Shapiro*, 127 Cal. App.2d Supp. 807, 273 P.2d 619 (1954), CPA Agran prepared returns, performed research, and represented his clients before the IRS. Agran's preparation of Shapiro's return involved extensive research—including more than 100 court cases, Code sections, and Regulations—concerning a question involving the proper treatment of a net operating loss. Upon completion of the work, the CPA presented his bill and, when he was not paid, sued Shapiro to collect. Agran was found by the court to have engaged in the unauthorized practice of law and, therefore, was unable to collect his fees. In its decision, the California Superior Court relied on *Gardner v. Conway* and rejected the "incidental to practice" test that Agran used in his defense. The court did not decide, however, whether the authorization to practice before the IRS preempted the right of the state to regulate tax practice.

In *Sperry v. Florida*, 373 U.S. 379, 83 S.Ct. 1322 (1963), the U.S. Supreme Court held that a Federal statute that admitted nonattorneys to practice before Federal agencies (in this case, the Patent Office) took precedence over state regulation. In late 1965, Congress enacted Public Law 89-332, amending prior law and allowing CPAs to practice before the IRS. Although this law added to the force of the Sperry decision as it applied to CPAs, Sperry still provides for the preemption of Federal regulations and statutes in matters of practice before other Federal agencies.

In 1981, the AICPA and the ABA held a conference for attorneys and CPAs to address some of these definitional questions relative to tax practice and the unauthorized practice of law. The stated purpose of this session was to "promote understanding between the professions in the interests of the client [taxpayers] and the general public." This National Conference of Lawyers and CPAs issued a statement in November 1981, reaffirming that clients [taxpayers] are best served when attorneys and CPAs work together in tax practice. The text of the statement identifies eight areas related to income taxation and three areas related to estate and gift planning in which such professional cooperation should be encouraged. The statement lacks any form of exclusionary language. Indeed, it asserts the following.[8]

> *Frequently, the legal and accounting phases (of tax practice) are so intertwined that they are difficult to distinguish. This is particularly true in the field of income taxation where questions of law and accounting are often inextricably intertwined.*

CPAs and Other Nonattorneys

Currently, CPAs and other nonattorneys who practice tax law before the IRS are in little danger of entering into the unauthorized practice of law provided they avoid providing general legal services. This can be accomplished if CPAs and other nonattorneys do not themselves engage in the following kinds of general law activities.

- Expressing a legal opinion on any nontax matter
- Drafting wills or trust instruments
- Drafting contracts
- Drafting incorporation papers
- Drafting partnership agreements

---

[8]For a complete discussion of this conference statement, see the *Journal of Accountancy* (August 1982).

Taxpayers can draft any of these documents themselves without the services of an attorney. If a CPA's client wishes to handle personal legal affairs in this manner, the CPA (exercising caution) can render professional advice without running afoul of the case law concerning the unauthorized practice of law.

As long as CPAs and other nonattorneys stay within the practice of tax, and do not cross over into the practice of general law, the control exercised by *Circular 230* and the AICPA Code should ensure that virtually all tax compliance, planning, and research activities that are provided by adequately trained nonattorney CPAs constitute the "authorized practice of law."

SUMMARY

In addition to the tax return preparation statutes that are discussed in Chapter 13, CPAs, attorneys, EAs, and others who practice before the IRS are faced with various sets of overlapping rules of conduct. *Circular 230* applies to anyone who practices before the IRS. Members of the legal and public accounting professions are subject to additional codes of ethics and conduct. Similarly, cultural codes of morality and social responsibility form general boundaries relative to acceptable behavior by a taxpayer or tax professional. When engaged in tax practice, one always must be aware of the appropriate rules of conduct and conduct oneself in accordance with those rules.

TAX TUTOR

Reinforce the tax research information covered in this chapter by completing the online tutorials located at the *Federal Tax Research* web site: **http://academic.cengage.com/taxation/raabe**

KEY WORDS

By the time you complete this chapter, you should be comfortable discussing each of the following terms. If you need additional review of any of these items, return to the appropriate material in the chapter or consult the glossary to this text.

Administrative Proceeding
American Bar Association (ABA)
American Institute of Certified Public Accountants
  (AICPA)
Circular 230
Closed Transaction
Contingent Fees
Enrolled Agent (EA)
Ethical Standards
Independence

More-likely-than-not
Open Transactions
Practice Before the IRS
Tax Avoidance
Tax Compliance
Tax Evasion
Tax Litigation
Tax Planning
Tax Research
Unauthorized Practice of Law

DISCUSSION QUESTIONS

1. In a modern, industrial society, the tax system is derived from several disciplines. Identify the disciplines that play this role in the United States. Explain how each of them affects the U.S. tax system.

2. The elements of tax practice fall into what major categories in addition to tax research?

3. What is tax compliance as practiced in the United States? Give several examples of activities that can be classified as tax compliance.

4. Several groups of individuals do most of the tax compliance work in the United States. Identify these groups and describe briefly the kind of work that each group does. In this regard, be sure to define the term "Enrolled Agent."

5. What is tax planning? Explain the difference between tax evasion and tax avoidance, and the role of each in professional tax planning.

6. Tax planning falls into two major categories, the "open" transaction and the "closed" transaction. Discuss each type of transaction, and describe how each affects tax planning.

7. What is tax litigation? What type of tax practitioner typically handles tax litigation on a taxpayer's behalf?

8. In tax litigation, what is usually the role of a Certified Public Accountant?

9. Define tax research. Briefly describe the tax research process.

10. Who issues *Circular 230*? Which tax practitioners are regulated by it?

11. CPAs must follow the rules of *Circular 230*. In addition, CPAs in tax practice are subject to two other sets of ethical rules. Give the name and the issuer of both of these sets of rules.

12. The term "practice before the IRS" includes the representation of clients in the United States Tax Court for cases being handled under the "small tax case procedure." True or false? Explain your answer. (IRS adapted)

13. The rules that govern practice before the IRS are found in *Circular 230*. Discuss what entails practice before the IRS, and state which section of *Circular 230* contains the definition.

14. There are two ways to become an EA. Briefly explain what they are and give the Subpart and section references in *Circular 230* where the details of becoming an EA are found.

15. EAs are subject to Continuing Education (CE) requirements. Briefly describe the CE requirements and give the reference to where the details can be found in *Circular 230*.

16. Leigh, who is not an EA, attorney, or CPA, is employed by Rose, a CPA. One of Rose's clients has been notified that his 2007 income tax return has been selected for audit by the IRS. Rose had prepared the return and signed it as

preparer. Rose has been called out of town on a family emergency and would like for Leigh to represent the client. Leigh cannot represent the client even if she has Rose's written authority to do so and has the client's power of attorney. True or false? Explain your answer. (IRS adapted)

17. Regular full-time employees are allowed to represent certain organizations before the IRS without being an attorney, CPA, or EA. Name the organizations that can be represented by full-time employees, and cite where you found that authority in *Circular 230*.

18. Jane's mother is in a nursing home and cannot travel. There is a problem with her mother's last year's tax return, and the IRS needs to discuss the matter with her at the local IRS office. Is it possible for Jane to handle this matter without having to hire professional tax representation? Reference your answer to the appropriate part of *Circular 230*.

19. A practitioner could be suspended from practice before the IRS if the practitioner employs, accepts assistance from, or shares fees with any person who is under disbarment or suspension from practice before the IRS. True or false? Explain your answer. (IRS adapted)

20. Tax practitioners must not sign a tax return under *Circular 230* if the return takes a position that does not have a "more-likely-than-not" chance of being sustained by the IRS.
    a. What is a more-likely-than-not chance, as defined by the IRS?
    b. Is it possible for a tax practitioner to sign a tax return that takes a position that does not meet the more-likely-than-not standard? If so, what must be done to allow the tax practitioner to sign the tax return?

21. Under *Circular 230*, may an attorney, CPA, or EA advertise on television? On the Internet? If so, what standards are applied to the advertisements?

22. Can a tax practitioner who is a CPA form a CPA partnership with an IRS agent who is also a CPA? What limits (if any) would be placed on such a partnership?

23. If a tax practitioner finds an error in a prior year's tax return, what action must he or she take (if any) under *Circular 230*? What subpart and section addresses this situation?

24. Is a tax practitioner required to adhere to the Best Practices standard under *Circular 230* §10.33? Explain.

25. What are the four Best Practices under *Circular 230* §10.33?

26. Explain the difference between a "reliance opinion" and a "marketed opinion" under *Circular 230* §10.35. How does *Circular 230* §10.36 apply the Covered Opinion requirement of §10.35?

27. A practitioner cannot give written advice under *Circular 230* §10.37 in what situations?

28. Practicing CPAs generally are subject to the AICPA Code of Professional Conduct. What is its stated purpose?

29. The rules under the AICPA Code of Professional Conduct are enforceable ethical standards. Broad in nature, they generally apply to all of the services that are performed by a CPA who is an AICPA member. Identify the two situations in which the application of the rules may be limited.

30. In what situation may a CPA under the AICPA Code of Professional Conduct accept a commission?

31. Under Rule 101 (Independence), a CPA (or CPA firm) in public practice must be independent of the enterprise for which professional services are being provided. Discuss situations in which the CPA's independence may be impaired.

32. Under Rule 102 (Integrity and Objectivity), a CPA who is engaged in tax practice may resolve a doubtful area in favor of his or her client. Explain.

33. A CPA must meet certain qualitative standards under Rule 201 (General Standards). Discuss the four general standards of this rule.

34. In each of the following independent situations, state which AICPA Code of Professional Conduct (if any) is violated by a CPA in public practice.
    a. The CPA opens a tax practice and names the new firm "Jill's Super Tax."
    b. In return for recommending a certain investment to an audit client, a CPA receives a 5 percent commission from the broker who sells the investments.
    c. A taxpayer is being assessed by the IRS for an additional $100,000 of tax. The CPA offers to represent the taxpayer for a fee that is equal to 25 percent of any amount by which he can get the IRS to reduce its assessment.
    d. A CPA places an advertisement in the local newspaper that states that she is the "Best CPA in the Western World." The advertisement further states that, because of her great skill, the CPA has considerable influence with the IRS and the United States Tax Court.
    e. A CPA partnership has eight partners, six of whom are members of the AICPA. On its letterhead, the firm designates itself as "Members of the AICPA."
    f. A CPA who is not in public practice is convicted of helping to run a large illegal drug operation.

35. Under Rule 301 of the AICPA Code of Professional Conduct, a CPA must not disclose confidential client data without the specific consent of the client. Under what conditions might a disclosure of confidential information without the client's consent be appropriate?

36. What are the SSTS? Who issues them? Discuss their principal objectives.

37. What guidelines does SSTS No. 1 provide for a tax practitioner regarding tax return positions?

38. According to SSTS No. 2, a tax return should be signed by a member only after reasonable effort has been made to answer all of the questions on the return that apply to the taxpayer. What are some of the reasonable grounds under which a member may sign a return as the preparer even though some of the pertinent questions remain unanswered?

39. What guidelines are provided by SSTS No. 3 as to the reliance by a member on information supplied by the taxpayer for use in preparing the taxpayer's return?

40. A member may use estimates in completing a tax return according to SSTS No. 4. When might the use of estimates be considered appropriate?

41. Last year a taxpayer was audited by the IRS and an item of deduction on the tax return was disallowed. On this year's tax return, the taxpayer would like to deduct a similar item. Discuss the circumstances under which a member may allow the taxpayer to take the deduction on the current year's return and still be in compliance with SSTS No. 5. Under what conditions must special disclosure be made by the member?

42. When a member learns of an error in a previously filed tax return or learns of an error during an audit, how is he or she to respond and still be in compliance with SSTS No. 6 and No. 7?

43. What situations are addressed by SSTS No. 8?

44. The Sarbanes-Oxley Act prohibits CPA firms from providing certain services to publicly traded corporate audit clients. Is doing tax compliance work for an audit client one of the prohibited transactions? If such tax work is allowed, who must approve it?

45. Differentiate between the ABA Model Code of Professional Responsibility and that organization's Model Rules of Professional Conduct.

46. Who sets ethical rules for attorneys in the various states?

47. What is an Ethical Dilemma?

48. The text discusses three types of ethical reasoning. Identify them and give a short description of each.

49. Ethical professional behavior is the interaction of several standards. Identify these standards and briefly describe each.

50. How does the term "the unauthorized practice of law" apply to CPAs?

51. List several services or products that a CPA or EA purposely should not make a part of a tax practice, so as to minimize exposure to a charge of the unauthorized practice of law.

EXERCISES

52. Summarize what is discussed in each of the following sections of *Circular 230*.
    a. Subpart A, §10.4(b)
    b. Subpart B, §10.21
    c. Subpart B, §10.26
    d. Subpart B, §10.32

53. Summarize what is discussed in each of the following sections of *Circular 230*.
    a. Subpart C, §10.51(b)
    b. Subpart A, §10.6(e)
    c. Subpart A, §10.2(e)
    d. Subpart B, §10.27

54. Summarize what is discussed in each of the following sections of *Circular 230*.
    a. Subpart A, §10.2(e)
    b. Subpart A, §10.7(c)(viii)
    c. Subpart B, §10.24
    d. Subpart B, §10.34

55. Summarize what is discussed in each of the following sections of *Circular 230*.
    a. Subpart B, §10.33
    b. Subpart B, §10.35
    c. Subpart B, §10.36
    d. Subpart B, §10.37

56. Which subpart and section of *Circular 230* discusses each the following topics?
    a. Solicitation
    b. Negotiation of a taxpayer's refund checks
    c. Depositions
    d. Authority to disbar or suspend from practice before the IRS

57. Which subpart and section of *Circular 230* discusses each the following topics?
    a. Conflicting interests
    b. Tax shelter opinions
    c. Disreputable conduct
    d. Assistance from disbarred or suspended persons

58. Which subpart and section of *Circular 230* discusses each of the following topics?
    a. Practice of law
    b. Information to be furnished
    c. Fees
    d. Who may practice before the IRS?

59. Which subpart and section of *Circular 230* discusses each of the following topics?
    a. Best Practices
    b. Covered Opinions
    c. Tax Return Positions
    d. Due Diligence

60. Summarize what is discussed in each of the following rules of the AICPA Code of Professional Conduct. Give a simple example of a transaction or an action relevant to each rule.
    a. Article VI, ¶ para 1
    b. Rule 201, ¶ .02 201-1
    c. Rule 502, ¶ .03 502-2
    d. Rule 504, ¶ .01

61. Summarize what is discussed in each of the following SSTS.
    a. SSTS No. 1
    b. SSTS No. 4
    c. SSTS No. 6

62. What is the precedent-setting value of each of the following cases?
    a. *Lowell Bar Association v. Loeb*

      b. *Bercu*

      c. *Sperry v. Florida*

63. Ms. E is an EA who prepared the tax returns for Mr. A and Mr. B (buyer and seller, respectively). Ms. E may not, under any circumstances, represent A and B before the IRS with regard to this buy and sell transaction. True or false? Explain your answer. (IRS adapted)

64. A full-time employee of a sole proprietorship may represent his or her employer in an examination by the IRS without being an EA, attorney, or CPA. True or false? Explain your answer. (IRS adapted)

65. An unenrolled tax preparer who has not prepared the tax return of John Gomez may represent John before an IRS revenue agent in the conduct of an examination, provided that the unenrolled tax preparer has written authorization from John. True or false? Explain your answer. (IRS adapted)

66. EAs, attorneys, and CPAs shall exercise due diligence in preparing or assisting in the preparation of documents and other papers relating to IRS matters. True or false? Explain your answer. (IRS adapted)

67. Which of the following statements may not be used when an EA advertises? Explain your answer. (IRS adapted)
    a. Name, address, and office hours
    b. Names of associates of the firm
    c. Claims of quality of service that cannot be verified
    d. Membership in professional organizations

68. The IRS Director of Practice may take into consideration a petition for reinstatement from any person disbarred from practice before the IRS after a period of how many years? Explain your answer. (IRS adapted)
    a. Never
    b. 2 years
    c. 3 years
    d. 5 years

69. Inclusion of which of the following statements in a CPA's advertisement is unacceptable under the AICPA Code of Professional Conduct? Explain your answer.
    a. Julie Adams, CPA, Fluency in Spanish and French
    b. Julie Adams, CPA, MBA, Big State University, 2005
    c. Julie Adams, CPA, Free Initial Consultation
    d. Julie Adams, CPA, I Always Win IRS Audits

70. Which of the following situations would most likely result in a violation of the practitioner's ethical standards? Explain your answer.
    a. A CPA is controller of a bank and grants permission to the bank to use his "CPA" title in the listing of the bank officers in the bank's publications.
    b. A CPA who is also a member of the bar represents on her letterhead that she is both an attorney and a CPA.
    c. A CPA, the sole shareholder in a professional accountancy corporation, uses the term "and company" in his firm's title.
    d. A CPA who writes a newsletter on financial management topics grants permission to the publisher to solicit subscriptions.

71. Which of the following situations would provide an acceptable case for using a taxpayer's estimated figure in the preparation of a Federal income tax return? Explain your answer.
    a. The taxpayer has the necessary data available, but is busy with a pressing public offering and has not had the time to look through her records for the information.
    b. The data are not available at the time of filing the return, and the estimated amounts appear reasonable to the CPA.
    c. The taxpayer has the data available at the time for filing the return but feels that the data do not fairly represent the results of her business operation and therefore desires to use an "estimate."
    d. The taxpayer, relying on the income tax regulations that allow the use of reasonable estimates under certain circumstances, desires to use an estimate to determine the amount of his deduction for entertainment expenses.

72. According to the AICPA Code of Professional Conduct, CPAs in tax practice who are representing a taxpayer in a formal controversy with the government are permitted to receive contingent fees because:
    a. this practice establishes fees that are commensurate with the value of the services rendered.
    b. attorneys who are in tax practice customarily set contingent fees.
    c. determinations by tax authorities are a matter of judicial proceedings that do not involve third parties.
    d. the consequences are based on the findings of judicial proceedings or the findings of a government agency.
    Explain your answer.

73. The AICPA Code of Professional Conduct states that a CPA shall not disclose any confidential information in the course of a professional engagement, except with the consent of the client. This rule should be understood to preclude a CPA from responding to an inquiry that is received from:
    a. an investigative body of a state CPA society.
    b. the Trial Board of the AICPA.
    c. a CPA-shareholder of the taxpayer corporation.
    d. an AICPA voluntary quality review body.
    Explain your answer.

74. A taxpayer's records are destroyed by fire. A CPA prepares the tax return based on estimates and other indirect information she has obtained. Under the SSTS, she should:
    a. disclose the use of estimates to the IRS.
    b. not disclose the use of estimates to the IRS.
    c. charge the taxpayer a double fee.
    d. not prepare a return based on estimates.
    e. have an attorney prepare the return.
    Explain your answer.

75. With regard to the categories of individuals who may practice before the IRS under *Circular 230*, which of the following statements is correct? Explain your answer. (IRS adapted)
    a. Only EAs, attorneys, or CPAs may represent trusts and estates before any officer or employee of the IRS.

b. An individual who is not an EA, attorney, or CPA and who signs a return as having prepared it for the taxpayer may, with proper authorization from the taxpayer, appear as the taxpayer's representative, with or without the taxpayer, at an IRS Appeals Office conference with respect to the tax liability of the taxpayer for the taxable year or period covered by the return.

c. Under the limited practice provision in *Circular 230*, only general partners may represent a partnership.

d. Under the limited practice provision in *Circular 230*, an individual who is under suspension or disbarment from practice before the IRS may not engage in limited practice before the IRS.

76. If an EA, attorney, or CPA knows that a client has not complied with the revenue laws of the United States with respect to a matter administered by the IRS, the EA, attorney, or CPA is required under *Circular 230* to:
    a. do nothing until advised by the client to take corrective action.
    b. advise the client of the noncompliance.
    c. immediately notify the IRS.
    d. advise the client and notify the IRS.
    Explain your answer. (IRS adapted)

77. Answer each of the following questions.
    a. What is found in Subpart A, §10.7(a) of *Circular 230*?
    b. In *Circular 230*, where are the rules on tax shelter opinions found?
    c. Describe the requirements of Rule 301 of the AICPA Code of Conduct.
    d. Which SSTS discusses the use of estimates in preparing a tax return?
    e. Under SSTS No. 1, a member must have a good-faith belief that a recommended position has a _____ chance of being sustained if challenged. (Fill in the blank.)

78. Answer each of the following questions.
    a. What is found in Subpart C, §10.51 of *Circular 230*?
    b. In *Circular 230*, where are the rules on knowledge of client omissions found?
    c. Describe the requirements of Rule 503 of the AICPA Code of Conduct.
    d. Which SSTS discusses the requirements for verifying a tax client's information?
    e. Under SSTS No. 8, a member must use judgment that reflects and serves the taxpayer's needs. (Fill in the blank.)

79. The exam to become an EA has four parts. Go to the IRS web site (**http://www.irs.gov**) and determine what is tested on each part of the exam. Describe the content of each part.

80. Go to the NAEA web site (**http://www.naea.org**). Who is the current president of the NAEA and in what city is the headquarters located?

81. Go the AICPA web site (**http://www.aicpa.org**). Find SSTS No. 2 and print out the complete statement.

82. Go to the IRS web site (**http://www.irs.gov**). What is the form number of the Application for Enrollment to Practice before the IRS? Print out a copy of the form to hand in.

83. Go to (the IRS web site (**http://www.irs.gov**). Do a publications search and find the most recent *Circular 230*. Print out the title page of the *Circular 230* you found to hand in.

84. Many states have an ethics education requirement to become a CPA. Determine your home state's ethical education requirements to become a CPA. If your state does not have an ethics requirement, state so.

RESEARCH CASES

85. Professor Andy Accrual works for a big state university. The state has negotiated a set of special airfares with various airlines for state employees to use when traveling on state business. These fares are lower, and they do not have restrictions on changing, cancellation, etc. Andy is aware that the airlines never check to see if he is on state business when he books such a fare. He has decided that he would like to go to Hawaii on short notice for a well-earned mini-vacation. When he checks the web for airfares he discovers that the cheapest fare he can find is $700 per person. However, the fare for state employees for traveling on business to Hawaii is only $400. Although he is traveling for personal reasons, in your opinion is it ethical to use the special state employee airfare for his vacation? Would this qualify as an ethical dilemma?

86. Donna Deduction is a staff accountant for Dewey, Cheatham, and Howe, LLP. She and other staff raid the office supply cabinet for office supplies to take home to use. In addition to the standard paper, pens, paper clips, etc., the staff takes home inkjet cartridges and other high-cost supplies. During the year Donna takes home supplies worth over $500. In your opinion is this ethical behavior? If Donna does a significant amount of work for the firm at home, would your opinion change?

87. You are a CPA in practice who has just obtained a new client. Another CPA did the tax returns for the prior three years. The client has operated his business as an S corporation during the three-year period. After starting work on this year's tax return, you notice that the S corporation has an October 31 fiscal year-end. After examining the file, you discover that three years ago, when the S corporation adopted the fiscal tax year, a §444 election was not made. In addition, the S corporation has not maintained the proper required "minimum deposit account" with the IRS.

    The client wants your advice on what to do now. You determine that there are three options: (1) you can do nothing and hope the IRS doesn't find out, (2) you can notify the IRS of the mistake and pay any interest and penalties, or (3) you can elect a calendar year and hope the IRS doesn't notice the current invalid fiscal year. What potential nonregulatory ethical issues do you see in this situation that could influence your decision on any recommendation?

88. You are a CPA in practice and have a long-term client who is involved in a nasty divorce proceeding with her husband. The client has assets she deposited in a bank account in the Grand Cayman Islands. There is U.S.-taxable interest on the deposits. Because she does not want her husband to know about the deposits, she asks you to report the interest on her tax return in such a way that it

will not "tip off" her husband to the existence of the account. You can handle this request by reporting the interest through Schedule C (instead of Schedule B) on her tax return and thus avoid making the source of the income known. What potential nonregulatory ethics issues do you see in this situation?

89. Ahi Corporation is one of your clients in Hawaii. The company had a good year last year and owes the IRS $100,000,000, due on March 15. There are no penalties or interest due to the IRS. One of Ahi's employees approaches you with the following plan to benefit from the so-called "float" on the large payment due to the government. First, Ahi Corp. will courier its tax return and payment to the U.S. Virgin Islands. There, the tax return will be mailed to the IRS Service Center in Fresno by certified mail on the return's due date, March 15. By doing this, the employee thinks it will take at least six days for the tax return to reach the IRS and for them to cash the $100,000,000 check. Ahi can earn 7 percent after tax on its money, so the interest earned during these six days because of the float is $19,178 per day [($100,000,000 × .07/365 days]. Thus, the total interest earned on the float for six days would be $115,068 ($19,178 × 6 days).

    a. Would you recommend Ahi complete this transaction?
    b. What potential ethics issues do you see in this situation?

90. John Haddock owns 75 percent of Haddock Corporation. The other 25 percent of the stock is held by John's wife, Marsha. You are a tax manager assigned to prepare the corporate tax return for Haddock. While working on the return, you note that Haddock Corp. pays rent to John for a building he owns with his son, John, Jr. The rent being paid is at least three times the normal rate for rentals of similar property in that area of town. You report this observation to the partner on the engagement. She tells you that it is alright to deduct the payments because Haddock Corp. has been doing it for several years, and the IRS never has objected. Under your firm's policy, managers sign the tax return for clients.

    a. Would you sign this tax return?
    b. What potential ethics issues do you see in this situation?

91. You are negotiating a transaction for your client, Shark Corporation. Parties on the other side of the deal ask you for information about the structural stability of a building, which is a significant part of the transaction. Coleman, Shark's tax director, tells you to say "everything is OK," when, in reality, the building has substantial hidden damage. Coleman tells you to say this because it would be more favorable to Shark's position in the transaction.

    a. How would you respond to Coleman's request?
    b. What if you have already told the other side that the building is OK when you learn about the problems?
    c. What other potential ethics issues do you see in this situation?

92. Big CPA Firm has many partners in one of its local offices. Two of these partners are Tom, a tax partner, and Alice, an audit partner. Because of the size of the office, Tom and Alice do not know each other very well.
    Tom has a tax client, Anchovy Corporation, that is in severe financial trouble and may have to file for bankruptcy. Anchovy is a customer of Sardine Corporation, one of Alice's audit clients. Accounts receivable on Sardine's books from Anchovy are significant. If Anchovy goes bankrupt, it could cause serious

problems for Sardine. Alice is unaware of the bad financial condition of Anchovy.

a. Can Tom disclose to Alice the problems at Anchovy?

b. What if Anchovy goes under and takes Sardine with it?

c. What potential ethics issues do you see in this situation?

93. You are the tax manager in a CPA office. One of your clients, Snapper Corporation, is also an audit client of the firm. The CFO of Snapper invites you and the audit manager for a one-week deep-sea fishing trip to Mexico, all expenses to be paid by Snapper. The audit manager says that you both should go and just not tell your supervisor at the CPA firm any details (like who paid the expenses) about the trip.

a. Would you go on the trip?

b. Would you tell your supervisors at the CPA firm if the audit manager went on the trip without you?

c. What other potential ethics issues do you see in this situation?

94. Clara comes to an attorney's office in need of assistance with her husband's estate. Her husband, Phil, a factory worker, had been a saver all his life and owned approximately $1,500,000 in stocks and bonds. Clara is relatively unsophisticated in financial matters, so the attorney agrees to handle the estate for 17 percent of the value of the estate. The normal charge for such work is 3–5 percent of the estate. The widow agrees to the 17 percent arrangement. The attorney then hires CPA Charles for $10,000 to compute Phil's estate tax on Form 706 and to prepare other appropriate documents.

a. Does Charles have any responsibility to inform the widow that she is being significantly overcharged by the attorney?

b. What potential ethics issues do you see in this situation?

95. Darlene works for Big CPA Firm. When she was being interviewed, Darlene was told by a partner in the firm that she was not to underreport her time spent on various engagements. However, after working for a few months, she discovers that everyone in her office "eats time." Because she is not eating time like everyone else, Darlene is always over budget. She is beginning to get a reputation as a "budget buster." As a result, none of the senior tax staff wants her on their engagements. She is getting the worst clients and bad reviews from the people for whom she works. It appears that unless she starts eating time, Darlene's future with the firm is limited.

a. What would you recommend Darlene do?

b. What potential ethics issues do you see in this situation?

96. Freya is an accountant working on the tax return of a high-tech client. After reviewing the work papers, she discovers that there is a pattern of double billing the U.S. Navy for various projects done by the tax client. She brings this to the attention of her manager on the job, and he tells her that it is not the CPA firm's business what the client does since this is not an audit engagement.

a. What would you recommend Freya do at this point?

b. What potential ethics issues do you see in this situation?

97. Jenny is an accountant for an international energy corporation. She oversees the accounting for certain associated offshore entities. The amount of funds involved in the entities is substantial. At the end of the year she notices that the

accounting information from the offshore entities is not included in the consolidated financial statements of the corporation, but is reported on the consolidated tax return. She inquires about this and she is told that the corporation does not report the financial information from the offshore entities since it would lower the earnings of the main corporation. Jenny is sure that this is not the proper accounting and tax treatment for the entities.
a. What would you recommend Jenny do at this point?
b. What potential ethics issues do you see in this situation?

98. Eric is a tax manager for a national CPA firm that audits Penny-Pinching Bank (PPB). Eric and his staff prepare and review the tax return for PPB. One day, at an alumni football tailgate party, he meets another alumnus who Eric discovers is on the Audit Committee of PPB. The Audit Committee member/alumni was unaware that Eric's CPA firm is doing PPC's tax return.
a. What would you recommend Eric do at this point?
b. What potential ethical and practice issues do you see in this situation?

99. Dodger Corporation has been in the manufacturing business in the United States for over 100 years. A tax consultant has proposed that Dodger use a "corporate inversion" to nominally move its headquarters to an island in the Atlantic Ocean. The operating headquarters will remain in the United States, along with all of its employees, its plant and equipment, and most of its customers. By undertaking this corporate inversion and technically moving its headquarters offshore, Dodger can defer or avoid paying U.S. corporate income tax. However, for all practical purposes, it remains a U.S.-based company.
a. What would you recommend Dodger do about the proposed corporate inversion?
b. What potential ethics issues do you see in this situation?

Tax Research Methodology

Chapter Outline

Learning Objectives

- Recognize the importance of a systematic approach to tax research.

- Delineate and elaborate on the steps of the tax research process.

- Appreciate the importance of gathering pertinent facts and identifying research issues.

- Discuss the sources of the Federal tax law.

- Identify how computer resources affect the conduct of tax research.

Tax research is the process undertaken to answer taxation questions relevant to the researcher's needs. The tax research process is a multistep process, which includes an algorithm discussed in this chapter. The tax researcher should become efficient at tax research since these professional services can be very expensive for the client, or the time spent on research can take away valuable time that could be used for other activities of the tax practitioner. Unnecessary time spent doing tax research could be used by the tax practitioner to produce additional tax revenue, or to give him or her additional personal time for other activities.

SPOTLIGHT ON TAXATION

The Complexity of Taxation

The complexity of the tax system (and thus tax research) can be shown in a quote related from Pam Olson, the Treasury's Assistant Secretary for Tax Policy. When speaking to a group of tax specialists, she quoted an e-mail sent to her by a tax attorney, who said:

It is difficult to predict the future of an economy in which it takes more brains to figure out the tax on our income than it does to earn it.

The tax research process is similar to that of traditional legal research. The researcher must find authority, evaluate the usefulness of that authority, and apply the results of the research to a specific situation. One can identify two essential tax research skills. The first is the ability to use certain mechanical techniques to identify and locate the tax authorities that relate to solving a problem. The second entails a combination of reasoning and creativity and is more difficult to learn. A tax researcher must begin with native intelligence and imagination and add training and experience properly to apply the information found. Creativity is necessary to explore the relevant relationships among the circumstances and problems at hand to find a satisfying (and defensible) solution. In many cases, no legal authority will exist that is directly on point for the problem. If such a situation exists, the researcher must combine seemingly unrelated facts, ideas (including those that he or she has derived from previous research work), and legal authority to arrive at a truly novel conclusion. This creative ability of the researcher often spells the difference between success and failure in the research process.

Outline of the Tax Research Process

As the tax problems of the client become more significant, the related tax research can become time consuming and thus expensive to the client. A moderate tax research problem often takes up to eight or ten hours of research time, and the bill for these services may approach or even exceed $5,000. Because of the costs that are involved, the tax researcher must work as efficiently as possible to obtain the solution to the client's problem. The researcher needs a framework for the research process, so that he or she does not waste time and effort in arriving at a solution to the problem.

The tax research process can be broken down into six major steps (Exhibit 2-1). Tax researchers (especially those without a substantial amount of experience at the task) must approach the resolution of a tax problem in a structured manner, so that the analysis of the problem will be thorough and the solution complete.

Exhibit 2-1: Steps in the Tax Research Process

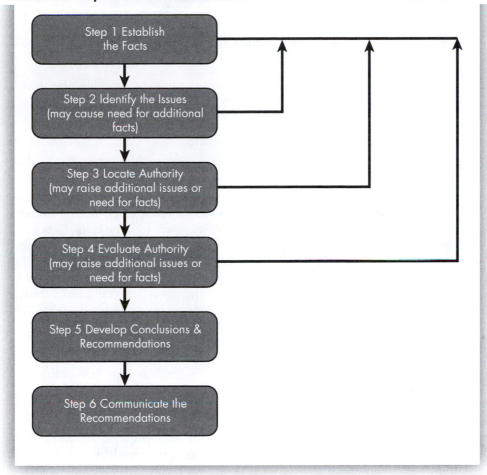

Step 1: Establish the Facts

All tax research begins with an evaluation of the client's factual situation. To find the solution to a problem, the researcher must understand fully all of the facts that could affect the related tax outcome. Many beginning tax researchers make the mistake of attempting to research a problem before they completely understand all of the relevant facts and circumstances.

Moreover, a tax researcher may approach the tax research process so rigidly that he or she ignores new factual questions that arise during the other steps of the research task. The tax researcher may engage in several rounds of fact gathering, including those necessitated by additional tax questions that arise as he or she is searching for or evaluating pertinent tax authority. These research "feedback loops" are not endless, although they might seem to be. The best tax researcher is one who can balance the need for efficiency against the need for thoroughness.

Significant tax facts that often influence the client's situation include:

- the client's tax entity, for example, individual, corporation, trust;
- the client's family status and stability;
- the client's past, present, and projected marginal tax rates;

- the client's place of legal domicile and citizenship;

- the client's motivation for the transaction;

- relationships among the client and other parties who are involved in the transaction;

- whether special tax rules apply to the taxpayer due to the type of business in which the taxpayer is engaged (he or she is a farmer, fisherman, or long-term contractor); and,

- whether the transaction is proposed or completed.

Fact gathering can present many practical problems for the researcher. Often, the client will (wittingly or not) omit information that is vital to a solution. He or she may not believe that the information is important or may have personal reasons for not conveying the information to the practitioner. In such cases, the researcher must persist until all of the available information is known. In some cases, facts that initially appear to be irrelevant may prove to be important as the research project progresses. The researcher, therefore, should pay attention to and record all details that the client discloses. Efficient tax research cannot be completed until the factual situation is clear; without all of the facts at hand, the researcher could make costly false starts that, when additional pertinent facts become known, must be discarded or redone, often at the client's (or, worse, at the researcher's) expense.

In gathering facts relative to a research problem, the researcher also must be aware of the nontax considerations that are pertinent to the client's situation. For example, the client may have economic constraints (such as cash flow problems) that could preclude the implementation of certain solutions. In addition, the client may have personal preferences that will not accommodate the best tax solution to the problem. For instance, assume that the client could reduce his own income and estate tax liability by making a series of gifts to his grandchildren. However, because the client does not trust the financial judgment of the grandchildren, he does not want to make any such gifts to them during his lifetime. Accordingly, the researcher must look for alternative methods by which to reduce the client's total family tax burden.

Step 2: Identify the Issues

A combination of education, training, and experience is necessary to enable the researcher to identify successfully all of the issues with respect to a tax problem. In some situations, this step can be the most difficult element of a tax research problem.

Issues in a closed-fact tax research problem often arise from a conflict with the IRS. In such a case, one can easily ascertain the issue(s). Research of this nature usually consists of finding support for an action that the client has already taken.

In most research projects, however, the researcher must develop the list of issues. Research issues can be divided into two major categories, namely, fact issues and law issues. **Fact issues** are concerned with information having an objective reality, such as the dates of transactions, the amounts involved in an exchange, reasonableness, intent, and purpose. **Law issues** arise when the facts are well established, but it is not clear which portion of the tax law applies to the issue. The application of the law might not be clear because of an apparent conflict among code sections, because a genuine uncertainty as to the meaning of a term as used in the *Internal Revenue Code* may exist, or because there are no provisions in the law that deal directly with the transaction at hand.

When undertaking a research project where the issue may end up being challenged in court, the researcher must be sure to address all of the issues in the tax return. The legal concept of *collateral estoppel* bars relitigation on the same facts or the same issues. Therefore, the practitioner must make sure that his or her case is researched fully, and that no issues that could be resolved in the client's favor have been overlooked. If such an issue is not addressed in the original case, it may be lost forever.

In many situations, a research project may encompass several tax years. The researcher must be aware of any fact or law changes that occur during the period that might affect the results of the research project. The pertinent facts or law may be subject to changes that will cause the researcher to arrive at different conclusions and recommendations, depending on the tax year involved. Seemingly simple situations can often generate many tax research issues. In the process of identifying tax issues, the researcher might discover that additional facts are necessary to provide sufficient answers for the new questions. The taxpayer in the following example is used to illustrate the potential for complexities in merely identifying tax research issues.

> **Example 2-1** The KML Medical Group of Houston would like to hire a new physician from Atlanta. However, the new physician owns a home in Georgia on which she will sustain a loss if it is sold in the current housing market. KML approached the Happy Care Hospital, the institution at which the group practices, and asked whether they would reimburse the new physician for the loss to facilitate her move to Texas. The hospital agreed to reimburse the physician this year for her $20,000 realized loss.

A tax researcher might address or clarify at least the following issues in making recommendations concerning tax treatment of the reimbursement.

- Why did the hospital reimburse the physician?

- Is there any parent-subsidiary relationship between the hospital and the KML Medical Group?

- Do any members of the KML Medical Group have an equity or debt interest in the hospital?

- Does the reimbursement constitute gross income to the physician?

- If the reimbursement does constitute gross income to the physician, is it treated as active, passive, or investment income?

- Is the new physician classified as an employee of the hospital?

- Should the hospital report the payment to the physician on a Form 1099 or W-2?

- Should the hospital withhold any income or FICA tax on the reimbursement?

- Can the hospital deduct the reimbursement as a trade or business expense?

- Should the physician consider the reimbursement and/or the loss on the sale of her residence in computing her moving expense deduction?

- If the reimbursement is considered gross income to the physician, when should the amount be included in the physician's income?

- Is the reimbursement subject to any restrictions such as the physician's continued employment? For how long?

- Is the reimbursement to the physician considered an additional amount realized on the sale of her residence?

- Can the reimbursement be considered a gift from the hospital to the physician?

Imagine how the question concerning whether the physician's gross income (if any) was ordinary income might lead to further questions concerning her potential employee status, income tax and FICA withholding, and reporting issues.

Tax Research as an Iterative Process The process of tax research is iterative in the sense that, once an answer is found, it often causes a new issue to appear and thus requires the gathering of more information. In other words, the tax research process is not strictly linear. This relationship between facts, issues, and answers is illustrated in Exhibit 2-2. The tax research process requires *mechanical skills* and *critical thinking*. Mechanical techniques are gained and sharpened through both knowledge and experience. *Knowledge* is usually gained through education in universities and other formal class work. *Experience* is obtained through working in the field and dealing with real tax problems on a recurring basis. Critical thinking is the hardest skill for the researcher to develop. To some extent, it depends on native ability, but a person can be taught the elements of logical analysis and can learn to watch for common pitfalls in evaluating information. Being able to analyze and solve a problem is something the tax researcher must master if he or she is to earn a living in this field. Knowledge is useless when it cannot be applied to solve the problem at hand. The following example illustrates how both mechanical skills and critical thinking are used to solve a tax research problem.

Exhibit 2-2: Interaction among Research Facts, Issues, and Solutions

Example 2-2 This year, Chris Lee, a client of your CPA firm, sold stock in Slippery Bank (a publicly traded company with a limited market) to Kolpin Corporation for $100,000. Chris has records that show the stock was acquired ten years ago and has a basis of $135,000. He personally owns 30 percent of Kolpin Corporation. At first glance, the tax researcher would conclude that Chris would have a capital loss of $35,000, which would be deductible against his current-year long-term capital gains of $50,000. This situation appears to be very straightforward. The problem could become complex, though, if someone at the CPA firm asked questions about the other owners of Kolpin. What if Chris's wife, Judy Lee, owns Kolpin stock? The researcher must back up in the research process and gather more facts to determine how many shares she owns.

Suppose Judy Lee owns 25 percent of the Kolpin stock. Now the tax practitioner (you) is faced with new facts and issues; §267 of the *Internal Revenue Code* suggests that the loss might be disallowed. By looking at §267(b)(2), you would find that losses between an individual and a corporation are disallowed if "more than 50 percent in value of the outstanding stock of which is owned directly or indirectly, by or for such individual." You then need to know what "indirect ownership" is. Looking further in the Code, you would find in §267(c), "An individual shall be considered as owning the stock owned, directly or indirectly, by or for his family." Finally, in §267(c)(4), you would discover, "The family of an individual shall include only his brother and sisters (whether by whole or half blood), spouse, ancestors, and lineal descendants."

Armed with this new information, it becomes clear that Chris is a related party to Kolpin Corporation within the meaning of §267. He owns more than 50 percent of the stock, 30 percent directly and 25 percent indirectly through his wife. As a result, the $35,000 capital loss is not allowed to Chris, and he cannot use it to offset his other capital gains.

Step 3: Locate Authority

Once facts have been gathered and the issues defined, the tax researcher must locate legal authority that relates to the issue(s). Authority comes from many sources, including Congress, the courts, and the IRS. Since the inception of the 1913 tax law, several hundred thousand pages of such authority have been produced. To solve a given problem, the researcher must find the appropriate authority in this massive amount of information.

In general, tax authority can be classified as either primary or secondary authority. **Primary authority** is an original pronouncement that comes from statutory, administrative, and judicial sources. **Statutory sources** include the U.S. Constitution, tax treaties, and tax laws passed by Congress. Statutory authority is the basis for all tax provisions. The Constitution grants Congress the power to impose and collect taxes, and authorizes the creation of treaties with other countries. The power of Congress to implement and collect taxes is summarized in the *Internal Revenue Code*, the official title of U.S. tax law. The *Internal Revenue Code* constitutes the basis for all tax law and, therefore, the basis for arriving at solutions to all tax questions.

The other primary sources of the tax law, administrative and judicial authority, function primarily to interpret and explain the application of the provisions of the *Internal Revenue Code* and the intent of Congress. **Administrative sources** include the various rulings of the Treasury Department and the IRS. These are issued in the form of Regulations, Revenue Rulings, and other pronouncements. **Judicial**

sources consist of the collected rulings of the various courts on Federal tax matters. The primary sources of the tax law will be discussed in detail in Chapters 3, 4, and 5. **Secondary authority** consists of interpretations of primary authority and is an unofficial source of tax information. Examples of secondary authority include tax services, journals, textbooks and treatises, and newsletters. The distinction between primary and secondary sources of authority has become more important since the enactment of §6662, which imposes a penalty on substantial understatements of tax, except where the taxpayer has "substantial authority" for the position taken on the return. The regulations under §6662 specify the sources of "substantial authority" to include the provisions of the *Internal Revenue Code*, temporary and final Regulations, court cases, administrative pronouncements, tax treaties, and congressional intent as reflected in committee reports. This list also includes Proposed Regulations, Private Letter Rulings, Technical Advice Memoranda, Actions on Decisions, General Counsel Memoranda, Information or Press Releases, Notices, and any other similar documents published by the IRS in the *Internal Revenue Bulletin*. Treatises and articles in legal periodicals, however, are not considered substantial authority under this statute.

Secondary authority is useful when conflicting primary authority exists, when there appears to be no extant primary authority, or when the researcher needs an explanation or clarification of the primary authority. During the past fifteen years, as the support staff of government agencies and (especially) federal courts have decreased in number or otherwise become inadequate, more dependence has been placed on the secondary authorities of the tax law, even by the IRS, the Treasury Department, and the court system. The beginning researcher must be careful, though, not to rely too heavily on secondary authority, and always to read any pertinent primary authority that is referred to in the secondary sources.

Because of the vast amount of tax authority that is available, the tax researcher would have a tremendous problem in undertaking a tax research problem for a client if it were not for commercial **tax services** and treatises. Several publishers have produced coordinated sets of reference materials that organize the tax authority into a usable format, making the *Internal Revenue Code* much more accessible. These commercial tax services are useful in that they often provide simplified explanations with footnote citations, as well as examples illustrating the application of the law. These tax services may lead the tax researcher, via the footnote references, to the primary source that is pertinent to the question at hand.

Traditionally, tax services have been classified as either annotated or topical. The annotated services are organized in *Internal Revenue Code* section order, while the topical services are arranged by topic, as defined by the publisher's editorial staff. However, the use of computers has significantly blurred the differences between the organization of commercial tax services. With hypertext linking, any of the tax services can be used from a Code or topical orientation. Exhibit 2-3 includes a listing of the current major commercial tax services. The tax services are discussed in detail in later chapters.

Court decisions are published in sets of bound volumes called *court reporters*. Examples of publishers and court reporters would include those produced by the Government Printing Office (GPO): *Tax Court of the U.S. Reports*, West Publishing Company: *Federal Reporter*, Research Institute of America (RIA): *American Federal Tax Reports*, and Commerce Clearing House: *United States Tax Cases*. Chapter 5 discusses in detail the means by which to find court cases in these (and other) reporters.

Exhibit 2-3: Major Tax Services

Publisher	Title of Tax Service	Orientation
Research Institute of America (RIA)	*Tax Coordinator 2d*	Topic
Research Institute of America (RIA)	*United States Tax Reporter*	Code
Commerce Clearing House (CCH)	*Standard Federal Tax Reporter*	Code
Commerce Clearing House (CCH)	*Federal Tax Service*	Topic
Bureau of National Affairs (BNA)	*Tax Management Portfolios*	Topic
West Group	*Mertens Law of Federal Income Taxation*	Topic

Both CCH and RIA provide "citators" as part of their tax services. A citator is a reference source that enables the researcher to follow the judicial history of court cases. The citators are discussed in detail in Chapter 8. The GPO prints many of the pronouncements of the IRS. The primary publication for IRS authority is in a set of bound volumes titled the *Cumulative Bulletin*. Chapter 4 includes a detailed discussion concerning the use of this authority.

Tax journals are another source of information that can be useful to the tax researcher. By reading tax journals, a tax practitioner can become aware of many current problem areas in taxation. She can also increase her awareness of recent developments in the tax law, tax compliance matters, and tax planning techniques and opportunities. Numerous journals, ranging from law reviews to *Cosmopolitan*, publish articles on current tax matters. The tax researcher typically is interested in publications devoted to scholarly and professional discussions of tax matters. Among these publications, each tax journal usually is written for a specific group of readers. Exhibit 2-4 lists several useful tax journals, their publishers, and the target readership of each.

Exhibit 2-4: Selected Tax Journals

Journal	Publisher	Target Readership
Journal of Taxation	Warren, Gorham & Lamont—Thomson RIA	Sophisticated tax practitioners
Practical Tax Strategies	Warren, Gorham & Lamont—Thomson RIA	Tax practitioners in general practice
Estate Planning	Warren, Gorham & Lamont—Thomson RIA	Practitioners who are interested in estate and gift tax matters
The Tax Adviser	American Institute of CPAs	Members of AICPA and other tax practitioners
TAXES	Commerce Clearing House	General tax practitioners

Step 4: Evaluate Authority

After the researcher has located authority that deals with the client's problem, he or she must evaluate the usefulness of that authority. Not all tax authority carries the same precedential value. For example, the Tax Court could hold that an item should be excluded from gross income at the same time that an outstanding IRS Revenue Ruling asserts the item is taxable. The tax researcher must evaluate the two authorities and decide whether to recommend that his or her client report the disputed item.

In the process of evaluating the authority for the issue(s) under research, new issues not previously considered by the researcher may become known. If this is the case, the researcher may be required to gather additional facts, find additional pertinent authority, and evaluate the new issues. This interaction is illustrated in Exhibit 2-1.

Step 5: Develop Conclusions and Recommendations

After several iterations of the first four steps of the tax research process, the researcher must arrive at his or her conclusions for the tax issues raised. Often, the research will not have resulted in a clear solution to the client's tax problems, perhaps because of unresolved issues of law or incomplete descriptions of the facts. In addition, the personal preferences of the client must also be considered. The "ideal" solution for tax purposes may be entirely impractical because of other factors that are integral to the tax question. In any of these cases, the tax practitioner must use professional judgment in making recommendations based on the conclusions drawn from the tax research process.

SPOTLIGHT ON TAXATION

Changing a Research Conclusion

The changing nature of a tax research conclusion can be illustrated as follows. When Congress created Roth IRAs, a procedure was set up for taxpayers to convert a regular IRA into a Roth IRA by paying the tax on the conversion over a four-year period. In spite of this, after making the conversion many taxpayers reexamined their tax situation and found that the Roth conversion was not as good a deal as originally thought. In this case, however, there was a way out. The tax law gave taxpayers a "second chance" by allowing them to "recharacterize" the Roth IRA conversion back to a regular IRA (within a certain period). Many taxpayers opted to change their converted Roth IRA back into a regular IRA.

Where unresolved issues exist, the researcher might inform the client about alternative possible outcomes of each disputed transaction and give the best recommendation for each. If the research involved an open-fact situation, the recommendation might detail several alternative courses of future action (e.g., whether to complete the deal, or how to document the intended effects of the transaction). In many cases, the researcher may find it appropriate to present his or her recommendation of the "best" solution from a tax perspective, as well as one or more alternative recommendations that may be much more workable solutions. In any case, the researcher will want to discuss with the client the pros and cons of all reasonable recommendations and the risks associated with each course of action.

Step 6: Communicate the Recommendations

The final step in the research process is to communicate the results and re-commendations of the research. The results of the research effort usually are sum-marized in a memorandum to the client file and in a letter to the client. Both of these items usually contain a restatement of the pertinent facts, as the researcher understands them, any assumptions the researcher made, the issues addressed, the applicable authority, and the practitioner's recommendations. An example of the structure of a simple tax research memo is shown in Exhibit 2-5. The memor-andum to the file usually contains more detail than does the letter to the client.

Exhibit 2-5: Tax Research Memo Sample Format

Raabe, Whittenburg & Sanders
Certified Public Accountants
San Francisco, CA

Relevant Facts:

Specific Issues:

Conclusions:

Support:

Actions to Be Taken:

_____ Discuss with client. Date discussed: _____

_____ Prepare a memo or letter to the client.

_____ Explore other fact situations.

_____ Other action. Describe:

Preparer: _____

Reviewer: _____

In any event, the researcher must temper his or her communication of the research results so that it is understandable by the intended reader. For instance, the researcher should use vastly different jargon and citation techniques in preparing an article for the *Journal of Taxation* than in preparing a client memo for a businessperson or layperson who is not sophisticated in tax matters. Chapter 11 provides additional guidelines and formats for client memoranda and other means of delivering the results of one's research. In addition, an excellent web site to help the tax researcher improve his or her written tax communication is **http://www2.gsu.edu/~accerl/home.html.**

OVERVIEW OF COMPUTERIZED TAX RESEARCH

The body of knowledge that encompasses the field of taxation grows at a phenomenal pace. Since 1975, Congress has enacted more than two dozen major tax and revenue bills that have had a significant effect on U.S. taxpayers. In addition, each year hundreds of new Treasury Regulations, court decisions, Revenue and Private Letter Rulings, Revenue Procedures, and Technical Advice Memoranda are issued.

The avalanche of tax-related information is not expected to decrease during the foreseeable future. The abundance of available information, as well as the complexity of the tax laws that have been enacted since 1975, has made it even more difficult and time consuming to conduct thorough and effective research concerning a tax-related issue.

Whenever a diligent tax professional is providing advice or other services to a client, he or she must be cognizant of the latest legislative changes and judicial decisions. Furthermore, he or she must be able to draw upon, and sort through, the vast body of established tax knowledge and to apply statutes and administrative and judicial rulings to the current tax issue.

Most tax professionals conduct a significant portion of their tax research using computer resources. The vast amount of storage available on a computer, coupled with the computer's fast retrieval of information, has made electronic tax research invaluable for the tax profession. The tax practitioner has two chief ways to find computer information for tax research purposes: (1) **online** subscription systems and (2) online free (nonsubscription) **Internet** sites.

Computerized tax online services are accessible through the Internet and several public telecommunications networks. The materials that are available with these services are contained in databases that are stored at centralized computer locations. These databases may be accessed from remote locations with the use of a variety of compatible video display terminals and keyboards. Usually, they can be accessed via compatible handheld devices and computers that the user already owns. Some popular computer subscription systems are shown in Exhibit 2-6, and examples of online free Internet sites are shown in Exhibit 2-7.

Electronic online tax research systems are relatively simple to operate. Normally, the user will have no trouble utilizing the system after he or she has devised an effective search command or query. Once the user is satisfied with the composition of his or her search query in an online system, it is transmitted over the Internet or a commercial network to a central computer, where it is processed and documents are identified that satisfy the search request. The text of the retrieved documents is then transmitted to the user and displayed for reading, printing, or saving. After the documents are received, the user must evaluate them and decide whether further research is required. As in using the tax research methodology

Exhibit 2-6: Examples of Online Tax Resources

Name	Description
RIA Checkpoint	A web-based computerized tax research service that contains all the RIA material on Federal, state, local, and international taxation. Checkpoint contains all RIA analytical material such as the *Tax Coordinator 2d* and the *United States Tax Reporter*. All public domain information such as the Code and Regulations, U.S. tax treaties, IRS publications and pronouncements, and court cases are available on Checkpoint.
CCH Tax Research Network	A web-based Internet system that contains all of CCH's tax services and other Federal and state legal and tax information. All government documents (IRS publications, court cases, etc.) are available on this system.
Kleinrock's	The Code, the Regulations, *Cumulative Bulletins*, Tax Court Regular decisions (since 1954), Tax Court Memo decisions and other court cases (since 1987), and all IRS publications.
Tax Analysts	The Code, the Regulations, *Cumulative Bulletins*, Court Regular decisions (since 1954). Tax Court Memo decisions and other court cases (since 1985), *Circular 230*, and all IRS publications.
LexisNexis	The largest of the commercial computer-based information systems. Besides containing all Federal and state legal and tax research material, Lexis has extensive libraries of newspapers, magazines, journals, patent records, and medical, economic, and accounting databases.
Westlaw	Offered by the major legal publisher, this system contains all Federal and state legal sources including court cases, administrative releases, and statutory information. All government documents (IRS publications, court cases, etc.) are also available on this system.
Practitioners Publishing Company	A practitioner-oriented service that also contains a good free tax newsletter. Part of Thomson Publishing.

Exhibit 2-7: Examples of Online Free Tax-Related Internet Sites

Site Name	Internet Address	Description
Tax Sites	http://taxsites.com	Indexes to other tax, accounting, and legal web sites. Links to commercial, Federal government, state, local, and international web sites.
Internal Revenue Service	http://www.irs.gov	Taxpayers can find tax forms, instructions, publications, and other IRS information.
Ernst & Young	http://www.ey.com	A web site that contains a large amount of tax and accounting information from the staff of E&Y.
Deloitte Tax LLP	http://www.deloitte.com	The Deloitte Tax LLP web site contains a large amount of tax and accounting information from the staff of Deloitte Tax LLP.
Thomas	http://thomas.loc.gov	Legislative information from the Library of Congress.
Will Yancey's Home Page	http://www.willyancey.com	Indexes to other tax, accounting, and legal web sites. Links to commercial, Federal government, state, local, and international web sites.

itself, electronic searching requires a combination of technical knowledge, experience, and creativity in approach.

Benefits of Using a Computerized Tax Service

Historically, tax research usually began with the consultation of topical and annotated tax services or tax-related text. In most instances, the user first had to consult a topical index to locate the appropriate page or pages on which to begin his or her research. However, any time that a tax service is accessed by way of its topical index, the user is relying on someone else's judgment (i.e., the service's editors) or performance (e.g., the staff of the database or library for proper treatment of update material) as to what is important with respect to the specific topic. Moreover, the desired information may not be located, even if it exists in the proper place in the database, because the keyword for which the user is looking is not the same word that was used by the editor in the index to discuss the issue that is the subject of the search. It is also possible that, when the index was prepared, the topic of the search was ignored because it was not as important a topic as it is today.

The primary benefit of using a computerized tax service is that such a resource makes it possible for the *user* to index any significant term, that is, by using it as a search term in a query. By creating his or her own indexes, the researcher is not bound by the limitations that are imposed by a third-party editor or data processor. Once the central computer is accessed with a proper search request, the service's software will electronically scan the designated files and retrieve all of the documents that contain the word or words included in the query. Thus, the user is able to bypass the predefined list of topics that constitute the subject's index and perform his or her search directly on the documents themselves.

Another benefit of using a computerized tax research system is that the user can tailor his or her query to fit the requirements of a specific tax problem. Because the user defines the precise specifications of the query, computerized research is exceptionally flexible. Each search request can be made as specific or as broad as desired, depending on the issue to be researched. If they are properly structured, computerized search queries can result in the research process being conducted with greater speed and thoroughness, and they can reduce the amount of time spent on that phase of the research task.

Such speed and flexibility are best realized as the researcher moves among pertinent tax documents. Most of the electronic services allow this capability through **hypertext** linking. Generally, when a hypertext link is indicated, typically through a different color for the text, the user can move to the related document so indicated with a click of the mouse or keyboard. For instance, the researcher could be reading a court case that refers to §2032A. By clicking on the hypertext link character, he or she is taken directly to the text of the Code section for direct perusal of the statutory language. Similarly, links can be made to pertinent Regulations or to similar court documents in a manner that the researcher could not accomplish by hand. As the number of available tax documents becomes more voluminous, the importance of moving among the documents quickly is met only with an electronic tax research tool.

Online services are updated many times a day. A researcher generally is able to retrieve recent court decisions and administrative rulings from a computerized service almost immediately upon release by the source of the document. In addition, the computerized services include one or more of the daily tax news summaries, such as BNA's *Daily Tax Report* or Tax Analysts' *Tax Notes Today*. In this regard, a computerized tax service allows a tax researcher to stay on top of the latest news and developments without incurring additional subscription costs for the stand-alone services.

Computerized services are particularly useful in researching case law. Every word that is contained in a case is included in the database of the computerized service. Thus, the user can save time by directly accessing only those cases that contain the key terms of his or her search. For example, all of the cases that deal with unreasonable compensation can be accessed within seconds, simply by using *unreasonable compensation* as a search request.

An additional benefit of using a computerized tax service is that certain documents no longer are available in print. For example, full printed transcripts of Actions on Decision and slip opinions normally are not published. However, these documents often may be obtained from the databases of an electronic tax service.

A computerized research service also can be used to obtain regularly published documents to which the researcher does not have access. For example, the full text of Private Letter Rulings is available on most computerized tax research databases. Thus, by using a target or filter feature in a computerized service, a tax practitioner can obtain only the ruling needed, without subscribing to an expensive loose-leaf service for the entire year.

Because of all its inherit advantages, the web-based tax service has become the standard source for current and archival tax research material.

Factors in Choosing a Computerized Tax Service

In *Computer-Assisted Legal and Tax Research* (Prentice-Hall), Thomas and Weinstein propose that a potential subscriber consider the following factors when choosing a computerized tax database.

- *Database contents:* Does the service provide specialty libraries that will be important in the researcher's work and that are unavailable elsewhere?

- *Search capabilities:* While the search commands and requirements are similar among the commercial tax services, some of the electronic services allow direct reviews of editorial information, and others encompass the Shepard's citations service.

- *Training:* Each of the services offers some level of educational training, either at the user's office or at a regional training center. The proximity, depth, and quality of such seminars may differ among services and across the country.

- *Customer support:* Other forms of contact with the user, such as to develop more sophisticated search techniques or to provide necessary repair services, should be available to the subscriber.

- *Price:* One must consider the cost of the time required to perform the research itself, as well as that of necessary equipment or special software.

Using a Computer in Tax Research

In the first part of this chapter, we presented a model of the tax research process. In this model, steps 1 and 2 of the tax research model are (1) to establish the facts and (2) to identify the issues related to the research question(s). The next step in the research model is to locate tax authority with which to solve the research question. In most situations, the tax researcher uses a computer in step 3 of the model in order to find the required authority (or to conclude that there is no authority on

Exhibit 2-8: Steps in the Computer Research Process

the subject). The process of finding tax authority using a computer can be broken down into several steps, as shown in Exhibit 2-8.

Step 1: State the Issue as a Question

After the tax researcher has established the facts and identified the issues that he or she needs to resolve, the issues should be stated as a question to be answered. For example, suppose the researcher has a client who is a self-employed attorney. As part of her trade or business, the attorney incurs substantial travel expenses during the year. She has learned that if she buys airline tickets in advance and extends her visit over a Saturday night, she will receive a large savings on airfare. Usually, an extra day of meals and lodging can save many hundreds of dollars in her airfare travel expenses. In the current year, she has spent $4,000 in extra Saturday night expenses to save $12,000 in airfare. The research question in this situation could be stated as:

> *Are the additional travel costs (primarily meals and lodging) of staying over a Saturday night in order to save substantial amounts on the business airfare deductible?*

Step 2: Identify the Keywords

Once the research question has been stated, the researcher must next identify the keywords to construct a proper query in the next step. In the preceding research question, the keywords would be as follows.

- meals and lodging

- travel

- Saturday

- deductible

- airfare

The researcher is looking for words that, when entered into a computer, will find tax authority that is "on point." If the correct keywords are not identified, tax researchers cannot find the authority needed or could be led down blind alleys.

Step 3: Construct a Computer Research Query

Computer tax research systems use a **query** in order to begin the search for the authority needed by the researcher. The construction of the query varies for each commercial computer tax research system; however, there are many similarities between the systems. All tax computer research systems recognize various types of connectors to construct a research query. Generally, computer tax services, such as **RIA Checkpoint**, have ten to fifteen search connectors available, but most tax research searches can be accomplished by using several basic connectors. The syntax of the four most useful connectors in RIA Checkpoint is shown in Exhibit 2-9.

In addition, the tax services allow the use of wildcard (universal) character(s). For example, in RIA Checkpoint, an "*" (asterisk) at the end of a root word finds all variations of that word. Thus, the word "deduct*" will find deduct, deducted, deduction, deductible, and so on. Other computer tax services use similar methods to construct tax research queries.

Computer tax services are continually being updated. Users should check the appropriate help menu of whichever computer tax service is being used to determine how to construct a query and to find other new features.

Step 4: Select a Database and Execute the Search

Once the query is constructed, the researcher must log on to and choose a database to search. Each computer tax research system contains numerous databases. As an example, RIA Checkpoint contains the following databases (among many others).

- All Federal Databases

- Federal Editorial Material

- *Federal Tax Coordinator 2d* (a tax service)

Exhibit 2-9: Selected RIA Checkpoint Search Connectors

Connector	Example	Description
And	stock and securities	Finds documents with both the term stock and the term securities in them.
Or	stock or securities	Finds documents with either the term stock or the term securities in them.
/n	stock/15 securities	Finds documents where the term stock is within fifteen words of the term securities.
Not	stock not securities	Finds documents with the term stock, but not the term securities.

- Source Material: Cases

- Source Material: Code, Committee Reports, Regulations, Tax Treaties

- Source Material: IRS Rulings and Releases

- Source Material: Tax Court and Federal Procedural Rules

- WG&L Journals

Continuing our example of the deductibility of Saturday night expenses, we could choose to search *"All Federal Databases"* using a query such as *travel/25 Saturday*. See Exhibit 2-10. If we executed this search on RIA Checkpoint, we would find several references to the fact that the IRS has issued Private Letter Ruling 9237014 that states the extra expenses for staying over a Saturday to get a lower airfare are deductible as part of the expenses of the business trip.

Step 5: Interpret and Refine the Search

After executing a computer tax search, often the query produces too little or too much information. If there is too little information, the search query must be broadened. For example, other keywords may be used or proximity connectors may be relaxed. On the other hand, if the query generates too much information, the search should be tightened. For example, fewer libraries or more unique keywords may be used or proximity connectors may be used or narrowed.

Each computer tax service (e.g., Lexis, Westlaw, Kleinrock's, CCH Tax Research Network) uses its own format for conducting tax searches. However, all services (including those conducted on Google or Yahoo) use the same basic steps in executing such searches. In all computer tax systems, the researcher must state the

Exhibit 2-10: RIA Checkpoint Query and Database Selection Screen

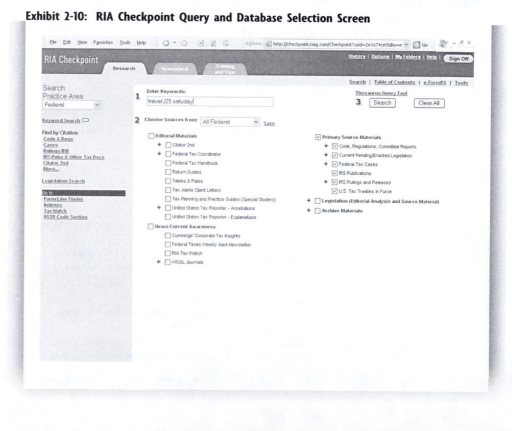

Exhibit 2-11: IRS Web Site Connectors

Boolean Connectors	http://www.irs.gov Shortcuts
OR	Space
AND	+
NOT	–
ADJ	"enclose in quotes"

issue, select the keywords, construct a query, choose a database, execute a search, and interpret and refine the search.

IRS Web Site Research

The IRS maintains an excellent web site where someone interested in tax information can conduct limited tax research. While the IRS web site is not a full-service tax research resource, it does contain searchable and downloadable tax information such as tax forms, instructions, publications (e.g., Publication 17), and other IRS information. The IRS web site also has a limited search engine that uses several of the basic connectors and recognizes wildcard characters as shown in Exhibit 2-11.

The wildcards "*" and "?" are also allowed by the IRS search engine. Using these wildcards, you can find documents that contain words that have similar spellings but are not stemmed variants. For example, air* finds documents that contain air, airline, and airhead. Entering "?at" finds documents that contain cat and hat, while "??at" finds documents that contain that and chat. For complete information on how to do IRS web site searches, go to **http://www.irs.gov/help/search_help.html**

> **Example 2-3** Last year, Doris's daughter and her (worthless) husband moved into her home. This year, Doris has supported both of them for the entire year. Doris would like to know if she can claim a dependency exemption for her son-in-law. Doris could go to the IRS web site (**http://www.irs.gov**) and click the search button. She could then search terms such as "son-in-law" and "dependent." See Exhibit 2-12. The IRS search engine should return several IRS publications (e.g., Pub. 501) that will inform Doris she can claim a deduction for her son-in-law.

Tax Research on the CPA Exam

The CPA exam is the examination that all individuals must pass if they wish to obtain a CPA license in one of the fifty states and other jurisdictions (e.g., Puerto Rico) of the United States. The exam is prepared by the American Institute of CPAs and is administered through the National Association of State Boards of Accountancy (NASBA). NASBA information can be found at the following web site: **http://www.nasba.org/**

NASBA contracts with testing centers around the United States, which actually give the exam. The CPA exam is a computer-based exam that tests accounting knowledge (e.g., financial accounting, taxation, auditing, etc.) and a set of supporting "soft" skills deemed to be important to the practice of public accountancy. The skills required for the CPA Exam include the abilities to communicate, perform research, and analyze information, as well as other higher-order skills such as judgment and understanding [The CPA Exam Alert, AICPA (January/February

Exhibit 2-12: IRS Site Search Page

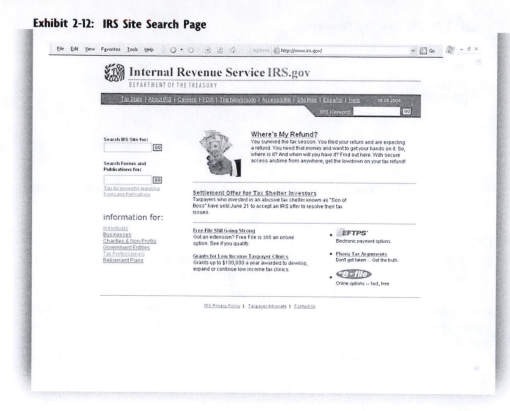

2003) p. 3]. The necessary skills as defined by the Board of Examiners are as follows:

1. **Communication** is the ability to effectively elicit and/or express information through written or oral means.

2. **Research** is the ability to locate and extract relevant information from available resource material.

3. **Analysis** is the ability to organize, process, and interpret data to provide options for decision making.

4. **Judgment** is the ability to evaluate options for decision making and provide an appropriate conclusion.

5. **Understanding** is the ability to recognize and comprehend the meaning and application of a particular matter.

CPA exam candidates are required to demonstrate their ability to apply these skills in each section of the Uniform CPA Examination in the context of the content knowledge.

The CPA exam, which is fourteen hours in total, is given in four parts. These parts can be taken separately as long as all four parts are in all passed within certain time limitations. The CPA Exam parts are

1. **Auditing and Attestation (AUD).** This section covers knowledge of auditing procedures, generally accepted auditing standards and other standards related to attest engagements, and the skills needed to apply that knowledge. [four hours and 30 minutes exam session]

2. **Business Environment and Concepts (BEC).** This section covers knowledge of general business environment and business concepts that candidates need to know in order to understand the underlying business reasons for and accounting implications of business transactions, and the skills needed to apply that knowledge. [two hours and 30 minutes exam session]

3. **Financial Accounting and Reporting (FAR).** This section covers knowledge of generally accepted accounting principles for business enterprises, not-for-profit organizations, and governmental entities, and the skills needed to apply that knowledge. [four-hour exam session]

4. **Regulation (REG).** This section covers knowledge of Federal taxation, ethics, professional and legal responsibilities, and business law, and the skills needed to apply that knowledge. [three-hour exam session]

Currently, each part of the CPA Exam (except Business Environment and Concepts) contains two types of questions: (1) multiple choice (standard objective questions) and (2) simulations (short multipart cases). With simulations the candidates demonstrate an ability to research professional and legal databases, identify relevant authority, and draw conclusions, to solve a problem. In addition, when completing a CPA exam simulation the candidate must show the writing skills necessary to communicate the solution to the client or other interested parties.

The format of CPA Exam simulations can be demonstrated in the following computer screen shots. Exhibit 2-13 shows the general "Directions" tab, which gives information for completing a CPA Exam simulation. The tabs across the top are how the candidate navigates to the various parts of the simulation. The general information about the problem to be solved is delineated under the "Situation" tab

Exhibit 2-13: Simulation General Instructions

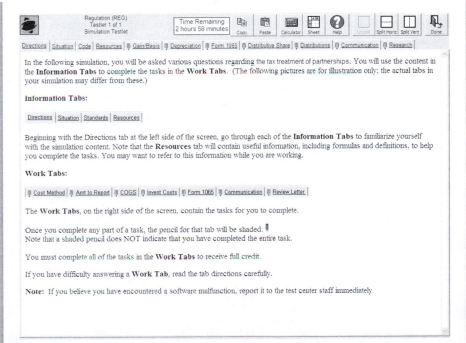

Exhibit 2-14: The Simulation Situation

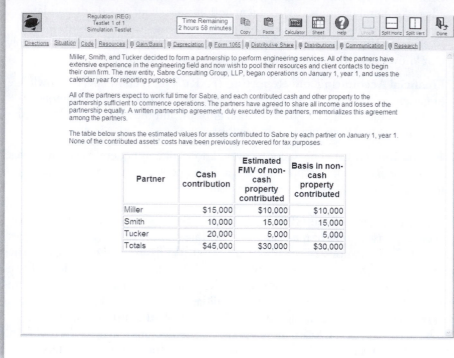

Exhibit 2-15: Simulation Requirement to be Completed

Complete the shaded cells in the following table by entering the gain or loss, if any, recognized by each partner in year 1 on the property contributed to Sabre Consulting Group, LLP, the partner's basis in the partnership interest, and Sabre's basis in the non-cash contributed property as of January 1, year 1. Loss amounts, if any, should be recorded as negative numbers. Note: To use a formula in the spreadsheet, it must be preceded by an equal sign, e.g., = B1+B2.

	A	B	C	D
		Partner's gain or loss, if any, on property transferred	Partner's basis in partnership interest	Partnership's basis in non-cash property contributed
1				
2	Miller			
3	Smith			
4	Tucker			

Exhibit 2-16: Simulation Requirements to be Completed

| Regulation (REG) Testlet 1 of 1 Simulation Testlet | Time Remaining 2 hours 55 minutes | Copy | Paste | Calculator | Sheet | Help | Unsplit | Split Horiz | Split Vert | Done |

Directions | Situation | Code | Resources | Gain/Basis | Depreciation | Form 1065 | Distributive Share | Distributions | Communication | Research

Sabre Consulting Group, LLP, is a limited liability partnership for tax purposes. Complete the income section of the year 1 IRS Form 1065 for Sabre Consulting Group, LLP using the following information:

Ordinary income from other partnerships	$5,200
Net gain (loss) from Form 4797	2,400
Consulting fees earned	120,000

K21

Form **1065**		U.S. Return of Partnership Income		OMB No. 1545-0099

Department of the Treasury
Internal Revenue Service

For calendar year 1 or tax year beginning .... , year 1, and ending .... year .....
► See separate instructions.

YEAR 1

A Principal business activity	Use the	Name of partnership		D Employer identification number
Engineering	IRS	Sabre Consulting Group, LLP		22-9999999
B Principal product or service	label.	Number, street, and room or suite no. (If a P.O. box, see page 14 of instructions.)		E Date business started
Consulting	Other-	1210 Industry Blvd		1/1/year 1
C Business code number	wise print	City or town, state, and ZIP code		F Total assets (see page 14 of the instructions
541330	or type	New York, NY 10011		$ $40,000

G Check applicable boxes: (1) X Initial return   (2) O Final return   (3) O Name change   (4) O Address change   (5) O Amended return

H Check accounting method: (1) O Cash   (2) X Accrual   (3) O Other (specify) ► ....

I Number of Schedules K-1. Attach one for each person who was a partner at any time during the tax year: ► ..... 3 ....

Caution: Include only trade or business income and expenses on lines 1a through 22 below. See the instructions for more information.

1a	Gross receipts or sales	1a			
b	Less returns and allowances	1b		1c	
2	Cost of goods sold (Schedule A, line 8)			2	
3	Gross profit. Subtract line 2 from line 1c			3	
4	Ordinary income (loss) from other partnerships, estates, and trusts (attach schedule)			4	
5	Net farm profit (loss) (attach Schedule F (form 1040))			5	

Exhibit 2-17: Research Question and Memo

| Regulation (REG) Testlet 1 of 1 Simulation Testlet | Time Remaining 2 hours 56 minutes | Copy | Paste | Calculator | Sheet | Help | Unsplit | Split Horiz | Split Vert | Done |

Directions | Situation | Code | Resources | Gain/Basis | Depreciation | Form 1065 | Distributive Share | Distributions | Communication | Research

In addition to preparing the partnership's federal return, you prepare Smith's personal income tax return. Smith incurred a substantial amount of medical expenses in year 2 and also received a small amount of reimbursements from medical insurance coverage in year 2 for these expenses. Write a letter to Smith explaining the rules regarding the deductibility of medical expenses. In your letter you should discuss the different types of expenses that would qualify as medical expenses, the proper treatment of medical expense reimbursements received in the same year, and the percentage of adjusted gross income limitation that would reduce the net amount of medical expenses allowed as a deduction.

Type your communication in the response area below the horizontal line using the word processor provided.

REMINDER: Your response will be graded for both technical content and writing skills. Technical content will be evaluated for information that is helpful to the intended reader and clearly relevant to the issue. Writing skills will be evaluated for development, organization, and the appropriate expression of ideas in professional correspondence. Use a standard business memo or letter format with a clear beginning, middle, and end. Do not convey information in the form of a table, bullet point list, or other abbreviated presentation.

| Spelling | Undo | Redo | Cut | Copy | Paste |

Mr. Smith
232 Pine Street
Anytown, NB

Dear Mr. Smith:

as shown in Exhibit 2-14. Generally, this should be the first screen the candidate goes after reading the "Directions" tab. Exhibits 2-15 and 2-16 show examples of the kinds of questions the candidate must answer in the simulation. Exhibit 2-15 is a table with various gain or loss questions to be answered, while Exhibit 2-16 is a Form 1065 Partnership tax return to be filled in. The research question and memo for this simulation are shown in Exhibit 2-17, which is found under the "Research" tab. This is where the candidate has to show his or her ability to answer a research question and properly document the solution in writing. Links to research sources such as the Code for candidates to use in solving the research question are in other tabs across the top of the screens. The material in this book will educate the candidate on how to effectively and efficiently complete the research simulations on the CPA Exam.

SUMMARY

Tax research is a complex process. The researcher must complete all of the steps in the research process to arrive at a solution to or recommendation for the client's tax problem. Moreover, the steps delineated in Exhibit 2-1 (or iterations of them) must be completed in their proper order to minimize the possibility of errors in evaluating the authority, arriving at conclusions, or making recommendations. If the process is abbreviated, the researcher risks failure to properly serve the client. This could result in the payment of unnecessary taxes by the client, or in the payment of damages by the tax practitioner to the client.

TAX TUTOR

Reinforce the tax research information covered in this chapter by completing the online tutorials located at the *Federal Tax Research* web site: **http://academic.cengage.com/taxation/raabe**

KEY WORDS

By the time you complete this chapter, you should be comfortable discussing each of the following terms. If you need additional review of any of these items, return to the appropriate material in the chapter or consult the glossary to this text.

Administrative sources
Collateral estoppel
Fact issues
Hypertext
Internal Revenue Code
Internet
Judicial sources
Law issues

Online
Primary authority
Query
RIA Checkpoint
Secondary authority
Statutory sources
Tax journals
Tax services

DISCUSSION QUESTIONS

1. What is the purpose of tax research?

2. What are the basic steps in conducting tax research? Briefly discuss each step in the tax research process.

3. What are the two chief tax research skills, as identified in this text? Explain the importance of each basic skill.

4. The tax researcher must find the facts as the first step in tax research. Give examples of the kind of information that a tax practitioner might want to obtain.

5. What are some of the potential pitfalls in the first step of the tax research process?

6. In each of the following independent situations, indicate whether the item generally would be a tax (T) or a nontax (NT) consideration in solving a tax research or tax planning problem.
    a. The taxpayer would like to set up a private foundation to reduce her annual income tax liability.
    b. The taxpayer has a very poor cash flow because of prior investments; therefore, he has a limited ability to make "tax-advantaged" investments.
    c. The taxpayer wants to transfer as much of her property to her grandchildren as possible. However, she does not want any of the property to fall into the hands of the grandchildren's mother (her daughter-in-law).
    d. The taxpayer lived through the Great Depression of the 1930s and does not like investments with any risk, such as owning stocks or bonds.
    e. The taxpayer likes to maintain highly liquid investments, such as money market funds and certificates of deposit in insured banks and savings and loan institutions.
    f. The taxpayer hates to pay Federal taxes. He will take any legal action to avoid paying any Federal income, estate, or gift taxes.

7. Identify and briefly describe the two major types of tax research issues.

8. What is *collateral estoppel*? How does it affect tax research and planning?

9. Tax law provisions tend to change over time. Explain how this might affect tax research and planning.

10. In the tax research process, the researcher has an obligation to the client to evaluate authority. Do the precedents in all tax authority carry the same value? Explain.

11. Primary tax authority can be classified as statutory, administrative, or judicial. Briefly describe each.

12. Classify each of the following items as a primary (P) or secondary (S) tax research authority.
    a. The *Internal Revenue Code*
    b. A Tax Court case
    c. A textbook on corporate taxation

d. Treasury Regulations

     e. An IRS Revenue Ruling

     f. An article in *Journal of Taxation*

     g. *Taxes on Parade* (a newsletter)

     h. A Supreme Court decision on a tax matter

13. Classify each of the following items as a primary (P) or secondary (S) tax research authority.
    a. A U.S. District Court Case
    b. An IRS Revenue Procedure
    c. Code §162
    d. *The Daily Tax Report* newsletter
    e. An article on recent tax rulings on inventory valuation in *Practical Tax Strategies*
    f. The U.S./Australia Income Tax Treaty
    g. A discussion on earnings and profits in the RIA Tax Coordinator 2d Tax Service
    h. A partnership tax treatise

14. Briefly characterize and distinguish between annotated tax services and topical tax services.

15. Classify each of the following commercial tax services as either an annotated service (A) or a topical service (T).
    a. CCH's *Standard Federal Tax Reporter*
    b. RIA's *Tax Coordinator*
    c. BNA's *Tax Management Portfolios*
    d. *Mertens Law of Federal Income Taxation*
    e. CCH's *Federal Tax Service*

16. What is a court reporter? Name three organizations that produce court reporters.

17. Who publishes each of the following court reporters?
    a. *United States Tax Cases*
    b. *Federal Reporter*
    c. *American Federal Tax reports*
    d. *Tax Court of the U.S. Reports*

18. What kind of information can be found in a citator?

19. Name the primary bound publication where IRS pronouncements can be found.

20. Tax practitioners use the term "tax service" all the time. What is a tax service?

21. What is the target readership of each of the following tax journals?
    a. *TAXES*
    b. *Journal of Taxation*
    c. *Practical Tax Strategies*
    d. *The Tax Adviser*
    e. *Estate Planning*

22. Specific items of tax authority have different "values" in helping the tax researcher to solve his or her problem. Explain this statement and describe how it applies to the tax research process.

23. Step 5 in the tax research process is concerned with reaching a conclusion or making a recommendation. If one has not found a clear answer to a tax research problem, how is a conclusion or recommendation to be reached?

24. The final step in the research process typically involves a memorandum to the client file and/or a letter to the client communicating the results of the research. List the items that should be found in the body of both of these documents.

25. It has been said that the tax research process is more circular than linear. Do you agree with this statement? Explain your answer.

26. What is deemed to be substantial authority under the §6662 Regulations? Why is this important?

27. Describe an online tax research system. What are the two advantages of such a system over a standard printed tax service?

28. Give the web address of three free online Internet sites where someone could find information on various aspects of taxation.

29. What is computerized tax research, and why is it necessary for the tax professional to be able to use computerized techniques to conduct tax research?

30. Briefly describe what is contained in each of the following tax services.
    a. RIA CheckPoint
    b. CCH Tax Research Network
    c. LexisNexis
    d. Westlaw

31. What are the disadvantages of using a computerized tax service?

32. List four benefits of using a computerized service to conduct your tax research.

33. What are the major steps in developing an effective computerized tax research query?

34. If you were researching an issue and the computer informed you that it had located 1,000 pertinent documents, what would you do to reduce the number of retrieved documents to a more reasonable number?

35. What are the search connectors discussed in the text used by RIA Checkpoint? Describe how each operates.

36. For the following RIA Checkpoint databases state if they generally contain primary or secondary authority: (1) *Federal Tax Coodinator 2d*, (2) Source Material Cases, (3) Source Material IRS Rulings and Releases, and (4) WG&L Journals.

37. What is the Internet address of the Internal Revenue Service's server?

38. What are the connectors used by the IRS web site search engine?

39. What are the two "wildcards" used by the IRS web site search engine? Explain how each operates.

40. Where can someone find additional information on searching techniques available for use on the IRS web site?

41. The computerized Uniform CPA exam has four parts. Identify them and briefly state what is covered in each part.

42. The Uniform CPA exam has a stated set of "supporting skills" that it tests. What are these skills? Do you think they should be tested on the Uniform CPA exam?

EXERCISES

43. Use your university's tax library (or other library assigned by your instructor) to discover the breadth of tax journal offerings. List any five tax journals and the publisher of each.

44. The purpose of this exercise is for you to locate publications that frequently are used in tax research. Give the call number and location (i.e., floor, room, stack, etc.) in your library, and the major color of the binding of the publication, for each of the following references. If a publication is not available, state that it is not.
    a. RIA's *United States Tax Reporter*
    b. CCH's *Standard Federal Tax Reporter*
    c. BNA's *Tax Management Portfolios*
    d. *Mertens Law of Federal Income Taxation*
    e. RIA's *Tax Coordinator 2d*

45. Find out whether each of the following court reporters is available in your library. Give the call number and location (i.e., floor, room, stack, etc.) for each reference. If a reporter is not available, state that it is not.
    a. *American Federal Tax Reports*
    b. *United States Tax Cases*
    c. *Tax Court of the U.S. Reports*
    d. *Federal Reporter*

46. Determine if each of the following tax journals is available in your library. What is the most current issue in your library? List the author(s) and title of any two articles from the most recent issue.
    a. *Journal of Taxation*
    b. *Practical Tax Strategies*
    c. *Journal of International Taxation*
    d. *The Tax Adviser*
    e. *TAXES*

47. Is the *Internal Revenue Code* found in separate volumes in each of the following tax services? If so, in how many volumes?
    a. CCH's *Standard Federal Tax Reporter*
    b. BNA's *Tax Management Portfolios*
    c. RIA's *Tax Coordinator 2d*

48. Find a copy of the *Cumulative Bulletin* in your university's library. By looking in a volume, list three different tax research sources published in a *Cumulative Bulletin*.

49. Locate a copy of the *American Federal Tax Reports* in your library. List two courts that have decisions published in this court reporter.

50. Locate a copy of CCH's *United States Tax Cases* in your library. List two courts that have decisions published in this court reporter.

51. In your university's library, locate the CCH and RIA citators. How many volumes does each contain?

52. Determine if your campus has any of the following online tax research services available for student use. If a service is available on your campus, describe how you would gain access to that system for research projects in your tax classes. If a service is not available on your campus, state where you might be able to find it.
    a. Kleinrock's
    b. Lexis
    c. RIA Checkpoint
    d. Westlaw
    e. CCH Tax Research Network

53. Go to the IRS web page (**http://www.irs.gov**) and print out a copy of the most recent Instructions for Form 3903 of Form 1040.

54. Go to the IRS web page (**http://www.irs.gov**) and print out a copy of the most recent Instructions for Form 4952 of Form 1040. You may first need to download the Adobe Acrobat Reader software to be able to view or print the form. The software is provided free of charge by Adobe through a link on the IRS page.

55. Go to the IRS web page (**http://www.irs.gov**). What IRS publication number addresses tax rules that apply to personnel in the armed forces? Print the first page of the IRS publication to hand in.

56. Go to the IRS web page (**http://www.irs.gov**). What IRS publication number addresses tax rules for pension and annuity income? Print the first page of the IRS publication to hand in.

57. Go to the IRS web page (**http://www.irs.gov**). Find information on abusive tax shelters. Give an example of an abusive tax shelter listed by the IRS.

58. Go to the IRS web page (**http://www.irs.gov**). Find a copy of Form 1040-PR, the Puerto Rico individual tax return. Print out and turn in page 1 of the 1040-PR Form.

59. Go to the IRS web page (**http://www.irs.gov**). Find a copy of Form 1040-C (PDF) U.S. Departing Alien Income Tax Return. Print out and turn in page 1 of the 1040-C Form.

60. Go to **http://taxsites.com** and give the complete web address for each of the following sites:
    a. The California Franchise Tax Board
    b. The New York Department of Taxation and Finance
    c. The American Institute of CPAs (AICPA)

61. Go to **http://www.willyancey.com** and give the complete web address for each of the following sites:
    a. The Hawaii Department of Taxation
    b. The Vermont Department of Taxes
    c. The American Taxation Association

62. Go to the Practitioners Publishing Co. web site (**http://www.ppc.thomson.com**) and locate the most recent Practitioners *Tax Action Bulletin*. Print out a copy of the bulletin.

63. Go to the IRS web page (**http://www.irs.gov**) and find the most recent IRS Publication 1542, Per Diem Rates. What is the maximum per diem rate for lodging and meals and incidental expenses (M&IE) for each of the following towns?
    a. Miami, Florida
    b. Palm Springs, California
    c. San Antonio, Texas

64. Go to the IRS web page (**http://www.irs.gov**) and find the most recent IRS Publication 1542, Per Diem Rates. What is the maximum per diem rate for lodging and meals and incidental expenses (M&IE) for each of the following towns?
    a. Buffalo, New York
    b. Honolulu, Hawaii
    c. Spokane, Washington

65. Locate and print out the web site home page of each of the following CPA firms.
    a. Ernst and Young LLP
    b. Deloitte Tax LLP
    c. BDO Seidman LLP
    d. PricewaterhouseCoopers LLP

66. Locate the web site home page of each of the following CPA firms. Give the city location of the firm's main (home) office.
    a. KPMG LLP
    b. Grant Thorton LLP
    c. CBiz LLP
    d. Moss Adams LLP

67. Jennifer owns 200 acres of land on which she grows flowers for sale to local nurseries. Her adjusted basis in the land is $30,000. She receives condemnation proceeds of $20,000 from the state for ten acres of her land on which a new freeway will be built. The state also pays her $30,000 for the harmful effects that the increased auto exhausts might have on her flowers. List as many tax research issues as you can to determine the tax consequences of these transactions. Do not attempt to answer any of the questions you raise. Simply identify the research issues.

68. Joey parked his car on the top of a hill when he went to watch the X games in San Diego. He did not properly set his brakes or curb the wheels when he parked the car. When he returned from the games, he found his car had rolled down the hill, smashed into Nick's house, and injured Nick, who was watching

TV in his den. Joey does not have car insurance. List as many tax research issues as you can to determine the tax consequences of this accident. Do not attempt to answer any of the questions you raise. Simply identify the research issues.

69. John and Marsha are married and filed a joint return for the past year. During that year, Marsha was employed as an assistant cashier at a local bank and, as such, was able to embezzle $75,000, none of which was reported on their joint return. Before the defalcation was discovered, Marsha disappeared and has not been seen or heard from since. List as many tax research issues as you can to determine the tax consequences of this crime. Do not attempt to answer any of the questions you raise. Simply identify the research issues.

70. In the current year, Dave receives stock worth $125,000 from his employer. The stock is restricted and cannot be sold by Dave for seven years. Dave estimates the stock will be worth $300,000 after the seven years. List as many tax research issues as you can to determine the tax consequences of this transaction. Do not attempt to answer any of the questions you raise. Simply identify the research issues.

71. On December 1, 20X1, Ericka receives $18,000 for three months' rent (December, January, and February) of an office building. List as many tax research issues as you can to determine the tax consequences of this transaction. Do not attempt to answer any of the questions you raise. Simply identify the research issues.

72. Formulate a search query to determine whether your client is required to include in gross income the proceeds from a redemption of a tax-exempt bond, purchased in 1988 and called by the school district this year. Redemption proceeds were $90,000, and the 1988 purchase price on the secondary market was $76,000. Give an example of a computer search query using only the following RIA Checkpoint connectors: "and," "or," "/n," and "not."

73. Formulate a search query to determine the provisions of the United States' treaty with Germany relative to fellowship income received by a business student during a summer internship with the German Department of Price Controls. Give an example of a computer search query using only the following RIA Checkpoint connectors: "and," "or," "/n," and "not."

74. Formulate a search query to determine whether your client is required to capitalize fringe benefits and general overhead that is attributable to employees who are building an addition to your client's factory during a "slack time" at work. Give an example of a computer search query using only the following RIA Checkpoint connectors: "and," "or," "/n," and "not."

75. Formulate a search query to determine whether your client can retroactively elect to change its accounting method. Give an example of a computer search query using only the following RIA Checkpoint connectors: "and," "or," "/n," and "not."

76. Formulate a search query to find all of the cases in which the word *constructive* occurs within ten words of the word *dividend*. Give an example of a computer query using only the following RIA Checkpoint connectors: "and," "or," "/n," and "not."

77. Go the AIPCA web site (**www.aicpa.org**) and "drill-down" to the Uniform CPA exam simulation section. Find an example of a tax simulation situation. What is the subject of the simulation that you located? Print out the web page showing the simulation to turn in.

78. Go the AIPCA web site (**www.aicpa.org**) and "drill-down" to the Uniform CPA exam simulation section. Find an example of a nontax simulation situation (e.g., financial accounting or auditing). What is the subject of the simulation that you located? Print out the web page showing the simulation to turn in.

RESEARCH CASES

79. Sam Manuel has been employed on a full-time basis as an electrical engineer for the past three years. Prior to obtaining full-time employment, he was self-employed as an inventor of complex electronic components. During this period of self-employment, most of his projects produced little income, although several produced a significant amount of revenue.

    Due to the large expenditures necessary and the failure of the majority of the products to produce a profit, Sam was forced to seek full-time employment. After obtaining full-time employment, he continued to work long hours to perfect several of his inventions. He continued to enjoy relatively little success with most of his products, but certain projects were successfully marketed and generated a profit. For the past two years, Sam's invention activity has generated a net loss.

    a. List as many possible tax research issues as you can to determine whether the losses may be deducted.

    b. After completing your list of tax research issues, list the keywords you might use to construct a computer tax research query.

80. Matthew Broadway was a partner in the law firm of Johnson and Smith, a partnership of twenty partners, for the past ten years. Without the knowledge or consent of the other partners, Matthew worked on a highly complicated acquisition and merger project for six months, at all times using the resources of the law firm. Several months later, the firm for which Matthew provided the professional services made out a check for $300,000 to the firm of Johnson and Smith. Matthew insisted that the fee should rightly be his, while the firm disputed his claim. Because of the dispute, the fee was held in escrow until the following year when the dispute was settled.

    The dispute was settled with Matthew agreeing to withdraw from the partnership. Included as part of the withdrawal agreement was a clause that specified he would receive $45,000 of the $300,000 fee, with the law firm retaining the remainder. Six months later, Matthew received a total payment of $125,000, which included the $45,000 fee, from Johnson and Smith.

    a. List as many possible tax research issues as you can to determine the tax treatment of the $125,000 payment received by Matthew.

    b. After completing your list of tax research issues, list the keywords you might use to construct a computer tax research query.

81. Juanita Sharp purchased a large parcel of property for $120,000. A short time after purchasing the property, Sharp submitted plans for the division of the

parcel into six lots and the construction of three single-family residences on three of the lots. The city permits required that the property be divided into six lots and that street improvements and water and sewer access be provided. Sharp spent $22,000 for the street, water, and sewer improvements. As a result of the improvements, the value of each of the three vacant lots increased by $1,000, based on an appraisal completed subsequent to the completion of the improvements. The costs of constructing the three single-family residences totaled $200,000.

a. List as many possible tax research issues as you can to determine how the original purchase price of $120,000, the $22,000 cost of the improvements, and the $200,000 cost of the construction of the homes should be allocated to the basis of each of the lots for purposes of determining gain or loss on the sale of the lots.

b. After completing your list of tax research issues, list the keywords you might use to construct a computer tax research query.

82. Tom and Donna were divorced three years ago. At the time of their divorce, they owned a highly appreciated residence. Tom remained half-owner of the house, but moved out and allowed Donna to continue living in the house. In the current year, Tom and Donna sold the house for $300,000. Last year, Tom purchased a new house for $190,000.

a. List as many possible tax research issues as you can to determine tax treatment(s) available to Tom on the sale and purchase of the residence.

b. After completing your list of tax research issues, list the keywords you might use to construct a computer tax research query.

83. Vincent Vineyard, MD, is a very successful physician in Temecula, California. He earns approximately $800,000 per year from his medical practice. His two children have graduated from college and he and his wife are now "empty-nesters." Vincent, Jr., is an officer in the Navy and his daughter Valerie is an engineer in Texas. Vinny has had an interest in wine and grape growing for many years. Now, with more time to devote to other activities, Vinny recently started a winery with an initial investment of $1,000,000. Since the winery is new, he expects it to be eight to ten years before the winery makes a profit. Vinny would like your advice as to any potential tax problems he might have with his new winery investment.

a. What additional information might you want in this situation?

b. Where might that information come from?

c. Are all the given facts pertinent? Which (if any) are irrelevant?

d. What is the primary research question you would try to answer?

e. Are there any additional research question(s) you want to address?

84. Ned Naive operated several franchised stores, and at the home office's suggestion, consolidated its payroll and accounting functions with Andy the Accountant. Andy is not a CPA. Last year, Andy began embezzling taxpayer's escrowed tax withholdings and failed to remit required amounts for the four quarters. The IRS assessed Ned penalties for failing to make the proper withholding deposits during the year.

a. What additional information might you want in this situation?

b. Where might that information come from?

c. Are all the given facts pertinent? Which (if any) are irrelevant?

d. Where might that information come from?

e. What is the primary research question you would try to answer?

f. Are there any additional research question(s) you want to address?

85. Dr. Diego Dissolution is recently divorced and has some questions regarding payments he is making to his ex-wife (Mrs. D.). Diego is forty-five years old and has a successful dental practice. Mrs. D. was divorced from her first husband six years ago. Diego is paying $12,000 per month to Mrs. D. He wants to know if the tax payments on the $12,000 per month are deductible.

a. What additional information might you want in this situation?

b. Where might that information come from?

c. Are all the given facts pertinent? Which (if any) are irrelevant?

d. Where might that information come from?

e. What is the primary research question you would try to answer?

f. Are there any additional research question(s) you want to address?

86. Phred Phortunate won his state lotto two years ago. His lotto ticket was worth $10,000,000, which was payable in twenty annual installments of $500,000 each. Phred paid $1.00 for the winning ticket. The lotto in Phred's state does not allow winners to receive their payout in a lump-sum. Phred wanted all of his money now, so he assigned his future lotto winnings to a Happy Finance Company for a discounted price of $4,500,000. Assignment of lotto winnings is permitted by Phred's state lotto. Phred filed his tax return and reported the assignment of the lotto winnings as a capital gain ($4.5M–$1.00) taxable at a 15 percent rate.

a. List as many possible tax research issues as you can to determine whether Phred correctly reported his lotto winnings.

b. After completing your list of tax research issues, list the keywords you might use to construct a computer tax research query.

87. The Mucho Oro Indian Tribe operates a casino on its reservation in Arizona. The casino is very profitable and therefore the tribe has excess money to invest. The tribe is approached by an entrepreneur who wants to build an outlet mall next to the casino. The entrepreneur would like to operate the outlet mall as an S corporation. Both he and the tribe would be shareholders in the new S corporation.

a. List as many possible tax research issues as you can to determine whether this plan of organization would be allowed under the current tax law.

b. After completing your list of tax research issues, list the keywords you might use to construct a computer tax research query.

88. Your client, Barney Green, and his wife, Edith, attended a three-day program in Honolulu, entitled "Financial, Tax, and Investment Planning for Investors." The Greens went to Hawaii several days early so that they could adjust to the jet lag and be ready for the seminar. The $3,000 cost of the trip included the following expenses.

First-class airfare	$1,200
Hotel (seven days)	800
Program fee	300
Meals and other expenses	700

The Greens have records to substantiate all of the above expenditures in a manner that is acceptable under §274.

   a. List as many possible tax research issues as you can to determine whether the Greens can deduct any or all of the $3,000 of expenditures on their current-year tax return.

   b. After completing your list of tax research issues, list the keywords you might use to construct a computer tax research query.

   c. Execute a computer search using your query. For simplicity, select the IRS Taxpayer Information Publications (TIPS) database from whichever computer tax service you use. Summarize your findings.

89. Ban Vallew has a son, Katt, by a previous marriage, who is in the custody of his ex-wife. Katt Vallew has a history of emotional disturbance. He has been sent to a psychiatrist for several years for this problem. This year he has become so disturbed, manifesting violence at home and school, that he had to be sent to a special school in Arizona for problem children. This school is very expensive ($2,000 per month), the cost of which Ban pays for. Ban would like to determine whether he is entitled to the medical expenses deduction (over 7.5% of adjusted gross income) for the cost of sending his son to this special school.

   a. List as many possible tax research issues as you can to determine tax treatment(s) available to Ban on the payments to the special school.

   b. After completing your list of tax research issues, list the keywords you might use to construct a computer tax research query.

   c. Execute a computer search using your query. For simplicity, select the IRS Taxpayer Information Publications (TIPS) database from whichever computer tax service you use. Summarize your findings.

90. Linda Larue suffered from arthritis. Her chiropractor advised her that she needed to swim daily to alleviate her pain and other symptoms. Consequently, Linda and her husband, Philo, purchased for $100,000 a new home that had a swimming pool, after selling their old home for $85,000. If the Larues had constructed a pool at their former residence, it would have cost $15,000 to build, and it would have increased the value of their home by $8,000.

   a. List as many possible tax research issues as you can to determine whether the Larues can deduct any of their current-year expenditures for Linda's arthritis.

   b. After completing your list of tax research issues, list the keywords you might use to construct a computer tax research query.

   c. Execute a computer search using your query. For simplicity, select the IRS Revenue Rulings database from whichever computer tax service you use. Summarize your findings.

91. Gwen Gullible was married to Darrell Devious. They were divorced two years ago. Three years ago (the year before their divorce), Darrell received a $250,000 retirement plan distribution, of which $50,000 was rolled over into an IRA. At the time, Gwen was aware of the retirement funds and the rollover. The distribution was used to pay off the couple's mortgage, purchase a car, and for living expenses. Darrell prepared the couple's joint return, and Gwen asked him about the tax ramifications of the retirement distributions. He told her he had consulted a CPA and was advised that the retirement plan proceeds used to pay off a mortgage were not taxable income. Gwen accepted that explanation and signed the return. In fact, Darrell had not consulted a CPA.

One year ago (after the divorce), Gwen received a letter from the IRS saying they had not received the tax return for the last full year of marriage. On advice from a CPA, Gwen immediately filed the return (she had a copy of the unfiled return). The Internal Revenue Service notified Gwen that no estimated payments on the retirement distribution had been paid by Darrell, and that she owed $60,000 in tax, plus penalties and interest.

a. List as many possible tax research issues as you can to determine whether Gwen is liable for the tax, interest, and penalties.

b. After completing your list of tax research issues, list the keywords you might use to construct a computer tax research query.

c. Execute a computer search using your query. For simplicity, select the IRS Revenue Rulings database from the computer tax service you use. Summarize your findings.

Primary Sources of Federal Tax Law

PART

II

Constitutional and Legislative Sources

Chapter Outline

Learning Objectives

- Outline the primary and secondary sources of the Federal tax law.

- Describe in detail the nature and structure of the statutory sources of the tax law, including the Constitution, tax treaties, and the Internal Revenue Code.

- Delineate how statutory tax law is created and how tax research resources are generated in this process.

- Determine how to locate the statutory sources of the tax law.

- Discuss how the tax researcher can carefully interpret the Internal Revenue Code.

Q UESTIONS ABOUT INCOME TAXATION, unlike many other areas of law, are primarily based in the underlying statute. As a result, the first step in locating potential authority in a tax matter usually consists of identifying the pertinent Code section(s). The current statutory source is in the *Internal Revenue Code* (IRC) of 1986. In addition, a tax researcher may need to examine the legislative history of a tax provision. Furthermore, it may be necessary to understand the constitutional foundation and associated tax treaties that may affect the Code section(s) in question.

In this chapter, we take a closer look at the tax research process and how the primary tax law sources are used to help the tax researcher arrive at a solution to his or her client's tax problems.

Tax professionals utilize three primary sources of the tax law, mirroring the constitutional division of the function of the Federal government.

- Statutory sources, or the legislative branch.

- Administrative sources, or the executive branch.

- Judicial sources, or the judicial branch.

Thus, the constitutional and legislative tax sources often are referred to as the **"statutory sources."**

Sources of Federal Tax Law

As mentioned in the previous chapter, the sources of the Federal tax law can be classified as **primary authorities** or **secondary authorities**. Chapters 3 through 8 of this text include detailed examinations of these various sources, discussing their nature, location, and use in the tax research process. The sources of the Federal tax law to be examined here are presented in outline form in Exhibit 3-1. In particular, we will examine the statutory sources of the U.S. Constitution, tax treaties, and the *Internal Revenue Code*. The reader should refer to this outline while reading this text to maintain perspective as to the relationships between each of the sources discussed.

History of U.S. Taxation

Although the Massachusetts Bay Colony enacted an income tax law in 1643, the first U.S. income tax was not created until the Civil War. An income tax law was passed at that time to help the North pay for the cost of fighting the war. This Federal income tax law was passed on August 5, 1861. The tax was not generally enforced, but some limited collections were made under the law.

This first Federal income tax was levied at the rate of a modest 3 percent on income between $600 and $10,000, and 5 percent on marginal incomes in excess of $10,000. Later, in 1867, the rate was a flat 5 percent of income in excess of $1,000. The Civil War income taxes were allowed to expire in 1872. In 1894 another income tax act was passed by Congress. By this time, however, the income tax had become an important political issue. The southern and western states generally favored the tax, and the eastern states generally opposed it—the tax had developed into an important element of the Populist political movement. In *Pollock v. Farmers' Loan and Trust Co.*, 157 U.S. 429, 15 S.Ct. 673 (1895), the Supreme Court held that the income tax was unconstitutional because it was a constitutionally prohibited "direct tax."

Exhibit 3-1: Framework of Primary and Secondary Sources of Federal Tax Law

Primary Sources (Original Pronouncements)	Secondary Sources (Interpretations of Primary Authority)
Statutory Sources (Chapter 3)	
U.S. Constitution	**(Chapters 6–8)**
Tax Treaties	
Internal Revenue Code	***Tax Services***
Administrative Sources (Chapter 4)	*Annotated Services*
Treasury Regulations	*Topical Services*
Revenue Rulings	
Revenue Procedures	***Tax Citators***
Other written determinations	
Miscellaneous IRS publications	***Tax Journals***
Judicial Sources (Chapter 5)	
Supreme Court	***Tax Newsletters***
Courts of Appeals	
District Courts	***Tax Textbooks***
U.S. Court of Federal Claims	
Tax Court	***Tax Treatises***
Tax Court, Small Cases Division	

The supporters of the income tax decided to amend the Constitution so that there would be no question as to the constitutionality of a Federal income tax, applying progressive rates to diverse sources of income. The proposed amendment was sent to the states on July 12, 1909, by the Sixty-First Congress; it was ratified on February 3, 1913. The new Sixteenth Amendment to the Constitution stated:

The Congress shall have the power to lay and collect taxes on incomes, from whatever source derived, without apportionment among the several States, and without regard to any census or enumeration.

A copy of a 1913 individual tax return (Form 1040) is shown in Exhibit 3-2. It should be noted that individual taxpayers were allowed a $3,000 ($4,000 for married taxpayers) "specific exemption" before they had to start paying income tax at a 1 percent rate. The 1 percent bracket went up to $20,000 of taxable income before a surtax of an additional 1 percent was added. The surtax eventually reached 6 percent at a taxable income of $500,000. Thus, the maximum marginal tax rate in 1913 was 7 percent (1% regular tax plus 6% surtax).

The 1913 specific exemption is similar to the current standard deduction. If $3,000 in 1913 were price-level adjusted into today's dollars, it would be more than $63,000. Thus, an individual taxpayer would not pay any Federal income tax until he or she showed taxable income of over $63,000 if an equivalent exemption were in place today.

Before the Sixteenth Amendment was ratified, Congress passed a corporate income tax in 1909. This tax also was challenged at the Supreme Court level, in *Flint v. Stone Tracy Co.* 220 U.S. 107, 31 S.Ct. 342 (1911). The Court held that this tax was constitutional because it was a special form of excise tax on the privilege of operating in the corporate form, using income as its base, rather than a (prohibited) direct income tax.

Exhibit 3-2: 1913 Individual Form 1040

TO BE FILLED IN BY COLLECTOR.

Form 1040.

TO BE FILLED IN BY INTERNAL REVENUE BUREAU.

List. No. ....

.... District of ....

Date received ....

INCOME TAX.

THE PENALTY
FOR FAILURE TO HAVE THIS RETURN IN
THE HANDS OF THE COLLECTOR OF
INTERNAL REVENUE ON OR BEFORE
MARCH 1 IS $20 TO $1,000.
[SEE INSTRUCTIONS ON PAGE 4.]

File No. ....

Assessment List ....

Page .... Line ....

UNITED STATES INTERNAL REVENUE.

RETURN OF ANNUAL NET INCOME OF INDIVIDUALS.

(As provided by Act of Congress, approved October 3, 1913.)

RETURN OF NET INCOME RECEIVED OR ACCRUED DURING THE YEAR ENDED DECEMBER 31, 191 ....

(FOR THE YEAR 1913, FROM MARCH 1, TO DECEMBER 31.)

Filed by (or for) .... of ....
                              (Full name of individual.)   (Street and No.)

in the City, Town, or Post Office of .... State of ....

(Fill in pages 2 and 3 before making entries below.)

1.	Gross Income (see page 2, line 12)	$			
2.	General Deductions (see page 3, line 7)	$			
3.	Net Income	$			

Deductions and exemptions allowed in computing income subject to the normal tax of 1 per cent.

4.	Dividends and net earnings received or accrued, of corporations, etc., subject to like tax. (See page 2, line 11) . . .	$		
5.	Amount of income on which the normal tax has been deducted and withheld at the source. (See page 2, line 9, column A)			
6.	Specific exemption of $3,000 or $4,000, as the case may be. (See Instructions 3 and 19)			

	Total deductions and exemptions. (Items 4, 5, and 6)	$		

7.	Taxable Income on which the normal tax of 1 per cent is to be calculated. (See Instruction 3) .	$			

8.   When the net income shown above on line 3 exceeds $20,000, the additional tax thereon must be calculated as per schedule below:

				INCOME.			TAX.		
1	per cent on amount over $20,000 and not exceeding $50,000 . .	$				$		
2	"	"	50,000	"	"	75,000 .			
3	"	"	75,000	"	"	100,000 .			
4	"	"	100,000	"	"	250,000 .			
5	"	"	250,000	"	"	500,000 .			
6	"	"	500,000						

Total additional or super tax	$		
Total normal tax (1 per cent of amount entered on line 7) . .	$		
Total tax liability	$		

SPOTLIGHT ON TAXATION

Who Pays the Income Tax?

The 1913 income tax was strictly a tax on wealthy and high income taxpayers (i.e., a "select tax"). The original post–Sixteenth Amendment income tax applied to less than 1 percent of the population (i.e., 1 in every 271 adults). It wasn't until the end of World War II that the income tax became a broad-based tax that applied to the majority of the population (i.e., a "mass tax").

In recent years, the income tax has been attacked in the courts on the basis that it is unconstitutional. For instance, some protesters have asserted that, since the U.S. currency no longer is based on the gold standard, the Sixteenth Amendment's measure of income, and therefore the tax itself, is invalid. Others have asserted that the Federal income tax law forces the taxpayer to surrender his or her Fifth Amendment rights against self-incrimination. Federal courts, however, have denied virtually all of the protesters' challenges.

Congress has passed several laws to discourage tax protesters. For instance, a taxpayer is subject to a $5,000 fine if he or she files a "frivolous" tax return as a form of protest against the IRS or the U.S. budgetary process. This fine would be levied, for example, when the taxpayer files a blank tax return accompanied by a note suggesting that the Federal income tax is unconstitutional or that the taxpayer wishes to protest against tax revenues going to the creation of nuclear weapons. A number of lower courts have upheld the constitutionality of this fine [e.g., *Schull*, 842 USTC ¶ 9529 (D.C., Va.)].

The Tax Court can impose a penalty, not to exceed $25,000, if the taxpayer brings a "frivolous" matter before the Court. Under §§6673 and 6702, a frivolous matter is where the intent is to delay the revenue collection process and where the proceedings are found to be groundless, or where the taxpayer unreasonably failed to pursue available administrative remedies. Sanctions can also be imposed against tax practitioners who participate in the litigation of frivolous tax return positions.

U.S. Constitution

The Constitution of the United States is the source of all of the Federal laws of the country, including both tax and nontax provisions. In addition to the Sixteenth Amendment, however, the Constitution contains other provisions that bear upon the taxation process. For example, the Constitution provides that Congress may impose import taxes but not export taxes. Moreover, the constitutional rights of due process and of the privacy of the citizen apply in tax, as well as nontax, environments.

The Constitution also requires that taxes imposed by Congress apply uniformly throughout the United States. For instance, it would be unconstitutional for Congress to impose one Federal income tax rate in California and another rate in Vermont. Moreover, except as provided by the Sixteenth Amendment, the Constitution still bars per capita and other direct taxes, unless the revenues that are generated from these taxes are apportioned to the population of the states from which they were collected.

The Federal courts have upheld the constitutionality of the estate and gift taxes because they are in the form of excise taxes on (the transfer of) property, rather than direct taxes on individuals. Thus, one can conclude that, for better or worse, most future judicial challenges to the constitutionality of the elements of the Federal tax structure probably will be fruitless.

One can find copies of the U.S. Constitution in many textbooks, encyclopedias, dictionaries, and in publications such as *The World Almanac* and *Wikipedia*. The Constitution is also reproduced in Volume One of the *United States Code*, as published by the Government Printing Office.

An excerpt from the U.S. Constitution can be found in Exhibit 3-3. The Constitution can also be found at various Internet sites. An example of such a site is:

http://www.archives.gov

Exhibit 3-3: United States Constitution Excerpt (with original spelling)

WE THE PEOPLE of the United States, in Order to form a more perfect Union, establish Justice, insure domestic Tranquility, provide for the common defence, promote the general Welfare, and secure the Blessings of Liberty to ourselves and our Posterity, do ordain and establish this Constitution for the United States of America.

Article I

Section. 1. All legislative Powers herein granted shall be vested in a Congress of the United States, which shall consist of a Senate and House of Representatives.

Section. 2. The House of Representatives shall be composed of Members chosen every second Year by the People of the several States, and the Electors in each State shall have the Qualifications requisite for Electors of the most numerous Branch of the State Legislature.

No Person shall be a Representative who shall not have attained to the Age of twenty five Years, and been seven Years a Citizen of the United States, and who shall not, when elected, be an Inhabitant of that State in which he shall be chosen.

Representatives and direct Taxes shall be apportioned among the several States which may be included within this Union, according to their respective Numbers, which shall be determined by adding to the whole Number of free Persons, including those bound to Service for a Term of Years, and excluding Indians not taxed, three fifths of all other Persons. The actual Enumeration shall be made within three Years after the first Meeting of the Congress of the United States, and within every subsequent Term of ten Years, in such Manner as they shall by Law direct. The Number of Representatives shall not exceed one for every thirty Thousand, but each State shall have at Least one Representative; and until such enumeration shall be made, the State of New Hampshire shall be entitled to chuse three, Massachusetts eight, Rhode-Island and Providence Plantations one, Connecticut five, New-York six, New Jersey four, Pennsylvania eight, Delaware one, Maryland six, Virginia ten, North Carolina five, South Carolina five, and Georgia three.

When vacancies happen in the Representation from any State, the Executive Authority thereof shall issue Writs of Election to fill such Vacancies.

The House of Representatives shall chuse their Speaker and other Officers; and shall have the sole Power of Impeachment.

Section. 3. The Senate of the United States shall be composed of two Senators from each State, chosen by the Legislature thereof, for six Years; and each Senator shall have one Vote.

Immediately after they shall be assembled in Consequence of the first Election, they shall be divided as equally as may be into three Classes. The Seats of the Senators of the first Class shall be vacated at the Expiration of the second Year, of the second Class at the Expiration of the fourth Year, and of the third Class at the Expiration of the sixth Year, so that one third may be chosen every second Year; and if Vacancies happen by Resignation, or otherwise, during the Recess of the Legislature of any State, the Executive thereof may make temporary Appointments until the next Meeting of the Legislature, which shall then fill such Vacancies.

No Person shall be a Senator who shall not have attained to the Age of thirty Years, and been nine Years a Citizen of the United States, and who shall not, when elected, be an Inhabitant of that State for which he shall be chosen.

The Vice President of the United States shall be President of the Senate, but shall have no Vote, unless they be equally divided.

TAX TREATIES

Tax treaties are agreements negotiated between countries concerning the treatment of entities subject to tax in both countries. The United States has entered into treaties with most of the major Western countries of the world. The overriding purpose of such treaties (also known as *tax conventions*) is to eliminate the "double taxation" that the taxpayer would face if his or her income were subject to tax in both countries. In such a case, a U.S. citizen who has generated income from an investment in the United Kingdom (U.K.) usually would be allowed a credit on her U.S. income tax return to the extent of any related U.K. taxes that she paid.

Any tax matter can be covered in a tax treaty with another country. Many times, there are multiple tax treaties with a given country. For example, one treaty will address income tax issues, while another treaty covers estate tax, and a third treaty addresses excise taxes. An example of a portion of a tax treaty is shown as Exhibit 3-4.

In addition to the tax treaties, the U.S. government enters into nontax international agreements that are not formal tax treaties; however, in many respects they function like one. Along with other provisions, these agreements address tax issues involving the parties associated with the agreement. Examples of such international agreements include the North American Free Trade Agreement (NAFTA) and the General Agreement on Tariffs and Trade (GATT). Other agreements might address the exchange of tax, banking, and securities information among citizens of one or more countries.

Treaties are an important source of Federal law. Most treaties do *not* address tax issues, but the ones that do have a far-reaching effect. When dealing with a research problem that has international connotations, the researcher must locate, read, and evaluate any tax treaty that applies to the client's problem. The researcher cannot rely on the more typical sources of tax research information because these

Exhibit 3-4: Tax Treaty Excerpt

File Edit View Favorites Tools Help   Address http://checkpoint.riag.com/Checkpoint?usid=2e16282b2c8&n=   Go

RIA Checkpoint

Research   Newsstand   Training and Tips

Search | Table of Contents | e-FormRS | Tools

Full Text - Ukraine: Income tax 1994
U.S. Tax Treaties in Force

Income Tax Treaty with Ukraine. The treaty entered into force on June 5, 2000.

CONVENTION BETWEEN THE GOVERNMENT OF THE UNITED STATES OF AMERICA AND THE GOVERNMENT OF UKRAINE FOR THE AVOIDANCE OF DOUBLE TAXATION AND THE PREVENTION OF FISCAL EVASION WITH RESPECT TO TAXES ON INCOME AND CAPITAL

The Government of the United States of America and the Government of Ukraine, confirming their desire to develop and strengthen the economic, scientific, technical and cultural cooperation between both States, and desiring to conclude a convention for the avoidance of double taxation and the prevention of fiscal evasion with respect to taxes on income and capital, have agreed as follows:

ARTICLE 1 General Scope

1. This Convention shall apply to persons who are residents of one or both of the Contracting States and to other persons as specifically provided in the Convention.

2. The Convention shall not restrict in any manner any exclusion, exemption, deduction, credit, or other allowance now or hereafter accorded:

a) by the laws of either Contracting State; or

b) by any other agreement between the Contracting States.

3. Notwithstanding any provision of the Convention except paragraph 4, a Contracting State may tax, in accordance with its domestic law, residents (as determined under Article 4 (Residence)) of that State, and in the case of the United States, its citizens and former citizens.

4. The following benefits shall be conferred by a Contracting State notwithstanding the provisions of paragraph 3:

a) under paragraph 2 of Article 9 (Associated Enterprises), paragraph 1 of Article 19 (Pensions) and Articles 24 (Relief from Double Taxation), 25 (Non-discrimination) and 26 (Mutual Agreement Procedure); and

b) under Articles 18 (Government Service), 20 (Students, Trainees and Researchers), and 28 (Diplomatic Agents and Consular Officers) for individuals who are neither citizens of that State nor, in the case of the United States of America, individuals having immigrant status therein.

ARTICLE 2 Taxes Covered

Add to My Folders   Print   Export   Contents references usually address only domestic tax precedents. Tax treaties often address issues such as the following.

- How to treat the business and investment income of the visiting taxpayer

- When the visitor is subject to the host country's tax laws

- How to offset the possibility of taxing the same income or assets more than once

- How to compute the taxable amount in the host country

- To what extent host-country withholding taxes are applied to the visitor's transactions

- How taxes levied by a state/province/canton are treated by the taxpayer

- What tax disclosures must be made by the visitor

The Constitution provides that "Laws of the United States which shall be made in pursuance thereof; and all Treaties made, or which shall be made, under the Authority of the United States, shall be the supreme Law of the Land." An *Internal Revenue Code* provision and a provision under a treaty will sometimes conflict. In such a case, both of the provisions cannot represent the law; the one adopted later in time generally controls.

> **Example 3-1 Treaty Override.** Prior to 1980, the United States negotiated treaties with several countries that allowed foreign taxpayers to sell U.S. real estate and not pay tax on gains. Under these treaties, nonresident aliens and foreign corporations could avoid U.S. taxes on real estate if the gains were treated as capital gains and were not effectively connected with the conduct of a U.S. business. Because of this favorable treatment for foreign investors, many U.S. farmers felt foreign investors were bidding up the price of farmland in the United States. This and other concerns led Congress to pass the Foreign Investment in Real Property Tax Act (FIRPTA) of 1980. Under §897, FIRPTA makes gains and losses by nonresident aliens and foreign corporations taxable by treating such transactions as effectively connected with a U.S. trade or business. This provision overrides any treaties in effect at that time by making foreign capital gains on real property taxable for transactions after 1984. If an existing treaty was renegotiated prior to 1985, the new treaty could designate a different effective date for §897; however, the designated effective date could not be more than two years after the signing of the renegotiated treaty.

This later-in-time rule appears to be a simplistic approach to the complex interaction of the Code and treaty provisions. The courts have presented interpretive guidelines to be used in resolving interstatutory conflicts. One such guideline is that, where possible, equal effect should be given to both statutes; congressional intent to repeal a statute should not be assumed. A significant judicial history also exists for the interaction of treaties and the Code. In fact, as with conflicts between statutes, courts usually attempt to reconcile the apparent conflict in a way that gives consideration to both the treaty and the Code provisions.

The equality of the two types of provisions is indicated in §7852(d) of the Code, which provides that neither a treaty nor a law shall be given preferential status by reason of its being a treaty or a law. The language of both the Code and the Constitution make this clear. The only codified exception to this rule is that treaty provisions in effect in 1954 and which conflicted with the 1954 Code as originally enacted are given precedence over the existing provisions of the 1954 Code, but not over later amendments to the Code. Section 894 states that due regard shall be given to any treaty obligation of the United States that applies to the taxpayer when applying the provisions of the *Internal Revenue Code*.

Treaties are authorized by the U.S. Constitution. Under Article II, Section 2, of the Constitution, the President of the United States is allowed to enter into treaties with other countries after receiving the advice and consent of the Senate. The President may also enter into other international agreements that have effects on the Federal tax structure. Such agreements need not be ratified by the Senate; however, they are implemented by Congress in accordance with existing Federal laws. But tax treaties usually are initiated by the State Department, not the Treasury. Generally, tax treaties do not address the U.S. state and local tax effects of the citizens and transactions covered by them.

Treaties may be terminated in several ways. They may expire because of a specific congressional time limitation, be superseded by a newer treaty, or be terminated by the countries' mutual actions.

Tax researchers often find it necessary to examine the provisions of tax treaties. Tax treaties can be found in both the online and printed versions of most tax services, at the government web sites of many countries, and in many legal publications such as West's *United States Code Annotated*.

THE LEGISLATIVE PROCESS

To understand how to research tax issues, the tax researcher must have a grasp of the Federal legislative process. The tax law of the United States, like automobiles and hot dogs, is created in a multistep process. At each stage in the creation of a tax law, Congress generates additional items of information, each of which may be useful in addressing a client's tax problem.

Most tax legislation begins in the House of Representatives. In the House, tax law changes are considered by the Ways and Means Committee. Upon approval by this committee, the bill is sent to the full House of Representatives for its approval. The bill then is sent to the Senate, where it is referred to the Finance Committee. When the Finance Committee approves the bill, the proposal is considered by the entire Senate.

If any differences between the House and Senate versions of the tax bill exist (which is almost always the case), the bill is referred to a Joint Conference Committee, where these differences are resolved. The compromise bill must be approved by both houses of Congress before it is forwarded to the President. If the President signs the bill, the new provisions are incorporated into the *Internal Revenue Code*. If the bill is vetoed by the President, however, it is not enacted, unless Congress overrides the veto with a sufficient revote. Exhibit 3-5 summarizes the usual steps of the legislative process as it is encountered relative to tax legislation.

At each step in the legislative process, the appropriate committee of Congress produces a **Committee Report**, which explains the elements of the proposed changes and the reasons for each of the proposals. These Committee Reports are an important tool for tax researchers. In many situations where the tax law is unclear, or when recent legislation has been passed, they can provide insight concerning the meaning of a specific phrase of the statute or of the intention of Congress concerning a certain provision of the law. Committee Reports typically result from the deliberations of the Ways and Means Committee, the Finance Committee, and the Joint Conference Committee. A "General Explanation" of tax legislation occasionally is prepared by the Joint Committee on Taxation (the "Blue Book"). Exhibit 3-6 reproduces a portion of such a Committee Report.

Exhibit 3-5: Legislative Process to Amend the Tax Law

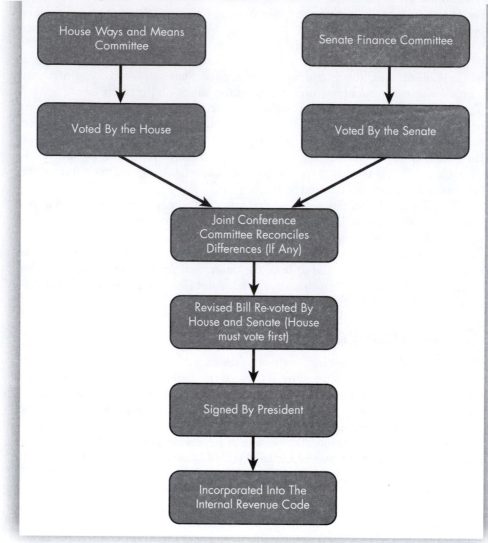

Committee Reports generally are referred to by Public Law number. Every bill that Congress passes is assigned such a number. For example, the Tax Reform Act of 1986 was designated as P.L. 99-514. Public Law is abbreviated as "P.L." in this context. The prefix of the numerical designation (here, 99) refers to the session of Congress that passed the law. The suffix of the Public Law number (here, 514) indicates that this was the five-hundred-fourteenth bill that this session of Congress adopted.

Congressional sessions last for two years; therefore, the researcher may find it useful to construct a method by which to identify the two-year period in which a tax law was passed. The recent sessions of Congress are identified as follows.

Congressional Sessions	Years
One-hundred-seventh	2001–02
One-hundred-eighth	2003–04
One-hundred-ninth	2005–06
One-hundred-tenth	2007–08
One-hundred-eleventh	2009–10
One-hundred-twelfth	2011–12

Exhibit 3-6: Committee Report

Conference Report 107-84: ECONOMIC GROWTH AND TAX RELIEF RECONCILIATION ACT OF 2001, PL 107-16

PRESENT LAW

Under the Code, gross income means, "Income from whatever source derived" except for certain items specifically exempt or excluded by statute (sec. 61). There is no explicit statutory exception from gross income provided for amounts received by Holocaust victims or their heirs.

HOUSE BILL

No provision.

SENATE AMENDMENT

The Senate amendment provides that excludible restitution payments made to an eligible individual (or the individual's heirs or estate) are: (1) excluded from gross income; and (2) not taken into account for any provision of the Code which takes into account excludable gross income in computing adjusted gross income (e.g., taxation of Social Security benefits).

The basis of any property received by an eligible individual (or the individual's heirs or estate) that is excluded under this provision is the fair market value of such property at the time of receipt by the eligible individual (or the individual's heirs or estate).

The Senate amendment provides that any excludible restitution payment is disregarded in determining eligibility for, and the amount of benefits and services to be provided under, any Federal or federally assisted program which provides benefit or service based, in whole or in part, on need. Under the Senate amendment, no officer, agency, or instrumentality of any government may attempt to recover the value of excessive benefits or services provided under such a program before January 1, 2000, by reason of failure to take account of excludible restitution payments received before that date. Similarly, the Senate amendment requires a good faith effort to notify any eligible individual who may have been denied such benefits or services of their potential eligibility for such benefits or services. The Senate amendment also provides coordination between this bill and Public Law 103-286, which also disregarded certain restitution payments in determining eligibility for, and the amount of certain needs-based benefits and services.

Eligible restitution payments are any payment or distribution made to an eligible individual (or the individual's heirs or estate) which: (1) is payable by reason of the individual's status as an eligible individual (including any amount payable by any foreign country, the United States, or any foreign or domestic entity or fund established by any such country or entity, any amount payable as a result of a final resolution of legal action, and any amount payable under a law providing for payments or restitution of property); (2) constitutes the direct or indirect return of, or compensation or reparation for, assets stolen or hidden, or otherwise lost to, the individual before, during, or immediately after World War II by reason of the individual's status as an eligible individual (including any proceeds of insurance under policies issued on eligible individuals by European insurance companies immediately before and during World War II); or (3) interest payable as part of any payment or distribution described in (1) or (2), above. An eligible individual is a person who was persecuted for racial or religious reasons by Nazi Germany, or any other Axis regime, or any other Nazi-controlled or Nazi-allied country.

EFFECTIVE DATE

The provision is effective for any amounts received on or after January 1, 2000. No inference is intended with respect to the income tax treatment of any amount received before January 1, 2000.

continued

Exhibit 3-6: (continued)

CONFERENCE AGREEMENT

The conference agreement follows the Senate amendment, with three changes. First, the definition of eligible individuals is expanded to also include individuals persecuted on the basis of physical or mental disability or sexual orientation. Second, interest earned by enumerated escrow or settlement funds are also excluded from tax. Third, the provision disregarding excludible restitution in determining eligibility for and the benefit calculation of certain Federal or Federally assisted programs is deleted.

To convert a session number into the second year of the applicable congressional session, multiply the session number by 2 and subtract 212 (the number of years from 1788 to 2000). For example, the second year of the one-hundred-ninth Congress is 2006 $[(109 \times 2) - 212 = 06]$.

Where to Find Committee Reports

When a new tax law is passed, the pertinent Committee Reports are released in the Internal Revenue Service's weekly *Internal Revenue Bulletin*. The texts of the 1954 Committee Reports relative to the **Internal Revenue Code** are found not in the *Cumulative Bulletin*, but in the *United States Code Congressional and Administrative News*. All of the pre-1939 Revenue Act Committee Reports are reprinted in the 1939 *Cumulative Bulletin*.

The Committee Reports and other legislative items can also be found in most subscription online tax services (e.g., RIA Checkpoint) and on various nonsubscription Internet sites such as:

http://thomas.loc.gov

http://waysandmeans.house.gov/

http://www.senate.gov/~finance/

Commerce Clearing House and the Research Institute of America both publish, usually in paperback form, a collection of Committee Reports (or excerpts thereof) whenever a major new tax law is passed. If a tax researcher wants to find the Committee Reports that underlie a statutory provision, he or she also can use reference materials that are included in the bodies of most of the commercial tax services or in the index to the *Cumulative Bulletin*.

The Committee Reports Findings List in Commerce Clearing House's *Citator*, Volume M–Z, is a good place for the tax researcher to locate Committee Reports by P.L. number. See Part 3 of this text for a detailed review of the use of citators.

In addition to the Committee Reports, the Floor Debate Report may be of value to the tax researcher. The Floor Debate Report includes a summary of what was said from the floor of the House or Senate concerning the proposed bill. It may include some detailed or technical information that is excluded from the Committee Report. The Floor Debate Report is included in the *Congressional Record* for the day of the debate.

INTERNAL REVENUE CODE

After the Sixteenth Amendment was ratified in 1913, Congress passed a series of self-contained revenue acts, each of which formed the entire income tax law of the United States. For about two decades, Congress passed such a free-standing revenue act every year or two. By the 1930s, however, this series of revenue acts, and the task of rewriting the entire tax statute so often, had become unmanageable. Thus, in 1939, Congress replaced the revenue acts with the *Internal Revenue Code of 1939*, the first fully organized Federal tax law.

Although the concept of a free-standing tax Code, as part of the entire *United States Code*, was a good idea, the organization of the *Internal Revenue Code of 1939* left little room to accommodate subsequent changes to the law. Accordingly, the 1939 Code was replaced with a reorganized, more flexible codification in 1954. Due to extensive revisions to the Code that were made as part of the Tax Reform Act of 1986, the statute was renamed the *Internal Revenue Code of 1986*. Thus, although the statute still follows the 1954 numbering system and organization, the official title of the extant U.S. tax law is the *Internal Revenue Code of 1986, as Amended*.

The principal sources of tax laws of the United States since 1913, then, have been identified as follows.

Period	Principal U.S. Tax Law
1913–39	*Periodic Revenue Acts*
1939–54	*Internal Revenue Code of 1939*
1954–86	*Internal Revenue Code of 1954*
1986–Present	*Internal Revenue Code of 1986*

Many provisions of the 1939 Code were carried over to the *Internal Revenue Code of 1954* without substantive change; some of these sections were adopted into the Code verbatim, although all of the sections were renumbered as part of the 1954 reorganization.

SPOTLIGHT ON TAXATION

Growth of the Code

If you think the tax law is getting more complex, you're correct. According to the Tax Foundation, in 1955 the *Internal Revenue Code* contained 106 Code sections and 409,000 words. Today there are about 1,000 Code sections containing more than 2,139,000 words.

The *Internal Revenue Code* is part of the *United States Code*, which is a codification of all of the Federal laws of the United States. The elements of the *United States Code* are organized alphabetically and assigned title numbers. Accordingly, the *Internal Revenue Code* constitutes Title 26 of the *United States Code*; its neighbors in the *U.S. Code* at one time included "Insane Asylums" and "Intoxicating Liquors."

Organization of the Internal Revenue Code

The *Internal Revenue Code* is organized into an outline form with multiple levels or subdivisions. The primary levels found in the Code are as follows.

Subtitles

  Chapters

    Subchapters

      Parts

        Sections

          Subsections

Subtitles of the Code are assigned a capital letter to identify them (currently A through K are used). Generally, each subtitle contains all of the tax provisions that relate to a well-defined area of the tax law. Exhibit 3-7 identifies the subtitles of the current Code. The tax researcher spends most of his or her time working with Subtitles A, Income Taxes; B, Estate and Gift Taxes; and F, Procedure and Administration. The other subtitles typically are used only from time to time for special research problems.

Each subtitle contains a number of chapters, numbered, although not continuously, from 1 through 100. These chapter numbers do not start over at each subtitle; rather, they are used in ascending order throughout the Code. Thus, for example, there is only one Chapter 11 in the *Internal Revenue Code*, not eleven of them. Each chapter contains the tax provisions that relate to a more narrowly defined area of the tax law than is addressed by the subtitles. Most of the subtitles include several chapters. Exhibit 3-8 examines the numbering system of the chapters of the *Internal Revenue Code*, concentrating on selected important chapters.

The chapters of the *Internal Revenue Code* are further divided into subchapters. Typically a subchapter contains a group of provisions that relates to a fairly specific area of the tax law. Subchapters sometimes are divided into parts, which may be divided into subparts. Letters are used to denote subchapters, and the lettering scheme starts over with each chapter. Thus, there may be a Subchapter A in each chapter.

Many times, tax practitioners use the subchapter designation as a shorthand reference to identify a certain area of taxation. For example, Subchapter C of

Exhibit 3-7: Subtitles of the *Internal Revenue Code*, as Amended

Subtitle	Tax Law Included
A	Income Taxes
B	Estate and Gift Taxes
C	Employment Taxes
D	Miscellaneous Excise Taxes
E	Alcohol; Tobacco; Miscellaneous Excise Taxes
F	Procedure and Administration
G	Joint Committee on Taxation
H	Presidential Election Campaign Financing
I	Trust Funds

Exhibit 3-8: Key Chapters of the *Internal Revenue Code*

Chapter	Subjects Included
1	Normal Taxes and Surtaxes
2	Self-Employment Tax
6	Consolidated Returns
11	Estate Taxes
12	Gift Taxes
61	Administration/Information
79	Definitions

Chapter 1 of Subtitle A of the *Internal Revenue Code* includes many of the basic corporate income tax provisions. Thus, when a tax practitioner wants to refer to a corporate tax matter, he or she often simply identifies it as a "Subchapter C" issue.

Most of the Code's subchapters are divided into parts. The parts provide a natural grouping of provisions that address essentially the same issue. Not all subchapters are divided into parts, and occasionally the parts are not numbered consecutively. For instance, the parts of Chapter 1, Subchapter A (i.e., normal income taxes), are:

Part I	Tax on Individuals
Part II	Tax on Corporations
Part III	Changes in Rates during a Taxable Year
Part IV	Credits against Tax
Part V	Not Used
Part VI	Alternative Minimum Tax
Part VII	Environmental Tax

Exhibit 3-9 shows the Table of Contents to Subtitle A (Income Taxes) of the Code with the "Parts" level shown for Subchapters A, B, and C. To save space, the "Parts" level is not shown for the other subchapters.

Exhibit 3-9: Subtitle A: Table of Contents Excerpt

Subtitle A Income Taxes §§1-1564
   Chapter 1 Normal Taxes and Surtaxes §§1-1400t
      Subchapter A Determination of Tax Liability §§1-59b
         Part I Tax on Individuals §§1-5
         Part II Tax on Corporations §§11-12
         Part III Changes in Rates During a Taxable Year §§15-15
         Part IV Credits Against Tax §§21-54
         Part VI Alternative Minimum Tax §§55-59
         Part VII Environmental Tax §§59a-59a
         Part VIII Supplemental Medicare Premium [Repealed]§§59b-59b
      Subchapter B Computation of Taxable Income §§61-291
         Part I Definition of Gross Income, Adjusted Gross Income, Taxable Income, Etc. §§61-68
         Part II Items Specifically Included in Gross Income §§71-90
         Part III Items Specifically Excluded from Gross Income §§101-140
         Part IV Tax Exemption Requirements for State and Local Bonds §§141-150
         Part V Deductions for Personal Exemptions §§151-153
         Part VI Itemized Deductions for Individuals and Corporations §§161-199
         Part VII Additional Itemized Deductions for Individuals §§211-224
         Part VIII Special Deductions for Corporations §§241-249
         Part IX Items Not Deductible §§261-280h
         Part X Terminal Railroad Corporations and Their Shareholders §§281-281
         Part XI Special Rules Relating to Corporate Preference Items §§291-291
      Subchapter C Corporate Distributions and Adjustments §§301-385
         Part I Distributions by Corporations §§301-318
         Part II Corporate Liquidations §§331-346
         Part III Corporate Organizations and Reorganizations §§351-368

continued

Exhibit 3-9: (continued)

Part IV Insolvency Reorganizations [Repealed] §§370-374
Part V Carryovers §§381-384
Part VI Treatment of Certain Corporate Interests as Stock or Indebtedness §§385-385
Part VII Miscellaneous Corporate Provisions [Repealed] §§386-386
Subchapter D Deferred Compensation, Etc. §§401-436
Subchapter E Accounting Periods and Methods of Accounting §§441-483
Subchapter F Exempt Organizations §§501-530
Subchapter G Corporations used to Avoid Income Tax on Shareholders §§531-565
Subchapter H Banking Institutions §§581-597
Subchapter I Natural Resources §§611-638
Subchapter J Estates, Trusts, Beneficiaries, and Decedents §§641-692
Subchapter K Partners and Partnerships §§701-777
Subchapter L Insurance Companies §§801-848
Subchapter M Regulated Investment Companies and Real Estate Investment
      Trusts §§851-860L
Subchapter N Tax Based on Income from Sources within or without The United States
      §§861-999
Subchapter O Gain or Loss on Disposition of Property §§1001-1111
Subchapter P Capital Gains and Losses §§1201-1298
Subchapter Q Readjustment of Tax between Years and Special Limitations §§1301-1351
Subchapter R Election to Determine Corporate Tax on Certain International Shipping …
      §§1352-1359
Subchapter S Tax Treatment of S Corporations and Their Shareholders §§1361-1379
Subchapter T Cooperatives and Their Patrons §§1381-1388
Subchapter U Designation and Treatment of Empowerment Zones, Enterprise …
      §§1391-1397e
Subchapter V Title 11 Cases §§1398-1399
Subchapter W District of Columbia Enterprise Zone §§1400-1400c
Subchapter X Renewal Communities §§1400e-1400j
Subchapter Y Short-Term Regional Benefits §§1400l-1400t
Chapter 2 Tax On Self-Employment Income §§1401-1403
Chapter 3 Withholding of Tax on Nonresident Aliens and Foreign Corporations
      §§1441-1464

The most important division of the *Internal Revenue Code* for the tax researcher is the section, because the Code is arranged so that its primary unit is the section number. The sections currently are numbered 1 through 9833, although not all of the numbers are used. Each section number is used only once in the Code. The researcher can refer to a specific provision of the *Internal Revenue Code* by its section number and not be concerned about duplication in another part of the law. Indeed, the most common element of the jargon of the tax practitioner community is the Code section number, and tax researchers must learn to identify important tax provisions merely by the corresponding section number.

Code sections can be divided into various smaller elements for the convenience of the drafter or user of the section. A section can contain subsections, paragraphs, subparagraphs, and clauses. Sections are denoted by numbers (1, 2, etc.), subsections by lowercase letters (a, b, etc.), paragraphs by numbers, sub-

Exhibit 3-10: Interpreting a Code Section Citation

Section 121(b)(2)(A)(ii)

	Section number 121
	Subsection b
	Paragraph 2
	Subparagraph A
	Clause ii

Section 121	SEC. 121. EXCLUSION OF GAIN FROM SALE OF PRINCIPAL RESIDENCE
Subsection(a)	(a) Exclusion
	Gross income shall not include gain from the sale or exchange of property if, during the 5-year period ending on the date of the sale or exchange, such property has been owned and used by the taxpayer as the taxpayer's principal residence for periods aggregating 2 years or more.
Subsection(b)	(b) Limitations
Paragraph(1)	(1) In general
	The amount of gain excluded from gross income under subsection (a) with respect to any sale or exchange shall not exceed $250,000.
Paragraph(2)	(2) Special rules for joint returns
	In the case of a husband and wife who make a joint return for the taxable year of the sale or exchange of the property—
Subparagraph(A)	(A) $500,000 Limitation for certain joint returns
	Paragraph (1) shall be applied by substituting "$500,000" for "$250,000" if—
Clause(i)	(i) either spouse meets the ownership requirements of subsection (a) with respect to such property;
Clause(ii)	(ii) both spouses meet the use requirements of subsection (a) with respect to such property; and
Clause(iii)	(iii) neither spouse is ineligible for the benefits of subsection (a) with respect to such property by reason of paragraph (3)

paragraphs by capital letters (A, B, etc.), and clauses by lowercase roman numerals (i, ii, etc.). In citing a Code section, one uses parentheses for each division that occurs after the section number.

There are some exceptions to the general formatting of Code section citations. For example, Congress has inserted Code sections in between other consecutive

Exhibit 3-11: Some Important Code Sections

Section Number	Contents
1	Individual Tax Rates
11	Corporate Tax Rates
61	Definition of Gross Income
62	Deductions for Adjusted Gross Income
162	Trade or Business Deductions
163	Interest Deduction
164	Deduction for Taxes
165	Losses
167, 168, 179	Depreciation, Cost Recovery
212	Production-of-Income Expenses
312	Corporate Dividends
351	Forming a Corporation
368	Mergers, Acquisitions, Corporate Break-Ups
469	Passive Activities
501	Tax-Exempt Status
721	Forming a Partnership, LLC
861	Sourcing of International Income and Deductions
904	Foreign Tax Credit
1245	Depreciation Recapture
1504	Consolidated Taxable Income
6662	Penalties for Inaccurate Tax Filings

sections and has had to use a capital letter [e.g., Section 25A(b)(1) or Section 280F (a)(1)] to accomplish this. The Code skips the subsections in certain cases, such as Section 212(2). Exhibit 3-10 provides a specific interpretation of a Code section citation.

Although there are nearly a thousand Code sections, certain ones contain basic principles that affect most tax situations (Exhibit 3-11). The tax researcher should be familiar with this group of Code sections for efficient analysis of his or her clients' tax problems.

Where to Find the Internal Revenue Code

The amended *Internal Revenue Code* can be found in several places. National publishers such as Research Institute of America (RIA), West, and Commerce Clearing House (CCH) publish paperback versions of the Code for use by tax practitioners. In addition, the text of the Code may be found in most commercial tax services and as Title 26 of the *United States Code*.

The type of tax service will indicate the probable location of the original language of the Code in the service. Typically, an annotated tax service (refer to Chapter 2 to review this definition) will include the text of the Code with the related section's discussion. On the other hand, a topical tax service typically reproduces the text of the Code in an appendix to pertinent chapters or volumes of the service.

The *U.S. Code* and the *Internal Revenue Code* (which is Title 26 of the *U.S. Code*) can also be found at various Internet sites. An example of such a site would be:

http://uscode.house.gov/

Exhibit 3-12: Examples of 1986 Code Sections Derived from the 1939 Code

1986 Code Section	1939 Code Section
§61, Gross income defined	§22(a)
§71, Alimony and separate maintenance payments	§22(k)
§103, Interest on state and local bonds	§22(b)(4)
§151, Allowance of deductions for personal exemptions	§25(b)
§162, Trade or business expenses	§23(a)(1)
§172, Net operating loss deduction	§122
§212, Expenses for production of income	§23(a)(2)
§301, Distributions of property	§22(e), 115(a), (b), (d), (e)
§316, Dividends defined	§115(a) and (b)
§701, Partners, not partnership, subject to tax	§181

Occasionally, a tax researcher needs to refer to a source that originated from the *Internal Revenue Code of 1939*. Many of the provisions of the 1986 (and 1954) Code can be found in the 1939 Code. Exhibit 3-12 gives examples of 1986 Code sections and their 1939 Code equivalents.

Other useful indices to the Code itself are provided by the editors of the tax services. For example, several useful tables are included in the Code volumes of the Commerce Clearing House tax service. In Cross-Reference Table 1, 1939 Code sections are cross-referenced to their 1954 (and 1986) counterparts. In Table 2 of the CCH service, current Code sections are cross-referenced to the 1939 Code.

Table III of this feature cross-references the Code sections within the current Code. These three tables can be useful to the tax researcher when he or she needs to find a 1939 Code section number, perhaps in interpreting a court case that addresses a pre-1954 Code issue, or in identifying situations where a Code section is referred to elsewhere in the current Code, or perhaps to find out whether other Code sections provide information bearing on the section being reviewed.

Most tax services also contain information about the history of each Code section. Typically, at the end of the text of each Code section, or as a related page that can be accessed by linking, the editors include a list of the Public Laws that have altered or amended the section. This listing generally includes a reference to the section as it existed prior to amendment, as well as the effective date of the amendment to the law. The tax researcher must be careful to consider the impact of any such amendments. Exhibit 3-13 illustrates the Public Law history with respect to a specific Code section.

Exhibit 3-13: Recent Amendments to Section 121

In 2003, P.L. 108-121, Sec. 101(a), redesignated para. (d)(9) as (10) and added para. (d)(9), effective for sales and exchanges after 5/6/97. For special rules, see Sec. 312(d)(2)-(4) of P.L. 105-34, reproduced below.

—P.L. 108-121, Sec. 101(b)(2), of this Act, provides:

"(2) Waiver of limitations. If refund or credit of any overpayment of tax resulting from the amendments made by this section is prevented at any time before the close of the 1-year period beginning on the date of the enactment of this Act by the operation of any law or rule of law (including res judicata), such refund or credit may nevertheless be made or allowed if claim therefore is filed before the close of such period."

continued

Exhibit 3-13: (continued)

In 2002, P.L. 107-358, Sec. 2, added subsec. (c) in Sec. 901 of P.L. 107-16 [see below], effective 12/17/2002.

In 2001, P.L. 107-16, Sec. 542(c), added para. (d)(9), effective for estates of decedents dying after 12/31/2009.

—P.L. 107-16, Sec. 901, of this Act [as amended by Sec. 2 of P.L. 107-358, see above], reads as follows:

"Sec. 901. Sunset of provisions of Act.

"(a) In general. All provisions of, and amendments made by, this Act shall not apply—

"(1) to taxable, plan, or limitation years beginning after December 31, 2010, or

"(2) in the case of title V, to estates of decedents dying, gifts made, or generation skipping transfers, after December 31, 2010.

"(b) Application of certain laws. The Internal Revenue Code of 1986 and the Employee Retirement Income Security Act of 1974 shall be applied and administered to years, estates, gifts, and transfers described in subsection (a) as if the provisions and amendments described in subsection (a) had never been enacted.

"(c) Exception. Subsection (a) shall not apply to section 803 (relating to no federal income tax on restitution received by victims of the Nazi regime or their heirs or estates)."

One other publication will prove to be valuable if the researcher is addressing issues that predate the 1954 Code. *Seidman's Legislative History of Federal Income Tax Laws* details the historical evolution of the early tax law. It explains how certain provisions evolved into their current form in the Code.

INTERPRETING THE INTERNAL REVENUE CODE

One of the greatest problems for a tax researcher is the interpretation of the *Internal Revenue Code*. Often, Code provisions are long, interrelated, and confusing. For example, several sentences in the Code exceed 300 words; one of them exceeds 400 words. In researching a client's tax problem, one must read each Code section that might apply. Many times, a single phrase or clause in the section may prevent the client from being subject to the provision or may contain other unexpected implications for the client's situation.

A researcher, in his or her initial review, may find the topical index, which is included by most publishers of the Code, a useful tool in locating a starting point or the relevant Code section. In reading, interpreting, and evaluating a selected Code section, the tax researcher must be especially critical of the language used throughout the section. Many, if not most, Code sections contain a general rule, followed by specific conditions that must be satisfied in order to apply the provision, and situations under which the taxpayer is excepted from the general rule. In some cases, the exceptions to the general rule are further modified to provide for exceptions to the general exceptions. Moreover, some exceptions to a Code section are addressed not within the same section, but in another section of the Code. Therefore, all relevant provisions must be read carefully.

In addition to being aware of the required conditions for application of a section, as well as the exceptions thereto, the researcher must be aware of the definitions of terms used in the section; pertinent definitions may be given within the section or in some other provision of the Code. These definitions may be significantly different from the common use of the term.

In §7701, the text defines many of the terms used throughout the Code, but these definitions may be superseded by material contained within the applicable Code section. In addition, the researcher may need to look beyond the Code, such as to the Regulations or other authority, to determine the conditions that a specific term may encompass. In all cases, the researcher should avoid jumping to premature conclusions until a thorough analysis of all relevant Code sections has been completed.

The tax researcher must be careful not to overlook words that connect phrases, such as "and" and "or." These words have very different logical meanings, and, even when the words are "hidden" at the end of the previous clause or subparagraph, they may significantly change the outcome of a research project. The word "and" is conjunctive; the word "or" is disjunctive. If the word "and" lies between two phrases, both of them must be true for the provision to apply to the client's problem. However, if the word "or" lies between two phrases, then only one of them must be true for the provision to apply.

The researcher also must be careful with words that modify percentage or dollar amounts. The phrases "less than 50 percent," "more than 50 percent," and "not less than 50 percent" have very different meanings in determining whether the provisions of a section apply. The researcher also must distinguish between such terms as "thirty days" and "one month," because they usually identify different time periods.

> ### Example 3-2 Conflicting Code Sections.
> Paul is a roofing contractor and has a truck he uses 100 percent of the time in his business. The truck cost $35,000 three years ago, and Paul has claimed cost recovery deductions of $24,920 on the truck, which leaves him an adjusted basis of $10,080. Paul sells the truck for $22,080 resulting in a gain of $12,000 on the truck. How is he to treat this gain for tax purposes?

In the *Internal Revenue Code*, Paul finds that when depreciable property used in a trade or business [§1231(b)] is sold, the gain is treated as a long-term capital gain [§1231(a)]. Thus, he might report the gain on his tax return as a long-term capital gain. However, in §1245(a), Paul discovers that gain on depreciable personal property (in this case, the truck) is ordinary income to the extent of depreciation claimed since 1961. Thus, §1245 would indicate the gain is ordinary, not long-term capital.

How is the problem resolved? In §1245(d), Paul finds a directive that the recapture provision "shall apply notwithstanding any other provision of this subtitle [of the Code]." As a result, he must report the gain as ordinary income on his tax return, not long-term capital gain.

If Paul had read only §1231 of the Code and not §1245, he would have arrived at a different conclusion about the gain. In many situations, when Code sections conflict, the resolution of the conflict may not be as easy as in this example.

When analyzing a provision that recently has been changed by Congress, a researcher must be very careful to cross-reference all of the uses of terms whose definitions have been affected by the new law. Often, Congress does not use the care necessary to ascertain that all of the "loose ends" of the new provisions have been tied up. In recent years, almost every major change in the tax law has been followed by a "technical corrections act" to remove errors in implementing and interpreting the new provisions of the law, as well as to clarify problems that arise in integrating the new provisions with the existing provisions of the Code. Most of these corrections are identified by practitioners whose clients' situations are adversely affected by a given reading of the amended law; thus, the typical technical corrections act testifies as much to the thoroughness of the practitioners' research as to shoddy drafting of the law by Congress.

Because the provisions of the *Internal Revenue Code* change frequently, the researcher must be aware of the effective dates of the various changes to the law. A provision may not go into effect immediately upon its adoption by Congress. The date of the act with which the change in law is passed is not always indicative of the effective date of the provision. Often, various provisions under the same tax law will become effective on different dates and, in fact, may have effective dates that precede the date of the tax act. Similarly, when a provision of the tax law is deleted from the Code, the provision may be left in effect for a designated period of time before it actually expires. Transitional rules may also apply. The effective date for a change in the tax law usually may be found in the explanation of the Public Laws, which follows the pertinent Code section (see, e.g., Exhibit 3-13). In some cases, the researcher may need to look to the explanation under another Code section for the effective date of a provision. The researcher must be careful to align the client's facts with the effective law at the pertinent dates, or a serious mistake could be made in the research conclusion.

Finally, the tax researcher must be aware that not *all* of the answers to a tax question will be found in the Code. The Code may be silent concerning the problem at hand, the application of Code language to the fact situation at hand may not be clear, or Code sections may appear to be in conflict. Thus, the researcher must look for an answer from other sources, such as tax treaties, administrative rulings (see Chapter 4), judicial decisions (see Chapter 5), or secondary sources of the law (see Chapters 6 through 8). Alternatively, the controlling law may be found in other parts of the Code, such as tariff or bankruptcy laws. Exhibit 3-14 lists examples of Federal laws other than the Code that affect specific tax matters.

Exhibit 3-14: Examples of Federal Laws Other Than the *Internal Revenue Code* That May Affect a Tax Transaction

Administrative Procedure Act

Alaska Native Claims Settlement Act

Atomic Energy Act Tax Provision

Bank Holding Company Act of 1956

Civil Rights Attorneys' Fees Awards Act of 1976

Financial Institutions Reform, Recovery, and Enforcement Act of 1989

Metric Conversion Act of 1975

Merchant Marine Act: Capital Construction Fund

New York City Pension Act

Organic Act of Guam

SUMMARY

The three major sources of statutory tax law are the Constitution, tax treaties, and the *Internal Revenue Code*. The tax researcher must thoroughly understand each of these sources and the interrelationships among them. The Constitution is the basis for all Federal laws. The tax treaties are agreements between countries, negotiated by the President and approved by the Senate, that cover taxpayers subject to the tax laws of both countries. The authority of a tax treaty may equal or exceed that of a Code section. The greatest volume of tax statutes is found in the *Internal Revenue Code*, which is Title 26 of the *United States Code*. The Code contains the tax laws that Congress has passed, and it is the basic document for most U.S. tax provisions.

TAX TUTOR

Reinforce the tax research information covered in this chapter by completing the online tutorials located at the *Federal Tax Research* web site: **http://academic.cengage.com/taxation/raabe**

KEY WORDS

By the time you complete this chapter, you should be comfortable discussing each of the following terms. If you need additional review of any of these items, return to the appropriate material in the chapter or consult the glossary to this text.

Committee Report
Internal Revenue Code
Primary authorities

Secondary authorities
Statutory sources
Tax treaties

DISCUSSION QUESTIONS

1. What are the three primary statutory sources of U.S. Federal tax law?

2. Discuss the effect of *Pollock v. Farmers' Loan and Trust Co.* on the development of U.S. income tax laws.

3. The Sixteenth Amendment to the Constitution had a significant effect on the U.S. income tax. What was it?

4. Discuss briefly the events leading to the passage of the Sixteenth Amendment to the U.S. Constitution.

5. What did the U.S. Supreme Court hold in *Flint v. Stone Tracy Co.* in 1911?

6. Tax protesters who file "frivolous" tax returns or bring "frivolous" proceedings before the U.S. Tax Court are subject to certain fines or other penalties. What are the grounds for imposing each penalty? What is the maximum amount of each penalty?

7. Discuss the powers of taxation that are granted to Congress by the U.S. Constitution. Are any limits placed on the powers of Congress to so tax?

8. Have the Federal courts ever held Federal estate and gift taxes to be unconstitutional?

9. What is a tax treaty? Explain the purpose of a tax treaty. What matters generally are covered in a tax treaty?

10. How is a tax treaty terminated?

11. When an *Internal Revenue Code* section and a tax treaty provision appear to conflict, which usually prevails?

12. Describe the ratification process for a tax treaty between the United States and another country.

13. The tax researcher must be able to find descriptions of tax treaties to solve certain tax problems. List different locations where a tax researcher might find a tax treaty.

14. Briefly summarize the usual steps of the legislative process for development of Federal tax legislation.

15. As a bill proceeds through Congress, various Committee Reports are generated. List the three Committee Reports that typically are prepared for a new tax law.

16. When are Committee Reports useful to a tax researcher?

17. What is a Public Law number? In P.L. 100-203, what do the "100" and the "203" indicate?

18. Where would a tax researcher find pertinent Committee Reports? List at least four publications and their publishers that include tax-related Committee Reports. Is there an index that would help a tax researcher locate a specific Committee Report? If so, where might such an index be found?

19. In addition to the Committee Reports, which are a by-product to the development of tax legislation, what other report may be of value to the tax researcher analyzing a new provision of the tax law? Why?

20. Discuss the evolution of today's *Internal Revenue Code*.

21. The *Internal Revenue Code* is Title 26 of the *United States Code*. How is the *Internal Revenue Code* subdivided?

22. How are the subtitles of the *Internal Revenue Code* identified? What generally is contained in a subtitle?

23. In the citation §101(a)(2)(B), what does the "a" stand for? What do the "2" and the "B" indicate to a tax researcher?

24. In the citation §1031(a)(3)(B), what does the "a" stand for? What do the "3" and the "B" indicate to a tax researcher?

25. Are there any exceptions to the general formatting rules for a Code section? Give examples.

26. In what subchapter of Chapter 1, Subtitle A are located the Code sections relating to:
    a. corporations?
    b. mutual funds?
    c. tax-exempt organizations?

27. What Code section contains the statute for the definition of:
    a. gross income?
    b. the interest deduction?
    c. depreciation and cost recovery?

28. The tax researcher must be careful not to overlook connecting words such as "and," "or," "at least," and "more than." Explain why this is important.

29. Not all statutory tax laws are found in the *Internal Revenue Code*. Is this statement true or false? Discuss briefly.

EXERCISES

30. Locate the Committee Reports associated with each of the following Code sections using a tax service such as RIA Checkpoint. Give the Public Law (P.L.) number of the most recent committee for each Code section.
    a. Section 25A
    b. Section 117
    c. Section 162

31. Locate the Committee Reports associated with each of the following Code sections using a tax service such as RIA Checkpoint. Give the Public Law (P.L.) number of the most recent committee for each Code section.
    a. Section 24
    b. Section 243
    c. Section 222

32. Log on (**http://waysandmeans.house.gov**) to the Ways and Means Committee of the U.S. House of Representatives web site and answer the following questions.
    a. Who is the chair of the committee?
    b. What is the total number of members on the committee?
    c. How many of the members are from your home state? If none, say so.
    d. The Ways and Means Committee has several subcommittees. Name three of these subcommittees and indicate who chairs each subcommittee.

33. What is found in each of the following subtitles of the *Internal Revenue Code*?
    a. Subtitle B
    b. Subtitle F
    c. Subtitle A
    d. Subtitle C

34. Each subtitle of the *Internal Revenue Code* contains several chapters. How are chapters identified? What generally is included in a chapter of the Code?

35. Identify the general content of each of the following chapters of the *Internal Revenue Code*.
    a. Chapter 11
    b. Chapter 61
    c. Chapter 1
    d. Chapter 12

36. Chapters of the *Internal Revenue Code* are subdivided into subchapters. How are subchapters identified? What generally is contained in a subchapter?

37. Correctly cite the italicized sentence indicated by the dart (▶) in the following passage from the Code.

    SECTION 74. PRIZES AND AWARDS
    a. General rule
       Except as otherwise provided in this section or in section 117 (relating to qualified scholarships), gross income includes amounts received as prizes and awards.
    b. Exception for certain prizes and awards transferred to charities
       Gross income does not include amounts received as prizes and awards made primarily in recognition of religious, charitable, scientific, educational, artistic, literary, or civic achievement, but only if—

       1. the recipient was selected without any action on his part to enter the contest or proceeding;

       2. ▶ *the recipient is not required to render substantial future services as a condition to receiving the prize or award; and*

       3. the prize or award is transferred by the payor to a governmental unit or organization described in paragraph (1) or (2) of section 170(c) pursuant to a designation made by the recipient.

38. Correctly cite the italicized sentence indicated by the dart (▶) in the following passage from the Code.

    SECTION 263A. CAPITALIZATION AND INCLUSION IN INVENTORY COSTS OF CERTAIN EXPENSES
    a. Nondeductibility of certain direct and indirect costs
       1. In general—In the case of any property to which this section applies, any costs described in paragraph (2)—
          A. in the case of property which is inventory in the hands of the taxpayer, shall be included in inventory costs, and
          B. ▶ *in the case of any other property, shall be capitalized.*
       2. Allocable costs

39. What is the general content of each of the following subchapters of Chapter 1, Subtitle A, of the *Internal Revenue Code*?
    a. Subchapter C
    b. Subchapter K
    c. Subchapter S
    d. Subchapter E

40. What is found in each of the following subchapters of Subtitle A, Chapter 1 of the *Internal Revenue Code*?
    a. Subchapter B
    b. Subchapter E
    c. Subchapter L
    d. Subchapter F

41. Which subchapter of Subtitle A, Chapter 1 of the *Internal Revenue Code* contains the provisions related to:
    a. Deferred Compensation
    b. Partners and Partnerships
    c. Corporate Distribution and Adjustments
    d. Banks

42. Which *Internal Revenue Code* sections are found in each of these subchapters of Subtitle A, Chapter 1?
    a. Subchapter J
    b. Subchapter A
    c. Subchapter I
    d. Subchapter P

43. Which *Internal Revenue Code* sections are found in each of these parts of Subtitle A?
    a. Subchapter A, Part IV
    b. Subchapter C, Part II
    c. Subchapter B, Part VIII
    d. Subchapter A, Part I

44. What is covered in Subtitle A, Chapter 2 of the *Internal Revenue Code*? What *Internal Revenue Code* sections are included in Chapter 2?

45. What is found in each of the following subchapters of Chapter 1, Subtitle A, of the *Internal Revenue Code*?
    a. Subchapter D
    b. Subchapter H
    c. Subchapter P
    d. Subchapter L

46. What is the official name of P.L. 108-27? What year was that law enacted? Where did you find your answer?

47. What is the official name of P.L. 99-514? What year was that law enacted? Where did you find your answer?

48. The most important division of the *Internal Revenue Code* is the section. Sections usually are subdivided into various smaller elements. Name several of these elements and state how they are denoted.

49. Do section numbers repeat themselves or is each one unique?

50. Identify the general contents of each of the following *Internal Revenue Code* sections.
    a. §61
    b. §162

    c. §1

    d. §212

51. Identify the general contents of each of the following *Internal Revenue Code* sections.

    a. §62

    b. §163

    c. §11

    d. §164

52. Locate Section 217 of the Code. It is found in the:

    a. Subtitle of the Code

    b. Chapter

    c. Subchapter

    d. Part

53. Locate Section 2036 of the Code. It is found in the:

    a. Subtitle of the Code

    b. Chapter

    c. Subchapter

    d. Part

54. Use a tax service (e.g., RIA Checkpoint, Lexis, Westlaw, etc.) to answer the following questions.

    a. Which service did you use?

    b. What is the general content of *Internal Revenue Code* §28?

    c. What is the general content of *Internal Revenue Code* §141?

    d. What is the general content of *Internal Revenue Code* §166?

    e. Print a copy (maximum of one page) of any one of the above Code sections and attach it to your answer.

55. Use a tax service (e.g., RIA Checkpoint, Lexis, Westlaw, etc.) to answer the following questions.

    a. Which tax service did you use?

    b. What is the general content of *Internal Revenue Code* §117?

    c. What is the general content of *Internal Revenue Code* §165?

    d. What is the general content of *Internal Revenue Code* §304?

    e. Print a copy (maximum of one page) of any one of the above Code sections and attach it to your answer.

56. Use a tax service (e.g., RIA Checkpoint, Lexis, Westlaw, etc.) to answer the following questions.

    a. Which tax service did you use?

    b. What is the general content of *Internal Revenue Code* §25A?

    c. What is the general content of *Internal Revenue Code* §67?

    d. What is the general content of *Internal Revenue Code* §280G?

    e. Print a copy (maximum of one page) of any one of the above Code sections and attach it to your answer.

57. Name several locations where a tax researcher would find the text of the current *Internal Revenue Code*.

58. If a tax researcher wants to know if there is an equivalent 1939 Code section for a specific 1986 Code section, how would he or she locate it?

59. One important problem that faces a tax researcher is interpretation of the *Internal Revenue Code*. Comment on each of the following interpretation problems.
    a. Exceptions to a Code section
    b. Words that connect phrases, such as "and" and "or"
    c. Recent changes in the Code
    d. Effective dates
    e. Words that modify percentages, dollar amounts, or time

60. Comment on the statement, "All tax questions can be answered using the *Internal Revenue Code*."

61. Does the United States have an income tax treaty with any of the following countries? If it does, in what year was the treaty signed? State where you found this information.
    a. Japan
    b. United Kingdom
    c. Egypt
    d. Germany

62. Does the United States have an estate tax treaty with any of the following countries? If it does, in what year was the treaty signed? State where you found this information.
    a. Canada
    b. Finland
    c. Hungary
    d. Italy

63. Does the United States have an estate tax treaty with any of the following countries? If it does, in what year was the treaty signed? State where you found this information.
    a. Ukraine
    b. Brazil
    c. Kenya
    d. Kazakhstan

64. Use a tax service (e.g., RIA Checkpoint, Lexis, Westlaw, etc.) to locate §117 of the *Internal Revenue Code*. Answer the following questions.
    a. Which tax service did you use?
    b. How many subsection(s) does §117 include?
    c. How many paragraph(s) does §117(b) include?
    d. How many subparagraph(s) does §117(d)(2) include?
    e. Print a copy (maximum of one page) of this section and attach it to your answer.

65. Use a tax service (e.g., RIA Checkpoint, Lexis, Westlaw, etc.) to locate §385 of the *Internal Revenue Code*. Answer the following questions.
    a. Which tax service did you use?
    b. How many subsection(s) does §385 include?

c. How many paragraph(s) does §385(b) include?

d. Print a copy (maximum of one page) of this section and attach it to your answer.

66. Use a tax service (e.g., RIA Checkpoint, Lexis, Westlaw, etc.) to locate §280C of the *Internal Revenue Code*. Answer the following questions.

a. Which tax service did you use?

b. How many subsection(s) does §280C include?

c. How many paragraph(s) does §280C(b) include?

d. How many subparagraph(s) does §280C(b)(2) include?

e. Print a copy (maximum of one page) of this section and attach it to your answer.

67. When was each of the following sections originally enacted? State how you obtained this information.

a. §843

b. §131

c. §469

d. §263A

68. In which subtitle, chapter, and subchapter of the 1986 Code are each of the following sections found?

a. §32

b. §172

c. §2039

d. §6013

69. List the first three section numbers and titles of each of the following sub-chapters of Chapter 1 of the *Internal Revenue Code*.

a. Subchapter B

b. Subchapter E

c. Subchapter J

d. Subchapter S

70. Identify the equivalent section of the current Code for each of the following sections of the 1939 Code. If there is no equivalent section, say so.

a. §1

b. §113(a)

c. §22(a)

d. §115(a)

e. §181

71. Use a computer tax service (e.g., RIA Checkpoint, Lexis, Westlaw, etc.) to lo-cate the following Code sections. What other Code sections reference each of the sections you found? State which computer tax service you used to complete this assignment.

a. §72

b. §307

c. §446

72. Name the article and section of the U.S. Constitution that gives Congress the power to levy a tax.

73. Enumerate the Code sections that contain the chief tax law provisions on the following topics.
    a. S corporations
    b. Personal holding company tax
    c. Gift tax
    d. Tax accounting methods

74. Use a nonsubscription Internet site to determine how many Senators are on the Senate Finance Committee. Who is the Chair of the Finance Committee? State where you found this information.

75. Use a nonsubscription Internet site to determine how many Representatives are on the House Ways and Means Committee. Who is the Chair of the Ways and Means Committee? State where you found this information.

76. Use a nonsubscription Internet site to determine what is contained in each of the following. State where you found this information.
    a. U.S. Const. art. I, §9 cl. 3
    b. U.S. Const. art. I, §8 cl. 1
    c. U.S. Const. art. II, §2 cl. 2

77. Locate and print the first page of a House Ways and Means Committee Report using only a nonsubscription Internet site. State where you found this information.

RESEARCH CASES

78. Private G.I. Jane was a soldier in the Iraq War. Her salary was $1,800 per month, and she was in the war zone for eight months. How much of her salary is taxable for the eight months? In answering this case, use only the *Internal Revenue Code* for your research. *Computer search keywords:* combat, pay, officers, enlisted

79. Carol received a gift of stock from her favorite uncle. The stock had a fair market value of $30,000 and a basis to the uncle of $10,000 at the date of the gift. How much is taxable to Carol from this gift? In answering this case, use only the *Internal Revenue Code* for your research. *Computer search keywords:* gift, gross income, exclusion

80. Maria is an independent long-haul trucker. She receives a speeding ticket for $500, which she pays. Can Maria deduct the ticket on Schedule C? In answering this case, use only the *Internal Revenue Code* for your research. *Computer search keywords:* fines, penalties, deduction

81. Julie loaned her friend Nathan $2,500. Nathan did not repay the debt and skipped town. Can Julie claim any deduction? In answering this case, use only the *Internal Revenue Code* for your research. *Computer search keywords:* loss, bad debt, worthless

82. In December of 20x1, Ann's twelve-year-old cousin, Susan, came to live with her after Susan's parents met an untimely death in a car accident. In 20x2, Ann provided all normal support (e.g., food, clothing, education) for Susan. Ann

did not formally adopt Susan. If Susan lived in the household for the entire year, can Ann claim a dependency exemption for her cousin for the tax year? In answering this case, use only the *Internal Revenue Code* for your research. *Computer search keywords:* dependent, household, support

83. John and Maria support their twenty-one-year-old son, Bill. The son earned $10,500 last year working in a part-time job. Bill went to college part time in the spring semester of the current year. To complete his degree, Bill started school full time in the fall. The fall semester at Bill's college runs from August 20 to December 20. Can John and Maria claim Bill as a dependent on the current year's tax return, even if Bill earns this level of gross income? Assume any dependency test not mentioned has been met. In answering this case, use a computer tax service with only the *Internal Revenue Code* database selected. State your keywords and which computer tax service you used to arrive at your answer.

84. George and Linda are divorced and own a house from the marriage. Under the divorce decree, Linda pays George $3,000 per month alimony. Since the real estate market has collapsed in the area where they live, George and Linda cannot sell the house. Since they are still friends, they decide to live in separate wings of the house until the real estate market recovers. If George and Linda live together for the entire current year, can Linda claim a deduction for the alimony paid to George? In answering this case, use a computer tax service with only the *Internal Revenue Code* database selected. State your keywords and which computer tax service you used to arrive at your answer.

85. Juan sold IBM stock to Richard for a $10,000 loss. Richard is the husband of Juan's sister, Carla. How much of the loss can Juan deduct in the current year if Juan's taxable income is $55,000 and he has no other capital transactions? In answering this case, use a computer tax service with only the *Internal Revenue Code* database selected. State your keywords and which computer tax service you used to arrive at your answer.

86. Tex is a rancher. This year her herd of cattle was infested with hoof-and-mouth disease and had to be destroyed. Tex's insurance policy reimburses her for an amount in excess of the tax basis in the cattle, thereby creating an "insurance gain." After receiving the insurance proceeds, Tex buys a new herd of cattle. Can Tex defer the recognition of this insurance gain on the destroyed herd? In answering this case, use a computer tax service with only the *Internal Revenue Code* database selected. State your keywords and which computer tax service you used to arrive at your answer.

87. Betty owed Martha $5,000. In payment of this debt, Betty transferred to Martha a life insurance policy on Betty, with a cash surrender value of $5,000. The face value of the policy is $100,000. Martha names herself as beneficiary of the policy and continues to make the premium payments. After Martha has paid $15,000 in premiums, Betty dies and Martha collects $100,000. Is any of the $100,000 Martha received taxable? In answering this case, use a computer tax service with only the *Internal Revenue Code* database selected. State your keywords and which computer tax service you used to arrive at your answer.

88. On May 1, Rick formed a new corporation, Red, Inc. He spent $3,000 in legal fees and paid the state $600 in incorporation fees to set up Red Corporation.

Red Corporation started operating its business on May 10. Can Rick or Red Corporation deduct either of these organizational fees? In answering this case, use a computer tax service with only the *Internal Revenue Code* database selected. State your keywords and which computer tax service you used to arrive at your answer.

89. This year, there were massive brush fires in the interior of Mexico. Amy gave $10,000 to the Mexican Relief Foundation, which is organized in Mexico City. The funds were used to provide food, clothing, and shelter to the victims of the Mexican fires. Is Amy's charitable contribution deductible for income tax purposes? In answering this case, use a computer tax service with only the *Internal Revenue Code* database selected. State your keywords and which computer tax service you used to arrive at your answer.

90. Curtis is fifty years old and has an IRA with substantial funds in it. His son, Curtis, Jr., was accepted to Yale University upon graduating from high school. Curtis had not planned for this and needs to draw $25,000 per year out of his IRA to help pay the tuition and fees at Yale. What are the tax consequences of the withdrawals from the IRA? In answering this case, use a computer tax service with only the *Internal Revenue Code* database selected. State your keywords and which computer tax service you used to arrive at your answer.

91. Cathy Coed is a full-time senior student at Big Research University (BRU). Cathy is considered by most as a brilliant student and has been given a $35,000 per year scholarship. In the current year, Cathy pays the following amounts to attend BRU:

Tuition	$26,000
Required Lab Fees	$300
Required Books and Supplies	$1,000
Dorm Fees	$7,500

What are the tax consequences (i.e., how much is income) of the $35,000 current year's scholarship to Cathy? In answering this case, use a computer tax service with only the *Internal Revenue Code* database selected. State your keywords and which computer tax service you used to arrive at your answer.

92. Dennis is an executive of Gold Corporation. He receives a one-for-one distribution of stock rights for each share of common stock he owns. On the date of distribution the stock rights have a fair market value of $2 per right and the stock has a fair market value of $20 per share. Dennis owns 10,000 shares of the stock with a basis of $5 per share. If Dennis does not make any special elections with regard to the stock rights, what is his basis in the rights?
   a. Locate the Code section(s) that deals with this situation. State the section number(s).
   b. Review the Code section(s). Does it raise a need for new information to solve this question?
   c. Are you able to reach a conclusion about the research question from this Code section? If so, what is your conclusion(s)?

93. Kurt purchased a new Toyota hybrid automobile that gets 50 miles per gallon of gasoline. Determine if Kurt gets any special Federal tax breaks for purchasing this energy-saving car. If so, how are such tax breaks calculated?

a. Locate the Code section(s) that deals with this situation. State the section number(s).
b. Review the Code section(s). Does it raise a need for new information to solve this question?
c. Are you able to reach a conclusion about the research question from this Code section? If so, what is your conclusion(s)?

94. Monica purchased two acres of land with an old building on it for $1,000,000. The purchase was made to acquire the land for a new store she wanted to open on the property. Shortly after completing the purchase, Monica pays $80,000 to have the old building demolished. How does Monica treat the $80,000 demolition payment for tax purposes?
a. Locate the Code section(s) that deals with this situation. State the section number(s).
b. Review the Code section(s). Does it raise a need for new information to solve this question?
c. Are you able to reach a conclusion about the research question from this Code section? If so, what is your conclusion(s)?

95. Lihue, Inc. sells timeshares in Hawaii. Gene buys a timeshare out of the inventory of timeshares for sale by Lihue, Inc. Gene agrees to pay them $10,000 down and Lihue, Inc. will finance a seven-year note for the balance of the purchase price at the current market rate of interest. Can Lihue, Inc. use the installment method to report their gain on the sale of the Hawaiian timeshare to Gene?
a. Locate the Code section(s) that deals with this situation. State the section number(s).
b. Review the Code section(s). Does it raise a need for new information to solve this question?
c. Are you able to reach a conclusion about the research question from this Code section? If so, what is your conclusion(s)?

96. Sara Student is a full-time freshman at Small State University (SSU). Her tuition for the year is $42,000, which is paid by Sara's mother, Susan. Sara also has a job earning substantial money as a model; therefore, Sara does not qualify as Susan's dependent. Can Sara's mother claim the HOPE Education credit for the tuition she paid? Can Sara claim the HOPE credit on any unused portion of the tuition?
a. Locate the Code section(s) that deals with this situation. State the section number(s).
b. Review the Code section(s). Does it raise a need for new information to solve this question?
c. Are you able to reach a conclusion about the research question from this Code section? If so, what is your conclusion(s)?

Administrative Regulations and Rulings

Learning Objectives

- Identify the most important administrative sources of the Federal tax law.

- Distinguish among the structure, nature, and purpose of Regulations, Revenue Procedures, and IRS Rulings.

- Describe how to locate, and how to interpret the precedential value of administrative sources of the tax law.

- Explain the elements of common citations for Regulations and other IRS pronouncements.

- Detail the contents and publication practices of the *Internal Revenue Bulletin* and the *Cumulative Bulletin*.

Chapter Outline

THE INTERNAL REVENUE SERVICE (IRS), part of the U.S. Treasury Department, is responsible for the administration of the income tax law. The administrative process consists of both interpreting and enforcing the tax laws. The IRS interprets the law by issuing various pronouncements, examples of which include Treasury Regulations, Revenue Rulings, Revenue Procedures, and Private Letter Rulings requested by taxpayers. Enforcement of the tax law by the IRS consists primarily of the systematic audits of tax returns and administering an appeals process for taxpayers to arbitrate disagreement with audit results (see Chapters 13 and 14). In addition, the IRS administers a collection process to collect overdue taxes. The Treasury Secretary delegates the ongoing administrative responsibilities for the tax law to the Commissioner of the IRS, who is a presidential appointee.

To facilitate the IRS's administration of the tax laws, the Code authorizes the Treasury Secretary (or his or her delegate) to prescribe the Rules and Regulations necessary to administer the Code. According to §7805(a),

> *Except where such authority is expressly given by this title to any person other than an officer or employee of the Treasury Department, the Secretary shall prescribe all needful rules and regulations for the enforcement of this title, including all rules and regulations as may be necessary by reason of any alteration of law in relation to internal revenue.*

This Code section gives the IRS general authority to issue binding Rules and Regulations concerning Title 26 of the *United States Code*. In practice, most of the IRS's pronouncements are written by IRS staff or by the Office of the Chief Counsel of the IRS, who is an Assistant General Counsel of the Treasury Department.

The tax researcher must be especially familiar with the four major types of pronouncements that may be forthcoming under this authority, namely, Regulations, Revenue Rulings, Revenue Procedures, and Letter Rulings. Each of these categories of rulings is issued for a different purpose and carries a different degree of authority. The first three of these categories generally are published by the IRS, while the Letter Rulings (and other pronouncements) typically are not published by any government agency. The remainder of this chapter addresses the nature and location of each of these administrative pronouncements.

REGULATIONS

The **Regulations** constitute the IRS's and, thereby, the Treasury's official interpretation of the *Internal Revenue Code*. Regulations are issued in the form of **Treasury Decisions (TDs)**, which are published in the *Federal Register* and, sometime later, in the *Internal Revenue Bulletin*, discussed later in this chapter. At least thirty days before a TD is published in final form, however, it must be issued in proposed form, allowing interested parties time to comment on it. As a result of the comments received during this process of public hearings, the IRS may make changes in the TD before its final publication.

Before and during the hearings process, the TDs are referred to as **Proposed Regulations** and, unlike Final Regulations, do not have the effect of law. After the hearings are completed, and changes (if any) have been made to the text of the TD, the TD is published in final form. Final Regulations are integrated with previously approved TDs and constitute the full set of IRS Regulations. After this integration has occurred, the TD designation usually is dropped, and the pronouncement simply is referred to as a "Regulation."

Observers have identified two distinct categories of Regulations, general and legislative. **General Regulations** are issued under the general authority granted to the IRS to interpret the language of the Code, usually under a specific Code (or Committee Report) directive of Congress, and with specific congressional authority. An example can be found under §212, Expenses for the Production of Income. This short Code section has many pages of interpretive Regulations, providing taxpayers with operational rules for applying this provision to tax situations.

With respect to **Legislative Regulations**, the IRS is directed by Congress to fulfill effectively a law-making function and to specify the substantive requirements of a tax provision. Regulations that are ordered by the Code in this manner essentially carry the authority of the statute itself and are not easily challenged by taxpayers. Such authority is granted because, in certain (especially technical) areas of the tax law, Congress cannot or does not care to address the detailed or complex issues that are associated with an otherwise-defined tax issue. Accordingly, Congress directs the IRS to pronounce Regulations on the matter. For example, Congress delegated to the IRS the authority to prescribe Regulations necessary to carry out the provisions of §135, which grants an exclusion for interest on certain U.S. savings bonds used for higher education expenses, including Regulations requiring record keeping and information reporting. Another example of this legislative authority is found in §385, which directs the IRS to prescribe Regulations to distinguish debt from equity in "thinly capitalized" corporations. Legislative Regulations bear the greatest precedential value of any IRS pronouncement.

Temporary Regulations

In addition to Proposed and Final Regulations, the IRS periodically issues **Temporary Regulations** in response to a congressional or judicial change in the tax law or its interpretation. Temporary Regulations are not subject to the public-hearings procedure that typifies the development of a Final Regulation, and they are effective immediately upon publication. Although they are effective immediately, the IRS must simultaneously issue the Regulations in proposed form; the Temporary Regulations expire three years after issuance pursuant to the statute.[1] Temporary Regulations are issued to provide the taxpayer with immediate guidance concerning a new provision of the law, perhaps concerning filing requirements that must be satisfied immediately or the clarification of definitions and terms.

Until a Temporary Regulation is replaced with the Final Regulation under a Code section, the tax researcher should treat the Temporary Regulation as though it were final. Thus, Temporary Regulations are fully in effect and must be followed until they are superseded, whereas Proposed Regulations, having been issued only to solicit comments and to expose the IRS's proposed interpretation of the law, need not be followed as if they were law.

Effective Date of Regulations

In general, a new Regulation can be effective on the date on which such Regulation is filed with the *Federal Register*.[2] However, there are certain situations in which a Regulation can be effective retroactively. These are

- The Regulation is filed or issued within eighteen months of the date of the enactment of the statutory provision to which the Regulation relates.

- The Regulation is designed to prevent abuse by taxpayers.

---

[1] IRC §7805.
[2] IRC §7805(b).

- The Regulation corrects a procedural defect in the issuance of a prior Regulation.

- The Regulation relates to internal Treasury Department policies, practices, or procedures.

- The Regulation may apply retroactively by congressional directive.

- The Commissioner also has the power to allow taxpayers to elect to apply new Regulations retroactively.

In situations where a Regulation applies retroactively, it technically can apply starting with the date of the underlying Code section to which it relates. However, the statute of limitations may limit the application of a retroactive Regulation in many situations.

Citing a Regulation

Tax practitioners use a uniform system for citing specific Regulations. Each Regulation is assigned a unique number by the Treasury, which is broadly based on the Code section being interpreted in that Regulation. An example of this citation system appears in Exhibit 4-1.

Exhibit 4-1: Interpreting a Regulation Citation

Reg. § 1.162-21 (a) (2)

⟶	*Type of Regulation (1 = income tax)*
⟶	*Related Code Section (162)*
⟶	*Regulation Number (21)*
⟶	*Regulation Paragraph (a)*
⟶	*Regulation Subparagraph (2)*

Regulation number	SEC. 1.162-21 FINES AND PENALTIES.
Paragraph →	(a) In general.
	No deduction shall be allowed under section 162(a) for any fine or similar penalty paid to—
Subparagraph →	(1) The government of the United States, a State, a territory or possession of the United States, the District of Columbia, or the Commonwealth of Puerto Rico;
Subparagraph →	(2) The government of a foreign country; or
Subparagraph →	(3) A political subdivision of, or corporation or other entity serving as an agency or instrumentality of, any of the above
Paragraph →	(b) Definition.
Subparagraph →	(1) For purposes of this section a fine or similar penalty includes an amount—

The number to the left of the period in a Regulation citation indicates the type of issue that is addressed in the pronouncement. The most commonly encountered types of Regulations include the following.

1. Income Tax

20. Estate Tax

25. Gift Tax

31. Employment Tax

301. Procedural Matters

By being familiar with this arbitrary numbering system used by the Regulations, the tax researcher immediately can identify the general issue that is addressed in a pronouncement. Note that these numbers indicating the type of issue addressed in the Regulation do not necessarily correspond to the chapter numbers of the Code sections that address the same issues.

The number to the immediate right of the period in the citation of a Regulation indicates the Code section to which the Regulation relates. In the Exhibit 4-1 example of a full citation, one can determine that this is an income tax Regulation dealing with §162 of the *Internal Revenue Code*. The numbers and letters to the right of the section number denote the Regulation number and smaller divisions of the pronouncement. Regulation numbers typically are consecutive, starting with 0 or 1, and follow the general order of the issues that are addressed in the corresponding Code section. The Regulation numbers, paragraphs, and so on do not necessarily correspond, however, to the subsection or other division designations of the underlying Code section.

The numbering system for Temporary Regulations is similar to the numbering system for the Final and Proposed Regulations; however, usually the reference to or citation of a Temporary Regulation will include a "T" designating the temporary nature of the Regulation. An example of a citation for a Temporary Regulation under Code §280H is **Reg. §1.280H-1T(b)(3).**

Assessing Regulations

In the course of tax practice, the researcher occasionally is faced with a question concerning the validity of a Regulation. If the practitioner disagrees with the scope or language of the Regulation, he or she bears the burden of proof of showing that the Regulation is improper. This can be difficult. Many Regulations simply restate the Code or congressional Committee Reports; they are known as "hard and solid" Regulations. Moreover, because of the authority delegated to the IRS, Legislative Regulations have the full force and effect of law. Finally, the Supreme Court views General Regulations as also having the force and effect of law, unless they conflict with the statute.[3] Thus, a taxpayer challenge to a Regulation typically must assert an improper exercise of IRS power, or an overly broad application of a rule.

In questioning the provisions of a Regulation, the tax researcher must be aware of several accuracy-related penalties Congress has enacted in the *Internal Revenue Code*. For example, a penalty is assessed equal to 20 percent of any underpayment of tax where the underpayment is found to be due to "negligence" on the part of the taxpayer.[4] Generally, negligence includes any failure to make a reasonable attempt to comply with the Code or any evidence of disregard of Treasury Rules or Regulations. Thus, if a practitioner chooses to ignore an administrative element of

---

[3] *Maryland Casualty Co. v. U.S.*, 251 U.S. 342 (1920).
[4] IRC §6662.

Exhibit 4-2: Sources of Administrative Tax Law

Computer Sources

RIA Checkpoint	Research Institute of America
Westlaw	West Publishing Co.
CCH Tax Research Network	Commerce Clearing House
Kleinrock's	Kleinrock Publishing Co.
Lexis	LexisNexis

Printed Sources

Tax Coordinator 2d	Research Institute of America
United States Code Annotated	West Publishing Co.
Standard Federal Tax Reporter	Commerce Clearing House
Cumulative Bulletin	Government Printing Office
Public Law Legislative History	Commerce Clearing House
Primary Sources (since 1968)	Bureau of National Affairs

the tax law, he or she must possess substantial authority to do so to avoid this penalty or others of its kind. See Chapter 14 for a more detailed examination of these provisions.

Locating Regulations

When TDs are final, they are published in the *Internal Revenue Bulletin*, a weekly newsletter of the IRS. Twice a year, the IRBs are indexed and bound into a set of volumes titled the *Cumulative Bulletin*, which becomes the permanent IRS location of the Regulations.

Most commercial tax services also reproduce the Regulations in their materials; annotated services usually include the text adjacent to the language of the Code and the related court case notes, and topical services usually provide an appendix that includes the edited Regulations for the volume or chapter that discusses the pertinent issue. Paperback or hardbound editions of the tax Regulations also are available from several commercial publishers, including Research Institute of America (RIA) and Commerce Clearing House (CCH), typically as a companion to a similar edition of the Code. Exhibit 4-2 shows common places where the tax researcher can find the Regulations and most other sources of administrative tax research material.

REVENUE RULINGS

Revenue Rulings are second to Regulations as important administrative sources of the Federal tax law. A Revenue Ruling is an official pronouncement of the National Office of the IRS; it deals with the application of the Code and Regulations to a specific factual situation, usually one that has been submitted by a taxpayer. Thus, many Revenue Rulings indicate how the IRS will treat a given taxpayer transaction. In addition, Revenue Rulings provide taxpayers needed information such as the short-term, mid-term, and long-term applicable Federal interest rates. These rates are used for complying with required tax law calculations.

Revenue Rulings do not carry the force and effect of Regulations. Revenue Rulings provide excellent sources of information; in fact, they are published chiefly for the purpose of guiding taxpayers. Therefore, even for a tax researcher whose client did not submit the original request for the Ruling, the result of the Ruling is of value if it concerns a transaction similar in nature, structure, or effect to the client's situation. Reliance should, however, not be placed on a Revenue Ruling if it has been affected by subsequent legislation, Regulations, Rulings, or court decisions.

Revenue Rulings adhere to a general internal structure, as illustrated in Exhibit 4-3. The typical structure is as follows.

Issue: A statement of the issue in question.

Facts: The facts on which the Revenue Ruling is based.

Law and analysis: The IRS's application of current law to the issue in the Revenue Ruling.

Holding: How the IRS will treat the transaction.

Exhibit 4-3: Revenue Ruling

REV. RUL. 2007-1

ISSUES

1. If a credit card issuer becomes entitled to a fee if it refuses to honor a credit card convenience check that, if honored, would leave the cardholder over the cardholder's credit limit, is the fee interest income for federal income tax purposes?

2. When is the credit card fee that is described in Issue (1) includible in gross income by the card issuer?

FACTS

X, a taxpayer that uses an overall accrual method of accounting for federal income tax purposes, issues a credit card to A. The credit card allows A to access a revolving line of credit to make purchases of goods and services and to obtain cash advances, including cash advances obtained through A's use of a convenience check made available through A's credit card account (an "account check").

There is a written agreement between X and A that sets forth the terms and conditions governing A's use of the credit card (the "Cardholder Agreement"). Under the terms and conditions of the Cardholder Agreement, X is not required to honor one of A's account checks if, when the account check is presented to X for payment, either A is overdrawn on A's line of credit or payment of the check would cause A to become overdrawn. Under the agreement X is entitled to impose a $25 fee (the "Credit Card NSF Fee") on A if an account check is presented to X that, if honored, would leave A overdrawn and X does not in fact honor the check (the "NSF Event").

A writes an account check and uses it to make a payment to a third party. X does not honor A's account check when the third party presents it for payment because A would be overdrawn on A's line of credit if X honored the account check at that time. X is therefore entitled to impose a $25 Credit Card NSF Fee on A in accordance with the terms of X's Cardholder Agreement with A.

LAW AND ANALYSIS

For federal income tax purposes, interest is an amount that is paid in compensation for the use or forbearance of money. Deputy v. DuPont, 308 U.S. 488 (1940); Old Colony Railroad Co. v. Commissioner, 284 U.S. 552 (1932). Neither the label used for the fee nor a taxpayer's treatment of the fee for financial or regulatory reporting purposes is determinative of the proper

continued

Exhibit 4-3: (continued)

federal income tax characterization of that fee. See Thor Power Tool Co. v. Commissioner, 439 U.S. 522, 542-43 (1979); Rev. Rul. 72-315, 1972-1 C.B. 49.

When X determines that it will not honor A's account check that the third party has presented for payment because A would be overdrawn on A's line of credit, X is denying A the use of X's funds. Thus, the $25 Credit Card NSF Fee does not compensate X for the use or forbearance of money, and it is not interest income for federal income tax purposes.

Under §451(a) of the Internal Revenue Code, the amount of any item of gross income is includible in gross income for the taxable year in which it is received by the taxpayer, unless that amount is to be properly accounted for in a different period under the method of accounting used by the taxpayer in computing taxable income.

* * *

HOLDINGS

1. The Credit Card NSF Fee is not interest for federal income tax purposes.

2. The Credit Card NSF Fee is includible in gross income for federal income tax purposes when the NSF Event occurs.

DRAFTING INFORMATION

The principal authors of this revenue ruling are Jonathan Silver and Tina Jannotta of the Office of Associate Chief Counsel (Financial Institutions & Products). For further information regarding this revenue ruling, contact the principal authors at (202) 622-3930 (not a toll-free call).

About seventy-five Revenue Rulings are released by the IRS each year (e.g., sixty-three in 2006). Each is identified by the year in which it was released and the consecutive number of the Ruling for that year. The IRS publishes them in the weekly *Internal Revenue Bulletin* and, later, in the *Cumulative Bulletin*.

Revenue Ruling Citations

Revenue Rulings bear both a temporary and a permanent citation. The temporary citation is structured as follows.

Rev. Rul. 2005-7, 2005-9 I.R.B. 712, where

> 2005-7 is the Revenue Ruling number (the seventh Revenue Ruling of 2005).
> 2005-9 is the weekly issue of the *Internal Revenue Bulletin* (the ninth week of 2005).
> I.R.B. is the abbreviation for the *Internal Revenue Bulletin*.
> 712 is the page number where the Ruling starts in the *Internal Revenue Bulletin*.

The permanent citation for the same Revenue Ruling would be as follows.

Rev. Rul. 2005-7, 2005-1 C.B. 712, where

> 2005-7 is the Revenue Ruling number (the seventh Revenue Ruling of 2005).
> 2005-1 is the volume number of the *Cumulative Bulletin* (Volume 1 of 2005).
> C.B. is the abbreviation for the *Cumulative Bulletin*.
> 712 is the page number where the Ruling starts in the *Cumulative Bulletin*.

Once the pertinent *Cumulative Bulletin* is published, the temporary citation is normally no longer used. The page number in the I.R.B. is the same as that in the C.B. Before 2000, Revenue Rulings were given a two-digit identification number instead of the current four-digit number (e.g., Rev. Rul. 98-23).

Locating Revenue Rulings

Generally, the tax researcher must examine every applicable Revenue Ruling before a tax research project is complete. Revenue Rulings can be found at most of the locations (i.e., commercial tax services, the *Cumulative Bulletin*, and some Internet sites) shown in Exhibit 4-2. Prior to 1953, Revenue Rulings were known by different names, including Appeals and Review Memorandum (ARM), General Counsel's Memorandum (GCM), and Office Decision (OD). These early rulings still may have some application in client situations if the IRS has not revoked them or modified them in any way. A tax researcher cannot ignore such rulings simply because they are old.

The current status of a Revenue Ruling or other IRS ruling can be checked in the most current index to the *Cumulative Bulletin*. In addition, several of the printed commercial tax services (i.e., RIA and CCH) present a variety of finding lists and other references with which to examine the status of a ruling.

REVENUE PROCEDURES

Revenue Procedures deal with the internal practice and procedures of the IRS in the administration of the tax laws. They constitute the IRS's way of releasing information to taxpayers. For example, when the IRS releases specifications for facsimile tax forms generated by a computer service, or informs the public about areas in which it will no longer issue Revenue Rulings, it issues a Revenue Procedure to that effect. Although a Revenue Procedure may not be as useful as a Regulation or a Revenue Ruling in the direct resolution of a tax research problem, the practitioner still should be familiar with all of the pertinent Procedures.

Revenue Procedures are issued in a manner similar to that for Revenue Rulings. They are first published in the weekly *Internal Revenue Bulletin* and later are included in the bound edition of the *Cumulative Bulletin*. The IRS issues approximately seventy-five Revenue Procedures per year (e.g., there were fifty-six in 2006).

SPOTLIGHT ON TAXATION

Factoid

Between 1954 and 2007, the IRS has issued approximately 20,000 Revenue Rulings and Revenue Procedures. This is an average of about 400 Rev. Ruls. and Rev. Procs. per year. But the average since 2000 has been less than one-half of that.

A Revenue Procedure is cited using the same system as that for Revenue Rulings, that is, adopting first a temporary and then a permanent citation. In this regard, the temporary citation refers to the location of the Procedure in the *Internal Revenue Bulletin*, and the permanent citation denotes its location in the *Cumulative Bulletin*. Thus, a typical Revenue Procedure would have the following permanent citation.

Rev. Proc. 2005-78, 2005-2 C.B. 1177

A Revenue Procedure is reproduced in Exhibit 4-4. Revenue Procedures can be found in the same publications in which Revenue Rulings are located.

Exhibit 4-4: Revenue Procedure Excerpt

Rev. Proc. 2004-22, 2004-15 I.R.B. 727

SECTION 1. PURPOSE

This revenue procedure provides transition relief from Revenue Ruling 2004-38 for determining an "eligible individual" under section 223 who may make contributions to a Health Savings Account (HSA). The transition relief covers the months before January 1, 2006, in the case of an individual who is covered by both a high deductible health plan (HDHP) and by a separate plan or rider that provides prescription drug benefits before the minimum annual deductible of the HDHP is satisfied.

SECTION 2. BACKGROUND

Section 1201 of the Medicare Prescription Drug, Improvement, and Modernization Act of 2003, Pub. L. No. 108-173, added section 223 to the Internal Revenue Code to permit eligible individuals to establish HSAs for taxable years beginning after December 31, 2003. Generally, an "eligible individual" is an individual who is covered by an HDHP and no health plan that is not an HDHP. Revenue Ruling 2004-38, clarifies that an individual who is covered by a health plan that provides prescription drug benefits before the minimum annual deductible of an HDHP has been satisfied, is not an "eligible individual" under section 223(c)(1)(A) and may not make contributions to an HSA. Because of the short period between the enactment of HSAs and the effective date of section 223, many employers and health insurance providers have been unable to modify the benefits provided under their existing health plans to conform to the statutory requirements for an HDHP. Thus, it is appropriate to provide transition relief to allow individuals to contribute to an HSA who would otherwise qualify as eligible individuals but for coverage by a prescription drug benefit provided under a separate plan or rider that is not an HDHP.

SECTION 3. APPLICATION

For months before January 1, 2006, an individual who would otherwise be an "eligible individual" under section 223(c)(1)(A), but is covered by both an HDHP that does not provide benefits for prescription drugs and by a separate health plan or rider that provides prescription drug benefits before the minimum annual deductible of the HDHP is satisfied (i.e., the separate prescription drug plan is not an HDHP), will continue to be an "eligible individual" and may make contributions to an HSA based on the annual deductible of the HDHP.

SECTION 4. EFFECT ON OTHER DOCUMENTS

The holding of Revenue Ruling 2004-38 is suspended in part and replaced by the transition relief provided in this revenue procedure for months before January 1, 2006.

DRAFTING INFORMATION

The principal author of this notice is Shoshanna Tanner of the Office of Division Counsel/ Associate Chief Counsel (Tax Exempt and Government Entities). For further information regarding this notice, contact Ms. Tanner at (202) 622-6080 (not a toll-free call).

LETTER RULINGS

The tax researcher is also interested in the *letter rulings* that are issued by the IRS in several forms, including Private Letter Rulings, Determination Letters, and Technical Advice Memoranda. The IRS does not publish these items in any official collection, but they are available from several commercial sources, as will be discussed later in this chapter.

Private Letter Rulings

The National Office of the IRS issues **Private Letter Rulings** in response to a taxpayer's request for the IRS's position on a specified tax issue. The IRS has the authority to decline to issue Letter Rulings under certain conditions, such as where the problem is one of an inherently factual nature. The content, format, and procedures that are used for Revenue Rulings apply with respect to Private Letter Rulings. The IRS does not publish its reply in the *Internal Revenue Bulletin* or *Cumulative Bulletin*. Rather, it sends its response only to the taxpayer who submitted the request. An excerpt of a Private Letter Ruling is shown in Exhibit 4-5.

Exhibit 4-5: Private Letter Ruling

LTR 200703016 COMPANY GRANTED EXTENSION TO FILE S CORP ELECTION.

Dear * * *:

This responds to a letter dated February 28, 2006, submitted on behalf of X, requesting relief under §1362(b)(5) of the Internal Revenue Code.

FACTS

According to the information submitted, X was incorporated on D1 under the laws of State. X intended to be treated as an S corporation for Federal tax purposes effective D2, but the election was not timely filed.

LAW AND ANALYSIS

Section 1362(a) provides that a small business corporation may elect to be an S corporation. Section 1362(b) provides the rule for when an S election will be effective.

Section 1362(b)(2) provides that if an S election is made within the first two and one-half months of a corporation's taxable year, then the corporation will be treated as an S corporation for the year in which the election is made. If the election is made after the first two and one-half months of a corporation's taxable year, then the corporation will not be treated as an S corporation until the taxable year after the year in which the S election is made.

Section 1362(b)(5) provides that if no election is made pursuant to section 1362(a), or, if made, the election is made after the date prescribed for making such an election, and the Secretary determines there was reasonable cause for the failure to timely make the election, then the Secretary may treat such election as timely made for such taxable year and effective as of the first day of that year.

X did not file a timely election to be treated as an S corporation under section 1362(a) effective D2. X has, however, established reasonable cause for not making a timely election and is entitled to relief under section 1362(b)(5).

CONCLUSION

Based solely on the facts submitted and representations made, and provided that X otherwise qualifies as a subchapter S corporation, and that within 60 days from the date of this letter, X submits a properly completed Form 2553, with a copy of this letter attached, to the appropriate service center, we conclude that X will be recognized as an S corporation effective D2.

    Except as expressly provided herein, no opinion is expressed or implied concerning the tax consequences of any aspect of any transaction or item discussed or referenced in this letter. Specifically, no opinion is expressed or implied concerning whether X is, in fact, an S corporation for federal tax purposes.

continued

Exhibit 4-5: (continued)

This ruling is directed only to the taxpayer requesting it. Section 6110(k)(3) of the Code provides that it may not be used or cited as precedent.

Sincerely,
Dianna K. Miosi
Chief, Branch 1
Office of the Associate Chief Counsel
(Passthroughs & Special Industries)

The process is as follows. The taxpayer asks the letter ruling application IRS to disclose its interpretation of the Code, Regulations, and pertinent court cases for a transaction the taxpayer describes; the description should include a statement of the business purpose for the transaction. For instance, if two corporations plan to merge, one of them might request a Private Letter Ruling to find out whether the IRS believes that the Code's tax-favored reorganization provisions will apply to the anticipated merger. In many cases, if the IRS asserts that the transaction will not receive a treatment favorable to the taxpayer, it will suggest means by which the transaction could be restructured to obtain the favorable treatment.

As mentioned, a Private Letter Ruling is issued only to the taxpayer who requested the ruling. However, Private Letter Rulings are included in the list of authorities constituting "substantial authority" upon which a taxpayer may rely to avoid certain statutory penalties.[5] Letter Rulings are, in any case, an important source of information, because they indicate how the IRS may treat a similar transaction.

Private Letter Rulings also constitute an important IRS stimulus for new Revenue Rulings. When the IRS comes across an unusual transaction that it believes to be of general interest, or when it receives a flurry of Letter Ruling requests concerning very similar factual situations, a Private Ruling may be converted into Revenue Ruling form and published in official administrative sources. The IRS must notify the taxpayer of its intention to disclose the ruling, and the taxpayer has the right to protest such disclosure. Before publication, all aspects of the new ruling, including the statement of facts, are purged of any reference to the taxpayer's name or other identifying information.

SPOTLIGHT ON TAXATION

Factoid

The IRS has issued almost 100,000 Letter Rulings and Technical Advice Memoranda since 1980. As a result, a tax researcher is faced with an average of over 3,000 new research documents every year just from this one source of authority.

Technical Advice Memoranda

A **Technical Advice Memorandum** is issued by the IRS's National Office, making it similar in this regard to the Private Letter Ruling and different from the Determination Letter. The Technical Advice Memorandum, however, concerns a

---

[5]Reg. §1.6662–4(d)(3)(iii).

completed transaction. Whereas a Private Letter Ruling typically is requested by a taxpayer prior to completing a transaction or filing a tax return, a Technical Advice Memorandum usually is requested by an agent when a question arises during an audit that cannot be answered satisfactorily by the local office.

Similar to the Private Letter Ruling, a Technical Advice Memorandum applies strictly to the taxpayer for whose audit it was requested, and it cannot be relied on by other taxpayers. However, again, the information that is contained in the memorandum may be useful to the tax researcher for the insight that it gives concerning the thinking of the IRS relative to a given problem area in taxation.

These memoranda are not included in any official IRS publication, but they are open for public inspection, as we will discuss next. If the facts or the holding of a Technical Advice Memorandum are felt by the IRS to be of general interest, the memorandum may be converted into Revenue Ruling format and published by the IRS in the *Internal Revenue Bulletin* and the *Cumulative Bulletin*.

Determination Letters

A **Determination Letter** is similar in purpose and nature to a Private Letter Ruling, except that it is issued by a local office of the IRS, rather than by the National Office of the IRS. Because a Determination Letter is issued by a lower-level IRS official, it usually deals with issues and transactions that are not overtly controversial. For instance, the trustee of a pension plan might request a Determination Letter to ascertain whether the plan is qualified for the Code's tax-favored deferred compensation treatment.

Determination Letters usually relate to completed transactions rather than to the proposed transactions that typically lead to the issuance of a Private Letter Ruling. Determination Letters are not included in any official IRS publication, but they are available to the tax researcher from commercial and Internet sources.

Public Inspection of Written Determinations

The public can receive copies of any unpublished IRS Letter Rulings, e.g., in lieu of using a subscription commercial service.[6] Included under this provision are Private Letter Rulings, Determination Letters, and Technical Advice Memoranda. Before any public inspection is allowed, however, the IRS is required to remove the taxpayer's name and any other information that might be used by a third party to identify the taxpayer.[7] In addition, the IRS is required to purge the document of any items that could affect national defense or foreign policy, trade secrets, financial information, data relative to the regulation of financial institutions, geographical data, and items that could invade personal privacy. If the taxpayer opposes the disclosure of the written determination, he or she can bring the matter before the IRS and the Tax Court prior to the scheduled disclosure.

Once all of the required data have been removed from the written determination, it must be made open for public inspection online and at such places as the Treasury Secretary designates in the Regulations. Information of this type is available in Washington, D.C., and at selected other locations.

The precedential value of any of these written determinations is strictly limited.[8] Overall, such pronouncements may not be cited as authority in a tax matter by either the taxpayer or the IRS. However, Letter Rulings can be used as "examples" of IRS treatment of similar factual patterns when dealing with the IRS.

---

[6] IRC §6110(f).
[7] IRC §6610(c).
[8] IRC §6110.

For example, tax practitioners could suggest that a Letter Ruling be used as guidance in a similar situation during an audit. However, an IRS agent need not follow a Letter Ruling issued to a different taxpayer.

Taxpayers may rely on Private Letter Rulings, Technical Advice Memoranda, Actions on Decisions, General Counsel Memoranda, and other similar documents published by the IRS in the *Internal Revenue Bulletin*, to avoid certain understatement of tax penalties. But use of such pronouncements for this purpose does not expand the general precedential value of these pronouncements with respect to determining a taxpayer's tax liability.

Written Determination Numbering System

Because the IRS issues thousands of Letter Rulings per year, it assigns a nine-digit document number to each written determination for identification purposes. The first four digits indicate the year in which the ruling was issued, the next two numbers denote the week, and the last three digits indicate the number of the ruling for the week. Thus, a lengthy but unique identifier is created for each pronouncement. For example, the number of a Letter Ruling can be interpreted as follows.

Ltr. Rul. 200917024, where

> 2009 is the year the Ruling is issued.
> 17 is the week of the year the Ruling is issued.
> 024 indicates that this is the twenty-fourth Ruling issued that week.
> Before 2000, only a two-digit date was used to signify the year in which the ruling was issued (e.g., 9814026).

Locating Written Determinations

The tax researcher needs access to written determinations to complete many tax research projects. Selected written determinations can be found in summary form in the major tax services. However, if the tax researcher needs access to the full text of a large number of IRS pronouncements, an electronic database is the best approach. Consult Exhibit 4-2 for the online computer tax databases that contain the full text of IRS written determinations.

Other IRS Pronouncements

The IRS issues several other types of information that can be of value to the tax researcher, including acquiescences and nonacquiescences, the *Internal Revenue Bulletin*, Chief Counsel Memoranda, and other miscellaneous publications.

Acquiescences and Nonacquiescences

When the IRS loses an issue or decision in court, the Commissioner may announce an acquiescence or nonacquiescence to the decision. An **acquiescence** indicates that the court decision, although it was adverse to the IRS, will be followed in similar situations. The Commissioner determines, at his or her own discretion, the degree of similarity required before the IRS will follow the result that is unfavorable to itself.

A **nonacquiescence** indicates that the IRS disagrees with the adverse decision in the case and will follow the decision only for the specific taxpayer whose case resulted in the adverse ruling. If the IRS wishes to express agreement with only part of the decision that is settled in the taxpayer's favor, the Commissioner may nonacquiesce with respect to certain issues. Finally, an acquiescence or nonacquiescence is not issued if the IRS prevails in a court case, because it likely agrees with all pertinent holdings.

Nonacquiescence may indicate to the tax practitioner that the IRS is likely to challenge a similar decision for the taxpayer in a case that has a similar factual situation. However, the issuance of an acquiescence does not necessarily mean that the IRS agrees with the adverse decision, but only that it will not pursue the matter in a (similar and) subsequent case. Each of these items of information can be useful when the practitioner prepares for, or anticipates, a court challenge to the client's position in a tax matter.

As mentioned, if the IRS has acquiesced to a case, then the taxpayer can rely on that decision as a precedent that will be followed by agents for similar fact patterns. However, if the IRS has nonacquiesced, the taxpayer must evaluate whether to pursue a similar fact pattern in court. Such factors as the cost of litigation plus the probability of winning must be appraised before proceeding with a case similar to one with which the IRS has nonacquiesced.

Occasionally, the IRS changes (with an attendant retroactive effect on taxpayers) its acquiescence or nonacquiescence position by withdrawing the original pronouncement. For example, in *U.S. v. City Loan and Savings*, 287 F.2d 612 (CA-6, 1961), the court allowed the IRS to withdraw an acquiescence on an issue-by-issue, but not taxpayer-by-taxpayer, basis. This change may occur after only a short time passes or many years later. Such a change in the IRS's position typically is accompanied by a brief explanation of the reason for the change—for example, because of a contrary holding in a subsequent court case or a change in the agency's policy concerning the issue.

IRS acquiescence decisions are driven by related litigation costs, revenue effects, and administrative and policy directives. The Service issues acquiescences/nonacquiescences as **Actions on Decision (AOD)**, relative to the following court decisions.

- Regular Tax Court

- Memorandum Tax Court

- District Court

- Court of Federal Claims

- Courts of Appeal

IRS Actions on Decision are published in the *Internal Revenue Bulletin* and thereafter, in the *Cumulative Bulletin*. They are prepared by the office of the Associate Chief Counsel (Litigation). AODs are public documents, and they generally include:

- The issue decided against the government,

- The pertinent facts,

- A discussion of the reasoning supporting the acquiescence/nonacquiescence decision.[9]

Exhibit 4-6 reproduces an acquiescence from the *Cumulative Bulletin* in which the IRS indicates its position on a case. A citator (see Chapter 8) also can be used to locate and interpret acquiescence and nonacquiescence decisions.

After the IRS issues such a pronouncement, any reference to the citation for the case includes either the abbreviation "Acq" or "Nonacq" (or, occasionally,

---

[9]*Taxation with Representation Fund v. IRS*, 485 F. Supp. 263 (DDC, 1990).

Exhibit 4-6: Action on Decision

ACTION ON DECISION 2003-01
January 10, 2003

SUBJECT: Doyle, Dane, Bernbach, Inc. v. Commissioner., 79 T.C. 101 (1982).

ISSUE: Whether an accrual method taxpayer must include in its gross income for 1975 amounts representing claimed refunds of New York State franchise taxes and New York City general corporate taxes paid for 1972 which became refundable by virtue of a net operating loss incurred in 1975 and carried back to 1972.

DISCUSSION: The Service issued an action on decision that non-acquiesced in the decision of Doyle, Dane, Bernbach, Inc. v. Commissioner, 1 C.B. 1. In a revenue ruling published elsewhere in this issue of the Internal Revenue Bulletin, the Service has concluded that New York State's approval of corporate franchise tax refund claims resulting from net operating loss carrybacks is not ministerial but involves substantive review. Accordingly, a New York State corporate franchise tax refund attributable to a net operating loss carryback is includible in the income of a taxpayer using the accrual method of accounting when the taxpayer receives payment or notice that the refund claim has been approved, whichever is earlier. SEE Rev. Rul. 2003-3.

RECOMMENDATION: Acquiescence. The action on decision approved on June 27, 1988 is withdrawn and replaced with this action on decision.

Reviewers:
NORMA ROTUNNO
Attorney Branch 2
Associate Chief Counsel
(Income Tax & Accounting)

Approved:
By B. JOHN WILLIAMS, JR.
Chief Counsel

"NA") to indicate the subsequent development. The AOD itself should not be cited as an IRS precedent, though.

Internal Revenue Bulletin

The IRS's official publication for its pronouncements is the *Internal Revenue Bulletin*. Most IRS Revenue Rulings and Revenue Procedures, and the agency's acquiescences and nonacquiescences to regular Tax Court decisions, first are published in the IRB. This reference bulletin also includes the following information, all of which can be useful to the tax researcher.

- New tax laws, issued by Congress as Public Laws

- Committee Reports underlying tax statutes

- Procedural rules

- New tax treaties

- TDs (which become Regulations)

- Other notices

Interested parties can subscribe to the *Internal Revenue Bulletin* by contacting the IRS. Alternatively, some of the commercial tax services include subscriptions to, or reproductions of, all of the issues of the *Internal Revenue Bulletin*. The *Internal Revenue Bulletin* is available by subscription in hard copy, and online in html and pdf formats.

The semiannual publication of the IRBs into the *Cumulative Bulletin* provides a permanent, bound, and indexed collection of the IRS documents. Citations to written determinatons should be changed to the permanent version when the corresponding CB is printed.

Chief Counsel Memoranda

The office of the IRS's Chief Counsel periodically generates memoranda that may be of use to the tax researcher. Although the IRS does not publish these memoranda in any official document, they are available from commercial publishers. A **Technical Memorandum (TM)** is prepared in the production of a Proposed Regulation. A GCM is generated upon the request of the IRS, typically as a means to assist in the preparation of Revenue Rulings and Private Letter Rulings. In addition, the Chief Counsel's office gives various forms of advice to IRS offices and personnel. IRS Chief Council Pronouncements are summarized in Exhibit 4-7.

These documents are available for public inspection and can be found on most computer-based tax services.

Announcements and Notices

The IRS issues **Announcements and Notices** concerning items of general importance to taxpayers. Announcements are public pronouncements that have immediate or short-term value such as an approaching deadline for making an election. Notices contain guidance involving substantive interpretations of the Code or other provisions of the law that usually have long-term application. Exhibit 4-8 reproduces a typical Notice. Both Notices and Announcements are published in the weekly *Internal Revenue Bulletin*.

Exhibit 4-7: IRS Chief Counsel Pronouncements

Document	Purpose
Technical Memorandum (TM)	TMs are prepared in the production of a Proposed Regulation.
General Counsel's Memorandum (GCM)	GCMs assist in the preparation of Revenue Rulings and Private Letter Rulings.
Action on Decision (AOD)	AODs are prepared when the IRS loses a case in a court. They convey the IRS decision to acquiesce/nonacquiesce.
Field Service Advice (FSAs)	FSAs are nonbinding advice, guidance, and analysis provided by IRS National Office attorneys to IRS field personnel.
Chief Counsel Notices (CCNs)	CCNs are temporary directives the IRS national office uses to disseminate policies, procedures, instructions, and/or delegations of authority to Chief Counsel employees.
Service Center Advice (SCAs)	SCAs are guidance provided by the IRS National Office to IRS service centers and related IRS functions concerning their tax administration responsibilities.

Exhibit 4-8: IRS Notice

Notice 2007-10

This notice announces that the Treasury and the Internal Revenue Service (IRS) will amend §301.7701-2(b)(8) of the Procedure and Administration Regulations to add the Bulgarian aktsionerno druzhestvo entity to the list of entities that are always treated as corporations under section 7701 of the Internal Revenue Code (Code).

BACKGROUND

The IRS and Treasury issued final regulations concerning the classification of business entities under section 7701 of the Code on December 18, 1996 (check-the-box regulations). See generally, TD 8697 (1997-1 C.B. 215; 61 FR 66584) and §§301.7701-1 through 3. Under the check-the-box regulations, a business entity generally can elect its classification for federal tax purposes. However, §301.7701-2(b)(8) provides a list of certain foreign business entities that are always classified as corporations for federal tax purposes (the per se corporation list).

On December 16, 2005, the IRS and Treasury published regulations (TD 9235, 2006-4 I.R.B. 338; 70 FR 74658) under section 7701 of the Code adding certain foreign business entities to the per se list of corporations. These regulations were in response to the adoption by the Council of the European Union of a Council Regulation (2157/2001 2001 O.J. (L 294)) (the EU Regulation) that recognized a new business entity, the European public limited liability company (Societas Europaea or SE).

The SE is a public limited liability company. The EU Regulation provides general rules that govern the formation and operation of an SE, and supplements those rules for specified issues and issues it does not otherwise address by reference to the laws with respect to public limited liability companies for the country in which the SE has its registered office. An SE must have a registered office in one of the Member States of the European Economic Area (which includes all Member States of the European Union plus Norway, Iceland, and Liechtenstein). For further background see TD 9197 (2005-1 CB 985; 70 FR 19697) and Notice 2004-68 (2004-2 CB 706).

As of January 1, 2007, Bulgaria will become a member of the European Union. Accordingly, an SE will be eligible to have its registered office in Bulgaria and those SEs with a registered office in Bulgaria will, to a certain extent, be subject to the laws of the public limited liability company in Bulgaria. As a result, and consistent with TD 9235, it is appropriate for the IRS and Treasury to add the public limited liability company for Bulgaria to the per se list.

DISCUSSION

The IRS and Treasury will issue temporary and proposed regulations that will modify §301.7701-2 to include the Bulgarian aktsionerno druzhestvo on the per se corporation list. This entity has been identified as the public limited liability company in Bulgaria.

EFFECTIVE DATE

The temporary and proposed regulations to be issued adding the Bulgarian aktsionerno druzhestvo to §301.7701-2(b)(8) generally will apply to such entities formed on or after January 1, 2007. However, they shall also apply to an entity formed before such date upon a 50 percent or greater change of ownership subsequent to such date.

The principal author of this notice is Ronald M. Gootzeit of the Office of Associate Chief Counsel (International). For further information regarding this notice contact Ronald M. Gootzeit at (202) 622-3860 (not a toll-free call).

Miscellaneous Publications

The IRS publishes numerous general and specialized documents to help taxpayers. Some of the more common ones include the following.

Publication 3, *Armed Forces' Tax Guide*

Publication 17, *Your Federal Income Tax*

Publication 225, *Farmer's Tax Guide*

Publication 334, *Tax Guide for Small Business*

Publication 463, *Travel, Entertainment, Gift, and Car Expenses*

Publication 519, *U.S. Tax Guide for Aliens*

Publication 520, *Scholarships and Fellowships*

Publication 589, *Tax Information on S Corporations*

Each of these documents is available directly from the IRS, both in print and electronic formats. See Exhibit 4-9 for an excerpt from an IRS publication from the IRS web site. In addition, several of the commercial tax publishers offer copies of these lay-oriented publications. Furthermore, any library that is designated as a government depository receives all of these documents in hard copy. Finally, many of the above publications can be ordered from the IRS in Spanish-language editions.

Although the IRS Publications contain useful information, the tax researcher must be careful when relying on them. IRS Publications typically do not cite the Code, Regulations, or other authority on which the information included therein is based. In fact, the IRS disclaims any responsibility for damages that the taxpayer may suffer in erroneously relying on its Publications, and it may, in fact, take

Exhibit 4-9: IRS Publication 3 (Armed Forces' Tax Guide) Excerpt

Armed Forces Reservists

If you are a member of a reserve component of the Armed Forces and you travel more than 100 miles away from home in connection with your performance of services as a member of the reserves, you can deduct your travel expenses as an adjustment to income on line 33 of Form 1040 rather than as a miscellaneous itemized deduction. The deduction is limited to the amount the federal government pays its employees for travel expenses. For more information about this limit, see Per Diem and Car Allowances in chapter 6 of Publication 463.

Member of a reserve component. You are a member of a reserve component of the Armed Forces if you are in the Army, Navy, Marine Corps, Air Force, or Coast Guard Reserve, the Army National Guard of the United States, the Air National Guard of the United States, or the Reserve Corps of the Public Health Service.

How to report. If you have reserve-related travel that takes you more than 100 miles from home, you should first complete Form 2106, Employee Business Expenses, or Form 2106-EZ, Unreimbursed Employee Business Expenses. Then include in the total on line 33 of Form 1040 your expenses for reserve travel over 100 miles from home, up to the federal rate, from line 10 of Form 2106 or line 6 of Form 2106-EZ. Write "RC" and the amount of these expenses in the space to the left of line 33 of Form 1040. Subtract this amount from the total on line 10 of Form 2106 or line 6 of Form 2106-EZ and deduct the balance as an itemized deduction on line 20 of Schedule A (Form 1040). See Armed Forces reservists under Miscellaneous Itemized Deductions, later.

positions that are contrary to those that are included in the Publications in certain court cases or appeals hearings.

These documents are prepared from the government's point of view. For instance, if a lower court has ruled against the IRS on a given matter that is addressed in a Publication, the text of the document probably will not mention the possibility that the IRS's official position will be found to be incorrect on appeal. Although IRS Publications can be the source of some basic information that is useful for laypersons, or in a tax compliance context, the tax researcher should not rely on or cite such a reference in a professional research report.

SUMMARY

Administrative pronouncements provide the tax researcher with a significant amount of information from and about the IRS. The primary IRS pronouncements that are of interest to the tax researcher include the Regulations, Revenue Rulings, Revenue Procedures, and Letter Rulings. The tax practitioner who performs competent research must be aware of the content and format of each of these items, know how to locate them, appreciate the precedential value of each, and understand how each might affect the client's tax problem. Exhibit 4-10 summarizes the most commonly encountered IRS pronouncements.

Exhibit 4-10: Common IRS Pronouncements

Pronouncement	Purpose
Regulation	The official Treasury or IRS interpretation of a portion of the *Internal Revenue Code*
Revenue Ruling	The IRS's application of the tax law to a specific fact situation
Revenue Procedure	A statement of IRS practice or procedure that affects taxpayers or the general public
Announcement	IRS release that has immediate or short-term value
Notice	Guidance involving substantive interpretations that has longer-term application
Private Letter Ruling	Statement issued by the National Office of the IRS at a taxpayer's request, applying the tax law to a proposed transaction
Determination Letter	Statement issued by the District Director in response to a taxpayer request, concerning the application of the tax law to a specific completed transaction
Acquiescence	Acceptance by the IRS of a court decision that was held in the taxpayer's favor. Published as an Action on Decision.
Nonacquiescence	Notice that the IRS still disagrees with a court decision that was held in the taxpayer's favor. Published as an Action on Decision.
Treasury Decision	A Regulation is promulgated or amended
Technical Advice Memorandum	A letter ruling issued on a completed transaction, usually during an audit

TAX TUTOR

Reinforce the tax research information covered in this chapter by completing the online tutorials located at the *Federal Tax Research* web site: **http://academic.cengage.com/taxation/raabe**

KEY WORDS

By the time you complete this chapter, you should be comfortable discussing each of the following terms. If you need additional review of any of these items, return to the appropriate material in the chapter or consult the glossary to this text.

Acquiescence
Actions on Decision (AOD)
Announcements and Notices
Cumulative Bulletin
Determination Letter
General Regulations
Internal Revenue Bulletin
Legislative Regulations
Nonacquiescence

Private Letter Rulings
Proposed Regulations
Regulations
Revenue Procedures
Revenue Rulings
Technical Advice Memorandum
Technical Memorandum (TM)
Temporary Regulations
Treasury Decisions (TD)

DISCUSSION QUESTIONS

1. What department and agency of the U.S. government has the responsibility to administer the Federal tax laws?

2. Section 7805(a) of the *Internal Revenue Code* authorizes the IRS to perform what activities?

3. The IRS issues numerous pronouncements. Name the four that are the most important in conducting Federal tax research.

4. Define the terms *Regulation* and *Treasury Decision*. Where are TDs published so that interested parties can comment on them?

5. "A tax researcher should not ignore Proposed Regulations." Comment on this statement.

6. Define and distinguish between *General* and *Legislative* Regulations.

7. In the citation, Reg. §1.212-3, what do the "1," the "212," and the "3" indicate?

8. Answer the following questions about this citation: Reg. §20.2039-1(a).
   a. What does the "20" stand for?
   b. What does the "2039" stand for?
   c. What does the "1" stand for?
   d. What does the "(a)" stand for?

9. Answer the following questions about this citation: Reg. §1.274-6T(a)(2).
   a. What does the "1" stand for?
   b. What does the "274" stand for?
   c. What does the "6T" stand for?
   d. What does the "(a)" stand for?
   e. What does the "(2)" stand for?

10. Give the number that is associated with each of the following categories of Regulations.
   a. Estate Tax Regulations
   b. Income Tax Regulations
   c. Gift Tax Regulations
   d. Procedural Regulations
   e. Employment Tax Regulations

11. Give the type of Regulation associated with each of the following Regulation numbers.
   a. 31
   b. 301
   c. 25
   d. 601
   e. 20

12. What are Temporary Regulations? What weight do they carry in the tax researcher's analysis?

13. The burden of proof is on the taxpayer to prove that a provision of the Regulations is improper. How could this affect one's tax research?

14. In general, what is the effective date of a new Regulation?

15. Give at least three locations where a tax researcher can find the complete text of a Regulation.

16. What is a Revenue Ruling?

17. Describe the structure of a typical Revenue Ruling.

18. Where are Revenue Rulings initially published by the IRS? Where are the rulings permanently published in hardbound editions?

19. Explain each of the elements of this citation: Rev. Rul. 2009-32, 2009-12 I.R.B. 621.

20. Explain each of the elements of this citation: Rev. Rul. 96-41, 1996-2 C.B. 8.

21. What is the correct citation for Revenue Ruling 2002-55, which is found on page 529 of the second *Cumulative Bulletin* volume for 2003?

22. What is the correct citation for Revenue Procedure 94-36, which is found on page 682 of the first *Cumulative Bulletin* volume for 1996?

23. What resources are available to help the tax researcher who wishes to check the current status of a Revenue Ruling?

24. Of what relevance to the tax practitioner is a Revenue Procedure?

25. Where can a tax researcher find copies of Revenue Procedures?

26. Construct the permanent citation for the fifth Revenue Procedure of 2009, which was published in the second week of the year. It is published on page 164 of the appropriate document.

27. Identify three types of Letter Rulings that are of interest to the tax researcher. Indicate whether each of these rulings is published by the IRS.

28. Which office of the IRS issues Private Letter Rulings? Who requests such a ruling? What kinds of issues are addressed therein?

29. Sometimes a Private Letter Ruling is generalized and included in an official IRS publication. What form does this recast private ruling take?

30. What is a Determination Letter? Which office of the IRS issues Determination Letters? What kinds of issues are addressed therein?

31. What is a Technical Advice Memorandum? Who requests it? What kinds of issues are addressed therein? Does the IRS include Technical Advice Memoranda in any official publication?

32. Discuss the precedential value of Private Letter Rulings, Determination Letters, and Technical Advice Memoranda. What role do these items play in conducting tax research?

33. Which IRS documents are open to public inspection under §6110?

34. What is the precedential value of an IRS written determination under §6110?

35. Explain each of the elements of this citation: Ltr. Rul. 9615032.

36. Where can a tax researcher find copies of written determinations?

37. The most important IRS publications are the *Internal Revenue Bulletin* and the *Cumulative Bulletin*. How often is each of these documents published? Name six items that typically are published in the *Cumulative Bulletin*.

38. Explain each of the elements of this citation: Rev. Proc. 2004-16, 2004-10 I.R.B. 559.

39. Explain each of the elements of this citation: Rev. Proc. 2009-41, 2009-2 C.B. 317.

40. Distinguish between a citation with "I.R.B." in it and one with "C.B." in it.

41. Discuss the difference between a Revenue Ruling and a Revenue Procedure.

42. In what publication(s) would a tax researcher find the official listing of the IRS acquiescences and nonacquiescences to a Tax Court decision?

43. Can the IRS change its position on acquiescences or nonacquiescences?

44. Must the IRS acquiesce or nonacquiesce to every issue in a court decision?

45. What is the purpose of each of the following?
    a. Technical Memorandum (TM)
    b. General Counsel's Memorandum (GCM)
    c. Action on Decision (AOD)

46. What is the purpose of each of the following?
    a. Field Service Advice (FSA)
    b. Chief Counsel Notices (CCN)
    c. Service Center Advice (SCA)

47. Give the title of each of the following.
    a. Publication 17
    b. Publication 225
    c. Publication 334

48. Give the title of each of the following.
    a. Publication 3
    b. Publication 463
    c. Publication 520

49. What is an IRS Notice? When is it used? In your opinion, could a tax practitioner rely on an IRS Notice as authority for a tax return position?

50. Why should the tax researcher exercise caution in relying on an IRS publication, such as published instructions to tax forms, in undertaking a research project?

EXERCISES

51. Locate Revenue Ruling 99-56. Explain the effect of that ruling on previous Treasury Department pronouncements.

52. Briefly describe the subject of each of the following Letter Rulings. State the type [Private Letter Ruling (PLR), Field Service Advice (FSA), Service Center Advice (SCA), etc.] of each Letter Ruling.
    a. 200034026
    b. 200113016
    c. 200113020
    d. 200113023

53. Correctly cite the italicized sentence indicated by the dart (▶) in the following passage from the Regulations.

    SEC. 1.162-21 FINES AND PENALTIES.
    a. In general.
       No deduction shall be allowed under section 162(a) for any fine or similar penalty paid to—
       (1) The government of the United States, a State, a territory or possession of the United States, the District of Columbia, or the Commonwealth of Puerto Rico;
       (2) ▶ *The government of a foreign country; or*
       (3) A political subdivision of, or corporation or other entity serving as an agency or instrumentality of, any of the above

54. Correctly cite the italicized sentence indicated by the dart (▶) in the following passage from the Regulations.
    SEC. 1.1362-1 ELECTION TO BE AN S CORPORATION.
    a. In general.
       Except as provided in section 1.1362-5, a small business corporation as defined in section 1361 may elect to be an S corporation under section 1362(a). An election may be made only with the consent of all of the shareholders of the corporation at the time of the election. See section 1.1362-6(a) for rules concerning the time and manner of making this election.
    b. ▶ *Years for which election is effective.*
       An election under section 1362(a) is effective for the entire taxable year of the corporation for which it is made and for all succeeding taxable years of the corporation, until the election is terminated.

55. Briefly describe the subject of each of the following Letter Rulings. State the type [Private Letter Ruling (PLR), Field Service Advice (FSA), Service Center Advice (SCA), etc.] of each Letter Ruling.
    a. 200414014
    b. 200235002
    c. 200411001
    d. 199950003

56. What is the subject of each of the following Revenue Rulings?
    a. Rev. Rul. 2007-4
    b. Rev. Rul. 2006-36
    c. Rev. Rul. 2003-73
    d. Rev. Rul. 95-29

57. What is the subject of each of the following Revenue Procedures?
    a. Rev. Proc. 2007-11
    b. Rev. Proc. 2005-78
    c. Rev. Proc. 2001-45
    d. Rev. Proc. 98-11

58. What is the subject of each of the following IRS Announcements?
    a. Announcement 2006-52
    b. Announcement 2004-90
    c. Announcement 99-27

59. What is the subject of each of the following IRS Notices?
    a. Notice 2007-2
    b. Notice 2007-91
    c. Notice 95-50

60. What is the subject of each of the following IRS Notices?
    a. Notice 89-114
    b. Notice 99-51
    c. Notice 2000-28

61. What is the subject matter of each of the following Technical Advice Memoranda?
    a. TAM 9015001
    b. TAM 199914034
    c. TAM 200050005

62. What is the subject matter of each of the following Technical Advice Memoranda?
    a. TAM 200703019
    b. TAM 200651033
    c. TAM 9853001

63. Briefly describe the subject matter of each of the following TDs.
    a. T.D. 8346
    b. T.D. 8780
    c. T.D. 8915

64. For each of the following Code sections, how many Treasury Regulations have been issued? Give the total number of such Regulations and the number of the last Regulation.
    a. §102
    b. §143
    c. §301
    d. §385

65. For each of the following Code sections, how many Treasury Regulations have been issued? Give the total number of such Regulations and the number of the last Regulation.
    a. §25A
    b. §119
    c. §180
    d. §305

66. What is the current status of each of the following Revenue Rulings?
    a. Rev. Rul. 95-35
    b. Rev. Rul. 94-17
    c. Rev. Rul. 87-34

67. What is the current status of each of the following Revenue Rulings?
    a. Rev. Rul. 2002-80
    b. Rev. Rul. 2001-31
    c. Rev. Rul. 98-13

68. Locate the pronouncement at 1989-1 C.B. 76.
    a. What is the number assigned to this written determination?
    b. What is the issue(s) addressed in this written determination?
    c. What is the holding in this written determination?

69. Locate the pronouncement at 2000-2 C.B. 333.
    a. What is the number assigned to this written determination?
    b. What is the subject matter discussed in this written determination?

70. Locate the pronouncement at 2004-10 I.R.B. 550.
    a. What is the number assigned to this written determination?
    b. What is the subject matter discussed in this written determination?

71. Locate the pronouncement at 2007-17 I.R.B. 990.
    a. What is the number assigned to this written determination?
    b. What is the subject matter discussed in this written determination?

72. Locate the pronouncement at 2006-40 I.R.B. 528.
    a. What is the number assigned to this written determination?
    b. What is the subject matter discussed in this written determination?

73. What is the current status of each of the following IRS pronouncements?
    a. Notice 2001-26
    b. Revenue Ruling 2000-41
    c. Revenue Procedure 89-31
    d. Announcement 99-110

74. What is the current status of each of the following IRS pronouncements?
    a. Notice 2004-29
    b. Revenue Ruling 2004-28
    c. Revenue Procedure 93-15
    d. Announcement 99-41

75. A member of a tax-exempt business league makes deposits into a strike fund. The contribution reverts to the taxpayer if the fund is terminated. Are these deposits tax deductible?
    Database to search: IRS Letter Rulings
    Keywords: business, league, strike, fund

76. Can proceeds from a life insurance policy be included in a decedent's gross estate if the policy was purchased by an S corporation for an employee-shareholder?
    Databases to search: the Code and IRS Letter Rulings
    Keywords: Sec. 2042, life, insurance, estate, inclusion

77. Is a veterinary medical corporation a "personal service corporation" for purposes of the required use of the flat 35 percent tax rate?
    Database to search: Revenue Rulings
    Keywords: veterinary, personal, service, corporation

78. Are homeowners who claim an itemized deduction for interest paid on adjustable rate mortgages and then receive refunds in a later year required to show the refunds as taxable income?
    Database to search: Notices
    Keywords: adjustable, rate, mortgage, refund

79. Are points paid by homebuyers on VA and FHA loans deductible in the year the house is purchased?
    Database to search: Revenue Procedures
    Keywords: loan, origination, fees, VA, FHA

RESEARCH CASES

80. Lance asks you to explain why his employer, the Good Food Truck Stop, an establishment that employs more than thirty waiters/waitresses, included $2,400 in tip income on his Form W-2 for the year. Lance always has kept track of the tips he actually received, and he has reported them in full on his tax return.
    Partial list of research material: §6053; Rev. Proc. 86-2, 1986-1 C.B. 560

81. Joe incurred $38,000 of investment interest expense in the current year. He also generated $35,000 in dividend income and had a $65,000 passive loss for the year. What is the amount of Joe's interest deduction?
Partial list of research material: §163; Reg. §1.163-8T; Announcement 87-4, 1987-3 I.R.B. 17

82. Georgia won the Massachusetts lottery, which means that she will receive $28,000 a year for the next thirty years. Georgia purchased the lucky ticket in March, and was selected the winner in June. Georgia regularly spent $100 a month on lottery tickets, one-third for Massachusetts tickets and two-thirds for Vermont tickets.
a. What is Georgia's gross income from this prize?
b. Is there any corresponding deduction?
Partial list of research material: §74; Rev. Rul. 78-140, 1978-1 C.B. 27

83. Dieter won the lottery this year, which means that he will receive $400,000 a year for the next thirty years. The present value of Dieter's prize is about $3,750,000. Conscious of the tax benefits of income shifting, Dieter irrevocably assigned one-fifth of every annuity payment to his daughter Heidi. What are the effects of these events on Dieter's taxable income?
Partial list of research material: §74; Rev. Rul. 58-127, 1958-1 C.B. 42

84. Ace High and Lady Luck live together and have pooled their funds for several months to purchase food and other household necessities and to buy an occasional state lottery ticket. Ace used part of these pooled funds to buy a lottery ticket that won $3,000,000. When they discovered that the lottery proceeds could be paid only to one recipient under state law, Ace and Lady executed a "separate ownership agreement." The agreement created an equal interest in the ticket for both Ace and Lady. Must Ace pay gift tax on the transfer of a one-half interest in the ticket to Lady? What is the value of the gift?
List of research material: Ltr. Rul. 9217004

85. Shaky Savings & Loan has a depositor named Olive who opened an account last year. At that time, Olive gave Shaky her Social Security number as a taxpayer identification number (TIN). The IRS notified Shaky that Olive's Social Security number was invalid. This year, Shaky asked Olive for a corrected number, which she provided. Later this year, the IRS notified Shaky that the new Social Security number also was invalid. What should Shaky do at this point about backup withholding on Olive's account? Prepare (in good form) a research memorandum to the file.

86. Alpine Corporation is a qualified small business corporation eligible to elect S corporation status. Albert is a shareholder in Alpine. On February 1 of the current year, Albert dies before signing the proper S corporation election form. The stock passes to Albert's estate. Ellen is appointed executor of Albert's estate on May 1 of the current year. On March 10 of the current year, Alpine filed Form 2553, the election form to be an S corporation, properly signed by all March 10 shareholders, and Ellen (the executrix) on behalf of Albert. Is this a valid S corporation election? Prepare (in good form) a research memorandum to the file.

87. Joe Bacillus, owns Bacillus's Italian Restaurant. A friend of Joe's who owns a sports bar comes to Joe and wants to form a partnership with Joe to buy an old

building, renovate it, and then move both the restaurant and the sports bar into it along with other tenants. Joe would like to make this investment. He needs approximately $200,000 for his share of the buy-in of the partnership that will purchase, renovate, and manage the building. However, because of other recent large expenses, Joe finds himself short of cash at the present time. His only large liquid asset is his self-directed IRA, which currently owns $225,000 in stock and bonds. Joe proposes that he direct the IRA to sell the securities and to use the proceeds to invest in the building renovation partnership. Conduct appropriate research (including a computer search) to determine if Joe's plan is workable. Prepare (in good form) a research memorandum to the file.

88. The Pima and Southern Railroad (PSRR) is a small railroad operating in rural Arizona. It exists by carrying freight to remote areas of the southwest. This year the PSRR needs to replace a thirty-mile section of its track. The PSRR has bids from a contractor to replace the track for the following amounts.

Cost of new track	$ 5,000,000
Installing new track	3,000,000
Road bed grading and improvements	2,500,000
Removing old track (net of salvage)	1,500,000
Total	$12,000,000

The old track is fully depreciated, and the cost shown is net of $200,000 salvage value received for the scrap metal. The new track is an improved type, and it is expected to last thirty-five to forty years. The controller of PSRR, Casey Jones, comes to you and wants to know the tax treatment of the above expenditures. He specifically wants to know if any costs can be deducted or if all must be capitalized and written off over a period of years. He is also concerned about any potential problems with the uniform capitalization rules under §263A. Prepare (in good form) a research memorandum to the file.

89. Your client, Ned Bovine, purchased a $2 million life insurance policy from the Nickel Life Insurance Co. (NLIC) of Dime Box, Texas. Ned's wife is the beneficiary of the policy. The policy was purchased ten years ago when Nickel Life Insurance was a mutual insurance company. In the current year, Nickel Life Insurance converted from a mutual company to a stock company in a tax-free reorganization. As part of the conversion, Ned received 800 shares of the new publicly traded (NASDAQ) Nickel Life Insurance Company. Three weeks after receiving the shares, Ned sold all his shares at $15 each. The total premiums paid by Ned on the policy before the conversion were $20,000.
   a. Locate the IRS pronouncement(s) that deals with this situation. State the pronouncement number(s).
   b. Review the IRS pronouncement(s). Does it raise a need for new information to solve this question?
   c. Are you able to reach a conclusion about the research question from this IRS pronouncement(s)? If so, what is your conclusion(s)?

90. At age sixty-five, Carlota's financial position was better than her health. She had a large balance in an IRA that she wanted to move to a different IRA. Carlota withdrew $100,000 from the IRA and planned to roll the funds over into another IRA. Unfortunately, she died before completing the rollover. Carlota's son, Andres, discovered, a week after her death, what his mother had done. Andres was both executor of Carlota's estate and beneficiary of her IRA.

Can Andres, in his role as executor, complete the rollover for his deceased mother by depositing the $100,000 in another IRA within the sixty-day rollover period?

a. Locate the IRS pronouncement(s) that deals with this situation. State the pronouncement number(s).

b. Review the IRS pronouncement(s). Does it raise a need for new information to solve this question?

c. Are you able to reach a conclusion about the research question from this IRS pronouncement(s)? If so, what is your conclusion(s)?

91. The Venganza Tribe is a Federally recognized Indian tribal government described in IRC §7701(a)(40)(A). The Venganza Tribe would like to invest some of its cash resulting from its newly opened casino in a real estate development, Vista de Basura, Inc. Vista de Basura, Inc. is an S corporation. Is the Indian tribal government an eligible shareholder for S corporation purposes?

a. Locate the IRS pronouncement(s) that deals with this situation. State the pronouncement number(s).

b. Review the IRS pronouncement(s). Does it raise a need for new information to solve this question?

c. Are you able to reach a conclusion about the research question from this IRS pronouncement(s)? If so, what is your conclusion(s)?

92. Fred Forgetful parks his personal car on a hill in sunny California and fails to properly set the brake or curb the wheels. As a result of Fred's negligence, the car rolls down the hill, damages Lucky's front porch, injures Lucky (who was sitting on the porch), and damages Fred's car. Due to the accident, Fred is forced to pay the following unreimbursed amounts.

Medical expenses for Lucky's injuries	$5,500
Repairs to Fred's car	7,000
Repairs to Lucky's porch	8,500
Fine for traffic violation	275

Using only the Regulations and Code, determine which of these payments, if any, would qualify for casualty loss treatment (before any percentage limitations) as to Fred.

93. Your client, Mustang Racing Parts, Inc. (MRP), is engaged in the production, transmission, distribution, and sale of racing headers for Ford Mustangs (inventory property). The client is also involved in the distribution of other racing parts manufactured by other suppliers (inventory property). During the tax year, MRP produces numerous identical dies and molds using standardized designs and assembly line techniques (noninventory property). The dies and molds are mass-produced. MRP uses the dies and molds to produce particular automobile racing components and does not hold them for sale. The dies and molds have a three-year recovery period for purposes of §168(c). The client wants to know if it can elect to use the "simplified service cost method" to calculate the amount capitalized under §263A on the dies and molds.

a. Locate the IRS Letter Ruling that deals with this situation. State the Letter Ruling number.

b. Review the IRS Letter Ruling. Does it raise a need for new information to solve this question?

c. Are you able to reach a conclusion about the research question from this IRS Letter Ruling ? If so, what is your conclusion(s)?

Judicial Interpretations

Learning Objectives

- Describe the structural relationship among the federal courts that hear taxation cases.

- Detail the constitution of, and procedures concerning, each element of the federal court system hearing tax cases.

- Use proper citation conventions for each of the courts that hear tax cases.

- State where Tax Court cases are published for use by tax researchers.

- Describe conditions under which the practitioner might choose each of the trial-level courts for a client's litigation.

- Work with the format and content of a court case brief.

Chapter Outline

W HEN A DISPUTE BETWEEN the Internal Revenue Service and a taxpayer cannot be settled through the administrative appeals process (see Chapter 13), the taxpayer can seek relief via the judicial system. The taxpayer may select one of three courts in which to initiate litigation with the IRS. These courts are the Tax Court, U.S. District Courts, and the U.S. Court of Federal Claims. If a taxpayer or the IRS disagrees with a lower court decision, an appeal may be made to the appropriate Court of Appeals and then finally to the U.S. Supreme Court. In this chapter, we will examine the federal court system, learn to locate various Federal tax judicial decisions, and discuss the use of those decisions in solving tax research problems.

FEDERAL COURT SYSTEM

When a taxpayer and the Internal Revenue Service cannot reach an agreement concerning a specific tax matter using the administrative review process (i.e., audits and appeals, which are discussed in Chapter 13), the dispute may be settled in the federal courts. Either the taxpayer or the IRS may initiate legal proceedings in the federal court system. A taxpayer may decide to initiate proceedings as a final attempt to recover an overpayment of tax the IRS refuses to refund or to reverse a deficiency assessment determined by the IRS. Alternatively, the IRS may initiate proceedings to assert its claim to a deficiency, to enforce collection of taxes, or to impose civil or criminal penalties on the taxpayer.

Judicial decisions are the third primary source of the tax law. The *Internal Revenue Code* is the chief statutory basis for Federal tax laws, and the administrative pronouncements of the IRS interpret provisions of the Code and explain their application. Frequently, however, additional issues and questions arise regarding the proper interpretation or intended application of the law that are not answered either in the law itself or in the administrative pronouncements. The judicial system is left with the task of resolving these questions. In this process, additional tax law is generated that can carry the full force of the statute itself. Often, recurring litigation in an area of innovative or unexpected judicial decisions regarding tax matters will result in Congress enacting legislation codifying certain judicial decisions. The practitioner must be familiar with the workings of this judicial system, which has the ability to stimulate tax laws and influence future legislative developments. In addition, in the event an issue is litigated in the court system, the tax practitioner must be familiar with the precedential value of court cases and the process for review of the court's decision.

Most disagreements with the Internal Revenue Service are resolved through the administrative process of appeals. Judicial decisions should be given significant weight in arriving at a conclusion or recommendation to a tax problem; however, caution should be exercised when it is apparent from the IRS's prior actions that a given position is almost certain to result in litigation. The costs of litigation, in terms of both money and time, may be prohibitive for certain taxpayers.

All litigation between a taxpayer and the government begins in a trial court. If the decision of the trial court is not satisfactory to one of the parties, the trial court decision may be appealed. The appellate court will review the trial court decision, often hear new evidence and arguments, and then either uphold the trial court's decision, modify it in some way, or reverse it.

The federal court system consists of three trial courts and two levels of appellate courts. The three trial courts are the U.S. Tax Court, the U.S. District Courts, and the U.S. Court of Federal Claims. The two appellate courts are the U.S. Court

Exhibit 5-1: Federal Tax System—Tax Cases

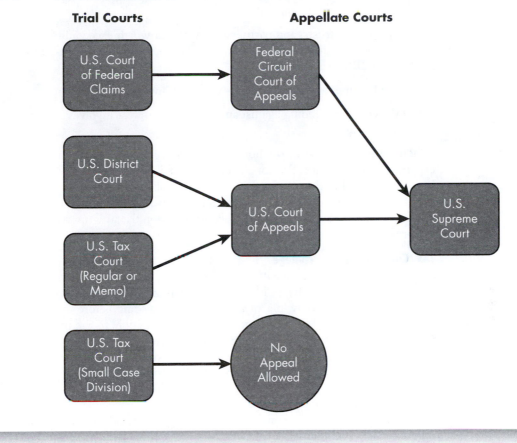

of Appeals and the U.S. Supreme Court. Each of the trial courts has different attributes and is designed to serve in a different capacity in the federal judicial system. Exhibit 5-1 diagrams the existing federal court system. An appeal from any of the three trial courts is to the appropriate U.S. Court of Appeals. The taxpayers and the IRS have no direct access to the Supreme Court or any Court of Appeals.

Legal Conventions

Burden of Proof   In most litigation, the party initiating the case has the burden of convincing the court that he is correct with respect to the issue. Historically, however, in most civil tax cases the *Internal Revenue Code* placed the burden of proof on the taxpayer, whether or not he or she initiated the case, except in cases of such items as hobby losses, fraud with intent to evade tax, and the accumulated earnings tax.

However, the burden of proof shifts to the IRS in a few situations.[1] The IRS has the burden of proof in any court proceeding on income, gift, estate, or generation-skipping tax liability with respect to factual issues, provided the taxpayer:

- Introduces credible evidence of the factual issue,

- Maintains records and substantiates items as presently required under the Code and Regulations, and

---

[1] IRC §7491.

- Cooperates with reasonable IRS requests for meetings, interviews, witnesses, information, and documents.

For corporations, trusts, and partnerships with net worth exceeding $7 million, the burden of proof remains on the taxpayer.[2] The burden of proof also automatically shifts to the IRS:

- If the IRS uses statistics to reconstruct an individual's income, or

- If the court proceeding against an individual taxpayer involves a penalty or addition to tax.

When reading a published opinion, the tax researcher should note whether the decision was based on the IRS's or the taxpayer's failure to meet a needed evidentiary burden, or whether the IRS or the taxpayer established the position with sufficient proof. The first situation should be considered a weaker precedent than the second. Understanding the "strength" of a court decision is an important part of tax research.

Tax Confidentiality Privilege   The attorney-client privilege of confidentiality also applies in tax matters to nonattorneys authorized to practice before the IRS (e.g., CPAs and enrolled agents), as identified in Chapter 1. The nonattorney-client privilege may be asserted only in a *noncriminal tax* proceeding before the IRS or federal court.[3] The confidentiality privilege usually does not apply to the preparation of tax returns, or the giving of accounting or business advice.

The nonattorney-client privilege does not extend to written communications between a tax practitioner and a corporation in connection with the promotion of any tax shelter. Nor does it apply to the client's workpapers used to determine tax expense for financial statements.

Certified public accountants and enrolled agents need to understand the rules regarding tax confidentiality as they have been applied to attorneys so as to be aware of the privilege limits. Usually, these rules are determined by state law, and the Federal confidentiality privilege cannot extend beyond the protection granted by state law, as it is currently interpreted.

Common Legal Terminology   Some of the common legal terms likely to be encountered by the tax researcher follow.

ad hoc For one particular or special purpose; for example, an ad hoc committee might be formed to solve a certain problem.

ad valorem According to value; used in taxation to designate an assessment of taxes based on property value.

appellant The party who appeals a decision, usually to a higher court.

bona fide In good faith and without fraud or deceit.

certiorari (writ of) The process by which the U.S. Supreme Court agrees to hear a case, based on the appeal of a lower court decision by one of the parties involved in that decision.

collateral estoppel When an issue of fact has been determined by valid judgment, that issue cannot be litigated again by the same parties in future litigation.

covenant An agreement or promise to do or not to do something.

---

[2]IRC §7491(a)(2)(C).
[3]IRC §7525(a)(1).

de facto In fact or reality; by virtue of accomplishment or deed.

de jure In law or lawful; legitimate.

defendant In civil proceedings, the party that is responding to the complaint; usually the one that is being sued in some matter.

deposition A written statement of a witness under oath, normally taken in question-and-answer form.

dictum (dicta) A statement or remark in a court opinion that is not necessary to support the decision.

en banc A decision by all the judges of a court instead of a single judge or a selected set of judges.

enjoin To command or instruct with authority; a judge can enjoin someone to do or not to do some act.

habeas corpus (writ of) The procedure for determining if the authorities can hold an individual in custody.

nolo contendere A party does not want to fight or continue to maintain a defense; the defendant will not contend a charge made by the government; "no contest."

non obstante veredicto (n.o.v.) Notwithstanding the verdict; a judgment that reverses the determination of a jury.

nullity Something in law that is void; an act having no legal force.

parol evidence The doctrine that renders any evidence of a prior understanding of the parties to a contract invalid if it contradicts the terms of a written contract.

per curiam A decision of the whole court, instead of just a limited number of judges.

plaintiff The one who initially brings a lawsuit.

prima facie At face value; something that is obvious and does not require further support.

res judicata The legal concept that bars relitigation on the same set of facts. Because of this concept, taxpayers must make sure that all of the issues they want (or do not want) to be litigated are included in a case. Once the case is decided, it cannot be reopened.

slip opinion An individual court decision published separately shortly after the decision is rendered.

vacate A reversal or abandonment of a prior decision of a court.

Tax Court

The U.S. **Tax Court** is a specialized trial court that hears only Federal tax cases. Established by the Code and not directly by the U.S. Constitution,[4] its jurisdiction is limited to cases concerning the various *Internal Revenue Codes* and Revenue Acts that were adopted after February 26, 1926. Before 1943, the Tax Court was known as the **Board of Tax Appeals** (BTA); it was an administrative board of the Treasury Department rather than a true judicial court. In 1943, the BTA became the U.S. Tax Court, an administrative court, and in 1969, its status was upgraded to that of a full judicial court, with enforcement powers.

---

[4]IRC §7441.

Nineteen judges hear Tax Court cases. Each judge is appointed to a fifteen-year term by the President of the United States, with the advice and confirmation of the Senate. This appointment must be based solely on the grounds of the judge's fitness to perform the duties of the office. A Tax Court judge may be removed from his or her position by the President, after notice and opportunity for public hearing, because of inefficiency, neglect of duty, or malfeasance in office, but for no other reason.

To alleviate the heavy caseload of the appointed Tax Court judges, the Chief Judge of the Court periodically designates additional special trial judges to hear pertinent cases for a temporary period. Limited primarily by the budget granted by Congress, these temporary appointments are useful in decreasing the waiting period for taxpayers who wish to be heard before the Court. The decisions of these special judges carry the full authority of the U.S. Tax Court. Senior judges are retired judges who still hear cases from time to time by invitation of the Chief Judge.

SPOTLIGHT ON TAXATION

U.S. Tax Court Judges (2007)

At the time this edition was prepared, the roster of Tax Court judges included the following.
(some positions may be vacant)

Judges:

* John O. Colvin, Chief Judge
* Carolyn P. Chiechi
* Mary Ann Cohen
* Maurice B. Foley
* Joseph H. Gale
* Joseph R. Goeke
* Harry A. Haines
* James S. Halpern
* Mark V. Holmes
* Diane L. Kroupa
* David Laro
* L. Paige Marvel
* Stephen J. Swift
* Michael B. Thornton
* Juan F. Vasquez
* Thomas B. Wells
* Robert A. Wherry, Jr.

Senior Judges:

* Renato Beghe
* Herbert L. Chabot
* Howard A. Dawson, Jr.
* Joel Gerber
* Julian I. Jacobs
* Arthur L. Nims, III
* Robert P. Ruwe
* Laurence J. Whalen

Special Trial Judges:

* Peter J. Panuthos

continued

* Robert N. Armen
* Lewis R. Carluzzo
* D. Irvin Couvillion
* John F. Dean
* Stanley J. Goldberg
* Carleton D. Powell

Tax Court judges are tax law specialists, not generalists. Typically, they have acquired many years of judicial or tax litigation experience before being appointed to the Tax Court. Thus, if a taxpayer wants to argue a technical tax issue with the IRS, the Tax Court usually is the best trial-level forum in which to try the case. Tax Court judges are better able to understand such issues than would be a judge in a more general court.

SPOTLIGHT ON TAXATION

Tax Law Complexity

We have from time to time complained about the complexity of our revenue laws and the almost impossible challenge they present to taxpayers or their representatives who have not been initiated into the mysteries of the convoluted, complex provisions affecting the particular corner of the law involved. . . . Our complaints have obviously fallen upon deaf ears.

—Arnold Raum, U.S. Tax Court Judge

The U.S. Tax Court is a national court, based in Washington, D.C. Its jurisdiction is not limited to a specific geographical region, as is the case with some other federal courts. Taxpayers need not travel to Washington, D.C., to have a case tried before the Tax Court because some of its judges travel throughout the country and are available to hear taxpayer cases in every major city of the United States several times every year. See Exhibit 5-2 for a map showing cities where the Tax Court occasionally holds trials.

When a case is heard before the Tax Court, it usually is presented before only one of the nineteen Tax Court judges. Taxpayers cannot request jury trials before this court. After the judge hears the case, he or she prepares a decision that is reviewed by the Chief Judge of the court. In most instances, the trial judge's opinion stands, but the Chief Judge can designate the opinion for review by the other members of the Tax Court. Upon their agreement with the decision, the opinion is released.

If the case involves an unusual, important, or novel issue, more than one judge, or the entire Tax Court, might hear the case. This rare occurrence is identified as an *en banc* sitting of the court.

For a case to be heard, the taxpayer must petition the Court within ninety days of the IRS's mailing of a notice and demand for payment of the disputed amount. The taxpayer need not pay the disputed tax liability before the case is heard.

Tax Court Decisions The Tax Court issues two kinds of decisions: regular and memorandum. A **Regular decision** (recently thirty to fifty cases per year) generally involves a new or unusual point of law, as determined by the Chief Judge of the

Exhibit 5-2: Tax Court Trial Locations

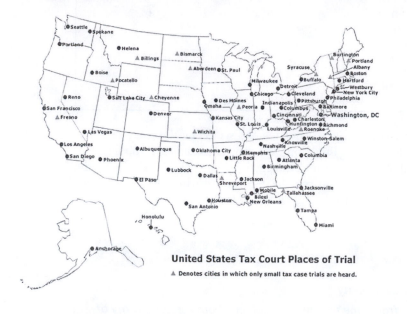

United States Tax Court Places of Trial

△ Denotes cities in which only small tax case trials are heard.

court. If the Chief Judge believes that the decision concerns only the application of existing law or an interpretation of facts, the decision is issued as a **Memorandum decision** (250–350 cases per year). Over the years, however, this classification scheme has not always been strictly followed by the Court. Many of its Memorandum decisions address significant points of law or other issues important to the tax researcher. Accordingly, the researcher should not ignore Memorandum decisions. If issues or points of law pertinent to the problem at hand are addressed, both Regular and Memorandum decisions of the Tax Court should be considered by the taxpayer.

Because the Tax Court is a national court, it hears cases that may be appealed to Courts of Appeals (discussed later in this chapter) in different geographical regions, or *circuits*. Because these Courts of Appeals occasionally disagree on tax issues, the Tax Court is faced with a dilemma. For example, one Court of Appeals may have held that a specific item is deductible in computing taxable income, while another has held against such a deduction. Which precedent should the Tax Court follow? Under *Golsen*,[5] the Tax Court will follow the Court of Appeals that has direct jurisdiction over the taxpayer in question. If the Court of Appeals that has jurisdiction over the taxpayer has not ruled on the matter, the Tax Court will decide the case on the basis of its own interpretation of the disputed provision. This *Golsen* **rule** means the Tax Court may reach opposite decisions, based on identical facts, for taxpayers differentiated solely by the geographical area in which they live. The tax researcher must be aware of the *Golsen* rule in analyzing cases that may be affected by it.

Small Cases Division   The Tax Court maintains a **Small Cases Division**, which is similar to a small claims court. If the amount of a disputed deficiency, including penalties, or claimed overpayment does not exceed $50,000, a taxpayer may be heard before the Small Cases Division, upon approval of the Tax Court. The hear-

---

[5] 54 T.C 752 (1970).

ing is conducted as informally as possible, and the taxpayer may represent him- or herself, that is, acting *pro se*. (Of course, the taxpayer may be represented by an attorney if he or she so desires.) Neither elaborate written briefs nor formal oral arguments are required in the Small Cases Division. Issues brought before this forum generally are fact-based; for example, does the taxpayer have the necessary documentation to claim the earned income tax credit?

At any time before a decision is final, the Tax Court may interrupt a Small Cases hearing and transfer the case to the regular Tax Court for trial. This might occur, for example, when important facts or issues of law, more suitably heard in the more formal Tax Court context, become apparent only after the Small Cases proceedings have begun.

Small Cases decisions, called Summary Opinions, are not officially published by the government. Nevertheless, they are available for review by tax researchers and taxpayers through commercial publishers. Small Cases Division decisions cannot be used as precedents when dealing with the IRS; however, they do provide insight into how the Tax Court has treated similar tax situations. The decision of the Small Cases judge is final and may not be appealed by the taxpayer or the government. An excerpt from a sample Summary Opinion is presented in Exhibit 5-3.

Exhibit 5-3: Tax Court Small Case (Summary Opinion) Excerpt

Estate of Stevens, Nicholas C., T.C. Summary Opinion 2003-163

Date Issued: 12/1/2003

Judge: Opinion by PANUTHOS

Pursuant to *Internal Revenue Code* Section 7463(B), this opinion may not be treated as precedent for any other case.

COUNSEL

Kim Patricia Bryan, pro se.

Clare J. Brooks, for respondent.

Opinion by PANUTHOS

This case was heard pursuant to the provisions of section 7463 of the *Internal Revenue Code* in effect at the time the petition was filed. The decision to be entered is not reviewable by any other court, and this opinion should not be cited as authority. Unless otherwise indicated, subsequent section references are to the *Internal Revenue Code* in effect for the year in issue.

Respondent determined a deficiency in decedent's Federal income tax of $1,324 and an addition to tax under section 6651(a)(1) of $121 for taxable year 2000. After respondent's concession, the issue for decision is whether decedent is taxable on unreported income of $12,154 from wages and interest during the 2000 taxable year.

BACKGROUND

Some of the facts have been stipulated, and they are so found. The stipulation of facts and the attached exhibits are incorporated herein by this reference.

Nicholas Charles Stevens, Jr. (decedent) died in Baltimore County, Maryland, in October 2001 at the age of 18 years. Decedent's mother, Kim Patricia Bryan (Ms. Bryan), was directed to serve as personal representative of decedent's estate. At the time the petition was filed, Ms. Bryan resided in Baltimore, Maryland.

During the year in issue, decedent received wages of $1,048 from Maryland Car Care, Inc. and $4,719 from Mangione Enterprises of Turf Valley. Also during the year in issue, decedent was credited with interest income of $7,435 from custodial accounts at Farmers and Mechanics

continued

Exhibit 5-3: (continued)

National Bank. Such accounts were established pursuant to the Maryland Uniform Transfers to Minors Act upon the death of decedent's father in 1992. Decedent, a minor, was 17 years old in 2000.

Decedent filed a Form 1040EZ, Income Tax Return for Single and Joint Filers with No Dependents, for the 2000 taxable year (2000 return). Decedent reported wages of $1,048 on his 2000 return. He did not report wages of $4,719 from Mangione Enterprises of Turf Valley. Nor did he report the interest income of $7,435 from custodial accounts.

Respondent issued decedent a notice of deficiency dated December 23, 2002, determining that decedent was taxable on unreported income of $12,154 from wages and interest during the 2000 taxable year. Ms. Bryan contends that a deceased person should not be liable for any tax deficiencies.

DISCUSSION

Decedent having filed his 2000 return after July 22, 1998, section 7491(a) is applicable in the instant case. However, neither party takes a position as to whether the burden of proof has shifted to respondent under section 7491(a). We conclude that resolution of the issue whether decedent is taxable on unreported income of $12,154 does not depend upon who has the burden of proof.

Gross income includes compensation for services. Sec. 61(a)(1). In the present case, decedent received wages of $4,719 from Mangione Enterprises of Turf Valley, and he did not report such amount in his 2000 return. Accordingly, we sustain respondent's determination that decedent received unreported income of $4,719 from wages in 2000.

Gross income also includes interest. Sec. 61(a)(4). In the present case, decedent was credited with interest income of $7,435 in 2000 from custodial accounts established pursuant to the Maryland Uniform Transfers to Minors Act (MUTMA). Under the MUTMA, interest income constitutes "custodial property" that generally transfers to a minor when he or she attains the age of either 18 years or 21 years, depending upon who originally transferred such property to the custodian. See Md. Code Ann., Est. & Trusts secs. 13-301(f), 13-320 (2001). While decedent was only 17 in 2000, he enjoyed the economic benefit of interest income from the custodial accounts, and therefore, such interest is taxable in the year earned and not in the year of actual receipt by him. See Anastasio v. Commissioner, 67 T.C. 814, (LEXIS through 2003 Sess.). 817-818 (1977), affd. 41 AFTR 2d 78-328, 78-1 USTC par. 9153 (2d Cir. 1977). We sustain respondent's determination that decedent was taxable on unreported interest income of $7,435 from custodial accounts in 2000.

Ms. Bryan nevertheless contends that a deceased person should not be liable for any tax deficiencies. "Death may be an avenue of escape from many of the woes of life, but it is no escape from taxes." Estate of Kahr v. Commissioner, 414 F.2d 621, 626 (2d Cir. 1969) (cited by United States v. Critzer, 498 F.2d 1160, 1163 (4th Cir. 1974)), affg. in part and revg. in part 48 T.C. 929 (1967).

Reviewed and adopted as the report of the Small Tax Case Division.

To reflect the foregoing, Decision will be entered for respondent with respect to the deficiency and for petitioner with respect to the addition to tax under Section 6651(a)(1).

Locating Tax Court Decisions   Tax Court regular decisions are published by the Government Printing Office (GPO) in a set of bound reporters called the *Tax Court of the United States Reports*. These volumes are cited as "T.C." The Board of Tax Appeals had its own reporter, called the *United States Board of Tax Appeals*, cited as "BTA."

Memorandum decisions are not published by the GPO. They are included in special-decision reporters that are published by Commerce Clearing House (CCH) and by Research Institute of America (RIA). The CCH reporter is titled *Tax Court Memorandum Decisions*, cited as "TCM," and the RIA reporter is known as *RIA Tax Court Memorandum Decisions*, cited as "RIA T.C. Memo." The Tax Court reporter is published twice a year, and both of the memorandum-case reporters are published once a year.

Because many months may elapse between the release of a Tax Court decision and its publication in a bound reporter, such decisions receive both a temporary and a permanent citation. The **temporary citation** is structured as follows.

Hillman, D. H., 114 T.C._____, No. 6 (2000), where

114 is the volume number.

T.C. is the abbreviation for the Tax Court Reporter.

_____ indicates the page number, which is to be determined later.

No. 6 is the number of the case.

(2000) is the year of the decision.

The temporary citation includes no page number for the case because the opinion has not yet been published. All proper citations either italicize or underline the name of the court case; major elements of the citation are separated by commas. The **permanent citation** for the same case is reported as follows.

Hillman, D. H., 114 T.C. 103 (2000), where

114 is the volume number.

T.C. is the abbreviation for the Tax Court Reporter.

103 is the page number.

(2000) is the year of the decision.

Most court case citations include the names of both parties involved. This convention is ignored for most Tax Court citations, however, because all such cases involve the taxpayer bringing suit against the government to avoid payment of disputed tax liabilities. Thus, a traditional citation for the above case would be *Hillman v. U.S.* (or, more precisely, *David H. Hillman v. Commissioner*). Nonetheless, common practice allows the tax researcher to omit the reference to the defendant in the action (i.e., the government or the IRS Commissioner), because such reference could be inferred from the notation for the court in which the lawsuit is heard.

Once the GPO publishes the decision in the permanent bound edition of the regular Tax Court cases, the temporary citation becomes obsolete. The same citation procedure is used with respect to Board of Tax Appeals cases, substituting "BTA" for the "T.C." identification. Indeed, this procedure for disclosing the citation for a case (i.e., Name–Volume Number–Reporter–Page Number–Year) is common among all American courts. Exhibit 5-4 is an example of a regular Tax Court decision, reproduced from the GPO Tax Court reporter.

Using the same citation conventions, the general and permanent citations, respectively, for a Tax Court memorandum decision would appear as follows.

General

Chi Wai, T.C. Memo 2006-179, where

T.C. Memo is a reference to a Tax Court Memorandum decision.

2006 is the year of the decision.

179 is the decision number.

Exhibit 5-4: Tax Court Regular Opinion-Excerpt

Campbell, Edwina D., 121 T.C. 290, Code Sec(s) 6015.

Date Issued: 11/24/2003.

By Final Notice of Determination dated Nov. 6, 2001, R determined that P was not entitled to relief from joint and several liability relating to 1989 because the request was, pursuant to Sec. 6015, I.R.C., filed more than 2 years after R's first collection activity against P. On Feb. 1, 2002, P filed, pursuant to sec. 6015(e)(1), I.R.C., a petition seeking review of R's determination. On Mar. 10, 2003, P filed a Motion for Partial Summary Judgment and on Mar. 31, 2003, R filed a Notice of Objection and Cross-Motion for Summary Judgment. The issue in both parties' motions is whether R's application of P's overpayment, relating to 1998, as a credit against P's 1989 tax liability is, pursuant to sec. 6015, I.R.C., a collection activity that bars P's request for relief relating to 1989.

Held: R's offset of P's overpayment is, pursuant to sec. 6015, I.R.C., a collection activity.
Held, further, P's Motion for Partial Summary Judgment is denied.
Held, further, R's Cross-Motion for Summary Judgment is granted. There is no genuine issue as to whether P is entitled to relief from joint and several liability relating to 1989 because P's election was, pursuant to sec. 6015, I.R.C., filed more than 2 years after R's first collection activity against P.

COUNSEL

Edwina Diane Campbell, pro se.Erin K. Huss, for respondent.

FOLEY, Judge

OPINION

This matter is before the Court on Petitioner's Motion for Partial Summary Judgment and Respondent's Notice of Objection and Cross-Motion for Summary Judgment pursuant to Rule 121. The sole issue for decision is whether respondent's application of petitioner's overpayment, relating to 1998, as a credit against petitioner's 1989 tax liability is, pursuant to section 6015, a collection action that bars petitioner's request for relief from joint and several liability relating to 1989.

BACKGROUND

On May 13, 1999, respondent applied, pursuant to section 6402(a), petitioner's overpayment, relating to 1998, as a credit against a portion of petitioner's 1989 tax liability and sent petitioner written notification thereof. On July 23, 2001, petitioner requested, pursuant to section 6015(b), (c), and (f), relief from joint and several liability relating to her 1989 joint Federal income tax return filed with Alvin L. Campbell.

By Final Notice of Determination dated November 6, 2001, respondent determined that petitioner was not entitled to relief from joint and several liability relating to 1989 because the request was, pursuant to section 6015, filed more than 2 years after respondent's first collection activity against petitioner.

On February 1, 2002, petitioner, while residing in Tucson, Arizona, filed a petition pursuant to section 6015(e)(1) seeking review of respondent's determination. Petitioner, on March 10, 2003, filed a Motion for Partial Summary Judgment, accompanied by a Memorandum of Points and Authorities, and Affidavit in support thereof. On March 31, 2003, respondent filed a Notice of Objection and Cross-Motion for Summary Judgment, accompanied by Declarations, and Memorandum of Law in support thereof. Petitioner, on April 16, 2003, filed an Opposition to Respondent's Cross-Motion for Summary Judgment.

continued

Exhibit 5-4: (continued)

DISCUSSION

An election pursuant to section 6015(b), (c), or (f) must be made within 2 years of respondent's first collection activity taken after July 22, 1998, against the individual making the election. Internal Revenue Service Restructuring and Reform Act of 1998, Pub. L. 105-206, sec. 3201(g)(2), 112 Stat. 740; sec. 6015(b)(1)(E), (c)(3)(B); Rev. Proc. 2000-15, sec. 5, 2000-1 C.B. 447, 449.

Petitioner contends that respondent's offset of her overpayment is not, pursuant to section 6015, a collection activity. We disagree. The offset of an overpayment is by its plain and ordinary meaning a collection activity pursuant to section 6015. See Perrin v. United States, 444 U.S. 37, 42 (1979) (stating that "A fundamental canon of statutory construction is that, unless otherwise defined, words will be interpreted as taking their ordinary, contemporary, common meaning"); Trent v. Commissioner, T.C. Memo. 2002-285 [TC Memo 2002-285] (stating that nonlevy collection actions include "offsetting overpayments from other tax years after the requesting spouse files for relief"). Because petitioner reported overpayments of tax on her 1998 return, she generally would be entitled to claim a refund. See sec. 6511(a), (b)(1); Commissioner v. Lundy, 516 U.S. 235, 240 [77 AFTR 2d 96-406] (1996). Pursuant to section 6402(a), however, respondent used petitioner's overpayment to partially satisfy her 1989 tax liability. Thus, respondent engaged, pursuant to section 6015, in a collection activity against petitioner. Because petitioner's election was filed more than 2 years after that collection activity (i.e., respondent applied the overpayment and sent petitioner written notification thereof on May 13, 1999, and on July 23, 2001, petitioner elected relief), there is no genuine issue as to whether petitioner is entitled to relief from joint and several liability relating to 1989. See Rule 121(b); Natl. Indus., Inc. v. Republic Natl. Life Ins. Co., 677 F.2d 1258, 1265 (9th Cir. 1982). Thus, Petitioner's Motion for Partial Summary Judgment is denied, and Respondent's Cross-Motion for Summary Judgment is granted.

Contentions we have not addressed are irrelevant, moot, or meritless.

To reflect the foregoing, An appropriate order and decision will be entered.

Permanent RIA

Chi Wai, RIA T.C. Memo ¶ 2006-179, where

RIA T.C. Memo is the RIA Tax Court Memorandum reporter.

2006-179 is the paragraph number.

Permanent CCH

Chi Wai, 92 TCM 181 (2006), where

92 is the volume number.

TCM is the CCH Tax Court Memorandum reporter.

181 is the page number.

(2006) is the year of the decision.

One can observe from the general and RIA citations that the opinion was issued in 2006 because all of the Tax Court Memorandum Decisions for that year are cited using paragraph numbers that begin with "2006." Thus, the reference in parentheses to the year of the decision is redundant and may be omitted. Again, the citation omits the reference to the government, typically "v. Comm.," as this is common among all Tax Court cases.

As we observed with respect to the regular Tax Court decisions, the temporary citation becomes obsolete when the permanent bound edition of the memorandum reporter is published.

Besides the traditional published sources for Tax Court decisions, these items also are available on computer tax services such as RIA Checkpoint, Lexis, and so on. All of the computer services reference the general citation, and most give the parallel RIA and CCH reporter citations.

Tax Court Rule 155   When a court reaches a tax decision, it normally will not compute the tax that is due to the government or the refund that is due to a taxpayer. The computation of this amount is left to be determined by the IRS and the taxpayer. The court will compute the tax only if the government and the taxpayer cannot agree. When the Tax Court reaches a decision without calculating the tax, the decision is said to be entered under *Rule 155*. See *Julie A. Toth*, 128 T.C. 1 (2007), for an example of how the Tax Court enters a decision under Rule 155. For Tax Court decisions prior to 1974, this practice was referred to as *Rule 50*.

Scope of Tax Court Decisions   The Tax Court may examine an entire tax return for a taxpayer whose case it is hearing. On the other hand, the District Court and Court of Federal Claims can address only the specific issue or issues that are involved in the case. If a taxpayer wants only a specific issue (or issues) litigated in a case, then the District Court or Court of Federal Claims may be a better forum than the Tax Court.

District Courts

The U.S. **District Courts** are another trial-level forum that hears tax cases. Unlike the Tax Court, however, the District Courts hear cases involving legal issues based on the entire U.S. Code, not just the *Internal Revenue Code*. District Court judges typically are generalists, rather than specialists in Federal tax laws. The same District Court judge might render opinions concerning matters of tax law, civil rights, bank robbery, interstate commerce, kidnapping, and fraud.

The District Courts are further distinguished from the Tax Court in that a taxpayer who disagrees with the IRS may take his or her case to the appropriate District Court only after paying the disputed tax liability; thus, in the typical District Court taxation case, the taxpayer sues the government for a refund of the disputed tax liability.

Numerous District Courts are located throughout the United States, each assigned a geographical area. The designated district can be as small as one city (New York City) or as large as the largest state (Alaska). Typically, the taxpayer will request a hearing before the District Court that has jurisdiction over the location in which he or she lives or conducts business.

District Court cases are heard before one judge, not a panel of judges. In the appropriate District Court, the taxpayer can request a jury trial concerning a tax case (or certain other Federal matters). This opportunity may be useful if the taxpayer wants to argue an "emotional" issue rather than a technical one, or if the taxpayer or his or her associates are particularly credible witnesses (and thus have a good chance of winning a jury trial). Limited to decisions concerning questions of fact, juries apparently occasionally can be persuaded in a tax case to hold for the taxpayer when a judge might not be so inclined.

Because the District Courts are general in nature and do not specialize in tax matters, over time, their decisions can vary significantly among the districts. Some of their decisions have important precedential value and can be relied on by the tax researcher; however, many of these decisions are poorly structured or poorly conceived from a technical standpoint, and represent candidates for overturn on appeal. The tax researcher must examine these decisions carefully to assess their probable use as a precedent before using them to help solve a client's tax problem.

Locating District Court Decisions   District Court tax decisions are published in three different reporters. West Publishing includes such cases in its *Federal Supplement Series*; citations for these cases include the "F.Supp." or the "F.Supp.2d." abbreviation. The series contains all decisions of the District Courts designated for publication, including those for the numerous nontax cases. Most university and law school libraries subscribe to the *Federal Supplement Series*. However, it is a waste of money for the tax researcher to subscribe to this series to obtain just the tax decisions that are rendered in the District Courts. Instead, the tax researcher can use special tax case reporters that include only tax decisions selected from all of the decisions of the federal courts except the Tax Court. (As we discussed earlier, the Tax Court's Regular and Memorandum Decisions are published in specialized reporters, so they do not present a budgeting problem of this sort.)

RIA's specialized tax reporter is titled *American Federal Tax Reports*, abbreviated in citations as **AFTR**. Currently, the second series of this reporter is in use, with "2d" added to indicate that the cases therein usually relate to the current *Internal Revenue Code*. Accordingly, the abbreviation AFTR2d is commonly used. CCH's specialized Federal tax case reporter is known as *United States Tax Cases*, which is abbreviated as **USTC** in traditional citations. Do not confuse this abbreviation with that for the U.S. Tax Court, which we have identified as "T.C." Occasionally, the West citation (F.Supp.) is referred to as the primary citation for a case, and the CCH and RIA reporters are used for secondary citations. The AFTR2d and USTC reporters each publish 1,000–1,500 tax cases in a typical year from courts other than the U.S. Tax Court.

Besides the traditional published primary and secondary court reporters, electronic court reporters are also available. The computer-based reporters have their own citations, and they usually cross-reference one or more of the standard printed reporters (West, RIA, and CCH). An illustration of various citations for a District Court case follows.

Court Reporters

West: *Barber, Lori,* 85 F.Supp.2d 967 (N.D.Ca., 2000)
RIA: *Barber, Lori,* 85 AFTR2d 2000-879 (N.D.Ca.)
CCH: *Barber, Lori,* 2000-1 USTC ¶ 50,209 (N.D.Ca.)

Each of these citations indicates both the specific District Court that heard the case and the year in which the opinion was issued. Given publication time lags, however, this may not match the year in which the reporter volume was published. Unless necessitated by such a delay, a proper citation need not include in the parentheses the year in which the opinion was issued, in all but a West citation.

Notice that more than one volume of the USTC reporter was published by CCH in 2000, as indicated by the volume number, and that this reporter uses paragraph numbers to organize the opinions. Other elements of the citations are familiar. A complete citation for this case, using traditional form, would appear as follows.

Barber, Lori, 85 F.Supp. 967; 85 AFTR2d 2000-879; 2000-1 USTC ¶ 50,209; (N.D.Ca.).

Court of Federal Claims

The U.S. **Court of Federal Claims** is the newest of the trial-level courts. It was created on October 1, 1982, by the Federal Courts Improvement Act (P.L. 97-164). In this act, the U.S. Court of Claims and the U.S. Court of Customs and Patent Appeals were reorganized into two new courts. The trial division of the U.S. Court of Claims became the new U.S. Claims Court, and the remaining divisions of both courts became the new Court of Appeals for the Federal Circuit, discussed later. The forum was renamed the U.S. Court of Federal Claims in 1992. Sixteen judges are appointed to the Court of Federal Claims. Its jurisdiction lies in hearing cases concerning all monetary claims against the Federal government, only one type of which is in the form of tax refunds. Thus, the taxpayer must pay the disputed tax and sue the government for a refund in order for the case to be heard in the Court of Federal Claims. Similarly, like the District Court but unlike the Tax Court, the Court of Federal Claims is composed of judges who, with only a few exceptions, are not specialists in technical tax law. The Court of Federal Claims does not allow jury trials on any matter.

The U.S. Court of Federal Claims is a national court located in Washington, D.C. However, because the Court of Federal Claims judges periodically travel to the major cities of the country and hear cases in these various locations, in a manner similar to that of the Tax Court, one need not go to Washington, D.C., to present a case before the Court of Federal Claims.

Moreover, because the Court of Federal Claims is a national court that must follow the decisions only of the Federal District of the Court of Appeals, it is not bound by the geographical Circuit Courts of Appeals that have ruled on similar cases, nor by the Court of Appeals for the circuit in which the taxpayer works or resides. This may be important to a taxpayer whose circuit has held adversely to his or her position on the disputed issue: if the case were presented to the appropriate District Court, or to the Tax Court (recall the *Golsen* rule), the precedent of the adverse ruling would be adopted by those trial courts, but the Court of Federal Claims is not so bound.

Locating Court of Federal Claims Decisions   Before October 1982, all U.S. Court of Claims decisions concerning both tax and nontax issues were published in West's *Federal Reporter*, second series (this reporter is now in its third series). Citations to the reporter use the abbreviations "F.2d" or "F.3d," as the case may be. Current decisions of the U.S. Court of Federal Claims can be found in West's primary reporter, *U.S. Court of Federal Claims*, which can be cited by using the abbreviation "Fed. Cl." In addition, tax decisions of the old U.S. Court of Claims and the new U.S. Court of Federal Claims are available through several secondary published and electronic reporters. U.S. Court of Federal Claims decisions are published in CCH's USTC, RIA's *American Federal Tax Reports* 2d (AFTR2d), and other places.

Examine the following proper primary and secondary citations for decisions of the U.S. Court of Federal Claims. All of the elements of these citations are familiar to us. As is most often the situation, when a decision is issued and published in the same year, one need not be redundant in identifying the given year in the body of the citation because the reader can infer the year from other aspects of the listing. A complete citation of the case would include references to all of the publications, in the form indicated previously.

Court Reporters

West: *Esposito v. U.S.*, 70 Fed. Cl. 558 (2006)
CCH: *Esposito v. U.S.*, 2006-2 USTC ¶50,434 (Fed. Cl.)
RIA: *Esposito v. U.S.*, 97 AFTR2d 2006-1733 (Fed. Cl.)

As a general tax court, the U.S. Court of Federal Claims has generated decisions that cannot easily be anticipated. Practitioners usually should pursue a case in the U.S. Court of Federal Claims when the applicable U.S. District and U.S. Tax

Court decisions are adverse to the taxpayer, or when a nontechnical matter lies at the heart of the taxpayer's case.

Courts of Appeals

The first level of Federal appellate courts is the U.S. **Courts of Appeals**. Like the District Court and Court of Federal Claims, the Courts of Appeals consider issues in both tax and nontax litigation, although the Courts of Appeals generally will hear only cases that involve a question of law. Seldom will a Circuit Court of Appeals challenge the trial court's findings as to the facts.

Congress has created thirteen Courts of Appeals: eleven are geographical, in that they are responsible for cases that originate in designated states; one is assigned to Washington, D.C.; and one is known as the Court of Appeals for the Federal Circuit. This last court hears tax and other cases that originate only in the Court of Federal Claims. The other Courts of Appeals consider tax and nontax issues brought from the Tax Court or a District Court for an assigned geographical region.

The eleven geographical Courts of Appeals are organized into geographical *circuits*, each of which is assigned a number. Practitioners commonly refer to the circuit courts by this number. For example, the Court of Appeals designated to hear cases that originate in Seattle typically is referred to as the Ninth Circuit Court of Appeals. Exhibit 5-5 shows the jurisdiction of each of the Courts of Appeals. Approximately twenty judges have been appointed to each of the circuit courts. Typically, a three-judge panel hears a Court of Appeals case. Jury trials are not available in these courts.

A Court of Appeals decision carries precedential weight because each circuit is independent of the others and must follow only the decisions of the U.S. Supreme Court. Because the Supreme Court hears only about a dozen tax cases annually,

Exhibit 5-5: Circuit and District Court Jurisdictions of the U.S.

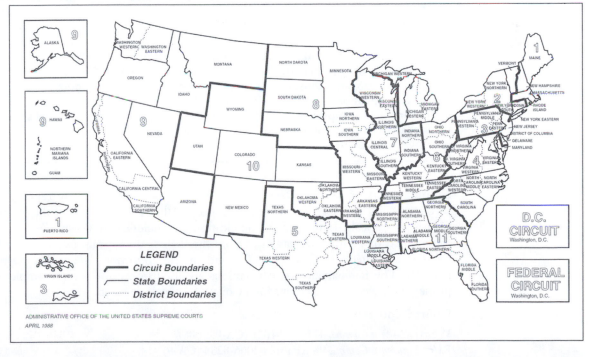

the Court of Appeals, in most situations, represents the final authority in Federal tax matters. Thus, a researcher generally must follow the holding of a tax decision issued by the Court of Appeals for the circuit in which the client works or resides if the controlling facts or issues of law are sufficiently similar.

Decisions by the circuit court in which the taxpayer works or resides should be given great consideration, even if the researcher has found that another circuit court has held in the taxpayer's favor in a similar case. For example, if a taxpayer lives in San Antonio, and the Fifth Circuit has held that an item similar to the taxpayer's does not qualify as a deduction, the deduction most likely should not be claimed, even if the Seventh or Eighth Circuit has held that the deduction is available. Under the *Golsen* rule, the unfavorable Fifth Circuit decision will apply to the taxpayer at the trial-court level, even though the U.S. Tax Court will be forced in this example to render opinions that are inconsistent among taxpayers.

If, in the same example, however, the Fifth Circuit had not yet ruled on the issue, and the favorable Seventh Circuit ruling is available, the researcher may be more comfortable in following the decision of the "outside" circuit. Prior decisions of Courts of Appeals are of great importance in the construction of subsequent decisions by another circuit, and the researcher rightly can place precedential value on the holdings of other circuits in anticipating the proper position for a client.

Therefore, in general, the Court of Appeals decisions most important to a given taxpayer are those issued by the circuit in which he or she works or resides. In addition, however, these observations can be made: Second, Ninth, and D.C. Circuit decisions are especially important, because of numerous innovative, unusual, and controversial judicial interpretations of the tax laws, and because their jurisdictions include the two most populous states in the nation and the nation's capital.

SPOTLIGHT ON TAXATION

Do We Need More Courts?

There is a proposal before Congress to add at least one more circuit to the Courts of Appeals, by splitting up the Ninth Circuit. Because of population migration in the past several decades, the Ninth Circuit is seen by some as "too big," constituting about 20 percent of the U.S. population. Another motivation for such a split-up might be political—the Ninth Circuit is historically the most progressive of the circuits, and this does not always sit well with citizens and their professional advisers in parts of the more conservative Western states.

Locating Court of Appeals Decisions   Court of Appeals decisions are reported in several general and specialized tax publications. All of the decisions of the various Courts of Appeals designated for publication are included in West's *Federal Reporter* (F.2d or F.3d). Most tax cases from the Courts of Appeals are published in the *United States Tax Cases* (USTC), and in the *American Federal Tax Reports* (AFTR). The familiar citation conventions are used in the following examples of primary and secondary citations for a Court of Appeals decision.

Court Reporters

West: *Hansen v Comm.*, 471 F.3d 1021 (CA-9, 2006)
RIA: *Hansen v Comm.*, 98 AFTR2d 2006-8234 (CA-9)
CCH: *Hansen v Comm.*, 2007-1 USTC ¶ 50, 167 (CA-9, 2006)

In the citations to *Hansen*, the CCH reporter first published this 2006 decision in its first 2007 volume. Thus, the year of issuance must be listed in parentheses. The appeal was from a 2004 Tax Court decision involving a 1991 tax return.

A tax decision from the Court of Appeals is reproduced in Exhibit 5-6.

Exhibit 5-6: Court of Appeals Decision

Cziraki, Imre and Gizella v. Commissioner, 87 AFTR2d 2001-308; 2001-1 USTC ¶ 50,141.

Appeal from a Decision of the United States Tax Court

Before: GOODWIN, HUG, and PREGERSON, Circuit Judges.

Imre and Gizella Cziraki (the "Czirakis") appeal the tax court's decision denying their casualty loss deduction in the amount of $220,000 for the 1992 tax year for damage to a dirt road on their farm land. Specifically, the Czirakis challenge the tax court's determination that this road was a "single identifiable property" (SIP) as this limits their casualty loss deduction to the road's basis. We have jurisdiction to review the final order of the tax court under 26 U.S.C. Section 7482, and we affirm. Because the parties are familiar with the factual and procedural history of the case, we will not repeat it here except as necessary to explain the disposition.

The question of whether a dirt road is a SIP or is part of the surrounding land is untechnical and factual and, thus, subject to our review for clear error. See *Condor Int'l. Inc. v. CIR,* 78 F.3d 1355, 1358 (9th Cir. 1996). Tax deductions are a matter of legislative grace, and as such the burden of proving a deductible loss and its amount is always upon the taxpayer. *Clapp v. Commissioner,* 321 F.2d 12, 14 (9th Cir. 1963). A casualty loss deduction is allowed under I.R.C. Section 165(a) for "any loss sustained during the taxable year and not compensated for by insurance or otherwise." In this context, the amount of loss taken into account is the lesser of (1) the difference between the fair market value of the property immediately before and after the casualty or (2) the taxpayer's adjusted basis of the property. I.R.C. Section 165(b); Income Tax Regs. Section 1.165-7(b)(1). A loss incurred in a trade or business is determined in this manner, but by reference to the "single identifiable property" damaged or destroyed. Income Tax Regs. Section 1.165-7(b)(2).

The Czirakis maintain that the dirt road had no basis and rather than being a SIP it was inextricably part of the land and so their casualty loss deduction for damage to the road should be limited by their basis in the land. The tax court characterized the dirt road as a SIP and accordingly limited the Czirakis' deduction to the basis in that road. In doing so, the tax court considered the time, effort, expense and resources spent on constructing the road. The court also correctly considered that a taxpayer may not borrow basis from unharmed property to increase the amount of a loss deduction for injury to other property. See *Rosenthal v. Commissioner,* 416 F.2d 491, 497-98 (2d Cir. 1969).

The tax court's finding that the dirt road was a SIP was not clearly erroneous. Accordingly, the decision of the tax court is AFFIRMED.

ENDNOTES

1. This disposition is not appropriate for publication and may not be cited to or by the courts of this circuit except as may be provided by 9th Cir. R. 36-3.

2. The Czirakis also contend that the tax court erred in commingling the basis in the dirt road and an adjacent asphalt road. If they are correct, then their entire deduction would be disallowed. Having noted that the Czirakis may have received a deduction to which they were not entitled, the Commissioner did not appeal the decision to allow the $6,844 deduction. Assuming the Czirakis prefer the limited deduction to no deduction at all, we leave the tax court's decision undisturbed.

Supreme Court

The U.S. **Supreme Court** is an appellate court and the highest court in the nation. Article III of the Constitution created the Supreme Court and extended to it judicial power "to all cases of law and equity, arising under this Constitution, the laws of the United States, and treaties. . . ." Thus, concerning all areas of Federal law, the Supreme Court is the final level of appeal and the sovereign legal authority.

The Supreme Court meets and hears cases only in Washington, D.C. If a taxpayer wants to have his or her case heard by the Supreme Court, the taxpayer and counsel must travel to the nation's capital to present the arguments. The Supreme Court is a nine-justice panel; all nine judges hear every case that the Court agrees to consider. The Court does not conduct jury trials.

A U.S. citizen has no automatic right to have his or her case heard by the Supreme Court. Permission to present the case must be requested by a **writ of certiorari.** If the Court decides to hear the case, then "certiorari is granted"; if the Court refuses, then "certiorari is denied." One must treat a Supreme Court decision as having the full force of the law; although Congress might repeal the challenged statute or the Federal administration might refuse to fund or enforce the underlying law and related activities, neither the citizen nor the government can appeal a Supreme Court decision.

As we have discussed, however, certiorari is granted in very few tax cases. Only about a dozen appeals relating to tax issues—state, local, and Federal; income, property, sales, estate, and gift; individual, corporate, and fiduciary—are heard by the Supreme Court in a typical year. In most cases, those petitions granted involve an issue at conflict among the Federal circuits or a tax issue of major importance. For instance, the Court might hear a client's case concerning the inclusion in gross income of life insurance proceeds, if many similar cases had been brought before the various federal courts and tremendous tax liabilities were under dispute, or if two or more of the circuits had issued inconsistent holdings on the matter.

In denying the petition for certiorari, the Supreme Court is not "upholding," or in any way confirming, a lower court decision. Rather, the Court simply does not find the appealed case to be interesting or important enough to consider during its limited sessions. The lower court's decision does stand, but one cannot infer that the decision necessarily is correct or that it should be followed in the future by other taxpayers whose situations are similar. These matters of open-fact tax planning must be analyzed using the tax researcher's professional judgment.

SPOTLIGHT ON TAXATION

The Supreme Court's Love Affair with Tax Law

If [a United States Supreme Court Justice is] in the doghouse with the Chief [Justice], he gets the crud. He gets the tax cases . . . .
—*Harry Blackmun, Supreme Court Justice*

Locating Supreme Court Decisions At least four different general and specialized reporters publish all of the tax-related Supreme Court decisions. CCH includes such cases in the *United States Tax Cases* service (USTC), and RIA publishes them in the *American Federal Tax Reports* (AFTR, AFTR2d, or AFTR3d). The GPO publishes the *United States Supreme Court Reports*, which contains all of the tax and nontax decisions of the Court. In common citation convention, references to this service are abbreviated as "U.S." In addition, West Publishing includes all Supreme Court decisions in the *Supreme Court Reporter* (S.Ct.).

In the following examples of proper citations, one can infer from the GPO and West citations that the case was heard by the Supreme Court, and any further reference to that forum (e.g., as United States Supreme Court (USSC) would be redundant). In addition, if a case involves an issue of pre-1954 Code tax law, the first series of the AFTR service would be cited. Exhibit 5-7 is an example of a tax decision of the Supreme Court.

Court Reporters

GPO:	*Chickasaw Nation v. U.S.*, 534 U.S. 84 (2001)
West:	*Chickasaw Nation v. U.S.*, 122 S.Ct. 528 (2001)
RIA:	*Chickasaw Nation v. U.S.*, 88 AFTR2d 2001-6967 (USSC)
CCH:	*Chickasaw Nation v. U.S.*, 2001-2 USTC ¶50,765 (USSC)

Exhibit 5-7: Supreme Court Decision Syllabus Excerpt

The Indian Regulatory Gaming Act (Gaming Act) provides, as relevant here, that Internal Revenue Code (Code) provisions "(including []1441, 3402(q), 6041, and 6050I, and chapter 35 ...) concerning the reporting and withholding of taxes" with respect to gambling operations shall apply to Indian tribes in the same way as they apply to States. 25 U.S.C. 2719(d)(i). Chapter 35 imposes taxes from which it exempts certain state-controlled gambling activities, but says nothing about tax reporting or withholding. Petitioners, the Choctaw and Chickasaw Nations, claim that the Gaming Act subsection's explicit parenthetical reference exempts them from paying those chapter 35 taxes from which the States are exempt. Rejecting that claim, the Tenth Circuit held that the subsection applies only to Code provisions concerning tax withholding and reporting.

Held: Section 2719(d)(i) does not exempt tribes from paying the gambling-related taxes that chapter 35 imposes. pp. 3-11.

(a) The subsection's language outside the parenthetical says that the subsection applies to Code provisions concerning reporting and withholding, and the other four parenthetical references arguably concern reporting and withholding. The Tribes nonetheless claim that the subsection's explicit parenthetical reference to chapter 35 expands the Gaming Act's scope beyond reporting and withholding provisions—to the tax-imposing provisions that chapter 35 contains—and at the very least gives the subsection an ambiguity that can be resolved by applying the canon that statutes are to be construed liberally in favor of Indians with ambiguous provisions interpreted to their benefit. Rejecting their argument reduces the chapter 35 phrase to surplusage, but there is no other reasonable reading of the statute. Pp. 3-4.

(b) The statute's language is too strong to give the chapter 35 reference independent operative effect. The unambiguous language outside the parenthetical says without qualification that the subsection applies to "provisions ... concerning the reporting and withholding of taxes"; and the language inside the parenthetical, prefaced with the word "including," literally says the same, since to "include" means to "contain." The use of parentheses emphasizes the fact that that which is within is meant simply to be illustrative. To give the chapter 35 reference independent operative effect would require seriously rewriting the rest of the statute. One would have to read "including" to mean what it does not mean, namely, "including ... and." To read the language outside the parenthetical as if it referred to (1) Code

continued

Exhibit 5-7: (continued)

provisions concerning tax reporting and withholding and (2) those "concerning ... wagering operations" would be far too convoluted to believe Congress intended it. There is no reason to think Congress intended to sweep within the subsection's scope every Code provision concerning wagering. The subject matter at issue—tax exemption—also counsels against accepting the Tribes' interpretation. This Court can find no comparable instance in which Congress legislated an exemption through a parenthetical numerical cross-reference. Since the more plausible role for the parenthetical to play in this subsection is that of providing an illustrative list of examples, common sense suggests that "chapter 35" is simply a bad example that Congress included inadvertently, a drafting mistake. Pp. 4-6.

(c) The Gaming Act's legislative history on balance supports this Court's conclusion. And the canons of interpretation to which the Tribes point—that every clause and word of a statute should be given effect and that statutes are to be construed liberally in favor of the Indians with ambiguous provisions interpreted to their benefit—do not determine how to read this statute. First, the canons are guides that need not be conclusive. Circuit City Stores, Inc. v. Adams, 532 U.S. 105, 115. To accept these canons as conclusive here would produce an interpretation that the Court firmly believes would conflict with congressional intent. Second, specific canons are often countered by some maxim pointing in a different direction. Ibid. The canon requiring a court to give effect to each word "if possible" is sometimes offset by the canon permitting a court to reject words as mere surplusage if inadvertently inserted or if repugnant to the rest of the statute. Moreover, the pro-Indian canon is offset by the canon warning against interpreting federal statutes as providing tax exemptions unless the exemptions are clearly expressed. Given the individualized nature of this Court's previous cases, one cannot say that the pro-Indian canon is inevitably stronger, particularly where the interpretation of a congressional statute rather than an Indian treaty is at issue. Pp. 6-11.

208 F.3d 871 (first judgment); 210 F.3d 389 (second judgment), affirmed.

BREYER, J., delivered the opinion of the Court, in which REHNQUIST, C.J., and STEVENS, KENNEDY, and GINSBURG, JJ., joined, and in all but Part II-B of which SCALIA and THOMAS, JJ., joined. O'CONNOR, J., filed a dissenting opinion, in which SOUTER, J., joined.

CASE BRIEFS

Most court reporters contain a brief case summary at the beginning of a case called a **headnote**. Headnotes are usually inserted by the court reporter editors. They are useful to the researcher by helping to quickly determine if a particular case is of interest. A court case may contain several issues; therefore, there may be several headnotes for any one case. In addition to using headnotes, tax researchers have found that the construction of a concise **case brief** is of great value to them, both when they return to a client's research problem or planning environment after a period of time passes and in using the given case in constructing a research analysis for another client. The reader should be careful, though, to distinguish this concise research tool from the case briefs required as part of the procedure of most court hearings. The latter is a lengthy collection of documents that includes a detailed analysis of all parts of the litigants' arguments.

A proper tax research case brief presents in summary fashion, ideally not exceeding one page, the facts, issue(s), holding, and analysis of the chosen court case. From such a brief, the researcher can discover in a very short period whether the

Exhibit 5-8: Court Case Brief Illustrated

CITATION	*U.S. v. Stephen W. Bentson*, 947 F.2d 1353; 92-1 USTC ¶ 50,048; 68 AFTR2d 5773 (CA-9, 1991).
ISSUE(S)	(1) Does the IRS's failure to comply with the Paperwork Reduction Act (PRA) preclude a taxpayer from being penalized for failing to file a tax return and cause charges against him to be dismissed?
	(2) Could the IRS penalties be avoided because the Form 1040 had not been published in the *Federal Register*?
	(3) Could the IRS penalties be avoided because of a lack of proof that Bentson had failed to file returns?
FACTS	For the tax year 1982, Bentson filed a "protest tax return." He refused to supply information other than his name, address, social security number, and signature. The rest of his Form 1040 was filled with asterisks, and he attached a statement asserting that to supply other information violated his Fifth Amendment constitutional right. No tax returns could be located for 1983 and 1984. Bentson was charged by the IRS with three counts of willful failure to file tax returns. A District Court bench trial was held. After the close of the government's case, Bentson moved for dismissal, relying on *U.S. v. Kimball*, 896 F.2d 1218, vacated, 925 F.2d 356 (CA-9, 1991).
HOLDING	The District Court granted Bentson's motion as to the first count only. He was found guilty on two counts and sentenced to eight months incarceration followed by three years' probation, and a $2,000 fine. The Ninth Circuit affirmed the lower court's decision.
ANALYSIS	(1) Bentson argued the IRS failed to comply with the Paperwork Reduction Act and relied on the original *U.S. v. Kimball*. This decision was reversed in 1991 (see 925 F.2d 356). The Ninth Circuit held that the public protection provision of the Paperwork Reduction Act is not a defense to prosecution.
	(2) Bentson argued that Form 1040 and the instructions constitute a "rule" for purposes of the Administrative Procedures Act (APA) and therefore must be published in the *Federal Register* to be valid. The Ninth Circuit ruled this argument had no merit.
	(3) Bentson argued the IRS had not proved he did not file tax returns for 1983 and 1984. This argument was rejected because Bentson had already made a binding judicial admission to the contrary.

full text of the case is of further use in the present analysis. If the briefed case does warrant further examination, the researcher can locate it (or any other cases that are cited in the brief itself) very quickly.

Study carefully the format of the case brief in Exhibit 5-8. Notice that the indicated tax research issues correspond with each of the analyses and holdings of the court, as indicated by the numbers of the brief's outline format. Finally, notice that citations to other cases, or to administrative proclamations, are complete and somewhat detailed, helping to facilitate further research.

THE INTERNET AND JUDICIAL SOURCES

The Internet and the World Wide Web provide another way for tax researchers to access judicial sources of tax law. Many law schools, journals, tax publishers, and individuals have set up their own home pages (web sites) on the Internet. While not as user friendly as a commercial service, these home pages allow anyone with access to the Internet to locate many court decisions. Examples of some of these home pages that have links to other judicial sources are as follows.

Emory U. School of Law	**http://www.law.emory.edu**
Cornell U. School of Law	**http://www.law.cornell.edu**
U. of Texas School of Law	**http://www.utexas.edu/law**
Practitioners Publishing Co.	**http://www.ppc.com**
Will Yancey's Home Page	**http://www.willyancey.com**

Computer Tax Service Example

The tax researcher can use a computerized tax service to find court cases of interest. If the researcher knows the case name or citation, he or she can enter it directly and obtain a copy of the case. However, if the case name or citation is not known, the researcher can use a computer query to find cases that have addressed the issue at hand.

Your client is involved in a dispute with the IRS over the valuation for estate tax purposes of a closely held business. In the process of getting ready to go to the Tax Court on this matter, you decide to hire an expert witness to justify the client's valuation of the business. During the interviews, one of the experts says that she will use the Capital Asset Pricing Model (CAPM) as the basis for her valuation. You are not sure what the CAPM is and how the courts will react to it. You therefore execute a computer search using RIA Checkpoint to see if there is any information available on the use of the CAPM in tax valuation. Exhibit 5-9 shows an example of a search query that could be used to find any court cases that have discussed the CAPM. Exhibit 5-10 shows a listing of Tax Court Regular and Memo decisions discussing the use of CAPM in valuing a closely held businesses. After reviewing these cases, you would conclude that there is a lot of controversy about using the CAPM in nonpublicly traded valuation situations. As a result, you should prepare your client's case using another method of valuation or be prepared to defend your use of the CAPM.

Exhibit 5-9: RIA Checkpoint CAPM Search Query

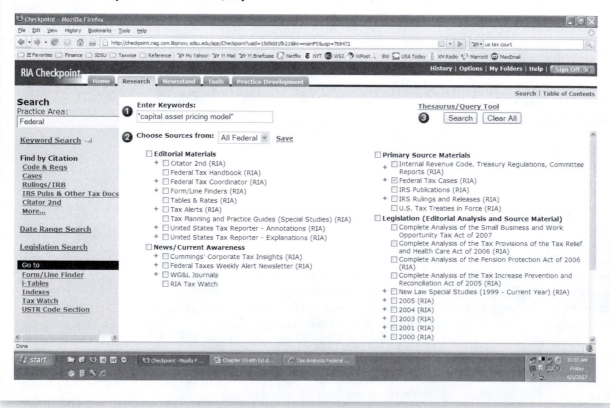

Exhibit 5-10: RIA Checkpoint CAPM Search Result (T.C. Memo Decisions)

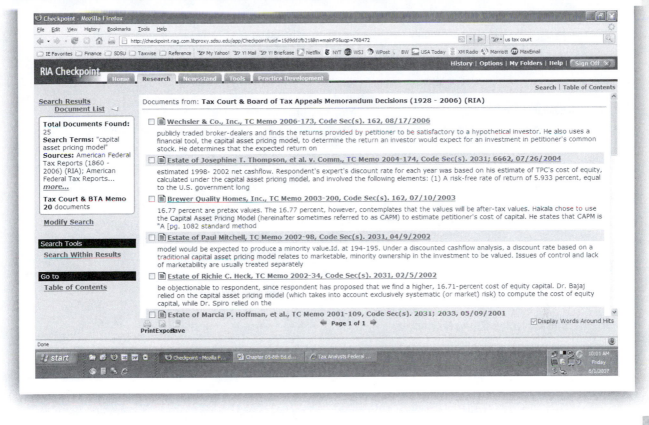

SUMMARY

The tax practitioner must possess a working knowledge of the federal court system to address tax research problems. The researcher must understand the role of the courts in generating Federal tax law, the relationship of the courts to one another, the Constitution, and the jurisdiction of each court, where to locate an appropriate decision, and how to interpret that decision.

Exhibit 5-11 offers a summary of some of the attributes of the trial-level and appeals courts discussed in this chapter. Because of differences among courts, the tax adviser may be inclined to choose one of the trial-level courts over the others to accommodate the special needs or circumstances of the client.

Exhibit 5-12 summarizes the decisions available in each of the tax case reporter services discussed in this chapter. With the variety of tax publications available, choices must be made so that the practitioner's tax research budget can be used effectively, without sacrifice of his or her ability to solve the client's problems.

Finally, a number of observations concerning citation conventions can be made. Review the citation examples given in this chapter to verify the list shown in Exhibit 5-13 and to add your own observations to it.

Exhibit 5-11: The Judicial Obstacle Course: Selected Attributes of Trial-Level Courts

Item	Tax Court	District Court	Court of Federal Claims
Jurisdiction	Tax cases only	Legal issues based on entire *U.S. Code*	Monetary claims against U.S. government
Judges	Tax law specialists	Tax law generalists	Tax law generalists
Domain	National court, but judges travel	Limited geographical area	National court, but judges travel
Jury trial available?	No	Yes, if question of fact	No
Number of judges	One, reviewed by chief judge; *en banc* hearing for certain issues	One	One to five hearing case
Small Cases Division	Yes	No	No available?
Payment of tax	Trial, then payment	Payment, then trial	Payment, then trial
Precedents court must follow	Supreme Court; pertinent circuit court; Tax Court	Supreme Court; pertinent circuit court; own District court	Supreme Court; Federal Circuit Court; Court of Federal Claims

Exhibit 5-12: Court Decision Reporter Summary

I. BY REPORTER

Publisher, Common	Reporter, Common	Decisions Included
Primary Reporters		
T.C. (B.T.A.)	GPO	Regular Tax Court (BTA) decisions
TCM	CCH	Tax Court Memorandum decisions
RIA T.C. Mem. Dec.	RIA	Tax Court Memorandum decisions
F.Supp	West	District court decisions
Fed. Cl.	West	Court of Federal Claims decisions
F.3d (F.2d)	West	Court of Appeals and pre-1982 Court of Claims decisions
U.S.	GPO	All Supreme Court decisions
S.Ct.	West	All Supreme Court decisions
Secondary Reporters		
USTC	CCH	Tax cases from all Federal courts except the Tax Court
AFTR series	RIA	Tax cases from all Federal courts except the Tax Court

II. BY COURT

Court	Publisher	Citation	Reporter
Supreme Court			
All cases	West	S.Ct.	*Supreme Court Reporter*
	GPO	U.S.	*U.S. Supreme Court Reports*

continued

Exhibit 5-12: (continued)

Tax only	CCH	USTC	*U.S. Tax Cases*
	RIA	AFTR series	*American Federal Tax Reports* *Kleinrock's Tax Cases*
Court of Appeal			
All cases	West	F.3d (F.2d)	*Federal Reporter, 3d (2d) series*
Tax only	CCH	USTC	
	RIA	AFTR series	
Tax Court			
Regular	GPO	T.C.	*Tax Court of the U.S. Reports*
Memo	CCH	TCM	*Tax Court Memorandum Decisions*
	RIA	RIA T.C.	*RIA Tax Court Memorandum*
		MemDec.	*Decisions*
District Courts			
All cases	West	F.Supp.	*Federal Supplement Series*
Tax only	CCH	USTC	
	RIA	AFTR series	
Court of Federal Claims			
All cases post-1982	West	Fed. Cl.	*U.S. Court of* *Federal Claims*
Tax only	CCH	USTC	
	RIA	AFTR series	

Exhibit 5-13:   Citation Conventions and Observations

- The common form of a citation is as follows: case name–volume–number–reporter–page number–court–year.
- The AFTR second series began with 1954 IRC cases.
- The B.T.A. became the U.S. Tax Court in 1943.
- The U.S. Court of Claims became the U.S. Claims Court in 1982, and the U.S. Court of Federal Claims in 1992.
- *Unless* the case was published in a year different from that in which it was heard, the USTC volume number (and many AFTR page numbers) includes a reference to the year, so the year need not be repeated in the citation.
- The S.Ct. and U.S. citations imply that the case was heard in the Supreme Court, so the court abbreviation need not be repeated in the citation.
- The government need not be mentioned in a typical Tax Court citation.
- Although they are not published in a printed court reporter, U.S. Tax Court Small Case Summary Opinions are available after 2000 on computer tax services (e.g., RIA and CCH).

TAX TUTOR

Reinforce the tax research information covered in this chapter by completing the online tutorials located at the *Federal Tax Research* web site: **http://academic.cengage.com/taxation/raabe**

KEY WORDS

By the time you complete this chapter, you should be comfortable discussing each of the following terms. If you need additional review of any of these items, return to the appropriate material in the chapter or consult the glossary to this text.

AFTR	Memorandum decision
Board of Tax Appeals	Permanent citation
Case brief	Regular decision
Court of Federal Claims	Small Cases Division
Courts of Appeals	Supreme Court
District Courts	Tax Court
En banc	Temporary citation
Golsen rule	USTC
Headnote	Writ of certiorari

DISCUSSION QUESTIONS

1. Who can initiate a court case that deals with a tax matter—the taxpayer or the IRS?

2. Explain the general organization of the federal court system for cases concerning Federal tax issues.

3. May a taxpayer take his or her tax case directly to the Supreme Court?

4. Who has the burden of proof in most cases involving the tax law? Why?

5. The U.S. Tax Court hears only certain types of cases. Identify those cases.

6. The U.S. Tax Court has undergone an evolution since it was founded. What happened to its structure in 1926, 1943, and 1969, respectively?

7. How many judges sit on the U.S. Tax Court? What is the length of time of the appointment of each judge?

8. The U.S. Tax Court is a national court that meets in Washington, D.C. Does this mean that the taxpayer and his or her attorney must travel to Washington to have a case heard?

9. May a taxpayer have a jury trial in the U.S. Tax Court?

10. What does the term *"en banc"* mean?

11. Distinguish among a Regular, Memorandum, and Summary decision of the Tax Court.

12. The U.S. Tax Court is a national court that hears cases of taxpayers who may appeal to various geographical Courts of Appeals. How does the Tax Court reconcile the opposite holdings of two or more of these Courts of Appeals for taxpayers who work or reside in different parts of the country?

13. What is the Small Cases Division of the U.S. Tax Court? What is the maximum amount of the deficiency that can be the subject of a Small Cases hearing? Comment on the trial procedures in the Small Cases Division.

14. Where are regular Tax Court decisions published? Illustrate the elements of both a temporary and a permanent regular Tax Court citation. Explain what each part of the citation means.

15. Tax Court Memorandum decisions are not published by the Federal government. However, commercial reporters include these decisions. Illustrate the elements of both a temporary and a permanent citation for a Tax Court Memorandum decision, using both the CCH and RIA reporters. Explain what each part of the citation means.

16. What is the jurisdiction of a U.S. District Court?

17. Can Tax Court Summary Opinions be cited as precedent? Discuss.

18. Must the taxpayer pay the disputed tax deficiency to the government before his or her case will be heard in a District Court? In the U.S. Court of Federal Claims? In the U.S. Tax Court?

19. Which of the trial courts is most appropriate for a taxpayer who wishes to limit the judicial review of the relevant year's tax return to the specific issue(s) involved in the case?

20. Which of the trial courts would best serve a taxpayer litigating an issue of a technical tax nature? Why?

21. Is a Federal District Court a national court? How many judges hear a case brought before a Federal District Court?

22. Name the three court case reporters that publish tax and nontax District Court decisions. Illustrate the elements of a citation that might be found in each reporter. Explain what each part of the citation means.

23. Differentiate between a primary and a secondary case citation.

24. What type of cases are heard by the U.S. Court of Federal Claims?

25. How many judges are appointed to the U.S. Court of Federal Claims?

26. Is the U.S. Court of Federal Claims a national court? Must a taxpayer go to Washington, D.C., to present a case to this U.S. court?

27. Name the three court case reporters that publish U.S. Court of Federal Claims decisions. Illustrate the elements of a citation that might be found in each reporter. Explain what each part of the citation means.

28. Are the U.S. Courts of Appeals national courts? What type of cases do they hear?

29. Identify the circuit court that would hear the case of a taxpayer who lives or works in each of the following areas.
    a. Texas
    b. New York
    c. California
    d. Colorado
    e. Illinois
    f. A case that is appealed from the U.S. Court of Federal Claims

30. Identify the circuit court that would hear the case of a taxpayer who lives or works in each of the following areas.
    a. Florida
    b. Ohio
    c. North Carolina
    d. Puerto Rico
    e. Guam

31. Identify the circuit court that would hear the case of a taxpayer who lives or works in each of the following areas.
    a. Arizona
    b. Alabama
    c. Vermont
    d. South Carolina
    e. Alaska

32. Each Court of Appeals has approximately twenty judges. How many of these judges hear a typical case?

33. Name the three court case reporters that publish Court of Appeals decisions. Illustrate the elements of a citation that might be found in each reporter. Explain what each part of the citation means.

34. Can a taxpayer have a jury trial before a Court of Appeals?

35. What is the highest court in the United States? What is its jurisdiction? Where does it hear cases?

36. How does one petition the Supreme Court to hear one's tax case?

37. How many justices are appointed to the Supreme Court? How many hear each case?

38. Why does the Supreme Court hear so few tax cases?

39. Differentiate between the Supreme Court's overturning of a lower court's decision, and its denial of a writ of certiorari.

40. Name the four court case reporters that publish Supreme Court decisions. Illustrate the elements of a citation that might be found in each reporter. Explain what each part of the citation means.

41. Is it possible for a taxpayer to have a jury trial before any of the trial courts? Before a Court of Appeals? Before the U.S. Supreme Court?

42. Discuss the precedential value of a Court of Appeals decision. Which Court of Appeals decisions are most important to a specific taxpayer?

43. In the (fictitious) citation *Gomez v. U.S.*, 104 T.C. 123 (2009), what does the "104" stand for? The "T.C."? The "123"?

44. Which court would have issued the (fictitious) *O'Dell v. U.S.*, 98 TCM 86 (2009) decision? What does each element in the citation mean?

45. In the citation *Simons-Eastern v. U.S.*, 354 F.Supp. 1003 (D.Ct., Ga, 1972), the "F.Supp." tells the tax researcher that the decision is from which court?

46. *By using only the citation*, state which court issued each of the following decisions. If you cannot determine which court by looking at the citation only, say so.
    a. *Davis v. U.S.*, 43 Fed. Cl. 92 (1999)
    b. *D.C. Crummey v. U.S.*, 68-2 USTC ¶ 12,541
    c. *U.S. v. Goode*, 86 AFTR2d 2000-7273
    d. *James v. U.S.*, 81 S.Ct. 1052 (1961)

47. What is a case headnote? How might it be useful to the tax researcher?

48. *By using only the citation*, state which court issued each of the following decisions. If you cannot determine which court by looking at the citation only, say so.
    a. *Douglas, Christopher*, T.C. Memo 1994-519
    b. *Takaba, Brian G.*, 119 T.C. 285
    c. *Botts, Roy R.*, T.C. Summary Opinion 2001-182
    d. *American Airlines, Inc.*, 40 Fed.Cl. 712

EXERCISES

49. Locate the court case *Central Labor's Pension Fund v. Heinz*, 541 U.S. 739 (2004). Using only the headnotes answer the following questions.
    a. What was the issue(s) addressed by the Court?
    b. What was the ruling of the court?

50. Locate the court case *Alemasov and Popov*, TC Memo. 2007-130. Using only the headnotes answer the following questions.
    a. What was the issue(s) addressed by the Court?
    b. What was the ruling of the court?

51. Locate the court case *Zimmerman, et al. v. United States*, 2001-1 USTC ¶50,107, 86 AFTR2d 2000-6701. Using only the headnotes answer the following questions.
    a. What was the issue(s) addressed by the Court?
    b. What was the ruling of the court?

52. Locate the court case *Anderson Columbia, Inc. V. U.S.*, 54 Fed. Cl. 756 (2002). Using only the headnotes answer the following questions.
    a. What was the issue(s) addressed by the Court?
    b. What was the ruling of the court?

53. Find the court decision located at 100 T.C. 32.
    a. What court heard the case?
    b. Who was the judge(s)?
    c. In what year was the case decided?
    d. What was the issue(s) involved?

54. Find the court decision located at 126 T.C. 47.
    a. What court heard the case?
    b. Who was the judge(s)?
    c. In what year was the case decided?
    d. What was the issue(s) involved?

55. Find the court decision located at T.C. Memo. 2001-71.
    a. What court heard the case?
    b. Who was the judge(s)?
    c. In what year was the case decided?
    d. What was the issue(s) involved?

56. Find the court decision located at T.C. Memo. 1992-204.
    a. What court heard the case?
    b. Who was the judge(s)?
    c. What tax year(s) is in question and in what year was the case decided?
    d. What Code section(s) was at issue?
    e. What was the issue(s) involved?
    f. Which party prevailed in the decision?

57. Find the court decision located at T.C. Summary Opinion 2003-168.
    a. What court heard the case?
    b. Who was the judge(s)?
    c. What tax year(s) is in question and in what year was the case decided?
    d. What Code section(s) was at issue?
    e. What was the issue(s) involved?
    f. Which party prevailed in the decision?

58. Find the court decision located at T.C. Summary Opinion 2006-20.
    a. What court heard the case?
    b. Who was the judge(s)?
    c. What tax year(s) is in question and in what year was the case decided?
    d. What Code section(s) was at issue?
    e. What was the issue(s) involved?
    f. Which party prevailed in the decision?

59. Find the court decision located at 2007-1 USTC ¶50,210.
    a. What court heard the case?
    b. Who was the judge(s)?
    c. What tax year(s) is in question and in what year was the case decided?
    d. What Code section(s) was at issue?
    e. What was the issue(s) involved?
    f. Which party prevailed in the decision?

60. Find the court decision located at 67 AFTR2d 91-718.
    a. What court heard the case?
    b. Who was the judge(s)?
    c. What tax year(s) is in question and in what year was the case decided?
    d. What Code section(s) was at issue?
    e. What was the issue(s) involved?
    f. Which party prevailed in the decision?

61. Find the court decision located at 98 AFTR2d 2006-8309.
    a. What court heard the case?
    b. Who was the judge(s)?
    c. What tax year(s) is in question and in what year was the case decided?
    d. What Code section(s) was at issue?
    e. What was the issue(s) involved?
    f. Which party prevailed in the decision?

62. If your last name begins with the letters A–L, read and brief the following cases.
    a. *Sorensen*, T.C. Memo. 1994-175
    b. *Keller*, 84-1 USTC ¶ 9194.
       If your last name begins with the letters M–Z, read and brief the following cases.
    c. *Washington*, 77 T.C. 601
    d. *Tellier*, 17 AFTR2d 633

63. If your last name begins with the letters A–L, read and brief the following cases.
    a. *Rownd*, T.C. Memo. 1994-465
    b. *Arnes*, 93-1 USTC ¶ 50,016.
       If your last name begins with the letters M–Z, read and brief the following cases.
    c. *Willie Nelson Music Co.*, 85 T.C. 914
    d. *Independent Contracts, Inc.*, 73 AFTR2d 94-1406

64. Read and brief the following cases.
    a. *Gregory v. Helvering*, 55 S.Ct. 266 (1935)
    b. *Hunt*, T.C. Memo. 1965-172

65. Read and brief the following cases.
    a. *Fulcher, Douglas R.*, T.C. Summary Opinion 2003-157
    b. *The Boeing Company and Consolidated Subs.*, 91 AFTR 2d 2003-1088 (123 S.Ct. 1099)

66. Read and brief the following cases.
    a. *Thornton v. Commissioner*, 2003-2 USTC ¶50,695
    b. *Stamoulis v. Commissioner*, T.C. Summary Opinion 2007-38

67. Use a tax service to give two parallel citations for the *U.S. v. D'ambrosia*, a Seventh Circuit Court of Appeals case decided in 2002. Using only the headnote(s), what was the issue(s) in this case?

68. Use a tax service to give three parallel citations for the *Baral v. U.S.*, a Supreme Court case decided in 2000. Using only the headnote(s), what was the issue(s) in this case?

69. Use a tax service to give three parallel citations for the *Falstone, Inc. v. Commissioner*, a Ninth Circuit Court of Appeals case decided in 2003. Using only the headnote(s), what was the issue(s) in this case?

RESEARCH CASES

70. Snidely Limited spent $1 million this year to upgrade its manufacturing plant, which had received several warnings from the state environmental agency about releasing pollution into the local river. Late in the year, Snidely received an assessment of $700,000 for violating the state's Clean Water Act. After he negotiated with the State, which cost $135,000 in legal fees, Snidely promised to spend another $200,000 next year for more pollution control devices, and the fine was reduced to $450,000. How much of these expenditures can Snidely Limited deduct for tax purposes?

    Partial list of research material: §162; Rev. Rul. 76-130, 1976-1 C.B. 16; *Tucker,* 69 T.C. 675.

71. Last year, only four of thirty-two professional basketball teams turned a nominal accounting profit. Betty purchased such a team this year. Her taxable loss therefrom properly was determined to be $950,000. Can she deduct this loss?

    Partial list of research material: §183; Reg. §1.183-2; *Brannen,* 722 F.2d 695.

72. Herbert, a collector of rare coins, bought a 1916 Spanish Bowlero for $2,000 in 1984. He sold the coin for $4,500 in January. Herbert retired from his loading dock job in June and began actively buying and selling rare coins. By December, Herbert's realized gain from such activities was $21,500. What type of taxable income was January's $2,500 gain?

    Partial list of research material: §1221; Rev. Rul. 68-634, 1968-2 C.B. 46; *Frankel,* 56 TCM 1156 (1989).

73. Steve is an usher at his local church. Can he deduct commuting expenses for the Sundays that he is assigned to usher for church services?

    Partial list of research material: §170; Rev. Rul. 56-508, 1956-2 C.B. 126; *Churukian,* 40 TCM 475 (1980).

74. A new member of the San Diego Chargers wants the team to transfer $1,000,000 into an escrow account, in his name, for later withdrawal. The player suggests this payment in lieu of the traditional signing bonus. When is this income taxable to him?

    Partial list of research material: §451; Rev. Rul. 70-435, 1970-2 C.B. 100; *Drysdale,* 277 F.2d 413.

75. Professor Stevens obtained tenure and promotion to full professor status many years ago. Yet, he continues to publish research papers in scholarly journals to satisfy his own curiosity and to maintain his professional prestige and status within the academic community. Publications are also necessary in order for Professor Stevens to receive pay raises at his university. This year, Dr. Stevens

spent $750 of his own funds to travel to southern Utah to collect some critical pieces of data for his work. What is the tax treatment of this expenditure?

Partial list of research material: §162; Zell, 85-2 USTC ¶ 9698; *Smith*, 50 TCM 904.

76. The local electric company requires a $200 refundable deposit from new customers, in lieu of a credit check. Landlord Pete pays this amount for all of his new-to-town tenants. Can he deduct the $200 payments on his tax return?

Partial list of research material: §162; Hopkins, 30 T.C. 1015; *Waring Products*, 27 T.C. 921.

77. High-Top Financing charges its personal loan holders a 2 percent fee if the full loan principal is paid prior to the due date. What is the tax effect of this year's $50,000 of prepayment penalties collected by High-Top?

Partial list of research material: §61; *Hort*, 41-1 USTC ¶ 9354.

78. Cecilia died this year, owning mutual funds in her IRA worth $120,000. Under the terms of the IRA, Cecilia's surviving husband, Frank, was the beneficiary of the account, and he took a lump-sum distribution from the fund. Both Cecilia and Frank were age fifty-seven at the beginning of the year.
   a. How does Frank account for the inheritance, assuming that he rolls it over into his own IRA in a timely manner?
   b. Would your answer change if Frank were Cecilia's brother?
      Partial list of research material: §408; Rev. Rul. 92-47, 1992-1 C.B. 198; *Aronson*, 98 T.C. 283 (1992).

79. During a properly declared U.S. war with Outer Altoona, Harriet, a single taxpayer, was killed in action. Current-year Federal taxable income to the date of Harriet's death totaled $19,000, and Federal income tax withholding came to $2,300.

   a. What is Harriet's tax liability for the year of her death?

   b. What documentation must accompany her final Form 1040?

   Partial list of research material: §692; Rev. Proc. 85-35, 1985-2 C.B. 433; *Hampton*, 75-1 USTC ¶ 9315.

80. Jerry Baker and his wife Hammi believe in the worship of the "Sea God." This is a very personal religion to Jerry and Hammi. To practice their beliefs, the Bakers want to take a two-week trip to Tahiti this year to worship their deity. The cost (airfare, hotels, etc.) of this religious "pilgrimage" is $5,250. Jerry wants to know if he can deduct the cost of this trip as a charitable deduction on the joint Form 1040, Schedule A.

   Partial list of research material: §170 and *Kessler*, 87 T.C. 1285 (1986).

81. Willie Waylon is a famous country-and-western singer. As an investment, Willie started a chain of barbecue restaurants called Willie's Wonderful Ribs. Willie's friends and associates invested $500,000 in this venture. The restaurant chain failed, and the investors lost all their money. Because of his visibility and status in the entertainment community, Willie felt that he personally had

to make good on the losses suffered by the investors, to protect his singing and business reputation. Consequently, he personally paid $500,000 to reimburse the investors for their losses. What are Willie's tax consequences (if any) from the reimbursement?

Partial list of research material: §162 and *Lohrke*, 48 T.C. 679.

82. Paul Preppie is an accountant for the Very Big (VB) Corporation of America, located in Los Angeles, California. When Paul went to work for VB, he did not have a college degree. VB required that Paul earn a B.S. degree in accounting, so he enrolled in a local private university's night school and obtained the degree. VB Corporation does not reimburse employees for attending night school, and because Paul attended a private university, the tuition and other costs were relatively expensive. Can Paul deduct any of the $5,500 he paid in tuition and other costs during the current tax year? Prepare (in good form) a research memorandum to the file (See Chapter 2 for an illustration of the structure of a tax memo.)

83. Several years ago, Carol Mutter, a cash-basis taxpayer, obtained a mortgage from Weak National Bank to purchase a personal residence. In December 2009, $8,500 of interest was due on the mortgage, but Carol had only $75 in her checking account. On December 31, 2009, she borrowed $8,500 from Weak Bank, evidenced by a note, and the proceeds were deposited in her checking account. On the same day, Carol issued a check in the identical amount of $8,500 to Weak Bank for the interest due. Is the interest expense deductible for the 2009 tax year? Prepare (in good form) a research memorandum to the file. (See Chapter 2 for an illustration of the structure of a tax memo.)

84. Phyllis maintained an IRA account at the brokerage firm ABC. On February 11 of the current year, she requested a check for the balance of her account. She received the check made out in her name and deposited it the same day in a new IRA account at the brokerage firm XYZ. Phyllis then requested a check on May 8 from XYZ, which was deposited in another new IRA account thirty-five days later. Is the May 8 distribution taxable to Phyllis? Prepare in good form a research memorandum to the file. (See Chapter 2 for an illustration of the structure of a tax memo.)

85. Crystal Eros is a devout Pyramidist and a member of the Religious Society of Yanni, a Pyramidist organization. She adheres to the fundamental tenets of Pyramidist theology, including the belief that the Spirit of God is in every person and that it is wrong to kill or otherwise harm another person. Crystal's faith dictates that she not voluntarily participate, directly or indirectly, in military activities. Because Federal income taxes fund military activities, Crystal believes that her faith prohibits her from paying such taxes. Is there any legal substantiation for Crystal's position? Prepare (in good form) a research memorandum to the file. (See Chapter 2 for an illustration of the structure of a tax memo.)

86. Last year, your client, Robert Dinero, mailed an automatic extension for his tax return on April 15. He enclosed a check for $10,000 with the extension request. The IRS cashed the check on April 28. Later, the IRS assessed Robert late filing penalties of $2,900 because they claim he did not mail the extension

request on time. On the same date, Robert mailed an income tax extension request and check to the state of California. The California check was cashed on April 16. You requested that the IRS send you a copy of the extension request envelope showing the postmark: however, the IRS has lost it. The IRS recently attached Robert's bank account for the $2,900, thereby seizing the funds directly. You have known Robert for years, and he could be described as a good, law-abiding, taxpaying citizen. He always pays his taxes on time, has never been in trouble with the IRS, and is not a tax protester. Robert asks you to recommend whether he should engage a tax attorney and sue for a refund, knowing that the legal fees for such an action will probably exceed $10,000. After appropriate research, write a letter to Robert explaining your findings. His address is 432 Lucre Street, Tecate, CA 91980.

87. Your client, Luther Lifo, is an auditing professor who runs a CPA review course. He comes to you with the following tax questions.

    Question One. Luther teaches CPA review courses on either a guaranteed or nonguaranteed basis. Under the guaranteed program, students pay higher tuition and, if they fail the CPA examination, are entitled to a full refund within two weeks of the release of the results. The CPA review course contracts require him to place the tuition in a set-aside escrow account until the students pass the exam; he established the savings account as a trust account for this purpose. The registration fee and tuition must be paid in full before the classes begin. Thus, students enrolled in the class that started in January 20x1 paid their tuition in December 20x0. In 20x0, Luther deposited registration fees and tuition, including $30,000 in guaranteed tuition payments for the winter 20x1 courses, into a checking account. Also during 20x1, he paid refunds to guaranteed students who failed the 20x1 exams from that account. Does Luther report the $30,000 as income in 20x0 or 20x1? How are the refunds paid in 20x1 treated for tax purposes? State the authority for your conclusion.

    Question Two. Luther is a majority shareholder in a corporation that owns an office building. He leases space in the building for use in his CPA review course. Luther pays approximately $20 per square foot in annual rent. The corporation leases the remaining space in the building to a LSAT, GMAT, SAT, and GRE review course run by other taxpayers for approximately $10 per square foot. Luther's main intent in negotiating the discounted lease was to secure the additional traffic generated by the other review courses in order to enhance the potential revenue for the CPA review course. What is the amount of rent that Luther can deduct in connection with the CPA review course? State the authority for your conclusion.

    After appropriate research, write a letter to Luther explaining your findings. The address is 321 Fifo Street, Temecula, CA 91980.

88. Austin Towers is a convicted former spy for the former Soviet Union. Austin received a communication from a Soviet agent that $2 million had been set aside for him in an account upon which he would be able to draw. Austin was told that the money was being held by the Soviet Union, rather than in an independent or third-party bank or institution, on the petitioner's behalf. Over the next few years, Austin drew approximately $1 million from the account. During that period, Austin filed annual tax returns with his wife showing taxable income of approximately $65,000 per year. Conduct appropriate research to determine Austin's tax liability for the $1 million in spy fees. After appro-

priate research, write a letter to Austin explaining your findings. His address is Lompoc Federal Prison, Cell #123, Lompoc, CA 93401.

89. The Reverend Shaman Oracle is an ordained minister in the Church of Prophetic Prophecy in Palm Desert, California. In the current year, Shaman receives payments from the church for his services of $150,000. Of this amount, the church designates $60,000 for compensation and $90,000 as a housing allowance. Shaman and his wife own a home and have actual expenditures during the year for the home of $72,000. The house is located in a well-established rental market, and the fair rental value of the home for the current year is $55,000. Shaman wants to know how he and his wife should report these amounts on their current year's tax return. After appropriate research, write a letter to Shaman explaining your findings. His address is P.O. Box 1234, Palm Desert, California 92211.

90. Your client, Teddy Chow and his wife Abby, filed a lawsuit to recover damages for personal injuries Teddy sustained in a 2000 auto accident. In 2004, a jury awarded Teddy $1,620,000 in damages. In addition, delay damages in the amount of $1,080,000 were then added to that award, resulting in a total judgment of $2,700,000. The defendants appealed the award, and while the appeal was pending, the parties reached a settlement, which provided for payment to Teddy of $2,550,000. In 2009, after attorney's fees of $850,000 were subtracted, Teddy received $1,700.000. Teddy wants to know how these amounts are treated for tax purposes. After appropriate research, write a letter to Teddy and Abby explaining your findings. Their address is 654 Hops Street, Golden, CO 78501.

91. Cabrito Ranch, Inc. is a family ranch owned and operated by two brothers, Billie and Bubba Cabrito. The corporation made in-kind bonus payments in the form of goats to its two officers (Billie and Bubba) in exchange for their performance of agricultural labor. The two brothers are the only employees to receive goat bonuses. The transfers of the goats to the officers occurred within days of the date Cabrito Ranch would have sold the goats within the ordinary course of its business. The two officers/brothers did not market their bonus goats separately from other Cabrito Ranch goats; rather, the bonus goats were loaded onto the same trucks and sold to the same goat buyer on the same terms as other Cabrito Ranch goats. The officer/brothers' goats were sold for $70,000 ($35,000 to each brother). Cabrito Ranch wants to know how to treat the cash from the goat bonuses for FICA purposes. After appropriate research, write a letter to Billie and Bubba explaining your findings. Their address is 247 Angora Road, Mohair, TX 77501.

92. Gwen Gullible was married to Darrell Devious. They were divorced two years ago. Three years ago (the year before their divorce), Darrell received a $250,000 retirement plan distribution, of which $50,000 was rolled over into an IRA. At the time, Gwen was aware of the retirement funds and the rollover. The distribution was used to pay off the couple's mortgage, purchase a car, and for living expenses. Darrell prepared the couple's joint return, and Gwen asked him about the tax ramifications of the retirement distributions. He told her he had consulted a CPA and was advised that the retirement plan proceeds used to pay off a mortgage were not taxable income. Gwen accepted that explanation and signed the return. In fact, Darrell had not consulted a CPA.

One year ago (after the divorce), Gwen received a letter from the IRS saying they had not received the tax return for the last full year of marriage. On advice from a CPA, Gwen immediately filed the return (she had a copy of the unfiled return). The Internal Revenue Service notified Gwen that no estimated payments on the retirement distribution had been paid by Darrell, and that she owed $60,000 in tax, plus penalties and interest. The deficiency notice provided that the retirement distribution, less the amount rolled, was income to the couple. After appropriate research, prepare (in good form) a research memorandum to the file. (See Chapter 2 for an illustration of the structure of a tax memo.) Then write a letter to Gwen explaining your findings. Her address is 678 Surprise Street, Houston, TX 77019.

93. Pealii Loligo owned and operated three "House of Calamari" restaurants from 1998 through 2000. His wife, Cleopatra Decacera, assisted with the management of the restaurants.

In May 1999, Ms. Decacera and Mr. Loligo purchased a $900,000 home. In relation to this home purchase, in 1996 and 2000 they signed mortgage loan applications indicating joint annual incomes of $235,000 and $321,000, respectively. On their 1998 joint Federal income tax return, however, Ms. Decacera and Mr. Loligo reported that they earned no salaries and had net losses of $55,000; and on their 1999 joint tax return, they reported that Mr. Loligo earned a salary of $23,000, and that they had net losses of $77,000.

During 1998–2000, Ms. Decacera and Mr. Loligo paid approximately $70,000 for home furnishings, $30,000 for a swimming pool, and $40,000 for Ms. Decacera's jewelry. In addition, they leased two Mercedes-Benz automobiles and took Ms. Decacera's parents on vacations to Florida and Nevada.

In 2003, Decacera and Loligo were indicted and charged with filing false tax returns in 1998–2000. Loligo pled guilty, while Decacera signed a deferred prosecution agreement and admitted filing false returns. The couple divorced in 2005, and in 2006, the IRS issued a deficiency notice for the 1998–2000 taxes. In September 2006, Ms. Decacera filed a petition in which she requested relief from joint and several liability for 1998–2000 income taxes. During January 2007, Mr. Loligo filed his "notice of intervention." In July, an IRS Appeals officer determined that Ms. Decacera did not qualify for Innocent Spouse relief under §6015(f).

After appropriate research, prepare in good form a research memorandum to the file. (See Chapter 2 for an illustration of the structure of a tax memo.) Then write a letter to Cleopatra explaining your findings. Her address is 4567 Whome Lane, Escondido, CA 92069.

94. Ned Naive (see research question Chapter 2, #84) operated several franchised stores, and at the home office's suggestion, consolidated its payroll and accounting functions with Andy the Accountant. Andy is not a CPA. Last year, Andy began embezzling taxpayer's escrowed tax withholdings and failed to remit required amounts for the four quarters. The IRS assessed Ned $10,000 in penalties for failing to make the proper withholding deposits during the year. After appropriate research, prepare (in good form) a research memorandum to the file. (See Chapter 2 for an illustration of the structure of a tax memo.) Then write a letter to Ned explaining your findings. His address is 4567 Brainless Street, Phoenix, AZ 91234.

95. Phred Phortunate (from Chapter 2), won his state lotto two years ago. His lotto ticket was worth $10,000,000, which was payable in twenty annual installments of $500,000 each. Phred paid $1.00 for the winning ticket. The lotto in Phred's state does not allow winners to receive their payout in a lump-sum. Phred wanted all of his money now, so he assigned his future lotto winnings to a Happy Finance Company for a discounted price of $4,500,000. Assignment of lotto winnings is permitted by Phred's state lotto. Phred filed his tax return and reported the assignment of the lotto winnings as a capital gain ($4.5M–$1.00) taxable at a 15 percent rate. After appropriate research to determine if Phred correctly reported his lotto winnings assignment, prepare (in good form) a research memorandum to the file. (See Chapter 2 for an illustration of the structure of a tax memo.) Then write a letter to Phred explaining your findings. His address is 2345 Ecstatic Street, White River Jct., VT 05001.

96. Your client, Gary Gearbox, wholly owned and worked full time for a C corporation in the business of repairing autos. His wife, Tammy, wholly owned and worked full time for another C corporation that provided mobile auto windshields repairs. Both corporations' offices were located in the Gearboxes' home. The corporations paid the Gearboxes rent for the use of this office space. In addition to renting this portion of their home, the Gearboxes also owned five rental properties. On their last three tax returns, the Gearboxes reported net income from leasing office space to their C corporations of $40,000, $24,000, and $22,000, respectively. During these years, the combined losses from the five other rental properties exceeded the income derived from their office leases. On their last three tax returns, the Gearboxes offset the losses from the rental properties against the income from the office leases and, as a result, paid no tax on the rental income paid to them by their corporation. After appropriate research to determine if Gary and Tammy correctly reported their rental income, prepare (in good form) a research memorandum to the file. Then write a letter to the Gearboxes explaining your findings. Their address is 7895 NASCAR Way, Anytown, Anystate 78501.

Research Tools

Tax Services and Periodicals

Chapter Outline

Learning Objectives

- Understand the advantages and disadvantages of Internet tax services.

- Apply the research process to actual Federal research problems.

- Become familiar with the major features of Internet tax services.

- Recognize the difference between annotated and topical tax services.

- Use the keyword, cite, and contents searches to find relevant materials in Internet tax services.

- Introduce the usefulness of tax periodicals and the role they play in the tax research.

- Master the correct citation forms for printed and Internet tax materials.

- Examine indexes to tax periodicals that can facilitate locating pertinent journal articles.

WITH EASY AND FREE access to virtually all primary tax sources via the Internet, one might wonder why tax practitioners are willing to bear the substantial costs associated with subscribing to commercial tax services. The reason is that, by organizing the copious assortment of primary and secondary tax law sources, these services facilitate more efficient, effective, and comprehensive searches for solutions to tax questions than a Google search would produce. Further, tax practitioners are being more closely scrutinized by the IRS and the Securities and Exchange Commission (SEC) as a result of the Sarbanes-Oxley legislation and other increases in regulation. This heightened oversight increases the importance of conducting quality tax research that is carefully documented. Tax services provide a vehicle for conducting this quality research.

The tax services provide editorial explanations and expert analysis of the primary tax sources. As the tax law can be quite complex, the plain English commentary alone can be worth the cost of the services. Thus, the value of a commercial tax service is to act as an index for and explanation of primary and secondary tax law source materials. Most tax practitioners avail themselves of the benefit of a tax service, as there are services priced to fit the needs (and pocketbooks) of even the smallest tax office.

While one of the main features practitioners appreciate in a tax service is the editorial explanation, only reckless (or inadequately trained) tax practitioners confine their analysis to this commentary. The tax services should efficiently direct the researcher to the germane primary sources of the controlling law. It is the ethical and professional duty of the researcher to undertake an evaluation of these primary sources, and to ascertain whether any developments have occurred recently that may change or alter the results of the research.

This chapter concretely applies the basic steps for developing effective and efficient tax research, based on the process introduced in Chapter 2, by utilizing the major tax services to find a solution to an actual tax question. The features of the tax services are explored on this journey. The end of the chapter investigates some of the important tax newsletters and periodicals that may be quite useful in finding solutions to tax problems. Tax services offering legal as well as tax products are examined in Chapter 7.

TAX SERVICES

Traditionally, commercial tax services are classified into two general types, annotated and topical. **Annotated tax services** are organized by *Internal Revenue Code* section number. They may also be called **Compilations** because they compile an editor's explanation and evaluation with the Code section, its recent committee reports, and Regulations, and they provide **annotations** (brief summaries) of related court cases and administrative rulings. **Topical tax services**, on the other hand, divide the tax law into transactions and related subject matter with underlying tax principles as an organizing format. Thus, the material follows logical threads that connect noncontiguous Code sections. Since the electronic services developed from published services, they are generally organized as topical and annotated databases; however, this structure may not be apparent.

One of the greatest benefits of any electronic tax service is the currency of the information provided. Most Internet services update in text on a daily or continuous basis. Still, daily updating does not necessarily mean that what happened yesterday will be accessible today. Processing time still is required. Daily updating does mean, however, that as soon as the information is processed it can be entered into the system.

There are numerous public domain resources and third-party services available to the tax professional. Some tax services simply compile primary source information obtained from the government, while others originate information and include substantial analysis. While practitioners can retrieve most primary tax sources at no cost, this free access does not translate into more effective research. The sheer volume of information, and the time needed to sort, read, and comprehend all of it, can lead to information overload and inefficiencies. All of this information must be managed; otherwise, using the Internet for tax research is not effective. Consequently, Internet access to primary sources cannot substitute for a subscription to comprehensive tax services. Besides checking the validity of primary tax sources, tax services furnish various methods of searching the tax sources, editorial analysis and comments, organization, and an integration of the tax resources.

SPOTLIGHT ON TAXATION

Tax Quote

The difference between tax avoidance and tax evasion is the thickness of a prison wall.

—Denis Healey

ILLUSTRATIVE RESEARCH EXAMPLE

The following research project is used to demonstrate the steps in tax research and to explore the essential features of the major tax services. It is important that *you* attempt the illustrative research project using the tax services available to you. The procedural knowledge necessary to use these tax services efficiently can be acquired only through hands-on practice. The remainder of this chapter is designed to guide you through the basic tax services and is *not* a substitute for your actually using the services. Performing the research along with the text presentation of the research steps is a highly effective method of learning this material.

Research Project 6–1. Our clients, Alfred and Agnes Zyzzic, have a sole proprietorship that develops and manufactures children's toys. Alfred is the inventor of the toys, and Agnes is the marketer of their products. However, Agnes has had serious medical problems for the past two years and has not been able to market their products effectively. Consequently, sales have plummeted and the business is in financial distress. The medical problems have also resulted in huge medical costs that were not covered by insurance. Thus, the Zyzzics also are experiencing serious personal financial difficulties. They feel that the best solution to their current predicament is to file for protection under the personal bankruptcy law. They have hired a lawyer to prepare and file all the necessary documents in the bankruptcy court. The Zyzzics would like to know how bankruptcy costs are treated for tax purposes.

Approaching the Research Problem

Regardless of the research method used, the starting point in approaching any tax research problem is to formulate various tax questions to be asked and develop the issues associated with the question. The tax question for Research Project 6–1 appears to be: What is the appropriate tax treatment of the legal fees incurred in filing for bankruptcy by the Zyzzics? This first formulation of the tax question should not be considered its final version. As the research progresses, other issues are likely to be identified, causing some refinement of the tax research questions and necessitating the development of new ones. Recall the iterative nature of tax research as discussed in Chapter 2 relative to Exhibits 2-1 and 2-2.

Gradually research questions are refined to their final states and all the associated issues are identified. However, this refinement does not guarantee that controlling authority will be found that provides a definite answer to the tax research question. The final conclusion may be that one solution appears more supportable than another, or that the IRS or the courts are more likely to interpret the facts and circumstances in a particular manner when making a decision. In most tax research engagements, professional judgment is required because the controlling law is imprecise and can be interpreted differently by the taxpayer and the IRS. Professional judgment is what taxpayers are seeking when they hire CPAs for tax assistance.

Based on the initial question formulated, the main issues in Research Project 6–1 appear to be the deductibility of bankruptcy legal fees as business expenses, as deductible personal expenses, or as nondeductible personal expenditures. Therefore, relevant keywords for this research include: *bankruptcy, legal, fees, business expenses, personal expenditures,* and *deduction.* It is wise to make an extensive list of possible keywords, to lessen the chance of omitting relevant terms.

Through a basic knowledge of the Code, we know that business expenses are governed by IRC §162, Trade or Business Expenses. Finally, in prior research of other topics, we have seen references to a 1963 Supreme Court case called *Gilmore* that developed the origin-of-claim test for determining whether legal expenses are deductible business costs or personal nondeductible expenses. The case specifically concerns legal costs associated with divorces, but it may have some bearing on this situation.

Accessing Tax Information

The key to effective tax research is finding the pertinent material necessary to formulate an informed conclusion about the optimum treatment of the transaction. How the tax services are entered will determine how efficiently the relevant materials are found. Most of the services allow researchers to choose whether to have retrieved documents presented in order of relevance to the search or listed by database sources. The former uses a complex software formula to determine relevance, whereas the latter lets the researchers themselves decide which documents should be examined first.

Regardless of the order in which the results are displayed, a researcher unfamiliar with the topic should start with an editorial explanation and overview of the applicable tax law. This commentary will help the researcher identify the most pertinent elements of the project and introduce the applicable primary tax law. Access to the primary sources from the explanation is easy because the primary sources are generally hyperlinked to their citations. This initial foray into the service is likely to identify other issues to investigate and more facts that should be collected. Remember that research is an iterative process.

From this initial analysis, a researcher may decide that a new, more targeted search is warranted. Once the relevant primary sources are identified, but before they are carefully read, it is necessary to determine which sources are still valid law by checking them through a citator (see Chapter 8 for a full discussion of citators). The fact that the tax service locates a document and places it high on the relevance list does not mean the researcher can assume it is still valid law. The last step is to read carefully the germane primary tax law sources. Only after evaluating these sources themselves can the researcher provide educated suggestions as to the optimum treatment for the items in question.

The commercial providers of tax services offer a plethora of tax products (databases) that can be bundled in a variety of ways. This chapter's description of the tax databases within any of the services may not be what is available by subscription to the reader. Each tax professional, firm, or library performs a cost–benefit analysis and purchases only those resources that it can afford and finds useful in its practice. In addition, the tax services are constantly updating their products to maintain their competitive edges. Therefore, the current appearance of the tax services and products offered may differ from those presented in this text. Nevertheless, the basic methodology described in this chapter should apply to whatever tax databases and products are available to the reader and whatever their visual presentation.

RIA Checkpoint

Tax services can be entered using three search methods: Keyword, Cite (using the citation of primary sources such as a Code section, case name, or ruling number), and Content (Table of Content and Index). How to use each method will be illustrated using **Checkpoint**, the Research Institute of America (RIA) Internet tax service. This is one of the most authoritative and well-known tax services available. The general methodology that applies to RIA Checkpoint also applies to other tax services.

RIA Checkpoint provides a full gambit of Federal tax information with several different product packages available. The most inclusive package includes all primary tax sources, **Federal Tax Coordinator** (FTC), **United States Tax Reporter** (USTR), Citator 2nd Series, Warren, Gorham & Lamont (WG&L) journals, WG&L textbooks and treatises, IRS publications, and so on. With so much information available, it is important to limit a search to only those databases that are pertinent to the research project; otherwise, too many irrelevant documents will be retrieved.

Exhibit 6-1 shows the opening search screen appearing after the RIA Checkpoint log-on screen. The screen is organized to facilitate quick access to the research methods most frequently used by the practitioners. As can be seen, the focus of Checkpoint is on Keyword searches; the Keyword entry box is center screen. A Table of Contents (TOC) search can be launched by clicking on the button so named at the top of the screen and Index searches started either through the TOC or the left window of the opening search screen. Cite searches are also accessed through the left window. The discussion of searching in Checkpoint will start with Keyword searching since this is Checkpoint's emphasis and then move to Contents and finally Cite searches. Before the searching can commence, a practice area needs to be selected. Among the choices are Federal, State & Local, Estate Planning, Pension & Benefits, International, and All Practice Areas. The default area is Federal, and therefore, no changes need to be made for Research Project 6–1, since it involves a Federal income tax problem.

Keyword Search

Checkpoint makes Keyword searching appear to be as easy as 1, 2, 3 (see Exhibit 6-1). First, enter keywords in the box provided. Second, select a database to search. Third, click on the "Search" button. If only it was that easy to find the perfect search terms, select just the right database, and have the pertinent search results appear with the click of the mouse! Probably the most difficult part of a keyword search is finding the

Exhibit 6-1: RIA Checkpoint Opening Search Screen

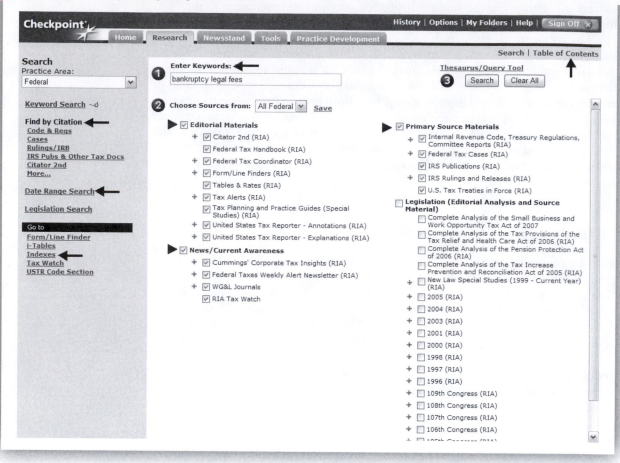

best words to use that are not so broad that too many irrelevant documents are retrieved and not so narrow that too few relevant documents are found.

For an initial search, the terms *bankruptcy legal fees* were entered in the Keywords box of Exhibit 6-1. Editorial Materials, News/Current Awareness, and Primary Source Materials databases were searched. Over 2,700 documents were retrieved on the Source Documents screen. A full-text search looks for each term appearing anywhere in the text of the documents. It does not consider our desire that the document be about the tax treatment of the incurred legal fees for bankruptcy. The program literally searches for a string of characters making up the words. Thus, every document addressing bankruptcy with the words *legal* and *fees* in it is identified. Court cases, for example, are most likely to contain the term *legal* somewhere in their text. If the cases discuss bankruptcy and any type of fees, it is included in the document list. Approximately 1,800 of the search results are court cases, the majority of which are not applicable to research project. Common words selected as keywords are likely to not be useful in discriminating relevant documents and should therefore be avoided if possible.

Due to the number of the documents retrieved, our search should be modified in two respects. First, the number of databases searched is reduced. A general understanding of the deductibility of bankruptcy legal fees is first necessary if the researcher is unfamiliar with the topic. Therefore, only editorial materials providing explanations of the tax law such as the FTC and the USTR—Explanations are selected. This modification is accomplished by selecting the "Modify Search" on the Source Documents screen in Exhibit 6-2. With this modification, approximately sixty documents were retrieved.

Another modification performed to reduce the number of documents retrieved is to place quotation marks around the words "legal fees" indicating that these words should be searched as a phrase. Again, from the Source Document screen, the "Search Within Results" Search Tools option is chosen to make this modification. This search option allows the researcher to further search the source documents already identified using additional terms or in our case altered terms. Running the search with the modified keyword terms and the new databases identifies a more reasonable number of documents. Through this iterative research process, our first set of search terms became *bankruptcy "legal fees."* The spaces between words are interpreted by Checkpoint as an "and" connection. Accordingly, only documents containing all of these words anywhere in its text are located. Notice that these terms were entered into the Keywords box in no particular order. However, if an order is desired, Boolean connectors may be used. A list of the RIA Boolean connectors is furnished in Exhibit 6-3. Not only can the researcher indicate order with these connectors, but relationships among words themselves. For our search, for example, indicating that the terms should appear within the same

Exhibit 6-2: RIA Checkpoint Document Sources

Source	Documents
Editorial Materials	
Federal Tax Coordinator (RIA)	
Analysis / Federal Tax Coordinator (RIA)	53
Checklists (RIA)	1
Client Letters (RIA)	1
Tax Alerts (RIA)	
Tax Alerts Developments (RIA)	1
Tax Alerts Archives (RIA)	3
Tax Planning and Practice Guides (Special Studies) (RIA)	1
United States Tax Reporter - Annotations (RIA)	
Annotations (Code Arranged – USTR) (RIA)	189
United States Tax Reporter - Explanations (RIA)	9
News/Current Awareness	
Federal Taxes Weekly Alert Newsletter (RIA)	25
WG&L Journals	
Business Entities (WG&L)	32
Journal of Corporate Taxation (WG&L)	11
Journal of Taxation (WG&L)	57
Practical Tax Strategies/Taxation for Accountants (WG&L)	38
Practical Tax Strategies Preview (WG&L)	2
Primary Source Materials	
Internal Revenue Code, Treasury Regulations, Committee Reports (RIA)	
Final, Temporary & Proposed Treasury Regulations (RIA)	8
Internal Revenue Code (RIA)	1
Internal Revenue Code History (RIA)	2
Preambles to Final and Temporary Treasury Regulations (Treasury Decisions) (RIA)	28
Preambles to Proposed Treasury Regulations (RIA)	1
Prior Final & Temporary Treasury Regulations (RIA)	4

Checkpoint

History | Options | My Folders | Help | Sign Off ✕

Home   Research   Newsstand   Tools   Practice Development

Search | Table of Contents

Search Results

Total Documents Found: 2,738
Search Terms: bankruptcy legal fees
Sources: Actions on Decisions (1967 - Present) (RIA); Advance Citator 2nd (RIA); Advance...
more...

Modify Search

Search Tools
Search Within Results
Save or Schedule Search

Go to
Table of Contents

☑ View hits only

Exhibit 6-3: RIA Checkpoint Boolean Connectors

Keyword Search Type	Connector to Use	Example
Containing all my keywords	Space, &, AND	earnings profits
Containing any of my keywords	|, OR	earnings OR profits
Contains one keyword but not the other	^, NOT	earnings NOT profits
Containing an exact phrase	" " (quotes)	"earnings and profits "
Containing variations of my keywords	* (asterisk)	deduct*
Showing order to perform commands	( ) (parentheses)	(earning profits) NOT retained
Within n words of other (any order)	/n (n equals a number)	consent /5 dividends
Within n words of other (in exact order)	pre/n	consent pre/5 dividends
Within same sentence (or 20 words) as other (in any order)	/s	consent /s dividends
Within same sentence (or 20 words) as other (in exact order)	pre/s	consent /s dividends
Within one paragraph (or 50 words) of other (in any order)	/p	consent /p dividends
Within one paragraph (or 50 words) of other (in exact order)	pre/p	consent pre/p dividends

sentence would have been useful. The keywords would be entered in the Keywords box as *bankruptcy /s "legal fees"*. Using this entry produces four documents in the FTC, all of which are relevant to our project. Variations in words may also be searched. If we want to search for the terms *expense, expensing,* and *expenditure*, we could enter "expen*" where the asterisk is a holder for zero or more characters at the end of a word. Documents containing any of the variations are retrieved. The list of connectors is available in Checkpoint by clicking on Thesaurus/Query Tool function (see Exhibit 6-1, at top right).

If the researcher is not sure of the best terms to use, synonyms can be added to the keyword search terms, by using the thesaurus built into Checkpoint. The researcher has the option of selecting which of the synonyms displayed are added to the search or of including all of the alternatives. By being able to select only some or one of the terms, researchers can customize the search to their particular research project. For Research Project 6–1, the term bankruptcy elicits synonyms of *receivership* and *"subchapter v."* By selecting the synonyms we prefer, Checkpoint automatically adds the terms to the keywords box with a vertical slash between each term indicating an "or" connection for the synonyms. More information on formatting keyword entries can be found in the "Help" feature appearing on every screen (see Exhibit 6-2).

Using the databases and search terms described, our search results in documents being identified in the FTC and the USTR—Explanations. Clicking on either of these titles will display the list of documents found in these services. The FTC, RIA's flagship service, is a topical service, whereas the USTR is an annotated service that provides explanations as well as annotations to cases and rulings. As Exhibit 6-4 demonstrates, the FTC document list provides the paragraph number, the title of each document, and shows the keywords in context with the keywords highlighted. The first document listed "Deductibility of fees incurred in connection with personal and business bankruptcy" appears to provide a promising start for our research project. Clicking on the title of the document will retrieve its full-text entry.

Notice that prior to the paragraph number is a column titled Score. This score is used for listing the documents in order of relevance. The relevance of documents is determined by an internal complex formula created by IRA that weighs factors such as density, commonality, and relativity of the search terms in the documents. Rather than being displayed by relevance, the documents may be listed by TOC order. The researcher may indicate display preferences through the Options function (see Exhibit 6-4, at the top right).

The Document Display screen (Exhibit 6-5) provides easy access to the other documents in the FTC by listing them in the left window. Documents in the FTC and all documents found by the search also are accessible through the Document arrow at the bottom (right) of the screen. Clicking on the arrow will scroll though the documents. The Content arrows change the left window to a Contents View, (Clicking on the Contents View button at the top of the left window will perform the same ordering.) This allows the researcher to know where in the TOC the current document is located. Also, through this view, the researcher can browse the service as one would flip through the pages of the published version. This is very handy when the researcher would like to read other explanations closely related to the topic of the research project.

Finally, the Keyword arrows (far right bottom) find the occurrences of the keywords in the documents. The keywords throughout the text are highlighted for

Exhibit 6-4: RIA Checkpoint Document List

Exhibit 6-5: RIA Checkpoint FTC Document

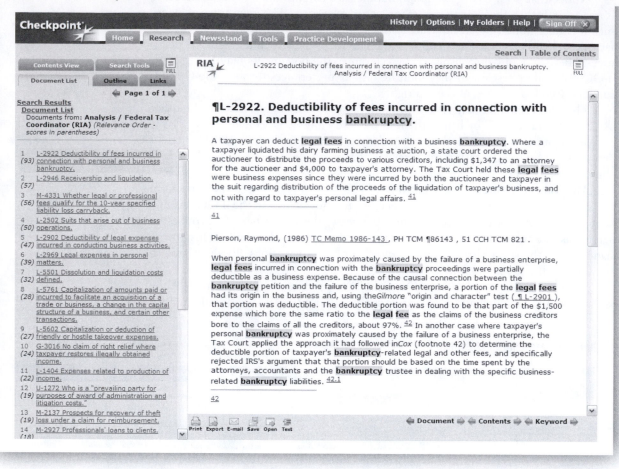

easy identification (see Exhibit 6-5). Citations that hyperlinked to their full-text documents are indicated by being underlined and in blue type. Clicking on the footnote numbers will jump to the citations. Since the FTC is a topical service, footnotes are utilized to provide substantiation for the editorial views expressed in this service. The discussion presented in such commentary is not the law, and the paragraph numbers of the FTC should not be cited as support by a tax professional. Primary sources, after being investigated and applying professional judgment, are usually the only appropriate documents to be used for supporting a taxpayer's position.

SPOTLIGHT ON TAXATION

Tax Service History

The United States Tax Reporter, the annotated tax service offered by RIA, didn't start out with this name. Prentice Hall published this tax service from 1924 to 1990 as the *PH Federal Taxes*. In November of 1989, Maxwell MacMillan bought the service and merely replaced Prentice Hall's

continued

continued

name as the publisher. Then, in September 1991, Thomson acquired Maxwell MacMillan. The *PH Federal Taxes* became part of the RIA offerings in 1992 when its name was changed to the United States Tax Reporter.

Through reading the documents currently identified, we realize that we need to revise our tax issues. We have learned that personal bankruptcy legal costs are not deductible. The revised tax issue becomes the deductibility of all or part of the bankruptcy legal costs as business expenses. To make sure that we find all of the pertinent documents addressing the deductibility of legal fees as a business deduction, we enter a different keyword search using the terms *business* and *"legal expenses"* or *"legal fees."* The Source Documents screen indicates sources available in the USTR–Explanations and USTR–Annotations, the two databases chosen for this search. One of the documents from Explanations, Expenditures connected with litigation, is reproduced in Exhibit 6-6. Note that the paragraph number, ¶1624.040, provides a reference to the Code section governing this issue, §162. The last number, 4, indicates that the paragraph is an explanation.

Exhibit 6-6: RIA Checkpoint USTR Document

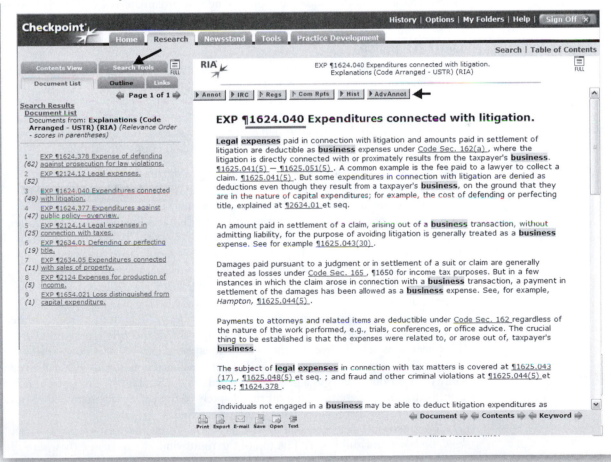

Directly above the paragraph number and document title in Exhibit 6-6 are a number of buttons that will lead the researcher to other documents related to this topic, such as annotations (Annot), the applicable Code sections (IRC), Regulations (Regs), committee reports (Com Rpts), history (Hist), and advance annotations (Adv Annot). When comparing this document with the FTC document in Exhibit 6-5, observe that these useful buttons are not present in the FTC. This is because the FTC is a topical service and the USTR is an annotated service. As in Exhibit 6-5, the left window of Exhibit 6-6 displays a list of the documents retrieved by the search.

Selecting the Document List tab (in left window) displays the long list of documents from the search appears in the left window. An easy way to narrow this list is to click on the Search Tools tab at the top of the left window, then select Search within Results, and enter *personal bankruptcy* into the Keywords box. The documents and annotations returned seem to be pertinent to our research. Since the annotations also are part of the USTR, the same buttons (IRC, Regs, Com Rpts, etc.) appear above the annotation titles. The Expl button replaces the Anno button and will take the researcher to the explanation portion of the USTR related to the annotation. Each annotation is hyperlinked to the related primary documents. Competent researchers always read the primary documents and never rely on these exceedingly brief annotations when resolving a tax question. The case of Herbert E. Cox, TC Memo 1981-552, indicates that the bankruptcy legal fees are deductible to the extent that the bankruptcy filing has its origin-of-claim in the taxpayers' business. The crucial factor is whether the bankruptcy filing was proximate result of the business failure.

Contents Search

One very important method of limiting the number of documents retrieved and guaranteeing their pertinence is to employ a contents search either in conjunction with a keyword search or as the only method of searching. This method treats electronic tax services as if they are their counterpart published services. Accordingly, researchers can "drill down" through either the TOCs or Indexes of the tax services just like they would "thumb through" these if they had books in front of them.

TOC Search   A TOC search is launched from the opening screen by selecting the Table of Contents option (see Exhibit 6–1). For the illustrative Research Project 6–1, we would review the Federal Editorial Materials and in particular the FTC. Scanning the chapters in the FTC, Chapter L Deductions: Business and Investment Expenses, Travel & Entertainment appears to be relevant. Clicking on the title will display the TOC for the chapter. The researcher can continue to drill down through the contents until pertinent individual entries are found. This drill-down method can be very efficient when the researcher has a good idea of where in the services the relevant documents are likely to be located.

At any point in the drilling-down process, a keyword search may be performed on up to fifteen topics by checking the box in front of the title (see Exhibit 6-7). This search is not limited to the TOC titles as might be presumed; rather it searches the documents within the titles. Thus, using this method will lead to the same relevant documents as a general keyword. The advantage of this option, however, is that the researcher can limit the chapters of the tax service searched to only those that are pertinent to the issue being researched.

The results of keyword search of Chapter L, using the terms *bankruptcy* and *legal*, is shown in Exhibit 6-7. The top of the right window shows exactly where the topics retrieved are located in the service (Federal Library, Federal Editorial Materials, FTC 2d, Currently in Chapter L). The numbers after the topic titles indicate

Exhibit 6-7:　RIA Checkpoint Table of Contents

Checkpoint

HISTORY | Options | My Folders | Help | Sign Off

Home　Research　Newsstand　Tools　Practice Development

Search | Table of Contents

Table of Contents

Jump To
Titles
Form/Line Finder
USTR Code Section

Browse
Display Level 1
Display Level 2
Display Level 3

☑ Show Only Hits

Search Results
Modify Search
Clear Search

Search Tools
Search Within Results
Save or Schedule Search

Go to
Source List

Checkpoint Contents　15
Federal Library　15
Federal Editorial Materials　15
Federal Tax Coordinator 2d　15
☐ Currently in: **Chapter L Deductions: Business and Investment Expenses, Travel & Entertainment**　15

+ ☐ L-1100 What is a Trade or Business?　2
+ ☐ L-1400 Expenses for Production of Income.　1
+ ☐ L-2500 Payment of Civil Judgments and Settlements.　1
+ ☐ L-2900 Legal and Accounting Expenses.　4
+ ☐ L-3900 Employees' Special Expenses.　1
+ ☐ L-4200 Miscellaneous Expenses.　1
+ ☐ L-4400 Which Taxpayer Is Entitled to Deduct Business and Investment Expenses?　1
+ ☐ L-5400 Treatment of Expenses Incurred in Connection With Reorganizations.　1
+ ☐ L-5500 Dissolution and Liquidation Expenses.　1
+ ☐ L-5600 Capital Expenditures.　1
+ ☐ L-5750 Expenditures to Acquire or Create Intangible Assets or Benefits　1

© 2007 Thomson/RIA. All rights reserved.

Enter Keywords:　Thesaurus/Query Tool

bankruptcy legal　[Search]　[Clear All]

how many documents were found containing the keywords. Legal and Accounting Expenses (¶ L-2900) has the most hits. Expanding this title leads to ¶ L-2922, Deductibility of fees incurred in connection with personal and business bankruptcy, which is the same document found using the keyword search and provided in Exhibit 6-5.

Index Search　An Index Search was one of the most efficient search methods when tax services were available only in published form. The advantage of an index search is that the tax meanings of the words are considered as well as the context in which the words are found. This is because the individuals create indexes. The researcher has the ability to use the expertise of the indexer in locating the primary documents of interest. This advantage of indexes holds for the electronic services as well. Some researchers find it beneficial to start with an index search to help them identify effective terms for their general keyword searches.

An Index search can be started from two different points in the RIA Checkpoint service. The first method is to select Indexes under the Go To heading in the left window of the opening screen (see Exhibit 6-1). Only the Federal databases with indexes appear on the displayed screen. These services include the following.

- FTC 2d Topic Index

- Code Arranged Annotations & Explanations (USTR) Topic Index

- RIA's Federal Tax Handbook Topic Index

- Current Code Topic Index

- Final & Temporary Regulations Topic Index

- Proposed Regulations Topic Index

Once a database is selected, the researcher has two options. Clicking on the database will display a listing of the alphabet. From this screen the researcher can select a letter and continue to drill down until the specific topic of interest and the documents are located. This method is similar to using an index for a published service.

The other method for starting an Index Search is through the TOC. Federal Indexes is one of the options listed for TOC Searches. As with other TOC searches, a keyword search is possible with any of the indexes. However, the keyword search is restricted to the index entries. This differs from other keyword searches in that it is the index entries themselves, and not the underlying documents, that are being searched. For example, selecting the letters B and L within the FTC index, keywords *bankruptcy* and *legal* are searched. Under the letter L, four topics are listed, one of which is legal expenses. Clicking on this topic (shown in Exhibit 6-8) leads directly to ¶ L-2922. This is the same document found through the original Keyword and TOC searches. However, the Index Search took less time.

Exhibit 6-8: RIA Checkpoint Index Listing

Tax professionals familiar with search engines such as Google and Yahoo often are inclined to use a Keyword Search when an Index or TOC Search may be more efficient and effective. Experienced tax researchers tend to use TOC, index, and citation searches much more frequently as they develop their skills.

Citation Search

A third approach to electronic searches is a Citation Search. To perform a search by Code section or case name, choose a title under Find a Citation in the left frame of the opening screen (see Exhibit 6-1). Citation Searches can be performed on the Code, Regulations, cases, various IRS rulings, and IRS publications. If the type of document you wish to find is not listed in one of these options, the More … heading contains an extensive list of documents that can be searched by citation. After selecting a type of document, Checkpoint provides templates for entering citations and examples for each template. These templates make entering a citation simple because the proper format is provided. Examples of Code and Case Searches are presented next.

Code Search   Research Project 6–1 concerns the possibility of deducting the bankruptcy legal fees. The most likely reason for these legal fees to be deductible is that they are associated with a trade or business, that is, they fall under the umbrella of §162. Entering the section number in the template for Current Code retrieves the full text of §162, Trade or business expenses, as shown in Exhibit 6-9. On careful

Exhibit 6-9: RIA Checkpoint Code Document

examination of Exhibit 6-9, you will see a symbol for the four compass directions. Placing the mouse pointer over or clicking on this symbol brings up a box in which the exact cite for the particular portion of the document is displayed. This small box is visible in Exhibit 6-9 for the §162(a)(3) paragraph. This unique feature is helpful when examining long Code sections or Regulations with complex paragraphing structures. If the researcher would like to know where the Code section fits within the *Internal Revenue Code*, the Contents View, in the left window, contains this information. As can be seen in Exhibit 6-9, the Contents view shows the exact placement by providing the subtitle, chapter, subchapter, part, and section number for the current Code section of interest.

Another useful feature offered in the left window is the Outline. This gives an outline of the Code section by listing the subsection titles and their associated letters. By clicking on the title, Checkpoint presents that part of the Code section on the screen. With Code sections like §162 that have numerous subsections (through subsection q), this is particularly helpful. It is easy to get lost as to where you are in sections that are as long as this one.

Using the Code section as the beginning point for identifying related documents is simplified by use of the buttons located above the Code section title and at each subsection or division thereof. These buttons will lead the researcher to explanations and annotations in the USTR (Expl and Annot), topical entries in the FTC, relevant primary sources (Regs and Com Rpts), history (Hist), and current developments (AdvAnnot and New Law Analysis). Through these links, the researcher eventually may find the relevant documents desired. However, relying exclusively on Code section searches may be more time consuming than contents or keyword searches when there are several Code sections involved in the research issue.

Case Search Unlike the other major services, Checkpoint allows the researcher to enter either the case name or its citation into one of the templates furnished (reproduced in Exhibit 6-10). This is quite convenient in situations such as ours for Research Project 6–1 when all we know is the name of the case. Entering the *Gilmore* name retrieves all of the court cases with Gilmore as a taxpayer. This produces over forty cases. Since we know that it is a Supreme Court case, we can use the Search Within Results tool to narrow the listed cases. Using the abbreviation for Supreme Court (S Ct) in the Keyword box substantially reduces the cases retrieved. Only one of these cases was decided in 1963.

In the case document listing, along with the proper citation for each case and its disposition, RIA lists the Code sections applying to the cases. The Code citations often help in identifying which case is relevant to the research project. Clicking on the case citation produces the full text of the case. The complete RIA citation is given as the title for the document and, again, the Code section applying to the case is listed. Since the Gilmore case is from 1963, we definitely should check this case through the Citator (using the citator button provided above the case name) to make sure that it is still valid law (see Chapter 8 for a detailed discussion of Citators). If we are interested in only newer cases, the Date Range Search, in the left window of the opening Screen (Exhibit 6-1), allows court cases to be searched using keywords with date restriction.

As was true for a Code section document, a case document may furnish entry into the tax services. The buttons offering annotations and explanations that appeared on the Code Section screen are also present on the Case screen. With these buttons, the researcher is led to the case's annotations in the USTR or explanations where the case is cited in the FTC service. Selecting either of these buttons leads to documents retrieved in the previous Keyword Searches.

Exhibit 6-10: RIA Checkpoint Case Templates

With a Citation Search, the text of a specific case, Code section, or other primary source is the end result of the search. Cite searches do not facilitate the retrieval of all documents that might be relevant to the research project. Case names or Code sections may be used as search terms in Keyword Searches to locate the relevant documents. It would be important in this type of search to include other keywords as well, to narrow the search and ensure that every document containing the case name or Code section number is not retrieved. These latter searches follow the same steps as any Keyword Search.

CCH TAX RESEARCH NETWORK

The Commerce Clearing House (CCH) Internet service, called **Tax Research NetWork** (NetWork), is visually quite different from RIA Checkpoint; however, the searching methods utilized with NetWork are similar to those applied in the Checkpoint section. The differences in the implementation of these methods will be illustrated in this section by again using Research Project 6–1. This will facilitate comparisons of the two tax services.

CCH is organized like a file cabinet with folder tabs for its major databases (see Exhibit 6-11). Since Network generally opens to the "My CCH" folder that

Exhibit 6-11: CCH Tax Research NetWork Federal-Opening Search Screen

CCH® Tax Research NetWork™

Preferences | Help | Log Out

[Search] ◄—

Main Menu   Clear Selections   Research History   Research Folders   [Check Citator] [Find by Citation] [Search Tools] ◄—

My CCH	Tax Tracker News	Accounting & Audit	Federal Tax		
State Tax	State Business Income Tax	Sales/Property Tax	Financial & Estate Planning	Wealth Management	Tax Practice Areas	Pension & Payroll
International Tax	perform plus III forms	ClientRelate	Capital Changes	Tax Tools	CPE	Training & Support

Federal Tax

Current Features and Journals — Select All ☐

☐ Federal Tax Day	☐ Journal of Retirement Planning	☐ Federal Estate and Gift Tax Report Letter
☐ CCH Federal Tax Weekly	☐ ADVANCE RELEASE Documents	☐ Tax Treaties Report Letters
☐ TAXES - The Tax Magazine	☐ Federal Excise Tax Report Letter	

Tax Legislation — Select All ☐

☐ CCH Legislation Newswire	☐ Tax Relief and Reconciliation Acts of 2006: Law & Explanation	☐ JCT Blue Books
☐ Bills Worth Watching	☐ Law, Explanation and Analysis Books (1989-2006)	☐ CRS Reports and Other Studies (2003-2007)
☐ CCH Tax Briefings	☐ Tax Bills and Reports: 110th Congress (2007-2008)	☐ Historical Legislative Documents (2003-2006)
☐ Small Business and Work Opportunity Tax Act of 2007: Law & Explanation	☐ Major Tax Acts and Reports (1986-2007)	☐ Historical Legislative Documents (1954-2002)

CCH Explanations and Analysis — Select All ☐ ◄—

☑ CCH Tax Research Consultant	☐ Fed Excise Tax Reporter	☑ Tax Practice Guides
☑ Standard Federal Income Tax Reporter	☐ Tax Treaties Reporter	☐ Employee Benefits Analysis
☑ Standard Federal Income Tax Reporter-- Explanations	☑ U.S. Master Tax Guide	☐ Social Security Benefits Explained
☐ Federal Estate and Gift Tax Reporter	☑ Practice Before IRS & Courts	

Primary Sources — Select All ☐ ◄—

☑ Current Internal Revenue Code	☑ Cases	☑ Internal Revenue Manual
☐ Last 1954 Code	☑ Letter Rulings & IRS Positions (including TAMs and FSAs)	☑ IRS Publications

contains current tax news, a folder must be selected before the researcher can begin searching. For Research Project 6–1, we will select the Federal folder and this will be the focus of the CCH section. The State and Sales Tax folders will be discussed in Chapter 9, and the International Tax tab is reviewed in Chapter 10.

SPOTLIGHT ON TAXATION

Tax Service History

The CCH service has been in existence since the first U.S. tax law was passed in 1913. Through this long history, CCH has become one of the most recognized publishers of tax products. In 1995, Wolters Kluwer, an international Dutch publishing corporation, acquired CCH from the majority shareholders, including the members of the Thorne family whose great-great grandfather founded the company. This $1.9 billion takeover was the world's largest publishing acquisition at the time.

Keyword Search

As with RIA Checkpoint, CCH NetWork emphasizes keyword searching. The Keyword search box appears in the tools bar and therefore is available from every screen (see Exhibit 6-11). The Search Tools button associated with the Keyword box enables the researcher to customize word searches. With this option, the researcher may select from the following search methods: all terms (the default setting), any term, near (terms to be within twenty words of each other), exact phrase, or Boolean connectors. The number of documents retrieved can be set from 1 to 9,999 with the default at 50 (generally more than enough to examine). NetWork sorts the list of documents retrieved by relevance unless the researcher selects to display the list of documents based on the TOC of each database selected.

NetWork automatically applies a thesaurus to all the keywords. This may not be beneficial in all research situations as it can cause numerous unrelated documents to be retrieved. This feature may be turned off on the Search Tools screen. Recall that with RIA Checkpoint, the researcher must select which words the thesaurus suggests to be added to the Keyword Search. Thus, the application of the RIA thesaurus is not automatic like it is with CCH.

From this same Search Tools screen, the searched databases can be restricted by date or by type of document. The Search by Date restriction option is especially convenient when updating a previous research project. Accordingly, only the most current documents would be designated for searching.

Once the keywords and search options are entered, the databases within the folder must be selected. Within the Federal folder there is a variety of resource groups, composed of numerous databases, from which to choose. Only a small portion of the available databases is seen in Exhibit 6-11. Researchers have the option of selecting all the databases within a resource group or only those databases applicable to their project. If a researcher decides to change the selection, using the Clear Selections option in the toolbar removes all choices, and the selection process starts over again. This clearing includes the choices made on the Search Tools screen. The researcher can also just unmark the database boxes not desired.

To locate documents related to Research Project 6–1, CCH Explanations and Analysis and Primary Sources databases is selected (see Exhibit 6-11). Within the former database those services such as Federal Estate and Gift Tax Reporter and Federal Excise Tax Reporter, which would not be useful in this research, were deselected. The same selective process was applied to the Primary Sources databases. As with RIA Checkpoint, CCH NetWork editorial materials provide a topical service, **Tax Research Consultant** (TRC), that is similar to the FTC, and an annotated service, **Standard Federal Income Tax Reporter** (SFITR). However, unlike RIA, CCH's premier service is its annotated service. If the researcher is only interested in explanations, the SFITR—Explanations can be selected. This is an abbreviated SFITR service, which does not include the Code, committee reports, or annotations that are contained in the full SFITR.

The result of the search is a document list presented in order of relevancy. The presentation may easily be changed to a TOC ordering, as in Exhibit 6-12, by selecting this option in a pull-down menu available (upper right). The TOC display is very helpful, as it organizes the results to make it easier to see at a glance which documents are not relevant to the research project based on the TOC titles. Clicking on the TOC titles expands the list to the individual documents. Examining Exhibit 6-12, the list is expanded to the relevant document in the CCH TRC. This is much more efficient than reading through the fifty document titles in the relevancy list. Notice that at the top of the document list screen, all of the terms

Exhibit 6-12: CCH Tax Research NetWork Table of Contents View

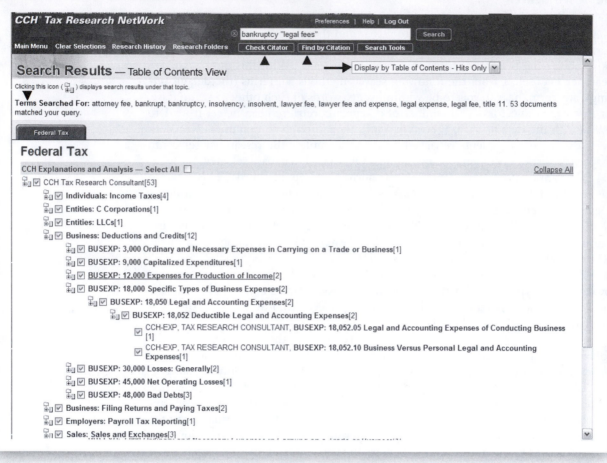

searched are listed alphabetically, including those added by the thesaurus. For our search, the terms *attorney fee, bankrupt, insolvency, insolvent, lawyer fee and expense, legal expense*, and *title eleven* were added.

Citation and Contents Searches

Citation To search by Code section, case name, or other primary source, the researcher uses the Find by Citation option visible at the top center of all NetWork screens (see Exhibit 6-11 and Exhibit 6-12). This option offers templates for every type of primary and secondary source available through NetWork. If the complete citation is known, it can be entered in CCH recognizable format in the citation general box; otherwise, one of the citation templates is completed. Unlike RIA Checkpoint, names of cases may not be entered in the templates. Fortunately, if only the name of the case is known, the proper citation for a case is obtainable by selecting the Check Citator option (next to Find by Citation) and entering the taxpayer's name (see Exhibit 6-12).

TOC NetWork does not have a separate button or folder for TOC searches. Rather, a database content search begins by clicking on the *title* of the database of interest. The next screen will furnish the TOC for the database. Continue to drill down in the same manner as in RIA Checkpoint until the documents of interest are found. As with RIA, a keyword search can be instigated at any point of the drill-down by marking boxes in front of databases. The same documents can be lo-cated using this method as were retrieved using only a keyword search.

Similar to RIA, NetWork, the documents offer hyperlinks to primary sources and provide buttons to access the Code, Regulations, CCH Annotations, CCH Explanation, and Related Topics, as seen in Exhibit 6-13. The Related Topics button yields a list of documents that would appear under the same heading in the indexes available in the CCH service. These documents will vary greatly as to their applicability to the research project at hand. To jump to the next (or previous) document from the search results list, the researcher may click on the Search Results icons. To browse the materials that would be in close proximity to your document if it were in a printed service, select the icons for Nearby Documents. This option gives the ability to "flip through the pages" of the service. Finally, to find the first point at which one of the keywords appears in the document, use the icon for first term. To return to the document list, click on the List icon under Search Results, and to get back to the opening search screen, click on Main Menu in the top left corner. All of these options are illustrated in Exhibit 6-13.

Index   At the bottom of the Federal opening screen, the Topical Indexes list all the services with indexes. The index entries can be searched using the keyword search method. Instead of using keywords, the researcher drills down through an index of the selected service in a manner similar to that used with the TOC.

Exhibit 6-13: CCH Tax Research NetWork Document

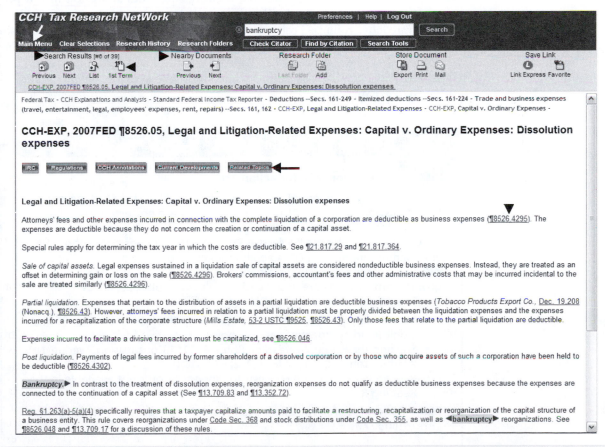

The statements in the RIA Checkpoint section regarding the usefulness of this searching method apply to CCH NetWork as well. Remember that indexes are created by individual employees of the publisher, and how one person would index a topic can be different from how another would. Topics may be indexed in RIA differently than they are in CCH.

| ATX/KLEINROCK

ATX/Kleinrock Publishing (Kleinrock) was originally known for its affordable, easy-to-use **Federal TaxExpert®** that was available on CD-ROM. It contained nearly a GB of tax law sources on a single CD. Thus, not only was it comprehensive, it was also very portable. Kleinrock now supplies Internet access to its TaxExpert® service, while still offering the CD version, and it still provides both at very affordable rates. Besides this Federal service, Kleinrock offers many other products, such as the Federal Tax Bulletin, multi- and individual state tax services, employment tax service, and a full range of compliance products. Kleinrock had filled a niche so successfully that in 2006 it was acquired by Wolters Kluwer NV to become part of the CCH business offerings. At the time of its acquisition it had over 48,000 subscribers. Since CCH is offered though LexisNexis, Kleinrock is one of the services available as part of the Tax Center database.

Kleinrock's Federal service includes twenty-five volumes of analysis and explanations that are similar to the CCH and RIA editorial tax services included in NetWork and Checkpoint. In addition, Kleinrock provides access to full-text primary sources such as the Code, Regulations, IRS pronouncements and publications, private letter rulings, Technical Advice Memorandums, and Federal tax cases (including Tax Court Memorandums). With the service, the subscribers receive biweekly issues of the *Federal Tax Bulletin* by e-mail. The CCH *U.S. Master Tax Guide: Kleinrock Edition* is also sent in printed form and available online to the subscribers of TaxExpert®.

SPOTLIGHT ON TAXATION

Freedom of Information Act

The **Freedom of Information Act** (FOIA), 5 USC §552, gave the public the right to access IRS records unless they are protected from disclosure. Under this provision, taxpayers have access to the nonpublished documents issued by the IRS such as Private Letter Rulings and Technical Advice Memorandums. The FOIA applies to records created by Federal agencies, yet records held by Congress and the courts are exempt. State and local government agencies are under each state's own public access laws.

The IRS complies with the FOIA by:

- Maintaining publicly available materials on the Internet in the IRS Electronic Reading Room of www.irs.gov
- Staffing the IRS Public Reading Room at 1111 Constitution Avenue, NW, Washington, D.C. 20224 [call (202) 622-5164]
- Responding to written requests for agency records not available in the Reading Room

Many IRS records are available for sale from the Government Printing Office. (**http://www.gpo.gov/**)

TAX PERIODICALS

Tax periodicals contain a variety of articles and news briefs that are designed to keep readers relatively knowledgeable of developments in specific or general areas of the tax law. These articles might contain, for example, an in-depth review of a recently decided court case, a broad analysis of the factors that should enter into the practitioner's decision on whether to make a certain tax accounting election, or a call for reform of a statute by a neutral (or biased) observer. Tax articles can suggest new approaches to tax problems, give guidance for solving complex problems, or just explain a new law in a readable form. All of these resources are very useful to tax practitioners.

With an article that is right "on point" with tax issues, the practitioner is able to, in effect, use the author of the article as a research associate by capitalizing on the author's expert judgments and references thereby saving hours of research time. Keep in mind, however, that tax periodicals are secondary sources of the tax law and therefore should not be cited as a controlling authority, especially when primary sources supporting the position are available. The article's references can lead the practitioner to the pertinent primary tax sources. With that caveat aside, researchers who ignore the tax periodicals might be accused, at best, of reinventing the wheel and, at worst, of professional malpractice.

Traditionally, citing articles in professional tax research is limited to two situations: (1) if the researcher is referring to the author's analysis and conclusions as stated in an article; and (2) if the researcher cannot find any controlling primary sources of law and a secondary source addresses the issues. Tax articles are now being cited more frequently in case opinions than was true in the past. When they are lacking both the appropriate primary law sources and adequate judicial staff, the authors of these case opinions may draw on tax articles to support the views of the court. In any event, it is imperative that researchers understand the practical implications of using secondary law sources.

Citing Articles

A citation to a printed tax journal article should take the following standard form.

> Banoff, Sheldon I., and Richard M. Lipton. 2007. Is Wikipedia Good Authority in the Tax Court? *Journal of Taxation* 106 (4): at 257.

Notice the proper placement of capital letters, periods, and commas in the citation. The denotation "at 257" indicates that the researcher is referencing or quoting from a specific portion of the article. If the entire article were being referenced, the citation would merely contain the beginning page number of the article. For the citation above, this would be "… (4) 256."

Unfortunately, the proper citation for articles found on the Internet is not as well established as for printed materials. A problem that complicates the matter is deciding how to characterize the Internet material to be cited. For example, is the material a journal article, a newsletter, a report, or a blog; who is the author, when was the resource generated? Once all this information is deciphered (and deciphering this may not be easy), a generally safe citation format to follow is that of a printed document with additions or deletions as necessary. The following would be an acceptable format for a journal article found on the Internet.

> Browne, Marlene M. 2007. When Bankruptcy Meets Divorce. Forbes.com (May 5). Retrieved June 28, 2007 at http://www.forbes.com/personalfi-nance/taxes-estates/2007/05/03/divorce-bankruptcy-debt-pf-estates-in_mb_0503money_inl.html

Site addresses on the Internet are generally case and punctuation sensitive. Therefore, one should ignore normal grammar rules when providing uniform resource locators (URLs) and place no punctuation (such as a period or a comma) at the end of a URL. It is important to indicate the date on which the document was retrieved, because documents and web site URLs may change or be removed over time.

Types of Periodicals

Tax periodicals can be categorized according to the depth of the coverage of their articles and the audience for which they are written. From the most extensive coverage to the least, they can be listed as follows.

- Annual proceedings
- Scholarly reviews
- Professional journals
- Newsletters

Although each publication has unique attributes, several general characteristics of each category will be identified. This discussion provides an initial introduction to the broad market of secondary source tax commentary.

Annual Proceedings   A number of annual conferences for tax practitioners and academics are conducted every year. Usually sponsored by a professional organization, law school, or educational agency, these conferences generally last from two to five days. The agenda at these conferences may include any of the following: lectures, paper presentations with or without discussion, panel discussions, seminars, demonstrations, and luncheon addresses. Often, the conference speakers allow the sponsoring agency to publish their presentations as proceedings of the meeting. These **annual proceedings** are distributed to the participants at the conference, and later to the general public in the form of a collection of articles. Most of these papers exhibit considerable depth of coverage and practical insight by the authors. They can be a valuable resource for the tax researcher. A few of the more established tax conferences include the following.

- New York University Institute on Federal Taxation had its first annual meeting in 1942.
- Penn State Tax Conference was established in 1946.
- University of Chicago's Annual Federal Tax Conference first met in 1947.
- University of Southern California's Tax Institute (formerly Major Tax Planning Institute) began in 1948.
- Tulane Tax Institute started in 1952.

The proceedings and indexes to these conferences are widely available. For example, CCH publishes the proceedings of the University of Chicago's Annual Federal Tax Conference as the March issue of *Taxes—The Tax Magazine*.

While some conferences select different areas of tax each year as the theme of the meetings, other annual conferences focus on a specialized area year after year. Examples of specialized tax conferences include the Nonprofit Legal and Tax Conference held in March in Washington D.C.; the Institute on Oil and Gas Law, which meets in Texas; the Great Western Tax and Estate Planning Conference of the National Law Foundation held in Las Vegas; the Asian Development Bank

Organization's International Taxation Conference held in Japan; and the University of Miami Law Center's Heckerling Institute on Estate Planning, held each January in Miami Beach.

Scholarly Reviews   All major law schools and a few business schools produce publications referred to as **law reviews** or **academic journals**. These publications are edited either by faculty members or by graduate students under the guidance of the school's faculty. Most law reviews also use an outside advisory board comprised of practicing attorneys and law professors at other universities to aid in selecting and reviewing articles. The articles appearing in these **scholarly reviews** are usually written by tax practitioners, academics, graduate students, or other noted commentators.

Some law schools produce journals that are limited to a specific area of law, such as constitutional or labor law, in addition to the regular multitopic law reviews. Most of the general law reviews feature one to three tax articles per year; however, some law reviews are dedicated exclusively to tax matters. The following are several of the law reviews that concentrate on taxation issues.

- *Akron Tax Journal* by University of Akron School of Law

- *Ohio Tax Review* by Capital University Law & Graduate Center

- *Florida Tax Review* by University of Florida College of Law

- *Tax Law Review* by New York University School of Law

- *The Tax Lawyer* and *The State and Local Tax Lawyer* by Georgetown University and the ABA.

- *Virginia Tax Review* by University of Virginia School of Law

Besides law schools, academic organizations such as the National Tax Association (NTA) and the American Taxation Association (ATA) publish scholarly journals. The articles appearing in the *National Tax Journal* (NTJ), and the papers from the NTA annual symposium tend to take an analytical or mathematical approach to identifying the broad economic and social implications of taxation on the population.

The ATA, a subdivision of the American Accounting Association, publishes two regular issues of *The Journal of the American Taxation Association* (JATA) and, like the NTA, the ATA prints a special supplement containing the papers presented at its yearly national conference. This journal is a research publication that offers a combination of taxation articles that employ (1) quantitative or analytical, (2) empirical, or (3) theoretical methodologies in analyzing issues considered of interest to the academic tax community.

Professional Journals   A wide variety of tax journals is published for the purpose of keeping tax practitioners abreast of the current changes and trends in the tax law. This category of journals, commonly referred to as **professional journals** or **practitioner journals**, includes publications by professional organizations as well as commercial companies. Examples of the former are the AICPA's *Tax Adviser*, the National Association of Tax Professional's *TAXPRO*, and journals published by state CPA or law societies.

Because the commercial publications are numerous, the tax coverage of these journals can accommodate the needs of the general tax practitioner and those who specialize in a specific area of tax law. For example, journals such as WG&L *Journal of Taxation* and *Practical Tax Strategies* or CCH's *Taxes—The Tax Magazine* cover a variety of tax areas, whereas journals such as BNA Tax Management's *The Compensation Planning Journal* or WG&L *Journal of Taxation of Investments* cover single topics. Further, the articles appearing in these journals also vary greatly in their coverage from very complex with an exceedingly narrow focus to extremely practical "how to" articles designed for immediate implementation. Since the editors of most professional journals presume that their readers have access to little, if any, other current tax resource material, any major change in the tax law or important Court tax decision spawns numerous articles in the various periodicals on the same or similar topics.

To accommodate the tax practitioner's need for timely information, most of the multitopic tax journals are published monthly, whereas the more specialized tax journals tend to be issued on a quarterly basis. Practitioners with subscriptions to Internet services may obtain their journals through their online services. For example, a subscriber to RIA Checkpoint may add subscriptions to the WG&L journals. The journals ensure the quality of their articles by accepting solicited and unsolicited articles prepared by appropriate tax experts. In each case, an editorial review board assesses the timeliness, accuracy, and readability of each article before it is accepted for publication.

Newsletters   The major tax services include a **tax newsletter** as part of their service. The Internet services tend to have daily newsletters, whereas the published services send the newsletters weekly. These newsletters help the subscriber keep abreast of important tax law developments. They are designed to give the practitioner both a capsulated summary of tax law modifications and a reference to the paragraphs in the compilation materials that contain a more detailed analysis. Some of these newsletters also publish information concerning tax seminars and professional meetings, short reviews of (or citations for) selected current tax articles, and editorial highlights concerning recent tax developments. Several of the most popular commercial tax newsletters are listed in Exhibit 6-14.

RIA   Opening the RIA Newsstand folder in Checkpoint generates the daily RIA Updates. On this screen, the practitioner may access the most recent news briefs for the following services.

- RIA Tax Watch
- Federal Tax Updates
- State & Local Tax Updates
- International Tax Updates
- Corporate Finance Updates
- Current WG&L Journals

The RIA Tax Watch specifically reports tax legislative developments. Infrequently it will also contain articles by expert practitioners, giving commentary on various aspects of proposed and potential tax legislation. Another RIA daily news service is Tax Alerts (listed with the editorial materials on the search screen). This service covers current tax developments affecting compliance issues. Besides supplying the news, it indicates which form(s) may be affected by the tax news, recommends actions to be taken for clients, and provides links to related materials in Checkpoint. It even contains a database of client letters, prepared to explain a specific recent tax event.

Exhibit 6-14: Selected Tax Newsletters from Major Publishers

Title of Newsletter	Frequency	Publisher
Daily Tax Report	Daily	Bureau of National Affairs
Federal Daily Tax Bulletin	Daily	Kleinrock
Federal Tax Bulletin	Biweekly	Kleinrock
Federal Tax Day	Daily	Commerce Clearing House
Federal Taxes Weekly Alert	Weekly	Research Institute of America
Focus on Tax	Monthly	Commerce Clearing House
International Taxes Weekly	Weekly	Research Institute of America
Multistate Tax Report	Monthly	Bureau of National Affairs
RIA Tax Watch	Daily	Research Institute of America
State & Local Taxes Weekly	Weekly	Research Institute of America
State Tax Notes Today	Daily	Tax Analysts
State Tax Notes Weekly	Weekly	Tax Analysts
State Tax Day	Daily	Commerce Clearing House
Tax News Headlines	Daily	Commerce Clearing House
Tax Notes	Weekly	Tax Analysts
Tax Notes International	Weekly	Tax Analysts
Tax Notes Today	Daily	Tax Analysts
Tax Tracker News	Daily	Commerce Clearing House
Tax Watch	Quarterly	Tax Foundation
TM Memorandum	Biweekly	Bureau of National Affairs
TM Weekly Report	Weekly	Bureau of National Affairs
Weekly State Report	Weekly	Bureau of National Affairs
Worldwide Tax Daily	Daily	Tax Analysts

CCH   Tax news is so important to CCH that the opening screen for Tax Research NetWork is My CCH. The Tax Tracker News appearing in My CCH can be personalized to focus on those areas of the tax law that are of particular interest to the practitioner. This time-saving feature alerts practitioners to tax law changes in their area of specialization, without requiring that they wade through all news articles for the day. The specialization can be for state news as well as Federal, as both are provided in Tax Tracker.

Other news sources furnished on My CCH are Today's Tax Highlights and Tax Briefing Special Reports. Today's Tax Highlights contains a combination of Federal and state tax news. The number of news briefs varies from day to day with usually far fewer on the weekends. The Tax Briefing Special Reports are more specialized articles on topics such as new tax acts or multistate issues.

Locating Relevant Tax Articles

The numerous published and computerized indexes available to tax researchers facilitate locating tax, business, and law journal articles that are pertinent to their research. However, the **CCH** *Federal Tax Articles* (FTA) and the **WG&L** *Index to Federal Tax Articles* (IFTA) are the two indexes specifically designed for locating tax articles. Unfortunately, both of these indexes are offered only in print and are not available on the Internet. There are also very useful periodical Internet indexes, such as ProQuest (ABI/INFORM), that can be employed in finding accounting and tax periodicals. Depending on the subscription, these search programs index thousands of periodicals, including most of the accounting professional and academic publications. Most Internet indexes focus on a Keyword Search strategy and allow the researcher to determine the connectors (and versus or) among the words or phrases. Since these indexes are not exclusively for tax research, they will not be covered here.

CCH FTA   The FTA index, published by CCH, has many outstanding features that make it one of the best tax indexes available. Because the FTA is only available in a published format, it is not offered as part of the CCH online tax service. This is frustrating for the subscribers to the CCH Tax Research Network, as the FTA would be most useful in an electronic format.

The FTA is known for the concise abstracts it furnishes for each article cited in the index. Reading these abstracts helps the practitioner reduce the false starts that commonly occur when trying to find pertinent articles based solely on their titles. The framework for organizing these abstracts is the *Internal Revenue Code*. This organization also facilitates finding articles addressing the Code section under investigation by the researcher. CCH updates this index monthly so the citations are timely. Because the FTA current volume is a loose-leaf service, the updates provide new pages that either replace existing pages or are added to the contents of the volume. Besides listing the filing instructions for the new pages, the Report Letter presents the highlights of the most interesting new developments, seminars, and tax conferences.

Prior to 2004, twice a year the updates were consolidated and assigned new paragraph numbers. The biyearly sections were maintained separately. Therefore, the researcher desiring articles published in the past three years would have to review as many as six sections of listings. Every four to seven years, the CCH cumulative biyearly reports fill the loose-leaf volume and require the start of a new volume. At this time the various indexes are consolidated for the entire period. As of 2004, each new update integrates all prior article summaries. Thus, there are not separate sections of biyearly summaries. This makes the current loose-leaf binder easier to use, and the researcher needs to look in only one place for articles on a particular Code section. In the bound volumes (prior to 1990), the cited articles with their abstracts are arranged alphabetically by title under each Code section heading. The article citations are preceded by a new paragraph number that is tied to the Code section. Subsequently, a new loose-leaf volume is issued for articles that are published after the issuance of the bound volume.

Approximately 250 journals, law reviews, papers, and proceedings are included in the index. The topics covered in the FTA include Federal income, excise, estate, gift, and employment taxation. The main division of the index, called Articles by Code Section, gives the full citation for each article and its abstract. This cumulative index gives Code section numbers with a brief description of the section as its headings.

Articles can also be located by using the topic and author indexes. Each of these indexes refers the researcher to the "Articles by Code Section" division, through a system of paragraph numbers. These paragraph numbers are located at the outside bottom corner of the pages. The numbers at the top of the pages are used solely for filing and should not be confused with the paragraph numbers. In the bound volumes, the index's main citation number (i.e., to the left of the decimal point) provides the Code section paragraph number, and the numbers to the right of the decimal point refer to the specific article abstract. The paragraph numbers for abstracts in the current binder have no relation to the Code section number.

As previously mentioned, the FTA is only available in print. As the loose-leaf volume accumulates years of monthly updates, it becomes more cumbersome to use. As with any published services, additions to the services processed by editors are printed, shipped, and then filed by the practitioner or an employee. This can result in a substantial time lag, especially if the updates are not filed on a timely basis. Further, there is the likelihood of human filing errors—and a page misfiled is information lost to the researcher. Providing this service online would eliminate these problems with using the FTA.

WG&L IFTA   The WG&L IFTA provides citations and occasional summaries for articles covering Federal income, gift, and estate taxation or tax policy that appear in more than 350 periodicals. The index surveys not only traditional tax journals, but also law reviews, major annual tax symposia, and certain economics, accounting, and finance journals. The IFTA is issued in bound quarterly volumes and includes permanent accumulations of references for the older periods. A paperback cumulative supplement augments the main index volumes. Because the supplements are cumulative, the researcher need only consult one supplement for recent articles.

Unlike the CCH index, both the topic and the author indexes contain full article citations. Using the full citations in the author index, the researcher can identify other current articles by the same author pertaining to a specific topic. Authors with several articles on the same topic are more likely to have an expertise in that field, and, thus, their analysis may be more effectual. Further, the custom of listing citations for each author and topic heading in reverse chronological order (rather than in alphabetical order) expedites finding the most recent publications.

The IFTA contains a user's guide that provides the following: explains how to use the index; lists the more than 1,500 topical index subject headings; supplies a key to abbreviations of periodical titles; and, lists the periodicals included in the first three volumes. Further, each cumulative volume and the current supplement also list not only the periodical titles but also the volumes and issue numbers covered by the supplement.

Whereas every citation in the CCH index is accompanied by an abstract, only articles judged by the WG&L compilers and Editorial Advisory Board to be of special interest are furnished with a brief summary in the IFTA. Very few articles receive this distinction.

SUMMARY

There are many commercial tax services available, and no one service is the best for all practitioners. While the services provide different features, all are most efficient when the organization of the service matches the issues in a client's tax situation. Thus, each tax service has its place in tax research, and practitioners must determine with which products they are most comfortable and which fit the research requirements of their firm. Changes in technology and the tax services happen on a continuous basis. The same changes occur in the practitioner's business. Consequently, the practitioner's comfort level with products and technology and the research needs will change over time. Practitioners should evaluate their tax resource choices often, at least once a year when it is time to renew their services.

The tax researcher should employ tax services as gateways to the primary sources and not as a substitute for primary source research. Tax services can make the research process more efficient and productive, but should not replace thorough review of primary sources and professional judgment.

Tax journals and other periodicals not only help researchers locate primary sources of the tax law, but they also enlighten the researcher as to other ways of analyzing a tax issue. Tax articles can synthesize information from the Code, Regulations, and pertinent court cases into a more logical presentation. These articles may help the practitioner identify relevant tax issues or precedents during the research process or in preparing for litigation on a client's behalf. Finally, such publications are an integral part of the means by which the tax professional remains current with respect to the evolution of the Federal tax law.

TAX TUTOR

Reinforce the tax research information covered in this chapter by completing the online tutorials located at the *Federal Tax Research* web site: **http://academic.cengage.com/taxation/raabe**

KEY WORDS

By the time you complete this chapter, you should be comfortable discussing each of the following terms. If you need additional review of any of these items, return to the appropriate material in the chapter or consult the glossary to this text.

Academic journals
Annotated tax services
Annotations
Annual proceedings
CCH Federal Tax Articles
Checkpoint
Compilations
Federal Tax Coordinator
Federal TaxExpert®
Freedom of Information Act
Law reviews

Practitioner journals
Professional journals
Scholarly reviews
Standard Federal Income Tax Reporter
Tax newsletter
Tax Research Consultant
Tax Research NetWork
Topical tax services
United States Tax Reporter
WG&L Index to Federal Tax Articles

DISCUSSION QUESTIONS

1. What is the function of commercial tax services?

2. Compare and contrast the general format of an annotated tax service with that of a topical tax service.

3. Why would a practitioner need a tax service when most primary tax sources are available for free on the Internet?

4. Internet services tend to be updated on a daily or continuous basis, therefore they are current up to the minute. Comment on this statement.

5. Formulating the research question is an iterative process. Once it is refined in its final state, will the researcher be able to find a solution to the tax question?

6. What is the key to effective tax research?

7. With what type of tax service documents should practitioners start if they are unfamiliar with the topic being researched?

8. Why is it important for you to actually try research projects with the various tax services?

9. Discuss whether it is likely that the appearance of the tax services as presented in the text is going to differ from what is available to you. How will this influence the effectiveness of the methodology presented in this chapter?

10. The fact that a tax service located a document and placed it high on the relevance list means you can assume it is still valid law. Comment on this statement.

11. What are the three methods for starting a research project with an electronic service? Which does RIA emphasize?

12. Explain how RIA Checkpoint makes Keyword Searching appear as easy as 1, 2, 3.

13. What functions do "Modify Search" and "Search Within Results" perform in RIA Checkpoint?

14. Explain the functions of the following special symbols in a keyword search in RIA Checkpoint: /s, " ", *.

15. Which annotated and topical tax services are included in RIA Checkpoint?

16. How does the thesaurus function work in RIA Checkpoint?

17. What is the purpose of the Contents View in RIA Checkpoint?

18. How do you perform a TOC search in RIA Checkpoint?

19. What are the two options for conducting an index search in RIA Checkpoint?

20. What is the function in RIA Checkpoint of the directional symbol (compass) found in reproduced Code sections or Regulations? Why is it useful?

21. How does RIA Checkpoint differ from other services with regard to case searches?

22. Which annotated and topical tax services are included in CCH Tax Research NetWork?

23. What is the difference in the application of the thesaurus in RIA Checkpoint and CCH Tax Research NetWork?

24. Explain the differences in conducting a TOC search using RIA Checkpoint and CCH Tax Research NetWork.

25. How is ATX/Kleinrock's TaxExpert® different from the other tax services discussed in this chapter?

26. What is the FOIA and how does it apply to IRS documents?

27. How can finding an article on-point with a practitioner's tax issue be like hiring someone to do the research?

28. Why are tax journals and newsletters generally not cited as authority in professional tax research? When would it appropriate to cite tax journals or newsletters as authority in professional tax research?

29. What does the denotation "at 407" indicate in a tax journal citation?

30. Briefly describe each of the following.
    a. Annual proceedings
    b. Scholarly reviews
    c. Professional journals
    d. Newsletters

31. Give the names of two academic organizations that publish scholarly journals. What are the titles of the journals they publish?

32. *Taxes—The Tax Magazine* publishes the conference proceeding from what annual meeting?

33. What type of articles would you expect to find in *Tax Advisor* versus the type you would expect to find in *Journal of Limited Liability Companies?* Which one of these would you expect to be published monthly and which quarterly?

34. How do newsletters of major tax services tie their stories to their service's editorial materials?

35. How is the news service on CCH's Tax Research NetWork different from RIA's Checkpoint news service?

36. What is the major obstacle to using either the CCH FTA or the WG&L IFTA?

37. What is one of the most outstanding features of the CCH FTA that is not available with most other journal indexes? How does the organizational framework of the CCH FTA differ from that of the WG&L IFTA?

38. What are three methods that can be used to locate articles in the CCH FTA? Can these same three methods of locating an article be used with the WG&L IFTA? Explain your answer.

39. How frequently are the journal indexes FTA and IFTA updated?

40. On what electronic services are the journal indexes FTA and IFTA offered?

EXERCISES

41. Use the RIA Checkpoint Federal opening screen to answer the following questions.
    a. Expand the FTC by clicking on the + before the title. What are the subheadings listed?
    b. What is the earliest Congress listed in the legislation materials available?

   c. What templates are available in the Form/Line Finder?

   d. What are the Practice areas available in Checkpoint?

42. Use the RIA Checkpoint to answer the following questions.
   a. What templates are available in the IRS Pubs & Other Tax Docs?
   b. What type of documents may have the Date Range Search applied to them? What are the oldest available dates for these documents?
   c. What tables are available in the "i-Tables" tool?
   d. Expand the IRS Rulings and Releases (RIA). What is the oldest available Revenue Ruling?

43. Use the RIA Checkpoint Indexes in the left window of the Federal opening screen to answer the following questions.
   a. What Federal editorial materials have indexes?
   b. In the FTC Topic Index, determine what paragraph addresses the deductibility of false teeth.
   c. In the Current Code Topic Index, determine what Code section discusses the depletion of Kyanite.
   d. In the Code Arranged Annotations & Explanations (USTR) Topic Index, determine which paragraph discusses rental pools.

44. Use the Home & Tool Tabs in RIA Checkpoint to answer the following questions.
   a. What are the different windows shown on the Home Tab?
   b. With the savings tool found on the Tool Tab, determine how much you need to start saving now (based on your current age) to have $1 million when you are sixty-five. Use an expected rate of return of 6 percent and expected inflation rate of 2.5 percent. Repeat the process adding ten years to your current age.
   c. With the auto tool found on the Tool Tab, determine whether it would be better to buy or lease an automobile. The cost of the car is $30,000 and the down payment is $1,000. Assume a rate of return and interest rate of 8 percent, sales tax rate of 7 percent, and depreciation rate of 20 percent. The loan would be for five years. The lease option would be for three years with $100 in fees and $500 for a security deposit. The residual value of the car would be 60 percent.

45. Use the RIA Checkpoint to answer the following questions.
   a. What are the thesaurus alternatives for "car"?
   b. Using the TOC, determine in what title education is listed in the Federal Employment Regulations (found in Payroll Library).
   c. What is the full citation for a Supreme Court case in 1977 involving GM Leasing?
   d. What Code section does Private Letter Ruling 200422053 involve?

46. Use the CCH Tax Research NetWork Federal Tab to answer the following questions.
   a. What are the major database categories provided?
   b. Select 2001 in the Federal Tax Achieves. What tax act is listed? When would it be useful to see what the IRC was in a prior year?
   c. What is the most recent Treasury Decision listed in Advance Release Documents?
   d. What bills does CCH think are worth watching?

47. Use the CCH Tax Research Network Topical Indexes Database to determine the following.
    a. The listings for the letter "K" in the *Internal Revenue Code* index.
    b. The number of listings under Bermuda in the Tax Treaties Reporter.
    c. The paragraph number at which quid pro quo contributions are discussed in the *U.S. Master Tax Guide*.

48. Use the Search Tools Options of CCH Tax Research NetWork to answer the following questions.
    a. What date range options are available?
    b. Select the CCH Explanations and Analysis database on the Federal opening search screen. Which parts of a document may be searched? Does your response change if only the SFITR is selected? Explain your response.
    c. Besides sorting results by relevance and indicating the maximum number of documents to show, what other options are in the Search Method section?

49. Use the CCH Tax Research NetWork to answer the following questions.
    a. Who were the staff members (not legislators) who participated in the issuance of the Joint Committee on Taxation "Blue Book" General Explanation of Tax Legislation Enacted by the 109th Congress, JCS 1-07 (January 19, 2007)?
    b. What is the most recent Private Letter Ruling listed in Federal Tax Day? Give the full citation of the PLR and section to which it pertains.
    c. Tax Practice Guides indicates that having doubts as to the collectibility of an IRS levy is grounds for requesting a compromise, in the section: How to Write Offers in Compromise. Upon what should this doubt be based?
    d. According to Circular 230, who may qualify to practice before the IRS? Give the citation substantiating your answer.

50. Use the CCH Tax Research NetWork Tool Tab and/or the Practice Aids database to answer the following questions.
    a. What is the current per diem maximum for meals and lodging for staying in Atlanta, Georgia?
    b. Using the Federal withholding calculator, determine the estimated tax due (or refund) for yourself based on what you expect your income and family situation to be five years from now. Print the calculated page to turn in.
    c. Using the Multistate Quick Answer Chart, determine the gasoline tax per gallon in Oregon.
    d. Are the tools offered in the Tool Tab the same as in the Practice Aids database?

51. Use the RIA Checkpoint Newsstand Tab to answer the following questions.
    a. For the WG&L Tax Journals, what articles are listed in the highlights for *Practical Tax Strategies* under the In This Issue heading?
    b. What is the title for the State Tax News brief for your state? If there is not a news brief for your state, select the closest state alphabetically and provide its news brief title.
    c. In the Newsletter Library, select the Cummings' Corporate Tax Insights. What is the title of the first article for January of the current year?

52. Use the CCH Tax Research Network My CCH Tab to answer the following questions.
   a. For Tax Tracker News, select the set up search option. What choices does the Narrow with Search Options allow?
   b. What is the title of the first article that is provided in Today's Tax Highlights?
   c. In the Tax Briefing, what is the most current tax act that has a special report provided?

53. Indicate the relevant information requested for CCH Tax Research Network SFITR, paragraph ¶ 12,623.025.
   a. What is the title for the paragraph and Code section?
   b. What Regulations apply to this paragraph? What are the paragraph numbers for these Regulations?
   c. What are the current developments for this paragraph?
   d. In what other databases (services) are related topics referenced for this paragraph?

54. Indicate the relevant information requested using RIA Checkpoint and §521.
   a. What FTC paragraphs discuss the exemption of farmers' cooperatives [§521(b)(1)]? Provide paragraph number and title.
   b. What Regulations were issued on this Code Section? What are their titles?
   c. In what years and by what public laws was this section amended?
   d. What are the titles of the committee reports associated with the public laws found in part c?

55. Find the following law journals and provide the title to the article by the author indicated.
   a. *Akron Tax Journal*: Volume 22 by Richard C. E. Beck.
   b. *Virginia Tax Review*: Volume 26 by Linda Sugin.
   c. *Florida Tax Review*: Volume 7 by Pamela Champine.
   d. *Tax Law Review*: Volume 59 by Anne L. Alstott and Ben Novick.

56. Use the RIA Checkpoint to perform a keyword search using the terms *bankruptcy "legal fees"* and *deduction* with the WG&L Journals database.
   a. What is the citation for the most recent article found in the *Journal of Corporate Taxation*?
   b. Does the article found in part a actually discuss the deductibility of legal fees, or do the keywords randomly appear in the article?
   c. Find the same article as in part a using a TOC search. Is the article a main article or found in the columns? What citation information is available that was not available from the keyword search?

57. Use the CCH Tax Research Network to perform a keyword search using the terms *bankruptcy* and *family limited partnerships* with the *Journal of Retirement Planning* as the database.
   a. What is the citation for the most recent article with either bankruptcy or family limited partnership in the title?
   b. Does a similar article appear in *Taxes—The Tax Magazine* in the same year?
   c. After performing the search using the Display by Document format, change to Display by TOC—Hits Only. Which method of display made it

easier to find the articles in *Journal of Retirement Planning* and *Taxes—The Tax Magazine*?

58. Use the CCH FTA index to answer the following questions.
    a. Provide the proper citation for the most current article listed discussing §382.
    b. What are the paragraph citation numbers for articles discussing the protection of individual retirement accounts (IRAs) from creditors of bankrupt individuals? What Code section are these articles under?
    c. Provide the proper citation for the most current article by Susan Kalinka.
    d. What is the date on the last update filed in your library's current binder of FTA. (Check behind the tab "Last Report Letter" to find the answer.)

59. Use the WG&L IFTA index to answer the following questions.
    a. Provide the proper citation for the most current article listed discussing §382 (Limitation on NOL loss carryforwards).
    b. Provide the proper citation for the most current article by Susan Kalinka.
    c. What is the most recent supplement in your library?

60. Use the CCH FTA index and the WG&L IFTA for the following tasks.
    a. Using both indexes, find a current article on U.S. citizens living abroad and provide the proper citation for the article. Describe the search strategies you used for each index. Which one proves easier to find the article?
    b. Using both indexes, find a current article on §6111, Registration of Tax Shelters, and provide the proper citation for the article. Describe the search strategies you used for each index. Which one proves easier to find the article?
    c. Using both indexes, find a current article by H. W. Wolosky and provide the proper citation for the article. Describe the search strategies you used for each index. Which one proves easier to find the article?

61. Find an article on using offshore integrated estate planning (§2001) that appeared in *Taxes—The Tax Magazine* between 1998 and 2002 using the CCH FTA index. Find the same article using the WG&L IFTA.
    a. Provide proper citation for the article.
    b. Provide full volume information and page number on which the citation was found in each of the indexes.
    c. What is the area of expertise of the author of this article?
    d. Compare the search strategies in using each index. Which one provides easier access?

62. Use the CCH FTA index and the WG&L IFTA for the following tasks.
    a. Using both indexes, find a current article on charitable giving and provide the proper citation for the article. Describe the search strategies you used for each index. Which one proves easier to find the article?
    b. Using both indexes, find a current article on §213, Medical Expenses, and provide the proper citation for the article. Describe the search strategies you used for each index. Which one proves easier to find the article?
    c. Using both indexes, find a current article by E. J. Schnee and provide the proper citation for the article. Describe the search strategies you used for each index. Which one proves easier to find the article?

63. Compare the CCH FTA and the WG&L IFTA regarding ease of locating articles when using the three methods of locating an article (by Code section, by author, and by topic).

64. Find an article on using offshore integrated estate planning (§2001) that appeared in *Taxes* between 1998 and 2002, using the ProQuest or any Internet periodical index available to you.
    a. Provide proper citation for the article.
    b. What is the area of expertise of the author of this article?
    c. What journal published most of this author's articles?
    d. Perform the searches requested in Question 61. Compare the search strategies in using published indexes with using an Internet index. Which one provides easier access?

65. Use any Internet periodical index available to you to find the most current article on the final regulations under §752 that discusses allocating liabilities to the owners of entities that are disregarded for Federal tax purposes.
    a. What index did you use?
    b. What is the proper citation for the article you found?
    c. Knowing the journal in which the article appears, would there be another index that could have been as efficient in finding the article?

RESEARCH CASES

66. Candidate Feldman ran for Congress in 2008, raising $4.7 million for the campaign, including $800,000 in Federal matching amounts. Five months after his opponent had been sworn into office, auditors discovered that Feldman had used $500,000 of campaign donations for a personal vacation, taken immediately after the unsuccessful campaign. What are the tax consequences of this use of election funds?

67. Ann is required under a divorce decree to pay alimony of $2,000 per month and child support of $3,000 per month. Ann has only been paying $4,000 per month because she thinks the child support requirement is too high. On Ann's tax return, what portion of the payments does she treat as alimony and what part is considered child support?

68. Which of the following items qualifies for the child care credit claimed by the Rodriguez family?

    - Salary for nanny.
    - Employer's share of FICA tax for nanny, paid by Rodriguez.
    - Employee's share of FICA tax for nanny, paid by Rodriguez.
    - Health insurance premiums on nanny, paid by Rodriguez.
    - One-half of nanny's hotel bill while on her own during a European vacation, paid by Rodriguez.
    - Dry cleaning bills for nanny's clothes soiled by youngsters and paid by Rodriguez.

69. Kenny has been a waiter at the Burger Pitt for four years. The Pitt treats its employees well, allowing them a 60 percent discount for any food that they

buy and consume on the premises. This year, the value of this discount for Kenny amounted to $2,500 for days on which he was working, and $1,500 for days when he was not assigned to work but still stopped by during mealtimes. How much gross income must Kenny recognize this year with respect to the discount plan?

70. Ollie died this year in September, after a long illness. His wages prior to death totaled $15,000, and his state taxes thereon came to $600.
    a. Who must file Ollie's last tax return?
    b. How is the return signed?
    c. Who collects Ollie's $440 Federal refund?

71. When Fifi, a sheriff's deputy, was injured on the job, she was allowed under her contract with the state to choose between a $1,000 weekly sick-pay distribution and an $850 weekly workers' compensation payment. Which one should Fifi select?

72. Willie was tired of cleaning up the messes that his wife made in their house. One morning, he found a crumpled Kleenex on the bathroom vanity, so he disgustedly flushed it down the toilet. Unfortunately, the Kleenex was wrapped around Barbara's engagement ring, which she had removed the previous evening after cutting her finger while shoveling snow. Is the couple allowed a deductible casualty loss for Federal income tax purposes under IRC §165?

73. Louella was born into a poor family that lives in a poor section of town. She recently landed a job as wardrobe consultant at High Fashions, Ltd., a retailer of expensive women's clothing at an Elm Grove shopping mall. Can Louella claim a §162 business expense deduction on her Federal income tax return for the cost and upkeep of the expensive Yves St. Laurent outfits that she is required to wear on the job?

74. Harriet purchased a variety of birth control devices during the year. To what extent, and under what circumstances, do such items qualify under §213 for a medical expense deduction?

75. Phyllis sued Martin's estate and won a $65,000 settlement. She showed the probate court that she carried out her end of a compensatory arrangement with her companion, where she provided "traditional wifely services" without benefit of matrimony during Martin's life in exchange for all of his estate. Martin left his entire estate to his faithful dog Sparky, via a trust. How much gross income is recognized by Phyllis?

76. How much gross income is recognized by Carol, who received $10,000 damages (two months' salary) for pain and suffering due to the school administration's critical reaction to her negative comments about ineffective recruiting of athletes who graduate with legitimate academic majors?

77. Carol and Jerry, LLP, pays the Good Eats Cafe each month for the lunches the two accountants eat there each work day because they always discuss some business. Often Carol and Jerry invite friends who work at other CPA firms to join them, so they can keep up with what is happening in the accounting community. Are these meals deductible?

78. Lila personally bought three insurance policies on her life. She borrowed $28,500 and prepaid the first five years' worth of annual payments on a whole life policy. In addition, she borrowed $4,200 and paid one of the two required premiums on a group term policy through her professional organization. Finally, she borrowed $3,000 and bought utilities mutual fund shares. The principal and interest of the fund's assets are to be appropriated in a timely fashion by Lila to make payments on a five-premium endowment contract. Interest charges for the three loans were $2,500, $420, and $310, respectively. How much of this interest can Lila deduct?

79. CPA Joe reimburses a client for a $75,000 tax liability that is traceable to Joe's bad tax advice. For fear of increasing his already steep malpractice insurance premiums, Joe does not file a claim with the insurer. Can Joe deduct the $75,000 loss?

80. Toni, a gardener, lent Harry, his friend, his new $500 lawn mower. Harry ruined the lawn mower, but replaced it with a $425 model. Later in the same year, Toni lent Harry $5,000 for bail, $3,000 to start a fencing operation, and $15 for a meal. According to Harry's parole officer, none of these items will ever be paid back. Can Toni deduct any of these losses?

81. Three years ago, Geraldine bought a Kandinsky for her art collection from a mail-order advertisement for $310,000. This year, Geraldine's art dealer told her that the painting was actually painted by Kansky and is not worth more than $310. What is her deductible loss upon discovery of the forgery?

82. Chickfer Cooperative is a horticultural cooperative located in Arkansas that markets fertilizers created by its members specially for use by commercial greenhouses. It grossed $25 million in sales for the current year. Is Chickfer able to qualify for the domestic production activities deduction?

83. It is 3 A.M. and your access to the university's tax services is down. Find a text version of the Code on the Internet and print §61. Where did you find the Code? Who maintains the site? Does the version of the Code you found use text hyperlinks? What happens when you click on a hyperlink? Download and print a copy of a page with hyperlinks, then click on several hyperlinks and print the pages to which they link.

84. Bob Carburetor is the new owner of Carburetor Cars. Bob's brother Bill has owned an auto dealership for years, Radiator Cars. Bob decides to adopt all of his brother's accounting methods. At Radiator Cars, when a vehicle is sold, the dealership tries to sell an auto service contract. The amounts received for these contracts are placed into an escrow account. The agreements grant the buyers the right to have parts or components covered by the contract repaired or replaced, whenever the covered parts experience a mechanical difficulty. The dealer will provide the services or will reimburse the car buyer for the reasonable cost of repair or replacement. Normally, the buyer returns the vehicle to the dealer for repair, but this is not required. In either case, the repairs or replacements must be authorized in advance by an administrator hired by Radiator Cars. Fees to the administrator of the contracts are paid out of the escrow account. Is this the proper tax treatment for these service contracts?

85. Betty Jo Harris lives in Maine with her son Rick and husband Walter Reed. Rick has Lou Gehrig's disease. Rick's physician encourages Betty Jo to go to a Caregivers of Lou Gehrig's disease conference at the Mayo Clinic in Rochester, Minnesota, so she can learn how to better take care of Rick. Betty takes the advice and flies to Rochester. Besides the cost of the plane ticket, Betty Jo incurs the following types of expenses: meals, lodging, phone calls home, dry cleaning (she dumped her taco salad on her lap at lunch), and conference registration fees. The leading speaker at the conference suggested that caregivers take their patients to destinations in warm climates to improve their state of mind and general condition. When Betty returns home, she arranges a two-month trip (January and February) to the Bahamas for Rick and herself. One week after they have arrived in the Bahamas, Rick's father, Walter, arrives and stays for a couple of weeks. Advise Betty Jo as to whether any of these expenses are deductible as medical expenses.

86. Several years ago, Agnes and Wyman Booth bought a home for $200,000. They lived in the home for ten years and then moved into an apartment. Unable to immediately sell the home, they rented it for two years earning $24,000 in rents and taking $14,000 in depreciation. After the two rental years, the Booths exchanged the house for $30,000 cash and a duplex worth $600,000. The Booths will hold the duplex as rental property. How much taxable income do the Booths have from the exchange?

87. King & Knight is a personal service corporation that has been in existence for five years. In the current year, it makes a §444 election to have its year-end become October 31. King & Knight incurs an NOL for the current year amounting to $100,000. How should King and Knight treat this NOL for tax purposes?

88. Clarence is a packrat. He has clothes from when he was in high school some twenty years ago that he would never wear. He also has household items that have accumulated over the past fifteen years. Some of these household items have not been used by Clarence in years and he is not sure if they even work. Clarence is buying a new home and wants to clean out his closets before he moves into his new house. He would like to give all of his old clothes and household items to local charities. What restrictions apply to charitable deductions of old clothes and household items?

EXTENSIVE CASES

89. Helen Hanks, who lives in San Francisco, California, has just been promoted to manager of the divisional office. However, the divisional office is located in Portland, Oregon. Helen's significant other, Tom Hunt, will be moving with her to Portland. Helen's children from a previous marriage will also be joining her in Portland. The children have been living with their father in Spain for the past year.

   Helen easily sells the San Francisco house in which she and Tom live. Helen is the sole owner of the house. However, she has a harder time finding the right home in Portland. Helen has to make several trips to Portland before buying a house under construction. It won't be available for occupancy for at least twenty days after she arrives in Portland. Tom accompanied Helen on the house hunting trips to give his opinion on the houses, and to look for a new job.

The actual move takes place as follows. The movers arrive on Wednesday to pack up Helen's and Tom's household items. Thursday, the movers pack up Helen's items from a storage unit located outside of the city, and her sailboat. The movers then leave for Portland. Helen hires a college student to drive her car to Portland; the driver leaves on Friday. On Saturday, after dropping Helen at the airport for her flight to Portland, Tom leaves to drive his car to Portland via Salt Lake City, Utah, where he also visits his brother. Helen and Tom stayed in a hotel Wednesday to Friday while still in San Francisco, and upon arriving in Portland until the house is ready for occupancy. The moving company stores their household items at its warehouse until Helen and Tom are ready to move in. Helen's children arrive two weeks after she and Tom have finally moved into the new house.

Helen pays for all of the costs involved in selling the San Francisco home and moving Tom, the children, and herself to Portland in November of the current year. Helen's employer eventually reimburses her (in March of the next year) for 75 percent of all costs of moving the household items (Helen's and Tom's), Helen's car, and two house hunting trips. The employer also reimburses Helen for 50 percent of the total hotel and meal costs while she and Tom were in Portland and waiting for the completion of their home. Advise Helen on the tax consequences of the above events.

90. Mark and Leslee Jones were married in 1995. Mark has an MBA from Harvard and worked in the financial markets in New York City. Leslee has a degree in Hotel Administration and worked for the Hilton Hotel until two years ago, when Mark and Leslee moved to California. They moved to California because Mark lost his job. He had been accused of embezzlement, and formal charges had been filed against him. However, the charges were dropped because the firm for which Mark worked did not want to be involved in a public scandal. Mark admitted the embezzlement to Leslee and promised that if they stayed married and moved, he would never embezzle again. In California, Mark obtained a job as the chief financial officer of a mid-size company. His salary, while about 60 percent of his former salary, was still over $200,000.

Mark likes to gamble. He does so by betting on horse races, going to Las Vegas, playing in the stock market, and buying speculative real estate. The reason he had embezzled the money at his former job was to cover his gambling and stock market losses. While in California, he continued to bet on horse races and visit Las Vegas to gamble. Leslee accompanied him to the race tracks and to Las Vegas. Since Mark was known as a big gambler, their rooms were always provided for free, as were any costs associated with their stays in Las Vegas. Leslee would watch Mark gamble for a while, get bored, and then go to see shows or go shopping. Leslee liked to shop and spent thousands of dollars at a time.

As to the investment speculations, Leslee did not help in the decisions to purchase stock or real estate. However, she did sign all purchase and sale agreements for real estate, as California is a community property state. Any proceeds from the sales were paid to both Mark and Leslee. She endorsed all checks, which were deposited in their joint checking account. Leslee and Mark both wrote checks out of this account. What Leslee did not know is that Mark had a separate bank account into which he deposited much of his gambling winnings and stock gains.

In the current year, the Jones's prior two tax returns are audited and material omissions are found. The embezzled money never had been reported, gambling gains were substantially understated, and gains on the sale of stock and real estate were omitted from the returns. Shortly after the notice from the IRS as to their findings regarding the audits, Leslee filed for divorce, for obvious reasons.

What tax-related advice do you have for Mark and Leslee? Leslee would like to apply for innocent spouse protection from the tax liabilities. She claims that she had no knowledge of any of the underreporting on their tax returns. Mark and Leslee always used a CPA to prepare their returns.

CHAPTER 7

Legal Services and Internet Sites

Chapter Outline

Learning Objectives

- Use the major features of legal tax research services.

- Apply the search methodologies that are available with each of the legal tax research services.

- Employ the connectors, universal characters, and proximity commands available for each legal tax research service.

- Know which legal tax research services are most appropriate for different research objectives.

- Identify the major tax newsletters and law reviews.

- Become familiar with Internet sources of tax information.

Taxation provisions are law and therefore fall under the purview of those in the legal profession. Consequently, research services created for tax attorneys can be used by other tax professionals in performing tax research. This chapter focuses on the two major legal services, LexisNexis and Westlaw, and two other publishers of tax materials, Tax Analysts and **Bureau of National Affairs (BNA)**. Since service providers are eager to increase the acceptance of their products by tax professionals in the accounting arena, these publishers are adapting their products to be user friendly to all tax practitioners. Both LexisNexis and Westlaw offer individual bundling of products, and for their larger accounting firm clients, create special web interfaces.

While there are numerous legal services that could be examined, the coverage in this chapter is limited to services to which tax practitioners are most likely to subscribe. Only the tax products offered by these services will be reviewed. Chapter 8 reviews the case law products of these services, and Chapters 9 and 10 provide more detailed information regarding the state and international products available through legal and tax services.

LexisNexis

The amount of information available on the **LexisNexis** system is staggering. With more than 5 billion searchable documents from 32,000 legal, business, and news sources included in LexisNexis, it is possibly the world's largest full-text information resource. About the only tax services not available on LexisNexis are the competitors RIA and Westlaw. **Lexis**, for legal (tax) sources, was started in 1973 and **Nexis**, for news, financial, and business information, was started in 1979. The LexisNexis services initially were offered on dedicated terminals because they were developed long before the universal use of personal computers. These services now are offered on the Internet with yearly, weekly, or daily subscriptions, and on a pay-for-document credit card system. Documents can be retrieved for a nominal cost, and conducting the search is free.

Tax Center

Realizing how important tax research has become, LexisNexis, in April 2006, uses a service created exclusively for tax practitioners called **Tax Center**. This service is designed to streamline tax research by having an interface separate from LexisNexis and giving the practitioner the ability to conduct a single search across the full content of this service. Prior to the development of Tax Center, a researcher could not access all the databases within LexisNexis in a single search, as is possible with the RIA and CCH services. Rather, LexisNexis is structured somewhat like a tree. The main libraries are located on the trunk of the tree, and the databases within the libraries are the various branches of the tree. At each level in the database selection process the branch is narrowing until the researcher reaches the end of the branch. For example, in LexisNexis the three areas of Legal, Business & News, and Public Records could not be queried in a single search. Three searches would need to be performed. Thus, allowing a single search across the entire contents of Tax Center does streamline searching in this LexisNexis product.

The tax materials currently available in Tax Center are primary sources (Code, regulations, cases, IRS pronouncements, and public records) and the analytical materials of CCH, BNA, Tax Analysts, Matthew Bender, and Kleinrock. Also provided are Shepard's citators for tax professionals (see Chapter 8 for discussion of citators), LexisNexis Company Dossier, and Industry Dossier. Practice Insights offer strategic analysis by leading tax practitioners and experts. LexisNexis plans to add additional services as Tax Center evolves. Different packages are available that can be specifically designed for the practice of the tax professional. Consequently, the package utilized in this chapter may vary from the service available to the student.

Tax Center's opening research option presents the practitioner with a wide variety of databases (see Exhibit 7-1). Each database category offers some choices that are combinations of several sources, while others are only a single source. For example, in the column for Cases, the first choice, Tax Cases, Federal and State, includes all of the other Case choices visible in Exhibit 7-1. Therefore, it is redundant to select Tax Cases, Federal and State and any of the other Cases options visible. As all of the possible databases for Primary Sources cannot be listed and still have the Analytical Sources visible on the opening screen (see Exhibit 7-1), an abbreviated list is shown initially. To see all of the options, the researcher would click on the More Sources button. Since the researcher is limited to a total of fifty sources, checking the boxes by the column headings (IRS, Code & Regulations, and Cases) will select more than the allowed sources and is unnecessary. It is preferable to select combined databases for searching efficiency.

Exhibit 7-1: LexisNexis Tax Center Federal Screen

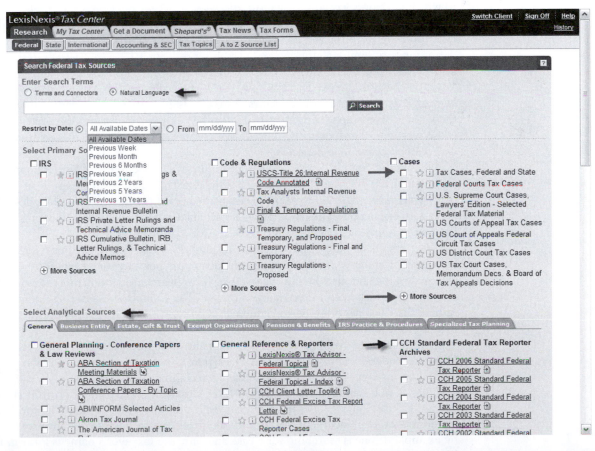

The Analytical Sources are divided into several topical areas as well as a general category. The General References & Reports contains the LexisNexis Tax Advisor, its topical tax service, plus the CCH tax services such as the Standard Federal Tax Reporter (SFTR), Kleinrock's Tax Expert Analysis and Explanations, and Rabkin & Johnson Federal Tax Guidebook. There is a separate category for CCH SFTR Archives (see Exhibit 7-1). The archives are useful if the researcher needs to know what the tax law was in a prior year, for instance, when a client is taking a tax issue to court.

Given the almost overwhelming number of database options, Tax Center includes an option to select databases as Favorites by clicking on the star in front of the title. This causes the database to be listed in the My Tax Center tab. Consequently, the researcher can customize Tax Center to support the type of searches most commonly performed. Within the My Tax Center tab, the practitioner may set preferences for the searches and results. For example, the researcher can choose to have the results sorted by relevance or by date. The default option is to sort the results list by Sources.

Tax Center offers the researcher a choice of **Natural Language** or **Terms and Connectors (Boolean)** types of searches (see Exhibit 7-1). With a natural language search, the tax question is entered in standard English (natural language) words, phrases (entered within quotation marks), or sentences. The program determines the key terms for searching and relationships among the words (i.e., connectors to apply). This type of search is useful when the researcher is unsure as to which keywords would be the most effective.

LexisNexis supports numerous search connectors and **wildcard (universal) characters** in its terms and connectors searches. Many of the connectors and their definitions are similar to those listed in Exhibit 6-3, for RIA. LexisNexis interprets a space between words as signifying a connection of words in a phrase and not as "and" in the usual sense. For example, if the researcher enters the words *kickback business deduction* with no connectors, LexisNexis identifies only documents with these three words appearing next to each other. To search for any occurrence of these words in the document, they must be entered with "and" between them— *kickback and business and deduction*.

Below the Search Term box is the option of Restriction by Date. As can be seen in Exhibit 7-1, the choices are All Available Dates, a previous period of time (e.g., previous week, month, year), or a specific period (from … to …). The default is no date restriction. The date option is particularly beneficial when updating earlier research or when trying to locate tax law for a prior tax year.

The results of a keyword search are displayed by Category and Sources, as can be seen in Exhibit 7-2. The number of documents per category is shown on the Category tabs and also in the main table. This search retrieved more than 300 documents, which likely is too many to review. Tax Center allows the researcher to reduce the documents by performing a FOCUS terms search within the original results (see Exhibit 7-2).

Another search option is Get a Document. Documents can be retrieved by Citation, Federal Citation, and State or Region Citation as shown in Exhibit 7-3. The citations must be entered in a format recognized by LexisNexis. If the researcher is not familiar with the LexisNexis format, the Help function (top right corner, Exhibit 7-3) includes in its index a listing for Citation Format. The formats for administrative document, cases, and tax or legislative documents are provided by example. If one is searching for a case and only the taxpayer's name is known, it is best to use a keyword search in the Research tab and select the level of court

Exhibit 7-2: LexisNexis Tax Center Document List Screen

LexisNexis® *Tax Center*

| Research | My Tax Center | Get a Document | Shepard's® | Tax News | Tax Forms |

Terms: **leases and AMT** (Edit Search)

FOCUS™ Terms ⟵   Search Within Original Results (1 -337) ▾ Go → Advanced...

View: Summary   ◄ 337 Results ►   Print | Download | Fax | Email

▼   ▼   ▼   ▼   ▼

| All Results - (337) | Cases - (90) ▸ | Statutes & Regulations (Legislative) - (61) ▸ | Agency Materials - (31) | Treatises & Analytical Materials - (91) ▸ | Law Reviews & Journals - | ◄ ← → ►|

Source: **Combined Source Set** ℹ

All Results - 337   Print Summary Table

Category	Sources
Cases - 90	Federal Courts Tax Cases - 64 US Tax Court Cases, Memorandum Decs. & Board of Tax Appeals Decisions - 26
Statutes & Regulations (Legislative) - 61	USCS-Title 26:Internal Revenue Code Annotated - 5 CCH Standard Federal Tax Reporter - 56
Agency Materials - 31	IRS Bulletins, Letter Rulings & Memoranda Decisions, Combined - 31
Treatises & Analytical Materials - 91	CCH Standard Federal Tax Reporter - 56 Rabkin & Johnson, Federal Tax Guidebook - 2 Kleinrock's TaxExpert Analysis and Explanation - 6 LexisNexis® Tax Advisor - Federal Topical - 27
Law Reviews & Journals - 87	Tax Law Review Articles, Combined - 87
Professional & Practice Materials - 89	CCH Standard Federal Tax Reporter - 56 ABA Section of Taxation Meeting Materials - 33

Note: Sources may appear in more than one category. All Results counts the number of documents from each source only one time even though the source and its results may appear under multiple categories.

LexisNexis® About LexisNexis   Terms & Conditions
Copyright © 2007 LexisNexis, a division of Reed Elsevier Inc. All rights reserved.

▲Explore   Page   ◄ Doc 1   of 337 ► ◄ Term   of

from the Cases column. When the researcher is unsure of the judicial level of the case, the combined Federal and state databases or just combined Federal Courts Tax Cases should be selected.

SPOTLIGHT ON TAXATION

The Huge Two

Two companies dominate the realm of providing legal and tax information, Reed Elsevier and Thomson. These corporations are two of the largest publishing and information providers in the world. Reed Elsevier, an Anglo-Dutch company, is the parent company of LexisNexis; Thomson owns Westlaw, RIA, and Warren, Gorham & Lamont (WG&L). Through LexisNexis and Westlaw, the tax practitioner can access virtually every major tax publication. While CCH is a separate company owned by Wolters Kluwer, CCH has a long-standing relationship and multiyear agreement with LexisNexis. It is the only source, other than CCH itself, to offer web access to CCH products. In addition, LexisNexis offers BNA, Tax Analysts, Matthew Bender, Shepard's, and Kleinrock. Westlaw also offers access to BNA products as well as all of the RIA and WG&L products.

Exhibit 7-3: LexisNexis Tax Center Get a Document Screen

LexisNexis® *Tax Center*   Switch Client | Sign Off | Help

Research | My Tax Center | Get a Document | Shepard's® | Tax News | Tax Forms   History

LexisNexis Get a Document

Retrieve a single document or validate an authority with *Shepard's®*.

Option 1: General Citation Entry
If you know the citation and format, enter it below, select an option, and click the Go button.

Retrieve by Cite or Validate Authority [?]

Enter Citation
506US 168

○ Retrieve Document
⊙ Validate Authority with *Shepard's®*   Go →

Option 2: Federal Citation Wizard
If you are unsure of the citation format, first select a source. The text box and example citation will update dynamically based on your selection. After entering your citation, select an option and click the Go button.

Retrieve by Cite or Validate Authority [?]

Select Federal Source
Internal Revenue Code   ▼

Enter Citation
IRC 162
(e.g. IRC Sec. 112)

⊙ Retrieve Document
○ Validate Authority with *Shepard's®*   Go →

Option 3: State Citation Wizard
If you are unsure of the citation format, first select a State or Region. Based on your selection, the list of sources, text box, and example citation will update dynamically. After entering your citation, select an option and click the Go button.

Retrieve by Cite or Validate Authority [?]

Select State or Region
Montana   ▼

Select Source
Montana Administrative Rules   ▼

Enter Citation
Mont. Admin. R.
(e.g. Mont. Admin. R. 1.2.101)

⊙ Retrieve Document
○ Validate Authority with *Shepard's®*   Go →

LexisNexis®   About LexisNexis | Terms and Conditions | Contact Us
Copyright © 2007 LexisNexis, a division of Reed Elsevier Inc. All rights reserved.

LexisNexis Academic

LexisNexis offers a customized version of its services to academic institutions and public libraries called **LexisNexis Academic**. While the complete LexisNexis flagship service provides full-text documents from over 6,000 publications, most library subscriptions do not carry all of the offerings. The resource categories in Academic include the following.

- National and regional newspapers, international news, wire services, broadcast transcripts, and non-English language sources.

- Federal and state primary sources such as case law, Code, Regulations, and rulings.

- Legal and professional journals, law reviews, and international information.

- Treatises and analytical materials from services such as Kleinrock and Tax Analysts.

- Shepard's citations.

- Business news journals, company financial information, SEC filings and reports, and industry and market news.

Exhibit 7-4: LexisNexis Academic Legal Screen

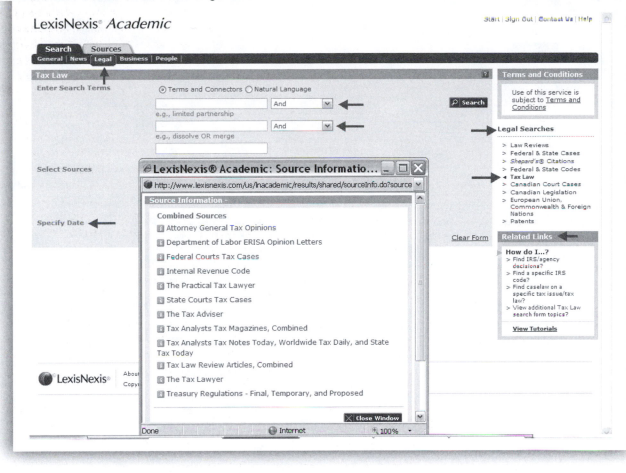

To perform tax research using Academic, select the Legal button from the category list on the Search tab as shown in Exhibit 7-4. Legal Searches, in the right panel, indicates the legal databases available for the subscriber. Choosing Tax Law provides access to primary sources, tax journals, newsletters, and tax law reviews as listed in the insert of Exhibit 7-4. These sources may be searched individually or in any combination desired by the researcher, by using either Terms and Connectors or Natural Language keywords. The entry boxes vary depending on the type of keyword search selected. As demonstrated in Exhibit 7-4, the connectors available in Academic are provided in pull-down menus. To enhance the relevancy of the documents retrieved, date limitations (Specify Date) can be imposed (options available are not visible in Exhibit 7-4). The Related Links, in the lower right panel, offers a variety of help options and links to related material depending on the screen visible.

To access specific sources that may not be included in the Tax Law database of the Search Tab, the Sources tab is used. As Exhibit 7-5 indicates, using the browse option is as easy as 1, 2, 3. First, select how the sources should be organized. Second, filter the sources by country (United States), topic (Taxation Law), and source types (multiple, single, or all sources). The final step is to select the sources and then perform a keyword search. As shown in Exhibit 7-5, Kleinrock's TaxExpert Analysis and Explanation permits further browsing using a table of contents approach to drill down to the document of interest.

Exhibit 7-5: LexisNexis Academic Browse Sources Screen

LexisNexis® *Academic*   Start | Sign Out | Contact Us | Help

Search | Sources
Browse Sources | Find Sources

Browse Sources   **Find a Source**

▶ 1 By ⦿ **Publication Type** ○ News & Business Topics ○ Industry ○ Area of Law

▶ 2 Filter by: Country   United States ▾   All Regions ▾   [   ] Go
            Topics   Taxation Law ▾   More Options
            Multiple/Single Source   All sources ▾

Trail: Publication Type > **Treatises & Analytical Material**

▶ 3 ↓ Select a category to view sources   06 🖹 Selected View ↪ OK - Continue

                              ⇧ **1-57 of 57 Sources** ⇨

🔼 [Up a level]

☑🖹 **ABA Section of Taxation Conference Papers - By Topic**	☐🖹 Tax Analysts Letter Ruling Review Magazine (1992 - 1996)
☐🖹 All State Tax Statutes, Regulations, Cases and Admin Decisions	☑🖹 **Tax Analysts Regs - Final, Temporary, Proposed & Comments**
☐🖹 Combined Kleinrock Bulletins	☐🖹 Tax Analysts State Tax Notes Magazine
☐🖹 Combined Kleinrock Tax Publications	☐🖹 Tax Analysts State Tax Regulations
☐🖹 Combined State Tax Publications	☐🖹 Tax Analysts State Tax Statutes
☐🖹 Cost of Capital: Estimation and Applications	☐🖹 Tax Analysts State Tax Statutes and Regulations
☐🖹 Financial and Accounting Guide for Not-for-Profit Organizations	☐🖹 Tax Analysts State Tax Today
☐🖹 Financial Valuation: Applications and Models	☐🖹 Tax Analysts State, Federal & International Tax Directories
☐🖹 Handbook of Budgeting	☑🖹 **Tax Analysts Tax Magazines, Combined**
☐🖹 Income Taxation of Estates and Trusts	☐🖹 Tax Analysts Tax Notes Today
☐🖹 Inside New York Taxes	☐🖹 Tax Analysts Tax Notes Today, Worldwide Tax Daily, and State Tax Today
☑🖹 **IRS Practice and Procedure Deskbook**	☐🖹 Tax Analysts Tax Notes Weekly
☐🖹 Kleinrock California Tax Bulletin	☐🖹 Tax Analysts Tax Practice and Controversies
☐🖹 Kleinrock Federal Tax Bulletin	☐🖹 Tax Analysts Tax Professionals Directory
☐🖹 Kleinrock New York Tax Bulletin	☐🖹 Tax Analysts Tax Publications
☑🖹 **Kleinrock's TaxExpert Analysis and Explanation** Browse	☑🖹 **Tax Analysts Tax Publications and Treaties**
☐🖹 Langer on Practical International Tax Planning	☐🖹 Tax Analysts Worldwide Tax Treaties In Force
☐🖹 Law of Tax-Exempt Organizations	☐🖹 Tax Cases, Administrative Decs., & ALR Annotations, All States
☐🖹 The Market Approach to Valuing Business	☐🖹 The Tax Law of Colleges and Universities

The results of an Academic search (see Exhibit 7-6) may be listed either by relevance or publication date. The results summary (left window, Exhibit 7-6) also may be personalized to present by category or publication name. If the documents retrieved are not on point, the researcher may use the Edit Search option to return to the original keyword entry box or if too many documents are returned, searching within the list may be accomplished with the Narrow Search option. Selecting one of the document titles displays the document as seen in Exhibit 7-7. Academic offers the **KWIC** (key words in context) view, which highlights the terms entered as keywords. If the narrow search option has been applied, only the words used for narrowing will be KWIC. The documents retrieved are full text and may be downloaded, e-mailed, or printed from the browser.

The improvements made by LexisNexis to Academic have dramatically increased the usefulness of this service for performing tax research. While there are remnants of the prior "tree" organization of the libraries that preempted comprehensive single searches, Academic is a more tax-research-friendly service than in the past.

Exhibit 7-6: LexisNexis Academic Results Screen

LexisNexis® Academic

General Search - Tax Analysts Tax... [] > ("charitable contributions" w/10 ... (85)

Search | Sources

Results

Result Groups

Sources by Category

All Results (85)
- Legal News (85)
- Treatises & Analytical Material (85)
- Newsletters (62)
- Magazines & Journals (23)

View List | Narrow Search | Go

Sort Relevance | 1-25 of 85 | Next Steps Edit Search | Go

Publication Date
View Relevance

No.	Results
☐ 1	2001 TNT 244-13 ISSUES TO CONSIDER WHEN MAKING AND ACCEPTING GIFTS OF RESTRICTED STOCK. (Section 170 -- Charitable Deduction) (Release Date: OCTOBER 31, 2001) (Doc 2001-30708 (19 original pages)), News, Commentary, and Analysis; Special Reports 6298 words, TAX NOTES TODAY, DECEMBER 19, 2001 WEDNESDAY
☐ 2	2000 TNT 34-39 COUPLE DISPUTES DISALLOWANCE OF STOCK CONTRIBUTIONS. (Kevin L. Woodbridge, et ux. v. Commissioner) (No. 869-00) (United States Tax Court) (Section 170 -- Charitable Deduction) (Release Date: JANUARY 18, 2000) (Doc 2000-3267 (19 original pages)), Court Documents; Court Petitions and Complaints 1795 words, TAX NOTES TODAY, FEBRUARY 18, 2000 FRIDAY
☐ 3	98 TNT 119-19 SHARES ARE QUALIFIED APPRECIATED STOCK. (Section 170 -- Charitable Deduction) (LTR 9825031) (Release Date: June 19, 1998) (Doc 98-19751 (9 pages)), IRS Letter Rulings (LTR) 3185 wordsIRS Letter Rulings (LTR) 3185 wordsIRS Letter Rulings (LTR)3185 wordsIRS Letter Rulings (LTR) 3185 words, TAX NOTES TODAY, JUNE 22, 1998 MONDAY
☐ 4	2001 TNT 58-14 PREVIOUS STOCK DONATIONS TO FOUNDATIONS INCLUDED IN FUTURE CONTRIBUTION LIMITATION CALCULATION. (Section 170 -- Charitable Deduction) (LTR 200112025) (Release Date: DECEMBER 19, 2000) (Doc 2001-8475 (9 original pages)), Administrative Rulings; IRS Letter Rulings 4134 words, TAX NOTES TODAY, MARCH 26, 2001 MONDAY
☐ 5	2001 TNT 58-13 PREVIOUS STOCK DONATIONS TO FOUNDATIONS INCLUDED IN FUTURE CONTRIBUTION LIMITATION CALCULATION. (Section 170 -- Charitable Deduction) (LTR 200112024) (Release Date: DECEMBER 19, 2000) (Doc 2001-8474 (9 original pages)), Administrative Rulings; IRS Letter Rulings 4123 words, TAX NOTES TODAY, MARCH 26, 2001 MONDAY
☐ 6	2001 TNT 58-12 PREVIOUS STOCK DONATIONS TO FOUNDATIONS INCLUDED IN FUTURE CONTRIBUTION LIMITATION CALCULATION. (Section 170 -- Charitable Deduction) (LTR 200112022) (Release Date: DECEMBER 19, 2000) (Doc 2001-8472 (9 original pages)), Administrative Rulings; IRS Letter Rulings 4135 words, TAX NOTES TODAY, MARCH 26, 2001 MONDAY
☐ 7	94 TNT 207-14 ABA TAX SECTION MEMBERS SUGGEST EXEMPT ORGANIZATION AREAS IN NEED OF PRECEDENTIAL GUIDANCE. (Section 501 -- Tax-Exempt Organizations) (Release Date: October 5, 1994)

Start | Sign Out | Contact Us | Help

Exhibit 7-7: LexisNexis Academic Document Screen

LexisNexis® Academic

General Search - Tax Analysts Tax... [] > /../ > (Exempt) (43) > **Document** (2/43)

Search | Sources

Results

View KWIC™ | Narrow Search | Go

2 of 43 | Next Steps Edit Search | Go

☐ © 2007, Tax Analysts, Tax Notes Today...

Copyright © 2007 Tax Analysts
Tax Notes Today

APRIL 16, 2007 MONDAY

DEPARTMENT: News, Commentary, and Analysis; Washington Roundup

CITE: 2007 TNT 73-44

LENGTH: 54343 words

HEADLINE: 2007 TNT 73-44 TRANSCRIPT OF THE JANUARY 20, 2007 ABA TAX SECTION EXEMPT ORGANIZATIONS COMMITTEE MEETING. (Section 501 -- Tax-Exempt Organizations) (Release Date: MARCH 13, 2007) (Doc 2007-9491)

CODE: Section 501 -- Tax-Exempt Organizations

ABSTRACT: A transcript of the January 20, 2007 meeting of the American Bar Association Section of Taxation's Exempt Organizations Committee, which took place in Hollywood, Fla., is provided.

REFERENCES:
Subject Area:
  Exempt organizations
Industry GRoup:
  Nonprofit sector
Principal Cited Reference:
  section 501;
  section 501(c)(3);
  section 4958

TEXT:

Transcript of the January 20, 2007 ABA Tax Section Exempt
Organizations Committee Meeting

Start | Sign Out | Contact Us | Help

Hits: 1 of 90

TAX ANALYSTS

Tax Analysts, established by Thomas F. Field in 1970, is a nonprofit entity whose mission is to be "respectfully disagreeable" and to defend the public interest. Tax Analysts works to promote a transparency of tax rules, fosters dialog between taxpayers and taxing authorities, and provides literary forums for education and tax policy debate. To further these objectives, Tax Analysts produces a variety of comprehensive state, Federal, and international news, analysis, and commentary publications for tax professionals on a daily, weekly, monthly, and quarterly basis. It also provides a document search service. However, what Tax Analysts is best known for in the tax community is its outstanding news publications *Tax Notes* and *Tax Notes Today* (TNT).

Research Library

Federal Research Library The **Federal Research Library** (FRL) has been enhanced to make searching easier and faster than before. It has moved from a library organization to a database grouping based on document type, similar to the format of the CCH Tax Research NetWork (see Chapter 6). The collection of documents within the databases includes the following.

- Code, Explanations, and Code Section Summaries.

- Regulations.

- IRS Documents such as Revenue Rulings and Procedures, Announcements, Publications, Notices, and *Circular 230*.

- IRS Written Determinations such as PLRs, TAMs, FSAs, and GCMs.

- Court Opinions, which includes over 100,000 Federal court opinions since 1913.

- The *Internal Revenue Manual*.

- Recent legislation, legislative histories, and Joint Committee on Taxation (JCT) Blue Books since 1981.

- Quick References and Other Documents such as tables, *Tax Practice* magazine, and Congressional Research Service Reports.

Any, some, or all of these databases and specific document types within each database may be searched using keywords as Exhibit 7-8 illustrates. The keyword options supported by FRL include treating words as a phrase (quotes connector), which is the default, all terms must be found ("and" connector), at least one term must be found ("or" connector), and terms within the same paragraph (proximity connector). The program searches for root words and finds common variations such as plurals, different tenses, and possessives. When searching for terms that include punctuation, quotes should be used, as Exhibit 7-8 indicates. The number of search documents retrieved may be limited by database rather than in total. They also may be sorted by database or by relevance.

Tax Analysts offers two editorial services. The first topical service is called Federal Tax Explanations, formerly Federal Tax Baedeker. This service is divided into twenty-six chapters that can be searched either by keyword, or using the table of contents drill-down method by clicking on the triangles preceding the topic heading. The explanations are basic plain English guides to key

Exhibit 7-8: Tax Analysts Federal Research Library Screen

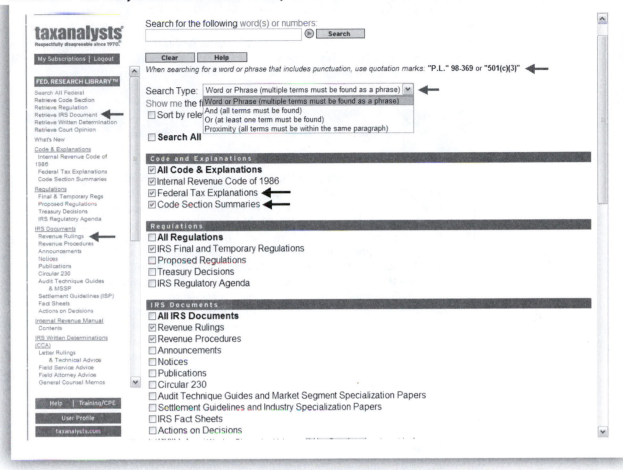

Federal tax law. The coverage is not as in-depth as CCH or RIA furnishes, but it is more in the nature of the Kleinrock service. The Explanations are updated monthly. The second editorial service is Code Section Summaries. This service also provides plain-English explanations of each Code section. These are very useful to read prior to tackling the legal verbiage in the Code itself.

Documents are retrievable by entering the citation in templates using the Retrieve tools (similar to the RIA Checkpoint), or by browsing a list of the documents of interest once the database is selected (see left window in Exhibit 7-8). The latter database also supports searches by citation. For example, to find a specific Revenue Ruling, the researcher may enter the ruling number in the template provided by selecting Retrieve IRS Documents (left window) or by selecting the Revenue Ruling database listed beneath IRS Documents.

Finally, the opening screen of FRL provides access to the most current legal tax sources including pronouncements by the IRS, Congressional Research Service Reports, Court Opinions, Treasury Decisions, and Proposed Regulations. These are available in a seven-day view and as revolving headlines of the most significant recent documents.

OneDisc Tax Analysts developed a single-disc tax product, **OneDisc Premium**, which contains an extensive list of primary Federal sources, tax treaties, IRS pronouncements, full-text court cases, Internal Revenue Manual, and the topical explanations of the FRL. Thus, this 3.3 GB DVD containing full-text source documents is quite handy for practitioners to take to client offices, or to use when Internet access is not reliable or unavailable. OneDisc has two updating options, quarterly and, for a slightly higher cost, monthly. A slimmed down version of OneDisc also is available. This version provides access to the text of fewer cases but still provides the editorial materials.

SPOTLIGHT ON TAXATION

Field Service Advice Memorandums

Field Service Advice (FSA) memorandums are available to the tax community thanks to Tax Analysts. In 1993, Tax Analysts filed a request under the Freedom of Information Act to have FSA memorandums become subject to public disclosure. The IRS declined this request, because these documents contained "return information" or were protected by the attorney-client privilege, and therefore were not available for public disclosure. Tax Analysts took the question to court and a 1996 District Court ordered the IRS to release the FSAs to the general public. The court indicated that FSAs are similar to General Counsel Memoranda (GCMs), also public information. They contain legal analysis and conclusions of the law and are not "return information" under any reasonable interpretation of §6103. Further, just because an IRS attorney declares FSAs to be "return information" does not make them so. FSAs are merely memoranda routinely used by the IRS as guidance in conducting audits and therefore are applied by the IRS in its dealings with the public.

Newsletters

Tax Analysts publishes an influential set of newsletters, including a daily tax news series and one of the most highly regarded weekly publications, *Tax Notes*. The daily news services, available only online, offer up-to-the-minute coverage of Federal (TNT), state *(State Tax Today)*, and worldwide *(Worldwide Tax Daily)* tax news. The weekly print series include *Tax Notes* and *State Tax Notes*, and *Tax Notes International*. The Tax Analysts newsletters also are available through LexisNexis.

TNT is updated continually throughout the day, not just once a day, so practitioners can be as up-to-date as they desire. The amount of information included in these newsletters is staggering. The TNT, for example, includes the following.

- Commentary and analysis by experts.

- IRS Private Letter Rulings (PLRs), Chief Counsel advice, Revenue Rulings, Revenue Procedures, FSAs, and Announcements.

- IRS Final, Temporary, and Proposed Regulations, as well as public comments on Proposed Regulations.

- All original full-text documents.

- White House budget proposals, tax bills introduced in Congress, and coverage of other congressional action, as well as reports by the Congressional Budget Office (CBO) and the JCT.

- IRS and congressional hearing transcripts.

- Court cases.

TNT also includes access to *Financial Reporting Watch*, a publication addressing the latest developments related to the post-Sarbanes-Oxley practice. It includes articles on financial reporting, original source documents, and continuously updated databases of tax documents found in SEC filings by public companies. To retrieve the articles in these reports, the subscriber selects the Document icon. Document icons within articles denote that the preceding citation is linked to its full-text document.

The content of the weekly *Tax Notes* publication is similar to TNT and the *Weekly Report* published by BNA (discussed later in this chapter). However, *Tax Notes* includes in-depth analysis of court decisions, regulatory pronouncements, and policy-oriented research submitted by tax professionals and academics, as Exhibit 7-9 illustrates. Special sections provide news and practice tips just for accounting and tax practitioners.

To obtain the full text of a document discussed and cited within a *Tax Notes* article, the subscribers use the *Tax Notes* unique document identification numbers (see Exhibit 7-9) through an online service such as LexisNexis.

Exhibit 7-9: Tax Analysts Tax Notes

tax analysts › news and analysis

Congress Adjourns Without Passing Tax Extenders, Estate Tax Reform

By Wesley Elmore — welmore@tax.org

Congress adjourned for a six-week preelection recess last week without passing a package of popular tax relief measures or more controversial estate tax reform legislation. Still, lawmakers remained hopeful that those issues would be addressed when they return November 13 for a lame-duck session.

While supporters of a permanent reduction in the estate tax had resigned themselves to the fact that action on the legislation was unlikely to occur before Congress adjourned, several taxwriters had been holding out hope that the so-called tax extenders package would be passed before the recess.

Senate Finance Committee Chair Chuck Grassley, R-Iowa, told reporters that at a Senate Republican caucus meeting last week, he raised the prospect of passing an extenders package, "but there wasn't much of a desire to discuss it."

Along with Finance Committee ranking minority member Max Baucus, D-Mont., Grassley had been one of the most vocal supporters of passing the tax extenders package before the recess, arguing that a failure to do so before November would cause administrative difficulties for the IRS and confusion for taxpayers. The state and local sales tax deduction, the research credit, and the work opportunity

The extenders were included — along with reforms to the estate tax and an increase in the minimum wage — as part of the House-passed "trifecta" legislation (H.R. 5970) that failed to advance in the Senate in early August. Senate GOP leaders have insisted that the extenders remain attached to any estate tax legislation to pull in more support for such a bill. (For prior coverage, see *Tax Notes*, Aug. 7, 2006, p. 463, *Doc 2006-14718*, or *2006 TNT 151-1*.)

Neither Grassley nor Lott was ready to dismiss the possibility that the Senate would once again take up the controversial trifecta bill in November, although both were pessimistic about its chances of passage this year thanks to overwhelming Democratic opposition. Even Baucus, who has supported estate tax reform efforts, told reporters that "the die is pretty much cast" on the estate tax.

Other supporters of the trifecta bill have a different outlook. For example, Senate Budget Committee Chair Judd Gregg, R-N.H., has said that the Senate might be more successful if it waits until after the elections to try again on the trifecta bill. At that point, Gregg has said, Democrats will be more likely to buck their leadership and vote in favor of the bill. (For prior coverage, see *Tax Notes*, Sept. 18, 2006, p. 1015, *Doc 2006-19167*, or *2006 TNT 177-1*.)

But Grassley said that as long as the estate tax reforms in the trifecta bill remain unchanged, nothing can be added to the bill to pull in more Democratic support. "Adding a, b, c, d, e, and f —

WESTLAW

The West Group, an authoritative legal publisher, offers tax research capabilities through its **Westlaw** service. This service is legally oriented because it was designed by attorneys for attorneys. Its orientation is evident in its structure and its emphasis on citators and citing. (The first two data entry boxes on the "Westlaw" opening screen are for finding documents by citation; see Exhibit 7-10.) Due to this orientation toward the legal profession, Westlaw is less represented than RIA and CCH in accounting firms. However, to capture more of the accounting tax practice market, the West Group, like LexisNexis, has developed products specifically for tax research such as the Tax Platinum Library and Tax Gold Library. Thus, most international, regional, and large local CPA firms subscribe to some portion of the Westlaw service, especially those that hire attorneys into their tax service groups. Virtually all law schools train their students on the Westlaw system.

Data and Access

Westlaw contains over 19,000 databases including BNA *Tax Management Portfolios*, all of the RIA products including the *Federal Tax Coordinator 2d* and its citator, the WG&L newsletters, journals, manuals, and treatises, law reviews, and various tax news services. The popular South-Western Federal Taxation textbook series and a topical tax service, called *Mertens Law of Federal Income Taxation*, also are included in Westlaw.

Exhibit 7-10: Westlaw Welcome Screen with Help Center

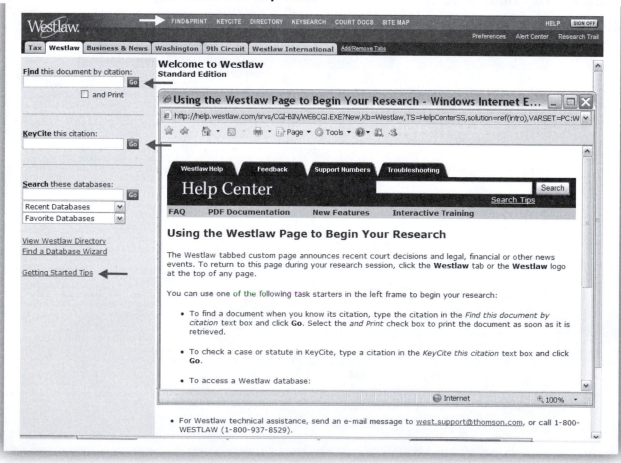

As with LexisNexis, when Westlaw began in 1975, it required a dedicated on-line terminal. Now Westlaw is accessible via the Internet or with wireless mobile devices (Westlaw Wireless). Westlaw offers tailored bundling of the databases to its customers and even provides access to its services without requiring a subscription. Using a pay-as-you-go system (credit card required), researchers can retrieve documents as necessary from Westlaw.

Customized Westlaw web sites can meet the specific professional needs of different Westlaw users. Consequently, the appearance of the Westlaw service demonstrated in this chapter may vary from the customized site available to you through your school or employer. The basic searching strategies discussed in this section, however, are similar in all versions of Westlaw.

Searching Westlaw

When logging on to Westlaw, it may be necessary to enter a client name to proceed with the research project. This feature, included for the benefit of the tax professional, is helpful in tracking the time spent on each search by client for billing purposes.

The Welcome to Westlaw screen shown in Exhibit 7-10 allows access to the major features of Westlaw. The immediate options facilitate searching for a document by citation, performing a citator search (KeyCite), or locating a database (see left window). Also available is information about Westlaw's new products, and interesting legal news (main window, not visible in Exhibit 7-10). If the researcher is new to Westlaw, the Getting Started Tips function may be a good place to begin. Not only does it offer advice on initiating research, it also gives access to the Westlaw Help Center that has been opened as an insert window in Exhibit 7-10.

The top toolbar is available from any of the library tabs. From this toolbar, the researcher may locate documents (Find&Print and Court Docs), perform a Key-Cite, KeySearch, or Directory search, and see a Site Map that provides access to all services available in Westlaw. With the exception of KeyCite, the Westlaw options are reviewed in this section. **KeyCite** is a citator and will be covered in Chapter 8, Citators and Other Finding Devices.

Westlaw allows the researcher to personalize the library tabs appearing at the top of the screen, to offer easy access to the practice areas frequently visited. For example, in Exhibit 7-10, the tabs are customized to facilitate performing international research and tax research specifically for the state of Washington and its applicable Ninth Circuit. Business & News has also been chosen to keep the illustrated user up-to-date. These six tabs (the maximum allowed) were added by clicking on the Add/Remove Tabs function appearing at the end of the tabs (see Exhibit 7-10). Since we are interested in tax research, utilizing the features on the Tax tab will be the focus for the remainder of this section.

The first type of search offered on the Tax tab is Find by Citation. A document can be retrieved by entering the appropriate citation, if its citation is known (Exhibit 7-11). Exact spacing and punctuation is not necessary, but the Westlaw recognized citation must be known. Most Federal documents, topical materials, and law review or journal articles may be retrieved by citation. When the citation is not known, select the Find a Federal Tax Document feature. Templates for the Code, Regulations, cases, administrative pronouncements, and tax services are available with examples similar to those supplied by other services.

Another starting point for research is the Search These Databases feature (Exhibit 7-11). Either Westlaw database abbreviations are entered or the researcher may select from Favorite Databases or Recent Databases (databases recently

Exhibit 7-11: Westlaw Tax Database Screen

searched). Since all the tax databases are listed in the right-hand window, it is just as easy to click on the title. The View Taxation Directory option lists the same databases as listed in the right-hand window. Since there are no boxes to check in front of the titles, the only method for searching more than one database at a time is to use the Search these Databases option and enter the database abbreviations. To discover what is contained in particular databases, the researcher clicks on the "i" ball (see Exhibits 7-11 and 7-12) and a scope description of the database with a full listing of the sources included will appear.

Once a database is selected, the Search screen appears. As Exhibit 7-12 illustrates, the database selected appears at the top of the Search screen. The researcher can search using a Template, Natural Language, or Terms and Connectors (Boolean) keyword query. A thesaurus is available to help in selecting the best words for the search. The thesaurus is not automatically applied; rather, the synonyms are added to the keywords by the researcher. When the Terms and Connectors search option is selected, the list of Westlaw connectors and expanders is furnished (see Exhibit 7-13). These are similar to those of other services, but here a space between two words is interpreted as an "or," not as an "and" or phrase connector. An "&" or the word "and" must be included to apply an "and" connection. Westlaw likewise supports an expansive list of field restrictions such as Judge, Attorney, and References. Finally, the date for the search documents can be limited either by selecting one of the period options provided, or by entering specific dates for a

Exhibit 7-12: Westlaw Tax Search Screen

Exhibit 7-13: Westlaw Term Connectors, Fields, and Date Restrictions

Connector	Sign	Search Restriction Fields			Date Restrictions
AND	&	Annotations	Dissenting	Opinions	Unrestricted
OR	space	Attorney	Docket Number	Prelim	Before After Between
Phrase	" "	Author	End	References	Specific LastToday
But Not	%	Caption	Full Text	Source	Last 30 days
Expander	!	Citation	Headnote	Summary	Last 60 days
Universal	*	Concurring	Historical Note	Text	Last 90 days
Same sentence	/s	Court	Index	Title	Year-to-date
Precede in sentence	+s	Credit	Judge	Topic	This year and last year
Same Paragraph	/p	Digest	Notes	Year	Last 3 years, Last 10 years
Within n terms	/n				

period restriction. A list of Westlaw connectors, fields, and date options is presented in Exhibit 7-13.

The Natural Language search option allows the researcher to type a description of the tax question in plain English using up to 640 characters. The spaces between the words are considered "and" rather than "or" connectors. Accordingly, if the search being performed is using only "and" connectors, it is quicker to use Natural Language than Terms and Connectors. Once the Natural Language search description is entered, the researcher can indicate which terms are required, and which terms should be excluded. Moreover, the number of times a term should appear in the retrieved document can be set separately for each required term.

The results of the search are presented with the key words highlighted as seen in Exhibit 7-14. The researcher can move from one highlighted term to another using the Term arrows at the bottom of the screen. A special feature, offered only by Westlaw, is the Best locator, also at the bottom of the screen. Selecting the Best arrow takes the researcher to the part of the document that is judged to be most relevant to the query. This can save valuable time, especially when the document is long and the search terms appear frequently within the document.

If the number of documents retrieved is large, the researcher can search within this list by selecting the Locate in Result option (see Exhibit 7-14). Only the words entered in the Locate in Result search are highlighted in the narrowed list. In addition, Westlaw includes in the search results its unique feature, ResultsPlus (see left panel, Exhibit 7-14). The results displayed in the main window are solely those documents found in the databases the researcher chose to search. The ResultsPlus is a list of suggested analytical materials relevant to the search

Exhibit 7-14: Westlaw Document Screen

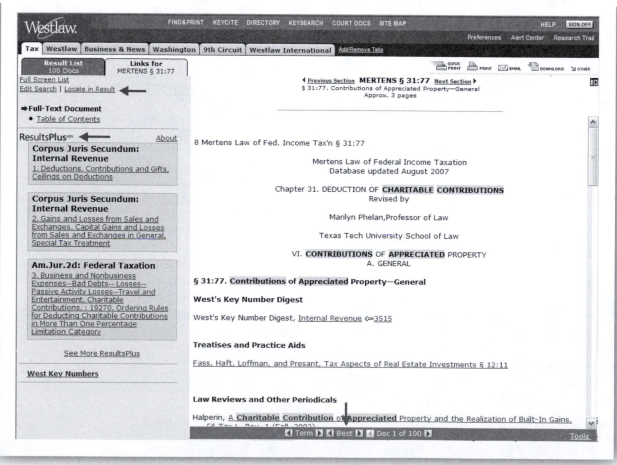

topic. The materials appear in law reports, treatises, law reviews, and topical publications such as the BNA Portfolios. As discussed in Chapter 6, finding an article (or Portfolio) on your research issue can save you from repeating the work that has been done by the authors and editors in preparing the article.

The Table of Contents (TOC) search option is offered on the Tax tab (Exhibit 7-11) and on the Search screen (Exhibit 7-12). As can be seen in Exhibit 7-11, an expandable list of services with TOC search capabilities is available. This list, however, is very limited. Therefore, if the service of interest is not on this list, a TOC may be available through the Search screen after the service of interest is selected in the right window of the Tax tab (Exhibit 7-11). For example, the Search screen for Mertens Law of Federal Income Taxation in Exhibit 7-12 may be searched by TOC through the option in the top right-hand corner. The researcher continues drilling down until a document of interest is identified. This is helpful when the researcher wants to read an entire chapter in a treatise, for example. Most publications that would have a TOC in print format may be accessed through the TOC option in Westlaw.

KeySearch uses the West Key Numbering System, which numbers key issues (topics) found in court cases, as the backbone of this searching mode. The practitioner identifies the legal topic within which the research problem lies either by searching the list of topics with the word search or by drilling down through the topics presented. KeySearch formulates a query based on the underlying terms for the topic and adds the key numbers associated with the topic. The researcher can determine what type of cases to search, or decide to search treatises or journals and law reviews. Only one of these categories may be searched at a time. Other search terms can be added at the researcher's option to ensure the results will be relevant. This type of search is especially effective when the researcher is unfamiliar with that particular area of the tax law.

Business & News

Westlaw's Business & News offers a comprehensive list of news, business, and financial information from more than 12,000 sources, only a few of which are visible in Exhibit 7-15. These sources include the following.

- Wall Street News compiled from numerous sources and updated continuously throughout the day.

- Top daily newspapers such as *The Los Angeles Times, New York Post, Chicago Tribune, USA Today*, plus thousands of international business sources.

- Newswires such as Associated Press, PR Newswires, MarketWatch, and Knight Ridder.

- Business magazines such as *Business Week, Forbes, The Economist, Harvard Business Review, Business Week, Time*, and *Newsweek*.

- Company profiles and business intelligence reports for more than 450,000 companies.

- Stock quotes from nearly 100 different exchanges with market indices from Dow Jones, AMEX, NASDAQ, and NYSE.

- Dun & Bradstreet Business Information Reports and full Edgar filings.

- Private Company Due Diligence Reports.

- Industry News including accounting, computer, government, real estate, science, and utilities.

Exhibit 7-15: Westlaw Business & News Screen

For a complete list of the Westlaw News offerings, select the View Westlaw Directory or View Business & News Directory (see Exhibit 7-15). These directories may be browsed or searched with the ALLNEWS Search option, utilizing either Terms and Connectors or Natural Language searches (see Exhibit 7-15).

Besides all of these news sources, Westlaw offers access to the WG&L, RIA, and the BNA journals and newsletters. The WG&L and RIA journals and newsletters are discussed in Chapter 6 and the BNA newsletters are discussed later in this chapter. With all of these news and business information sources, a practitioner cannot plead ignorance to what is currently happening in tax law due to lack of access to current data!

Mertens Service

Mertens Law of Federal Income Taxation (Mertens), originally published in 1934 (in six volumes and costing $60), was developed by Randolph Paul and Jacob Mertens. By its next edition in 1942, Paul had dropped off as an author but the service more than doubled in size (thirteen volumes) and became one of the foundation treatises on income taxation. It is now offered on Westlaw and in print. The **Mertens** service has three main components: Mertens Treatise, Mertens Rulings, and Mertens Current Tax Highlights. The Treatise is a comprehensive topical service organized in over sixty chapters. While Mertens is comparable in its coverage and depth to the RIA and CCH topical tax services (see Chapter 6), it is much more oriented toward the legal profession. Consequently, courts cite it more than the other tax services. This legal orientation is evidenced by the text material being heavily footnoted. On occasion there is more footnote material than text material on a Mertens printed page. These footnotes provide more than mere citations to the relevant primary tax law sources; often they annotate cases, quote freely from the Code, Regulations, and Committee Reports, or review legislative history. Its in-depth analysis explains the intent of Congress in drafting the Code, what the Code means, and how the Internal Revenue Service has been interpreting it. Unlike other Internet services, Mertens is updated monthly rather than daily.

As part of the service, Mertens includes the full text of every Revenue Ruling and Revenue Procedure since 1954. What makes this service unique is its indexing system, enabling a researcher to find every IRS document addressing an individual Code section. Thus, it is easy to determine the IRS's current position on a particular issue. In addition, the Code, Regulations, and Rulings volumes also contain Amendment Tables, which allow the researcher to trace the statutory or administrative evolution of any provision.

The Mertens Current Highlights component provides timely information on current developments in tax laws through newsletters, journals, and alerts. Feature articles of special interest, and materials on recent developments, such as Committee hearings, new legislation, and breaking news from Capitol Hill, are included, as well as summaries of Code changes, cases, and recent IRS releases.

Finally, Mertens includes a Code Commentary, which furnishes contextual explanations of Code provisions and has "snapshot" versions of previous years' Code, Regulations, and Rulings volumes. This extremely useful feature of the Mertens service facilitates the analysis of the evolution of a tax law. For a client whose prior year's tax returns are under audit or at trial, the tax practitioner can use this feature of Mertens to reconstruct the details of the primary law sources that applied at the date of the original return.

Bittker & Lokken Service

WG&L is the publisher of **Federal Taxation of Income, Estates, and Gifts (B & L Service)**, a treatise by Boris I. Bittker and Lawrence Lokken. Since WG&L is an affiliate of West, its products are offered online through Westlaw and RIA. The five-volume published B & L Service is less comprehensive and more conceptual than many of the other topical tax services on the market. Its stated objective is to "provide guidance and orientation [to income and transfer taxation] by emphasizing the purpose, structure, and principal effects of the *Internal Revenue Code*, without bogging down in the details." It is a blend of tax law synthesis with illustrative examples and authoritative commentary and expert reasoning. Due to its style, the service sometimes reads like a collection of essays and journal articles rather than a systematic analysis of the workings of the Code. However, it is considered to be a leading authoritative treatise by professionals, and it is cited in tax cases by the various courts. Its audience includes tax professionals, attorneys, judges, and government employees.

The B & L Service may serve as a good starting point for the researcher who needs to obtain an initial grasp of a selected area of the tax law. Its citations can provide easy access into the other tax services, books, and articles or immediately direct the practitioner to the primary sources of tax law. Currently, it stands somewhere between a one-volume treatise or textbook and a free-standing comprehensive topical tax service. The published service is updated three times a year, whereas the online version is updated as needed.

BNA

Tax Management, a subsidiary of the BNA, offers over 350 products covering all areas of Federal taxes. However, it is best known in the tax community as the publisher of the BNA Tax Management Portfolios and its newsletter, the *Daily Tax Report* (DTR). Both of these products are available on LexisNexis, Westlaw, RIA Checkpoint, and BNA's own online service.

SPOTLIGHT ON TAXATION

BNA

In 1926, David Lawrence started *The United States Daily* as the country's "first truly national newspaper." In 1929, Lawrence established BNA as a division for the purpose of reporting, interpreting, and explaining the workings of the Federal government and its impact on national economics. Since 1947, BNA has been wholly employee-owned, making it the oldest employee-owned company in the United States.

Portfolios

The over 400 BNA **Tax Management Portfolios** (Portfolios) are classified into four series: U.S. Income Tax; Estates, Gifts, and Trusts; Foreign Income; and State. The size of the Portfolio library varies as topics are added, deleted, or combined. While the number of Portfolios appears vast, the series is not truly comprehensive. As with any topical service, it would be impossible to cover every issue that a practitioner may encounter in the course of business. However, practitioners that identify a Portfolio on point with their research question generally have completed their searching, as the Portfolio will address the issue in a comprehensive manner.

Each BNA Portfolio begins with a Portfolio Description, which gives a brief overview of the topic and the order in which the materials are presented. The TOC follows this description. The remainder of the Portfolio contains three sections: (A) Detailed Analysis, (B) Working Papers, and (C) Bibliography and References. The printed page numbers of these sections are preceded by the letters (A, B, or C) to indicate which portion of the Portfolio is being examined. The Portfolio sections are updated in response to important tax developments, and when necessary, the complete Portfolio is rewritten.

The Detailed Analysis section is, as the title suggests, an extremely comprehensive examination of the topic (see Exhibit 7-16). It is written by one or more tax practitioners who are experts on the topic. Practitioners are the preferred authors because they are more sensitive to the information requirements of the subscribers. For this reason, Portfolios are a favorite research tool with practitioners. As with other topical services, the Code, Regulations, Rulings, and court case opinions are integrated into the analysis with citation footnotes, or the relevant portions are included in the text. In addition, the authors identify potential pitfalls, probable IRS positions, effective tax planning techniques, and alternative

Exhibit 7-16: BNA Tax Management Portfolio

TMFEDPORT No. 522 § IV (BNA)

BNA Tax Management Portfolios
U.S. Income Series
Income, Deductions, Credits and Computation of Tax
522-3rd: Tax Aspects of Settlements and Judgments
Copyright © 2007 Tax Management, Inc.

IV. Non-Personal Injury Cases

A. Ordinary Income or Capital Gain
B. Punitive Damages
C. Antitrust Recoveries
1. Taxation of Punitive Damages
2. Taxation of Compensatory Damages
3. Reduction of includible Antitrust Recoveries by a Special Deduction
a. Compensable Injury
(1) Patent Infringement
(2) Breach of Contract or Fiduciary Duty or Relationship
(3) Antitrust Law Violations
b. Compensatory Amount
(1) Interest on Compensatory Amount
(2) Settlement of Civil Action for Damages
c. Amounts Paid or Incurred in Securing the Award or Settlement
d. Unrecovered Losses
(1) Injury Period
(2) Net Operating Losses Attributable to Compensable Injuries
(3) Application of Losses Attributable to a Compensable Injury
e. Effect on Net Operating Loss Carryovers

Amounts received pursuant to a judgment or a settlement in cases where the taxpayer's lawsuit asserts a non-personal injury (i.e., a business injury) are includible in gross income. [FN356] The only situations where payments received in non-personal injury cases are excludible from gross income are those where such payments are a substitute for amounts which are excludible from gross income under a specific statutory provision (e.g., gifts, inheritances, etc.). Example : T, the residuary beneficiary of his father's estate, was assured on a number of occasions that inequities created by an inter vivos trust set up by his parents would be remedied. T brought suit claiming that he was entitled to a large share of the income of the trust. T received a lump sum in settlement of the suit. The lump sum is excludible from gross income as a payment received in lieu of a bequest. [FN357]

means of structuring transactions in a tax-favorable manner. The value of these insights varies by author.

The Working Papers section of the Portfolios is perhaps the service's most unique and useful feature. This material includes practitioner checklists; reproduced IRS forms (interactive for online version); occasionally filled in for an illustrative fact situation; computation worksheets; sample draft agreements and contract clauses; sample board or shareholder resolutions and employment contracts; reproductions of pertinent primary sources; and other practical materials that can assist the professional in implementing tax planning techniques and procedures.

The Bibliography section of a Portfolio has a comprehensive listing of the primary (Official) and secondary (Unofficial) sources of the tax law utilized by the author(s) in the preparation of the Portfolio. Finally, this section of the Portfolio often includes a listing of journal articles and treatises that are relevant to the Portfolio topic.

The published Portfolios have a comprehensive index to aid in the search process. For each series (Income, Foreign, etc.) the Master Index provides a list by topic and Portfolio number of all the Portfolios within the series. The topics section is a very broad-based index, whereas the numerical listing is like a table of contents for the series. The Master Index is updated at least quarterly.

The Index also contains a Code section guide that traces specific Code sections to the various Portfolios within which it is discussed. The asterisk in front of the Portfolio title indicates that it contains primary coverage of this Code section topic. Finally, Portfolios may by identified by IRS Forms and Publications Finding Table. This part of the Index identifies Portfolios discussing the item and/or reproducing the form. It is particularly useful when the practitioner has questions regarding the proper completion of a particular form.

News Reports

One of the most important tax newsletters available to practitioners is the BNA DTR. Showing both breadth in coverage and a quality of analysis similar to the Tax Analysts TNT, DTR offers up-to-date information concerning statutory, administrative, and judicial tax law developments that affect state, Federal, and international taxation. In addition, the newsletter provides interviews with government officials, articles reviewing the day's events, and the full text of key documents discussed in the newsletter. In some instances these documents are not available from other tax services. Monthly indexes, including PLR and Code Section indexing, are provided and are cumulated quarterly. The DTR is available through several Internet services, on wireless devices (summaries and table of contents with URLs to full text), and by paper subscription. Subscribers may also receive notification of breaking tax news as soon as it occurs with the *DTR Real Time* e-mail alerts. DTR offers the equivalent of thirty to fifty pages of single-spaced printed copy every weekday. Because this is clearly too much data to digest every day, the DTR is organized to facilitate accessing only the material of greatest interest to the subscriber. While the content section lists only the title of each note by category, the highlights provide brief paragraphs describing the notes. Through the Internet, the subscriber can access the actual government document on which the story is based.

To link directly to the full-text documents discussed in DTR, the subscription includes access to **TaxCore**, which is a web-based source of a wide variety of full-text primary tax materials that is updated daily. It provides a categorization of sources to facilitate retrieving the document of interest. The source categories include Congressional, Treasury, Court, IRS, State and Local, White House, and International. TaxCore may be obtained separately from the DTR.

As one would expect, receiving such extensive tax news on a daily basis is an expensive proposition. However, the DTR (as well as many newsletters produced by other publishers) is available online to subscribers of various electronic tax research services. Thus, by subscribing to one of the major tax database systems, the practitioner has access to the DTR at a small or zero incremental cost.

Similar to Tax Analysts, BNA publishes a weekly newsletter as well as a daily. The *Weekly Report* coverage is similar to the DTR but more in depth. In addition, it contains articles on news and emerging tax topics. The comprehensive index makes locating items of interest easy. Besides other weekly, biweekly, and monthly newsletters, BNA publishes journals in the areas of financial planning, real estate, compensation planning, international, and estates, gifts, and trusts. It also has a research service called Tax Practice Library that includes a topical service providing analysis, examples, and practice tools such as client letters, line-by-line form guidance, checklists, and interactive tax forms.

INTERNET SITES

A growing source of tax materials that literally changes daily is the Internet. There is so much information available on the Internet that it can be overwhelming. Therefore, performing a Google or other board search on a tax topic can return so many documents that the researcher is overwhelmed and does not know where to start. A more directed search, using a tax service, is usually more effective and efficient. The web sites for the tax services discussed in Chapter 6 and this chapter are listed in Exhibit 7-17. The web addresses in this list were accurate as of the date of publication. This list should by no means be considered a comprehensive list of tax services available to the practitioner through the Internet.

Exhibit 7-17: Web Sites for Commercial Tax Services

Commercial Services	Web Sites
Bureau of National Affairs (BNA)	http://www.bna.com
Tax Management Resources (BNA)	http://www.taxmanagement.bna.com/tm/index.html
	http://www.bnatax.com/tm/index.html
Commerce Clearing House	http://tax.cchgroup.com
CCH Tax Research NetWork	http://tax.cchgroup.com/network
	http://tax.cchgroup.com/primesrc/bin/login.asp
LexisNexis	http://www.lexisnexis.com
LexisNexis Academic	http://lexis-nexis.com/universe
LexisNexis Tax & Accounting	http://www.lexisnexis.com/accountant
Lexis	http://www.lexis.com
Nexis	http://www.nexis.com
Kleinrock	http://www.kleinrock.com
Research Institute of America	http://ria.thomson.com/
RIA Checkpoint	http://checkpoint.riag.com
Tax Analysts	http://www.taxanalysts.com
Thomson	http://www.thomson.com
Thomson Tax and Accounting	http://www.thomson.com/solutions/taxacct
West	http://west.thomson.com
Westlaw	http://web2.westlaw.com

As mentioned previously, most of the primary tax source documents are accessible free of charge on the Internet. The Federal government has numerous web sites to disseminate its documents to the general public. A list of web sites offering government documents is presented in Exhibit 7-18. There are also many web sites maintained by companies, organizations, and individuals that have links to the government sites to facilitate retrieval of primary sources of the tax law. One of the most useful of these sites is **Tax and Accounting Sites Directory** (Tax Sites) at **http://www.taxsites.com** and shown in Exhibit 7-19. Tax Sites is a comprehensive index including links to Federal, state, and international primary sources as well as to most secondary source providers. It is designed to be a jumping-off point for searching for tax information, products, and services. This site offers one-stop searching when looking for tax information.

SPOTLIGHT ON TAXATION

Humorous Quotes

"The nation should have a tax system that looks like someone designed it on purpose." —William Simon

"I am proud to be paying taxes in the United States. The only thing is —I could be just as proud for half the money." —Arthur Godfrey

"If you don't drink, smoke, or drive a car, you're a tax evader." —Thomas S. Foley

continued

continued

A tax loophole is "something that benefits the other guy. If it benefits you, it is tax reform." —Russell B. Long

"Taxation with representation ain't so hot either." —Gerald Barzan

"People who complain about taxes can be divided into two classes: men and women." —Unknown

"Next to being shot at and missed, nothing is really quite as satisfying as an income tax refund." —F. J. Raymond

"[A] tax lawyer is a person who is good with numbers but does not have enough personality to be an accountant." —James D. Gordon III

Exhibit 7-18: Selected Primary Source Internet Sites

Primary Source	Web Site
Circular 230	http://www.irs.gov/pub/irs-pdf/pcir230.pdf
Code of Federal Regulations	http://www.gpoaccess.gov/cfr/
Committee Reports	http://www.thomas.gov
Congressional Record	http://www.gpoaccess.gov/crecord/index.html
Federal Register	http://www.gpoaccess.gov/fr/index.html
Federal Tax Cases	http://www.legalbitstream.com/case_law.asp?pl=c1
FedWorld.Gov	http://www.fedworld.gov/
Financial Accounting Standards Board	http://www.fasb.org
Government Accounting Office (GAO)	http://www.gao.gov
Government Printing Office (GPO) Access	http://www.gpo.gov/
House Ways and Means	http://www.house.gov/ways_means
Internal Revenue Bulletin	http://www.irs.gov/irb/
Internal Revenue Code	http://www.access.gpo.gov/uscode/title26/title26.html
Internal Revenue Manual	http://www.irs.gov/irm/index.html
Internal Revenue Service	http://www.irs.gov/
	http://www.irs.ustreas.gov/
Internal Revenue Service Forms & Publications	http://www.irs.gov/formspubs/index.html
IRS Pronouncements	http://www.legalbitstream.com/irs_materials.asp?pl=i1
Joint Committee on Taxation	http://www.house.gov/jct/
Legislative Information	http://www.thomas.gov/
Regulations	http://www.gpoaccess.gov/cfr/
Securities and Exchange Commission	http://www.sec.gov/
Senate Finance Committee	http://www.senate.gov/~finance/
Social Security Administration	http://www.ssa.gov
Tax Division Department of Justice	http://www.usdoj.gov/tax/
Tax Forms	http://www.irs.gov/formspubs/index.html
U.S. House of Representatives	http://www.house.gov/
U.S. Senate	http://www.senate.gov/
U.S. Treasury Department	http://www.ustreas.gov/
White House	http://www.whitehouse.gov/

Exhibit 7-19: Tax and Accounting Sites Directory

TAXSites.com®
Tax, Accounting and Payroll Sites Directory

Google™ Custom Search | Search |
Get better results than generic Google Search

Find a local CPA,
Accountant or Tax Pro.
Database of 35,000.
Full Details, Free Consultations

Quick Access
IRS
Taxpayer Advocacy
Federal tax forms
State tax forms
State tax departments

Tools
W-4 calculator
Financial calculators
Payroll calculators
Tax calculators

Accountant/Tax Pro,
Promote your practice.
List your firm in one of the most
widely used online directories
of accountants.

Tax
Tax Topics
Academia
Federal Tax Law
Finance and Investing
Firms and Careers
Guides-Tips-Help
Internat'l Tax
IRS Links
News and Updates
Policy and Reform
Publishers and CPE
Rates and Tables
State and Local Tax
Tax Associations
Tax Bookstore
Tax Discussions
Tax Forms and Pubs
Tax Software

Accounting
Academia
Accounting Information Systems
Accounting Software
AICPA Links
Associations
Auditing and Fraud
Certification
Discussion
Financial Reporting
Firms and Careers
General Law Directories
Government and Data
Governmental and Not-for-Profit
Accounting
International Accounting
Managerial
On-Line Accounting News
Publishers and CPE
Regulatory Bodies
Web Search
Web Services

Payroll/HR
APA Links
Associations
Benefit Admin.
Discussions
Government Regulations
Federal Topics
Forms and Pubs
Govt and Regulation
Human Resources
IRS Links
Payroll Services
Payroll Software
Retirement Plans
State Topics
Tax and Compliance

Ads by Google   Accounting Tax | State Tax | Corporate Tax | Service Tax

Home | About | Awards | Legal Disclaimer | Privacy Policy

Copyright © 1995-2006 AccountantsWorld, LLC
E-Mail: webmaster@taxsites.com

SUMMARY

The market supports a variety of tax research products, all designed to facilitate locating relevant sources by practitioners. Whether the service is categorized as legal or tax, all have their place in tax research. The enormous databases of services such as LexisNexis and Westlaw make them very attractive. On the other hand, the ability to access materials on a single CD without having to connect to the Internet is appealing to many sole practitioners and small firms. There is a wide range of products between these extremes. Practitioners must decide which media and tax products best serve the needs of their business at a price they can afford. With technology and software advances occurring at a rapid pace, what seemed to be an innovative product when this text was written may be passé by the time it is read. The success of tax practitioners often is contingent on their information providers being flexible and quickly adjusting to the changing technology needs of a dynamic industry like tax and accounting.

TAX TUTOR

Reinforce the tax research information covered in this chapter by completing the online tutorials located at the *Federal Tax Research* web site: **http://academic.cengage.com/taxation/raabe**

KEY WORDS

By the time you complete this chapter, you should be comfortable discussing each of the following terms. If you need additional review of any of these items, return to the appropriate material in the chapter or consult the glossary to this text.

Bureau of National Affairs (BNA)
Daily Tax Report
Federal Research Library
Federal Taxation of Income, Estates, and Gifts
    (B & L Service)
KeyCite
KeySearch
KWIC
Lexis
LexisNexis
LexisNexis Academic
Mertens
Natural Language

Nexis
OneDisc Premium
Tax Analysts
Tax and Accounting Sites Directory
Tax Center
Tax Management Portfolios
Tax Notes
Tax Notes Today
TaxCore
Terms and Connectors (Boolean)
Weekly Report
Westlaw
Wildcard characters

DISCUSSION QUESTIONS

1. When were Lexis and Nexis started? What topic areas are covered by each?

2. What tax sources are not included in the LexisNexis offerings?

3. What is the tax service offered by LexisNexis and what advantage does it provide over the other LexisNexis services?

4. LexisNexis Tax Center includes CCH archives of the SFTR. When would the archives be useful to a tax researcher?

5. What is a natural language search and when is it useful?

6. How is a space between keywords interpreted by LexisNexis, Tax Analysts, and Westlaw?

7. When is it beneficial to use a date restriction on a search?

8. If a LexisNexis Tax Center search retrieves "too many" documents, what can a researcher do to reduce the results?

9. What information must the researcher know to use the Get a Document feature in the LexisNexis Tax Center?

10. If the researcher is searching for a case and only knows the taxpayer's name, what option should be used to locate the case in the LexisNexis Tax Center service?

11. What media companies dominate as providers of tax/law research services?

12. What is LexisNexis Academic?

13. When using the Search Tab in LexisNexis Academic, where are tax materials located?

14. What are the steps in using the browse option in LexisNexis Academic?

15. LexisNexis offers a KWIC document view mode. What is KWIC?

16. What is the Tax Analysts mission? Who started this nonprofit organization?

17. What is the keyword default treatment of a string of words in the Tax Analysts FRL?

18. What are the two editorial services offered by Tax Analysts FRL?

19. What is OneDisc Premium offered by Tax Analysts?

20. What organization sued the IRS to gain access to FSA Memorandums?

21. Tax Analysts is known for its two outstanding publications *Tax Notes* and TNT. Describe these two publications.

22. Who designed Westlaw? What is its target market?

23. What tax services are available through Westlaw? How does this compare with LexisNexis offerings?

24. The opening screen in Westlaw is oriented to what type of searches?

25. How and why would a practitioner want to select personalized tabs to add to Westlaw?

26. Explain what function the following connectors perform in Westlaw: %, +s, and !

27. Westlaw provides two unique features, the Best locator and ResultsPlus. Discuss each of these features.

28. What is KeySearch in Westlaw?

29. How does one locate news documents in Westlaw?

30. What makes the footnotes in Mertens unique?

31. Why is the Mertens Rulings service unique?

32. What is the scope or objective of the B & L Service?

33. When would a practitioner likely start a research project by using the B & L Service?

34. BNA is best known as a provider of what tax services?

35. How is each volume of the BNA *Tax Management Portfolios* arranged?

36. Describe the Working Papers section of a BNA *Tax Management Portfolio*.

37. Compare the contents of Tax Analysts TNT with BNA DTR.

38. What is the BNA TaxCore? What is its purpose?

39. What information is available on the Tax and Accounting Sites Directory web site?

40. Why would a practitioner pay for tax service when most tax primary sources are available through the Internet for free?

EXERCISES

41. Use the Federal area in LexisNexis Tax Center to answer the following questions.
    a. What sources are included in the IRS Bulletins, Letter Rulings, and Memoranda Decisions?
    b. Which law journals are listed in General Planning—Conference paper and Law Reviews?
    c. What Tax Analysts products are provided in General References and Reports?
    d. Select LexisNexis Tax Advisor Federal Topical under the General References & Reports databases. Perform a natural language search to determine the tax treatment of stock redeemed from a deceased shareholder. Perform the same search using terms and connectors. List your natural search question and the number of documents it retrieved. Provide the same information for the terms and connectors search. Explain why one was a more effective search.

42. Use LexisNexis Tax Center to answer the following questions.
    a. What is the difference in the function of the arrow that appears after the CCH SFTR and the arrow after the CCH SFTR Topical Index?
    b. Click on the More Sources button for Code & Regulations. What other source documents are listed that are not redundant sources of the Code, and Regulations?
    c. For the CCH SFTR, what is the earliest year in the Achieves?
    d. Select the Specialized Tax Planning tab. What chapter in the Farm Income Tax Manual discusses tax savings for farmers?

43. Use LexisNexis Tax Center to answer the following questions.
    a. Select the Tax New Tab. What are the service sources for the Top Tax New?
    b. Select the Tax New Tab. What journals are listed under Accounting with blue arrows after their titles?
    c. Select A to Z Source lists. What documents do you find under the letters Q and Z?
    d. Select Tax Topics. Which entries have Related Topics?

44. Use the LexisNexis Academic Legal Search option to answer the following questions.
    a. Perform a search of the Tax Law Review Articles, Combined for articles by *Yoram Keinan*. How many articles do you find? Which of these articles discusses spin-off reorganizations?
    b. What other methods besides keywords are available for searching the Federal & State case library?
    c. When using Terms and Connectors, what is the maximum number that may be used with the "w/#" connector? What are the approximate word numbers for a sentence and a paragraph?
    d. One of the sources in the Tax Law library is *The Tax Adviser*. What is the coverage period for this journal and how often is this journal published (Hint: use the "i" button)?

45. Use the LexisNexis Academic Legal Search option to answer the following questions.
    a. Discuss what information is available in the Related Links box when Tax Law library is chosen versus Federal & State cases?
    b. Select Federal & State Codes, and enter the terms *like-kind and exchange* using Terms and Connectors. What are the U.S. Code Service Title numbers and titles for the retrieved documents?
    c. Under the Federal & State Codes, how are Federal tax laws listed? What title does it list for the IRC?
    d. What types of sources are provided in the Tax Law library?

46. Use LexisNexis Academic, answer the following questions.
    a. Select the Business option and enter *Intuit* as the company name for the Dossier. What are Intuit's address, ticker symbol, and primary SIC number?
    b. Select the Business option and the Accounting library. Within the Accounting library select: GAAP Guide Levels A, B, C, D, then enter the terms: *capital leases* in a Natural Language search. Narrow the search by entering *improvements*. How many documents and at what levels (Level A, B, etc.) are retrieved? What are the dates of the articles?
    c. Select the News option. What index terms may be added to the search?
    d. Select the News option. Provide the title, author, and date of the most recent New York Times article on stock redemptions.

47. Use the Tax Analysts Federal Tax Explanations to answer the following questions.
    a. What chapter and section discusses the general tax treatment for feeder organizations of tax-exempt entities?
    b. In the Index, what chapter and section is listed as discussing wash sales?
    c. With a keyword search, find the chapters and sections listed for the key terms: *wash sale*. List the results.
    d. Explain why your responses to b and c above differ.

48. Using Tax Analysts, answer the following questions.
    a. With Federal Tax Explanations and Code Section Summaries databases perform a keyword search using the following words: *employee business expense*. Describe the results when the search type is: (1) word or phrase (2) and (3) or (4) proximity.

b. The Quick Reference Tables provide information on the per diem deemed substantiation. What Revenue Procedure is listed as a source document for the most current time period? What Code sections does this Rev. Proc. address?

c. For what does the IRS acronym COGS stand? (Hint: Look in the Tax Directory.)

d. What is the title of the first article in the most current issue of *Tax Practice*? Provide the date, volume, and number of the issue.

49. Using Tax Analysts, answer the following questions.

a. Examine the articles in the most recent issue of *Tax Notes* available to you. Is the information in any of these articles essentially the same as articles in TNT for the same period? Elaborate.

b. Select an article from the Analysis section in a recent *Tax Notes*. Provide a proper citation for the article and a brief synopsis.

c. Select an IRS Field Attorney Advice from a recent TNT. Provide the Code section to which it applies and a brief synopsis of the issue and conclusion. Provide the date of the *Tax Notes*.

50. Use the Westlaw Tax tab to answer the following questions.

a. What is the date and title of the most recent Spotlight Article found in the Weekly Tax Updates?

b. What is the Westlaw abbreviation for the IRS new releases (Hint: look in Find a Federal document)?

c. What services are listed under the Commercial Tax Services that are published by Thomson-West?

d. Provide the full citation for the most recent article in the *Journal of Corporate Taxation* that discusses consolidated returns.

51. Use Westlaw to answer the following questions.

a. What symbol is used for the connector "but not"? Explain the use of the universal characters "*" and "!". What does "+n" mean and how large can "n" be?

b. In the Directory under the What's New heading, what new database was added within the past month?

c. What is the abbreviation to enter in the Search these Databases box if you are interested in using the RIA complete Analysis of the Tax Act—Historical?

d. In the Directory of Professionals located in the Taxation Library, how many professionals are listed with the last name of Sanders?

52. Use the Westlaw Tax tab to answer the following questions.

a. What is the most current mid-term annual adjusted federal rate?

b. In what area of taxation does Zaritsky have the most WG&L tax treatise titles?

c. What is Saltzman: IRS Practice and Procedure?

d. What is the title of Chapter 12C in Mertens (Hint: Use TOC for Mertens found in More of Commercial Tax Services)?

53. Use the Westlaw service to answer the following questions.

a. What synonyms does the Westlaw thesaurus provide for the following terms: surgery, installment, and costume?

b. In what chapter of the White Collar Crime Thomson-West Tax Treatise is RICO the primary topic?

c. What Code section is discussed in PLR 200715002?

d. What is the most recent *New York Times* headline that has a foreign country listed as the location of the story?

54. Use the Mertens service to answer the following questions.

a. The sale of a patent by the original individual inventor generally is treated as a capital gain, even for a professional inventor. Search for substantiation of this statement, using all three keyword search options: Terms and Connectors, Natural Language, and Template. How many documents does each search return? In what chapter and section was the relevant discussion of the law found for each keyword search option?

b. What is the topic matter covered by Chapters 9, 18, and 62 (Hint: For the TOC of Mertens, use More in Commercial Tax Services of the Tax Tab)?

c. In a Template Keyword search, use the terms: foreign earned income. What chapter covers this topic? What BNA Portfolios and what Bittker & Lokken Service documents does ResultsPlus suggest?

d. When was the Mertens service last updated?

55. Use the BNA Internet web site (**http://www.bna.com**) to retrieve a sample of TaxCore (Hint: select Tax & Accounting in Product Information, then find TaxCore).

a. What is the most recent IRS transcript available? Provide the title, date of the transcript, and a brief description of its contents.

b. The TOC main view lists all of the documents available for the dates available. What is the most recent IRS News Release (IR) provided? Provide the citation, Code section to which it applies, and date it was issued by the IRS.

c. What is the most current PLR listed for the Code sections between §351 and §368? Provide its proper citation, Code section to which it applies, title, and date it was released by the IRS.

56. Use the BNA Tax Management Portfolios to answer the following questions.

a. What is the Portfolio number (and section) that discusses mineral property advance royalties?

b. In the Portfolio identified in part a, what is demonstrated in Worksheet 4?

c. What is the Portfolio number (and section) that discusses the deductibility of attorney's fees for bankrupt corporations?

d. In the Portfolio identified in part c, what is the state Tax Management Portfolio listed in the Unofficial Bibliography?

57. Use the BNA Internet web site (**http://www.bna.com**) to retrieve a sample of the DTR (Hint: select All Products and scroll down to DTR).

a. What is the date and number of the most recent sample available?

b. What is the title of the first article listed in the TOC under the category Federal Tax & Accounting? Provide the title and a brief summary of the article.

c. Use the Search All Issues function (top of the opening screen) to find the most recent Revenue Ruling cited within a heading. Provide the Revenue Ruling title as well as its citation.

d. What is the most recent Tax Court case reported? Provide the case's complete citation.

58. Use the Tax and Accounting Sites Directory (**http://www.taxsites.com**) to answer the following questions.
    a. Where does the tax link for timber in Tax Topics take you?
    b. What are the different headings under Tax Bookstore? Under what heading is this textbook listed?
    c. What is the latest IR discussed on the IRS Newsroom web site?
    d. Select Firms & Careers, then Career Search: Tax & Accounting. What location names are mentioned in the listings?

59. Surf the web and find three noncommercial tax sites that are not mentioned in this text. Provide the URL and a general description of the information provided on the site.

60. Visit the web sites of two commercial tax services discussed in this text. Describe the free news services they offer to the public. Evaluate the usefulness of these news services.

RESEARCH CASES

61. Three friends form a film production partnership. Will the operations of this partnership qualify for the domestic production activity deduction in the current year?

62. Can a business traveler to your town use the high-cost-city meal allowance for travel away from home overnight? What would the meal allowance be for a business trip to Washington, D.C.?

63. Nancy and Curtis had not spoken to each other since their mother's funeral in 1991. Nancy broke the family discord this year by selling Curtis a family heirloom, basis to her $14,000, for $1,700. What are the tax consequences of this transaction?

64. Zarco, a very profitable corporation, was owned by three shareholders, Julio, Tilly, and Martinez. Julio and Martinez purchased all of Tilly's Zarco Corporation stock for $50,000 and a $100,000 promissory demand note that was guaranteed by Zarco. Tilly demanded payment on the note, and Zarco, rather than Julio and Martinez, paid the note. What are the tax consequences of this transaction?

65. Dolores is a limited partner in the Houston Hopes partnership. This year, she was forced under the terms of the agreement to make a $50,000 contribution to capital because the general partners were unable to meet the operating expenses of the entity. Dolores's basis in the partnership prior to the contribution was $40,000, but her at-risk amount was zero because of her limited partner status and her prior-year pass-through losses. What is her at-risk amount after the $50,000 cash call?

66. Steve is a member of a local church. May he deduct as a charitable contribution the commuting expenses for the Sundays that he is assigned to usher?

67. Phil is a used-car manager. To obtain advanced skills in management and marketing, he enrolls in the weekend MBA program at State University, twenty

miles from his home. Does Phil qualify for an educational credit? What items associated with Phil's education are deductible as an employee business expense, assuming that he receives no reimbursements for any of them?

68. Frank and Sharon have been married for five years. Without Frank's knowledge, Sharon has been operating an escort service from the local pub. This year's operations were very profitable. In fact, if Sharon had reported any of the net escort income, their joint Federal income tax liability would have increased by $50,000. When Sharon finally is nabbed by the police, she is taken to jail. Frank is unable to locate any of Sharon's earnings in their personal bank or brokerage accounts. Can Frank fend off the IRS's charge that he should pay the $50,000 in tax, plus interest and penalties, from his salary as an engineer?

69. Maria has an unusually strong constitution, which produces the highest quality blood and plasma available for transfusion. She manages to stay healthy while donating blood at the hospital two or three times a week. For each blood donation, the hospital pays Maria $175. Maria drives forty miles round-trip to the hospital to make her donation. Moreover, she spends about $135 every month for vitamins and other pills prescribed by her physician to ensure that her general health and blood quality do not degenerate in light of her frequent donations. Last year, Maria quit all of her part-time jobs and now survives financially solely by these blood donations. Specify the tax consequences of this regular activity.

70. Chang, a brain surgeon, pays for the *Journal of Brain Research* under the three-year plan; he paid $3,000 this year for a three-year subscription to the weekly scientific journal, which charges $1,500 for an annual renewal. In what year(s) can Chang deduct this $3,000?

71. Handy Corporation assists its relocated executives by buying their homes if an acceptable sale cannot be completed before the move. Purchase is made at the appraised value. What is the nature of Handy's gain or loss on the subsequent sale?

72. Walt was convicted of murder and sent to prison for life. Walt continued to profess his innocence. His sister, Wanda, believed him. After spending three years in law school and two years gathering facts, she proved that he was innocent. Walt and Wanda assigned the book, movie, and photo rights concerning their story to Sundance Films for $500,000. How is this payment treated by Walt and Wanda?

73. Hugo was burying his (dead) dog when he unearthed 100,000 certificates of ITT bearer bonds, current value $4,000,000. He speculated that they had been placed there by the (also dead) former owner of Hugo's home, at a time when they were worth nearly $400,000. Hugo did not sell the bonds by the end of the year. Must Hugo recognize any gross income with respect to the bonds?

74. Karla is a single parent with two children ages seven and eleven. She is a full-time student and earns $12,000. Both of her children receive dividends and capital gains from mutual funds started for them by their grandparents. Karla has elected to include her children's income on her return for the kiddie tax computation. Since it is on her tax return, does her children's income affect the computation of Karla's earned income credit?

75. At gunpoint, Roger lent $2,000 from the cash register at his hardware store to four large youths who told Roger that they wanted a loan to set up their own business. Not having the phone number of any of the sprightly entrepreneurs, Roger could not recover any of the invested funds. Can Roger claim any deduction with respect to this loan? In what tax year?

76. Phyllis, a Virginia resident, owns some property in Florida. Every year, she travels to Florida (coincidentally, during baseball's spring training season) to inspect the property, initiate repairs, interview new tenants, and search for new properties in which to invest. She also attends about twenty ball games. Determine Phyllis's deductible travel expenses.

77. Bruce wanted to be an Olympic skater. His family paid $12,000 in 2006 and $14,000 in 2007 for travel and training expenses related to skating practices and competitions. Bruce made the 2008 U.S. Olympic team. The U.S. Olympic Committee is an exempt organization. How much of Bruce's expenses are deductible and when?

78. Harold installed a safe and an alarm system and bought a German shepherd dog to protect his vintage paperback and comic book collection. What are his deductible items?

79. Donna's and Albert's children attend a parochial grade school. The school charges $1,500 annual tuition and $200 for uniforms for Donna's children, but only $500 tuition and $100 for uniforms for Albert's children because he is a member of the congregation. Albert contributed $800 to the church this year. Can Donna and Albert withdraw amounts out of their children's Coverdell Educational Savings Accounts to pay for this private primary education? What is the amount of Albert's charitable contribution for the year?

80. Julie is a professional singer in the City Symphony Chorus (CSS). CSS requires that all members wear traditional formal wear (i.e., $500 tuxedos for the men and $300 long black gowns for the women) during performances. In addition, because of her annual $15,000 contribution to the CSS patron drive, Julie is a member of the symphony's board of directors. The board chooses the works to be performed, sites for the concerts, and the resident conductor. How much of Julie's $15,300 expenditures on behalf of the exempt orchestra this year can she deduct?

81. Tony, a single parent, spent $3,600 on after-school care for his six-year-old son. Tony received $1,200 as aid to families with dependent children from the State Department of Social Services (DSS) for child care as part of the welfare assistance program in which he is enrolled. In determining his child-care credit, how much of the DSS payments are included in gross income, and what is the amount of Tony's child-care costs for computing the child-care credit?

82. Carmella really wants to be an actor but she is having trouble getting that "big break" she so desperately needs. To keep food on the table, Carmella has a small tax preparation business and nets about $30,000 a year. She has received small parts in several movies and on television, earning about $10,000. However, she incurs substantial expenses associated with her acting career that amount to $15,000. Can Carmella deduct her acting expenses and/or can Carmella qualify for the qualified performing artist deduction?

83. Yukio was seriously injured when he fell through an open manhole. Yukio was awarded compensatory damages of $500,000 for his injuries, loss of current wages, reduced future earning ability, and for all of the suffering he incurred and may incur in the future. Is any of the settlement taxable to Yukio? Specifically is the amount for lost wages taxable?

84. The IRS acquires vast amounts of sensitive information about individual taxpayers. The government is required to keep this information confidential. May a state child support agency obtain access to an individual's Form 1040 information in determining one's ability to pay child support?

85. The farmers in Whitman County are concerned about the price they are receiving for their products. They have decided to create the Whitman County Farm Commission, whose purpose is to encourage farmers to band together when selling their products, educate the legislators on farming issues, and instruct farmers on methods to control pests and weeds in the most environmentally safe manner. Does this organization qualify for tax-exempt status?

ADVANCED CASES

These cases require that you have access to research materials other than the Federal tax law and related services. Consult with your instructor before beginning your work to be certain that the necessary research resources for these cases are available to you.

86. A friend of yours took a job in the air transportation industry. Knowing that you are taking tax courses, she asks you about the excise taxes that her firm must pay. Indicating that excise taxes for the air transportation industry are not generally covered in any of your classes, you tell your friend that you will see what you can find out about this for her. What did you learn about excise taxes for the air transportation industry?

87. Which of the following receipts are taxable to the state high school athletic association as unrelated business income?

- Ticket revenues from the basketball tournaments

- Advertising revenues from the programs sold at the tournaments

- Subsidy from the state budget for the tournaments

- Payment from Grand Central Limited to be the official sponsor of the tournaments

88. Heather had named Brenda the executrix of her estate. Brenda had no experience in this domain, but she filed the return, and the estate paid a Federal death tax of $2 million. This year, Heather's son Dylan, studying for a master's degree in taxation, discovered that Brenda had not reported any of Heather's realty in the gross estate and that an additional $250,000 in taxes and interest is due. The IRS then assessed various penalties, totaling $30,000. How can the estate, now administered by Dylan, avoid this penalty?

89. Last year, the Waltons were injured when an electrical cable that city workers were repairing landed in their swimming pool. The Waltons sued the city and were awarded damages as well as prejudgment interest. The state characterized all amounts paid to the Waltons as compensation for injuries. The Waltons assume that none of the amounts they received are taxable because of the state's treatment of the prejudgment interest as an element of the injury compensation. Are the Waltons correct in their assessment of the law?

90. Clyde Miller, a Mississippi resident, has lived with Lenora Waitsfield and her two children for the past five years. Clyde and Lenora are not married and her children are from a former relationship. The children have no legal relationship with Clyde, yet Clyde has supported the children and Lenora since they have been cohabiting. Clyde is claiming Lenora and the children as dependents on his tax return. He also has been claiming an earned income credit based on Lenora's children, who are both younger than age seventeen. Is Clyde correct in his treatment of Lenora and the children on his tax return? (Hint: State law considerations of the relationship between Clyde and Lenora are relevant.)

EXTENSIVE CASES

91. Thomas and Nicole Eirgo have been married for twenty years and have three children, Candice, age eighteen, and twin boys, Trevor and Julian, age twelve. Nicole has an undergraduate degree in accounting and worked in public accounting while Thomas was obtaining his law degree. Five years ago they quit their jobs and started TechKnow, a C corporation that develops legal and tax software specifically for accountants and lawyers with high-tech clients. Thomas and Nicole work more than full time at TechKnow and have received only modest salaries. No dividends have been paid. The business has finally started to make substantial profits, but success, unfortunately, has brought problems. Thomas and Nicole have very different opinions regarding TechKnow's future. Thomas would like to continue to reinvest most of the profits for the development of software for other specialties, whereas Nicole would like to focus on the lines they have and enjoy their success by distributing some of the profits. Since they cannot come to an agreement, the earnings are being retained, and no new software is being developed.

These business disagreements are having a disastrous effect on their marriage. The only solution Thomas and Nicole see is to divorce. As might be expected, Thomas and Nicole cannot decide on how to separate their ownership interests in TechKnow. Some options they are considering include redeeming Nicole's stock, having Thomas and/or the children buy the stock, or dividing the business in some manner between the two.

One thing Nicole has decided is to fulfill a lifelong dream of obtaining a doctorate degree in accounting. She will be entering a PhD program in the fall, at which time the divorce should be final. Since Candice also will be attending college, she will live in an apartment with her mother. Thomas will keep the house, and the boys will live with him. Thomas will pay Nicole alimony and child support while she and Candice are in school. The terms and amounts of these payments will be determined at the time the divorce is final.

Advise the Eirgos on the tax consequences of the above events. Support your conclusions with primary citations.

92. Chris and Sue are 50 percent shareholders in the BackBone personal service corporation. BackBone provides chiropractic services in four small towns: Troy, Union, Vista, and Willow. Chris is the main chiropractor in the Troy office, and Sue heads the Vista office. The two other offices have chiropractor employees running the practices. But that is where Backbone's trouble lies. Charlie, the main chiropractor in the Willow office, does not see eye-to-eye with Chris and Sue on management styles. Charlie does not take well to any interference in how he runs the office, the hours he keeps, or therapy techniques he employs.

Firing Charlie is not an option for two reasons. First, it is difficult to find chiropractors who want to work and live in small towns. Second, and most important, if Charlie were to leave BackBone, he would start his own practice in Willow. He is very good with patients and easily would be able to take at least 80 percent of the clients in Willow. Sue and Chris have noticed that some of the patients in Union drive to Willow because they prefer Charlie to Joe, the chiropractor in their Union office.

Chris and Sue do not want to compete with Charlie and would prefer that the parties would come up with some arrangement that would make everyone happy. They already pay Charlie handsomely, so more salary is not the main solution. For Charlie, it seems to be a matter of control. Chris and Sue may be willing to give up control of the Willow office, but they do not want to completely lose the profits this office adds to BackBone.

Chris and Sue have come to you for some suggestions on how to solve this problem with the lowest tax cost. Provide BackBone with several options and the tax consequences of each. Support your conclusions with primary citations.

Citators and Other Finding Devices

Chapter Outline

Learning Objectives

- Understand the function of the citator in the tax research process.

- Use the indexing systems in each of the most popular tax citators.

- Know the abbreviation and reference conventions used by the most popular tax citators.

- Update research by using materials in the most popular tax citators.

- Know the comparative strengths and weaknesses of the most popular tax citators.

- Understand the basic and advanced citator functions of Internet resources.

B ESIDES CONFRONTING THE TREMENDOUS volume of tax law, tax practitioners face the added dilemma that the tax law is in a constant state of change. Each year new laws are passed that amend the *Internal Revenue Code* (IRC) and new Regulations are issued to provide guidance and revise interpretations of the Code. Every day administrative pronouncements are issued and court cases are decided. This daily change in the tax law makes it very difficult for a tax practitioner to know what law is current and what has been superseded or overruled. This chapter provides the methodology for ensuring that the tax laws, cases, and administrative documents supporting a client's tax position are up-to-date and still controlling law.

Recall from the research process explained in Chapter 2, an evaluation of the relevant primary authority must occur before conclusions can be developed. The evaluation of tax authority includes not only determining whether the authority is still valid but also making judgments about the precedential value of the primary sources. How citators help in this evaluation process is the focus of this chapter.

CITATORS

Law relies heavily on the **precedential value** of cases, which can be defined as the legal authority established by the case. This legal authority of prior cases is considered when judges are writing opinions in subsequent cases that have similar facts or legal issues. Tax law also relies on the precedential value of tax cases and administrative rulings for guidance. The tax law attempts to maintain continuity in treatment of similar issues so taxpayers can anticipate the application of the law to their own situations. Each appellate opinion sets a precedent that applies to later cases.

What Is a Citator?

The law is constantly in a state of flux, and, again, tax law is no exception. The Code is changed frequently by passage of tax bills. Regulations are proposed, finalized, and withdrawn. Administrative rulings are issued, modified, superseded, and revoked or made obsolete by changes in the tax law. A case decided at one level may be appealed by one or both parties. The higher court can overrule the lower court's decision. Infrequently, a court may see a flaw in the reasoning it or another (equal or lower) court used in deciding an earlier case, or a court may use a different line of reasoning to reach a distinct decision in an area previously reviewed by other courts. When a court takes any action that relies on, rejects, or affects the holding of another case, the acting court refers to the affected case in its opinion. All of this results in a tangle of interreferences among vast numbers of cases.

Along with statutory law, practitioners rely on administrative rulings and court decisions to interpret tax law and argue the appropriate treatment of their clients' tax transactions. They must be able to determine if subsequent events have affected the legal standing of the sources upon which they rely. Thus, they need a tool to help them ascertain which legal sources provide strong precedents and which have little or no value. The tax professional could follow the reference threads from case to case or ruling to ruling, but this would be extremely tedious and would only identify earlier cases and not later cases that may have altered or overruled the case or ruling of interest. This latter information is critical for determining the validity of the case of interest. Fortunately, citators provide this service by following the threads in subsequent cases and summarize, in shorthand form, where the threads lead, and what they mean.

A citator is a tool through which a tax researcher can learn the history of a legal source and evaluate the strength of its holdings. Before a researcher relies on the opinion in a case or analysis in a ruling (or even commits the time to read the document), it is important to ascertain its legal standing. Thus, when a case or ruling relevant to a client's tax situation is found, it is imperative that a citator be examined to determine how later legal sources have considered the document of interest. Since the legal profession long has recognized the need for this specialized information, citators were developed in the late 1800s, a hundred years before computer searches were possible.

To avoid confusion, it is important to learn the specific terminology that describes references between cases. When one case refers to another case, it **cites** the latter case. The case making reference to another case is called the **citing case**. The case that is referenced is the **cited case**. The citing case will contain the name of the cited case and where the cited case can be found. The reference is called a **citation**. A **citator** is a service that indexes cited cases, gives their full citations, and lists the citing cases and where each citing case can be found. A significant older case, one that establishes an important legal principle, may have been cited by hundreds of other cases. Thus, its entry in a citator would be extremely long and complex. A very recent case, or one examining a narrow aspect of the law, would have few cites and thus a short entry.

A citator will not provide all types of information about a case or a ruling. For instance, it does not guide the researcher to documents related to a case or ruling that do not specifically cite it. Citators also may not always indicate when a case or ruling is no longer valid because of changes in the Code, unless the Code itself specifically identifies the case or a subsequent document makes a specific reference to the Code overriding the case. This is because citators are created by searching primary sources for cites to the case or ruling. A practitioner could perform the same search by using the case name or its official cite in a keyword search of databases containing all primary sources. Without access to a tax service, you might try a simple Google or Yahoo search on the case name. However, sifting through the results would be an arduous task and very inefficient.

Given the tremendous number of court cases and rulings issued annually, the citator is a vital tool in the research process. If the primary sources have not been checked through a citator, the research process is not complete. Thus, only careless or improperly trained practitioners rely on legal sources that have not been checked through a citator.

The various commercial citators organize the lists of citing cases in distinctive schemes. Depending on the researcher's purpose, one citator may be more appropriate than another. For example, one citator may only list citations that have a major impact on the logic or holding of the cited case. Another may list all citations. A researcher, initially checking to make sure a case has not been overruled, would prefer the former. The citations may be annotated to indicate the type of impact the citing case has on the cited case (e.g., modified, overruled, followed). A trial court case may be appealed, and each appellate court that hears the case creates additional citations. Because each of these decisions may be cited in other documents, a citator can organize cases by jurisdictional level. As each citator is discussed in this chapter, you should consider its suitability for specific research applications. Citators are not a one-size-fits-all type of research tool.

It is important for the researcher to consider a case in context, to trace its judicially derived decision, and to monitor the reaction of subsequent court cases. This is even more important when the opinion is innovative. By using a citator properly, the researcher can review subsequent courts' reactions and determine the strength of the precedent established by the opinion. However, before turning to a case, the Code and Regulations, the foundation for tax research, should be read and analyzed. Remember, cases and rulings are reviewed to provide guidance in interpreting the statutory and administrative tax law.

Changing the Tax Law—Courts and IRS

Tax Cases

There are ninety-four Federal District Courts. Each state has at least one district, and New York City and the District of Columbia have their own. Puerto Rico, the Virgin Islands, Guam, and the Northern Mariana Islands also have District Courts. These courts along with the other federal courts publish over 200 decisions in a year giving guidance on taxes. Besides these decisions, the Tax Court hands down about 450 memorandum and summary decisions in a year.

Revenue Rulings and Procedures

The IRS is releasing fewer published rulings currently than it did in the past. For example, in 2006, the IRS issued sixty-three Revenue Rulings and fifty-six Revenue Procedures. Looking back twenty years to 1986, the IRS was issuing more than 200 Revenue Rulings and Procedures in a year. This is about a 42 percent drop in the number of published guiding rulings. In the mid-1990s, the IRS decided to cut back on its issuances of Revenue Rulings, thus causing the reduction in administrative rulings.

With so much tax law being promulgated on a yearly basis, tax professionals need citators to help determine which cases and rulings are still valid and which have been modified, reversed, revoked, and superseded.

When a legal source has been identified as pertinent to a research question, the first step in reviewing the document is to check it through a citator. For instance, say that a tax researcher has identified *Corn Products Refining Company* (a 1955 Supreme Court holding) as pertinent to a research project. The holding in the case might help or hurt the client's case. The task, then, is to find out how strong the holding in the *Corn Products* case is. The researcher must determine how subsequent cases evaluated the legal reasoning and findings of the *Corn Products* decision. In addition, the researcher must determine if changes in the Code made the case obsolete.

Commercial Citators

Of the four citators examined in this chapter, three have editions that exclusively cover tax cases—Commerce Clearing House (CCH), Research Institute of America (RIA), and Shepard's—and one includes tax cases in its law citator—Westlaw. The CCH, RIA, and Shepard's commercial citators are available in published or electronic formats, although the published format is becoming used less frequently over time in the tax practice. Westlaw does not have a published counterpart. CCH provides its citator as part of its Standard Federal Tax Reporter tax service, whereas the RIA Citator 2nd is offered separately from its tax services. Shepard's Federal Tax Citator is offered through the Internet exclusively by Lexis. The accuracy of the case citations is very important; consequently, this will be the focus of the citators review in this chapter.

One of the advantages of the CCH and RIA citators is that they allow the researcher to enter case names or citations. Shepard's and Westlaw, on the other hand, accept only citations. All of the citators furnish templates and/or guidance for entering the citations for documents of interest to the researcher. The citations reproduced by CCH are *general*, directing the researcher to the first page of the citing case; the other citators give *local* citations (also called a pinpoint citation), directing the researcher to the exact page where the cited case is mentioned in the citing case. For example, *Gregory v. Helvering* (293 US 465) is cited in the Second Circuit Court of Appeals case *Bausch & Lomb Optical Co.*, on page 78 in the *Federal Reporter 2d Series* case reporter. The CCH citation indicating this citing is *Bausch & Lomb Optical Co.*, 267 F2d 75 (first page of the *Bausch & Lomb Optical Co.* case), whereas the RIA, Shepard's, and Westlaw citators have the cite as *Bausch & Lomb Optical Co.*, 267 F2d 78. Having local citations that pinpoint the discussion of the case of interest can be a real time saver when the citing case is long.

The discussion in this chapter concentrates on the Internet versions of the citators. The published versions are briefly reviewed to give a sense of the origins and evolution of citators, as well as some concept of the physical scope of the information contained in citators. While the Internet versions generally are no more than the paper publication in electronic form, this may not be evident to the user.

The *Nader Soliman* case (506 US 168, 113 S Ct 701, 71 AFTR 2d 93-463, 93-1 USTC ¶ 50,014, 121 L Ed 2d 634) will be utilized for demonstrating the various features of the citators. This case involves the deductibility of home office expenses (§ 280A). It has an interesting judicial history, as it started in the Tax Court and was affirmed by the Fourth Circuit Court of Appeals and then reversed by the Supreme Court. The Supreme Court case was then superseded by new congressional legislation causing § 280A to be amended.

Shepard's

Shepard's was the first major publisher to truly understand the commercial value of citators. It became the leading publisher of citators and thus its name has become synonymous with the act of citing. In fact, the process of evaluating the validity of a case and locating additional authority is called "**Sheparding**" a case. The **Shepard's Citators** (Shepard's) are currently available in print, on CD-ROM, and on the Internet through LexisNexis, who acquired Shepard's in mid-1990s. Many attorneys view Shepard's as *the* citator service and all other services as mere imitations. This may have been true at one point in time, but the current competitors have just as much to offer as the "original."

SPOTLIGHT ON TAXATION

Factoid

In 1873, Frank Shepard of Chicago introduced his first citator as an aid to legal research. This citator was actually printed on gummed labels, listing each case cited in another case. Before Shepard created these gummed labels, those reading a case that cited another case would jot a note in the reporter margins of the cited case, to signal that they might later need to rely on the cited case. In 1900, Shepard's began to annotate the cases by indicating the treatment of the case by the citing cases (i.e., explained, overruled, etc.).

Since that time, Shepard's has evolved into over twenty different citators that cover virtually every case reporter series, as well as for specialized areas of the law, such as *Shepard's Federal Tax Citator* (FTC) for tax research. Because of its dominance in citator publishing and the breadth of its coverage, legal researchers often refer to the process of evaluating the validity of a case as "Sheparding" a case. In 1996, LexisNexis purchased 50 percent of Shepard's and operated it in conjunction with Time Mirror. In 1998, LexisNexis acquired the remaining 50 percent to become the sole owner and Internet provider of Shepard's.

Shepard's Citator Shepard's is the only major tax citator that is organized by case reporter series. Accordingly, the practitioner must know the court reporter citation for the case of interest, regardless of whether the paper or electronic version is used. This can be a problem if only the name of a case is known. However, using a document searching tool, such as the Tax Law Search in LexisNexis Academic, the name of the case can be entered as a keyword search and the case retrieved. From the document (case) listing or the actual document, the citation is obtained. This can then be entered into the citation box. Since citations must be entered in the proper format, Shepard's provides an exhaustive list of examples of citation formats for every possible document that can be Shepardized (see Citation Formats tool).

There are two ways to locate the citation format, Browse Citations and Find Citations. Within the Browse Citations tool, there are so many sample entries that they are indexed themselves. When using the Find Citations tool, the publication name (reporter for cases) is entered as shown in Exhibit 8-1. Once the document of interest is found, clicking on its associated abbreviation displays a template for entering the citation. The templates are set up in the standard "volume, reporter, page" format. If the researcher knows these three elements of the citation, the program is forgiving of punctuation, internal spacing, and capitalization variations.

Exhibit 8-1: Shepard's Find a Citation Format Screen

LexisNexis® *Academic*   Start | Sign Out | Contact Us | Help

Search   **Sources**
General | News | Legal | Business | People

Shepard's® > Citation Formats

Find Citations \ **Browse Citations**

Enter a publication name and click **Find**. In the results, click an Abbreviation link to go to a customized citation search form.

Find a Citation Format   Tax Court   ◄   🔍 **Find**

15 Publications

Full Name	Abbreviation
Maryland Tax Court LEXIS cite [MD]	Md. Tax LEXIS
Minnesota Tax Court LEXIS cite [MN]	Minn. Tax LEXIS
New Jersey Tax Court LEXIS cite [NJ]	N.J. Tax LEXIS
New Jersey Tax Court Reports [NJ]	N.J. Tax
Oregon Tax Court Advanced Sheets [OR]	Or. Tax. Adv.
Oregon Tax Court LEXIS cite [OR]	Ore. Tax LEXIS
Reports of the United States Tax Court [US] ◄	► T.C.
Tax Court Memorandum (RIA)	T.C.M. (RIA)
Tax Court Memorandum Decisions	T.C. Memo
Tax Court Memorandum Decisions (CCH)	T.C.M. (CCH)
Tax Court of the United States Reports (by number) [US]	T.C. No.
Tax Court Summary Opinions	T.C. Summary Opinion
Tax Court Summary Opinions LEXIS cite	Tax Ct. Summary LEXIS
United States Tax Court LEXIS cite [US]	U.S. Tax Ct. LEXIS
United States Tax Court Memorandum LEXIS cite [US]	Tax Ct. Memo LEXIS

LexisNexis®   About LexisNexis | Terms and Conditions | My ID
Copyright © 2007 LexisNexis, a division of Reed Elsevier Inc. All rights reserved.

Shepard's displays the following information for the case of interest (see Exhibit 8-2).

- Case evaluation symbol.

- Case citation in proper format.

- Parallel citations.

- All prior case history.

- Treatment by citing cases.

- Citations to secondary citing sources such as law reviews.

In examining Exhibit 8-2, the first item listed is the case citation in proper format. Clicking on the citation produces the LexisNexis reporter full-text case document. Each commercial reporter provides information that varies by publisher before the text of the actual case, which is the same in each reporter. For example, LexisNexis includes a case summary (Procedural Posture and Overview) as well as headnotes and core terms. **Headnotes** are the paragraphs in which the editors of the court reporter summarize the court's holdings on each issue of the case. Since the editors

Exhibit 8-2: Shepard's Unrestricted List for Soliman Case

LexisNexis® *Academic*

Start | Sign Out | Contact Us | Help

Shepard's® > 506 us 168(1/1) - Unrestricted(Full)

Search   Sources

Results   ?

Restrict By Unrestricted

◁ 1-100 of 214 Total Cites ⇨

● Commissioner v. Soliman, 506 U.S. 168

Commissioner v. Soliman , 506 U.S. 168, 113 S. Ct. 701, 121 L. Ed. 2d 634, 1993 U.S. LEXIS 828, 61 U.S.L.W. 4053, 6 Fla. L. Weekly Fed. S 807, 93 Cal. Daily Op. Service 219, 93 D.A.R. 528, 71 A.F.T.R.2d (RIA) 463, 93-1 U.S. Tax Cas. (CCH) P50014 (1993)

SHEPARD'S SUMMARY Show Summary

PRIOR HISTORY (5 citing references) Hide Prior History

1. *Soliman v. Commissioner*, 94 T.C. 20, 1990 U.S. Tax Ct. LEXIS 3, 94 T.C. No. 3 (1990)

2. **Affirmed by:**
   Soliman v. Commissioner, 935 F.2d 52, 1991 U.S. App. LEXIS 11355, 67 A.F.T.R.2d (RIA) 1112, 91-1 U.S. Tax Cas. (CCH) P50291 (4th Cir. Va. 1991)

3. **Writ of certiorari granted:**
   Commissioner v. Soliman, 503 U.S. 935, 112 S. Ct. 1472, 117 L. Ed. 2d 616, 1992 U.S. LEXIS 1708, 60 U.S.L.W. 3652 (1992)

4. **Motion granted by:**
   Commissioner v. Soliman, 503 U.S. 969, 112 S. Ct. 1582, 118 L. Ed. 2d 302, 1992 U.S. LEXIS 2136, 60 U.S.L.W. 3687 (1992)

5. **Motion granted by:**
   Commissioner v. Soliman, 503 U.S. 969, 112 S. Ct. 1582, 118 L. Ed. 2d 302, 1992 U.S. LEXIS 2136, 60 U.S.L.W. 3687 (1992)

▸ **Reversed by (CITATION YOU ENTERED):**
   Commissioner v. Soliman, 506 U.S. 168, 113 S. Ct. 701, 121 L. Ed. 2d 634, 1993 U.S. LEXIS 828, 61 U.S.L.W. 4053, 6 Fla. L. Weekly Fed. S 807, 93 Cal. Daily Op. Service 219, 93 D.A.R. 528, 71 A.F.T.R.2d (RIA) 463, 93-1 U.S. Tax Cas. (CCH) P50014 (1993)

SUBSEQUENT APPELLATE HISTORY (1 citing reference) Show Subsequent Appellate History

CITING DECISIONS (123 citing decisions)

1ST CIRCUIT - COURT OF APPEALS

of each reporter analyze the legal points of a case differently, the headnotes for a specific case will not likely correspond across the various reporters. Tax cases may address several issues, and the headnotes help the researcher identify how their particular issue of interest was treated. If the researcher is examining the case document and wants to Shepardize it, links to Shepard's are easily accessible.

Preceding the case citation is an easy-to-recognize symbolic case evaluation. Thus, the researcher quickly can determine the legal standing of a case at-a-glance. Note that the *Soliman* case has a stop sign shape (see Exhibit 8-2). The symbols used by Shepard's to indicate the precedential status of the citing cases are as follows.

- Red stop sign shape: Warning—Negative Treatment. The case has a history of negative treatment such as being overruled or reversed on one or more of its issues.

- Yellow triangle: Caution—Validity Questioned. The case's validity is questioned by citing cases.

- Green diamond with a "+" in the center: Positive Treatment. The citing cases have affirmed or followed the case.

- Blue circle with an "A" in the center: Analysis Available. The citing cases have analysis of the case.

- Blue circle with an "I" in the center: Information Available. The citing material has citation information available. Law review or treatise discussion would be an example of this information available.

Shepard's furnishes an extensive list of parallel citations. It includes all of the government and major commercial citations along with several unofficial or lesser known reporter versions. Parallel citations all refer to the same case, thus the text of the case is the same regardless of which citation is utilized to retrieve the case. Therefore, it is not necessary for researchers to list every parallel citation in file memos or client letters; one citation usually is sufficient. This can be either the government or one of the major commercial citations (RIA, CCH, or West). Lexis citations are not supported with templates by CCH and RIA, and tax professionals generally do not use them.

The prior direct history developed by Shepard's lists the complete judicial proceeding for the case of interest. For example, the prior direct history of the *Soliman* case includes its original Tax Court opinion that was affirmed on appeal by the Fourth Circuit Court of Appeals, the motion for writ of certiorari granted, and the reversal by the Supreme Court. Cases may have prior direct histories with more than two lower court citations when the case has been remanded or other judicial proceedings were required.

The researcher can restrict the citing cases retrieved by Shepard's to all positive, all negative, or any analysis, or the restriction can be customized by type of court or headnote paragraph number. This allows the researcher to quickly locate citing cases that address the particular tax issue of interest and in the geographical location of the taxpayer. For our case, we used an unrestricted search, which retrieved 123 citing decisions. In addition to the citation of the citing case (and its parallel citations), Shepard's hyperlinks the specific page where the citing case discusses the case of interest and indicates which headnote is linked to the discussion.

Since the numbered headnotes for a specific case do not necessarily correspond among the various reporters, when using headnote numbers to restrict retrieved cases, the researcher must be cognizant of which court reporter headnote numbers are pertinent to each citator service. Shepard's also evaluates the discussion of the citing case and categorizes its treatment (e.g., affirmed, cited by, criticized, distinguished, explained, followed, etc.) and the operation (amended, extended, revoked, etc.) of the citing cases. These evaluated citing cases are listed beginning with any Supreme Court citing cases and continuing with Federal jurisdiction (Appeals Courts in number order and then District Courts), followed by the U.S. Court of Federal Claims, Tax Court, various state courts, statutes, law reviews and periodicals, treatises, and other secondary sources. Within each of these citing groups, the citations are listed in reverse chronological order (newest first).

Shepard's Table of Authorities   Shepard's **Table of Authorities** (TOA) is a type of citator service, but it has a different purpose than regular citators. Rather than furnishing a history of a case and a list of cases citing it, the TOA lists the cases that are cited by the case of interest and to what extent it relied on these cases. This saves the researcher from having to enter each of these cases in the regular citator and consequently is a tremendous time-saving tool. For our research, the TOA would list the cases the Supreme Court cited and relied upon in reaching its opinion in *Soliman*. Examining the cases cited in *Soliman* is useful in tracing the logic of the court's decision, whether or not *Soliman* supports our client's preferred tax treatment. If *Soliman* relies on other cases with negative or weak histories, then some of the reasoning in *Soliman* may be flawed. Accordingly, a case that itself has no negative history when checked in the regular citator may appear to be sound law when, in fact, it may be weak as precedent because it relies on cases that have been overruled or have other negative connotations. Thus, less reliance should be placed on the case's findings in this situation.

The TOA lists the cited cases by jurisdiction (Circuit Court of Appeals, District Court, etc.). For each of these cases, the TOA furnishes the same information that the researcher would obtain if each case was separately checked through the regular Shepard's citator. Thus, for each cited case, the TOA lists the full case name, its citation (with parallel citations), and the ultimate disposition of the case. It also provides an assessment of how your case of interest evaluated the cited cases and the page in your case on which the cited case is discussed. The cited cases themselves are evaluated based on their history and assigned a Shepard's at-a-glance symbol (stop sign, triangle, etc.) indicating their current status.

Lexis

Besides the Shepard's Citators, Lexis contains the Auto-Cite citator and the LEX-CITE search system. Each of these is a useful tool for the researcher when verifying a case's value as precedent.

Auto-Cite   LexisNexis developed its own citator, **Auto-Cite**, before it offered Shepard's. Since Auto-Cite was first offered in 1979, it was originally available only through Lexis dedicated terminals. Now it is part of the Lexis Internet service. Auto-Cite was designed by Lawyers Cooperative Publishing to help their editors check the validity of citations. Therefore, its primary objectives are to provide absolutely accurate citations, and to do so within twenty-four hours of receipt of each case. Not only is Auto-Cite beneficial in determining whether a case is still good law, it also allows researchers to check the standing of Revenue Rulings and Revenue Procedures.

The information retrieved by Auto-Cite includes the correct spelling of the case name, its official citation, the year of the decision, and all official and most unofficial parallel cites. The prior and subsequent case history shows the full litigation history of a case, whereas the subsequent treatment history focuses on opinions that have lessened or negated the case's precedential value. Thus, the service lists citing cases that have overruled, criticized, or in some manner devalued the case of interest. To help quickly analyze whether a case is still good law, Auto-Cite uses at-a-glance symbol designations similar to those of Shepard's. Finally, an interesting feature of Auto-Cite that is not offered in Shepard's is a listing of documents that have had their precedential value negatively affected by the case of interest.

Auto-Cite is updated at least daily, and it provides accurate information on cases that affect the strength of the cited case. Whereas Shepard's focus is on furnishing a comprehensive history of the case, Auto-Cite is a selective list of citing cases having a significant impact on the validity of the case of interest.

LEXCITE   When researchers want to search the most current legal documents for references to their case of interest, **LEXCITE** is the tool to choose. Lexis prides itself on LEXCITE being more current than even Shepard's. As with Shepard's and Auto-Cite, the citation for the case (not the name) must be entered in the standard "volume-reporter-page" convention. LEXCITE ascertains the case's parallel citations, and then it searches for all of the embedded cite references in documents including case law, the Code, Federal Register, IRS pronouncements, and secondary sources such as law reviews and journals. Once the case cite has been located in a document, LEXCITE will identify and highlight subsequent *id*. and *supra* references.

The LEXCITE feature actually searches the full text of the documents available in Lexis, which covers more than 1,700 reporters and authorities. Accordingly, the researcher is able to see the references to the case of interest in context and make a personal determination of how the case was evaluated by the document's author. One limitation should be mentioned, however; LEXCITE will not find references to case names only—a court reporter citation must be present for LEXCITE to identify the document as a source.

An advantage of using LEXCITE is that the practitioner can customize the search to retrieve documents that address only a particular point of law in the cited case by using other search terms in addition to the citation. The jurisdiction, such as only Circuit Court of Appeals or only Missouri state court cases, can be specified. Date restrictions are very helpful when updating previous research, and one could examine all of the decisions written by a specific judge. This ability to customize the search is particularly useful when assisting a client in litigating a tax issue.

Westlaw Citator System

As discussed in Chapter 7, Westlaw is structured for legal research. It was designed by attorneys for attorneys. Since case law is very important in most areas of law, taxation included, the citation applications are the centerpiece of the Westlaw service. Westlaw's citators are also very effective for validating statutes, regulations, and administrative rulings. Besides its own citators, Westlaw also offers the RIA Citator 2nd. As its operation is essentially the same as when accessed through the RIA Checkpoint service, discussion of the RIA Citator 2nd is deferred until the next section of this chapter.

KeyCite   Westlaw launched its own major citator, called **KeyCite**, in 1997, while still offering other citator services such as Shepard's. With the loss of Shepard's in 1999, Westlaw reorganized its citators and developed KeyCite into a comprehensive proprietary service. Since it was developed solely for use by Westlaw customers, there is no published version of KeyCite. Westlaw also created a KeyCite especially for tax. As Exhibit 8-3 shows, this citator offers templates and examples (below the templates) illustrating the proper format for entering citations. Besides the templates for the Code, Regulations, and administrative pronouncements that are visible in Exhibit 8-3, templates also are provided for all tax case reporters. The

Exhibit 8-3: Westlaw KeyCite Tax Templates

templates simplify entering the citations, especially when the researcher is unfamiliar with the acceptable Westlaw format.

KeyCite for Tax has the same drawback as the previously discussed citators, that is, only a citation and not the case name can be entered into the templates. However, by using the Find&Print feature in the Westlaw toolbar (see top of Exhibit 8-3), the option of locating a court case by the taxpayer's name (Find a Case by Party Name) is available. The jurisdiction of the case may be used to narrow the search. Once the case is found, KeyCite may be applied to retrieve the citator information. As seen in the left frame of Exhibit 8-4, the KeyCite citator offers several display options to the researcher. Those that we will examine are Direct History, Citing References, Full-Text Document, ResultsPlus, and TOA. Demonstrating just how "key" the KeyCite service is to Westlaw, it is accessible directly on the Westlaw Welcome screen (see Chapter 7, Exhibit 7-10) by entering a citation, or by clicking on the KeyCite button in the Welcome screen and then entering a citation.

As with Shepard's Citator, the system has been designed to be flexible as to citation formats. Most formats are accepted as long as the general form of "volume-reporter-page" is used. If the researcher does not know the proper citation format for a document of interest, a publication list is available. Since the list contains over 4,400 documents, it can be scanned by either entering words contained in the document title or entering letters or words with which the document title starts. Unlike the Shepard's list, clicking on the title does not produce a template for

Exhibit 8-4: Westlaw KeyCite Full History for Soliman Case

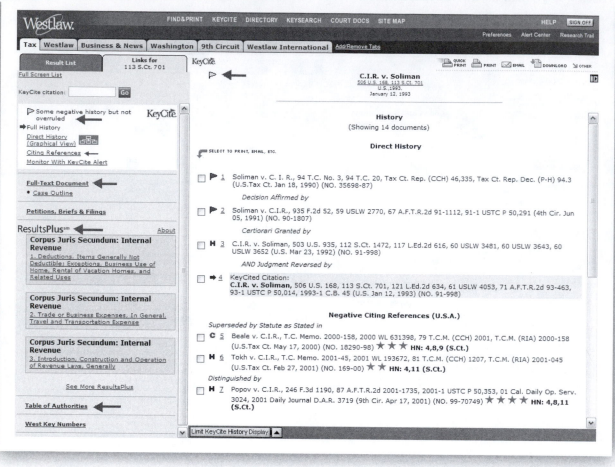

entering the citation. The researcher must enter the citation in the KeyCite box, using the abbreviation discovered in the publication list.

History The Direct History and Negative Citing References are retrieved when the case citation is initially entered into KeyCite. The case's chronological progress through the courts is listed first in the Direct History section, as Exhibit 8-4 illustrates for *Nader Soliman* (506 US 168). The chronological progress also can be graphically displayed. The editors indicate the effects of this progression with words and symbols. Although the symbols employed are different from Shepard's, their meanings are similar. KeyCite's symbols are as follows.

- Red Flag: Warning—Negative Treatment. The case or administrative decision is no longer good law for at least one of the points of law it contains. For statutes or regulations, the law has been amended recently or repealed, superseded, or held unconstitutional or preempted in whole or in part.

- Yellow Flag: Caution—Some Negative Treatment. The case has negative history but has not been overruled. The statute or regulation has been renumbered, reinstated, corrected, or transferred recently, or its validity has been called into doubt.

- Blue "H": Neutral Analysis. The case has some direct history but it is not known to be negative.

- Green "C": Information Available. The case or administrative decision has citing references but no direct or negative history. For statutes and regulations there are citing references, but no updating documents.

After the direct history, KeyCite presents the Negative Citing References section, which includes citing cases that adversely affect the precedential value of the case of interest. Phrases indicate whether the cases have criticized, distinguished, limited, questioned, or overruled the cited case's logic or holding. Notice in Exhibit 8-4 that KeyCite indicates that the *Soliman* case has been superseded by statute as indicated in two citing cases. The negative cases are also evaluated as to whether they are still good law, using the same symbols as for the direct history (see Exhibit 8-4).

Besides this evaluation, KeyCite determines the extent to which the citing cases discuss the cited case of interest. This feature is unique to KeyCite and greatly facilitates determining which citing cases should be reviewed. The symbols range from four stars to one star, with four denoting an extended examination of the case (usually more than a printed page in length) and one denoting a brief reference (such as in a string of citations). The final unique symbol supplied by KeyCite is quotation marks, indicating that the citing case has quoted the cited case. This symbol does not appear in the negative citing references but is utilized in the Citing References and the Table of Authorities (Exhibit 8-5).

Exhibit 8-5: Westlaw KeyCite Table of Authorities for Soliman Case

Citing References To look at a comprehensive list of citing cases, select the Citing References option. KeyCite retrieved 579 documents for the *Soliman* case, almost all of which are positive cites. The listing starts with the negative cases presented in the Negative Citing References, with the most recent cases presented first. The Positive Cases section is organized by the depth of coverage, starting with the four-star examinations and leading to the one-star citing cases. Next is administrative pronouncements, such as IRS Rulings and Notices, and the last section contains secondary source references by journals, law reviews, Bureau of National Affairs (BNA) Portfolios, tax services, and so on. Since the number of documents retrieved can be overwhelming, KeyCite allows the researcher to limit those retrieved by headnotes (key numbers), location, type of jurisdiction, date, type of document, and depth of treatment (number of stars). A keyword search is possible if the KeyCite list is less than 2,000 documents.

As discussed previously, the headnote paragraphs represent a summary of each significant legal issue in the case. The interpretation of "significant issues" varies by the editorial staff of each court reporter. The editors of the court reporters analyzed the judicial opinions to different degrees of detail. For example, the West *Supreme Court Reporter* editors for the *Soliman* case required thirteen headnotes to evaluate the law, whereas the RIA editors of the AFTR2d series needed just one. The drafting of headnotes and the breadth of the issue that each headnote addresses are a matter of style and editorial policy of the entity that publishes the reporter. In KeyCite, the West headnotes discussed by each citing case are listed after the "star" designations in the citation (see Exhibit 8-4).

SPOTLIGHT ON TAXATION

Supreme Court Justices

The U.S. Supreme Court is made up of nine justices who are nominated by the President and approved by the Senate. Approximately 8,000 petitions are filed with the Supreme Court in the course of one year. In addition, some 1,200 applications of various kinds are filed each year that are acted upon by a single justice. As Supreme Court justices reside on the bench for life, the ability to nominate a Supreme Court justice accords the President tremendous power to influence future Supreme Court decisions by virtue of the person selected for nomination. This is especially true if that person is relatively young (by Supreme Court standards), such as John Roberts, who was fifty when nominated by George W. Bush to be the Chief Justice. The following is a list of the Supreme Court justices as of the beginning of 2008. It is likely that this list will change in the next few years.

Name	Date and Place of Birth	Nominating President	Year Installed
John G. Roberts, Jr. (Chief Justice)	January 27, 1955 Buffalo, New York	G. W. Bush	2005
John Paul Stevens	April 20, 1920 Chicago, Illinois	Nixon	1970
Antonin Scalia	March 11, 1936 Trenton, New Jersey	Reagan	1986
Anthony M. Kennedy	July 23, 1936 Sacramento, California	Reagan	1988

continued

continued

David H. Souter	September 17, 1939 Melrose, Massachusetts	G. H. W. Bush	1990
Clarence Thomas	June 28, 1948 Pinpoint, a community near Savannah, Georgia	G. H. W. Bush	1991
Ruth Bader Ginsburg	March 15, 1933 Brooklyn, New York	W. Clinton	1993
Stephen Breyer	August 15, 1938 San Francisco, California	W. Clinton	1994
Samuel A. Alito	April 1, 1950 Trenton, New Jersey	G. W. Bush	2006

The West headnote system has a particularly valuable feature for finding law, the **West Key Number System**. The points of law articulated in a case are classified by the editors into Key Numbers that create an extensive system for organizing case law called the West Key Number Digest. The key number for a topic of interest can be found by drilling down through the Key Numbers alphabetical list. Internal Revenue, for example, is Key 220 and Home Office Expenses are 220k3355.

Full-Text Document Selecting Full-Text Document displays the text of the selected case. The full citation (all official cites and numerous unofficial cites) of the case, geographical location, and date of judgment are provided as well. After a summary of the case, the headnotes and key numbers assigned by the case reporter editors appear, and then the official full text of the document. Rather than retrieving the full text, the researcher can select the outline option. With this option, the researcher can jump to the synopsis, headnotes, or opinions (concurring and dissenting) for the case.

ResultsPlus As discussed in Chapter 7, **ResultsPlus** displays a list of suggested analytical materials relevant to the search. For the *Soliman* case, ResultsPlus suggests discussions of the IRC related to the issues in *Soliman* (see Exhibit 8-4). The materials appear in legal encyclopedias (Corpus Juris Secundum and American Jurisprudence), legal reports (American Law Reports), treatises, law reviews, and topical publications such as the *BNA Portfolios* and *Mertens*.

Table of Authorities The Westlaw TOA performs the same function as the Shepard's version. However, the Westlaw TOA reports more information. As Exhibit 8-5 demonstrates, not only does the TOA indicate where the case of interest cites other cases in supporting its reasoning, Westlaw also denotes how much discussion was given to the case using its four-star depth of treatment symbols. Further, if the case of interest quotes other cases, this is designated with the quotation marks symbol. The cases listed in the TOA with negative history, or those that have been reversed or overruled, are marked with a yellow or red flag, making it easy for researchers to determine the strength of the cases relied on by the case of interest.

RIA Citator 2nd

The RIA **Citator 2nd** is a comprehensive tax citator. Along with District Court, Court of Federal Claims, Court of Appeals, and Supreme Court cases reported in RIA's tax court reporter series, American Federal Tax Reporter series (AFTR and

AFTR 2d), and the Tax Court cases (regular, memorandum, and unpublished), the RIA citator evaluates administrative pronouncements (hereafter referred to as rulings) issued by the IRS and Treasury Decisions.

Using the RIA Citator 2nd The Citator 2nd is accessible from the opening Checkpoint screen (see Chapter 6, Exhibit 6-1, left window). It supports citator searches by case (taxpayer) name, citation, or keyword (see Exhibit 8-6). For case name searches, as in Exhibit 8-6, the court may be indicated through a list supplied by RIA. This is an optional entry; thus, if only the taxpayer name is known, the search still can be successful. When the citation is known, templates, similar to those provided by Westlaw, are furnished to ensure that citations are entered in the proper format.

The researcher has the option of retrieving a list of cases and rulings that cite the case of interest (Cited) or a list of cases and rulings cited by the case of interest (Citing). This latter option is similar to the Shepard's and Westlaw's TOA, but less extensive information is provided. The score rating supplied is based on the number of times the citation appears in the case in relation to other documents, applied with a "complex formula" developed by RIA. This method of scoring probably does not provide much information to the researcher, however.

The result of the *Soliman* Cited search is a list of all the tax cases citing *Soliman*. Thus, the major difference between the RIA Citator 2nd and Shepard's or KeyCite is that RIA only lists citing tax cases. This is beneficial to a tax researcher

Exhibit 8-6: RIA Citator 2nd Case Name Template

because it reduces the number of citations retrieved to only those citing the case of interest based on its analysis of tax issues. Clicking on the citation of any of the citing cases listed will take the researcher directly to the place in the citing case where *Soliman* is cited and discussed.

The AFTR court reporter's full-text reproduction of the *Soliman* case is in Exhibit 8-7. The main advantages of the AFTR court reporter for tax research are that its headnotes address only the tax issues of the case, and that it adds the Code sections addressed in the case to its Case Information summary, which includes the level of the court, docket number, date decided, prior history, tax year, disposition of the case, and parallel citations. Knowing the tax year for the case can be very beneficial when the tax law is amended after the tax year but before the case is decided. This is possible, when, as the *Soliman* case illustrates, it can take ten years for the final decision by the courts (tax year 1983 and Supreme Court decision 1993). Knowing the disposition of the case before starting to read the case also may help practitioners to focus their reading of the opinion. It can be hard to determine the final result of the case merely by reading an opinion from beginning to end!

The three buttons just above the *Soliman* case name and citation, in Exhibit 8-7, access annotations of the case in the United States Tax Reporter (Annot), paragraph references of the case in the Federal Tax Coordinator 2d (FTC), or the case's listing in the Citator 2nd (Citator). References to the annotations also are listed between the headnotes and the opinion (not visible in Exhibit 8-7).

Exhibit 8-7: RIA Soliman Case and Citator 2nd Links

RIA Conventions   When the plaintiff in a tax case is the U.S. Government, Commissioner of Internal Revenue, Secretary of the Treasury, or an IRS employee, the RIA citator does not catalog the case under the plaintiff's name, as is the traditional legal convention. This is because there are thousands of cases in which Eisner, Helvering, Burnet, or other Commissioners or Secretaries of the Treasury initiated the litigation. Rather, the RIA Citator 2nd catalogs all cases by the taxpayer's name. This convention greatly facilitates the researcher's search by case name.

The *Soliman* case was first decided in 1990 by the Tax Court (94 TC 20), which found for the taxpayer, allowing the home office deduction. The IRS appealed to the Court of Appeals for the Fourth Circuit. This case, decided in 1991 (67 AFTR2d 91-1112), again found for the taxpayer. The IRS appealed again, this time to the U.S. Supreme Court. The Supreme Court decided the case in the IRS's favor in 1993 (71 AFTR2d 93-463). Consequently, there are three separate entries in the Citator 2nd for this case, because each of these courts wrote an opinion that can be cited by other cases (see left frame, Exhibit 8-7).

The Supreme Court opinion is the most cited, since it is the final judicial decision on the issue. However, this is not the final word for the tax researcher because Congress amended the Code to reject the findings of the Supreme Court, as Exhibit 8-8 clearly indicates in the *Soliman* judicial history. Note that the Tax Court decision is not shown in the Judicial History, but two relevant rulings are listed.

Compare the data provided in Exhibit 8-8 to that of Exhibits 8-2 and 8-4. Shepard's and KeyCite list more parallel citations and more extensive judicial

Exhibit 8-8: RIA Citator 2nd for Soliman Case

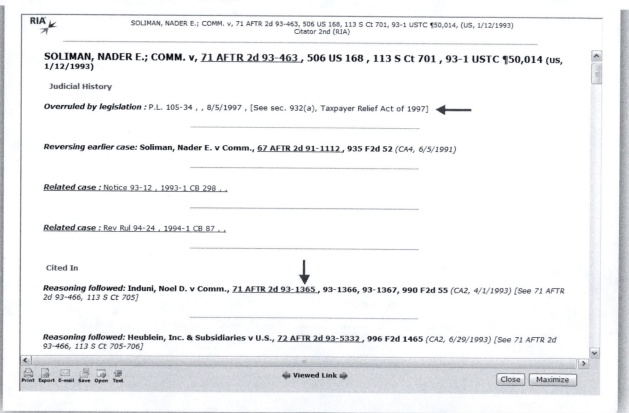

(prior) histories than Citator 2nd. The question for the researcher is which service provides the information essential to the project at hand. More information is not necessarily more useful to assessing current law.

Following the judicial history, the Citator 2nd first lists the citations for cases that are in complete agreement with the cited case. Next, citing cases are listed that discuss the holdings or reasoning of the cited case but do not refer to a specific paragraph or headnote. Finally, cases are listed in order of the headnote issue that they address. The headnote number references allow the researcher to restrict a search to only those citing cases with issues that are relevant to the client's factual situation. The Citator 2nd bases its headnote designations on the AFTR series, as that reporter also is an RIA product. For the *Soliman* Supreme Court case, AFTR2d provides only one headnote. The researcher needs to make sure that with the Citator 2nd the AFTR headnotes numbers are utilized and not headnotes numbers from other reporters, such as those published by West.

Within any of the citing groupings—complete agreement, no specific headnote, Headnote 1, Headnote 2, and so on—citing cases and rulings are listed in the following order.

- U.S. Supreme Court

- U.S. Courts of Appeal

- U.S. Court of Federal Claims (or predecessor court)

- U.S. District Court

- U.S. Tax Court (or predecessor court—BTA, regular then memorandum decisions)

- State courts

- Treasury Rulings and Decisions

Citing cases within any court or ruling group are arranged in chronological order.

The Citator 2nd includes tax citing cases that discuss or even just cite the case of interest in a list of citations. Therefore, the listings for important cases, such as *Soliman*, can be several screens long. Rather than using symbols to indicate how each of these citing cases treated the case of interest, the Citator 2nd uses short, easy-to-understand, descriptive phrases.

Many researchers prefer to start their analysis of a case with the most recent citing cases and work backward to earlier cases. Using this method, they can quickly identify the current status of the cited case. For example, a steady stream of recent favorable references probably indicates that the precedent of the original case is still valid and strong, whereas either a list of negative comments or a scarcity of references may indicate a weak or out-of-date decision. The citator portion of a research project is complete when the researcher is satisfied that the status of the case is sufficiently confirmed.

At this point, some of the citing cases should be examined, especially if the cases found initially support the client's position but the facts are somewhat different. The citing cases may provide support with more similar facts. Hence, those citations designated as "case reconciled," indicating that their facts or opinions are different from those of the cited case and require reconciliation, should be consulted. If the initial cases found have holdings adverse to a client's position, the practitioner should search for cases marked "case distinguished," to identify what factors are relevant to the issuance of an adverse opinion.

The "distinguished" cases usually have facts that are actually different from those of the cited case, thus supporting a different holding. Some of these facts may resemble the facts of the practitioner's client and thus provide the desired support. Similarly, a case denoted as "citing generally" limits the holding of the cited case to a narrow set of facts. This may occur when a higher court has ruled differently on a case with somewhat similar facts or there has been a change in the tax law. Thus, the holding of the cited case may be inapplicable to the client's factual situation.

RIA Citator: Rulings Upon identifying administrative rulings (Revenue Ruling, Revenue Procedure, Notice, General Council Memorandums, etc.) that appear to support a client's tax position, it is critical for a researcher to determine if they are still in effect and represent the current view of the IRS. Rulings are continually clarified, modified, superseded, or revoked, as Exhibit 8-9 illustrates. What is good law at one point (e.g., Rev Rul 2006-36 issued August 14, 2006) may not be so a few months later (modified by Notice 2007-22 on February 15, 2007).

The steps in checking the validity of rulings are the same as with a court case. The Citator 2nd furnishes templates for most IRS administrative rulings. The search results for rulings provide a hyperlink to the actual ruling and then its judicial history. In this case, the judicial history shows the effect the ruling of interest had on other administrative pronouncements, and/or the effect subsequent administrative pronouncements had on the ruling of interest. If there are any citing court cases, these are listed after citing rulings and before lesser pronouncements (such as Notices). As Exhibit 8-9 demonstrates, it is always important to check pertinent pronouncements through a citator.

CCH Citator

The Commerce Clearing House Tax Citator **(CCH Citator)** is available in print as an integral part of CCH's Standard Federal Tax Reporter (discussed in Chapter 6). It also is accessible through CCH's Internet service Tax Research NetWork (NetWork). The NetWork version is merely the paper version in electronic form.

The CCH Citator Attributes The CCH Citator differs dramatically from the other citators. First, the CCH Citator lists only those citing cases that the CCH editors believe will serve as useful guides in evaluating the cited case's effectiveness as precedent. Thus, the tax researcher is directed to those cases that may be most likely to develop, explain, criticize, or otherwise evaluate a rule of law. This is in contrast to the other citators, which provide all of the cases mentioning the cited case. Although the latter practice provides a level of thoroughness that may be useful, the CCH editorial screening procedure guards against the possibility of being overwhelmed by the sheer volume of citing cases presented. The more selective CCH approach, of course, forces the researcher to rely on an editor's evaluation concerning the usefulness of the citing cases.

Second, as discussed at the beginning of this chapter, the CCH Citator uses a general citation rather than a specific location citation. This means that the citation for the citing case is the first page of the citing case and not the point in the case of interest where the citing case is discussed. If the citing case is long, the researcher can waste valuable time identifying where the citing case discusses the case of interest.

Third, as Exhibit 8-10 illustrates, the CCH Citator acts as a Finding Table as well as a citator, by listing paragraph references as to where the case is reviewed in the Standard Federal Income Tax Reporter. This feature reduces the searching time

Exhibit 8-9: RIA Citator 2nd for Notice 2007–22

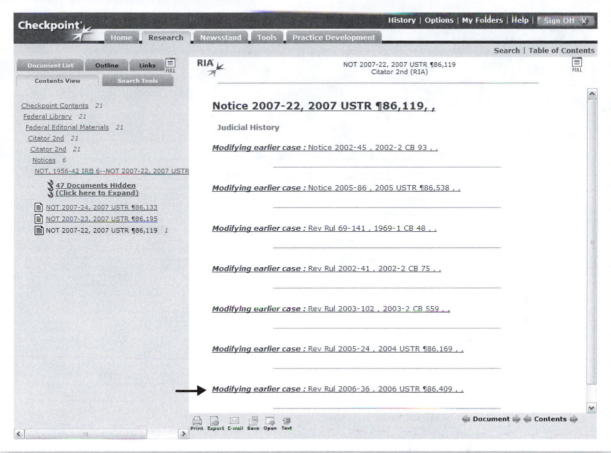

required to locate supplemental information regarding a case or ruling of interest. The tax service discussions help the researcher evaluate the case or ruling in the context of relevant Code sections, Regulations, and administrative sources of tax law.

Fourth, while the CCH Citator provides parallel citations, it does not list as many other citations. Specifically missing are references to the RIA AFTR court reporter series and the Lexis reporter series (see Exhibit 8-10). It may be understandable that the competitor AFTR series is not represented, but Lexis cites should be present, given the relationship between the two companies.

Finally, the CCH Citator does not provide evaluations of the citing cases (see Exhibit 8-10), nor references to headnotes. While the CCH court reporter, United States Tax Cases (USTC), provides headnote information and back references to its tax service, it does not number or label this analysis. Thus, there is no available method to reference this evaluation in the Citator. The omission of these evaluation sources is a significant drawback of the CCH Citator. With cases having numerous issues and lists of citing cases as long as *Soliman*'s, for example, knowing how each citing case interpreted the different tax issues substantially could reduce the number of cases the researcher reads. The only information that can be gleaned by glancing at the *Soliman* Citator entry is that *Soliman* is an important case, given the number of cases citing it. One cannot even tell if the Supreme Court decision is still valid, which is critical when relying on the *Soliman* case.

Exhibit 8-10: CCH Citator for Soliman Case

CCH® Tax Research NetWork™

Preferences | Help | Log Out

[Search]

Main Menu   Clear Selections   Research History   Research Folders   [Check Citator]   [Find by Citation]   [Search Tools]

Document List [#1 of 1]   Nearby Documents   Research Folder   Store Document   Save Link
Previous Next List 1st Term   Previous Next   Last Folder Add   Export Print Mail   Link Express Favorite

CCH-CITATOR, 2007FED, Main Citator Table, Soliman, Nader E.

CCH-CITATOR, 2007FED, Main Citator Table, Soliman, Nader E.

Soliman, Nader E.

ANNOTATED AT ... 2007FED ¶12,523,477; ¶14,854,027; ¶14,854,94; ¶39,651G,305; ¶39,652,34 ◄——

  ——► ● SCt--(rev'g CA), 93-1 USTC ¶50,014; 506 US 168; 113 SCt 701; Ct. D. 2054, 1993-1 CB 45

    Sorrentino, CA-10, 2004-2 USTC ¶50,372, 383 F3d 1187

    Textron, Inc., CA-1, 2003-2 USTC ¶50,571, 336 F3d 26

    Tokh, CA-7, 2002-1 USTC ¶50,128, 25 FedAppx 440

    Popov, CA-9, 2001-1 USTC ¶50,353, 246 F3d 1190

    Kurzet, CA-10, 2000-2 USTC ¶50,671, 222 F3d 830

    True Oil Co., CA-10, 99-1 USTC ¶50,364, 170 F3d 1294

    Fingar, CA-11, 99-1 USTC ¶50,392, 176 F3d 493

    EWC, Inc., CA-10, 97-1 USTC ¶50,475, 114 F3d 1071

    Sierra Club, Inc., CA-9, 96-2 USTC ¶50,326, 86 F3d 1526

    Rakosi, CA-9, 95-1 USTC ¶50,133

    Putnam, CA-5, 94-2 USTC ¶50,466, 32 F3d 911

    Heublein, Inc., CA-2, 93-2 USTC ¶50,397, 996 F2d 1455

    Induni, CA-2, 93-1 USTC ¶50,200, 990 F2d 53

CCH Conventions   Similar to the RIA Citator 2nd, the CCH Citator accepts the taxpayer's name, the complete citation, if known, and it furnishes templates for entering the citation of the case or ruling of interest. For illustrative purposes, Exhibit 8-11 has entered the case name, complete citation, and cites using the case templates for the *Soliman* case. A researcher would actually input data for only one of these searches. Notice that the CCH Citator does not support AFTR (RIA Federal court reporter) citations with a template, nor will it recognize them as complete citations, whereas the RIA Citator does include templates for USTC (CCH Federal court reporter) citations. This can cause problems when a journal article, published by WG&L, for example, contains an AFTR 2d cite for a case with a common taxpayer name, but the practitioner has access only to the CCH Citator and CCH court reporters.

Rather than listing the judicial history, the first entry after the name of a cited case is the annotation paragraph number references to the Standard Federal Tax Reporter compilations (see Exhibit 8-10). Bold black bullets are used to designate the cases in the direct history. The highest level court to address the case is listed first, and the trial-level court is listed last. Hence, the citation for the *Soliman* Supreme Court case is listed first, followed by all of its citing cases, then several screens later the Fourth Circuit case followed by its citing cases, and finally the

Exhibit 8-11: CCH Check Citator with Soliman Case Citation

Tax Court case. Consequently, the court path chosen by the parties is not as quickly identifiable as with other citators. Examining the entries in Exhibit 8-10, the citing cases are listed by court level and generally in reverse chronology (most recent first), although this is not consistent for all cases. Unlike Shepard's, the CCH Citator does not list Appeals Court cases in order, or the Circuit or District Court by geographical location. Rather, within Appeals Courts, the cases are listed by date. After listing all court citations, pronouncements are listed by type in a random date order.

The CCH Citator provides limited information about the judicial history of the case. The reference for the Supreme Court case for *Soliman* denotes that it reversed the Fourth Circuit's holding, and the Fourth Circuit reference indicates it affirmed the Tax Court decision. Since the CCH Citator does not denote citing case evaluations, the researcher cannot determine if, for example, the *Sorrentino* case followed, or explained, or distinguished itself from the *Soliman* case (see Exhibit 8-10).

Finally, the Check Citator button in CCH Tax Research Network is available from all screens, as it is part of the toolbar that is constantly visible. Thus, while viewing a case on screen, selecting the Check Citator button will display the Citator entries for the case being examined.

SUMMARY

The tax researcher's job of sorting through the thousands of potentially pertinent Federal tax authorities is facilitated by citators. When familiar with these research tools, the current status and precedential value of a specific case or ruling can be determined effectively and quickly. This determination is necessary for the researcher to evaluate the judicial and administrative sources of the tax law that pertain to a client's tax issue. The Internet services automate virtually all of the tedious mechanical aspects of Shepardizing cases and validating the formal correctness of citations. Further, they make the retrieval of cited and citing cases seamless. The overview of citators and the act of citing presented in this chapter demonstrate that research is not complete until all primary sources upon which the researcher is relying are found to be currently "good law."

TAX TUTOR

Reinforce the tax research information covered in this chapter by completing the online tutorials located at the *Federal Tax Research* web site: **http://academic.cengage.com/taxation/raabe**

KEY WORDS

By the time you complete this chapter, you should be comfortable discussing each of the following terms. If you need additional review of any of these items, return to the appropriate material in the chapter or consult the glossary to this text.

Auto-Cite
CCH Citator
Citation
Citator
Citator 2nd
Cited case
Cites
Citing case
Full-Text Document

Headnotes
KeyCite
LEXCITE
Precedential value
ResultsPlus
Shepardizing
Shepard's Citators
Table of Authorities
West Key Number System

DISCUSSION QUESTIONS

1. Why does the researcher need to determine the precedential value of a case?

2. Why are subsequent cases important to the value of a prior case?

3. Describe the function of a citator in the tax research process.

4. Distinguish between the following terms: cited case, citing case, citation, and cites.

5. Citators do not provide all information related to a case. What kind of information do citators *not* provide?

6. How many federal judicial districts are there, and where are they located?

7. Name three commercial citators that focus exclusively on tax cases. Indicate whether the citations are sold as part of a commercial tax service.

8. Explain the difference between a general directing and a local directing cite. Which service uses local directing cites?

9. What does "Shepardizing" mean?

10. Compare the coverage and organization of Shepard's with the RIA and CCH citator services.

11. Explain whether a researcher can locate a case either by the case name or by its citation when using the Shepard's Citator.

12. What are headnotes? Explain whether the headnotes for a given case are set by the court and are consistent across court reporting services.

13. What is the equivalent of the Shepard's Green Diamond symbol in Westlaw?

14. What is the function of a TOA? Why is it a useful research tool?

15. What is Auto-Cite, who developed it, and what is its primary objective?

16. What is LEXCITE, and when would a researcher use this Lexis service?

17. What is KeyCite, and what event in 1999 caused a reorganization of KeyCite?

18. How does the information provided by KeyCite History differ from that retrieved using KeyCite Citing Reference?

19. What information regarding citing cases is provided by KeyCite that is not available from the other citation services discussed in this chapter?

20. Who is the Chief Justice of the Supreme Court? Who is the most recent addition to the Supreme Court?

21. When is the West Key Number System useful to a researcher?

22. Compare the Shepard's TOA with the Westlaw KeyCite version.

23. Why is the responsibility of nominating Supreme Court justices an important presidential power? Which President appointed the greatest number of the current Supreme Court justices?

24. What company was the first to introduce citators as legal aids?

25. What is the tax court reporter series that is associated with the RIA Citator 2nd?

26. What types of citator searches are supported by the RIA Citator 2nd?

27. What Internet service besides Checkpoint provides access to the RIA Citator 2nd?

28. What type of case searching does the RIA Citator support that is unavailable with Shepard's, Auto-Cite, LEXCITE, or KeyCite?

29. What feature does the RIA Citator 2nd offer that is similar to the TOA in Shepard's and KeyCite?

30. What is the major difference in the focus of the citing cases found with a RIA Citator 2nd search and those cases found using Shepard's or KeyCite?

31. The RIA Citator 2nd does not follow the traditional legal convention of listing cases under the plaintiff's name. What convention does it use? Why are the cases listed in this manner?

32. In what order does the RIA Citator list citing cases?

33. What symbols does the RIA Citator 2nd use to indicate the treatment of citing cases of the cited case?

34. When is the citator portion of a research project finished?

35. Why must Revenue Rulings identified through a keyword search be checked in a citator?

36. What different Internet services offer access to the CCH Citator?

37. How is the CCH Citator different from the other citators discussed in this chapter?

38. How does the CCH Citator act as a Finding Table?

39. How is the direct history for a case of interest presented in the CCH Citator?

40. When viewing a document in CCH NetWork, how does one check the document through the CCH Citator?

EXERCISES

41. Use Shepard's to answer the following questions.
    a. Provide the full citation for a 2007 article on Sarbanes-Oxley in the *Akron Law Review*. What is the Shepard's abbreviated citation?
    b. What topic is addressed in the sixteenth Technical Advice Memorandum (TAM) issued in the twenty-seventh week of 2007 (a TAM is cited the same as PLR)? Provide its Shepard's abbreviated citation.
    c. What is the Shepard's abbreviated citation for the twentieth Chief Counsel Advice Memorandum issued in the thirtieth week of 2007?
    d. What is the Shepard's abbreviated citation for the Lexis reproduction of Field Service Advice 199952041?

42. Shepardize *C. G. Services Corp.*, found in volume 73 of the Tax Court Reporter on page 406.
    a. What Shepard's evaluation symbol is associated with the case? What does the symbol mean?
    b. Give either the AFTR or the USTC citation for the 1997 District Court case citing *C. G. Services Corp.*
    c. What is the subsequent appellate history of this case?
    d. There is an article in the 1989 *Tennessee Law Review* on page 661 that cites *C. G. Services Corp.* What is the title of the article and the name of the author(s)?

43. Locate *Stange* (282 US 270) using the Shepard's Citator.
    a. What are the parallel citations for this case? What precedence symbol is associated with this case?
    b. What is the highest court to have heard this case, and in what year was this case decided?
    c. On what page does the case, *Aiken v. Burnet*, 75 L. Ed 339, cite the *Stange* case? What page would this be if you were using the United States Supreme Court Reports (US)?
    d. The Alaska Supreme Court has cited the *Stange* case. Provide the citation for the case.

44. Shepardize *Fritz W. Hintze* (879 F2d 121) using the Shepard's Citator.
    a. What are the parallel citations for the *Hintze* case? What precedence symbol is associated with this case?
    b. How many headnotes does the *Hintze* have? How many of the headnotes concern civil procedures?
    c. Who were the judges who heard *Hintze* case? Which judge wrote the opinion?
    d. What was the Supreme Court's view of the *Hintze* case? In what case did the Supreme Court indicate this viewpoint?

45. Use the Shepard's Citator to answer the following questions regarding the *Hinck* (127 S CT 2011) case.
    a. Which Supreme Court justice wrote the *Hinck* opinion? Explain whether the other Supreme Court justices agreed with the written opinion.
    b. What was the court of original jurisdiction for the *Hinck* case, and what court heard the appeal?
    c. What are the parallel citations for the *Hinck* case? What precedence symbol is associated with this case?
    d. What Code section is involved in the *Hinck* case? When was the case argued and when was it decided?

46. Use the LexisNexis Auto-Cite to locate *City of New Britain*, 1954 US Lexis 2751.
    a. What Lexis precedent symbol is associated with this case? What event caused the New Britain case to receive this symbol?
    b. What is this case's judicial history?
    c. What U.S. Code Service (USCS) sections cite City of New Britain?
    d. What citing cases are listed in the subsequent treatment history section?

47. Use the LexisNexis LEXCITE and enter the following citation: 5 L Ed 2d 128 and select Combined Federal Courts as the Jurisdiction.
    a. What is the name of the case with the citation you entered? When was it decided and by what court?
    b. In the "Enter more terms" type "sweepstakes" into the box. There is a 1965 Tax Court case and its Second Court of Appeals case in the citing list. What is the name of this case?
    c. Remove the "sweepstakes" term and select Secondary Sources as the Jurisdiction. What is the full citation for the *University of Colorado Law Review* article citing the case of interest?

48. Use the LexisNexis TOA and enter the following citation: 347 US 81.
    a. What are the parallel citations for this case? In what year was this case decided?
    b. How many cases did it cite in developing its decision? Which cited cases have some type of warning associated with them?
    c. What are the jurisdictional levels in which the cases are divided?
    d. On which pages in 347 US 81 are the cases in the TOA cited?

49. State the proper Westlaw KeyCite citation for the following documents.
    a. An article in *New York University Law Review*, volume 81 starting on page 148.
    b. The forty-third Private Letter Ruling issued in the twenty-ninth week of 2007.
    c. The second section of article 16 of the Arkansas State Constitution.
    d. The thirty-fourth Field Service Advice issued in the forty-seventh week of 2002.

50. Use Westlaw KeyCite to locate *Hinck*, 95 AFTR 2d 2005-873.
    a. What are official parallel citations for this case? In what year was this case decided?
    b. Using KeyCite History, list each court hearing the case. How did the appeals court treat this case? Did the Supreme Court grant certiorari?
    c. Where is this case discussed in the FTC 2d?
    d. Select Full-Text Document. What are the titles of the headnotes for this case?

51. Use the Westlaw TOA to find the following information for *Stange*, 28 US 270.
    a. How many cases does *Stange* cite in its decision? What year was the most recent cited case decided?
    b. What case does *Stange* (28 US 270) quote? What does the quote discuss?
    c. How many of the cases cited in *Stange* have warning or caution symbols? How does this make you feel about the reasoning in this case?
    d. How many different pages have discussion of cases?

52. Use Westlaw to answer the following questions.
    a. Locate the 2006 *David Bruce Billings* Tax Court case (Hint: use Find& Print). What was the tax issue and what was the decision of the court?
    b. Find the 2007 *David Bruce Billings* Tax Court case. Why are the results of this case different from those of the 2006 case?

    c. What is the KeyCite Key Number for the issue in the 2007 case?

    d. How useful do you think the KeyCite Key Numbering system is in locating cases on income tax issues?

53. Use the RIA Checkpoint Citator to locate the 1958 *Knetsch* case.

    a. What is its citation? Provide the citations for all the cases generally citing the *Knetsch* case.

    b. What are the citations for the cases that constitute the direct history for the *Knetsch* case?

    c. How many headnotes does the case show? What does each headnote address?

    d. How many Eleventh Circuit Court of Appeals cases cite the *Knetsch* Supreme Court case? List the names of the taxpayers in these cases. What was the easiest method to find this information?

54. Use the RIA Checkpoint Citator 2d to locate the 2002 *Gwendolyn A. Ewing* Tax Court case.

    a. What is its citation and what tax issues does the case address?

    b. What is the case's direct judicial history?

    c. Where is the case annotated in the United States Tax Reporter?

    d. The *Robert Haag* case cites the 2002 *Ewing* case at 94 AFTR 2d 2004-6667. What is the *Haag* case's treatment of the *Ewing* case?

55. Use the LexisNexis Academic Shepard's and the RIA Checkpoint Citator 2d to Shepardize *Deluxe Check Printers, Inc.* 15 Cl Ct 175.

    a. Explain the difference in the AFTR citation listed by the RIA Citator 2d and that listed in Shepard's.

    b. Do RIA and Shepard's link to the same case documents? Explain your response.

    c. Discuss whether the two citators display the same citing cases and other citing documents.

    d. Which citator do you find easier to use? Explain your response.

56. Use the RIA Checkpoint Citator 2d to locate the Revenue Ruling 2001-60.

    a. What is the ruling's complete citation?

    b. What was the effect of Rev Rul 2001-60 on Rev Proc 99-49 and Rev Rul 55-290?

    c. Which IRS Revenue Procedures favorably cite Rev Rul 2001-60?

    d. What issue does Rev Rul 2001-60 address?

57. Use the CCH Citator to locate the 1956 *William George* Tax Court case.

    a. What is the citation for the case?

    b. What is the title of the paragraph where *George* is annotated?

    c. What Code section is related to the *George* case?

    d. A Revenue Ruling cites the *George* case. What is the citation and title? How does the Revenue Ruling evaluate the *George* case?

58. Use the CCH Citator to locate the 290th Revenue Ruling issued in 1955.

    a. What is its complete Cumulative Bulletin citation? Is this Revenue Ruling still valid?

    b. What tax issue does the Revenue Ruling address?

c. List the citations of any cases that cite Revenue Ruling 1955-290.

d. In what paragraph of the CCH service was this ruling initially discussed?

59. Use the CCH and the RIA Citators to locate the *Estate of Edward Kunze* Seventh Circuit case.

a. What method did you use to find this case?

b. Do the citators list the same citing cases? Explain your response.

c. How did the citing cases generally treat the *Kunze* case? Which citator did you use to determine this?

d. What issues appear to be involved in this case? Which citator did you use to determine this?

60. Use the CCH Citator to locate the 2006 *Gwendolyn A. Ewing* case.

a. What is its citation and what tax issues does the case address?

b. What is the case's direct judicial history?

c. Where is the case annotated in the Standard Federal Income Tax Reporter?

d. The *Robinette* case (2006-1 USTC ¶ 50,213) cites *Ewing*. What is the *Robinette* treatment of the *Ewing* case?

e. Compare the information retrieved using the CCH Citator and the RIA Checkpoint Citator 2nd (question 54). Which was easier to use, and which provided more relevant information?

RESEARCH CASES

61. Jamie is an elementary school teacher, and her adjusted gross income is $31,000. For 2007 and 2008, she spent $350 of her own funds on special school supplies for those children who could not afford to purchase the necessary supplies. She bought these supplies during a seventy-mile round trip to a specialty educational store. Can she deduct any portion of these amounts?

62. Ted's sister, April, was injured while performing her duties as a police officer. She was in the hospital for three weeks before she died from her wounds. The city paid directly to Ted the workers' compensation benefits due to April before she died, as he is April's only surviving relative. How much gross income does Ted recognize upon receiving the benefits?

63. Peggy had been a heavy tobacco user until she joined the Norwood Tobacco Free Program. She had spent a substantial amount of money on nicotine patches and other nonprescription treatments without much success. Her father recently died from lung cancer, and his death made her realize that to kick the habit she would need to get professional help before her smoking created serious medical problems. While she is very pleased at being tobacco free for the first time in ten years, she is wondering whether any of the vast amounts spent on the cure are deductible?

64. Sally sells her home to Bob and pays $9,000 in points for Bob's mortgage, by receiving $9,000 less in sale proceeds. Determine the tax effects on both parties.

65. Ethel and Rick spent $4,500 in allocable interest and taxes and $1,100 in advertising and maintenance for their "bed and breakfast" inn. This year's rental

income from the inn came to $4,900. Determine the tax effects of conducting the B&B using one-third of Ethel and Rick's residence.

66. Carline's son, Leon, who is 10, is a musical prodigy. Carline, also a musical person, has spent a significant amount of time teaching Leon music and promoting his possible career. When Leon finally receives a recording contract, Carline is designated in the contract to receive one-half of Leon's total earnings. Discuss the proper recognition of gross income and related deductions concerning this arrangement.

67. Barbara owns an incorporated consulting business, for which she has spent years building up its respectable reputation. However, business recently has dropped dramatically due to the unprofessional behavior of Cliff, Barbara's husband. Barbara feels that the only way to protect her business is to divorce Cliff. Cliff demands 50 percent of the stock in Barbara's business. The divorce will be costly because Cliff and Barbara cannot reach an agreement about the business's stock. Are the costs of the divorce deductible to Barbara or to Cliff?

68. Newark Marine Food Service (NMFS) sells hot lunches and snacks to the crews of ships that dock at the Port of Newark. According to custom, the officers of the visiting ships receive a 5 percent "commission" from all sales, so that NMFS can retain its "exclusive rights" to the seamen's business. Are the commissions deductible by NMFS?

69. Clara, a community college graduate, works at the Pamper U Hotel in Lake Tahoe. Clara's job is to provide relaxation demonstrations, teach yoga, provide massage therapy, and give lectures on stress management. Since Clara possessed no formal training in any of these subjects, she decided to attend seminars all over the United States on the topics related to her job. She also attended the local university and took physiology classes to learn more about the body and how it functions. Can Clara receive any tax benefits from these educational expenses?

70. John accompanied his wife, Ling, on a business trip to San Diego because Ling is paralyzed from the waist down and confined to a wheelchair. John was not associated with Ling's business directly, but he performed services such as helping Ling overcome architectural barriers, carrying Ling's luggage, facilitating security inspections of Ling at airports, and helping Ling gain access to airplanes. What is the tax treatment of the incremental expenses for John accompanying Ling on the trip?

71. After his divorce, Brown paid the expenses of maintaining the family home, which continued to be the principal residence of his ex-wife and their three children. Thus, he owns the house, but he no longer lives there. Instead, Brown maintains another home as his principal residence. Can Brown claim head of household status, assuming that the divorce decree grants him the dependency exemptions for his children?

72. Alice, the chair of the School of Accountancy, entertains the faculty at her home each semester and has a holiday party at the end of December for the faculty and their families. When a faculty member is promoted or has a paper published in an exceptionally prestigious journal, Alice hosts a "social hour" at her house. She also sponsors a picnic for the faculty and graduate students at

the start of the fall semester to let them get acquainted with each other. To what extent are these expenses deductible?

73. Cambro Construction Company hires union carpenters for home building. Cambro requires, as a condition of employment, that the carpenters provide and maintain various tools of their trade. Cambro pays each carpenter a set amount per hour as a "tool allowance" to cover the costs of the tools. This amount is determined quarterly based on national complied data on the costs of carpenter tools. How should this employee reimbursement be treated for tax purposes?

74. Buddy was injured by Matt in an automobile accident. The court awarded Buddy $30,000 in damages, but Matt was only able to pay Buddy $12,000. They both then considered the matter closed, under these terms. Compute the amount of gross income to Buddy, and to Matt, from this event.

75. Con man Floyd sold Larry the Library of Congress for $150,000. Since Larry didn't have that kind of money, he embezzled the $150,000 from his employer to make the purchase.
    a. How much gross income should Larry and Floyd report as a result of this event?
    b. For tax purposes, how will Larry treat any repayment of the embezzlement to his (former) employer?

76. Reverend Ruth receives a yearly salary of $50,000 and a parsonage allowance of $12,000. She paid $9,000 in rent for the house where she lives, and she spent $1,500 on housing-related purchases. What is her gross income from these items?

77. Jill received a research grant from the University of Minnesota in amounts of $10,000 for her time and $3,000 for related supplies and expenses. She purchased a $28,000 Audi the day after depositing the university's check. Jill is a candidate for a master's degree in philosophy and ethics. What is her gross income from the grant?

78. Earl is a golf course superintendent. He recently was hired by the Jack Nicks Corporation to construct an eighteen-hole course in Wyoming. There will be substantial earthmoving costs in creating the landscape desired for the course. The fairways will have planted grass, but the greens will be "modern greens" containing sophisticated drainage systems. The greens must be replaced when the underlying drainage systems are replaced. Earl would like to know what costs are expensed and what costs capitalized either as part of the land or as depreciable assets.

79. Barry's wife, Terra, died in an accident, leaving him with four young children to raise. Shortly after Terra's funeral, Barry and the children move from the house that Barry and Terra owned for eight years, mainly because they needed a change. Barry buys a new house with the help of Lisa, a realtor. Lisa and Barry start dating and, within one year, Barry and Lisa are married. Lisa has four children of her own. Given that neither Lisa's or Barry's homes are large enough for the combined family of eight children, Lisa and Barry both sell their homes and buy a new six-bedroom house. Lisa owned her home for six years but Barry has owned his most recent house for only one year. All of the

houses show realized gains on the sales. How are these sales of personal residences treated for tax purposes?

80. To what extent should Professor Dodd include in gross income the value of examination copies of text books that he receives without charge from book publishers, if he donates them to a local library and takes a charitable contribution deduction?

State Tax Services

Chapter Outline

Learning Objectives

- Apply the tax research process to state and local issues.

- Know the major features of state tax services.

- Understand the similarities and differences in Federal and state tax research.

- Use the search methodologies that are available for each of the state tax services.

- Know which tax services are most appropriate for different research objectives.

Chapter Outline (continued)

THE STATE AND LOCAL tax environment is becoming increasingly complex and challenging to navigate, due to the states' ever-increasing expansion of their taxing systems. Taxpayers are therefore finding it more difficult to stay abreast of and comply with these evolving state requirements. Thus, state and local tax planning and compliance has become big business for accounting and tax law firms. In today's market, practitioners who service their clients successfully recommend tax solutions that are not only consistent with the client's overall financial goals, but also help the client minimize their state and local tax burdens. Consequently, the tax professional must stay current in this area of tax law, even though this specialized area can represent an additional burden on the practitioner's already tightly scheduled time.

There are numerous reasons for emphasizing state and local tax planning. For many businesses this is an untapped planning opportunity in which practitioners can offer an expertise. This is especially important as many of the most productive Federal tax planning opportunities for businesses have been limited by tax law changes, and exhausted by prior consulting work. While the amount of any one tax paid to individual states may be small, total state and local tax obligations can be almost 50 percent of a business's tax bill. Coordinated state tax planning can substantially reduce this percentage, especially where the taxpayer operates in a variety of state and local taxing jurisdictions and has some flexibility as to where its property and labor force are located.

The power to tax is an inherent authority that all states possess. Generally, local governments must be specifically authorized to impose taxes by state statutory or constitutional provisions. These authorizing provisions, in turn, regulate the rates and operation of local government taxes. Courts in some states, however, have ruled that the power to impose taxes can be implied from broad "home rule" provisions. These rules grant partial autonomy to local government authorities under general state constitutional provisions.

This chapter explores state and local taxation and the resources available for state tax research. Since state and local taxing systems are separate from the Federal tax domain, an overview of state and local taxation is presented before delving into the tax products available to practitioners. Research projects then are then used to demonstrate the major tax services.

IMPORTANCE OF STATE AND LOCAL TAXES

State and local taxes are playing an ever-increasing role in the tax planning of business and individuals alike. While Federal tax rates have remained constant in the past several years, some state and local taxes and rates have been increasing. Often, greater revenues are needed to meet the demands of constituents, so states often must raise the tax burdens of citizens. Tax increases for state and local governments can be especially critical when the economy is in a downturn. During these times, the demands for social programs such as welfare and Medicaid build, while the tax bases for states are reduced due to the slow economy. Since most states constitutionally cannot operate at a deficit, the state and local tax obligations become more of a burden for the taxpaying businesses and individuals. Exhibit 9-1 illustrates the increase in the state taxes over time. In 1970, the tax collected by states was $48 billion, whereas by 2006 the amount rose to over $706 billion. This is more than a 1,370 percent increase in collections in thirty-six years!

Businesses take the level of state and local taxation into consideration when deciding where to locate a new plant or headquarters. This analysis includes not only business taxes but also the individual taxes of the personnel relocating to the new location. Exhibit 9-2 ranks states based on the individuals' per capita state

Exhibit 9-1: State Tax Collections

Year	Collections ($B)	Year	Collections ($B)
1970	48.0	1990	307.1
1975	80.1	1995	393.2
1980	136.9	2000	551.9
1985	214.9	2006	706.3

Sources: U.S. Bureau of the Census.

Exhibit 9-2: State and Local Individual Income Tax Collections per Capita 2005

Rank	State	Dollar Amount	Rank	State	Dollar Amount
	United States	$2,190	26	Virginia	$2,104
1	Vermont	$3,600	27	Ohio	$2,094
2	Hawaii	$3,478	28	Nevada	$2,075
3	Wyoming	$3,418	29	Illinois	$2,069
4	Connecticut	$3,300	30	Idaho	$2,054
5	Delaware	$3,229	31	Indiana	$2,049
6	Minnesota	$3,094	32	Kansas	$2,040
7	Massachusetts	$2,815	33	Montana	$2,004
8	Alaska	$2,799	34	Iowa	$1,939
9	California	$2,724	35	Oklahoma	$1,933
10	New Jersey	$2,631	36	Louisiana	$1,910
11	New York	$2,607	37	Florida	$1,905
12	Rhode Island	$2,443	38	Utah	$1,897
13	Wisconsin	$2,430	39	Mississippi	$1,860
14	Maryland	$2,410	40	Arizona	$1,854
15	West Virginia	$2,367	41	Oregon	$1,791
16	Washington	$2,360	42	Georgia	$1,728
17	Arkansas	$2,358	43	South Carolina	$1,720
18	Michigan	$2,324	44	Alabama	$1,711
19	Maine	$2,323	45	Tennessee	$1,678
20	New Mexico	$2,319	46	Missouri	$1,645
21	North Dakota	$2,203	47	Colorado	$1,640
22	Pennsylvania	$2,193	48	New Hampshire	$1,544
23	Kentucky	$2,178	49	Texas	$1,434
24	Nebraska	$2,158	50	South Dakota	$1,430
25	North Carolina	$2,147			

Sources: State Government Tax Collections: 2005, U.S. Bureau of the Census, available at http://ftp2.census.gov/govs/statetax/05staxss.xls

Exhibit 9-3: State and Local Corporate Income Tax Collections per Capita 2005

State	Collections Per Capita	Rank	State	Collections Per Capita	Rank
U.S. Total	$145	–	Rhode Island	$106	26
Alaska	$888	1	Montana	$105	27
New Hampshire	$365	2	Maine	$103	28
New York	$362	3	Florida	$100	29
Delaware	$296	4	Oregon	$100	30
New Jersey	$256	5	Arkansas	$100	31
West Virginia	$255	6	Idaho	$ 98	32
California	$240	7	Hawaii	$ 97	33
Massachusetts	$207	8	Mississippi	$ 97	34
Michigan	$189	9	Kansas	$ 90	35
Minnesota	$182	10	Alabama	$ 87	36
Illinois	$171	11	Virginia	$ 80	37
Connecticut	$164	12	Louisiana	$ 78	38
North Carolina	$147	13	Georgia	$ 78	39
Maryland	$144	14	Utah	$ 76	40
Wisconsin	$142	15	Colorado	$ 68	41
Pennsylvania	$137	16	South Dakota	$ 63	42
Tennessee	$135	17	Iowa	$ 63	43
Indiana	$132	18	South Carolina	$ 58	44
New Mexico	$126	19	Oklahoma	$ 48	45
North Dakota	$120	20	Missouri	$ 41	46
Arizona	$118	21	Nevada	$ 0	—
Ohio	$117	22	Texas	$ 0	—
Kentucky	$115	23	Washington	$ 0	—
Nebraska	$113	24	Wyoming	$ 0	—
Vermont	$111	25	District of Columbia	$342	

Sources: U.S. Department of Commerce, Bureau of the Census.

and local tax burdens and Exhibit 9-3 shows rankings for state corporate income taxes per capita. The national average for personal state taxes, as a percentage of income, is 11 percent, and the average for Federal and state taxes is about 33 percent (see Exhibit 9-4). However, the state tax burden varies across states, with Vermont having the highest percentage (14.1%), Alaska having the lowest (6.6%) and Indiana, South Carolina, and Utah about in the middle (10.7%).

Many state constitutions constrain the types of taxes that may be imposed within the state and/or set upper limits on tax rates. Therefore, states may be forced to resort to alternative methods for generating revenues, such as trying to increase compliance and imposing substantial penalties. As failure to comply with state and local tax laws becomes more costly, businesses and individuals are requesting additional research from their tax professionals to help manage this significant tax burden.

Exhibit 9-4: Tax Burdens by State and Level of Tax

State and Local Tax Burdens

2007

Combined State and Local Tax Burdens by Rank			Adding Federal Taxes to State/Local Changes Rankings		
State	State and Local Tax Burden	Rank	State	State, Local, and Federal Tax Burden	Rank
Total	11.0%			32.7%	
Vermont	14.1%	1	Vermont	35.1%	5
Maine	14.0%	2	Maine	33.9%	10
New York	13.8%	3	New York	37.1%	2
Rhode Island	12.7%	4	Rhode Island	35.1%	6
Ohio	12.4%	5	Ohio	32.4%	18
Hawaii	12.4%	6	Hawaii	33.0%	16
Wisconsin	12.3%	7	Wisconsin	33.3%	13
Connecticut	12.2%	8	Connecticut	38.3%	1
Nebraska	11.9%	9	Nebraska	31.8%	22
New Jersey	11.6%	10	New Jersey	35.6%	3
Minnesota	11.5%	11	Minnesota	33.9%	11
California	11.5%	12	California	34.3%	8
Arkansas	11.3%	13	Arkansas	30.7%	32
Michigan	11.2%	14	Michigan	31.9%	21
Kansas	11.2%	15	Kansas	31.0%	27
Washington	11.1%	16	Washington	34.0%	9
Louisiana	11.0%	17	Louisiana	29.1%	44
Iowa	11.0%	18	Iowa	30.6%	33
North Carolina	11.0%	19	North Carolina	31.3%	24
Kentucky	10.9%	20	Kentucky	30.4%	34
West Virginia	10.9%	21	West Virginia	29.8%	40
Illinois	10.8%	22	Illinois	33.2%	14
Maryland	10.8%	23	Maryland	33.1%	15
Pennsylvania	10.8%	24	Pennsylvania	31.9%	20
Indiana	10.7%	25	Indiana	30.8%	30
South Carolina	10.7%	26	South Carolina	30.3%	35
Utah	10.7%	27	Utah	30.3%	36
Massachusetts	10.6%	28	Massachusetts	34.4%	7
Mississippi	10.5%	29	Mississippi	28.1%	47
Colorado	10.4%	30	Colorado	31.8%	23
Arizona	10.3%	31	Arizona	31.3%	25
Georgia	10.3%	32	Georgia	30.9%	28
Virginia	10.2%	33	Virginia	32.9%	17
Missouri	10.1%	34	Missouri	30.2%	38
Idaho	10.1%	35	Idaho	29.6%	42
Nevada	10.1%	36	Nevada	35.2%	4
Oregon	10.0%	37	Oregon	30.7%	31
Florida	10.0%	38	Florida	33.6%	12
North Dakota	9.9%	39	North Dakota	30.2%	37
New Mexico	9.8%	40	New Mexico	28.8%	45
Montana	9.7%	41	Montana	29.8%	39
Wyoming	9.5%	42	Wyoming	32.1%	19
Texas	9.3%	43	Texas	29.8%	41
South Dakota	9.0%	44	South Dakota	29.3%	43
Oklahoma	9.0%	45	Oklahoma	27.8%	50
Alabama	8.8%	46	Alabama	28.0%	49
Delaware	8.8%	47	Delaware	31.2%	26
Tennessee	8.5%	48	Tennessee	28.8%	46
New Hampshire	8.0%	49	New Hampshire	30.8%	29
Alaska	6.6%	50	Alaska	28.1%	48
District of Columbia	12.5%	-	District of Columbia	36.4%	-

Source: Tax Foundation calculations based on data from the Bureau of Economic Analysis.

HISTORICAL PERSPECTIVE

Since the time of the early American colonies, payments were made by citizens to their local governing units. Whether these payments were voluntary or required, the purpose of the collections was the same, that is, to support community needs. These early taxing systems were based on the characteristics of the local economy. Accordingly, in the southern states, where cotton was the main commodity, taxes were based on imports/exports, whereas taxes in the northern states were based on an economy of farmland products. By the end of the eighteenth century, property taxes were becoming popular, and by the mid-nineteenth century, property taxes were the cornerstone of the state and local tax systems. In 1890, state tax collections reached the $100 million mark.

States relying on property taxes then needed to supplement these revenue sources with other kinds of taxes. State income taxes were introduced in Wisconsin, in 1911, and gradually spread to most other states and several municipalities. State sales taxes made an appearance in the early twentieth century, with the first city sales tax imposed by New York in the 1930s. The growth of tax base diversification helped to stabilize state and local governments' revenue yields over time.

In 1945, states were collecting almost $6 billion per year, and by 2000 this amount had risen to over $550 billion (see Exhibit 9-1). Some state and local governments' financial burdens have also escalated due to cutbacks in Federal aid. These cuts come at a time when citizens are demanding more public services. The combination of these effects has caused the state and local tax burdens to increase substantially over the past fifty years.

SPOTLIGHT ON TAXATION

Tax Freedom Day

Every year the Tax Foundation determines "Tax Freedom Day," the hypothetical day when taxpayers have earned enough money to pay all of their taxes and now can "work for themselves." In 2007, the National Tax Freedom Day was April 30. There has been a steady increase in the number of days until Tax Freedom Day since 2003. The latest Tax Freedom Day was in 2000 (May 5) when the economy was booming and the dot-com bubble had not yet popped. The earliest Tax Freedom Day since the introduction of Federal income taxes was in the 1930s, when it was in mid-February.

The Tax Foundation determines a Tax Freedom Day for each state as well. In 2007, the earliest dates were for Oklahoma & Alabama (April 12) and Alaska & Mississippi (April 13). The latest state dates were for Connecticut (May 20), New York (May 16), New Jersey (May 10), and Vermont (May 9). For details, go to **http://www.taxfoundation.org/taxfreedomday**

LEGAL PERSPECTIVE

Federal and state constitutional provisions play an integral role in state tax planning. The constitutional validity of state tax laws still is challenged in the courts today, whereas the Federal taxes are rarely questioned on their constitutionality any more. State and local tax challenges address not only whether the taxes fall within the purview of the state constitution, but also whether the laws are federally constitutional. The Federal clauses most frequently providing the basis for state taxation disputes are Supremacy, Commerce, Due Process, Equal Protection, and Privileges and Immunities.

Supremacy

The Supremacy provision in the Federal constitution confers superiority to Federal laws over state laws. That is, Federal laws are "the supreme law of the land" and trump state laws. If a state's constitutional provisions or laws are in conflict with a Federal law, the state provisions are invalid. The **Supremacy Clause** generally is applied to tax conflicts involving the Federal commerce clause, discussed later.

Another important application of the Supremacy Clause concerns the taxation by the states of Federal government operations. If states were permitted to tax the Federal government, Federal supremacy would be impinged. Thus, the Supremacy Clause in the Constitution immunizes the Federal government from taxation by the states.

Commerce

The Federal Constitution **Commerce Clause** states that Congress shall have the power to regulate commerce with foreign nations, among states, and with Native American tribes. This clause contains the most significant Federal limitation on a state's capacity to impose taxes. It grants powers to Congress and places constraints on the states' ability to tax interstate trade.

The commerce clause has a long history of Supreme Court actions. The interpretation of the clause as it now stands is based on the case *Complete Auto Transit Inc. v. Brady*, 430 US 274 (1977). The case involved a tax being imposed on companies for the privilege of conducting interstate transportation businesses. Corporations involved in intra- and interstate commerce were all subject to the tax. In unanimously deciding that the tax was valid, the Supreme Court established the four criteria now regarded as controlling as to whether a state may tax interstate commerce without the tax becoming an unreasonable burden. A tax may be imposed if:

- The activity includes a substantial connection (nexus) with the taxing state

- The tax burden is fairly apportioned

- The tax does not discriminate against interstate commerce

- The tax fairly relates to the services provided by the state

Thus, businesses involved in interstate commerce should be subject to a tax burden related to their fair share of the state's costs of providing benefits to the taxpayer.

Due Process

The Supreme Court also has applied the Federal **Due Process Clause**, found in the Fourteenth Amendment, to limit the territorial scope of a state's taxing authority in interstate commerce cases. States have lost cases in two key situations.

- States seek to tax out-of-state businesses whose connections with the state are not sufficient to satisfy the Due Process Clause.

- The tax imposed does not fairly reflect the taxpayer's activities in the state.

To be successful in applying a tax, states must prove that the business has more than a de minimis existence within the state, and that the taxing base for the interstate enterprise includes only amounts fairly apportioned to its activities within the state. The *Complete Auto Transit* interpretation of the commerce clause also contains these two criteria for successful taxation of interstate commerce. However, the level of a business's existence within the state required to meet the Due Process clause is different from that required by the Commerce Clause.

A landmark case in determining the states' ability to have jurisdiction over out-of-state businesses under the Due Process and Commerce Clauses is *Quill Corp. v. North Dakota*, 504 US 298 (1992). In this case, North Dakota wanted Quill Corporation to collect use tax for North Dakota on its mail order sales within the state. The U.S. Supreme Court held that Quill's mail order business, with its substantial contacts in North Dakota, met the nexus requirement inherent in the Due Process Clause. The Due Process Clause does not require a physical presence by the out-of-state entity for a state to have taxing jurisdiction. Thus, an economic presence rising above a de minimis level is sufficient to tax under the Due Process Clause. However, this same level of customer contact might not be sufficient to create the substantial nexus within a state as required by the Commerce Clause. Since Quill did not have a Commerce-Clause substantial nexus within North Dakota, it could not be required to collect use tax. Thus, this case established that the business presence requirements for the Due Process and Commerce Clauses are not identical.

The Due Process Clause is directed toward the fairness of governmental activities. This "fairness" test is satisfied when an out-of-state entity "purposefully avails itself of the benefits of an economic market in the foreign State." The Commerce Clause, on the other hand, is concerned with the effects of state regulations on the interstate economy. Accordingly, the Commerce Clause requires more than the existence of customers to rise to the level of a nexus within the state, but a physical presence such as an office is not necessary. For example, direct marketing through retail outlets or personnel can create a Commerce-Clause nexus for an out-of-state business. The courts also consistently have ruled that out-of-state entities cannot skirt a state's taxing jurisdiction by contracting with in-state persons to conduct company business that would otherwise create a nexus if the out-of-state company had used its own employees.

In the same year as the *Quill* case, the Supreme Court addressed a related nexus issue in *Wisconsin Department of Revenue v. William Wrigley, Jr., Co.*, 505 US 214 (1992). Wisconsin considered Wrigley's business activities (selling chewing gum) within the state to be sufficient for the imposition of the state franchise tax. Wrigley argued that the business was protected from Wisconsin taxation under the Interstate Income Law.

The Interstate Income Law (Public Law 86-272; 15 USC §§381–384) prevents the income taxation of interstate commerce if a company's only business within the state is the solicitation of orders for sales of tangible personal property. In the *Wrigley* case, the Supreme Court clarified that the definition of "solicitation of orders" goes beyond merely making requests for sales—it includes the entire process associated with requesting orders by out-of-state businesses. Activities that are ancillary to obtaining orders are considered part of the solicitation. Further, activities that are beyond solicitation of orders, but are trivial, are considered de minimis and do not violate the solicitation of orders protection. Having an office located in a state, even if solely for the solicitation of orders, is not de minimis, and can subject a business to state taxation.

Finally, the Due Process Clause does not guarantee that the benefits received by an interstate enterprise will have any direct relationship to the amount of taxes paid to that state. To be fairly related to the services provided by a state, the last test from *Complete Auto Transit*, the tax need only be assessed in proportion to the business's activities within the state. As articulated in *Commonwealth Edison Co. v. Montana*, 453 U.S. 609 (1981), "(A) tax … is a means of distributing the burden of the cost of government. The only benefit to which the taxpayer is constitutionally entitled is derived from his enjoyment of the privileges of living in an organized society, established and safeguarded by the devotion of taxes to public purposes."

SPOTLIGHT ON TAXATION

Streamlined Sales Tax Project

Requiring out-of-state and Internet businesses to collect sales taxes on remote sales might impose an overwhelming burden that could severely restrict interstate commerce. There are over 7,500 different taxing jurisdictions in the United States. Texas alone has over a thousand, when considering its local and special taxing districts. In hopes of someday having businesses collect sales/use taxes, the Streamlined Sales Tax Governing Board, Inc. was created. The mission of its Streamlined Sales Tax Project is to develop measures to implement a radically simplified sales/use tax system. The Project's proposals include tax law simplifications, more efficient administration, and an embracing of emerging technologies to substantially reduce the burden of tax collection. Almost all states that impose sales taxes are involved with the project in some manner. To keep up-to-date on the progress of the Streamlined Sales Tax Project, visit the Governing Board's web site at **http://www.streamlinedsalestax.org**

Uniformity and Equal Protection

The Federal and most state constitutions include an **Equal Protection** and/or a **Uniformity Clause.** These two concepts are closely related for tax purposes, and state courts often treat them as being interchangeable. These rules require that similarly situated taxpayers or property be treated, for tax purposes, in a similar manner. Although the Fourteenth Amendment Equal Protection Clause does not reference taxation specifically, it has been relied upon to determine whether tax provisions treat different taxpayers equally.

The Supreme Court has construed the Equal Protection Clause as barring states from creating arbitrary classifications for taxation, and in particular, for non-resident or out-of-state businesses.[1] Yet, when the only Federal question is equal protection, the Supreme Court gives states a wide latitude in delineating classifications in taxing systems. The state legislature is considered to be in a superior position for designing its taxing system on an equitable and uniform basis. As long as the legislature can justify treating classes of taxpayers differently, the courts typically do not second-guess the wisdom of state legislatures. Accordingly, the Supreme Court's approach to applying this Fourteenth Amendment clause insulates state taxes from most challenges under the Federal Equal Protection Clause.

---

[1]*Metropolitan Life Insurance Co. v. Ward*, 470 U.S. 869 (1985); *WHYY, Inc. v. Glassboro*, 393 U.S. 117 (1968); *Atlantic Refining Co. v. Virginia*, 302 U.S. 22 (1937); *Hanover Fire Ins. Co. v. Harding*, 272 U.S. 494 (1926), *Southern R. Co. v. Greene*, 216 U.S. 400 (1910); *Atlantic Refining Co. v. Commonwealth of Virginia*, 302 U.S. 22 (1937).

Privileges and Immunities

Finally, the Federal constitution grants the citizens of each state all privileges and immunities of citizens in every other state. This means that a nonresident business has the right to engage in commerce within the state, without being subject to different or greater taxes than resident businesses. The main application of this clause has been to invalidate laws that imposed higher tax burdens on out-of-state businesses. Note that the **Privileges and Immunities Clause** applies only to "citizens" of states. Since a corporation is considered a "person" but not a "citizen" under the law, this clause largely protects individuals, while corporations, for the most part, are covered by the Equal Protection Clause instead.

STATE TAX STRUCTURE

The states have modeled their income tax structures on the Federal tax system. All of the states have adopted constitutions and typically use three branches of government: legislative, executive, and judicial. Tax statutes are enacted by the state legislatures. These statutes are signed by the state governor, just as Federal tax laws are signed by the President. Regulatory agencies similar to the IRS issue pronouncements on tax matters and administer the tax law. Finally, state courts hear cases regarding tax matters.

Constitution

While each state's taxing system is unique, they are all constrained by the U.S. Constitution and Federal laws. As discussed in the prior section, many clauses of the U.S. Constitution are applied to state taxation, yet only two clauses explicitly restrict state's taxation: the Import/Export Clause and the very specific Duty of Tonnage Clause. Both of these prohibit states from charging taxes on imports or exports without the consent of Congress. As import/export taxes have become less important at the Federal level, so have these clauses.

Although the Federal laws may appear to dominate state tax issues, it is actually each state's own constitution that is considered the fundamental taxing law, because a constitution places the most relevant restrictions on the state's authority to assess taxes. Generally, state constitutions limit the rates and types of taxes that can be imposed, and they require that tax laws show uniformity, equal protection, and have a public purpose. Since elected legislative bodies enact taxes, there is an eminent presumption of validity for a state's taxing laws. It is the ultimate role of the courts to ensure that the legislature acts within the restraints of Federal and state constitutions.

Requiring that tax revenues be generated only for a **public purpose** is a lofty sounding limitation on a state's ability to tax. However, the definition of "public purpose" is rarely included in constitutions, so the courts have rendered (sometimes vague and broad) interpretations in their decisions for specific taxes. Since the legislature represents a state's citizens, Federal and state courts generally accept the legislative interpretation of the concept.

Legislative

State legislatures are responsible for enacting laws regarding state revenue sources and consequently pass bills amending and augmenting their state's taxing code. While Federal revenue bills constitutionally must start in the House of Representatives, this is not a requirement in all state legislatures. In fact, the jurisdictions of the legislative houses vary from state to state, and there tends to be a significant overlap in their functions. One state, Nebraska, avoids this duplication by having only one legislative body. Once the tax bills are passed by the legislatures and signed by the Governor, they are incorporated into the state's statutory structure.

State tax codes can provide research challenges for tax practitioners. Each state organizes its tax code based on different criteria and has a different numbering system for its tax law. This means that the practitioner who knows that corporate tax laws are found in the 300 sections of the Federal *Internal Revenue Code* (IRC) must conduct a new search for the state corporate income tax laws, if they even exist!

States place varying reliance on the IRC. Some states piggyback most of their individual and business income taxes on the IRC, whereas other states have adopted substantial differences. A current trend in state tax law is selectively to enact changes made by Congress, especially when the Federal changes reduce the state's tax base in a manner the state can ill afford; for instance, some states have refused to adopt the §199 domestic production activities deduction, simply because they cannot afford the resulting loss of revenue. Therefore, the practitioner must be diligent in finding possible differences in state and Federal law when providing tax planning or advice to clients.

Income tax is not the only tax that states utilize, and income taxes may not be the most important revenue generator for the state. In fact, there are several states that do not assess any income taxes. Rather, states rely on a multitude of other taxes, including sales/use, real and personal property, excise on products, severance on natural resources, gaming/gambling, estate/inheritance, and gift taxes. Many states are enacting taxes that are assessed on assets or transactions of service industries, communication and computer operations, and financial enterprises. The mix of taxes varies greatly from state to state. Exhibit 9-5 summarizes the major taxes imposed by each state.

Administrative

Once tax statutes are enacted, they must be interpreted and enforced. These duties fall to administrative agencies created by either statute or constitutional provisions. In most states, the Department of Revenue (Department of Taxation, State Tax Commission, etc.) is the main administrative agency for this purpose. Other smaller agencies administer the more specialized taxes such as employment, tobacco, or fuel taxes. California is an exception in that it has two revenue agencies, the Franchise Tax Board (income and franchise taxes) and the State Board of Equalization (most other taxes).

It has been said that whoever has authority to interpret the law is really the lawmaker, and it is the state revenue agencies that play this role for the state tax laws. These agencies publish regulations, rulings, and various other authoritative pronouncements as aids in interpreting and applying the law to a specific situation. As in the Federal system, it is the courts' duty to ensure that the administrative agencies do not overstep their authority.

Most state revenue agencies issue rulings for specific taxpayers, similar in nature to Private Letter Rulings (PLRs) issued by the IRS. As with PLRs, the letters are for the exclusive use of the taxpayer requesting the guidance and usually cannot be relied upon by other taxpayers as authority. These private rulings, however, may provide taxpayers with hints as to the revenue agency's position on a particular issue and, therefore, are useful to the practitioner.

Exhibit 9-5: Selected Taxes Imposed by Each State

State	Income		Franchise[1]	General Sales	Tangible Property	Estate & Inheritance	Gift	Severance
	Ind.	Corp.						
Alabama	Yes	Yes	Yes	Yes	Yes	Yes	No	Yes
Alaska	No	Yes	No	No	Yes	Yes	No	Yes
Arizona	Yes	Yes	No	Yes	Yes	Yes	No	Yes
Arkansas	Yes	Yes	Yes	Yes	Yes	Yes	No	Yes
California	Yes	Yes	No	Yes	Yes	Yes	No	Yes
Colorado	Yes	Yes	No	Yes	Yes	Yes	No	Yes
Connecticut	Yes	Yes	Yes	Yes	Yes	Yes	Yes	No
Delaware	Yes	Yes	Yes	No	No	Yes	No	No
District of Columbia	Yes	Yes	No	Yes	Yes	Yes	No	No
Florida	No	Yes	Yes	Yes	Yes	Yes	No	Yes
Georgia	Yes	Yes	Yes	Yes	Yes	Yes	No	No
Hawaii	Yes	Yes	Yes[2]	Yes	No	Yes	No	No
Idaho	Yes	Yes	No	Yes	Yes	Yes	No	Yes
Illinois	Yes	Yes	Yes	Yes	No	Yes	No	No
Indiana	Yes	Yes	No	Yes	Yes	Yes	No	Yes
Iowa	Yes	Yes	No	Yes	No	Yes	No	No
Kansas	Yes	Yes	Yes	Yes	Yes	Yes	No	Yes
Kentucky	Yes	Yes	Yes	Yes	Yes	Yes	No	Yes
Louisiana	Yes	Yes	Yes	Yes	Yes	Yes	Yes	Yes
Maine	Yes	Yes	No	Yes	Yes	Yes	No	No
Maryland	Yes	Yes	No	Yes	Yes[3]	Yes	No	No
Massachusetts	Yes	Yes	No	Yes	Yes	Yes	No	No
Michigan	Yes	Yes	No	Yes	Yes	Yes	No	Yes
Minnesota	Yes	Yes	No	Yes	Yes	Yes	No	Yes
Mississippi	Yes	Yes	Yes	Yes	Yes	Yes	No	Yes
Missouri	Yes	Yes	Yes	Yes	Yes	Yes	No	No
Montana	Yes	Yes	No	No	Yes	Yes	No	Yes
Nebraska	Yes	Yes	Yes	Yes	Yes	Yes	No	Yes
Nevada	No	No	No	Yes	Yes	Yes	No	No
New Hampshire	Yes[4]	Yes	No	No[5]	No	Yes	No	No
New Jersey	Yes	Yes	No	Yes	Yes	Yes	No	No
New Mexico	Yes	Yes	No	Yes	Yes	Yes	No	Yes
New York	Yes	Yes	Yes	Yes	No	Yes	No	No
North Carolina	Yes	Yes	Yes	Yes	Yes	Yes	Yes	No
North Dakota	Yes	Yes	No	Yes	Yes	Yes	No	Yes
Ohio	Yes	Yes	Yes	Yes	Yes	Yes	No	Yes
Oklahoma	Yes	Yes	Yes	Yes	Yes	Yes	No	Yes

continued

[1]Franchise taxes based on net income are listed here as an income tax and not a franchise tax.
[2]On financial institutions only.
[3]Only on property connected with business.
[4]Tax on interest and dividends only.
[5]Sales tax on meals, rooms, rentals, and telecommunications only.

Exhibit 9-5: Selected Taxes Imposed by Each State (Continued)

State	Income		Franchise[1]	General Sales	Tanqible Property	Estate & Inheritance	Gift	Severance
	Ind.	Corp.						
Oregon	Yes	Yes	No	No	Yes	Yes	No	No
Pennsylvania	Yes	Yes	Yes	Yes	No	Yes	No	No
Rhode Island	Yes	Yes	Yes	Yes	Yes	Yes	No	No
South Carolina	Yes	Yes	Yes	Yes	Yes	Yes	No	No
South Dakota	Yes	No	No	Yes	No	Yes	No	Yes
Tennessee	Yes	Yes	Yes	Yes	Yes	Yes	Yes	Yes
Texas	No	Yes[7]	Yes	Yes	Yes	Yes	No	Yes
Utah	Yes	Yes	Yes	Yes	Yes	Yes	No	Yes
Vermont	Yes	Yes	Yes	Yes	Yes	Yes	No	No
Virginia	Yes	Yes	No	Yes	Yes	Yes	No	No
Washington	No	No	No	Yes	Yes	Yes	No	No
West Virginia	Yes	Yes	Yes	Yes	Yes	Yes	No	Yes
Wisconsin	Yes	Yes	No	Yes	Yes	Yes	No	Yes
Wyoming	No	No	No	Yes	Yes	Yes	No	Yes

[6]Part of franchise tax.

Federal regulations and rulings may be pertinent to state tax issues. For states that piggyback income, estate, or other taxes on Federal statutes, guidance in interpreting the law will come from the Federal pronouncements. As previously stated, the degree to which states follow Federal law varies greatly.

Judicial

State judicial systems are, for the most part, patterned on the Federal system. Most states use three levels of courts: supreme courts, appeals (appellate) courts, and trial courts. However, some states have only one appeals level court, whereas others have four levels by adding a county or district trial court with limited jurisdiction. The functions of the levels of state courts are similar to the Federal functions. The trial courts establish the facts and apply the law to these facts. The appeals courts review the trial court's application of the law to the set of facts. They generally rely on the trial court's account of the facts. The state's Supreme Court usually holds powers corresponding to the Federal Supreme Court; it is the final interpretation of an extant law of the state, but its precedents apply only to the state in which it is located. For those states that use only two levels of courts, the functions of the appeals and supreme courts are conjoined.

While most states do use a three-tier judicial system, it may not be inherently obvious from the court names what their precedential values are. A "superior court" is likely to be a trial court or can be an appellate court, but it probably is not the highest court of the state. Most of the intermediate courts have the words "appeals" or "appellate" in their names. However, the highest court of a state can also be called the "Court of Appeals." In New York, for example, the Supreme Court is its trial court and its highest court is called the Court of Appeals. The most diversity among states is with the trial courts. There are county, municipal, circuit, district, and superior trial courts, just to name a few. Each state has organized its trial courts to meet the needs of its citizens and judicial system.

Whereas the Federal judicial system includes a court specifically for tax cases, the Tax Court, most states do not have an equivalent. Rather, there may be administrative (quasi-judicial) tribunals authorized to expedite settlements of tax disputes. The decisions of these tribunals generally are available to the public, but they tend to have little precedential value. The findings generally apply only to the taxpayer bringing the dispute. As with other such documents, they can shed light on the state's position on a particular issue.

None of the tax services cull the tax cases from state court reporters and accumulate them into a state tax court service, like the CCH USTC or the RIA AFTR reporters. The tax cases are intermixed in the state reporters with all the other types of cases that state courts hear. Fortunately, the ability to search electronically eliminates any inconvenience that not having dedicated reporters might cause.

Multistate

Companies conducting business in more than one state are subject to multistate taxation. The income of the company must be apportioned among the states in which it conducts business. To create a greater uniformity and consistency in the measurement of business income, the **Uniform Division of Income for Tax Purposes Act (UDITPA)** was drafted by the **National Conference of Commissioners on Uniform State Laws** in 1957. This exercise received a mixed reception among the states.

Then, in 1967, the **Multistate Tax Commission (MTC)**[2] was created through an organization of state governments called the **Multistate Tax Compact**. The MTC adopted the UDITPA as part of its Articles and issued regulations interpreting the UDITPA in 1971 and 1973. It continues to issue apportionment rules. Special industries that have been addressed include construction, interstate trucking, airlines, television and radio broadcasters, publishers, and financial institutions. The MTC has strongly encouraged states to adopt the uniform tax laws and abide by its regulations. It has been successful in this endeavor as forty-seven states (as of 2007) are members or participants in MTC. The states not associated with MTC are Delaware, Nevada, and Virginia.

The purposes of MTC are to:

- Facilitate determination of state and local tax liabilities through equitable apportionment and settlement of apportionment disputes.

- Promote uniformity and compatibility across the state taxing systems.

- Improve taxpayer convenience and compliance in filing returns and other phases of tax administration.

- Avoid double taxation.

The MTC believes that greater uniformity in multistate taxation will ensure that interstate commerce is more fairly taxed, lessen compliance costs for taxpayers and revenue agencies, and reduce the potential for congressional intervention in state fiscal authority.

Participating states may take advantage of the **Joint Audit Program**, which allows the MTC to perform a comprehensive audit of a business's taxes for several states simultaneously. This can save the states and the taxpayer time and compliance costs. Over the past five years the Joint Audit Program has completed over 1,600 audits.

Another program offered by MTC is the **National Nexus Program**. The central function of this program is to facilitate information sharing among partici-

---

[2]http://www.mtc.gov

pating states and, accordingly, to increase state tax compliance by multistate businesses. For taxpayers, the MTC provides the **Multistate Alternative Dispute Resolution Program**. This unique program affords taxpayers the opportunity to resolve common tax issues with several states at once. Further, the MTC assists taxpayers with negotiations and drafting settlement agreements to be submitted to participating states.

SPOTLIGHT ON TAXATION

Quotation

The thing generally raised on city land is taxes.

—Charles Dudley Warner

ILLUSTRATIVE RESEARCH EXAMPLES

Sample research projects will be used to demonstrate effective state tax research methods. It is important that *you* attempt this research project using the various tax services available to you. The procedural knowledge necessary to perform state tax research effectively can be acquired only through hands-on practice. The remainder of this chapter is designed to guide you through the basic tax services—it is *not* a substitute for your actually performing the research yourself.

Research Project 9–1 Vincent Lopez is opening a new bowling establishment in Virginia. Vincent would like to know the sales tax implications for this business. Specifically, on which assets purchased for his business must Vincent collect sales taxes, and which will be exempt? Is bowling considered to be rendering a service, or is it the renting of tangible personal property, or a combination of both?

Research Project 9–2 Desiree Ward is considering starting an outdoor gear manufacturing plant. She is trying to decide which state would be best for tax purposes—South Dakota, Montana, or Wyoming. Her main concern is with regard to personal and corporate income taxes, state sales tax rates, franchise taxes, and property taxes on inventory.

These two projects are very common types of state research projects. The first requires locating specific tax information for a single state. The second involves a comparison among multiple states on a number of taxes. While each can be researched using the same services, the method for searching the services will be quite different for each project.

RIA STATE AND LOCAL SERVICE

Research Institute of America's **RIA Checkpoint State & Local Tax (SALT)** service is a comprehensive analysis of state and local taxes for all fifty states and the District of Columbia (D.C.). The service is designed to let the researcher designate the states, type of taxes, and documents to be searched. Any or all of the states' taxes and documents may be searched simultaneously. Essentially all of the taxes imposed by states and most enacted by localities are covered in this service. For a complete list of the taxes and documents included in the RIA SALT service, see Exhibit 9-6. A practitioner would be hard pressed to find another service that affords better access to state and local tax materials.

Exhibit 9-6: RIA Search States Tax Type & Document Selection Screen

As with the Federal Checkpoint materials, editorial explanations and annotations are an integral part of this service. The explanations are particularly useful when investigating a state's taxes with which you are unfamiliar, such as the Ohio commercial activity tax (CAT) or the business and occupation (gross revenue) tax of Washington State. The explanations contain links to all the supporting materials, making retrieval a seamless process. The annotations for court and agency decisions also are linked to their primary sources.

Special Features

RIA SALT has many features that were especially developed for this service. These options enhance the effectiveness and efficiency of researching state and local tax issues.

StateNet StateNet is a database consisting of all proposed and current enacted legislation in full text. For proposed legislation, the current status of bills can be tracked through StateNet. This is extremely valuable when a proposed change in the state tax law could have a major impact on the practitioner's clients. Status reports for legislative bills, executive orders, and ballot measures are furnished for each state. Within the Current Calendars heading is the Effective Date Calendar database, which lists each state's legislative enactment conventions. For example, California's effective date for newly enacted legislation is the following January 1 or as provided in the Act, whereas South Carolina is twenty days after the Governor's approval, or as specified in the Act. Lastly, current legislative calendars are reproduced in StateNet.

All State Tax Guide   The **All State Tax Guide** is a concise state-by-state analysis of all major taxes, with citations to state materials. The Guide covers interstate law, income allocation and apportionment, uniform acts, and the MTC. It offers numerous tables, charts, and checklists for a variety of tax data, as well as calendars for important reporting dates and monthly listings of recently approved state and local tax laws. The list of official state contacts makes it easy to find an address or phone number for taxing authorities. Also included is the *State & and Local Taxes Weekly* newsletter.

State Newsletters and Journals   The latest news on state tax developments is available through the *State & Local Taxes Weekly* newsletter. This newsletter offers practice-oriented analysis from national experts and breaking news, organized by state, making it easy to identify what is of interest to the practitioner. Also included with the SALT service is the *Journal of Multistate Taxation and Incentives*. The full-length articles in this journal generally report on multistate tax issues with an emphasis on practical planning opportunities, whereas the short technical comments focus on emerging tax issues for particular states.

Create-a-Chart   The **Create-a-Chart** feature facilitates the building of multistate charts that can cut across a variety of taxes and/or states. These convenient summary charts can be exported to a word processing or spreadsheet document. The product supports linking information on the charts to controlling authority and/or RIA's explanation paragraphs. These links are maintained when the chart is exported. The practitioner can designate the type of tax (income, etc.), a chart type (tax rates, starting point for computing taxable income, etc.), and which states to include in the comparison. Over 100 chart types are offered in Create-a-Chart.

Compare It   The RIA feature, **Compare It**, enables the researcher to compare the tax treatment of an item in one state to the treatment in another state or with the Federal treatment. This makes it easy to compare the tax treatment of an item in multiple states, and it eliminates the need to return to the list of documents when performing multiple state searches as would be necessary with Research Project 9–2. In Exhibit 9-7, for example, first locate the RIA sales tax explanations for Wyoming, click on Compare It, and then you can easily find the Montana and South Dakota sales tax explanations by merely clicking on the state names. Compare It is available only for explanatory materials, and not for state statutes or regulations.

As with the Federal databases, the SALT databases can be entered using the three search methods: keyword search, citation, and contents. The multistate search option is different, though. As a variant of a keyword search, it is demonstrated under the Keyword Search heading.

Keyword Search

The opening screen for RIA Checkpoint (see Exhibit 6-1, Chapter 6) allows the researcher to choose a practice area. Upon selecting "State & Local," Checkpoint offers a list of the states. All the states or any number of separate states may be designated for the search. At this juncture, one cannot enter keywords. Checkpoint requires that a type of tax and document be specified before a keyword search may occur. Exhibit 9-6 displays the choices for taxes and documents. The offerings ap-

Exhibit 9-7: RIA State & Local Document Screen and Compare It

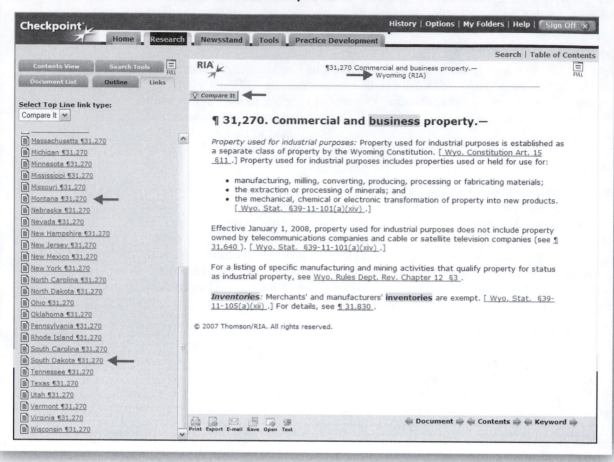

pearing on this screen are customized to the state(s) selected in the previous screen. Accordingly, this full list of taxes would not be offered for every state. Again, any or all of the taxes and document databases may be marked for the search.

With respect to Research Project 9–1, Virginia was selected in the list of states, sales tax was checked for the taxes, and several document types were marked in the document type section (see Exhibit 9-6). The search results link to explanations, regulations, and rulings pertaining to the sales taxes on bowling establishments in Virginia. By reading these documents, Research Project 9–1 can be fully analyzed. Rather than designating taxes and documents, the Search Other State Products option is available (see Exhibit 9-6). This accesses secondary sources such as RIA newsletters and journals in addition to StateNet and Federal cases on state topics. These databases may be searched using keywords or citations, depending on the nature of the database.

Multiple Sources Search   As can be seen in Exhibit 9-8, one of the search choices offered is Search Multiple Sources. A comparison of Exhibits 9-6 and 9-8 reveals that the document categories are not similar for these two keyword search functions. In fact, the Search Multiple Sources is designed for entering keywords (1) selecting document sources (2), and then searching (3). This closely resembles the Federal Practice Area keyword search format (see Exhibit 6-1, Chapter 6), and the same thesaurus and query tool functions are available.

Along with primary sources, editorial materials, current newsletters, and journals, the Multiple Sources offers the Miscellaneous Multistate Materials database. This database consists of materials from the Multistate Tax Compact, the Multistate Tax Commission, and the Federation of Tax Administrators. It also contains numerous multistate agreements and acts, formulas for apportionment and allocation of income, and Federal laws on state taxation.

Since the Search Multiple Sources option lacks a tax type indicator, the type of state tax being investigated must be included as a keyword, to narrow the results to the particular tax of interest. As can be seen in Exhibit 9-8, for Research Project 9–1, the terms *bowling* and *sales tax* were entered as keywords, and Virginia was selected from the State and Local Taxes list. The documents identified using Search States were also located by Search Multiple Sources.

Citation Search

Unlike the Federal Practice Area, the SALT materials do not allow state citation searches directly on the opening screen. Rather, only Federal cases on state tax issues may be searched without selecting a state. The Federal cases may be searched by name of the plaintiff or defendant, citation, or keyword. Since customized templates for the different court reporters are not furnished, the researcher must know the proper format for the citation.

Exhibit 9-8: RIA Search Multiple Sources Screen

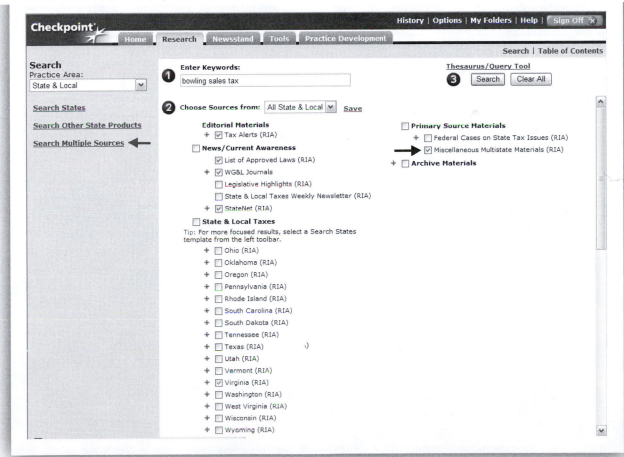

State statutes, regulations, rulings, and cases may be located by citation, but a state must be chosen before these options appear. The citation templates are customized based on the state selected (see Exhibit 9-9), and only one state's citations may be searched at a time. If more than one state is chosen in Search States, the Find by Citation option is not offered.

State Searches also supports a keyword search for courts and rulings using date restrictions. These two searches, Cases by Court/Date and Rulings by Date, also require a state to be selected before the options are accessible, because the listing of courts and ruling types are also customized by state. While these are technically keyword search options, the taxpayer's name may be entered as the keyword, thus functioning similar to a citation search. The ability to restrict the search by date is particularly useful when updating a previously searched tax issue.

Contents Search

The RIA SALT service supports Table of Contents (TOC) and Index searches. These methods allow the researcher to treat the tax service as if it were in a printed book. Thus, as in a book, the TOC and Index can be browsed for the topic of interest. In many cases, this methodology for searching is more efficient than the keyword search. By narrowing the search through focusing on the contents of

Exhibit 9-9: RIA Find by Citation Search Screen

databases, fewer extraneous documents are retrieved when a keyword search is performed. The limitation with this type of search is that only those databases containing tables of contents or indexes are searchable.

The Checkpoint TOC option is available from all screens. Therefore, the researcher does not need to be in the State and Local Practice Area to begin a TOC search. The methodology that is effective in a Federal TOC search also would be appropriate for the SALT search. Besides the editorial materials, StateNet, and newsletters, each state has a listing in the TOC.

One of the most useful subheadings listed for each state is the Index. By drilling down through the Index, the same documents previously identified for Research Project 9–1 can be found. Starting with Sales/Use in the Virginia Index, *bowling alleys* is one of the terms listed. Since the listing under Sales/Use is quite long and the keyword search is not permitted, using the "Ctrl-F" command to bring up the "Find" box and entering "bowling" quickly displays the entries desired. These drill-down techniques are efficient in locating pertinent documents; however, the drawback is that each subheading must be examined separately. Access to each state's index is also furnished when it is the only state selected for the Search States option.

Research Project 9–2 requires the comparison of various taxes in three states. By using the drill-down method in RIA SALT, Montana, South Dakota, and Wyoming can be selected. Performing a keyword search with terms such as *corporation "income tax" rates*, the rates for each state (or no rates) are easily identified. Applying this same method for the other taxes of interest brings up all the essential information necessary to resolve Research Project 9–2.

CCH NetWork State Service

Like RIA Checkpoint, Commerce Clearing House's Tax Research NetWork includes a complete state tax service. Unlike RIA, CCH features Sales/Property Tax and State Business Income Tax as practice area Tabs available from its opening window (see Exhibit 6-11, Chapter 6). The State Tax Tab provides access to the databases in these two tabs and all of the other state materials offered by CCH. This makes the initial screen of the State Tab quite lengthy. Due to this length, the very useful search option, Topical Indexes, located at the bottom of the screen, may be overlooked by researchers. Since all of the state materials are retrievable through the State Tax Tab, the focus in this section is solely on the State Tax Tab.

State Tax Tab

News Services   The State Tax Tab begins with the Current Features and Journals (News) heading to stress the importance of keeping up-to-date on current state tax issues (see Exhibit 9-10). The state news database also is accessible from any of the state tabs. CCH's daily news update is *State Tax Day*. The prior twelve months of issues may be searched by keyword or by TOC by clicking on the title. The TOC is organized by state and, within a state, by type of taxes the state imposes. News items that are not related to a specific state are found under the All States heading.

State Tax Review is a weekly newsletter that covers current changes in laws, new administrative rulings, and pertinent court decisions in every state. It also contains articles from experts on the CCH State Tax Advisory Board and contributing

Exhibit 9-10: CCH NetWork State Tax Opening Screen

editors. CCH has a series of Tax Alert newsletters and Cases and Rulings in the News by States. The latter are cases and rulings that have been promulgated in the past few months.

State Tax Reporters   The backbone of the CCH state tax service is the **State Tax Reporters**. This service combines detailed explanations, primary source materials, and practical compliance guidance. All of the major taxes imposed by states and localities are covered by the service. Although the CCH explanations are organized by tax type, with links to related primary sources, state material is retrieved by selecting the state(s) of interest. RIA requires the researcher to identify the type of documents to be searched, but CCH assumes all materials are of interest. The list of document types searched can be reduced in the Search Tools feature. A list of what is being searched is summarized in the Search Tools window. (Search Tools is in the top Tool Bar; see Exhibit 9-10.) The State Tax Reporters may be searched using keywords, TOC, or a combination of the two.

Keyword Search: Searching the State Tax Reporters for a solution to Research Project 9–1 begins by selecting Virginia on the opening State Tax Tab Screen as shown in Exhibit 9-10. Always click Clear Selections (in the top Tool Bar; see Exhibit 9-10) before starting a new search to make sure only the databases of interest are included. In case there are any current cases, rulings, or final or pending legislation with regard to bowling, these databases also are selected (see Exhibit 9-10). CCH automatically applies a thesaurus to the keywords entered, unless it is turned off in Search Tools. In this search, there are no synonyms for the word *bowling*. Search Tools is also where the type of keyword search may be changed to all terms, any terms, near, exact phrase, or Boolean if preferred.

Exhibit 9-11 is one of the Virginia documents retrieved by a CCH search. The buttons supplied above the annotation have links to the Statutes, Regulations, Explanations, Cases and Rulings, and Related Topics—State. This last button is the state version of the Federal Smart Relate feature and functions similar to the Compare It in RIA Checkpoint. Clicking on the button displays a list of related topics for each of the other states.

Content Search: Rather than checking the box before a state in the State Tax Reporters, clicking on the title displays a list of the three databases available for the state: State Tax Reporters, Smart Charts and Tools, and Topical Index. The contents of the State Tax Reporters and the Topical Index are organized by types of taxes and also contain other germane topics. This makes it possible for the user to pick a state and tax type, and then perform a keyword search. Using

Exhibit 9-11: CCH Document Search Results

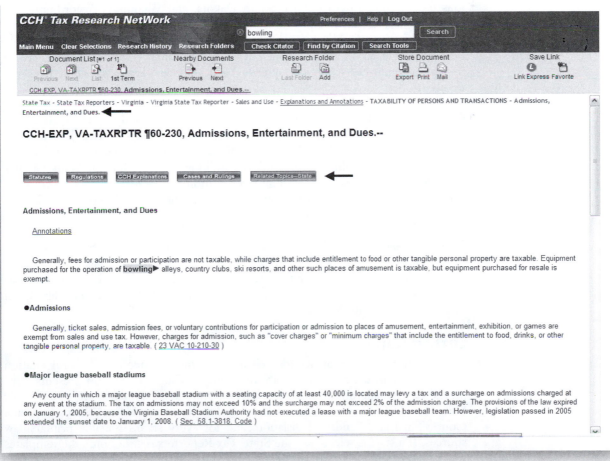

this method in the State Tax Reporters, checking Virginia, Sales and Use taxes, and entering the term *bowling* results in the same document list as a keyword search from the opening screen. The Topic Index may be searched in the same manner as the State Tax Reporters or using the drill-down method until bowling is found.

Multistate Publications   CCH offers several multistate databases including corporate income tax, property tax, and sales tax guides. Each is designed to be an all-in-one guide emphasizing multistate planning yet delivering state-by-state details for every topic. Cost-effective planning ideas are presented, and the "at-a-glance" charts are effective in finding quick answers to each state's treatment of key taxes.

Included with the specialized multistate databases is the State Tax Guide. This is similar to the Master Tax Guide, as it is intended for finding quick answers to everyday questions on taxes levied in every state. Thus, its treatment of tax issues is very concise—state tax statutes and pronouncements are summarized rather than reproduced. Each state has a page (Taxes by State heading) listing its major taxes, tax base and rates, and due dates. There also are charts (Charts heading) for most taxes that provide each state's imposition and rates. This publication can be an extremely efficient tool when all that is needed is a short answer to a simple question or a comparison among a few states on a particular tax.

The information needed for Reseach Project 9–2 includes the rates for various taxes imposed by Montana, South Dakota, and Wyoming. Accordingly, the Quick Answer Charts in the Multistate Quick Answer Charts database or Charts in the State Tax Guide provides the data desired. These charts list each state that levies the tax of interest, the rates imposed, and/or the tax base to which the tax is applied. A chart can quickly be developed for the client of Research Project 9–2.

Practice Aids   The latest in state legislation actions is found in the Practice Aids section of the State Tax Tab. This Week's Legislative Activity, Regulatory Activity, Current Year's Final and Pending Legislation, and Prior Year's Enacted Legislation are located in the Practice Aids. In addition, the Tax Law by State contains primary tax law for each state. The Constitution for each state, its revised (consolidated) statutes, city and/or county ordinances, and uncodified (unconsolidated) statutes are obtainable through Tax Law by State.

Topical Indexes   As previously mentioned, the last feature on the State Tax Tab is the Topical Indexes to the Multistate tax guides. Each state also has its own index, but these are accessed through the State Tax Reporter TOC for the state. The major advantage of using an index is that the definition of the term is considered, not just its occurrence in the document.

Citation Search

State citation searches are conducted in the same manner as a Federal citation search. Once in the State Tax Tab, the Find by Citation function presents templates that are appropriate for state citation searches. Templates are supplied for State Tax Day, Standard Federal Income Tax Reporter, United States Supreme Court, Final and Pending legislation, and for every state's possible primary law sources. If a state is selected in the State Tax Reporters section, only the templates for that state will appear, as can be seen in Exhibit 9-12.

SPOTLIGHT ON TAXATION

Disposable Income

The Bureau of Economic Analysis computes per capita personal income. For 2005, the top five states by disposable income are located in the Northeast, and the lowest five states are in the Southeast and West. Louisiana's entrance into the bottom five is due to the hurricanes that brought severe destruction to the state.

Ranking	State	Per Capita Income
1	Connecticut	$39,974
2	New Jersey	37,817
3	Massachusetts	37,711
4	Maryland	35,986
5	New Hampshire	34,399
46	New Mexico	25,045
47	West Virginia	24,761
48	Arkansas	24,264
49	Mississippi	23,246
50	Louisiana	22,813
Average	United States	35,509

U.S. Bureau of Economic Analysis, **http://www.bea.gov**.

LEXISNEXIS ACADEMIC

The state tax data included in the LexisNexis Academic service is offered through both of the searching engines, Search and Sources. The libraries presented in each are, to some extent, singular. Accordingly, the Search and Sources Tabs each are visited to make a thorough search of the documents available in Lexis Nexis Academic.

Search

As with Federal tax research, state tax libraries are located at the Legal button on the Search Tab. Exhibit 9-13 illustrates that the two primary state tax sources are cases (Federal & State Cases) and statutes (Federal & State Codes). The pull-down menu for the cases is visible for the Select Sources. Notice that a particular state may be selected to search. Cases can be searched for by using keywords, plaintiff and/defendant names, citation (examples of proper format are supplied in Citation Help), judge's name, and counsel or firm name. Date restrictions also are possible. The entry boxes for these search options cannot be seen in Exhibit 9-13 as they are behind the pull-down menu. Any cases retrieved may be run through the Shepard's Citator to determine their precedential value.

The state code searching is more limited in the number of databases offered. All state constitutions, statutory provisions, court rules, and so on are in a single library. Date restrictions are not permitted.

Sources

When Sources, Taxation Law is selected as the Area of Law in Step 1 and United States is the Country Filter in Step 2, the sources can be filtered further by select-

Exhibit 9-12: CCH Find by Citation

CCH® Tax Research NetWork™   Preferences | Help | Log Out

Search

Main Menu   Clear Selections   Research History   Research Folders   Check Citator   Find by Citation   Search Tools

Find by Citation

Type the citation number in the appropriate box and click on Search.

[Search]   Enter a complete citation: [   ]

State Tax

New York

[Search]   [   ]
[Search]   CCH ¶ [   ]
[Search]   N.Y. Tax Law § [   ]
[Search]   N.Y. Real Property Tax Law § [   ]
[Search]   N.Y. Cons. Laws, Ch. [   ] , § [   ]
[Search]   Reg. § [   ] (N.Y. State)
[Search]   TSB-M- [   ] Example: 99(3)C
[Search]   TSB-A- [   ] Example: 99(51)S
[Search]   ALJ and TAT: DTA No. [   ]
[Search]   Important Notice: N- [   ] - [   ]
[Search]   Guidance: [   ]
[Search]   [   ] N.Y.2d [   ]
[Search]   [   ] N.Y.3d [   ]
[Search]   [   ] N.Y. [   ]

ing a region or specific state from the pull-down menu shown in Exhibit 9-14. The categories of sources (Step 3) are customized to the region or state chosen. The sources offered are more expansive than in the Search Tab. Besides the state cases and regulations available through the Search Tab, Sources may contain state revenue decisions, newsletters, journals, IRS pronouncements, and even Kleinrock materials and newspaper articles. The selection of sources varies greatly by state or region. However, state constitutions are not one of the sources included in these sources. Therefore, the Search Tab would need to be accessed for any research on constitutional questions.

WESTLAW STATE SERVICES

Westlaw contains an extensive library of databases for state tax research. Exhibit 9-15 shows only part of the list of these databases. Note that the list includes the Bureau of National Affairs (BNA) Tax Management Portfolios devoted exclusively to state taxes, and the RIA state series. Besides furnishing access to all state tax statutes, regulations, court cases, and administrative pronouncements, Westlaw enhances the tax practitioner's ability to stay ahead of the curve on new state legislation by providing

Exhibit 9-13: LexisNexis Academic Legal Search

databases to track current, pending, and proposed state bills. Newsletters such as the BNA Daily Tax Report and the RIA State and Local Taxes Weekly also help keep the practitioner up-to-date.

Find and KeyCite

The Find a State Tax Document, on the opening Tax Tab screen (see Exhibit 7-11, Chapter 7), allows the researcher to enter the citation for state primary sources. Since the templates for entering citations are based on the state chosen, searching for a specific state document is easy if the general citation is known.

Another method for entering state law citations is to use **KeyCite**. The citation, however, must be in a format recognized by Westlaw. If the researcher does not know the format, the Publication List can be referenced. Unlike Find by Citation, the KeyCite publication list is not linked to templates for entering the citations.

Directory

There are two ways to access the state databases in the Directory. The first method is through the Topical Materials by Area of Practice and selecting Taxation. The

Exhibit 9-14: LexisNexis Academic Browse Sources

State Tax Materials is one of the files in the list. It contains the complete list of state databases found in Exhibit 9-15.

The second Directory heading leading to state tax materials is the U.S. State Materials. Since a taxation subheading is not displayed as one of the library options, a comprehensive search of state tax materials is not possible. By selecting the Other U.S. States subheading, however, access to tax materials is available through each state because Tax Materials is one of the legal topics offered for each state. Thus, each state's tax databases must be searched separately. To search across states, the researcher would select from libraries such as Case Law or Statutes & Legislative Services. Drilling down through these libraries, the researcher arrives at databases covering taxation.

Tax Tab

The Tax Tab lists several headings for state taxation (see Exhibit 7-11, Chapter 7). Expanding the More … headings presents an extended list of the state tax materials and databases (Statutes, Regulations, Cases, and Administrative Decisions) by individual state. Whether selected on the Tax Tab opening screen or after expanding the list, the databases may be searched using either natural language (all terms searched) or terms and connectors. Field filters are available, as is a thesaurus.

Exhibit 9-15: Westlaw State Databases

One can search some of the state tax databases by TOC. The State Tax Portfolios are listed in the TOC pull-down menu (see Exhibit 7-11, Chapter 7). Further, RIA products and some of the treatises have TOCs that can be browsed.

Practitioners performing state research frequently will want to create state and/or federal circuit case tab(s) for easy access to these databases. Unfortunately, there are not state tabs dedicated solely to taxation.

BNA State Services

The BNA complements its U.S. Tax Management Portfolios with a State Tax Series. As with the other BNA Portfolios, the state series is topic-driven and features analysis, insights, and guidance from leading state and local tax authorities on a variety of state issues. Some of the Portfolios offer an overview of a tax topic, while others focus on complex income, sales and use, or property tax issues. For topics such as credits and incentives or income taxation, it may take several Portfolios to cover all of the states. The state taxes and a sampling of the types of issues covered by the more than sixty State Portfolios are presented in Exhibit 9-16.

Exhibit 9-16: BNA State Portfolio List

BNA State Portfolio Topics

Taxes and Issues Covered	Issues Covered
Corporate Income & Franchise Taxes	Procedures and Administration
Gross Receipts Taxes	Managing State Tax Audits
Personal Income Taxes	State Tax Appeal Systems
Property Taxes	State Tax Audit and Collection Procedures
Sales and Use Taxes	Definition of a Unitary Business
Excise Taxes	State Formulary Apportionment
Special Industry Taxes	Choice of Entity
State Environmental Taxes	State Taxation of Pass-Through Entities
State Taxation of Electronic Commerce	Consolidated Returns and Combined Reporting
State Taxation for Specific Industries	Mergers and Acquisitions
State Taxation for Specific States	Business Credits and Incentives
State Environmental Taxes	State Tax Aspects of Bankruptcy
State Taxation of Compensation and Benefits	Doing Business Across State Lines
Limitations on States' Authorities to Taxes	Unclaimed Property

Source: http://www.bna.com.

The State Portfolios have the same format as the U. S. series. Each State Portfolio begins with a Portfolio Description, which gives a brief overview of the topic and the order in which the materials are presented. The Portfolios contain the three usual BNA sections: (A) Detailed Analysis, (B) Working Papers, and (C) Bibliography and References. The Portfolio sections are updated in response to state tax changes, and, when necessary, the complete Portfolio is rewritten. BNA has been adding new Portfolios to cover emerging issues and to round out the State Portfolios offerings.

When unfamiliar with a state topic, the overview Portfolios furnish a thorough but easy-to-comprehend introduction to the topic. Those Portfolios focusing on a specific technical state topic may assume a certain level of practitioner sophistication and therefore are more difficult for the state research novice. As with the U.S. portfolios, the state statutes, regulations, rulings, and court case opinions are integrated into the analysis with citations footnoted or included in the text. The critical documents cited are reproduced in the working papers section. Other useful aids furnished in the State Portfolios include the following.

- Interactive state forms

- Reproductions of model acts

- Sample sales and use certificates

- Tables, charts, and lists

- State tax administrations' addresses and telephone numbers

- Keyword indexes, state-by-state indexes

Although BNA does not offer a full state tax service like RIA, CCH, or Westlaw, the State Portfolios and its news reports can compete with any provided by other services. If the practitioner can find a Portfolio that covers the state tax issue of interest, BNA has performed the key research, and all that needs to be done is to apply the results to the facts of the client's situation.

OTHER RESOURCES

Warren, Gorham & Lamont (WG&L/RIA) publishes the *State Taxation* treatise by Jerome R. Hellerstein and Walter Hellerstein. This two-volume treatise, currently in its third edition, is possibly the most comprehensive single work on state and local taxation. The authors have undertaken the ambitious task of assembling a comprehensive review of all state and many local tax laws plus the court decisions interpreting those laws. Because few published works address state taxation in such a thorough manner, *State Taxation* has been cited by many state courts and even the U.S. Supreme Court as the authority on state taxation. Westlaw and RIA offer this treatise as part of their SALT services and it is also available in print.

The *Multistate Corporate Tax Guide* is another useful treatise. The two volumes (or CD ROM) concentrate on key corporate tax issues in sales and use taxation and income-based taxes for all states and some localities such as New York City and D.C. The treatise provides quick access to each state's position statements on tax issues through numerous charts. Much of the analysis is based on data collected through questionnaires completed by the top state officials who interpret and apply the state laws. To assure timeliness and relevancy of the information, the treatise is updated mid-year with a supplement.

PERIODICALS AND INTERNET SITES

State tax journals and newsletters contain a variety of articles and news briefs that are designed to keep readers current with regard to developments in general areas of state and local taxation and tax issues specific to a given state. These articles may contain, for example, an in-depth review of a recently decided court case, a broad analysis of state tax factors that should be considered in tax planning, or a call for reform of a statute by a neutral (or biased) observer. The articles can suggest new approaches to tax problems, give guidance for solving complex problems, or just explain a new law in a readable form.

Journals

Two important state taxation journals are the *Journal of Multistate Taxation and Incentives* (WG&L/RIA), with ten issues per year, and *Journal of State Taxation* (CCH), published bimonthly. Both of these journals focus on practical solutions to state and local taxation, as well as creative planning strategies for multistate business operations and individuals with multistate tax liabilities. These journals keep the subscriber informed on critical areas of state and local taxation nationwide and provide expert assessments of important cases and their potential impacts. Generally there are reviews of current state legislative issues to keep the reader up-to-date on state proposed, pending, or enacted legislation. Articles may cover legal, accounting, and business aspects of multistate entities. Both journals also focus on incentives offered by states to encourage business growth and expansion.

Newsletters

Tax Analysts publishes two influential state tax periodicals, *State Tax Notes* and *State Tax Today*. Like the Tax Analysts flagship, *Tax Notes* (see Chapter 7), *State*

Tax Notes is an authoritative source for news and commentary on state and local taxation. This weekly publication provides the latest news from all fifty states and D.C. plus in-depth analysis from leading experts in state taxation. Summaries of all judicial, administrative, and legislative developments are also included in *State Tax Notes*.

The purpose of *State Tax Today* is to furnish the most current state tax news on a daily basis. It covers every state, D.C., and U.S. territories. There are links to full-text state documents and U.S. Supreme Court, State Supreme Court, and appellate court decisions. Beside news briefs, *State Tax Today* has in-depth analytical articles, commentaries, and special reports.

Many of the other tax publishers provide state newsletters. For example, the *Tax Management Weekly State Tax Report* is the BNA analog to the Tax Analysts *State Tax Notes*. It gives a state-by-state analysis of state code and regulations, state administrative, judicial court decisions, and state administrative pronouncements as does *State Tax Notes*. Other state newsletters and reports published by BNA include:

- State Tax Legislation Monitor
- State Insights & Commentary
- State Tax Regulation Monitor
- Weekly State Tax Report
- Multistate Tax Report (print only)
- E-mail Highlights notification of the week's state tax highlights

The CCH newsletter is called *State Tax Day*, and RIA's is *State & Local Taxes Weekly*. Both are offered through the publishers' Internet tax services.

Internet Sites

As described in Chapter 7, the *Tax and Accounting Sites Directory* web site (**http://www.taxsites.com**) contains links to numerous tax resources on the web. The state and local listing has links to each state's taxing agency, legal information, organizations, and government sites. In addition, links to general locators, sales/use tax, news topics, organizations, tax rates and data, state tax guides, and e-commerce tax are included in the state and local screen.

SUMMARY

With so much of a business's tax bill being composed of nonfederal taxes, planning for state and local taxation has become more important to taxpayers and therefore to tax researchers. The research service industry has responded to this escalating need, creating a greater variety of more sophisticated tax research products that are designed to improve the practitioner's efficiency and effectiveness in state and local research. As SALT consulting becomes more of a mainstay for practitioners, tax services will provide more options for research. Consequently, state and local tax research tools likely will be among the fastest changing components of the major tax services.

TAX TUTOR

Reinforce the tax research information covered in this chapter by completing the online tutorials located at the *Federal Tax Research* web site: **http://academic.cengage.com/taxation/raabe**

KEY WORDS

By the time you complete this chapter, you should be comfortable discussing each of the following terms. If you need additional review of any of these items, return to the appropriate material in the chapter or consult the glossary to this text.

All State Tax Guide
Commerce Clause
Compare It
Create-a-Chart
Due Process Clause
Equal Protection
Joint Audit Program
KeyCite
Multistate Alternative Dispute Resolution Program
Multistate Corporate Tax Guide
Multistate Tax Commission (MTC)
Multistate Tax Compact

National Conference of Commissioners on
    Uniform State Laws
National Nexus Program
Privileges and Immunities Clause
Public Purpose
RIA Checkpoint State & Local Tax (SALT)
State Tax Reporters
State Taxation
StateNet
Supremacy Clause
Uniform Division of Income for Tax Purposes
    Act (UDITPA)
Uniformity Clause

DISCUSSION QUESTIONS

1. Why are taxpayers emphasizing state and local tax planning?

2. Why have state and local taxes been increasing over recent years?

3. Approximately what percentage of the national tax burden is made up of state and local taxes?

4. On what were the early taxing systems based in the southern states? The northern states?

5. What state was the first to introduce an income tax? In what year? What was the first city to have a sales tax? In what year?

6. What is Tax Freedom Day? What organization computes Tax Freedom Day?

7. Describe the different constitutionality challenges with regard to Federal and state taxes.

8. Discuss the supremacy provision in the Federal Constitution.

9. Which clause in the Federal Constitution contains the most significant limitation on state taxing authority?

10. What are the four criteria for imposition of state taxation set forth in *Complete Auto Transit Inc.?*

11. List two situations where the Due Process Clause has limited the scope of a state's taxing authority.

12. What is the importance of the *Quill* and *Wrigley* cases?

13. What do the Equal Protection and the Uniformity Clauses of most state constitutions require?

14. Why are corporations not covered by the Privileges and Immunities Clause?

15. What are the two clauses of the U.S. Constitution that specifically restrict state taxation?

16. What is the definition and purpose of "public purpose" for state tax law?

17. Explain how the passage of a state tax bill is similar to the passage of a Federal law.

18. When would Federal rulings be pertinent to state tax issues?

19. What is UDITPA and what is its significance with regard to the Multistate Tax Compact?

20. What is the Joint Audit Program that the MTC offers?

21. What is included in the RIA Checkpoint StateNet?

22. What is the function of the Compare It feature in RIA?

23. Compare the Multiple Sources search with the State and Local Taxes initial search option in RIA.

24. Discuss the citation search capabilities in the RIA state and local tax practice area.

25. When the keyword search option is not offered, such as with the RIA State Index, what is another method of performing this type of search?

26. What are the differences between the CCH news sources *State Tax Day* and *State Tax Review?*

27. In the CCH Network State Tax service, how can a researcher reduce the list of documents searched? How is this different from the RIA method?

28. What is the CCH equivalent to the RIA Compare It function?

29. Describe the differences in locating the TOC for a data set in RIA and CCH.

30. What is the function of the State Tax Guide offered by CCH?

31. Explain whether one can search the same libraries with the LexisNexis Academic Search engine and its Sources engine.

32. What tax service may be offered as one of the state databases in the LexisNexis Academic service?

33. Describe the two methods that work through the Westlaw Directory to search state tax documents.

34. Are the BNA State Portfolios organized by state? If yes, is there a portfolio on each state? If no, what is the organization?

35. What are the different sections in a BNA State Portfolio? How similar are these to the sections provided in the U.S. Income series?

36. Comment on the coverage and usefulness of the treatise *State Taxation*.

37. How does the *Multistate Corporate Tax Guide* gather its data?

38. Name two state taxation journals and indicate who publishes each.

39. Compare the state tax newsletters published by Tax Analysts and BNA.

40. Why does this chapter not provide a listing of state and local tax web sites?

EXERCISES

41. Locate the web site for the MTC.
    a. Define the three levels of membership in the MTC.
    b. Provide a brief summary of one of the latest articles in the *Multistate Tax Commission Review*. (Hint: Publications are found in Resources.)
    c. What is the Nexus Program? When was it founded?
    d. How does a taxpayer initiate joint audits?
    e. The MTC provides a link to the Federation of Tax Administrators (FTA). What is the title and date of the most recent FTA Meeting?

42. Use the RIA Checkpoint State & Local Practice area to locate the 1990 *Alamo Rent-a-Car, Inc. v. Sarasota-Manatee Airport Authority* case, using the Federal Cases in the State Taxes option.
    a. What is the citation for the case, and what court heard this case?
    b. What clauses of the U.S. Constitution is Alamo alleging were violated?
    c. Must the plaintiff and defendant names in the case be entered to find the case? Explain your response.
    d. Read this case. Perform a keyword search to locate the case without using the plaintiff or defendant names. If necessary, use the Search Within Results feature. What keywords did you use for the general search and (if necessary) for your follow-up search?

43. Use the RIA Checkpoint State & Local Practice Area to answer the following questions.
    a. Select the state in which the university you are attending is located and go to the next screen. What corporate items are provided in the tax type list? Is there a tax on intangibles, mortgages, or stock transfers?
    b. Select Washington as the state of interest and go to the next screen. What is the first tax type listed? What corporate items are provided in the tax type list? What is the database title for individual income taxes?

   c. Select the state in which the university you are attending is located. What is the rate of tax per pack of cigarettes? Compare your state's rate to that of Washington State.

   d. In what order are the Tax Types listed? In what order are the Document Types listed?

44. Use the RIA Checkpoint State & Local Practice Area to answer the following questions.

   a. For the state of your choice, compare the listing of documents available under the option Select Document Types in the Search States (SALT) with the list for the same state in the TOC.

   b. Using the Index in the TOC for the state of Illinois, what are the listings for the letter "H" under the "stamp" heading?

   c. In the Vermont TOC, what annotation is addressing the constitutionality of land gain taxes found in Recordation?

   d. In the Miscellaneous Multistate Materials TOC, what are the U.S. statute titles listed for Federal Laws on State Taxation?

45. Use the CCH NetWork State Tax to answer the following questions regarding the state in which the university you are attending is located.

   a. What is the title of the most recent article in State Tax Day related to this state?

   b. What is the most recent court case for this state?

   c. In the State Tax Reporters, perform a keyword search using the term "escheat." What does this term mean and to what does it apply? In what paragraph did you find the answer?

   d. Using the Topical Index for Multistate Property Tax Guide, perform a keyword search for "dining car." Under what headings are there entries for this term?

46. Use the CCH NetWork State Tax to answer the following questions.

   a. Does Hawaii allow estates a personal exemption? If yes, what is the amount, and what is the state statute allowing such amount?

   b. Use the tab Related Topics—States while in the document found in part a of this question. Which states seem to give standard deductions or personal exemptions to estates?

   c. Select all states to determine which states provide a personal exemption for estates. Use the keywords *estate "personal exemption"* in your search. Was this method as effective as the method used in part b of this question? Explain your response.

   d. Turn on the Thesaurus (use Search Tools). Select a state and perform a keyword search using the term *Devise*. What synonyms are also searched?

47. Use the CCH NetWork State Tax to perform a TOC search and answer the following questions.

   a. Did Alaska ever have a personal income tax? If yes, what was the last year Alaska collected the tax?

   b. Use the Multistate Quick Answer Charts to determine the diesel fuel tax for the state in which your university is located. Which state has the highest gasoline tax?

   c. Which state had the most tax legislation enacted since the beginning of the year?

   d. Using the State Tax Guide Topical Index, determine which states have Jai Alai taxes.

48. Using the LexisNexis Academic, Sources option, select New York as the Filter and Taxation as the Area of Law to answer the following questions.
    a. Perform a keyword search for "*use tax*" (as a single term) with the *New York Times* as the source. What is the title of an article published in the last three years that addresses a use tax issue?
    b. At what date does the Kleinrock New York Tax Bulletin coverage begin in this service? How frequently does this bulletin get published?
    c. What are the title and author of the most recent article in the *New York University Tax Law Review* with these three separate keyword terms: *property*, *tax*, and *abatement*? Did you use a natural language or terms and connector search?

49. Use LexisNexis Academic, Search option, Legal to answer the following questions.
    a. Locate the *International Business Machines v. State Board of Equalization*. What is its citation, what court heard it, and when was it decided?
    b. Explain whether the *International Business Machines v. State Board of Equalization* case is one upon which a practitioner should rely.
    c. Apply the Shepard's Citator to the *International Business Machines v. State Board of Equalization* case. How many citing decisions are there for this case? How many headnotes?

50. Use LexisNexis Academic to answer the following questions.
    a. Select Sources, By Area of Taxation—Taxation, Filter by—West. Which states does LexisNexis Academic consider to be western states?
    b. Using the same data set in part a of this question, what treatises and analytical materials are provided for the western states?
    c. Select Search, Legal. In what year was the Missouri constitution adopted?

51. Use Westlaw to answer the following questions regarding the *Village Bank and Trust Co.* (471 A.2d 1187) case.
    a. What year was the case decided and by what court?
    b. Clicking on the KeyCite Notes located in the West Headnotes provides access to three cases. What are the three cases and what KeyCite "flags" are associated with each?
    c. Using KeyCite, is the list of citing cases presented the same as that found in part b of this question? What KeyCite "flag" is associated with the *Village Bank* case?
    d. What are the cases listed in the Table of Authorities for the *Village Bank* case? How much reliance does it place on these cases?

52. Use the Westlaw Tax Tab to answer the following questions.
    a. What is the title of Chapter 22 in Hellerstein on State Taxation? (Hint: TOC is available on the search screen)
    b. Use the TOC for RIA State Tax Guide to determine what state violated the Commerce Clause by allowing an exemption from tax for products made from a native plant. (Hint: RIA State Tax Guide is found in the More heading.)
    c. Use the Multistate Taxation—Combined Primary Materials to determine in which states morticians are subject to collecting sales taxes on their products and services.

53. Use the Westlaw Tax Tab to answer the following questions.
    a. Through Directory, U.S. State materials, select a state. What topics are covered in the Tax Materials for the state?

b. Determine whether boarding a pet with a veterinarian is subject to sales tax in Wisconsin.

c. For the search performed in part b of this question, what is the first article suggested in ResultsPlus that appears in the American Jurisprudence 2d edition?

d. Select Directory, Topical Practice Areas, Taxation, State Tax Materials Complete List. Under the Key Number Service, what number is assigned to state taxation?

54. Use the service of your choice (RIA, CCH, LexisNexis, or Westlaw) to answer the following questions.

a. Locate *Complete Auto Transit, Inc. v. Brady*. What is the type of tax that was being examined in the case? Provide two parallel citations for the case and the name of the justice delivering the opinion.

b. Locate *Quill Corp. v. North Dakota*. What was the disposition of the case by the Supreme Court? Provide two parallel citations for the case and the name of the justice delivering the opinion. Name any judges that filed dissenting opinions.

c. Locate *Wisconsin Department of Revenue v. Wrigley*. What tax years are reviewed by the case? Provide two parallel citations for the case. Who were the attorneys for the respondent and petitioner? Were there any dissenting opinions?

d. Locate *Commonwealth Edition Co. v. Montana*. What is the type of tax that was being questioned in the case? Provide two parallel citations for the case. What two Federal clauses were addressed in the case?

55. Use the BNA Tax Management Portfolios, State Series to examine the following questions.

a. Is there a portfolio for each state? Which state has the most portfolios?

b. Generally, what are the Portfolio Series numbers for the portfolios that address state business entities and transaction issues?

c. What are the title and number of the Portfolio that addresses the court imposed limitations due to nexus issues?

d. Which portfolios were written by a team of professionals with no affiliation mentioned, rather than by authors identified by name and affiliation?

56. Use the BNA Tax Management Portfolios, State Series for the following questions.

a. What is the title of State Portfolio 1550? How many worksheets are included in this Portfolio?

b. Which Portfolio explains the QSSS election for S corporations?

c. How many parties are usually involved in a drop shipment transaction? In which Portfolio did you find your answer?

57. Locate state tax newsletters to answer the following questions.

a. What is the title of the most recent article in Tax Analyst *State Tax Today* discussing royalty trusts?

b. What is the most recent article in BNA *Tax Management Weekly State Tax Reporter* discussing the streamlining of sales taxes?

c. What is the title of the most recent article in CCH *State Tax Day* on gasoline taxes?

    d. What is the title of the most recent article in CCH *State Tax Review* that discusses sales tax obligations of telephone carriers? How many years of CCH *State Tax Review* are maintained in the Archives?

    e. What is the title of the most recent article in RIA *State & Local Taxes Weekly* newsletter on state renewable energy technology tax credits? How many years of RIA *State & Local Taxes Weekly* are archived?

58. Find an article in the *Journal of Multistate Taxation and Incentives* on the following topics. Provide the authors, title of the article, and date published.

    a. The ad valorem property taxes on a baseball stadium.

    b. Most recent economic incentives provided to the film industry.

    c. Credits and exemptions used by Mississippi to promote development of broadband technology.

    d. The most recent article on the dividends-received deduction.

59. Use the *Journal of State Taxation* to answer the following questions.

    a. What is the title of the most recent article on web-related activities and potential nexus problems?

    b. What are the volume and number of the most current issue? What is the lead article?

    c. Who is the current editor of the journal? Is there anyone on the advisory board that is from the university you attend? If yes, list the name(s).

    d. Who is the author of the article titled "Throwback of Foreign Sales"? What are the year, volume, and issue number in which the article appears?

60. Use Internet sites to answer the following questions.

    a. Provide the links to three News & Topics sites provided by Tax Sites for states (**http://www.taxsites.com**).

    b. Visit three national associations that are concerned with state tax issues. Provide their URLs.

    c. Visit the web site of your state's agency responsible for taxation (Department of Revenue for many states). Provide the URL for this agency. For California, provide both agencies' URLs.

    d. Select an adjacent state and give a summary of one of its taxes. (You could use Alaska and Hawaii as a pair.)

RESEARCH CASES

61. Tom and Verna are going to combine their fishing businesses to become more profitable. Tom currently lives in Mississippi and Verna lives in Louisiana. They would prefer to set up the business as an S corporation, but only if it will not be subject to state taxation. Since Verna and Tom live within twenty miles of each other, they don't have a preference as to the state of incorporation. Does it make a tax difference which state they choose?

62. NewCity, California, charged Rick a real estate transfer tax when his property was relinquished to the Federal Housing Administration (FHA) in its capacity as his loan guarantor. The amount charged was the same as the amount Rick was required to pay the county. Can Rick be required to pay this tax, or should the FHA pay it?

63. TimberCut Corporation transferred all the rights to timber growing on its land located in Spokane County, Washington, to its wholly owned subsidiary, PineCo. The Department of Revenue has imposed a real estate excise tax on TimberCut because PineCo transferred $1 million cash to TimberCut. Is TimberCut's transfer a sale of timber land subject to the taxes imposed?

64. WaterWorks Corporation has decided to sell off one of its amusement parks located in Texas. Several businesses have been identified as possible buyers. It is unlikely that one of these businesses will purchase all of the assets of the amusement park, but WaterWorks is confident that it can sell all of the assets to various parties within a six-month period. Is this sale subject to Texas sales tax?

65. A tribal nation in Kansas is considering building a gas station to accommodate travelers through their reservation. Before undergoing the considerable expense for construction, the tribal members want to know whether the fuel sold will be subject to state fuel taxes. This will make a difference in the profitability of the project. Is gasoline sold on a federally recognized reservation subject to the fuel tax imposed by Kansas?

66. A town in Vermont wants to charge property tax on a lot and building used by a not-for-profit organization as its administrative office. To be exempt from property taxes, the property must have the following characteristics.

   • Be dedicated to public use

   • Have its primary use directly benefit a class of persons who are part of the public

   • Be owned and operated on a not-for-profit basis

   Does administrative use of the building meet the definition for the exemption?

67. Iowa imposes a tax on the operation of slot machines. The rate is graduated, based on slot machine revenues. Can Iowa charge a higher maximum rate to racetrack owners than it does to riverboat owners, without violating the equal protection clause of the U.S. Constitution?

68. The Pluto Corporation has been mining ore in Oklahoma for many years. A new mine just developed is producing ore containing uranium. Pluto would like to know the rate of the severance tax on mined uranium, and upon what base the tax is assessed.

69. The Peppermint Partnership operates a successful candy business. It is considering taking the partnership public and becoming a master limited partnership. If it does so, will it be subject to the corporate franchise tax in New York, where its headquarters and operating plant are located?

70. Rodney has been in the South Carolina National Guard for the past twenty years. This is his last year as an active member. Since Rodney turns sixty-five in August of this year, he will begin collecting Social Security benefits and Guard retirement pay. His employer laid him off in January, and Rodney qualified for unemployment compensation. Rodney received severance pay of $50,000 when terminated by his employer. Which of these amounts are taxable to Rodney in South Carolina?

71. Poplar Inc.'s corporate headquarters, plants, and warehouses are located in Vermont. Until this year, all of Poplar's sales have been made in Vermont. Poplar's first out-of-state sale of $1 million (cost of sales, $300,000) is shipped by a common carrier trucking firm from its warehouse to the purchaser's dock in Indiana. The truck stops for gasoline in New York and Ohio, and its driver spends a night in Ohio. To which states must Poplar apportion income from the sale? How much income is taxed in each such state?

72. A religious organization is considering spreading its message into Illinois by opening several churches. As part of its ceremonies, wine is consumed by its members. The church would like to know the consequences for the alcoholic beverage tax if it ferments its own wine. What if, instead of making the wine, the church purchases it from an importing distributor?

73. The Ohio Government Employees Credit Union (Union) was created by merging the Ohio Teachers Bank, the Ohio Transit Credit Association, and the Federal Government Workers Credit Bank. The stock issued by the merged entity is held by those having deposits in Union. Union believes that it is not subject to the Ohio franchise tax (an income tax), because immunity is implied under the Supremacy Clause of the U.S. Constitution. Union believes it is closely connected with the government and thus should be exempt from taxation. Is Union correct in its conclusion that it is not subject to the Ohio franchise tax?

74. Travis Smith and Carmela Jones operate a successful law firm in Portland, Oregon. They are considering opening another office across the Columbia River, in Vancouver, Washington. Travis and Carmela would like to know if they then would be subject to any business or personal taxes in Washington. If they are subject to any taxes, can they use those taxes as a credit or a deduction on their Oregon income tax returns, as taxes paid to another state?

75. Jie Wang wants to open a new funeral parlor in Colorado. She would like to know the sales/use tax implications for this business. Are morticians considered to be rendering services, are they selling tangible personal property, or a combination of both? Specifically, Jie needs to know whether she should contract funeral services as one lump sum, or would it be more beneficial to itemize the charges for caskets, urns, and so on separately from the services offered?

76. Brock and David are equal shareholders of an S corporation that manufactures electric razors. They are interested in opening a plant in the south. They want to know whether Florida or Alabama would be the best state to move to, considering only tax consequences. The main concern is with regard to income taxes (corporate and personal), franchise taxes, and intangible asset property taxes. Brock and David expect the S corporation to generate $400,000 annual taxable income.

77. Melkry, an Ohio corporation, provides tugboat services on the Great Lakes to vessels weighing at least 800 tons. Each of Melkry's tugboats weighs approximately 100 tons. Michigan has assessed use tax on repair materials, fuel, and capital assets purchased by Melkry for its operations. Is Melkry subject to the use tax?

78. EmiLu Corporation is a private delivery company that hires independent contractors with their own trucks to deliver car parts to various auto repair shops in Pennsylvania. EmiLu contracts with the manufacturers of the car parts to make the deliveries, and then it hires the drivers in Pennsylvania to deliver the parts. EmiLu has no property, employees, or customers in Pennsylvania. EmiLu is incorporated in Delaware, where all the car part manufacturing customers are located. Is EmiLu subject to the corporate franchise tax in Pennsylvania?

79. Earl and Kathy live on the Big Island of Hawaii in the town of Captain Cook. Because the altitude is high, they have coffee plants growing on their property. Most of their neighbors grow coffee on their property as well. Earl and Kathy collect the coffee from their property and that of their neighbors, and then they dry the coffee in a special building they have constructed on their land. Does this activity affect their qualification for the home exemption for Hawaii property taxes?

80. Chuck Taylor owns a fish processing plant in Alaska. Some of the processing chemicals and fish remains could be considered hazardous wastes. What possible state and local taxes does Chuck need to be concerned about when disposing of these materials?

International Tax Services

Chapter Outline

Learning Objectives

- Apply the tax research process to international issues.

- Learn the major features of international tax services.

- Develop search methodologies applicable to each of the international services.

- Identify which tax services are most appropriate for different international research objectives.

THERE ARE MORE THAN 190 countries in the world today, and each can have its own tax rules and regulations. Consequently, global businesses must maneuver through a tangled web of tax laws that are likely to be unfamiliar to most tax professionals. Intricate (sometimes tax-motivated) intercompany transaction flows and transfer pricing further compound the complexity and create an international tax environment that can be an unmanageable labyrinth for many companies. Fortunately, international tax specialists can help with the perplexing compliance obligations and foster alignment of company tax strategies with its business needs. The ultimate tax planning goal of most companies, however, is quite simple—to reduce the company's overall global effective tax rate. Finding the road that leads to this goal is the challenge.

OVERVIEW OF INTERNATIONAL TAXATION

Global business transactions create distinctive tax concerns for both the native country and the temporary resident or transaction country. The native country is where the taxpayer is a citizen or legal resident, or where an entity is incorporated or organized (domestic corporation). The transaction country is where the income is earned or the transaction completed. International tax provisions generally are concerned with the two potential tax situations: the native country's taxation of its citizen's foreign-source income (outbound) and the transaction country's taxation of foreign taxpayers earning income within its borders (inbound).

From an economic perspective, the objective of the international tax rules of each country should be to ensure that the taxing systems interact efficiently and prevent, to the extent possible, a double taxation of income, while encouraging investment within the country's boundaries. At the same time, each country wants to promote global commerce but not erode its domestic tax base for generating revenues. Such tax objectives can be in conflict, and these conflicts are the cause of the complexity and often situation-specific rules found in international tax laws.

There are three chief models for developing international taxing systems: full inclusion, territorial, and blended (current U.S. model).

Full Inclusion Model

Under the **Full Inclusion Model**, a business pays taxes to its native country on all of the income it earns, regardless of the income's source. This would include income earned in other countries, and even income earned by foreign subsidiaries, whether or not the profits are distributed to the parent. All expenses associated with the earning of the foreign income are deductible currently. Since the foreign earned income also may be taxed by the transaction country, the native country would allow a foreign tax credit for taxes paid to other countries.

The full inclusion model generally ensures that a company pays the same amount of taxes whether its businesses are located within the resident country outside its borders. Thus, this taxing model does not encourage or discourage foreign operations. It is "capital export neutral" and theoretically should not have a negative effect on multinational companies or their ability to compete in the global market. Some argue, however, that the full inclusion model does interfere with a company's ability to compete in foreign markets, for example, when the native country's tax on income is higher than the transaction country's tax would be on the same income.

SPOTLIGHT ON TAXATION

International Tax Programs

Many businesses and CPA firms are struggling to attract and retain international tax personnel due to the shortage in high-quality individuals graduating from international tax programs at universities. Schools with specialized masters or law programs in international tax include the following.

Harvard Law School

New York University School of Law

Penn Foster College

Strayer University

University of Florida—Levine College of Law

University of Michigan Law School

Walter H. and Dorthy B. Diamond International Tax Program (online)

European Tax College (Netherlands)

Universität of Hamburg (Germany)

Universiteit Maastricht (Netherlands)

University of Sydney (Australia)

Universidad Torcuato Di Tella School of Law (Argentina)

Vienna University of Economics and Business Administration (Austria)

Territorial Model

With a **Territorial Model**, a local business is subject to the native country tax only on income earned within its boundaries. It would not be taxed on income earned outside the native country or income of its foreign subsidiaries, even when the income is repatriated to the parent. Since the foreign income is not taxed within the native country, there is no need for a foreign tax credit. Foreign income is taxed only once and that is by the foreign country. Accordingly, deductions associated with the foreign income are disallowed.

A territorial model generally permits companies with foreign operations to pay the same amount of taxes as companies whose residences are in those same foreign countries. This model is therefore "capital import neutral." Territorial tax proponents assert that native taxes on foreign income hinder a company's ability to compete in foreign markets by changing the profit margins. Opponents regard territorial taxes as eroding the native country's tax base by encouraging exporting of business and exacerbating transfer pricing problems.

Blended Model

The U.S. international taxing system is a blend of the full inclusion and territorial model, relying most heavily on full inclusion. In the **Blended Model**, foreign income is taxable to U.S. domestic companies when earned, and expenses associated with this income are currently deductible. However, the United States generally postpones taxing foreign subsidiary income until this income is distributed to the domestic parent. Since this repatriated income previously was taxed in the foreign country, a foreign tax credit for some or all of the taxes paid to other countries is available to the domestic parent company. This helps to mitigate the chances of double taxation. The amount of the foreign tax credit depends on the tax rates in the foreign country as compared to the U.S. rates.

U.S. tax law uses a territorial approach for taxing non-U.S. taxpayers. For instance, the income of a Ugandan citizen is subject to U.S. Federal income tax but only if that income is earned within the United States. The Ugandan's income attributable to sources outside the United States is not taxable within the United States. Thus, the current U.S. international taxing system applies both the full-inclusion (for citizens) and the territorial models (for nonresidents) concurrently.

The international tax structure developed by the United States reflects the tension between the full-inclusion capital export neutrality and territorial capital import neutrality. By allowing tax deferral on foreign subsidiary income, the blended model encourages domestic corporations to retain earnings in foreign countries and postpone repatriation as long as possible. This model also causes numerous opportunities for U.S. tax base erosion.

INCOME SOURCING

The geographical source of income has a direct bearing on its tax treatment. U.S. citizens are taxed on their worldwide income but income from other countries may receive tax relief through a number of Code provisions. Foreign taxpayers (also known as nonresident aliens), on the other hand, generally are subject to Federal taxes only on U.S. source income. Consequently, the sourcing rules often are the starting point in researching international tax issues.

Source Determination

The **source determination** of income is dependent on performance location and/or property location. Income from interest and dividends generally is sourced by the residency of the payor. Thus, dividends from a domestic corporation and interest from a state bond are sourced within the United States. For income from property, such as rents, royalties, or gains from property sales, it is the location of the property that is relevant. Sales of inventory often are sourced by the location of the transaction, not by the origin of the inventory. Thus, inventory purchased in a foreign country but sold within the United States produces domestic sourced income. Income for personal services usually is sourced according to where the services are performed, not the residency of the compensating entity or the citizenship of the personal service provider. Finally, sourcing rules apply to deductions as well as to income.

Deduction Apportionment

Since the U.S. tax is based on taxable income, deductions and losses must be apportioned between domestic and foreign-source gross income. **Deduction apportionment** for expenses and losses directly related to a transaction or activity can be easy to allocate. Thus, the cost of goods sold is apportioned to the sales income to which it relates.

Expenses that are either not attributable to any specific income source or are associated with more than one source must be apportioned. For example, interest expense is apportioned based on the theory that money is fungible. With limited exceptions, interest expense is attributable to all the taxpayer's leveraged transactions and activities, regardless of the specific purpose for incurring the debt.

SPOTLIGHT ON TAXATION

International Organizations

Three influential international organizations are the World Trade Organization (WTO), International Money Fund (IMF), and the Organization for Economic Co-operation and Development (OECD).

World Trade Organization

The WTO is a global organization that concentrates on developing agreements (known as multilateral trading systems) that become the legal ground rules for international commerce between nations. These agreements are negotiated and signed by the bulk of the world's trading nations after being ratified by their governments. Essentially, they are contracts, guaranteeing member countries important trade rights. They also bind governments to keep their trade policies in alignment with agreed-upon parameters for the benefit of the participating countries. The goal is to help producers of goods and services, exporters, and importers to conduct their business with the least amount of friction. In addition, the WTO wants to improve the welfare of the peoples within its member countries.

The WTO was established in January 1995 and is based in Geneva, Switzerland. As of January 2007, it has fifty member countries.

International Money Fund

The IMF was created to promote international monetary cooperation, exchange stability, and orderly exchange arrangements. Through these arrangements, the IMF fosters economic growth and high levels of employment. It also provides temporary financial assistance to countries needing help to ease the balance of payment adjustments. Since the IMF (and World Bank) was established in 1945 (after World War II), its purpose has remained unchanged. However, its operations have evolved to meet the changing needs of its 185 member countries in an ever-changing world economy.

The Executive Board consists of twenty-four member countries, of which sixteen seats are elected for two-year terms. The United States, United Kingdom, Saudi Arabia, Russia, Japan, Germany, France, and China have permanent seats. IMF headquarters are in Washington, D.C.

Organization for Economic Co-operation and Development

The OECD is an association of countries that believe in democratic governments and market economies. The goals of the OECD are to assist developing countries, support sustainable economic growth, boost employment, raise living standards, maintain financial stability, and generally contribute to world trade. Through its monitoring of world economics, the OECD has become known as one of the most reliable and prolific publishers of economic and social data/statistics. The OECD plays a prominent role in fostering good governance and helps to obtain multilateral economic agreements for individual countries wanting to participate in the global economy. It is a forum where peer pressure can act as a powerful incentive. This peer pressure incentive is demonstrated by the OECD's effect on tax havens. In 2000, the OECD issued a list of forty-one possible tax havens. There now are only five countries still classified as uncooperative tax havens.

The OECD started up in 1961 in Paris, France. It currently has thirty member countries and relationships with more than seventy other countries.

TAX TREATIES

International taxation is governed in the United States by the *Internal Revenue Code* (Code) and by tax treaties. **Tax treaties**, negotiated by the Treasury Department and signed by the President, are bilateral agreements regarding the treatment of residents (not necessarily citizens) of the foreign country and the United States. Generally, treaties are negotiated to prevent double taxation by providing reduced tax rates, or exempting certain types of income from taxation. The incomes receiving reduced rates and exemptions vary among countries. Most income tax treaties contain what is known as a "saving clause." These clauses prevent U.S. residents from using treaty provisions to avoid taxes on U.S. source income. The United States has tax treaties with over sixty countries, as enumerated in Exhibit 10-1.

The Code and tax treaties may provide conflicting treatment of some types of foreign sourced income. Unlike most countries, the United States does not consider treaty provisions to take precedence over the Code. Rather, to the extent possible, the Code and treaty should be applied in harmony with each other. If this is not possible, the most recently issued provision generally prevails. Some U.S. states do not honor the provisions of tax treaties, and U.S.-adopted tax treaties usually do not address state and local tax issues.

If there is no U.S. treaty covering income from a particular country, all taxable income from the country is includible in the tax base of the U.S. citizens and

Exhibit 10-1: U.S. Income Tax Treaty Countries*

Armenia	India	Portugal
Australia	Indonesia	Romania
Austria	Ireland	Russia
Azerbaijan	Israel	Slovak Republic
Bangladesh	Italy	Slovenia
Barbados	Jamaica	South Africa
Belarus	Japan	Spain
Belgium	Kazakhstan	Sir Lanka
Canada	Kyrgyzstan	Sweden
China	Korea	Switzerland
Cyprus	Latvia	Tajikistan
Czech Republic	Lithuania	Thailand
Denmark	Luxembourg	Trinidad/Tobago
Egypt	Mexico	Tunisia
Estonia	Moldova	Turkey
Finland	Morocco	Turkmenistan
France	Netherlands	Ukraine
Georgia	New Zealand	United Kingdom
Germany	Norway	Uzbekistan
Greece	Pakistan	Venezuela
Hungary	Philippines	
Iceland	Poland	

*IRS web site as of July 2007.

residents. This income also is likely to be taxed by the foreign country. To mitigate double taxation of this income, the foreign income exclusion, foreign tax credit, and other more specific provisions, were legislated.

TAX HAVENS

What is considered a **tax haven** varies depending on the observer's viewpoint. A rather neutral definition is that a tax haven is a location that imposes one or more of its taxes at a lower rate than the jurisdiction to which it is being compared. These beneficial (or no) tax rate areas encourage wealthy individuals and businesses to establish residency or a presence within the tax haven's boundaries. For example, a U.S. state with no sales tax or no corporate income tax meets this definition of a tax haven. Hence, different jurisdictions may be havens for singular taxes and for different types of taxpayers. Besides adopting a low tax rate, tax havens generally are viewed by the public as intentionally creating a tax structure that deliberately exploits the worldwide desire to engage in tax avoidance.

The **Organization for Economic Co-operation and Development** (OECD) suggests three key factors that identify a jurisdiction as a tax haven.

1. No or nominal taxes. This criterion might be applied with respect to income in general, or as to specific types or sources of income.

2. Effective information exchange lacking. Tax havens often adopt secrecy laws or administrative practices that protect individuals and businesses from the scrutiny of outside taxing authorities. Consequently, transactions within the tax haven jurisdiction remain private. This protection prevents an effective information exchange regarding taxpayers who are benefiting from locating within the tax haven.

3. Lack of transparency. Legislative, legal, or administrative provisions that are not transparent make it difficult to determine whether the laws are applied consistently. Information needed by taxing authorities, such as access to financial records, typically is legally restricted by a tax haven. These practices may make it impossible for outside tax authorities to determine tax obligations.

The OECD considers the first factor as necessary but not the deciding factor in defining a tax haven. Every jurisdiction, according to the OECD, should be able to determine whether it wishes to impose taxes and what rates are appropriate for which types of income and taxpayers. Therefore, one of the latter two factors also must be found for a jurisdiction to be considered a tax haven. Other observers believe that the first factor is sufficient for tax haven designation. The tax haven list appearing in Exhibit 10-2 is a composite from several different sources, with each country enumerated by at least two separate sources. Most of these countries would not meet the OECD's definition of a tax haven.

The remainder of this chapter reviews a sample of the commercial international tax service providers. As discussed in Chapter 6, these providers offer a plethora of tax products that can be bundled in a variety of ways. Thus, the tax services described in this chapter may not describe the set of resources available to the reader. Furthermore, the tax services constantly are updating their products to maintain their competitive edge, and this is especially true in the international arena. Therefore, the current appearance of the tax services may differ from those presented in this text. However, the research concepts still are applicable.

Exhibit 10-2: List of Tax Havens

The following is a composite list of countries considered as tax havens by at least two Internet sources. This list includes approximately 25% of the countries in the world.

Andorra	Liberia
Anguilla	Liechtenstein
Antigua and Barbuda	Luxembourg
Aruba	Maldives
Bahamas	Malta
Bahrain	Marshall Islands
Barbados	Mauritius
Belize	Monaco
Bermuda	Montserrat
British Virgin Islands	Nauru
Campione d'Italia	Netherlands Antilles
Canary Islands	Nevis
Cayman Islands	Niue
Cook Island	Panama
Costa Rica	Seychelles
Cyprus	St. Christopher
Dominica	St. Lucia
Gibraltar	St. Vincent
Grenada	Tonga
Grenadines	Turks and Caicos Islands
Guernsey	U.S. Virgin Islands
Hong Kong	Uruguay
Ireland	Vanuatu
Isle of Man	Western Samoa
Jersey	

BNA

The Bureau of National Affairs (BNA) has developed a myriad of products for the tax practitioner specializing in international taxation. Its international tax products can be divided into three major categories; (1) the U.S. tax treatment of foreign income or foreign taxpayers, (2) taxation by foreign countries, and (3) transfer pricing. BNA's signature publication, the **Tax Management Portfolios**, populates each of these categories. BNA also delivers in-depth news coverage, tax planning commentaries, journals, and detailed analysis through special tax services. The BNA products are so authoritative and of such quality that all of the major tax services (RIA, CCH, Westlaw, and LexisNexis) utilize BNA as the foundation of their international tax services.

BNA Foreign Income Library

The **BNA Foreign Income Library** includes approximately ninety Tax Management Portfolios written by leading experts in international taxation and business. The topics covered run the gamut from the foreign tax credit, to international aspects of social security taxes and foreign estates, to nontax issues such as the

Exhibit 10-3: BNA Working Paper Legal Certificate

TMFEDPORT No. 946 WS 14 (BNA)

BNA Tax Management Portfolios
Foreign Income Series
Provisions Applicable to U.S. and Foreign Persons
946-1st: U.S. International Taxation of Telecoms
Copyright © 2007 Tax Management, Inc.

Worksheet 14 **Sample** Exemption Certificate for Communications Excise Tax

Worksheet 14 **Sample** Exemption Certificate for Communications Excise Tax

Worksheet 14 **Sample** Exemption Certificate for Communications Excise Tax

EXEMPTION CERTIFICATE

FOR THE COMMUNICATIONS EXCISE TAX

IMPOSED PURSUANT TO SECTIONS 4251-4254

January 29, 2001
I certify that local telephone services have been furnished by U.S. Telco, Inc. to the United Nations; that the charges of $100.00 will be paid from United Nation's funds; and that the charges are exempt from tax under section 4253(c) of the Internal Revenue Code of 1986, as amended.

_____
(Signature of officer or employee)

_____
(Title of officer or employee)

_____
(Business Address of the officer or employee)
Note: Penalty for fraudulent use, $10,000 or imprisonment or both.
This document updated March 2007.
TMFEDPORT No. 946 WS 14

regulation of foreign investments and currency exchange controls. There are more than ten portfolios dedicated to transfer pricing and forty portfolios covering the taxation of business operations in specific countries. These Country Portfolios address not only income taxation but also indirect taxes such as the value-added tax (VAT) and other special taxes unique to the various countries.

As with the BNA U.S. Income Library, each Tax Management Portfolio contains excerpts from primary sources such as the Code, Regulations, and IRS pronouncements. For tax treaties, the portfolios furnish not only the text but all relevant materials for interpreting the agreements including technical explanations, legislative histories, and judicial interpretations. Practical advice for complying with the local business and tax laws is offered by notable practitioners in the Detailed Analysis Section. The Working Papers Section contains interactive and IRS forms, sample elections, official documents, and legal forms (some filled-in as examples). An example of a sample legal certificate is presented in Exhibit 10-3. These portfolios, which are updated regularly, are offered in print and electronic formats.

BNA International Service

BNA International Service (BNA IS) was developed to communicate accurate and detailed analysis of worldwide taxation as well as regular international news updates. Thus, in addition to the Country Portfolios, BNA IS offers a variety of news and analysis libraries to the international tax practitioner as illustrated in the left window of Exhibit 10-4. The table of contents (TOC) organization of these

Exhibit 10-4:   BNA International Service European Tax Service Opening Screen

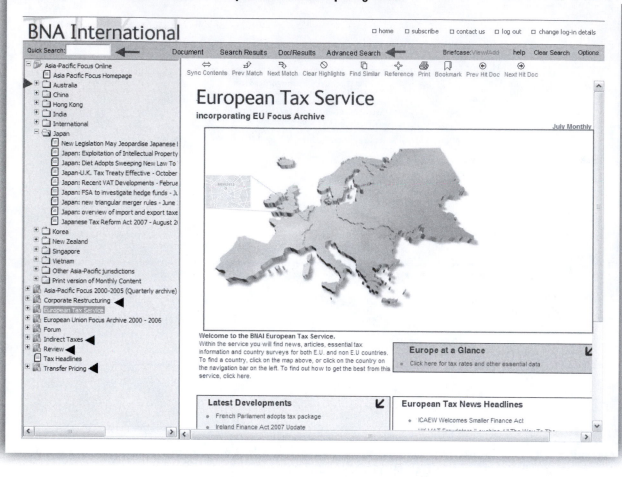

libraries is similar to that found in the CCH NetWork and RIA Checkpoint services discussed in Chapter 6. The library headings and document titles are displayed by expanding outlines, as can be seen for Japan in Exhibit 10-4. Each library in the BNA IS has its own opening page, as Exhibit 10-4 illustrates for the European Tax Service. The latest tax news and most recently added documents are highlighted on the opening page.

The Asia-Pacific Focus and the European Tax Service libraries both deliver news, in-depth articles on tax developments, legislative updates, and tax planning ideas that are country specific (see Exhibit 10-4). The European Union (EU) has a separate Tax Library and Focus Archive. For a practitioner whose expertise is international corporate restructuring, BNA IS maintains a separate Corporate Restructuring library covering mergers and acquisitions, capital raising, securitization, debt, and foreign investment. This global coverage is helpful when structuring cross-border transactions, as well as restructuring within a single foreign jurisdiction. While the Forum library contains quarterly issued articles on specific transactions that are written by experts, the Tax Planning International Review (Review in Exhibit 10-4) offers in-depth, practical analysis and focused monthly news reports on tax legislation, rulings, cases, and policies. Other specialty libraries available in BNA IS including Indirect Taxes (such as VAT, customs, stamp duties, etc.) and Transfer Pricing.

Table of Contents Search   Given the organization of the libraries, a TOC search can be quite efficient and effective. Simply expand the TOC by clicking on the + boxes preceding the headings (see Exhibit 10-4). However, a simple search of the entire service may be easily performed by entering keywords in the Quick Search box above the left window (Exhibit 10-4). This search retrieves documents containing any of the keywords. Thus, the fewer the number of the researcher's keywords, the shorter will be the list of documents retrieved.

Advanced Search   Rather than accepting Boolean term connectors, the Advanced Search option furnishes separate keyword boxes for the various types of searches, as seen in Exhibit 10-5. Accordingly, there are boxes for "and" (containing all of the words), "not" (not containing the word), "or" (containing one or more of the words), exact phrases, and proximity connectors (words that are used near each other). Advanced Search also allows the researcher to search for alternate word forms or apply a thesaurus to the search terms. Date restrictions are possible, and key word in context (KWIC) options of none, short, medium, and long are available.

The document list screen in Exhibit 10-6 shows the results of a search with keywords displayed in context (KWIC option was selected). If the researcher does not select the KWIC option on the search screen (Exhibit 10-5 screen), it can be

Exhibit 10-5: BNA IS Advanced Search Screen

turned on in the document list screen using the Document Excerpts option (Exhibit 10-6). Clicking on any of the highlighted keywords takes the researcher to where the word appears in the document. Based on the number of times the keywords appear in the document and other factors, the results are given a percentage score for ranking the document's relevance (see Exhibit 10-6).

Document Options   Exhibit 10-7 illustrates the various functions (at the top of the screen) that are available in the document screen. Most are self-explanatory; however, some may not be intuitive. For example, clicking on Sync Contents expands the entries in the left window to show where the documents retrieved by the search appear in the libraries. The Find Similar feature locates documents in the other libraries, previously not searched, that are on the same topic. This is very handy when trying to determine how various countries treat a particular transaction. Finally, when reviewing any document, clicking on Reference displays the location of the article in its library (see Exhibit 10-7).

LexisNexis

LexisNexis has built impressive international tax libraries by amassing documents and services developed by other publishers. The Tax Center and Academic services

Exhibit 10-6: BNA IS Document List Screen

BNA International

□ home   □ subscribe   □ contact us   □ log out   □ change log-in details

Quick Search: [____]

Document   Search Results   Doc/Results   Advanced Search   Briefcase:View/Add   help   Clear Search   Options

BNA International
Asia-Pacific Focus Online
Asia-Pacific Focus 2000-2005 (
Corporate Restructuring
(4) European Tax Service
European Union Focus Archive
Forum
Indirect Taxes
Review
Tax Headlines
Transfer Pricing

4 of 4 results   ⬚ Find Similar | ⬚Print Docs   Document Excerpts: Short ▾

Score	Title	Date	Location	Type	Briefcase/Print
1. 100% ☐	Russia: Expert Reports Valid For Determining Market Royalty Rates - June 2006	June 2006	European Tax Service		☐

... Reports Valid For Determining Market Royalty Rates Ruling of the Federal...
... an unreasonably high rate of royalty constituted a tax evasion scheme...
... Tver-Pivo. Afanasy-Pivo paid royalties to Tver-Pivo, and sought...
... round in a circle. The royalty rates in August and September...
... the average market rate for royalties associated with beverages is 2...
... as a source of market royalty rates. The company appealed, and...
... constitute proper evidence of market royalty rates. The tax authorities appealed...
... actually, it says that the royalty rates could be used as...
... source of information about market royalty rates, which does not make...

| 2. 64% ☐ | Russia: Participation Exemption Rules Proposed Under Draft Law - February 2007 | January 2007 | European Tax Service | | ☐ |

... and derivatives, the receipt of royalties, dividends and interest income. The...

| 3. 64% ☐ | Participation Exemption Rules Proposed Under Draft Law - January 2007 | January 2007 | European Tax Service | | ☐ |

... and derivatives, the receipt of royalties, dividends and interest income. The...

| 4. 45% ☐ | Transfer Pricing in the CIS Countries - August 2006 | August 2006 | European Tax Service | | ☐ |

... scope or proprietary rights (e.g., royalties) which are currently exempt from...

Save search as: [_____] save   ⬚ Manage Saved Searches

Exhibit 10-7: BNA IS Document

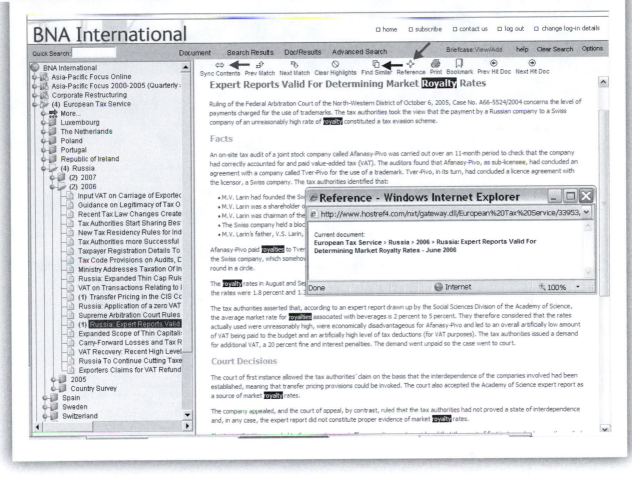

contain the international publications by BNA, CCH, Wiley, and Tax Analysts as well as publications written by recognized experts in the international field.

Tax Center

The International tab in the Lexis/Nexis Tax Center displays document sources in four categories as Exhibit 10-8 indicates. Foreign Tax Cases includes combined sources of international tax cases as well as cases from specific countries, such as Canada. The researcher may select one, some, or all of these sources and then perform keyword searches by using either the natural language or terms and connectors options. Date restrictions also are available. These restrictions are especially effective when the practitioner desires to merely update prior research or needs to know how the law stood in a prior year for such situations as tax audits or court proceedings.

The International Tax Planning heading offers the business primers, *Doing Business in ....,* for a variety of countries (see Exhibit 10-8). These portfolios provide an overview of the country's business environment, including its taxing structure. Clicking on the icon after the title will either access the document or display the document's TOC, as Exhibit 10-9 shows for the *Doing Business in Japan*

Exhibit 10-8: LexisNexis Tax Center International Tab Opening Screen

portfolio. Another document within International Tax Planning is the Ernst & Young (E&Y) *International GAAP* (see Exhibit 10-8). Written by the International Financial Reporting Group of E&Y, *International GAAP* contains the full text of every International Financial Reporting Standard (IFRS) and model IFRS financial statements. The Wiley *IFRS: Interpretation and Application of International Accounting and Financial Reporting Standards* (not visible in Exhibit 10-8) also is accessible within International Tax Planning.

The majority of the Tax Treaties & Analysis resources are products of the Tax Analysts organization. The **Tax Analysts Worldwide Tax Treaties** recently added several features to enhance the ability to compare, side by side, income tax treaties. Easy-to-read tables compare the tax rates on various types of income and withholding rates among over 170 worldwide taxing jurisdictions. The original, in-force, pending, terminated, and unperfected treaties can be viewed separately. The CCH Tax Treaties Reporter includes many of the same documents as the Worldwide Tax Treaties. Both have the income and estate tax treaties into which the United States has entered with foreign countries. In addition, the **CCH Tax Treaties Reporter** contains the exchange of information agreements between the United States and foreign countries, U.S. Regulations relating to treaty articles, reports from the Department of State and the Senate

Exhibit 10-9: LexisNexis Tax Center Document TOC Screen

Foreign Relations Committee, as well as administrative rulings and court cases pertinent to the treaties.

The last category of document offerings in the LexisNexis Tax Center is News. LexisNexis selected one of the most respected sources to supply its daily international news, the **Tax Analysts** ***Worldwide Tax Daily***. A sample of the *Worldwide Tax Daily* e-newsletter is presented in Exhibit 10-10. *Worldwide Tax Daily* offers international news on a daily basis, with news updates from around the world. It includes full-text PDF files of international tax documents and treaties discussed in its articles. The information is organized by countries and international organizations.

Tax Analysts also publishes ***Tax Notes International***. Similar to *Tax Notes* (see Chapter 7 for discussion), *Tax Notes International* is a weekly publication that provides tax news, commentary, and in-depth analysis of legislative, judicial, and administrative tax developments from over 180 countries. Full-text tax documents also are available with *Tax Notes International*.

Academic

The international content of LexisNexis Academic is similar to that found in the Tax Center. Academic also relies heavily on Tax Analysts for most of its sources, as

Exhibit 10-10: Tax Analysts Worldwide Tax Daily

Exhibit 10-11 demonstrates. Access to the international documents is easiest through the Sources Tab, as opposed to the Search Tab.

On the Sources Tab, the Browse Sources option requires three choices (numbered 1 through 3 in Exhibit 10-11) to be made before a search can be performed. First, the researcher selects Browsing by one of the following: Publication Type, News & Business Topics, Industry, or Area of Law. Second, Filters are applied by Country, Publication Type, and Multiple/Single Source. Each of the filters has a pull-down menu, and only one item may be selected. The Publication Type menu is illustrated in Exhibit 10-11. Finally, the researcher selects a Category to View Sources. The researcher may search any or all of the listed sources.

The next step is to click the OK Continue button, which produces the Power Search keyword entry box for natural language or terms and connectors keyword searches. The search then proceeds as discussed in Chapter 7.

RIA

Similar to LexisNexis, RIA also offers a variety of international products that may be bundled with RIA Checkpoint (see Chapter 6 for discussion) to meet the parti-

Exhibit 10-11: LexisNexis Academic International Libraries

cular needs of each practitioner's international research. In the International Practice Area, primary international law and treaties are supplied along with editorial materials (see Exhibit 10-12) by the International Bureau of Fiscal Documentation (IBFD), BNA, Warren, Gorham and Lamont (WG&L), the Practicing Law Institute (PLI), and RIA in-house editors. Three of RIA's international products are examined in this section.

International Tax Products

The **RIA Worldwide Tax Law (WTL)** service is one of the more comprehensive services in the International Practice Area (see Exhibit 10-12). It offers English translations of tax and commercial laws for approximately ninety countries. Similar to the search methodology used for the State & Local Checkpoint service (see Chapter 9), WTL requires the researcher to select one of eight geographical areas and at least one country, then the type of documents desired before a keyword search is performed (see Exhibit 10-13). From this point, the Checkpoint search and document retrieval proceeds in the same fashion as searching any other Practice Area, as illustrated in earlier chapters of this book.

Exhibit 10-12: RIA International Practice Area Opening Screen

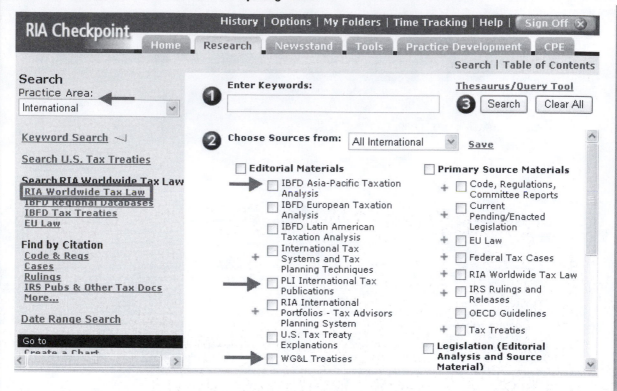

SPOTLIGHT ON TAXATION

IBFD

The International Bureau of Fiscal Documentation (IBFD) is a not-for-profit organization organized in 1938 to provide authoritative expertise to tax practitioners around the globe with regard to cross-border taxation. The IBFD relies on independent tax research as well as its research specialists to contribute international tax information and education materials to its customers. Originally the IBFD was simply a tax document repository, but now it focuses on research products, which it distributes to both the private and public sectors. Because it is an independent agency, the IBFD strives to produce objective and unbiased products including software, tax courses, personalized client research (for private and government use), daily newsletters, journals, and numerous books on international tax issues. Besides its publications, the IBFD has a library that is regarded as the world's leading resource for international and comparative taxation. Free online access to this library is available at **http://www.ibfd.org**.

Another useful service accessible through Checkpoint is the **RIA International Tax Library (ITL)**. Unlike other RIA tax products (see Chapters 6 and 9), ITL is a comprehensive set of analytical treatises and texts. A U.S. bilateral tax treaty database is included for accessing primary sources. Thus, the ITL lacks a

Exhibit 10-13: RIA Worldwide Tax Law Search Screen

central RIA editorial service such as the Federal Tax Coordinator. Newsletters and journals are included to keep the practitioner up-to-date on global taxation.

RIA offers International Portfolios, called the **RIA Tax Advisors Planning System**, that are written by expert practitioners currently in practice. These portfolios, updated monthly, focus on specific issues relevant to taxpayers with international business. Each portfolio includes commentary, advice supported by detailed explanations, integrated planning ideas, and the current rules with citations to the controlling authorities. In addition, practice aids similar in nature to those offered by the Tax Management Portfolios are furnished. The list of RIA portfolios is shorter than BNA's offerings, but the quality is outstanding.

All international subscriptions receive the **RIA International Taxes Weekly**. This is a weekly e-newsletter that covers current developments and emerging issues related to international taxation and is similar to the newsletter delivered with subscriptions to regular RIA Checkpoint.

Checkpoint offers the unique **RIA International Create-a-Chart** function that facilitates creating tax comparisons charts with links to controlling authority, detailed explanations, and analysis by WG&L treatises. These links are maintained when the chart is exported to a word processing file. The Create-a-Chart feature develops personalized charts of pertinent information for countries selected by the practitioner. There are currently over seventy-five chart types offered in Create-a-Chart on topics such as alimony, air and ship transport, capital gains, dividends, charitable contributions, and pensions.

WESTLAW

Westlaw offers two portals to international taxation materials, through a separate service, Westlaw International, and through the standard Westlaw subscription. Only the standard subscription is examined in this section.

Westlaw can be personalized, allowing the researcher to select up to six tabs to be displayed for those libraries most often searched. The Westlaw International Tab, shown in Exhibit 10-14, gives access to documents on a variety of international topics, one of which is Tax Law (located in Topical under the Westlaw International Subscriptions heading). The databases generally cover U.S. taxation and its treaties, with analysis supplied by the Law of Federal Income Taxation (Mertens) tax service.

Specific country headings, such as Australian and Canadian in Exhibit 10-14, have Tax as one of the Practice Areas and thus provide access to the country's tax

Exhibit 10-14: Westlaw International Directory

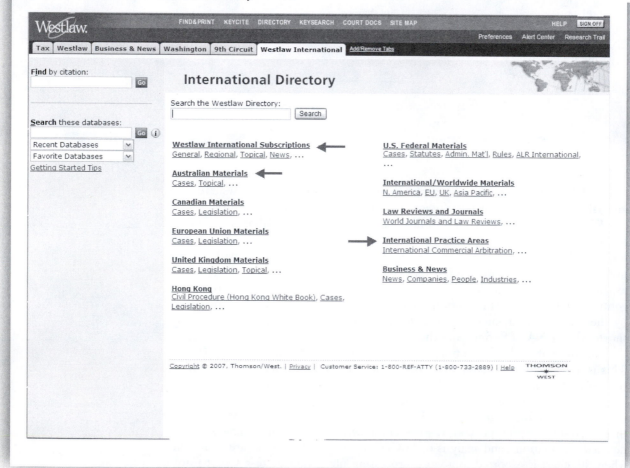

Exhibit 10-15: Westlaw International Tax Journal, Texts, and Treatise Offerings

This list is a sample and is not intended to be comprehensive.

Journals

British Tax Review

International Income Tax and Estate Planning

International Tax and Estate Planning: A Practical Guide for Multinational Investors

International Tax Journal

International Tax Review

Journal of International Taxation

Treatises

Conlon & Aquilino: Principals of Financial Derivatives: U.S. & International Tax

Dolan: U.S. Taxation of International Mergers, Acquisitions & Joint Ventures

Kuntz & Peroni: U.S. International Taxation

Langer on Practical International Tax Planning

Levey: U.S. Taxation of Foreign Controlled Businesses

Lowell & Governale: U.S. International Taxation: Practice and Procedure

Lowell, Tilton, Sheldrick & Donohue: U.S. International Taxation: Agreements

Streng: US International Estate Planning

Tilton: U.S. International Tax Forms Manual: Compliance and Reporting

laws. However, the countries available may be limited by the user's subscription. Finally, while International Practice Areas might appear a logical avenue for finding tax databases, taxation is not listed under this heading.

A more fruitful means of entry into Westlaw's international taxation resources is through the Tax library (Tax Tab) discussed in Chapter 7; it can be seen in Exhibit 7-11. This portal furnishes access to the RIA and BNA international materials (primary and editorial) discussed previously in this chapter, as well as international journals, WG&L treatises, and texts. Exhibit 10-15 is a partial list of these latter offerings. Most of the treatises, journals, and texts are not part of a basic subscription, so a premium charge applies to their access.

CCH

CCH offers numerous international tax products that offer timely and authoritative materials with practical analysis and understandable explanations written by experts in this field. To provide these products, CCH has teamed up with other publishers and authors. For example, CCH offers the BNA international publications and the **CCH *International Tax News***, which is created in conjunction with Horwath International. This newsletter is included with subscriptions to any of the CCH international tax services.

All of the CCH international tax services may be accessed through the Tax Research Network platform (see Chapter 6), thus simplifying the search process for those practitioners already familiar with this service. The International Tax tab, as shown in Exhibit 10-16, furnishes access to the U.S. Tax Treaties Reporter, which consolidates U.S. international primary and secondary tax sources into one library. This service contains all bilateral U.S. treaties (arranged by country), annotations, explanations, current developments, selected forms, publications, and primary sources that address international issues (see Exhibit 10-16).

Exhibit 10-16: CCH International U.S. Tax Treaties Reporter

CCH® Tax Research NetWork™   Preferences | Help | Log Out

Search

Main Menu   Clear Selections   Research History   Research Folders   Check Citator   Find by Citation   Search Tools

My CCH	Tax Tracker News	Accounting & Audit	Federal Tax		
State Tax	State Business Income Tax	Sales/Property Tax	Financial & Estate Planning	Wealth Management	Tax Practice Areas	Pension & Payroll
International Tax	perform plus III forms	ClientRelate	Capital Changes	Tax Tools	CPE	Training & Support

International Tax - Tax Treaties and Analysis - U.S. Tax Treaties Reporter - Tax Treaties Compilations -

Selected Laws and Regulations— Select All ☐

- ☐ Income not connected with United States business --Sec. 871 [3]
- ☐ Branch profits tax. --Sec. 884 [8]
- ☐ Income affected by treaty --Sec. 894 [32]
- ☐ Disposition of investment in United States real property --Sec. 897 [9]
- ☐ Withholding of tax on nonresident aliens --Sec. 1441 [20]
- ☐ Withholding of tax on foreign corporations --Sec. 1442 [7]
- ☐ Foreign tax-exempt organizations --Sec. 1443 [2]
- ☐ Withholding on Virgin Islands source income --Sec. 1444 [2]
- ☐ Withholding of tax on dispositions of United States real property interests --Sec. 1445 [20]
- ☐ Liability for tax withheld --Sec. 1461 [12]
- ☐ Treaty-based return positions --Sec. 6114 [4]
- ☐ Mode or time of collection --Sec. 6302 [3]
- ☐ Failure to make deposit of taxes --Sec. 6656 [3]
- ☐ Failure to disclose treaty-based return positions --Sec. 6712 [3]
- ☐ Definitions --Sec. 7701 [3]
- ☐ Certification required to obtain reduced tax rates --26 C.F.R. 601 [3]
- ☐ Other applicable rules --Sec. 7852 [18]
- ☐ Expatriated entities --Sec. 7874 [10]

Find help at http://support.cch.com, call Research Specialists at 800-344-3734, | Back to Top
or call Tech Support at 800-835-0105.

Service Offerings

The following is a list of some of the most useful resources offered within the CCH International Tax Service. Availability depends upon the level of the researcher's subscription.

Worldwide Tax Rates and Answers: Europe. Contains country-specific tax data, forms, and instructions for the European Union countries and Switzerland.

Global Transaction Library. A series of publications designed to provide guidance on tax planning and compliance for cross-border and international transactions by taking a transactional approach. This service includes publications by Tax Analysts (*Tax Notes International*) and CCH (*International Tax Journal*), treatises, the Transfer Pricing Library, and full text (in English) of all U.S. bilateral tax treaties.

International Tax Planning Library. This library consists of three comprehensive publications and a practical newsletter exploring tax planning issues from around the world. The three publications cover international tax planning for corporations, expatriates, and migrants, plus offshore financial centers for over forty countries.

International Tax Treaty Expert Library. Thousands of treaties (with amended language in context) and related documents, such as diplomatic notes and

Exhibit 10-17: CCH International Tax Treaty Expert Library

protocols, are available, and all are in English. The treaties cover income, estate and gift taxes, sea and air transport, and information exchange agreements. This service may contain the publications included in the International Tax Planning Library.

Exhibit 10-17 illustrates some of the treaties and analytical works included in the service. Model Tax Treaties by the OECD, United Nations, and United States are available. The Tax Treaty Withholding Rate Decision Support Tool is very useful; it is designed to simplify researching withholding tax rates for over fifty countries.

International Transfer Pricing Library. This library contains four authoritative commentaries on transfer pricing.

INTERNET SITES

As described in Chapter 7, the Tax and Accounting Sites Directory web site (**http://www.taxsites.com**) contains links to numerous tax web pages, one of which is designated for international tax topics. This is an excellent starting point for Internet international tax searches. Links to tax sites for over eighty countries are given, as well as references to international tax associations and IRS resources. A long list of other sources also is provided. Additionally, the international and regional businesses offer international tax information on their web sites.

SUMMARY

The world is shrinking as more companies enter the global economy. No longer do only the Fortune 500 companies maintain international offices. Now, many middle-market and owner-managed firms are expanding into the international markets of Europe and the Pacific Rim. In 2006, the U.S. exports grew to over $1.4 trillion, while U.S. imports reached about $2.2 trillion. Thus, it is no longer a luxury to employ staff knowledgeable about international taxation.

The demand for international tax services is rapidly growing, and the major players in the research service industry (CCH, LexisNexis, RIA, and Westlaw) appear to be relying on BNA and Tax Analysts for analysis and newsletters, and WG&L for texts and treatises. As the importance of international taxation continues to explode, the tax services will develop more targeted products to serve the needs of the tax practitioners. Consequently, international research tools will likely be among the fastest changing component of the major tax services.

TAX TUTOR

Reinforce the tax research information covered in this chapter by completing the online tutorials located at the *Federal Tax Research* web site. **http://academic .cengage.com/taxation/raabe**

KEY WORDS

By the time you complete this chapter, you should be comfortable discussing each of the following terms. If you need additional review of any of these items, return to the appropriate material in the chapter or consult the glossary to this text.

Blended Model
BNA Foreign Income Library
BNA International Service (BNA IS)
CCH *International Tax News*
CCH Tax Treaties Reporter
Deduction apportionment
Full Inclusion Model
Organization for Economic Co-operation
   and Development
RIA International Create-a-Chart
RIA International Tax Library (ITL)

RIA International Taxes Weekly
RIA Tax Advisors Planning System
RIA Worldwide Tax Law (WTL)
Source determination
Tax Analysts *Worldwide Tax Daily*
Tax Analysts Worldwide Tax Treaties
Tax haven
Tax Management Portfolios
Tax Notes International
Tax treaties
Territorial Model

DISCUSSION QUESTIONS

1. What is the ultimate tax planning goal of most companies?

2. What is the definition of a native country? What is the transaction country?

3. What are the three major models for developing international taxing systems?

4. What is the Full Inclusion Model of international taxation? Explain whether a corporation with only domestic income or a company with foreign income would pay more taxes under this model.

5. What are the two situations that international tax provisions generally address?

6. What is the Territorial Model of international taxation? Under this model, what rate of tax does a native corporation pay on its foreign income?

7. What problems does the Blended Model of international taxation cause for the United States?

8. How is the source of income from the sale of inventory and rental income typically determined?

9. Within the United States, what type of expenses are apportioned to determine the amount of their deductibility?

10. Describe the functions of the following organizations: WTO, IMF, and OECD?

11. If a provision of the *Internal Revenue Code* and a tax treaty are in conflict, which rule prevails?

12. What are the three factors that the OECD considers key in determining whether a jurisdiction should be listed as a tax haven?

13. The International BNA Tax Management Portfolios cover what three areas of international taxation?

14. What kinds of information are provided in the Working Papers Section of the International BNA Tax Management Portfolios?

15. In the BNA International Service, how is a TOC search performed?

16. In the BNA International Service, how is a Boolean search performed?

17. In the BNA International Service, how are the ranking percentages calculated, indicating "relevance?"

18. On what base has LexisNexis built its international tax services?

19. What are the four categories included in the international tab of LexisNexis Tax Center?

20. What type of information would you expect to find in the document *Doing Business in China*?

21. What organizations provide accounting and financial sources to LexisNexis Tax Center?

22. What organization provides the international news for LexisNexis Tax Center? What is the name of the news publication?

23. What is the easiest method to access the international documents on LexisNexis Academic?

24. What is the International Bureau of Fiscal Documentation?

25. How is the RIA International Tax Library different from other RIA services?

26. Describe the International Create-a-Chart function in RIA Checkpoint.

27. What are the two methods for accessing international tax resources in Westlaw? Which method is most effective?

28. CCH offers a newsletter with its international services. What is the name of the newsletter, and with whom is the letter created?

29. For international taxation, what categories of links does the Tax and Accounting Sites Directory web site (taxsites.com) employ?

30. Besides the Fortune 500 companies, what companies are expanding into the international markets of Europe and the Pacific Rim?

EXERCISES

31. Use the BNA International Service to answer the following questions.
    a. Who wrote the document *Doing Business in Austria*?
    b. What Latin American country has the most recent bankruptcy act listed in the Corporate Restructuring library?
    c. What type of business organization is a GmbH und Co KG? What countries recognize this business entity?

32. Use the BNA International Service to answer the following questions.
    a. What is the proper citation for the most recent article in the European Tax Service on the United Kingdom's VAT?
    b. Use the Advanced Search option to find a 2007 article on the transfer pricing for intellectual property in China. Give the article's proper citation.
    c. Use the Quick Search option to determine how many articles Bert Mesdom has written regarding the VAT.

33. Use the BNA International Service to answer the following questions.
    a. What is the title of the most recent Global Case Study in the Corporate Restructuring Library?
    b. What is the title of the most recent Featured Article on the Transfer Pricing Library opening page?
    c. What is the title of the August 2006 article by Professor Giampaolo Corabi and Roberto Scalia that discusses the European Commission request for Italy and other EU members to amend their tax legislation concerning outbound dividends?

34. Use the BNA International Service to answer the following questions.
    a. On what date was the Japanese Tax Reform Act of 2007 passed?
    b. What is the most recent article on European Court of Justice found in the European Tax Focus Archives? Give the proper citation of the article.
    c. Use the Advanced Search option to locate a 2005 article discussing German investment incentives for U.S. film production companies. Provide the title of the article and its author.

35. Use International Tax Law Sources of LexisNexis Academic to answer the following questions.

   a. Who is the publisher of International Tax Law and Estate Planning?
   b. What is the content of the Wiley IFRS: Interpretations and Applications of International Accounting and Financial Reporting Standards?
   c. Perform a Find a Source search using the key words transfer pricing. What sources are suggested?

36. Use International Tax Law Sources of LexisNexis Academic to answer the following questions.
   a. What is the address for the Ministry of Finance for Vanuatu (Use a Directory source)?
   b. Find the Canadian-French Social Security Agreement and Final Protocol. What is its date of publication and what is its effective date? What is the article number?
   c. In the Model Convention Documents, find the Commentary on the Articles of the OECD Model Income and Capital Tax Convention. Determine the article and paragraph number for the discussion of cross-border issues related to pensions. On what date was this Commentary issued?

37. Use the International Tax Law Sources of LexisNexis Academic to answer the following questions.
   a. What tax treatment do the Greece-Moldova treaties indicate for earnings of nonresident students? What is the effective date of the agreement?
   b. What is the title and date of the most recent article regarding Iceland in the Tax Analysts' *Worldwide Tax Daily*?
   c. What is the title and date of the most recent article on the European VAT found in the Tax Analysts' *Tax Notes International*?

38. Use RIA materials to answer the following questions.
   a. What international sources are included in the International News/Current Awareness source heading?
   b. What paragraph of the RIA Tax Treaty Editorial Explanations discusses rental, royalty, and realty income?
   c. What are the title and date of the most recent article in *International Taxes Weekly* that discusses charitable contributions of nonresident aliens?

39. Use RIA materials to answer the following questions.
   a. What are the title and date of the most recent article in the *Journal of International Taxation* on Belgium tax incentives?
   b. What International Create-a-Charts are available for the taxation of students and trainees?
   c. Who are the authors of the treatise titled *U.S. Taxation of International Mergers, Acquisitions & Joint Ventures*?

40. Use the Westlaw Tax Tab to answer the following questions.
   a. In which BNA Foreign Income Portfolio is there a discussion of enterprise investment incentives in Singapore?
   b. Perform a keyword search for the country of Ireland using the terms intangibles within ten words of royalties. Provide the article and paragraph number of where intangible royalties are discussed in a Treasury Technical Explanation? When were the documents issued?

c. What are the first and last names of the author of the WG&L treatise *Analysis of U.S. Income Tax Treaties*? What does Chapter 16 of this treatise cover? What subscription rate applies to this treatise?

41. Use the Westlaw International Tab to answer the following questions.
    a. What are the international practice areas listed in the International Directory?
    b. What South American countries are listed in the International/Worldwide Materials?
    c. What are the title and date of the most recent law review article on VAT tax evasion in the European Union found by searching World Journals and Law Reviews in the News and Periodicals of the Westlaw International Subscriptions?

42. Use the Westlaw Tax Tab to answer the following questions.
    a. How do the authors of the WG&L treatise, *U.S. International Taxation: Agreements, Checklists & Commentary*, suggest structuring an activity-specific foreign joint venture for intangible development arrangements?
    b. What are the title and date of the most recent article in the British Tax Review that addresses a U.S.-British tax issue?
    c. What are the numbers and titles of the BNA Foreign Income Portfolio that cover transfers under IRC §367?

43. Use the Westlaw International Tab to answer the following questions.
    a. Explain where tax-related documents are found in the United Kingdom Materials.
    b. What general terms does the thesaurus provide for VAT?
    c. What are the title and date of an article discussing the taxation of families with or without children?

44. Use the CCH International Tab to answer the following questions.
    a. What is the most recent Tax Treaties Report Letter? What does it discuss?
    b. What article of the Tunisia treaty discusses the U.S. taxation of students, apprentices, and trainees from Tunisia? At what CCH paragraph number does the article appear?
    c. Provide the IRS publication numbers listed in the Practice Aids in the Tax Treaties Compilations. (If there is no number, provide the name of the publication.)

45. Use the CCH to answer the following questions.
    a. How is a resident of Cyprus defined in its treaty with the United States?
    b. What is the Tax Treaties Report Letter from May 31, 2007 reporting? What is the letter number of this report?
    c. What is the title of Article 26 in the United Nations Model Double Taxation Convention Between Developed and Developing Countries?

RESEARCH CASES

46. VanDelay, a citizen of the United States but a resident of Dulcinea, is an important sculptor. This year, he came to the United States to appear at an exhibition of his work in San Francisco. The United States has no tax treaty with

Dulcinea. Does the $250,000 that VanDelay netted from the show qualify for the §911 earned income exclusion?

47. State University invites Dr. Byko, a Russian citizen, to become a member of the faculty for a three-year period to work on a large grant the university obtained from the National Aeronautics and Space Administration (NASA). Dr. Byko accepts the invitation and enters the United States on a J-1 visa. His university pay is entirely funded by the NASA grant. Based on the Russian treaty, Dr. Byko thinks his income is exempt because it is from a grant. Determine whether Dr. Byko is correct.

48. Haruo, a resident alien, obtained a U.S. divorce from his wife, Wakana, two years ago. Last July, Wakana returned to Japan; however, Haruo remained in the United States. For all of the current year, Haruo paid alimony to Wakana in the amount of $10,000 per month. Does Wakana have income subject to U.S. taxation or withholding?

49. Rainbow Corporation has a contract with the National Science Foundation to conduct research in Antarctica. Harriet, a U.S. employee of Rainbow, spent all of last year and part of this year working at McMurdo Station on Ross Island, Antarctica. When filing her return for last year, Harriet excluded her income from the contract, based on the fact that she worked outside of the United States Her income was not in excess of the excludible ceiling. Is Harriet correct in her treatment of last year's income?

50. Moonsoo, a Republic of Korea citizen, went to San Diego, California on a vacation. Since he liked San Diego, Moonsoo purchased five acres of land on which he wants to build luxury condominiums. He also bought the majority interest in a construction corporation that specializes in condominium construction. Moonsoo could not get the zoning clearance to build the condominiums, so he sold both the land and his stock in the construction corporation. Is Moonsoo taxed in the United States on his gains from these sales?

51. Ireland imposes a tax on the net market value (less certain deduction) of the taxable assets of those individuals residing in Ireland. Although she is a U.S. citizen, Katherine has been residing in Ireland for the past five years. She owns property located in Ireland and in the United States Much of her property consists of stocks and bonds, but she also has large holdings of land in both countries. Does this Irish tax qualify for the foreign tax credit, and/or as a deduction for U.S. tax purposes?

52. Paul Thomas and Karen Jackson are both in the Armed Forces and each receive combat zone pay. Karen is a commissioned officer, whereas Paul is enlisted personnel. How is each taxed on the combat zone pay? How does Paul treat his combat zone pay when computing his Earned Income Tax Credit?

53. Three international students are paid $1,000 a month to be teaching assistants in their university's Department of Accounting. The students from India and China have been in the United States for six years, and the student from Spain arrived one year ago. How is each of the students taxed in the United States for the current year?

54. A group of Russian tourists spent a week in Las Vegas. Kolzak, one of the tourists, was very lucky at the roulette table and won $50,000. Is Kolzak

subject to U.S. income tax, and is the casino required to withhold taxes on her winnings?

55. Which of the following payments by International Partners, Inc., a Montana corporation, qualifies for the foreign tax credit?

- Income tax paid to Germany, covered by an existing treaty.

- Income tax paid to Adagio, with which the United States has no income tax treaty.

- Value-added tax paid to Largetto, with which the United States has no income tax treaty.

- Oil extraction tax paid to Tedesco, with which the United States has no income tax treaty.

- Transportation tax paid to Santa Lucia, with which the United States has no income tax treaty. The tax is reduced dollar-for-dollar when International provides consulting services in designing Santa Lucia's new bullet train system. This year, International incurred $1 million in taxes, but it earned a $600,000 reduction for its services.

Implementing the Research Tools

Communicating Research Results

Learning Objectives

- Produce a standard format for the construction of a file memorandum to contain the results of one's research efforts and professional judgment.

- Develop skills in using other forms of communicating research results, including oral presentations and client letters.

ONCE THE PRACTITIONER HAS begun to develop effective tax research skills, he or she must hone them with practice—whether by working through tax research cases presented as a class exercise in a university course, or immediately beginning work for professional clients. Accordingly, the overriding purpose of this chapter is to provide the reader with guidance and opportunities to apply the research skills and examine the tax research resources that have been discussed in previous chapters.

In addition, this chapter will discuss the means by which the tax professional conveys the results of a tax research project—in other words, applying some of the judgment and communications skills required. Direction as to the proper format and content of memorandums to the file, of client letters, and of oral presentations is addressed, with development of professional skills the overriding goal.

COMMUNICATIONS AND THE TAX PROFESSIONAL

As we suggested in our initial discussions of the tax research process, illustrated in Exhibit 2-1, a tax research assignment often concludes with some form of communication by the tax professional. The audience for this communication often is the practitioner's supervisor or client, but tax-related communications can take many forms.

- A telephone call or instant message

- An informal discussion in person or via e-mail

- A letter prepared for reading by someone at least as familiar with the tax law as the writer

- A letter prepared for reading by someone less familiar with the tax law than is the writer

- A letter prepared for reading by someone who is essentially untrained in the tax law

- An article for publication in a newspaper or magazine directed at the general public

- An article for publication in a professional journal read by tax generalists

- An article for publication in a professional journal read by tax specialists

- A directed discussion among tax peers, for example, in a tax department meeting

- A speech to a general audience

- A speech at a conference of tax professionals

- A memorandum to be read in the future by the writer or by a peer with similar training

- An appearance on a news broadcast or program with a serious tone

- An appearance on a broadcast with a less serious tone

- A posting on a general, business, or tax-oriented blog

For the most part, the tax professional's preparation for these communications is similar. For the purposes of this chapter, we assume that all of the pertinent tax research techniques developed in earlier parts of this text have been planned and conscientiously applied, so that the practitioner is qualified and current enough with respect to prevailing tax law to address the audience in terms of the content of the communication. The challenge then becomes how to deliver this information in a manner that will be accepted and understood by the audience.

Actually, though, one's preparation for the delivery of tax communication must go far beyond obtaining control over the technical tax knowledge required for the assignment. As illustrated in Exhibit 11-1, communication truly occurs only when the message desired to be sent by the speaker or writer is received by the intended audience. Distractions of all sorts can make this process difficult to accomplish. Thorough research into the nature and expectations of the audience, factors that may interfere with the delivery of the message, and feedback and corrective measures must make up a critical part of the communicator's preparation.

Examples of "noise" that can disrupt the communications process include a mismatching of expectations as to the message, the chosen delivery method, the identity and nature of the sender and receiver of the message, other events competing for the attention of those involved, logistical difficulties, and technological problems. Feedback and corrective devices that can aid in accomplishing the delivery of the desired message include formal and informal evaluation processes, "real-time" opportunities such as question-and-answer periods and written comments received during the drafting of the document, and the sending and receiving of intended and unintended body language or other communicative signals.

Tax professionals generally are virtually untrained as to the application of communication methods in conveying tax messages, but this shortcoming can be remedied. The chief ingredients necessary to become an effective tax-content communicator are the desire to learn and improve as a communicator in general, and the use of every opportunity possible to obtain and develop skills in the delivery of tax information. Given the nature of today's competitive tax profession, plenty of such opportunities for practice exist, and pressures from others who are competing for clients and promotions provide most professionals with more than enough motivation to make improvements in their communication skills a lifelong process.

Exhibit 11-1: The Communication Process

Message

Noise

Feedback

Communicator   Audience

We begin a more detailed review of the communication process with an examination of the most commonly encountered written communications demanded in the tax practice. The chapter concludes with a discussion of skills needed in delivering spoken communications. In either case, the structure of the communication follows the basic format delineated in Exhibit 11-2.

THE HEART OF TAX RESEARCH COMMUNICATION: THE FILE MEMO

The tax researcher spends most of his or her time reviewing primary and secondary sources of the Federal tax law, redefining pertinent issues, and attempting to discover additional facts concerning the client's situation. On completion of this review, the researcher must integrate the disparate results of the research process into a more usable form. Thorough practitioners generate a memorandum to the client's file for this purpose. This **file memorandum** is designed to:

Exhibit 11-2: The Structure of Technical Tax Communications

Element of the Message	Purposes	Comments
Introduction	Provide a roadmap for what is to come.	**10% of allotted time/space.**
	Place the message in context.	Could include a story/anecdote, current news development, or "object lesson."
	Generate audience interest, if necessary.	
	Set the tone for the message.	
Body	Generally, the technical tax material is presented here.	**80% of allotted time/space.**
	Usually follows an order suggested by the hierarchy of the sources of the tax law.	Must be brief, to the point, hard-hitting; not trite or condescending.
	Alternative ordering methods: historical, strengths/weaknesses, cost/benefit.	Identify three to six key points that all readers/listeners must take away from the message.
Conclusion	Tie back to the introduction.	**10% of allotted time/space.**
	Reinforce key elements of the message. Bring the presentation to a climax. Indicate next steps and follow-up action.	Tip off the reader/listener that the conclusion is starting, with: "In closing," "To sum up," or "I'll conclude with …"

- organize the facts, issues, and conclusions of the project,

- facilitate a review of the research activities by the practitioner's supervisors or colleagues, and

- allow for a subsequent examination of the research issue, by the original researcher or by his or her successor, with respect to the same or another client's identical or related fact situation.

Accordingly, the file memo should be constructed in a general, usable format that lends itself to a quick perusal of the pertinent tax facts and issues. Many accounting and law firms impose a standardized file-memo format. If the reader's employer has enacted no such requirement, he or she should consider adopting the format illustrated in Exhibits 2-5 and 11-3. A template for this memo format is available at the Web site for this text, **http://academic.cengage.com/taxation/raabe**.

A file memo should include a brief introductory summary of the facts and issues that face the client. In all but the most complex instances, this statement should require no more than two paragraphs. Similarly, the rare footnote at this point of the memo should be restricted to current developments, for example, with respect to an appeal relative to one of the critical cases that is cited in the memo or a statutory amendment.

The file memo then includes a listing of the tax issues that are in dispute and a matching conclusion for each identified issue. This format allows the subsequent reader to determine quickly whether each issue is "pro" or "con" for the taxpayer and limits the time required to sort through a number of such memos. In the support section, a detailed review and evaluation of controlling laws is derived, with full citations presented in the standard forms. The "meat" of the memo is presented here, and the strengths and weaknesses of both sides of the tax argument are developed and discussed. Finally, recommendations for subsequent actions with the client may be enumerated, and other strategies as to tax return or audit positions are identified.

Often, the gathering of the pertinent facts is the most challenging of the tax professional's tasks. Tax engagements typically begin with client contact in the form of a phone call or meeting, followed by an exchange of copies of pertinent documents such as letters, spreadsheets, trusts or wills, contracts, life insurance or annuity agreements, employer handbooks, and diaries or logbooks belonging to the client. In reality, though, the initial determination of the facts is likely to be incomplete.

- Taxpayers tend to see the dispute only from their side, so that facts and circumstances may be hidden or "forgotten" if they would cast doubt on the ability to determine or document the pro-taxpayer position.

- Taxpayers are not trained in the details of the technical tax law, so they may be unable to determine which documents or other evidence of the facts are important in determining the controlling tax law.

- For tax research that requires the full professional judgment and experience of the practitioner, there may be no clearly controlling tax statute or precedent, facts may be truly incomplete, or they may unfold as the evaluation of tax law occurs. The researcher may discover that issues of taxpayer motive, knowledge, or other circumstances turn on facts that were not immediately known to be critical.

Moreover, fact gathering often turns on such intangible factors as the reliability of the memories of the taxpayers and key witnesses, the ability of witnesses to withstand scrutiny in the deposition and testimony phases of the case, the unanticipated death or disappearance of key parties, the destruction of records due to casualty or computer mismanagement, and the tendency of some taxpayers to "fix the truth" after the fact. Recalling our language in Chapters 2 and 3, more research engagements entail closed-fact settings than open-fact situations by far, but those facts may be fairly difficult to determine and support in a manner that will satisfy the Internal Revenue Service (IRS) or the courts. Such fact-gathering travails make for interesting anecdotes at conferences of tax practitioners, and they seldom are apparent from the clean, black-and-white statements of facts that accompany file memos and case briefs.

The tone and nature of the file memo should recognize that its readers will be restricted to fellow tax practitioners who are well versed in the Federal tax law. Thus, references to primary and secondary sources of the tax law should be frequent and complete, but usually limited to the tax case reporters that are available in the office of the researcher's firm. One must presume that the ultimate reader of the memo's comments will need no introduction to the hierarchy of the Federal tax system nor to statutory citation practices. In addition, it often is helpful to include pertinent references to one or more of the commercial tax services to which the researcher's firm subscribes, perhaps on a "sticky note" or other attachment to the memo, providing a clear paper trail to facilitate subsequent review and commentary concerning the tax issue.

Seldom will the researcher's efforts result in merely the preparation of a research memorandum to the file. In general, the memo will be accompanied in the file by links to and briefs of one or more pertinent court cases or administrative pronouncements. (Review Exhibit 5-8 and your related class exercises concerning the format and content of a well-constructed court case brief.) In addition, many practitioners append to the file memo photocopies of or network links to prior-year documents, in-house memos, various IRS rulings, and journal articles, much of which features "highlighting," that is, markup with a literal or virtual pastel marker. These practices are illustrated in Exhibit 11-3.

The authors recommend that practitioners restrict such appended material to only those resources that are of utmost importance to reduce both the associated client costs and the volume of the typical memo. In this regard, we believe that an effective statement of facts and issues, followed by a concise synthesis of the controlling law, is far more valuable than a mass of duplicated, small-print tax reference materials.

SPOTLIGHT ON TAXATION

The Tax Profession

The file memo and supporting documents also come under review by the audit department and others in the firm, so technical tax material might be accompanied by a set of nontechnical objectives and timetables for the client engagement. Information that could be used by those dealing with the creditors of the taxpayer also might be available in the file.

Exhibit 11-3: File Memorandum for Tax Research

Raabe, Whittenburg & Sanders, CPAs
San Francisco, CA
September 30, 20XX

Relevant Facts
The Browns live in South Dakota. They own their home and hold investments in the debt of several domestic corporations. The interest that they received on this debt was gross income to them. To diversify their portfolio, the Browns took out a sizable second mortgage on their home and applied a portion of the proceeds to some City of Chandler School Bonds. The remainder of the proceeds was used to expand the facilities of Mrs. Brown's dental clinic.

Specific Issues
How much of the mortgage interest paid can be claimed as an itemized deduction by the Browns?

Conclusions
That portion of the mortgage proceeds applied to the dental clinic generates an interest deduction to be claimed against clinic income on Schedule C. No other deduction is allowed.

Support
The Code disallows the deduction of interest on indebtedness that is incurred or continued to purchase or carry obligations, the interest on which is exempt from the Federal income tax. *IRC § 265(a)(2)*. This provision denies the double benefit that would be enjoyed by the taxpayer who would receive tax-exempt income while simultaneously claiming an investment interest deduction for the interest expense paid, for example, by incurring a bank loan and using the proceeds to purchase municipal bonds.

The IRS examines evidence to infer the intent of the taxpayer who is incurring the indebtedness. Under *Rev. Proc. 72-18, 1972-1 C.B. 740,* a taxpayer who purchases exempt bonds can claim an interest deduction if the debt in question has been incurred (1) for personal reasons (e.g., via a mortgage to finance the purchase of residential property) or (2) for valid business reasons, as long as the borrowing does not exceed legitimate business needs.

Several court decisions have emphasized that the existence of such business motives must be documented clearly, as to both presence and amount. *Wisconsin Cheeseman v. U.S., 388 F.2d 420 (CA-7, 1968);* Bradford, 60 T.C. 253 (1973); Israelson v. U.S., 367 F.Supp. 1104 (D.Md., 1973). However, if the taxpayer's holdings of tax-exempt securities are deemed to be immaterial in amount, the § 265(a)(2) disallowance will not be invoked.

Indian Trail Trading Post, Inc. v. Comm., 503 F.2d 102 (CA-6, 1974). Typically, if the average adjusted basis of the exempt bonds does not exceed 2 percent of the average adjusted basis of the entire investment portfolio, the entire interest deduction is allowed. *Batten v. U.S.,* 322 F. Supp. 629 (E.D.Va., 1971); *Ball,* 54 T.C. 1200 (1970).

Mortgage indebtedness is a classic illustration of an investment that will generate deductible interest expenses for the taxpayer who holds exempt bonds. However, the timing of such a mortgage transaction must be monitored to exhibit the proper motives for the benefit of the IRS. In one case, the taxpayer paid for his home with cash. Only later was an investment program (that included municipal bonds) initiated and a residential mortgage secured. The IRS inferred that the mortgage proceeds were in indirect support of the exempt indebtedness, and the deduction for the mortgage interest was disallowed. *Mariorenzi v. Comm., 490 F.2d 92 (CA-8, 1974), 32 TCM 681 (1973).* Had the taxpayer secured a mortgage before the home was

continued

Exhibit 11-3: (continued)

completed, purchasing the exempt bonds out of savings, it appears that the deduction could have been preserved. The IRS has applied this doctrine outside of the Eighth Circuit, in PLR 8631006.

Because the Browns live in the Eighth Circuit, the Mariorenzi doctrine prevails, and no itemized deduction is allowed at all, that is, for that portion of the loan that is applied to the school bonds. Rev. Proc. 72-18 is insensitive to portfolio diversification motives, and no personal motive appears to exist that supports any other possible deduction. According to the logic of these precedents, the Browns should have sold the exempt bonds and then used the proceeds to finance their portfolio acquisitions.

Actions to Be Taken
Prepare letter, review results with client.
Suggest changes in portfolio holdings to re-gain the deduction.
Preparer: Mary H. Polzin
Reviewer: Char E. Mano

EVALUATING THE SOURCES OF LAW

The tax researcher will have made a number of judgments and creative applications concerning the client's fact situation before preparing the file memo. For instance, the researcher may select and eliminate competing issues and direct the research process onto one or more pathways, to the exclusion of others. Nonetheless, in deriving an analysis of the various elements of the controlling sources of the tax law, the practitioner must choose from among a number of varied interpretations of the statute and of its (interpretive) regulations and court case opinions.

Often the researcher will be guided in this regard by the opinions of the most recent of the court cases discovered. Well-written case opinions typically provide a summary of the evolution of the pertinent tax law and a discussion of the competing interpretations thereof by the parties to the lawsuit. In this manner, the researcher regularly can obtain an indication of both the critical facts and issues that the court has identified in the present case and its interpretation as to the distinguishing features of seemingly relevant precedents. (In reality, most of these sections of the opinion are written by law clerks or law school students who obtain and retain their positions by preparing thorough and insightful file memos of their own!) Moreover, court case opinions often include lengthy dissenting or concurring opinions, from which the researcher can identify additonal facts and issues relative to the opinion. Logical and legal leads also might be found in a dissenting opinion that could be pertinent in building an appeal to overturn the majority opinion.

Lacking (or in lieu of) such judicial direction, the researcher's evaluation of the efficacy of a precedent or pronouncement often is guided by no more than a review of the hierarchy of the sources of the Federal tax law. (For a review of these sources, see Chapters 3 through 5.)

In addition, we offer the following points to be considered in the evaluation of a series of apparently conflicting tax laws.

- Regulations seldom are held to be invalid by a court. In the typical year, fewer than a dozen such holdings are issued. Thus, challenges to the provisions of a Regulation should be based on more than a simple challenge to the Treasury's authority or a self-serving competing interpretation of the statute offered by the taxpayer.

- Revenue Rulings and Revenue Procedures, however, are frequently modified or otherwise held to be invalid by a court. Accordingly, the taxpayer's attempted restructuring of the pertinent law in his or her favor with respect to such an administrative pronouncement is more likely to be heard openly by the court and, therefore, to be based on the weight of the competing arguments, rather than simply on the Treasury's preemptive interpretive rights.

- The decisions of courts that are higher in the judicial hierarchy should receive additional precedential weight. Given an adequate degree of similarity in fact situations, district and circuit court opinions have direct bearing on the taxpayer only if they were issued in the corresponding jurisdiction. On the other hand, opinions of the national courts like Court of Federal Claims and Tax Court are binding on the taxpayer, even though they were issued with respect to a taxpayer who works or resides in another jurisdiction, unless they are overturned in a pertinent appeal.

- Thus, a taxpayer who works in Wyoming is not bound by decisions of, say, the Seventh Circuit or Alaska District courts. The practitioner should not feel restricted in a trial or appeal hearing by the doctrine of *stare decisis*. Conversely, an Alaska taxpayer's Court of Federal Claims decision is binding on the Wyoming citizen's Court of Federal Claims case. If this Court of Federal Claims decision was held in a manner that is detrimental to the Wyoming taxpayer, another trial court should be pursued.

- Other factors being equal, decisions of the Second, Ninth, and Federal Circuits should be assigned additional precedential value. Among other reasons, this additional weight can be attributed to the inclusion of the cities of New York and Washington and the state of California in these circuits. Typically, the Ninth Circuit is the first to introduce an innovative or otherwise unusual interpretation of the law, and the Second and Federal Circuits are authoritative in a more traditional vein.

- Older court decisions should be assigned a geometrically declining degree of importance unless (1) they are Supreme Court cases, (2) they are Second, Ninth, or Federal Circuit cases, or (3) they are the only precedents available. The roster and philosophical makeup of a court change over time and often reflect the changing societal culture and philosophies. Thus, recent case opinions are more likely to identify issues that are held to be critical by the sitting judges that the taxpayer will face, and they are likely to be better predictors of the outcome relative to the current taxpayer's issues.

- Tax treatises and journal articles are a useful source by which to identify current, critical tax issues. They also can be utilized in the formation of the practitioner's research schedule, because they often include both a comprehensive summary of the evolution of the controlling law and a thorough list of citations concerning prior interpretive court decisions.

- IRS agents are bound only by the Code, administrative pronouncements, and Supreme Court decisions. Some of the most difficult decisions a tax practitioner must face include those in which one must determine whether the time, effort, and expense of litigation will generate a reward that is sufficient to justify, in essence, the construction of new (judicial) tax law, that is, to overcome this narrow scope of the agent's concern.

- Court decisions are never completely predictable. Thus, even if absolutely all of the judicial precedent that is available supports the taxpayer's position, the court still may hold against him or her. Negative decisions may be the result of a poor performance by the attorney, other tax adviser, or witnesses that are heard by the court; changes in the makeup or philosophy of the members of the court; changes in societal mores, as reflected by the court; or an incorrect interpretation of the law by the court that hears the present case. The practitioner, however, can do little more than conduct a thorough tax research analysis concerning the case, identify convincing witnesses, and trust that justice will prevail.

CLIENT LETTERS

Our discussion to this point in the chapter has concentrated on the communication of tax research by the practitioner to him- or herself or to other tax professionals in a fairly sophisticated document—a memorandum to the file. We now shift the focus for the communication to a different audience, namely, the client, and to a different setting, the written or oral presentation.

By far the most common form of substantive communication between the tax professional and his or her client is the telephone call. We must stress the danger inherent in placing too great a dependence on the phone call to convey the results of tax research, given the intricacies of both the fact situation and the (tax adviser's interpretation of) controlling law, in most professional situations. If the telephone must be used (perhaps because of time pressures or convenience) to convey tax research results, the practitioner should always send a fairly detailed follow-up **client letter**, in hard copy, not just e-mail, confirming his or her understanding as to the information that was conveyed and the actions that are to be taken as a result of the call.

Foremost among the attributes of the client letter is its brevity. Except in the most unusual circumstances, it should not exceed two pages. This rule should be violated only when the subject of the research is especially complex or grave, perhaps in anticipation of extended litigation or with respect to a more sophisticated client, where, for instance, one might be tempted to attach a copy (or a "client version") of the research file memo.

The brevity of the client letter is, most often, in response to the desire of the client for "the answer" that has been found concerning the extant tax issues. Clients do tend to see tax issues as black-and-white ones, and they want to know whether they will win or lose with the IRS. Of course, tax practitioners are aware of the colorful world that tax practice presents, and the various shades of emphasis and interpretation sometimes make the view quite murky. Thus, to accommodate the desire of the client, one typically must convey no more than the absolute highlights of the research process.

Another factor that leads to brief client letters is the tax practitioner's professional responsibilities. Responding to client questions is generally easier in a face-to-face meeting. Thus, most practitioners use the client letter to deliver the general conclusions of the research project and to request a follow-up meeting in which questions, comments, and the need for more detail can be addressed.

Exhibits 11-4 and 11-5 illustrate the format and content of typical client letters. The sole difference between these two letters is the degree of sophistication that is possessed by the receiving party.

Exhibit 11-4: Sample Client Letter—Sophisticated Client

Raabe, Whittenburg & Sanders, CPAs
San Francisco, CA
November 19, 20XX

M/M Dale Brown
2472 North Mayfair Road
Fillingham, SD 59990

Dear Dale and Rae,
Thanks again for requesting my advice concerning the tax treatment of your interest expenses. I am sorry to report that only a portion of your expenses can be deducted this year.

I have uncovered a series of court cases in which the IRS has prevailed over the taxpayer's requests for a deduction that is similar to yours. Unfortunately, the Tax Court's position is that interest such as yours is nondeductible, and additional litigation would be necessary to bring about a more favorable result for you.

My efforts have concentrated on the treatment of interest expenses that are incurred by taxpayers who hold exempt bonds while maintaining a bank loan that requires interest payments.

Over the past thirty years or so, a number of Circuit Court decisions have held that a taxpayer effectively must divest him- or herself of investments in such municipal bonds, regardless of portfolio diversification objectives, before a deduction for the interest payments to the bank is allowed. Fortunately, however, an exception exists relative to business-related loans, so that interest that is related to Rae's clinic will be allowed as a deduction. Conversely, that portion of the loan that relates to your school bond investment is nondeductible, even though it is secured by your residence.

You may wish to reconsider your use of the mortgage for this purpose, as your tax advantages therefrom are somewhat limited. This appears to be more palatable for you than would be the alternative of expensive further (and, probably, fruitless) litigation of the issue.

My conclusion is based upon the facts that you have provided me, and upon the efficacy of these somewhat dated court decisions. As you've requested, I've attached a copy of my research memo for you to read and from which you might develop subsequent inquiries.

I'm sorry that the news from me wasn't more favorable. I look forward to seeing you, though, at the firm's holiday reception!

Sincerely,
Mary H. Polzin
for Raabe, Whittenburg & Sanders, CPAs

In general, the client letter should be structured as follows, perhaps allowing one paragraph for each of the noted topics.

- Salutation/social graces/general conclusion

- Summary of the research project results

- Objective of the report

- Statement of facts and disclaimer as to the scope of the tax professional's knowledge base

- Summary of critical sources of law that lead to result

Exhibit 11-5: Sample Client Letter—Less Sophisticated Client

Raabe, Whittenburg & Sanders, CPAs
San Francisco, CA
November 19, 20XX

M/M Dale Brown
2472 North Mayfair Road
Fillingham, SD 59990

Dear Dale and Rae,

Thanks again for requesting my advice concerning the tax treatment of your interest expenses. I am sorry to report that only a portion of your expenses can be deducted this year.

My research has uncovered a series of successes by the IRS in convincing several important courts that interest such as yours should not be allowed as a deduction to reduce your taxes. Unfortunately, the court whose decision initially would prevail upon us would hold against you, and a series of court hearings, over two or three years or so, would be necessary for you to win the case.

This research has been restricted to situations that are similar to yours, that is, in which the taxpayer both owns a municipal bond and owes money to the bank from an interest-bearing loan.

It seems that the IRS would rather have you purchase the municipal bonds with your own money, rather than with the bank's. It maintains that you get a double benefit from the non-taxability of the school bond interest income and the deductibility of the interest expense that is paid to the bank. Thus, that portion of the interest that relates to the bond investment is not allowed. A business purpose for the loan salvages the deduction, however, so you can deduct the interest from the loan that relates to Dr. Rae's clinic.

You may just have to live with this situation, as the IRS has been winning cases like these for about thirty years. Yours is not likely to be the one that changes their mind, so you might reconsider your investment in the municipals in the near future.

My conclusion is based upon the facts that you have provided me, and upon the reliability of the court cases that I found.

I'm sorry that the news from me wasn't more favorable. I look forward to seeing you, though, at the firm's holiday reception!

Sincerely,
Mary H. Polzin
for Raabe, Whittenburg & Sanders, CPAs

- Implications of the results

- Assumptions/limitations

- Closing/reference to follow-up meeting/social graces

- Attachments, if any (e.g., engagement letter, file memo, illustrative charts, bibliography), on a separate page

Effective written business communication often makes use of the following guidelines. Notice that most of these elements are present in each of the two sample client letters that we have included in this chapter.

- Make your main point(s) in the first paragraph of the communication.

- State a well-defined purpose for the document, and stick to it.

- Avoid "filler" language, for example, "at the present time," "the fact that," "as you know," and "enclosed please find."

- Avoid cliches and trendy jargon, for example, "interface," "input," "seamless," "hands-on," "state-of-the-art," and any number of sports analogies.

- Follow the 10-80-10 rules of Exhibit 11-2.

- Don't be afraid to revise the letter several times to improve its format or to expand or narrow (as needed) its content. In this regard, allow enough time for the preparation of the document in a professional manner.

- Use the social amenities to your advantage by spelling names correctly, keeping current on the recipient's promotions and current title, and adding handwritten messages at the beginning or end of the document.

- *Practice writing* until it becomes easier and more enjoyable for you to do. Word processing programs, with the editing and proofreading capabilities that they provide, will aid you in this task.

COMPREHENSIVE ILLUSTRATION OF CLIENT FILE

Exhibit 11-6 provides a comprehensive illustration of the two major elements of a client file: a client letter and a file memo. Notice the degree of correspondence between the two documents, in that some portions of the client letter are no more than quotations or paraphrases of the file memo.

The remainder of the internal file for this hypothetical client would include, among many other possibilities:

- an engagement letter,

- a billing and collection history,

- case, regulation, and ruling briefs that are pertinent to the file memo, and

- links to important analyses of the client's prevailing tax issues from treatises, journal articles, and other resources.

Each consulting firm or tax department has its own formatting requirements with respect to client files. Because document and browser software is so easy to use, the temptation is for the tax researcher to reduce the thickness of the client file, as paper duplications of controlling law and other precedent are deemed unnecessary. This paper reduction movement constitutes a laudable goal. Yet one must not shortchange the importance of the client file as a roadmap by which to retrace the researcher's line of thinking that leads to the conclusions and recommendations evidenced in the file memo and client letter. Electronic equivalents of the mindmap of the researcher and of underlining or pastel highlighting of portions of lengthy legal documents must be developed.

Accordingly, every tax researcher must develop or work with a scheme by which to cross-reference the steps of the professional critical thinking model undertaken on the client's behalf. This might entail a listing of legal citations and computer files that would bear upon a reconstruction of the researcher's analysis,

Exhibit 11-6: Client File Illustration

CLIENT LETTER
Tax Jockeys Limited
Newport, RI
December 10, 20XX

Harold and Frieda van Briske
2000 Fox Point Heights
Whitefish Bay, RI 02899

Dear Harold and Frieda,

Congratulations on your recent marriage! I hope that you found your honeymoon at Club Med to be an enjoyable and memorable experience.

Thank you again for requesting my advice concerning the tax treatment of your prenuptial agreement. I understand that Frieda transferred some appreciated stock to Harold on the morning of the wedding, under the prenuptial agreement. I am happy to report that the transaction will not result in the imposition of any Federal tax for either of you.

My research has uncovered a series of successes by the IRS in convincing several important courts, including the Supreme Court, that an agreement such as yours is not supported by "full and adequate consideration," and, therefore, that it is to be treated as a gift. Although you did not intend for your property transfer to be a gift, the intent of the parties in such agreements does not control for Federal gift tax purposes.

Fortunately, however, the treatment of your transaction as a gift will result in the imposition of neither Federal income tax nor Federal gift tax upon you. Federal income tax is not imposed upon the transfer because gross income is not recognized by either the donor or donee when a gift is made. Although a gift has occurred, no gift tax is due, because the unlimited gift tax marital deduction neutralizes the transfer.

This research has been restricted to fact situations that are similar to yours, that is, in which, pursuant to a prenuptial agreement, a taxpayer surrendered his or her other marital rights in exchange for a sum of money or other property.

My conclusion is based upon the facts that you have given me and upon the reliability of the court cases that I found. I look forward to seeing you at the Christmas Charity Ball!

Sincerely,
Karen J. Boucher, CPA, JD, MST
for or Tax Jockeys Limited

FILE MEMO
December 10, 20XX
Tax Jockeys Limited
Newport, RI

Relevant Facts
On the morning of their wedding, Frieda gave to Harold $400,000 of appreciated stock, pursuant to a prenuptial agreement. Frieda's basis in the stock was $150,000. In exchange for these securities, Harold surrendered all other marital rights and claims to Frieda's assets, under the terms of the agreement. Harold and Frieda both are residents of Arizona.

Specific Issues
1. What are the gift tax consequences of this exchange?
2. What are the income tax consequences of this exchange?

Conclusions
1. Frieda incurs no gift tax liability as the agreement is executed and implemented.
2. Asset basis carries over to Harold, the new owner of the securities. Neither Frieda nor Harold recognizes gross income as a result of the exchange.

Support
Issue One
Donative intent on the part of the donor is not an essential element in the application of the gift tax. *Reg. § 25.2511-1(g)(1).*

The Supreme Court has held that prenuptial transfers in relinquishment of marital rights are not adequate and full consideration in money or money's worth for the transfer of property, within the meaning of IRC § 2512(b). *Merrill v. Fahs, 324 U.S. 308, 65 S.Ct. 655 (1945); Comm. v. Wemyss, 324 U.S. 303, 65 S.Ct. 652 (1945); Reg. § 25.2512-8.* However, the Second Circuit has held that a prenuptial agreement was acquired for valuable consideration and did not constitute a gift, for income tax (basis computation) purposes. *Farid-Es-Sultaneh v. Comm., 160 F.2d 812 (CA-2, 1947).* This decision is not critical to the present analysis, though, because the van Briskes do not live in the Second Circuit, and because the somewhat dated decision may be aberrational.

Although the van Briske transaction resulted in a gift, no gift tax is imposed due to the application of the annual exclusion and the unlimited gift tax marital deduction. IRC §§ 2503(b) and 2523; Reg. § 25.2511-2(a); Rev. Rul. 69-347, 1969-2 C.B. 227.

IRC § 2501 imposes a tax on the transfer of property by gift; the gift tax is not imposed, though, upon the receipt of property by the donee. Rather, it is the transfer itself that triggers the tax. Since the prenuptial agreement here is enforceable by state law only when consummated by marriage, the transfer has not taken place until after the marriage occurred. Thus, the transfer appears to be eligible for the gift tax marital deduction, regardless of the timing of the transfer relative to the marriage ceremony on the wedding day. Even if the securities had been physically transferred to Harold prior to the completion of the ceremonies, the agreement was only enforceable after the couple was married. The IRS likely would not need or attempt to establish the exact moments of both (1) the transfer of the securities, and (2) the consummation of the marriage. *C.I.R. v. Bristol, 121 F.2d 129 (CA-1, 1960); Bradford, 34 T.C. 1059 (1960, Acq.); Archbold, 42 B.T.A. 453 (1940, Acq. in result only); Harris v. Comm., 178 F.2d 861 (CA-2, 1949).*

Issue Two
Neither Harold nor Frieda recognize any gross income upon Harold's release of his marital rights. Gross income does not include the value of property that is acquired by gift. IRC §102(a); Reg. §1.102-1(a); Rev. Rul. 79-312, 1979-2 C.B. 29; Rev. Rul. 67-221, 1967-2 C.B. 63; *Howard v. C.I. R., 447 F.2d 152 (CA-5, 1971)* .

The transfer of securities is not deductible in any way by Frieda, but under the Farid decision, Harold's basis may be stepped up to fair market value. Recall our earlier comments, though, concerning the reliability of this precedent. *Illinois National Bank v. U.S., 273 F.2d 231 (CA-7, 1959),* cert. den. 363 U.S. 803, 80 S.Ct. 1237 (1960); *C.I.R. v. Marshman, 279 F.2d 27,* cert. den. 364 U.S. 918, 81 S.Ct. 282 (1960); Rev. Rul. 79-312. In the typical gift situation, the donee takes the donor's income tax basis in the transferred property. *IRC §§ 1015(a) and 1041(a)(1).*

Actions to Be Taken
Prepare letter, review results with client.
Place copy of prenuptial agreement in the client file.
Alert the New York and New Jersey offices that their conclusions may differ, under the Farid decision.

Preparer: *Karen J. Boucher*
Reviewer: *Lynne E. Schoenfeldt*

perhaps in the form of a decision tree or project management summary. Various software applications will be useful in this regard, not the least of which is the "research trail" feature of many electronic tax research products, which records the detailed sequencing of commands and decisions made during the online project. Regardless of the form this project diary takes, its importance for professional quality control cannot be overstated.

ORAL PRESENTATIONS OF RESEARCH RESULTS

Psychologists tell us that most people's greatest fear is speaking before groups of other people. Indeed, the thought of being the only one in the room who is standing, of having your listeners whispering their evaluations of you to each other, of having members of the audience taking notes on (or tape recording) your comments (certainly so that your errors of omission and commission can be parroted back at a later date), and of fielding extemporaneous questions is enough to bring many people to tears.

Yet public speaking is an important part of the tax practitioner's professional life. In many ways, it is the most accurate predictor of success. As politicians have long known, when one is delivering an oral presentation in an effective and professional manner, the audience becomes convinced that all of the other professional qualities that they desire from the speaker are also present. Conversely, an ill-prepared or ill-delivered message can do much to erode the audience's confidence in the speaker, not just with respect to the topic of the presentation, but in general.

Thus, it behooves the tax professional to develop skill in public speaking. In contexts that range from the presentation of an award to a colleague or the conduct of a staff meeting to the presentation of a keynote address at the annual tax conference of your peers, such skills can mean the difference between enhancing and damaging your reputation.

SPOTLIGHT ON TAXATION

Observation

Jerry Seinfeld noted that peoples' fear of public speaking is greater even than the fear of death. Under this ranking, he thought, someone attending a funeral would rather be in the casket than delivering the eulogy!

What is advised here is not a series of "tricks" to fool the audience into believing that you are more knowledgeable than you really are. Rather, we now convey some time-tested techniques leading to an effective communication of ideas—from one who has developed a secure base of knowledge in a subject to an audience with a specified background that has a desire to learn more about that subject. Whether making a presentation of one's results to a supervisor in one's own firm or elaborating on a research project with the client's board of directors, the communication of tax research results poses special problems that make a review of oral communications procedures all the more valuable. Specifically, we can make the following suggestions concerning **oral presentations** of tax research.

- General preparation for the talk should include a thorough, frank examination of the following set of questions by the presenter. Nearly all of these observations can be characterized as knowledge of the makeup of the audience.

    Why me? Why was I asked to speak? What knowledge or celebrity do I bring to the event?

    What do they want? What does the audience hope to take away from the presentation? Technical knowledge? Relief from stress? Inspiration? Skill development? Amusement or entertainment? Should I present an overview or a detailed technical update or analysis?

    What is their attitude? Is the audience coming to the event curious or anxious to hear from me, or must they be persuaded of the relevance or importance of my topics?

    From what should I stay away? Are there topics that are taboo for this audience, due to their age, experiences, or existing attitudes? One must not alienate the audience, wittingly or unwittingly, in any way if the message is to get across.

    What do they already know? What is the knowledge base of the audience? It would be ideal to speak to a homogeneous audience, especially in the level of knowledge that it brings into the event, but this seldom is the case. One must decide, then, whether to aim at the median knowledge base, above, or below. The stakes are high in exercising this judgment, though, and either repeating what is common knowledge to the group, or presenting information at a high level that is accessible to only a few in the audience, can make communication impossible.

    Who is the audience? Details as to the audience's demographic characteristics such as age, education and income level, political leanings, and so forth can be vital for tailoring one's style, presentation speed and media, references to literature and popular culture, and use of humor in an effective manner. Remember to play to as many members of the audience as possible, not just the majority of those in attendance or those who were involved directly in hiring or retaining your services.

- Be prepared in the technical aspects of your discussion, particularly the basic research. Spend most of your preparation time on your main points and conclusions rather than on the fine points. If you are caught without a piece of technical information, it is clearly better for you if that information is specific (so that you can refer the questioner to a more detailed reference or to a later, private conversation with you), rather than basic in nature.

- Resist the temptation to tell the audience all that you know about the subject. You almost certainly have neither the time nor the organizational abilities that are necessary to command the attention of the audience for that long a time. Direct your remarks to the highlights and general results of the research, and allow a questions-and-comments period in which more detailed subjects can be addressed. In this manner, you will provide the greatest amount of information to the greatest number of listeners in the audience.

- Use visual aids effectively. Handouts, slides, or videos can serve to clarify or emphasize your key points (and, not incidentally, to transfer the "spotlight" of the presentation away from you). Most advisers recommend that you not look at the screen repeatedly, or read the text of the visual aid word for word along with the audience, but, rather, that you use the visual aid as a means of keeping the audience focused on the discussion points by the use of a pointer or other highlighter. Avoid a sequence that allows a "blank screen" for more than a second or two. Inexpensive computer software will assist you in preparing and delivering electronic presentations, and in staying on schedule. Use your ink-jet or color laser printer to prepare your visual aids.

- If you are a frequent public speaker, purchase a moderately priced, easy-to-carry projector, so that you need not depend on conference center staff to present your slides.

Many speakers are tempted to overuse visual aids, especially because they are so easy to create, even at professional-quality levels, given today's software packages. Visual aids, though, generally should be used only for the following purposes.

- To illustrate things that are difficult to convey strictly with words by using a photograph, videotape, map, blueprint, or flowchart.

- To save time by consolidating ideas, committing to a time frame or strategy, or listing conflicting viewpoints or tactics.

- To create interest in a subject, perhaps by presenting the concept in a manner with which the audience is unfamiliar (e.g., an extra-large view, a view from "the other side of the issue," or an evolutionary time or growth line).

- To emphasize a point or concept by highlighting a graphic, picture, mnemonic, or list of key words or concepts.

- To organize the introduction, body, or conclusion of the presentation.

- To introduce humor to the event with a tasteful quotation or cartoon.

- To place ideas in the audience's memories, through a visual "take away" item.

A speaker's prepared slides should be designed with care and diligence. When using this technology, as opposed to the hand-drawn flip chart or on-the-fly smartboard drawing, one essentially is competing with professional graphic and television artists, and the audience will hold your efforts to these high standards. Most visual and graphic artists offer guidelines for presentation layouts, including the following.

- Use the slide to emphasize pictures, not text or numbers. Except to be able to point to a specific position on the page and keep the members of the audience in the same spot throughout the presentation, do not use your slideshow to duplicate pages of text or spreadsheets with voluminous numbers. Employ graphs, charts, arrows, and other pictorial devices instead.

- When text is involved, use the "six and six" rule: No more than six lines of type, and no more than six words on a line. This directive will help to dictate the font chosen and the corresponding size of print.

- Keep the font style simple. Use sans serif or newspaper-type fonts, not script or modern fonts, unless corporate logos or other protected styles are used. Most designers recommend that no more than two colors of text be used on a slide and that the color scheme of the graphics blend well with that of the text. Be conservative—stick to the primary colors, colors of local sports teams, and multiple shades of gray, so as not to frustrate the duplication process for related handout materials.

- Similarly, try to use some background music if your available technology will support it at a professional-quality level. In this regard, select audio clips that do not draw attention to themselves, but are memorable in a more subtle way. Music can signal the start or end of a presentation or its subunits, a change in direction, or a specific idea (e.g., a Frank Sinatra clip sends a different message than does one by Jimi Hendrix or a smooth jazz group).

- On the average, allow at least three minutes of spoken presentation for each slide. Accordingly, limit the number of your slides to the length of your talk in minutes, divided by three. In this way, you will not overproduce your number of slides. If you want to provide your audience with a content outline, use some other medium, not the slides.

- Prepare for the worst: E-mail yourself an extra copy of the slides in case of emergency, and carry your files to the site on a flash drive *and* on your portable music player. Bring a few sets of hard copy slides, as well.

Without exception, determine ahead of the presentation how long your talk is supposed to be and be absolutely certain not to exceed it. You need to be fair to the other speakers, if any, who follow your presentation. Moreover, with very few exceptions, the audience also is aware of the schedule for the session, and if the speaker exceeds the allotted time, the audience, at best, will stop paying attention and, at worst, will become restless or angry. Because of their technical nature, most tax presentations should not exceed forty-five minutes, and one-half of that time might be ideal for both speaker and audience.

Have an outline for your discussion that includes miniature versions of slides and your business address, phone and fax numbers, and your e-mail and Internet addresses. Use the visual aids to convince the audience that you are following the outline. This will (1) ensure that you will cover the material that you desire, (2) build confidence among the audience as to your speaking abilities, and (3) convince yourself that you are doing a good job in leading the discussion of the assigned topic.

Rehearse your presentation, word for word, at least once. The most effective means of preparing yourself in this manner probably is with a video recorder, because your distracting mannerisms (e.g., clearing the throat repeatedly, saying the words "ah" or "you know" too often, or pounding on the lectern) quickly will become apparent. Lacking such a device, use an audio recorder or webcam. Family members or colleagues should not be used for this rehearsal.

Be kind to yourself in evaluating your video performance, but be observant for the following "I didn't know I did that" items.

- In all but the very largest presentation venues, get as physically close to the audience as you can, ideally removing the lectern, stepping down from the stage or platform, and moving to a series of different spots in the room throughout your speaking time. Use a portable mouse device to control your slideshow, but practice using the device an hour before your presentation begins.

- Eliminate nervous and visual distractions, such as jingling coins, playing with pen and marker tops, and adjusting clothing. Minimize the use of crossing your arms, pounding the table, and finger-pointing, reserving them as means of emphasizing key points or declaring victory over competing viewpoints.

- Vary the pitch of your voice, avoiding both a dry monotone and a "classic actor" dramatic approach. Many speakers talk too fast or too loud; check yourself throughout the talk on these matters. Test the microphone system before the audience arrives, so that you don't need to ask, "Can you hear me in the back?"

- Don't be afraid of silence. Pauses invariably seem longer to the speaker than they do to the audience, so don't let natural breaks in the talk add to your anxiety. In fact, well-paced pauses can relieve tension (both yours and the audience's), signal changes of pace, and allow you to emphasize the importance of certain ideas.

- Don't read directly from your outline, except for a selected quote of three lines or so from the material once or twice in the presentation. Try not to have a separate set of note cards, because the tendency again is to break your contact with the audience and hide behind the scripting device. Disguise your notes in the form of comments on hard copies of your slides and flip charts and notes in the margin of your copy of the outline. Keep your eyes up and on the audience.

Avoid references to administrative or "housekeeping" aspects of the event—leave these to be conveyed by the host of the event. Be enthusiastic and positive about your comments—don't apologize for a lack of discussion on a tangential point, a logistical snafu, or a misstatement of fact or law. The audience generally wants you to succeed, so don't undermine this trust with self-destructive comments. Don't refer to the schedule for the event or other timing issues, because they can distract the audience or otherwise detract from conveying your message (e.g., "Only ten minutes to go," "We may be out of here early," "The previous speakers ran over into my time slot," or "I'll try to get through this quickly, so we can finish on time").

Rehearse the logistical aspects of the presentation, such as the lighting, projectors, or computer presentation software and terminals, before you begin to speak, ideally both the night before and one hour before your presentation. Have adequate numbers and varieties of markers, pointers, flip chart pads, and remote control devices. You don't want to encounter any surprises after it is too late to do anything about them! On your script, note cards, or slide masters, make notes to yourself as to when, for instance, to pass out the handout material, turn on or turn off the projector, or refer to a flip chart.

Avoid clichés, such as opening with a joke, or saying, "It's a pleasure to be here." Don't take the risk of boring or offending the audience with a joke that (1) they may have heard already or (2) you may not tell effectively under pressure. This is not to suggest that you avoid humor altogether, however. Audiences, and speakers' reputations, thrive on it. If you are sure of your skill in this area, you might venture a joke, but it would probably be wiser to open with a "punch line" summary of some of the most interesting of your results or fact situations.

Have a "Plan B" ready to go—flexibility is the watchword of the effective speaker. If the time actually allowed for your talk is shorter than you had thought, due to a misunderstanding or unanticipated events, have a list of topics, videos, or slides that can be eliminated without changing the nature of the talk. Practice your question-and-answer-session skills, especially for occasions where there is more time available than you had anticipated. Do not mention any of these on-the-fly adjustments to the audience—make the changes, don't talk about them.

Observe audience body language, and use signals conveying interest, enthusiasm, boredom, or restlessness to your advantage. Make consistent eye contact with the audience, smile when appropriate, and take a few seconds at the completion of the presentation to accept the audience's show of thanks and savor your job well done.

SUMMARY

The tax professional must become proficient in communicating his or her research results. Recipients of these communications might include oneself or one's peers, via the file memorandum; the client, via a brief letter; or a number of other listeners, via an oral presentation. In each case, the practitioner must be sensitive to the needs, backgrounds, and interests of the recipients of the messages, without sacrificing professional demeanor or responsibilities.

TAX TUTOR

Reinforce the tax research information covered in this chapter by completing the online tutorials located at the *Federal Tax Research* web site: **http://academic. cengage.com/taxation/raabe**

KEY WORDS

By the time you complete this chapter, you should be comfortable discussing each of the following terms. If you need additional review of any of these items, return to the appropriate material in the chapter or consult the glossary to this text.

client letter   oral presentations
file memorandum

TAX RESEARCH ASSIGNMENTS

As we have discussed them in this chapter, develop solutions and appropriate documentation for one or more of the problems that you have worked on in previous chapters or for the following fact situations. In this context, proper format and professional content are of equal importance, so that the development of the reader's tax research communication skills will be facilitated.

Specifically, as assigned by your instructor, prepare one or more of the following means of communicating your research results for your chosen problem or case. Be sure to apply the "10-80-10" rule of Exhibit 11-2.

- File memorandum
- Letter to tax-sophisticated client
- Letter to unsophisticated client
- Outline for a tax department meeting
- Article for local business news weekly
- Speech to local chamber of commerce
- Article for *Practical Tax Strategies*
- Speech to State Bar Association conference
- Presentation to client's board of directors
- Presentation to client's senior counsel

- Posting to the Internet Tax Blog for Practitioners
- Posting to the Internet Tax Help group for taxpayers

PROBLEMS

1. Sarah came home one day to find significant water damage in her home. Apparently one of the hoses to her washing machine had worn out and split, spilling water all over the place. Over the next month, mildew appeared as well. Is there any casualty loss deduction for Sarah? Ignore any computational floors and assume that she did not have any homeowners' insurance.

2. Richie is a wealthy rancher in Texas. He operates his ranch through a grantor trust set up by his grandparents. Richie does not like to get his hands dirty, so he hires a professional management company to run the ranch. The property generated a $500,000 loss this year. Can Richie deduct this loss on his Schedule E, given the material participation rules of § 469?

3. Maggie could not conceive a child using natural means, so she sought out a woman who would donate an egg to be surgically implanted in Maggie, so that Maggie could become a mother. Which of the following items are deductible by Maggie in her process to find an egg donor?
   a. Payment to a search firm to find donor candidates.
   b. Payment to Maggie's attorney.
   c. Payment of a fee to the egg donor.
   d. Payment to medical staff to run physiological and psychological tests on the prospective donor.

4. Larry and Mo were in the process of being divorced, and the decree as negotiated allowed alimony payments to Mo of $3,000 on the fifteenth of each month. The divorce was final on July 5, 2009, but Mo was short of cash, so Larry made the payments to her starting already in March. What is Larry's alimony deduction for 2009?

5. Sally incurred a ninety-mile round-trip commute every day, mainly because she could not get along with her supervisor at the sales office four miles from Sally's home. Sally works under a one-year contract, and her assignment to the nearer office is affirmed in the current year's contract, but management has allowed her to travel to the further location. How many deductible commuting miles does Sally accumulate on a work day?

6. Professor White operates a popular bar review course as a sole proprietor. He charges $2,000 tuition to each student, and he guarantees a full refund of the tuition if the student passes an in-course exam but does not pass the actual bar exam on the first try. White is bold enough to do this because the first-time-pass rate is more than 80 percent for the bar exam (as opposed to less than 15 percent for the certified public accountants [CPA] exam). He collected $150,000 tuition for his Fall 2008 review section, but he reported the gross receipts on his 2009 Form 1040, because the grades for those taking the fall review are not released until February 2009. Thus, White asserted that he had no constructive receipt of the tuition until February 2009. Is this treatment correct?

7. Lisa, usually a stay-at-home mother, went to the hospital one day for some outpatient surgery. She hired a babysitter for $35 to watch her four-year-old son while she was gone. What tax benefits are available to Lisa for this cash payment?

8. Same as 7, except that Lisa paid the sitter while she worked as a scout leader for the Girl Scouts.

9. Joan, a traveling sales representative, kept no formal books and records to summarize her gross receipts for the year, but she retained copies of all customer invoices and reported her gross income for the year from these totals. Is she liable for a negligence penalty under § 6662 for failing to keep any books and records?

10. Tex's credit union has provided him with financing to acquire his $200,000 home. The loan is set up as a three-year note with a balloon payment, but the credit union always renews the loan for another three years at the current interest rate. This year, the credit union renewed Tex's loan for the third time, charging $3,000 in points. In what year(s) can Tex deduct this $3,000?

11. Barb and Bob were one-fourth shareholders of a C corporation. When the entity had negative E&P, Barb and Bob secretly withdrew $200,000 in cash, hiding this fact from the other owners. How much gross income do Barb and Bob report?

12. Detail the tax effects to the Prasads of making the § 1(q)(7)(a)(iv) election to include their seven-year-old daughter's $10,000 unearned income on their current-year joint return.

13. Eighty percent of the Willigs' AGI comes from their submarine sandwich proprietorship. In 2009, the Willigs lost an IRS audit and owed $12,000 in 2007 Federal income taxes, all attributable to inventory computations in their business. Interest on this amount totaled $3,200. All amounts due were paid by the end of 2009. How much of the interest can the Willigs deduct on their 2009 Schedule C?

14. Al and Amy are divorced. In which of the following cases can legal fees be deducted?
    a. Al pays $5,000 to get the court to reduce his alimony obligation.
    b. Amy pays $5,000 to get the court to increase her alimony receipts.
    c. Al pays Amy's attorney fees in part b, as required by the original divorce decree.

15. Katie is a one-third owner of an S corporation. After a falling-out with the other shareholders, Katie signed an agreement early in January 2008. Under the terms of the agreement, Katie took $200,000 of her capital from the corporation and had eight months to negotiate a purchase of the stock of the other shareholders. She did not complete this task by the end of August 2008. Thus, contrary negotiations began and on March 1, 2009, Katie sold all of her shares to the remaining shareholders for a $2.5 million gain. For how many of these months does Katie report flow-through income from the S corporation?

16. Can an individual make a contribution to an IRA based on unemployment compensation proceeds received?

17. Duane paid his 2004 Federal income taxes in January 2007 in the amount of $10,000, and then paid $4,000 interest and penalties on this amount in May 2008. In April 2010, Duane filed a claim for refund of the $14,000, due to a sizable operating loss from his business in tax year 2009. Can he recover the 2004-related amounts?

18. After an audit was completed, IRS agent van Court informed Harris of the latter's $10,000 Federal income tax deficiency by leaving a summary memo on Harris's e-mail account. Harris shared this account with his mother, who read the mail first and in a panic confronted Harris with a two-hour "What's this all about?" interrogation. Did van Court violate Harris's right to privacy by using e-mail in this manner?

19. SlimeCo spent $250,000 to build storage tanks for its waste by-products. This is a recurring expenditure for SlimeCo, because once the tanks are filled, new ones must be built. When can SlimeCo deduct the $250,000?

20. Prudence was named a shareholder in her law firm, which operates as an S corporation. Her payments into the capital of the firm were to start in about nine months, when an audit would determine the full value of the firm and a new corporate year would commence. Paperwork with the pertinent state offices was completed, naming Prudence as a shareholder and director, and adding her name to that of the firm. But Prudence left the firm eight months after the announcement, that is, before she paid any money for shares. Is Prudence liable for tax on her share of the entity's earnings for the eight months?

21. Laura deducted $8,100 in state income taxes on her 2008 Federal income tax return. Her refund, received in 2009 after all credits and the minimum tax, was $7,800 for these taxes.
    a. How much 2009 gross income must Laura recognize?
    b. How does your answer change if Laura's 2008 deduction was limited to $7,200, due to the application of IRC § 68?

22. Cal's son has been labeled a "can't miss" NBA prospect since junior high school. This year, while the son is a college freshman and classified as an amateur under NCAA rules, Cal spent $14,000 for special clothing, equipment, camps, and personal trainers to keep improving his son's skills. Can Cal deduct these items?

23. CPA Myrna forgot to tell her client Freddie to accelerate the payment of state income and property taxes in a year when Freddie was in an unusually high tax bracket. Upon discovering the error, the parties negotiated a $15,000 payment from Myrna (and her insurance company) to Freddie to compensate Freddie for Myrna's inadequate professional advice. Is this payment gross income to Freddie?

24. How much of the $100,000 interest that is paid on a loan from Everett National Bank can Ben deduct if he invests the loan proceeds in the following? Consider each item independently.
    a. South Chicago School District bonds.
    b. AT&T bonds, paying $125,000 interest income this year.

    c. Computer Futures, Inc., shares, a growth stock that pays no dividend this year.

    d. A life insurance policy on Betty, Ben's wife.

25. Lilly leases a car that she uses solely for business purposes. The car would be worth $40,050 on the market, and Lilly paid $7,400 in lease payments this year. How are these items treated on her tax return?

RESEARCH CASES

26. Lizzie filed a gift tax return for a sizable transfer to her nephew. The value of the gift exceeded the annual gift tax exclusion and used up $1 million of her transfer tax exemption equivalent, so Lizzie's later gifts and taxable estate would have a more likely chance of being taxed.

    Four years later, another relative won a court case against Lizzie and the nephew. Uncle Joe prevailed in showing the court that the gift property was his, not Lizzie's. It seems that title to the property actually was held by Uncle Joe, not Lizzie, so the property was not hers to give away. Uncle Joe recovered the property and associated income from the nephew. But what about Lizzie? Is the $1 million of her exemption equivalent now wasted?

27. You served as an expert witness in taxation in a recent Tax Court case, charging $400 per hour for your services. The LLC client who employed you prevailed in the decision against the government, so now the client is filing to recover your fees from the Treasury under § 7430(c)(1)(B)(iii). How much can the client collect?

28. Pete is an engineering professor at State University. Under his contract, Pete's inventions while employed at the university are the property of the Board of Regents, but Pete receives an addition to his salary equal to one-third of the royalties received by the university on his patents. This year, Pete received $75,000 on top of his salary, as royalties allocated to him. Does Pete recognize this amount as ordinary income or capital gain?

29. Tobey was late in filing his Federal income tax refund claim, but he requested an extension of the statute of limitations, citing the financial disability exceptions of § 6511(h). Tobey's mother is chronically ill, and he must make four-day-a-week trips to another city to care for her. Will the IRS grant Tobey's request?

30. Dean and Robin owned a family business, each holding the shares as community property. When they were divorced in 2005, the court did not force them to split the shares, citing damage to the business that could occur if the public learned that ownership of the enterprise was changing. Now it is 2009 and Robin wants to remarry. She and her new husband want to have the business re-title one-half of the shares in Robin's name only. The original divorce court agrees in 2009. Is this an income taxable transfer? Is it a gift taxable event?

31. Dave took a $100,000 cash withdrawal from his IRA. He bought $100,000 of Microcraft stock and, within the rollover period, transferred the stock to another IRA. Does Dave report any gross income?

32. Gold Partners wanted to complete a like-kind exchange just before it liquidated. Accordingly, it sold the real estate it meant to transfer to the other party, and a qualified intermediary held the resulting cash. When the intermediary found acceptable replacement realty, the intermediary transferred cash and the like-kind property directly to the partners, thereby liquidating Gold. Does § 1031 apply?

33. HelpCo pays Hank two $100,000 salaries per year, one through its WestCo subsidiary and one through its EastCo subsidiary. How do Hank and HelpCo treat his Social Security tax obligations?

34. Zhang lived in Atlanta from 2005 through 2007 to carry out her duties as an employee of YourTV.com, receiving an annual salary of about $150,000. She was transferred to the San Jose office for 2008 through 2010, and then in 2011 she took an executive position with the Web2.2 LLC in Austin. Zhang owned a home in Atlanta, but she rented an apartment in San Jose. When she withdraws money from her IRA to submit a down payment on her Austin condo, is a 10 percent penalty due?

35. Give three examples of situations where the IRS would waive the two-year rule for applying the §121 exclusion of gain from the sale of a principal residence, due to "unforeseen circumstances."

36. LaFollette lives in a condo with Tourneau. The two are not married, but they each hold a one-half interest in the deed for their unit. In 2008, the condo association installed a solar water heater. The association paid for the water heating system, but it assessed LaFollette and Tourneau $7,500 for this expenditure, as it did for other unit owners. Tourneau was short of funds, so LaFollette paid the entire assessment before the end of 2008. Compute LaFollette's §25D credit against her Form 1040 liability for the year.

37. On December 6, Ed Grimely appeared on the game show, "The Wheel of Fate." As a result of his appearance, Grimely won the following prizes.

	Manufacturer's Suggested List Price	Fair Market Value	Actual Cost to the Show
All-expenses-paid trip to Hawaii	$8,432	$6,000	$5,200
One case of Twinkies	16	12	0
Seven music lessons for the calliope	105	35	0
One year of free haircuts	120	60	15

a. Assuming that Grimely received all of these prizes by the end of the year, compute his gross income from these prizes.
b. Will this amount change if Grimely refuses to accept the calliope lessons immediately after the program's taping session is completed?

38. Sing-Yi receives a $100 debit card every month from her employer, the Porter Group. The debit card is limited so that it only can be used to purchase fare cards and passes on the Metro Transit line that operates trains and subways in town. Sing-Yi throws away the card when it expires at the end of the month, and she is not required to provide any records to Porter about how the card

was used. The card logo says "American Airlines Visa," and Sing-Yi picks her own password for the card. Does the card represent $100 monthly gross income to Sing-Yi? Explain.

39. Ellie owned five apartment buildings, each worth $200,000. For three of the buildings, she worked with employees to keep the property in good repair. This entailed maintaining electrical and plumbing fixtures, common areas, and walls and roofs, and providing janitorial services such as garbage removal, vacuuming, and rest room supplies. For the other two buildings, Ellie's lease required the tenants to perform this work. Can her estate claim a § 6166 estate tax deferral for any of the buildings?

40. HardCo spent $4 million this year on a new graphic design for its product, a yo-yo. Under the prior design, HardCo's name and logo only appeared on the box and wrapping paper, which were discarded by most customers once they started using the product. The new design displayed HardCo's name and newer, flashier logo on both sides of the yo-yo, with a paint that also made it glow in the dark. When can HardCo deduct the $4 million?

ADVANCED CASES

These items require that you have access to research materials other than the Federal tax law and related services. For instance, you might need to refer to an international tax or multistate service or to access Internet sources to prepare your solution for these cases. Consult with your instructor before beginning your work, so that you are certain to have available to you all of the necessary research resources for the case(s) that you choose.

41. Tony received some nonqualified and incentive stock options when he worked for his employer in Oregon. But when he took a two-year assignment in another country, the corporation employing Tony there granted him some options, too. Does Tony have gross income in the other country upon receiving or exercising the non-U.S. options? Assume that Tony was assigned to a corporation based in:

    a. Belgium

    b. Germany

    c. Hong Kong

    d. Russia

    e. The Netherlands

42. Chico is a corporation operating in several states on the accrual basis. Chico received a state income tax refund this year, in 2010, in the form of a check from the state. Based on the following sequence of events, in which tax year does Chico recognize the refund as gross income?

    2007: Generated the operating loss.

    2008: Filed the loss carryback form with the state.

    2009: Received notice that the refund was approved.

    2010: Received the refund check.

43. Rosemary's house just did not sell, after her employer transferred her to another town. After two years of Internet listings, open houses, repairs and improvements, and price cuts, a buyer finally came along. By this time, the house had sat empty for twenty-five months before the closing occurred, and Rosemary rented it out just to help with the mortgage payments. Rosemary claimed a $40,000 Schedule C loss with respect to the house. Do you agree with this filing position?

44. Edna is a well-paid executive with ADley, a firm that uses stock options and deferred compensation as well as high salaries, to compensate its most successful employees. When Edna and Ron were divorced, Ron got the rights to a bundle of these deferred compensation rights. Complete the following table, indicating the required tax results.

Tax Year	Market Price for Edna's Option Transferred to Ron	Event	Tax Consequences to Edna	Tax Consequences to Ron
2004	$ 9	Divorce settlement		
2007	$14	Ron exercises options with $10 cash payment, then holds stock received.		
2010	$20	Edna terminates employment with ADley; $100 lump sum of deferred compensation is distributed to Ron.		
2012	$22	Ron sells shares received via option contracts.		

45. Wes and Donna were the only members of an LLC, and they fended off unwanted takeover suitors with a clause in the charter that shares could change hands only with unanimous approval from all of the other owners. Wes is now age seventy, so he wants to start phasing out of the business. He makes a gift of 10 percent of the LLC shares to his son Jeffrey as agreed to by Donna. The shares are worth $20,000. What is Wes's taxable gift in the year of the transfer to Jeffrey?

46. According to the Tax Foundation, what was the country's Tax Freedom Day in 2007? How much of this time was spent with respect to tax liabilities and how much in meeting tax compliance costs? Which states bear the heaviest tax burden? The lightest? Per capita, how much annual total income and total tax does the U.S. citizen generate? What is the average U.S. citizen's average tax rate?

47. Chan's only transaction in the United States this year was to sell the biggest office building in Denver at a $100 million gain. Chan has no assets, offices, or

employees in the United States. Can he be taxed on the gain? Why or why not?

48. As the result of a Federal audit, your 2009 Federal taxable income increased by $27,000. By when must you report this adjustment to your state's revenue department? What form is used for this purpose, where do you obtain it, and where is it to be filed?

49. Does your state provide a form with which to file for a manufacturer's exemption from sales/use tax? Which form is used for this purpose, where do you obtain it, and where is it to be filed?

50. For the current period, what is the short-term, quarterly compounded Federal AFR? Mid-term? Long-term exempt interest rate for computing loss carryforwards under § 382?

51. SalesCo sold Tom a prepaid phone card for $100 in 2008. Tom used the phone card for communications services in 2009. When can your state collect sales/use tax from SalesCo for the sale to Tom?

52. GoodCo donated $40,000 of goods from its inventory to the Red Cross. Does your state require GoodCo to collect or pay sales/use tax on these donated goods?

53. The Downtown Wellness Clinic, a tax-exempt organization, sells memberships to corporations so that their employees can work out before and after office hours. Three blocks away, the Power Up Fitness Center has similar facilities and also wants to sell memberships to corporate neighbors. Is the Clinic subject to Federal income tax on its membership sales?

54. Does America Online owe any corporate income tax to your state? Don't compute the tax, but determine whether AOL is subject to any obligation for the current year. Hint: apply the concept of *nexus*.

55. How much state and local income tax did New York Yankee Alex Rodriguez owe to your state last year?

56. Find two government documents that discuss potential solutions to the so-called marriage penalty characteristic of the Federal income tax.

CHAPTER 12

Tax Planning

Learning Objectives

- Identify several fundamental tenets of tax planning for optimizing tax liabilities.

- Gain perspective as to the role of tax planning in tax practice.

- Define and apply several key terms with respect to tax rate schedules.

- Illustrate effective tax planning as found in today's tax profession.

I N THIS CHAPTER, WE return to that element of the tax practice consisting of tax planning, as it was introduced in Chapter 1. A working knowledge of tax planning concepts is imperative for the researcher, because tax avoidance constitutes both (1) an important part of tax practice and (2) a prime motivation in the "open-fact" research context.

For most practitioners, tax research and planning represent the "glamor" end of the business. Properly accomplished tax planning:

- Forces the client to identify financial goals and general means by which to achieve them.

- Allows the tax professional to exercise a higher degree of creativity than in any other part of the practice.

- Affords the practitioner the greatest possible degree of control over the prescribed transactions and the tax consequences.

The tax planning process finds the tax professional in the roles of technical expert, friend, seer, and confessor priest for the client. It offers an opportunity for the most psychologically and financially rewarding work possible, in the context of a tax practice.

ECONOMICS OF TAX PLANNING, AVOIDANCE, AND EVASION

From both the Treasury and the taxpayer viewpoint, taxes can modify individual decisions. Taxes represent an additional cost of doing business or of accumulating wealth. Assuming that economists are correct in speaking about the ways in which a rational citizen makes day-to-day decisions, taxpayers employ tax planning techniques to accomplish the overall goal of wealth maximization.[1] Because taxes deplete the wealth of the taxpayer, planning behavior is designed to reduce the net present value of the tax liability. This is not the same as a simple reduction of taxes in current, nominal dollar terms, an objective that is so often assumed by laypeople, the media, and others, including too many tax advisors.

> **Example 12-1** Sharon can choose between two business plans. One will cost her enterprise $1,000 in taxes today. The other will cost the business $2,000 in taxes ten years from now. The plans are identical in all other ways. Prevailing interest rates average 10 percent. Because the present value of the taxes levied with respect to the second alternative are about $800, Sharon should choose the latter plan, that is, the one with the higher nominal dollar tax cost.
>
> If prevailing interest rates average 5 percent during the ten-year planning period, the present value of the taxes levied under the second alternative would be about $1,225, so the first plan, the one that requires an immediate tax payment, should be adopted.

In one important sense, the Federal income tax is its own worst enemy. Taxpayers are rewarded more for finding ways to save taxes than for earning an equal amount in the marketplace. This incentive for tax planning is the result of two rules of tax law.

---

[1]We use "wealth" in its broadest sense here; that is, an individual may choose increased leisure time or other forms of so-called psychic income over traditional forms of wealth. Wealth, the accumulation of which constitutes the overall goal for the specified time period, thus can include measures of happiness, satisfaction, investment, and control over time and other resources.

The first such rule is that the Federal income tax itself is not allowed as a deduction in determining taxable income. Consequently, reducing the amount of income taxes that are paid does not decrease one's allowable deductions and, hence, does not trigger any further increase in taxable income. Instead, the full amount of any tax that is saved increases after-tax income; that is, the tax savings themselves do not constitute taxable income. Unlike most profit-seeking activities, tax planning produces benefits that are completely exempt from income taxation.

The second such rule allows a deduction for any business-related expenses that are incurred in connection with the determination of a tax. Most tax planning costs are deductible by business owners and sole proprietors, but only a few employee-individuals qualify for such a deduction. The net cost of a tax planning project, then, is its gross cost minus the amount of the reduction in the tax liability that is generated by the attendant deduction. In concise terms, the after-tax cost of tax planning can be expressed as follows.

$$\textbf{ATC} = \textbf{BTC} \times (1 - \textbf{MTR}) \text{ where}$$

$$\textbf{ATC} = \text{after-tax cost}$$

$$\textbf{BTC} = \text{before-tax cost}$$

$$\textbf{MTR} = \text{marginal tax rate}$$

In relating both rules to tax planning projects, one can see that such endeavors enjoy an economic advantage over most other profit-seeking activities. In evaluating most other investment projects, the decision maker must compare after-tax benefits with after-tax costs. Yet, for tax planning projects, the payoffs are tax free, while the costs usually remain tax-deductible. Thus, for tax planning activities, one effectively compares pretax benefits with after-tax costs.

> **Example 12-2** Shull Corporation, subject to a marginal state and Federal income tax rate of 40 percent, is considering two mutually exclusive alternatives. Alternative A is to hire a university accounting major for the summer at a cost of $2,000; his task would be to undertake research on a tax avoidance plan. If it is successful, the plan would save the corporation $1,600 in Federal income taxes. The probability of success for the plan is estimated at 80 percent. Alternative M is to hire a university marketing major for the summer at a cost of $1,800; her task would be to undertake research on a marketing plan. If it is successful, this plan would generate new revenues of $2,000. The probability of such success is estimated to be 85 percent. Which, if either, alternative should Shull pursue?
>
> | | Alternative A | Alternative M |
> |---|---|---|
> | Before-tax cost | $2,000 | $1,800 |
> | Tax reduction (40%) | –800 | –720 |
> | After-tax cost | $1,200 | $1,080 |
> | | | |
> | Possible pretax payoff | $1,600 | $2,000 |
> | Probability of success | ×.80 | ×.85 |
> | Expected pretax payoff | $1,280 | $1,700 |
> | Tax on expected payoff (40%) | –0 | –680 |
> | Expected after-tax payoff | $1,280 | $1,020 |
> | | | |
> | Excess of after-tax payoff over after-tax cost | $ 80 | $ (60) |

Decision: Even though Alternative M offers a higher pretax payoff, a lower before-tax cost, and a higher probability of success, Alternative A should be accepted.

The facts of this example illustrate the apparent built-in economic bias of current tax law for tax planning projects, relative to other, seemingly more productive activities.

The analysis of Example 12-2, like most of the illustrations in this book, is based on a "marginal" viewpoint. Its purpose is to determine the effect of the transactions at issue, assuming that all other characteristics of the situation do not change. When it is viewed from this perspective, the after-tax cost of any deductible expenditure decreases if the marginal tax rate is increased. This fact may explain why lower-income taxpayers, who are subject to lower marginal tax rates, engage in tax planning activities less often than do higher-income taxpayers.

Example 12-3 Assume the same situation and opportunities as in Example 12-2, except that Shull's marginal tax rate is 20 percent.

	Alternative A	Alternative M
Before-tax cost	$2,000	$1,800
Tax reduction (20%)	–400	–360
After-tax cost	$1,600	$1,440
Possible pretax payoff	$1,600	$2,000
Probability of success	× .80	× .85
Expected pretax payoff	$1,280	$1,700
Tax on expected payoff (20%)	–0	–340
Expected after-tax payoff	$1,280	$1,360
Excess of after-tax payoff over after-tax cost	$ (320)	$ (80)

Decision: Accept Alternative M, because it generates the lesser after-tax loss, or undertake neither (seemingly profitable) project. The change in the marginal tax rate alone resulted in a different decision by Shull.

SPOTLIGHT ON TAXATION

Observation

Sometimes it is difficult to get a taxpayer to think in "after-tax" terms, so "bad" decisions can be made. For other taxpayers, there is an impression that the government fully reimburses a deduction, that is, a $1 "write-off" means that there is no cost to the taxpayer. The tax planner often must act as educator to eliminate both of these mistaken impressions.

TAX RATE TERMINOLOGY

The basic formula for computing a taxpayer's liability is

$$\text{Tax Liability} = \text{Tax Base} \times \text{Rate}$$

Thus, in many respects, the function of a legislative body is to define adequately the appropriate tax base and construct a schedule of tax rates, so that the ensuing liabilities will be in accordance with the prevailing revenue and nonrevenue objectives of the tax system. Once a tax has been included in a society's tax structure, legislative efforts seem to focus on slight modifications of the existing tax base and rates; major overhauls, additions, or deletions to the structure rarely are considered. Tax reform legislation thus usually takes the form of "fine-tuning" the system rather than "changing channels" altogether.

Tax Base

The income tax is the most modern of the taxes that are commonly found in contemporary industrialized societies. Allowing for the difficulties in constructing a definition for a virtually imaginary concept, most policymakers believe that a tax that is based on "ordinary taxable income," allowing deductions for the costs of earning such income and for certain personal expenditures, best reflects the capacity of the taxpayer to support government finance.

Previous efforts to base taxation on ability to pay have included taxes on individual consumption and wealth. Consumption taxes are supported by the rationale that the taxpayer receives personal benefit from society in accordance with the amount of goods and services that he or she exhausts during the period; thus, the government should appropriate its share of finances from what people take out of society's "kitty" for personal reasons, not from what they put into it, as is the case under income taxation.

Wealth or property taxes also have been structured to base levies on one's capacity to support the government. Most often, wealth taxes take the form of levies against the net holdings of tangible assets that are controlled by the taxpayer at a given time. In accounting terminology, the tax on the net tangible assets is assessed on what appears on the taxpayer's balance sheet at the end of the taxable year.

Tax Rates

Most tax scholars identify three distinct tax rate structures: proportional, progressive, and regressive, as illustrated in Exhibit 12-1. The classification of a rate structure depends on the trend of the tax rate as the tax base increases. Under a **proportional tax rate** system, the tax rate is constant; for example, it might stand at 29 percent of net wealth, over all possible values of the tax base. Most American sales and property taxes employ a proportional rate structure. Under a tax system with **progressive tax rates**, the applicable tax rate increases as the tax base grows larger. American income, estate, and gift taxes typically use nominally progressive rates. Finally, the tax rate decreases as the tax base grows larger under a system of **regressive tax rates**. Using the present scheme of classification, no significant American tax to date has employed a system of nominally regressive tax rates.

> **Example 12-4** In the typical year, Social Security taxes are imposed on employees at a flat rate (before credits), say, of 8 percent on all wages up to $110,000. For wages in excess of $110,000, there is no additional tax. Technically, this tax is proportional, because all covered wages (the tax base) are subject to the same rate of tax. However, many people regard Social Security taxes to be regressive, presumably because they tend to relate their analysis to all of one's income and not just to the statutory tax base. Under this view, because the marginal tax rate is zero on wages in excess of $110,000 for the year, the tax is both effectively and nominally regressive.

Many taxpayers confuse the appropriate meaning of their **marginal tax rate**. Typically, they assume that if a taxpayer is subject to a 36 percent marginal tax rate

Exhibit 12-1: Alternative Tax Rate Structures: Graphic Illustrations and Applicable Schedules

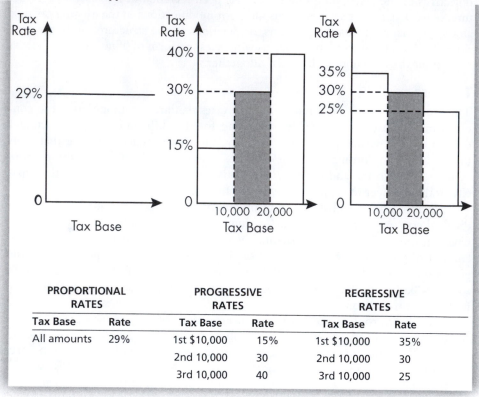

PROPORTIONAL RATES		PROGRESSIVE RATES		REGRESSIVE RATES	
Tax Base	**Rate**	**Tax Base**	**Rate**	**Tax Base**	**Rate**
All amounts	29%	1st $10,000	15%	1st $10,000	35%
		2nd 10,000	30	2nd 10,000	30
		3rd 10,000	40	3rd 10,000	25

(i.e., 36 cents is payable in tax on the next dollar of taxable income), he or she owes 36 percent of the *entire* taxable income. One often hears people fall victim to this fallacy, when they state, "I wish I hadn't gotten that raise, because it threw me into a higher tax bracket!" The truth is that even under a system of progressive tax rates, one is never left worse off by earning more money. The higher marginal rates that apply to additional income affect only those increments; the tax liability on the original income layers does not change.

Such comments reflect a confusion on the part of the taxpayer concerning marginal tax rate and average tax rate. The **average tax rate** is a simple division of the total tax liability by the corresponding tax base.

> **Example 12-5** Lydia earned $50,000 this year. After applying various deductions, exclusions, and exemptions, though, Lydia's statutory taxable income is $41,000; further, the middle tax rate system of Exhibit 12-1 is in effect. Lydia's tax is computed as follows.
>
> 15% × $10,000 = $ 1,500
> 30% ×   10,000 =   3,000
> 40% ×   21,000 =   8,400
> Tax liability $12,900
>
> Lydia's marginal tax rate is 40 percent, but her average rate is only 31.5 percent ($12,900 tax due ÷ $41,000 taxable income).

The reader should make sure that he or she understands this distinction between marginal and average tax rates, because all tax planning analyses should be based on

Exhibit 12-2: Various Tax Rate Computations Illustrated

Lydia files a tax return for $50,000 of economic income and $9,000 of exemptions, exclusions, and deductions. Taxable income is $41,000. Tax liability is $12,900 under the prevailing rate system.

Marginal tax rate	40% (from tax rate schedule, middle system, Exhibit 12-1)
Average tax rates	Nominal average rate: $12,900/$41,000 = 31.5%
	Effective average rate: $12,900/$50,000 = 25.8%

the marginal tax that the individual will pay or save by adopting a particular course of action. The average tax rate is an interesting statistic, but it is solely the marginal rate that affects the change in tax liability and any corresponding changes in taxpayer behavior.

Of course, this definition of statutory taxable income allows for certain deductions, exemptions, and exclusions from total receipts in determining the tax base for the year. Often, because one has received tax-exempt income during the period and because of the tax base's exemptions and standard deduction, an individual controls more receipts than he or she legally must report as taxable income. In this case, the distinction between the nominal and effective average tax rates becomes important. The **nominal average tax rate** can be computed in Example 12-5 as the division of total tax liability by taxable income (i.e., 31.5 percent). However, before considering Lydia's exclusions, exemptions, and deductions, effectively she had command over $50,000 of income during the year, even though only $41,000 of this amount was defined technically as taxable income. Thus, Lydia's **effective average tax rate** of tax for the year can be found by dividing the total tax liability by "total," or economic, income. Here, the effective average rate of tax is only $12,900 ÷ $50,000 = 25.8 percent. Exhibit 12-2 summarizes the various tax rate computations that have been introduced in this section.

TAX PLANNING IN PERSPECTIVE

The entrepreneurial tax professional should not see tax planning as an end in itself. Rather, especially when dealing with individual clients, tax planning must be seen as part of two sets of major services provided by the practitioner, as illustrated in Exhibits 12-3 and 12-4. As we discussed in Chapter 1, tax planning is part of the

Exhibit 12-3: Tax Planning in the Typical Tax Practice, by Time and Effort of the Professional Staff

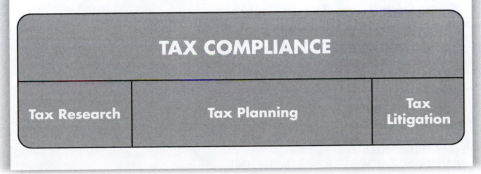

Exhibit 12-4: Tax Planning in the Client's Wealth Planning Process

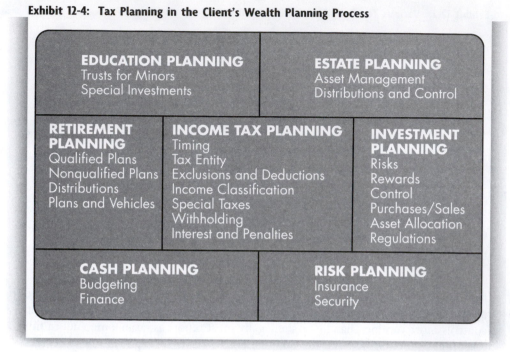

entire menu of tax services that the tax professional makes available. Although the compliance and litigation aspects of the profession increasingly are shared with paraprofessionals (who prepare the bulk of tax returns for many professional firms) or attorneys (when a seemingly irresolvable conflict arises, usually between the client and the IRS [Internal Revenue Service]), tax planning rightly is initiated by the well-educated and experienced tax practitioner.

Similarly, tax planning is but one of the various types of planning services that a tax professional offers to clients. As the U.S. population collectively ages, the importance of portfolio, estate, and retirement planning has increased. As the "baby boom echo" materialized in the early part of the twenty-first century, education planning again took center stage. Planning for cash and risk contingencies is mandatory for business clients, but even the most modestly endowed of individual clients can benefit from an introduction to such planning.

Thus, to the extent that the tax professional offers tax planning and counseling services, he or she must be facile with the rudiments of the planning process and with the dynamic nature of the evolution of the tax law as it affects planning engagements.

FUNDAMENTALS OF TAX PLANNING

As we noted in Chapter 1, tax planning is a completely legal means for saving taxes.[2] The basic objective of such planning is to arrange one's financial activities in a way that will reduce the present value of tax costs, such that maximum wealth accumulation can occur in the time period specified.

---

[2]Portions of this section are adapted from William A. Raabe and James E. Parker, *Tax Concepts for Decision Making* (St. Paul, MN: West Publishing Co., 1985).

Opportunities for effective tax planning almost always are greater when tax effects are given consideration before transactions are finalized, rather than after they are completed. Decision makers should constantly be alert for tax-optimizing alternatives in the everyday conduct of their affairs. In other words, the first requirement for effective tax planning is **tax awareness** on the part of decision makers, rather than tax expertise by tax professionals.

Example 12-6 Russell and Phyllis Cohen, a married couple subject to a 30 percent marginal tax rate, currently are negotiating the purchase of their first home with the Hacienda Heights Construction Company, a land developer. The company has offered to sell the Cohens a selected house and lot at a price of $60,000, with a 20 percent down payment and 10 percent interest on annual payments over a five-year period. Under these terms, payments would be as follows.

Year	Beginning Balance	Interest	Principal	Total payment
0	$60,000	$ —	$12,000	$12,000
1	48,000	4,800	7,862	12,662
2	40,138	4,014	8,648	12,662
3	31,490	3,149	9,513	12,662
4	21,977	2,198	10,464	12,662
5	11,513	1,151	11,513	12,664
Totals		$15,312	$60,000	$75,312

The Cohens are aware that mortgage interest payments are tax-deductible and that the purchase price of a home is not. Thus, they make a counter-offer to purchase the home at a price of $54,445, with $12,000 down and 15 percent interest on annual payments over a five-year period. Under these new terms, Hacienda Heights receives the same cash payments (and gross income) as it did under the original terms. However, the amount of allowable deductions to the Cohens would be increased, with no change in total cash payments.

Year	Beginning Balance	Interest	Principal	Total payment
0	$54,445	$ —	$12,000	$12,000
1	42,445	6,367	6,295	12,662
2	36,150	5,423	7,239	12,662
3	28,911	4,337	8,325	12,662
4	20,586	3,088	9,574	12,662
5	11,012	1,652	11,012	12,664
Totals		$20,867	$54,445	$75,312

These results are not uncommon in a robust tax planning context. Often, decision makers can benefit by recognizing how the rearrangement of a planned transaction can produce tax savings, even if the economic substance of the transaction is left unaltered (or altered very little). The key, of course, is to pay close attention to the structural and transactional categories that have been established by Congress and the courts. In Example 12-6, by reclassifying a portion of their housing expenditures as (deductible) interest rather than (nondeductible) principal, the Cohens were able to increase their allowable deductions and save taxes. Stated differently, the taxpayer's ability to conceptualize actions or events within stated legal definitions is of utmost importance.

Exhibit 12-5: Goals of Tax Planning Behavior

- Avoiding statutory income, obtaining deductions and credits
- Postponing income recognition, accelerating losses, deductions, and credits
- Changing tax jurisdictions
- Controlling the classification of income
- Spreading income among related taxpayers

Tax planning behavior can be characterized as falling into one or more of the general categories enumerated in Exhibit 12-5. Virtually every tax planning technique employed by the tax professional fits one or more of these overriding planning objectives.

SPOTLIGHT ON TAXATION

Radical Tax Planning

"A well-timed death is the acme of good tax planning, better even than a well-timed marriage."
—(Former IRS Commissioner) Donald C. Alexander

Avoiding Income Recognition

Taxpayers often can reduce their exposure to taxation by avoiding the accumulation of gross income that must be recognized. This is not to suggest that a taxpayer should avoid accumulating real economic income. As long as marginal tax rates remain less than 100 percent, few people would be willing to go to that extreme. Rather, one usually should strive to obtain economic wealth in some manner that does not create recognized income under the tax law.

> **Example 12-7** Julie earned $3,500 when she sold the crop of fruits and vegetables that she grew, and she was subject to income tax on the full amount. Warren also grew a crop of produce of the same size, but he and his family ate the food. Thus, Warren recognized no gross income and paid no income tax relative to his gardening activities, but his family enjoyed $3,500 worth of fruits and vegetables.
>
> Another method by which one can avoid obtaining recognized income is through the use of debt. Since neither the borrowing of money nor the receipt of funds that previously were lent generates gross income, taxpayers sometimes can use loans to avoid the recognition of taxable income on appreciated investments and enjoy the temporary use of the cash.

> **Example 12-8** Doug owns a tract of land that he acquired many years ago for $10,000. Currently, the land is worth $100,000. Doug needs $50,000 cash for a business venture. He is considering two alternatives: one is to sell half of the land and the other is to borrow the $50,000 by giving a mortgage on the land.

If Doug sells one-half of the land, he will recognize a $45,000 ($50,000 − 1/2 of $10,000) taxable gain. However, Doug recognizes no taxable income if he borrows the money, even though the amount that he borrows will be in excess of the basis of the land.

> **Example 12-9** Barbara Ward formed a new corporation by investing $100,000 cash. Following the advice of her tax consultant, Barbara designated $60,000 to be used for the purchase of corporate stock and $40,000 as a loan to the corporation. In this way, if Barbara wants to receive large amounts of cash back from the corporation in the future, the entity simply will repay part or all of the loan principal to her, tax free, rather than making a large (taxable and nondeductible) dividend payment. Barbara also can direct the corporation to pay interest on the loan; such payments are deductible by the corporation. Of course, both interest and dividends are taxable to Barbara when she receives them.

Still another, and perhaps more obvious, way in which one can avoid the recognition of income for tax purposes is to take advantage of the many exclusions that the law permits. For example, an employee might arrange to receive certain nontaxable fringe benefits (such as health insurance) from the employer, in lieu of an equivalent value in (taxable) cash salary. This relationship should affect all negotiations as to compensation arrangements: the employer is indifferent between the two choices because both salary and fringe benefit payments are fully deductible against gross income, but the employee's after-tax wealth increases more where tax-free benefits are received.

> **Example 12-10** Lee Schrader, who is subject to a 40 percent overall marginal tax rate, is better off if she receives a tax-free fringe benefit than if she receives an equivalent raise in her salary.
>
> | | If Salary Increases | If Fringe Benefit Is Chosen |
> |---|---|---|
> | Value of compensation received | $2,000 | $2,000 |
> | Tax on employee's compensation | − 800 | |
> | After-tax increase in employee's wealth | $1,200 | $2,000 |

Postponing Income Recognition

By delaying the recognition of income, one also delays the payment of the tax and, hence, can continue to enjoy the use of that tax money. Given the relatively high interest rates that are anticipated in coming years, this delay takes on increased importance. At 6 percent annual interest, the present value of a $1,000 tax that is postponed for ten years is only $558, a "forgiveness" of almost one-half of the tax "cost." For longer periods and/or higher interest rates, the economic significance of the delay would be even greater. Appendix A includes a series of tables computing factors to reflect the time value of money.

> **Example 12-11** Agatha Fraser paid $1,000 for 750 Euros. At the same time, her sister, Betty, put $1,000 into a U.S. bank savings account. By the current year, the value of Agatha's Euros had increased to $1,800, and Betty's bank account had increased, due to interest accumulations, to the same amount. Since the increase in the value of the Euros was unrealized, Agatha had not been taxed yet on her $800 increase in economic wealth. On the other hand, Betty's increase was realized from interest that was credited annually to her account.

Under the tax doctrine of *constructive receipt*, Betty had recognized gross income, accumulated over the nine-year planning period, of $800.

Example 12-12 Janie Heller owns land adjacent to her home that appreciated in value by $5,000 this year. However, because she did not sell the land, the appreciation in market value was not realized in a market transaction or recognized for income tax purposes. Janie has no recognized income from the land for that year.

Example 12-13 Janie Heller, of Example 12-12, paid interest of $4,000 on a mortgage that was used to finance her home and land investment. Janie can deduct the interest amount to offset the income that she derived from other investment sources in computing her taxable income. In effect, Janie is able to achieve a deliberate mismatching of current-year costs and unrealized revenues.

Example 12-14 Janie Heller, of Example 12-12, constructed an apartment building on her land, at a cost of $500,000, of which $475,000 was borrowed. By electing accelerated depreciation, which is based on the total $500,000 cost of the building rather than on Janie's $25,000 equity therein, Janie is able to take a depreciation deduction of about $12,000 in the construction year alone, nearly equal to about one-half of her entire cash outlay for the current year.

Changing Tax Jurisdictions

Tax systems are not universal in breadth, nature, or application. Taxes are adopted by governmental jurisdictions, to be collected from those who live and do business within their boundaries. Often, by moving assets or income out of one tax jurisdiction into another, tax reductions can be effected. Over time, governments tend to modify their tax systems to prevent the "leakage" of tax revenues through such cross-border transactions. Yet, in an effort to attract businesses and resulting jobs into their jurisdictions, governments often retain or create border incentives in the form of tax reductions that are limited in time or scope.

Example 12-15 The island country of Ricardo meets its revenue needs with tariffs on the fishing industry. Ricardo never has adopted an income tax system. Harris, a U.S. corporation, could build its new assembly plant through a wholly owned subsidiary incorporated and doing business only in Ricardo, thereby reducing its costs of conducting business because there is no income tax on executive salaries or annual profits. Perhaps by design, Ricardo has attracted new business, profits, jobs, and other benefits through its tax policies.

Example 12-16 State A includes in its statutory definition of taxable business income the interest paid on U.S. Treasury obligations. OneBank holds billions of dollars in Treasury notes, bills, and bonds, so, in an effort to reduce its tax costs, it creates a wholly owned subsidiary incorporated and doing business only in State B, which does not tax interest income. The subsidiary "repatriates" the interest to OneBank through quarterly dividend distributions, not taxed under the laws of State A. The economy of State A has been depleted because of its tax policy, but the taxpayer has responded with rational behavior in accord with its overall financial goals through judicious tax planning techniques.

Controlling Classification of Income

For Federal income tax purposes, several distinct categories of income, deductions, and credits are recognized. The most important of these are (1) ordinary income, which is fully taxable, and ordinary deductions, which decrease the tax base dollar for dollar; (2) investment or "portfolio" income, which usually is fully taxable except for tax-exempt state and local bond interest, and related expenses, which typically can be subtracted only against investment income; and (3) income from passive activities, such as the ownership of rental or "tax shelter" assets, which usually is fully taxable, and related expenses, which can be subtracted only against passive income.

In addition, a fourth classification of income and expenses should be identified. If the taxpayer is subject to the alternative minimum tax (AMT), preference and adjustment items, such as accelerated depreciation deductions, may be included, and other expenditures may not be available as deductions.

Effective tax planning often includes the proper identification or reclassification of income or expenditure items, using these statutory definitions.

> **Example 12-17** Phil Jankowski is the sole shareholder of a management consulting corporation. In addition, he has invested in tax shelter entities that are generating $40,000 per year in passive losses for him. According to the Code, such losses from passive activities cannot be applied as deductions to offset fully taxable income, for example, from Phil's salary or capital gain transactions. Accordingly, Phil cannot reduce current taxable income by the $40,000 passive loss from his tax shelter.
>
> As the dominant shareholder of his corporation, however, Phil may be in a position to salvage the $40,000 deduction. If he reduces his salary from the corporation by $40,000 and takes instead from the corporation a $40,000 properly structured lease payment for the use of specified personal or real property that he owns but the corporation uses, such as office equipment or automobiles, he may be able to create $40,000 in passive income from rental activities, against which the tax shelter loss can be offset.

> **Example 12-18** Matt Young Eagle is subject to the AMT for the first time ever this year because he exercised the incentive stock options of his employer. Nonbusiness taxes paid and miscellaneous itemized deductions, among other familiar items, are not allowed as deductions when computing AMT income. Only certain tax credits are allowed against the AMT. Accordingly, Young Eagle should defer the payments of his fourth-quarter state income tax estimates and of the real estate tax on his home until next year, when the usual definitions of taxable income will apply to him again.

Spreading Income among Related Taxpayers

Because different types of legal entities are taxed separately and at different rates, an individual often can produce an overall tax savings by conducting various business and investment activities within separate taxpaying entities. The progressive nature of the various tax rate schedules further tends to increase the advantage of income splitting. This benefit might result from shifting income, either among different economic entities that are owned by the same individual or among the individual's family members. Accordingly, tax considerations often play an important role both in the selection of organizational forms for a business enterprise and in family financial arrangements.

Example 12-19 Bob and Lorraine Whitehead are currently providing for Lorraine's parents' retirement out of after-tax income. Given the Whiteheads' marginal income tax rate of 30 percent, $1,000 of pretax income is needed to produce $700 of savings [$1,000 − (0.30 of $1,000) = $700]. Assuming that the parents have a marginal income tax rate of only 18 percent, a transfer to them of $1,000 of pretax income, say, by the placement of income-producing assets into an appropriate trust, would raise the after-tax contribution to the parents' retirement to $820 [$1,000 − (0.18 of $1,000)].

Example 12-20 Sally Campbell is the sole shareholder and only employee of the Newark Corporation. The corporation's operating income this year is expected to be $125,000. Sally is subject to an overall marginal income tax rate of 30 percent. Sally wishes to know, considering only the Federal income tax, what amount of salary payments to her would produce the smallest combined tax for both herself and the corporation. Sally's income from other sources is sufficient to meet her living expenses and it precisely equals her total income tax deductions, so her taxable income is exactly equal to any salary that she receives from the corporation.

Currently, marginal corporate income tax rates do not exceed the 30 percent marginal individual tax bracket until corporate taxable income is greater than $75,000. Accordingly, the tax adviser should be certain to plan the corporation's compensation policy so that a corporate taxable income of at least $75,000 exists every year.

Departing from the Fundamentals

The general principles of tax planning that have been presented usually produce an optimal tax liability for the taxpayer. However, unusual circumstances may dictate that such principles should be violated purposely, to produce a desired effect. Again, however, the tax awareness of the parties is utmost in proper planning activities.

Example 12-21 Gretchen's manufacturing business is unincorporated. It has generated an operating loss of $265,000, which Gretchen can deduct on her tax return. Although there may be other tax uses for this loss, Gretchen may want to accelerate the recognition of other gross income into the current year, for example, by selling appreciated investments, exercising more sophisticated tax accounting elections, or simply sending out bills to customers in a more timely fashion. Economically, such income has been earned gradually by Gretchen, but it has had no tax effect yet because it has not been realized. Realization this year, however, will result in no tax liability for Gretchen because of the loss, so income acceleration should be considered.

Example 12-22 Brian's gross income is lower than he expected because of an unanticipated decrease in the sale of his homemade sandals. From a tax standpoint, it may be better to delay deductible expenditures of a discretionary or personal nature (e.g., advertising, medical expenses, and charitable contributions) until business picks up again. In this manner, the value of such deductions will increase, as will the marginal income tax rate to which he is subject.

Example 12-23 Dolores is subject to the AMT this year, so her marginal tax rate is 24 percent, not the usual 36 percent. She might consider accelerating some gross income into the current year to take advantage of this structural decrease in her marginal tax rate. The tax adviser must be certain, though, to compare the present values of the resulting taxes, not just the nominal dollar amounts (i.e., the proper tax planning comparison is between the $32,400 and the $24,000), and Dolores should accelerate the gross income in this setting.

	If Regular Tax Applies, Taxed Next Year	If AMT Applies, Taxed This Year
Nominal tax liability	$36,000	$24,000
Present value of tax liability	32,400	24,000

SPOTLIGHT ON TAXATION

Fruits of Tax Planning

"Tax planning is driven by the fact that under a non-neutral tax law, transactions or arrangements whose economic differences are minor can have significantly different tax consequences."

—James W. Wetzler

EXPLOITING INCONSISTENCIES IN THE STATUTE

Sometimes, especially when the tax planner can affect the behavior of more than one taxpayer, the tax planning goals can be accomplished by exploiting perceived inconsistencies in the tax system. Multiple taxpayers can exist in the form of family members or related corporations and their shareholders. Several types of systemic inconsistencies can be identified and used by the tax planner.

Inconsistencies between Transactions

Most forms of self-provided in-kind income go unrecognized for tax purposes. Often, the same items are not deductible, however, when they are purchased in market transactions. Thus, providing for one's own needs can be an important technique in managing the recognition of taxable income.

Example 12-24 Jerry has $50,000 in savings. If the money were invested in securities, the yield on his investment would be taxable, although no deduction would be allowed for his "personal" expense of renting a home. If the $50,000 were invested in a home for his own use, however, the net rental value of the home would escape taxation, since such in-kind value is not recognized as gross income under the law.

Inconsistencies between Taxpayers

Inconsistencies often exist between Code sections that control the recognition of income and those that control the allowance of deductions for the same items. When a transaction is between related taxpayers, such inconsistent treatments sometimes can be used to the taxpayers' advantage. The objective in such a situation usually is to structure the terms of the transaction so as to decrease taxable income to the taxpayer group as a whole.

> **Example 12-25** Marilyn is the sole owner-employee of a corporation. To the extent that the corporation pays dividends to Marilyn, she will recognize gross income, but the corporation will receive no deduction. To the extent that Marilyn is paid a reasonable salary, she will recognize gross income and the corporation will receive a deduction. To the extent that she receives certain employee fringe benefits, such as medical insurance, Marilyn is not required to recognize taxable income, and the corporation is allowed an ordinary business expense deduction. In summary, the payment of dividends increases combined taxable income of a shareholder and the corporation, the payment of salary does not change combined taxable income, and providing qualified fringe benefits reduces combined taxable income.

> **Example 12-26** Don and Ann Evans operate a farm, producing a net taxable income of about $30,000 per year. Their nondeductible expenses for housing average $12,000 per year.
>
> The Evanses should consider forming a corporation and making a tax-free transfer of all of the farm property to the corporation, including their personal living quarters. As shareholders of the corporation, they could hire themselves as employees, with a requirement that they live on the business premises. The value of the lodging would not be taxable to the Evanses as individuals, under §119 of the Code, but it would be deductible as a business expense of the corporation, thus reducing the corporation's taxable income before salaries to $18,000 ($30,000 − $12,000).
>
> The Evanses then should have the corporation pay them reasonable salaries totaling $18,000. In this manner, taxable income of $18,000 would be taxed directly to them as individuals, and the corporation's taxable income would be reduced to zero, thus avoiding any double taxation. By using this combination of income splitting and an employee fringe benefit, the Evanses could effectively reduce their taxable income (i.e., from $30,000 to $18,000) by the amount of their lodging costs ($12,000), even though such costs are generally nondeductible by both self-employed persons and employees.
>
> This result is based on the assumptions that $18,000 is a reasonable salary for the work that they perform, and that the requirement for living on the farm is for a bona fide business purpose (other than merely for tax avoidance).

Inconsistencies between Years

Another form of inconsistency concerns timing differences in the recognition of income and deductions. Such inconsistencies may relate to the transactions of one taxpayer, or they may concern two taxpayers engaging in a single transaction. In both cases, careful planning to take advantage of tax law inconsistencies can result in a considerable delay in the payment of taxes.

> **Example 12-27** Sarah Carter uses borrowed funds to acquire nondividend-paying corporate stocks. Appreciation on the stocks is not taxed until it is realized on the sale of the shares; yet, Carter might be able to claim investment-interest deductions for the interest that she pays on the borrowed funds.

Example 12-28 Harry Fischer is a 40 percent shareholder and junior executive of Able Corporation. Harry's performance incentive bonus is set at 30 percent of the corporation's pretax earnings for the year. It is payable on January 31 of the following year.

Because the corporation is an accrual-basis taxpayer, the bonus is deductible in the year in which it is earned. As a cash-basis minority shareholder, however, Harry need not recognize the income until the following taxable year (i.e., when he receives it). To the extent of Harry's bonus, the recognition of combined corporate and shareholder income thus is delayed for one year.

Example 12-29 Jane Summer is an employee of Orange Corporation and is covered by the company's qualified pension plan. The corporation makes a contribution to the plan for Jane's retirement, which will occur in thirty years. Although Jane will not receive any gross income from the pension benefits until her retirement in thirty years, the corporation is entitled to a current-year business expense deduction.

AVOIDING TAX TRAPS

Ever since the enactment of the first income tax law, taxpayers have been trying to find ways to avoid such taxes. Likewise, Congress, the IRS, and the courts have enacted rules and doctrines to prevent, or at least restrict, various avoidance schemes. As a result, current tax law includes a maze of tax traps for the unwary.

Statutory Tax Traps

Many of the statutory provisions encountered in a tax planning context can best be understood when they are viewed as preventive provisions, that is, as rules designed by Congress to prevent certain techniques of tax avoidance. However, remember that any transaction that falls within the scope of a given provision, whether or not it is intended as part of a tax avoidance scheme, is subject to that provision. Thus, a basic knowledge of the tax system is necessary for the tax planner if certain disastrous pitfalls are to be avoided.

As we noted earlier in this chapter, income splitting between related taxpayers often can generate significant tax savings. To be effective for tax purposes, though, the income actually must be earned by the separate entities and not merely assigned by means of artificial transactions between them. Section 482 gives the IRS the power to reallocate both income and deductions among certain related taxpayers so as to reflect "true taxable income."

In applying §482, the regulations indicate that the IRS's right to determine true taxable income is not limited to fraudulent or sham transactions, but also situations where income inadvertently has been shifted between controlled parties. The courts have held, however, that there truly must be a "shifting" of income before the IRS's power comes into play. Bona fide business transactions that bring tax advantages in their wake should not subject the related parties to reallocation. In concept, at least, §482 can be applied by the IRS only where there has been some manipulation of income or deductions by the taxpayers.

Thus, while its boundaries are, in practice, both broad and sometimes hazy, §482 does not prohibit the use of multiple entities for the purpose of earning income. It does, however, give the IRS a potent weapon with which to combat the artificial shifting of income between those entities.

Example 12-30 X and Y are two corporations that are fully owned by the same individual. X operates an international airline, and Y owns several hotels that are located in cities served by X. In conjunction with the advertising of its airlines, X often pictures Y's hotels. Although the primary benefit of the advertising is to X's airline operations, Y's hotels also obtain patronage by travelers who respond to the ads. X does not charge Y for the advertising. Because an unrelated hotel operator presumably would have been charged for such advertising, the IRS may make an allocation of income from X to Y to reflect the fair market value of the advertising services that were provided.

The Code restricts the amount of unearned income that can be taxed at the (lower) marginal rates of one's dependent nonstudent child who has not yet attained age nineteen to less than $1,800 per year, an amount indexed for inflation. Any unearned income of the child that exceeds this amount is taxed to the child, but at the (higher) marginal rates of his or her parents. The purpose of this portion of the *Internal Revenue Code* is not to discriminate against children (who probably cannot vote in congressional elections), nor to place a higher tax burden on interest and dividend income, nor even to make the family the chief taxable unit in this country. Rather, the provision was enacted simply to discourage the shifting of taxable income from the higher tax brackets of the parent, through a temporary trust or some other accepted income-shifting vehicle, to the more favorable rates of the child, without any permanent loss by the parent of control over the use of the asset. Such tax planning techniques had been undertaken for many years, as a means (similar to that of Example 12-19 for older related individuals) of accumulating after-tax contributions to an educational fund, by transferring income to the lowest marginal tax rates that were available within the family.

Whereas the objective of this part of the statute may be defensible by some, the broad provision that was enacted to implement it may create undue hardships in some circumstances, because it affects all taxpayers, not only those with the now-forbidden income-shifting motivation.

Example 12-31 Jimmy, age seven, received an inheritance from his grandmother's estate last year. Grandmother wanted Jimmy to attend a good graduate program in taxation someday, so she invested in high-income securities that produce about $22,000 in interest income annually. Jimmy's parents are to see that he accumulates this income for his education. The interest will be taxed at the parents' 40 percent marginal rate, however, and not at Jimmy's (zero and) 15 percent rate, so a smaller after-tax amount of this income will be available for this laudable educational purpose.

Judicial Tax Traps

In the final analysis, the words of the tax law mean only what the courts say that they mean. Often, judicial decisions must be consulted to determine the allowable limits of various Code provisions.

Example 12-32 An employee-shareholder of a 50 percent family-owned corporation received an annual salary in excess of $1 million, an amount greater than that then paid to the heads of such corporations as General Motors and Sears.[3] Yet, despite IRS arguments to the contrary, the Tax Court upheld the

---

[3] *Home Interiors and Gifts, Inc.*, 73 T.C. 92 (1980).

entire amount paid as "reasonable" under the circumstances of the case because of the special talents and abilities that the employee brought to the corporation.

Example 12-33 A widow changed her will to disinherit her relatives and leave her assets to her attorney and his wife.[4] When the widow died, her relatives brought suit against the attorney, alleging that he had influenced the widow improperly through a personal relationship with her. The attorney paid them $121,000 to withdraw their litigation and deducted the payment as a business expense. The Tax Court upheld the deduction on the grounds that the payment was made for the purpose of maintaining the professional reputation of the attorney.

On appeal, the Tax Court's decision was overturned. According to the appeals court, a taxpayer's reasons for paying do not determine whether the payment is deductible. Because the lawsuit arose from the attorney's personal relationship with the widow, the $121,000 settlement was deemed to be a personal, nondeductible cost.

Example 12-34 Housing is expensive in Japan. A unit of a large oil company owned the house that was used by its president, at his discretion, when he stayed in Japan[5] The house would have rented for $4,400 a year in the United States, but in Tokyo its annual rental value was $20,000. The executive included it in income and paid tax on $4,400, the U.S. rental value. However, the IRS asserted that the full $20,000 should have been included in his gross income.

The U.S. Court of Claims agreed with the taxpayer, holding that the excess rental value was primarily of benefit to the company, rather than to the individual. The home's prestige value was held to be important to the employer because of social values that were peculiar to Japan, where, in the words of the court, "'face' is an almost tangible reality."

Two pervasive judicial doctrines that often limit the taxpayer's ability to employ effective planning techniques are the concepts of *business purpose* and *substance over form*. To be upheld for tax purposes, transactions must possess some nontax, or "business," purpose in addition to that of tax avoidance. Moreover, there is always the possibility that the court may ignore the form of a transaction if it perceives that such structural false colors cloud the actual substance of the arrangement.

Whenever a series of transactions results in significant tax savings, the IRS may attempt to apply the concept of substance over form by "telescoping" or "collapsing" several transactions into one. If it is upheld by a court, this *step-transaction doctrine* sometimes can negate what had been a good tax plan (where the steps were viewed as separate transactions). To guard against this possibility, the taxpayer should have a bona fide business purpose for each individual step in the transaction. Of course, documenting nontax purposes is usually much easier if the various transactions are separated by reasonable time spans, since they are then less likely to be viewed as component parts of an overall plan.

Example 12-35 Sandra is the sole shareholder of a real estate development corporation. On January 15, she purchased ten additional shares of stock from her corporation for $100,000. On the same day, she sold a tract of undeveloped

---

[4]*William J. McDonald, Jr.*, 592 F.2d 635, 78-2 USTC ¶ 9631, 42 AFTR2d 78-5797 (CA-2).
[5]*Faneuil Adams*, 585 F.2d 106, 77-2 USTC ¶ 9613, 40 AFTR2d 77-5607 (Ct.Cl.).

land to the corporation for its fair market value of $100,000. To the corporation, the land will be inventory. For Sandra, it had been a capital asset, having been held for investment purposes since its purchase ten years previously for $20,000. If these events are viewed as two separate transactions, Sandra will have increased the basis of her investment in the corporation by $100,000 and realized a fully taxable capital gain of $80,000 ($100,000 – $20,000). The corporation's basis in the land will be $100,000. Thus, if the corporation were to sell the land for, say, $110,000, its income therefrom would be only $10,000 ($110,000 – $100,000).

Alternatively, if these events are collapsed into a single transaction, Sandra's payment and receipt of cash would be ignored. Instead, she would be viewed as having given a tract of land in exchange for ten shares of stock of a corporation that she already controls. Under this single-transaction view, Sandra would recognize no taxable capital gain, and the corporation's basis in the stock would be the same as her prior basis, $20,000. Thus, if the corporation were to sell the land for $110,000, its ordinary income would be $90,000 ($110,000 – $20,000).

Taxpayers are restricted to the actual legal forms of the transactions in which they engage, but the IRS has the option of employing the step-transaction doctrine. Thus, the lack of any time lapse between the two transactions effectively gives the IRS its choice as to which interpretation it wishes to follow.

TAX PLANNING ILLUSTRATIONS

Consider several other examples of tax planning that are found in today's tax practice. Usually, a tax planning technique manifests at least one of the planning goals as listed in Exhibit 12-5. The best techniques meet two or more of those goals.

Example 12-36 Albert contributes the maximum amount for the year to a §529 education plan for his daughter. No immediate deduction is allowed, but the earnings in the account never are taxed. Withdrawals similarly are excluded from gross income when they are used for education-related expenses. Result: *Avoiding statutory income.*

Example 12-37 Phil designates a portion of his monthly paycheck for medical and child care expenses. No payroll taxes are due on these amounts. Phil's employer reimburses him from these funds when it receives documentation from Phil that he incurred medical and babysitting expenses for the period. By using a "flexible spending plan" such as this one, Phil reduces his total tax liability and has more discretionary income for the year. Result: *Avoiding statutory income.*

Example 12-38 Mary Jane uses a depreciable asset in her business to generate net sales at a profit. The depreciation deductions shelter current sales income from tax, but because the tax basis of the asset is reduced accordingly, there is a greater gain computed when Mary Jane sells or retires the income-producing asset. Result: *Postponing income recognition.*

Example 12-39 Judy keeps a log of her travels so that she can document that she is a resident of Texas, not New York. As a result, Judy's state income tax liability is reduced significantly every year. Result: *Changing tax jurisdictions.*

Example 12-40   Because she is a citizen of the Cayman Islands and not the United States, Ingrid is subject to very low marginal estate and gift tax rates on her extensive portfolio and collectible holdings. Result: *Changing tax jurisdictions.*

Example 12-41   Fizzy Corporation holds some vacant land for potential expansion of its operating plant. By paving asphalt over the land and turning it into a parking lot, charging its executives a nominal fee so that they can park closer to their offices, Fizzy converts portfolio gain into passive income, which frees up deductions now suspended under the passive activity rules. Such passive income is taxed, however, only when Fizzy unilaterally decides to sell the vacant land. Result: *Controlling income classification. Postponing income recognition.*

Example 12-42   Ralph forms a partnership that borrows money and purchases an office building in Texas, which is the home state of none of the partners. The entity passes through net operating losses, made up chiefly of interest and depreciation deductions, which the partners use to offset their passive income from other sources. When the building is sold, state and local income and property taxes are relatively low under Texas law. Result: *Avoiding statutory income. Postponing income recognition. Changing tax jurisdictions. Controlling the classification of income. Spreading income among related taxpayers.*

Example 12-43   Carolyn sets up a charitable lead trust, under which the museum receives the trust's distributable net income for fifteen years. Carolyn receives an immediate charitable contribution deduction, equal to the present value of the income stream that she has transferred to the museum. Then, the income-producing property of the trust is deeded to Carolyn's daughter, thereby likely deferring any estate tax on the property for another twenty-five years. Result: *Avoiding statutory income. Postponing income recognition (and transfer tax). Spreading income among related taxpayers.*

Example 12-44   George renovates a downtown warehouse and turns it into condos and apartments. Because the building has some historic significance, George undertakes the rehabilitation so as to maximize his state and Federal tax credits for rehabilitation expenditures. Result: *Controlling income classification. Avoiding statutory income (creating tax credits).*

Example 12-45   Richie makes certain that he makes gifts every year of $12,000 to each of his relatives, thereby using the entire statutory annual gift tax exclusion. Result: *Avoiding statutory income (using transfer tax exclusions). Spreading income among related taxpayers.*

SUMMARY

The study of taxes can be viewed as an examination of various ways to optimize one's tax liability. Tax rules that otherwise might seem as dry as a mouthful of sawdust have a way of becoming interesting, stimulating, and challenging when one realizes their economic significance and the resulting implications on human behavior. Tax optimization, therefore, can be viewed both as the heart of professional tax work and as the most important aspect of taxation for nontax specialists.

TAX TUTOR

Reinforce the tax research information covered in this chapter by completing the online tutorials located at the *Federal Tax Research* web site: **http://academic .cengage.com/taxation/raabe**

KEY WORDS

By the time you complete this chapter, you should be comfortable discussing each of the following terms. If you need additional review of any of these items, return to the appropriate material in the chapter or consult the glossary to this text.

Average tax rate
Effective average tax rate
Marginal tax rate
Nominal average tax rate

Progressive tax rates
Proportional tax rate
Regressive tax rates
Tax awareness

EXERCISES

1. Using the following codes, identify the basic approach(es) to tax avoidance that are used in each of the cases described below.

   Av = Avoiding income recognition

   Cl = Controlling the classification of income or expenditure

   Ju = Changing tax jurisdictions

   Po = Postponing income recognition

   Sp = Spreading income among related taxpayers

   None = None of the above

   a. Albert invests his savings in tax-exempt state bonds.
   b. Betty invests in nondividend-paying corporate stocks by using borrowed funds.
   c. Chuck lends $100,000 to his daughter on an interest-free demand note.
   d. Doris lends $10,000 to her son on a five-year note, bearing interest at the annual rate of 65 percent.
   e. Ed invests $100,000 of his savings in a home for his own use.
   f. Frankie invests in a mutual fund that purchases only the indebtedness of the state in which he lives.
   g. Grace invests in a mutual fund that purchases only the shares of U.S. corporations that pay no dividends, but whose share prices increase in value over a five-year time period.

2. Using the codes from Exercise 1, identify the basic approach(es) to tax avoidance that are used in each of the cases described below.

   a. Annie invests in a mutual fund that purchases only the shares of Colonnia corporations, a country that has no tax treaty with the United States.
   b. Burt moves his manufacturing plant to Mexico. Mexico has a tax treaty with the United States, but its labor and utility rates are much lower than is the case where Burt's Ohio plant now operates.

   c. Cheryl moves her manufacturing plant to Allegro. Allegro has no tax treaty with the United States, and its labor and utility rates are much lower than is the case where Cheryl's Ohio plant now operates.

   d. Donna fails to report on her tax return the interest earned on her savings account.

   e. Evelyn has her controlled corporation pay her a salary instead of a dividend during the current year.

   f. Flip operates his business as a regular corporation because of his high marginal tax rate. He plans to sell the corporation in five years.

   g. Georgia grows most of her own food instead of taking a second job.

3. With respect to the system of coding used in Exercises 1 and 2, create one new illustration in each tax planning category.

4. How do taxes fit into the general economic goals of most taxpayers?

5. How might a tax adviser ignoring the present value approach to tax planning arrive at an improper conclusion? Illustrate.

6. Give some examples of U.S. taxes that employ proportional, progressive, and regressive rate structures.

7. Give an example of a transaction between two taxpayers in which an inconsistent treatment is afforded the two taxpayers. Explain how related taxpayers might structure a transaction to take advantage of this inconsistency.

8. Give an example to show when a taxpayer might consider shifting income from the ordinary classification to capital.

9. Name two types of tax traps and give an example of each.

10. How does the typical tax practitioner divide his or her time among planning, compliance, research, and litigation?

11. What planning engagements can the tax professional offer? Why is he or she in an ideal position to offer these services?

12. Summarize the most important planning services that a tax professional can offer to a client.

13. Why does tax planning analysis focus on the marginal tax rate?

14. When might a taxpayer undertake transactions seemingly opposite to the usual tax planning principles?

15. Higher-income taxpayers tend to engage in tax planning more than do lower-income taxpayers. Why?

16. Is the objective of tax planning always to minimize taxes? Explain.

PROBLEMS

17. Examples 12–2 and 12–3 in the text concern a decision between the same two mutually exclusive alternatives under identical conditions, except for the

corporation's marginal tax rate. In Example 12-2, where the marginal tax rate was 40 percent, the conclusion was to accept Alternative A. In Example 12-3, where the marginal tax rate was 20 percent, the conclusion was to accept Alternative M.

Determine the marginal tax rate at which the two alternatives would be economic equivalents, that is, they would "break even" and generate the same excess after-tax payoff over after-tax cost. Your answer should be based on all of the conditions and assumptions as stated in Examples 12–2 and 12–3.

18. On creating a new 100 percent owned corporation, Ben was advised by his tax consultant to treat 50 percent of the total amount that was invested as a loan and 50 percent as a purchase of corporate stock. What tax advantage does this arrangement have over structuring the entire investment as a purchase of stock? Explain.

19. Julia currently is considering the purchase of some land to be held as an investment. She and the seller have agreed on a contract under which Julia would pay $1,000 per month for sixty months or $60,000 total. The seller, not in the real estate business, acquired the land several years ago by paying cash of $10,000. Two alternative interpretations of this transaction are (1) a price of $51,726 with 6 percent interest and (2) a price of $39,380 with 18 percent interest. Which interpretation would you expect each party to prefer? Why?

20. George, a high-bracket taxpayer, wishes to shift some of his own taxable income to his 25-year-old daughter, Debra, and is considering two alternative methods of doing so. One is to make a gift of the interest on some corporate bonds that he owns. The other is to make her a gift of the full principal amount of the bonds. Evaluate the pros and cons of each alternative.

21. Betty Smith has two sons, Bob and Jack. List several tax planning techniques that would allow Betty to transfer her full ownership in the family dry cleaning business to Bob and Jack, maximizing the wealth of all four taxpaying entities (Betty, Bob, Jack, and the company).

EXTENDED CASES

22. Should Ferris Corporation elect to forgo the carryback of its $60,000 year 2008 net operating loss? Ferris is subject to a 15 percent cost of capital. Corporate tax rates are as in IRC §11.

a.

Tax Year	Actual or Projected Taxable Income
2007	$700,000
2009	700,000

b.

Tax Year	Actual or Projected Taxable Income
2007	$ 70,000
2009	700,000

c.

Tax Year	Actual or Projected Taxable Income
2007	$ 70,000
2009	(70,000)
2010	(70,000)
2011	(70,000)
2012	700,000

23. Should Harris Corporation accelerate gross income into 2009, its first year subject to the AMT? Harris is subject to a 14 percent cost of capital. The corporate AMT rate is a flat 20 percent, and Harris exceeds the annual AMT exemption phase out.

a.

Tax Year	Actual or Projected Taxable Income
2010	Regular Tax $700,000
2011	Regular Tax $700,000

b.

Tax Year	Actual or Projected Taxable Income
2010	AMT $700,000
2011	Regular Tax $700,000

c.

Tax Year	Actual or Projected Taxable Income
2010	AMT $700,000
2011	AMT $700,000
2012	AMT $700,000
2013	AMT $700,000
2014	Regular Tax $700,000

24. Paris Corporation holds a $100,000 unrealized net capital gain. Should Paris accelerate the recognition of this gain, given a net capital loss carryforward in each of the following amounts? Paris is subject to a 14 percent cost of capital. Its marginal tax rate is 40 percent.

   a. $40,000

   b. $10,000

   c.   Repeat parts a and b, but assume that Paris is subject to a 6 percent cost of capital

25. Maris Corporation put into service $100,000 of equipment that qualifies for its state's 10 percent research credit. To the extent that the credit is claimed, no cost recovery deductions are allowed. Maris is subject to a 14 percent cost of capital. If the credit were not claimed, the property would qualify for cost recovery deductions using a three-year life, straight line with no salvage value, and a half-year convention. The state's flat income tax rate is as follows.

   a.   2 percent

   b.   4 percent

   c.   8 percent

CHAPTER 13

Working with the IRS

Learning Objectives

- Understand the organizational structure of the IRS and administrative procedures relative to the audit and appeals process.

- Advise clients as to audit selection factors and probable litigation success.

- Develop decision guidelines as to audit etiquette, working through the appeals system, and constructing taxpayer defenses.

Chapter Outline

WE HAVE DISCUSSED VARIOUS aspects of tax practice throughout this text, including both the principles of tax research and the structure of the judicial decision-making process. In this chapter, we will examine in more detail the workings of the **Internal Revenue Service** (IRS) and the **Treasury Department**, with an eye on an overview of the elections and other opportunities and pitfalls that face the practitioner in working with these administrative bodies.

After all, when the researcher has decided that his or her client should prevail with respect to a specified tax issue, a challenge to the IRS must be issued and implemented. In this chapter, we present some of the procedural aspects of this course of action.

ORGANIZATION OF THE IRS

The Department of the Treasury is responsible for administering and enforcing the internal revenue laws of the United States. However, most revenue functions and authority have been delegated by the Secretary of the Treasury to the **Commissioner of Internal Revenue**. The Commissioner is the chief executive officer of the IRS and is appointed by the President of the United States. The Commissioner holds the responsibility for overall planning and for directing, coordinating, and controlling the policies and programs of the IRS.

The IRS is one of about a dozen bureaus within the Department of the Treasury. It was established by Congress on July 1, 1862, to meet the fiscal needs of the Civil War. At that time, the name of the agency was the Bureau of Internal Revenue. In 1953 the name was changed to the IRS.

Since 1962 the agency has undergone a period of steady growth as the means for financing government operations shifted from the levying of import duties on outsiders to one of internal taxation on U.S. citizens and businesses. This expansion increased substantially after 1913 with the ratification of the Sixteenth Amendment, which authorized the modern income tax on noncorporate entities.

Until 1951 the agency was organized on a type-of-tax basis (i.e., with income, alcohol and tobacco, etc., divisions), with jurisdictionally separate departments that were responsible for administering these different revenue sources. Since 1952 the agency has undergone five major reorganizations, including one in 1998 aimed at reengineering the organization. The most important aspects of these structuring exercises have been the reorganization of the IRS along functional lines (i.e., into administration, operations, technical, planning, and inspection divisions), and the abandonment of the system of political appointments to positions other than that of the Commissioner and the Chief Counsel.

The latest restructuring effort was initiated as a response to perceived abuses by the agency. Recognizing that most Commissioners serve only a short tenure and that the Treasury Department carries myriad duties, Congress wants to use third parties to improve the chances for the development of consistent long-term IRS strategies and priorities. Private sector input is provided through the **IRS Oversight Board**, which functions as part of the Treasury Department. The Board has no authority to affect tax policy, to intervene in IRS personnel or procurement matters, or to affect the processing of individual tax cases. Its major duties include the following.[1]

- Review and approve IRS mission, strategic plans, and annual planning documents.

---

[1] §7802.

- Review IRS operational functions, including modernization, outsourcing, and training efforts.

- Recommend to the President candidates for Commissioner.

- Review the process of selecting, evaluating, and compensating senior IRS executives.

- Review and approve the IRS annual budget request.

- Ensure the proper treatment of taxpayers.

The Board is designed to function like a corporate board of directors. It is made up of six members of the private sector, appointed to five-year terms by the President, and of the Treasury Secretary, the IRS Commissioner, and a representative of IRS employees.

SPOTLIGHT ON TAXATION

Observation

It is difficult to obtain a proper balance in setting strategic and operational goals for the IRS, given its sometimes conflicting missions of compliance, enforcement, education, and customer service. So many tax returns are filed that a customer-friendly approach seems right; however, since "a little" cheating on returns is allowable under societal norms, a "get tough attitude" might be needed by the IRS.

IRS National Office

The IRS processes about 135 million Forms 1040 every year, about 80 million of which are filed electronically. It collects almost $2.5 trillion in tax revenues and pays refunds to about 110 million taxpayers every year, about 70 percent of which are deposited directly into taxpayer bank accounts. Today, the IRS is an organization of about 90,000 employees. With the exception of the Departments of Defense and Homeland Security, it is the largest agency of the Federal government. It consists of a national office in Washington, D.C., and a large decentralized field organization. Its current mission statement is as follows, reflecting the more aggressive enforcement orientation that the agency now has implemented.

Provide America's taxpayers top quality service by helping them understand and meet their tax responsibilities and by applying the tax law with integrity and fairness to all.

Guiding Principles

- Understand and solve problems from taxpayers' point of view.

- Enable IRS managers to be accountable to taxpayers.

- Use balanced measures of performance to measure taxpayer satisfaction, business results, and our employees' satisfaction.

- Foster open, honest communications.

- Insist on total integrity.

Exhibit 13-1: IRS National Office (Selections)

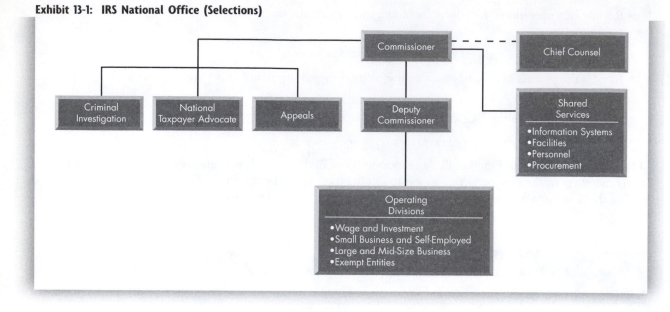

Strategic Plan Goals

- Improve taxpayer service

- Enhance enforcement of the tax law

- Modernize the IRS through its people, processes, and technology

Exhibit 13-1 illustrates that the IRS is organized to facilitate both the processing of tax returns and the carrying out of its broader goals, using a "shared services" model like that used by most large businesses.

The IRS's national office is located in the District of Columbia. It is staffed by the office of the Commissioner of Internal Revenue, which includes a Deputy Commissioner and various chief officers and assistants to the Commissioner. The IRS Commissioner is appointed by the President to a renewable five-year term. He or she is the chief executive officer of the agency and is charged to administer, manage, conduct, direct, and supervise the execution of the Federal tax laws.[2] The Commissioner's nomination is reviewed by the Senate. He or she advises the President as to the person who should be named Chief Counsel. The Commissioner is the agency's final authority as to the interpretation of tax law.

The **Chief Counsel** is the agency's highest ranking legal adviser. He or she is appointed by the President and reports to the Commissioner, relative to the administration and enforcement of the tax laws. In effect, the Chief Counsel is the IRS's attorney. Rulings and other written determinations are prepared by the Chief Counsel's office.[3] The Chief Counsel represents the agency in Tax Court cases and often assists in preparing proposed legislation, treaties, regulations, and executive orders. Associate Chief Counsels are assigned duties relative to litigation, technical matters, international transactions, and finance and management.

The **National Taxpayer Advocate** administers a taxpayer-intervention system, which is designed to resolve a wide range of tax administration problems that

---

[2] §7803(a).
[3] §7803(b).

Exhibit 13-2: IRS Operating Divisions

Tax Year 2000 estimates	Wage and Investment	Small Business and Self-Employed	Large and Mid-Size Businesses (Assets >$5 million)	Exempt Entities (Charities, Retirement Plans, Governments)
Type of return filed	1040 with only wage and investment income (no Schedules C, E, F, or Form 2106)	1040 Schedules C and F, Forms 1120, 1120S, and 1065	1040 Schedules C and F, Forms 1120, 1120S, and 1065	Form 990 and 1120, various payroll forms
Number of Filers	90 million, 116 million taxpayers	45 million	210,000	3 million entities, 1.9 million pay tax
Annual Income Tax Liabilities	$265 billion	$816 billion	$466 billion	$94 billion
Payroll Taxes Withholdings Paid	$38 billion	$562 billion	$712 billion	$198 billion
Notes	Fewer than half use a paid tax preparer	Pay in over 40% of all cash received by the IRS	Further organized into industry segments to handle complex filing requirements	Control about $10 trillion in assets
	Only 2% earn >$100,000 per year, 85% earn <$50,000, 28% earn <$10,000	4–60 annual transactions with the IRS	About 10% are audited every year, some deal with IRS agents year-round	

are not remedied through the agency's normal operating procedures or administrative channels.[4] The Advocate reports directly to the Commissioner and works through a system of local Taxpayer Advocates, one of which is located in each state.

The operating divisions of the IRS reflect the major types of tax return that the agency processes. Exhibit 13-2 outlines the workload of each operating division.

The IRS also takes on national-level projects in working with taxpayers. Some of the most important of these recent initiatives include the following.

- Document matching, allowing a lower audit rate because deficiencies or refunds are sent out when data listed on a tax return does not match that on a corresponding source document, like a Form 1099 or W-2.

- Electronic filing, again to reduce error rates and improve compliance with the filing requirements and to enact a modernization of the agency's data processing functions.

---
[4]§7803(c).

- Extending the reach of the Earned Income Credit to more of the targeted low-income employees.

- Educating cash- and tip-oriented workers to comply fully with their filing requirements.

IRS Service Centers

The first **Internal Revenue Service Center** was established in 1955 in Kansas City on a pilot basis. Additional service centers were established during the 1960s to meet the processing needs of the various geographic regions of the country. A few were redeployed after 2000 to reflect the increase in electronic filing. Today, IRS service centers are located at:

- Andover, MA

- Atlanta, GA

- Fresno, CA

- Kansas City, MO

- Memphis, TN

- Philadelphia, PA

The primary function of the service centers is to process and perform mathematical verifications of the massive volume of Federal tax returns. **Computing Centers**, located in Detroit; Martinsburg, WV; and Memphis, manipulate data collected from tax returns at **Processing Centers** in Austin, Cincinnati, Kansas City, and Ogden. About twenty-five **Customer Service Sites** deal with telephone and electronic contacts from taxpayers, in working with electronic filing of returns, and in answering telephone and online taxpayer inquiries.

SPOTLIGHT ON TAXATION

Observation

More closings and downsizing of IRS processing facilities will be called for in the future, to better manage the agency's cost structure as electronic filing and deposits become the norm. Resisting these redeployments surely will be the personnel unions associated with IRS employees, attempting to slow down technology and protect their jobs, much as did those in print publishing before the document processing revolution was brought about by copy machines, faxes, and computers.

Taxpayer Assistance Orders

The National Taxpayer Advocate can issue a **Taxpayer Assistance Order** (TAO) to suspend, delay, or stop actions where, in the determination of the Advocate, the taxpayer is suffering or about to suffer a significant hardship as a result of the manner in which the IRS is administering the revenue laws.[5] "Hardships" refer to any circumstance that includes an immediate threat of adverse action for the taxpayer,

---

[5] §7811.

his or her irreparable injury, a delay of more than thirty days in settling the taxpayer's account, or the incurring of significant costs (such as professional advisory fees) to handle the dispute.[6] The IRS action that is the subject of a TAO must be such that it would offend one's sense of fairness, given all the related facts.

Typically, the TAO requires remedial actions, such as a release from the IRS's levy of specific property or the cessation of a collection activity, or it gives the IRS a deadline for action. A TAO is binding on the IRS, short of its rescission by the Advocate, the Commissioner, or a Deputy Commissioner.

A taxpayer applies for a TAO by filing Form 911, Request for Taxpayer Advocate Service Assistance, reproduced as Exhibit 13-3.

Local Taxpayer Advocates

The IRS uses local Taxpayer Advocates in a system designed to help resolve taxpayer problems or complaints that are not being satisfied through regular agency channels. The primary objective of the Advocate system is to provide taxpayers with a representative within the IRS who has access to the pertinent regional, district, or service center official. In addition, the program enables the IRS to identify its own organizational, procedural, and systematic problems and to take corrective action as needed.

The system is not intended to circumvent the existing IRS channels of managerial authority, established administrative procedures, and formal avenues of appeal. Rather, it is designed to ensure that taxpayer problems or complaints that have not been resolved adequately through such normal procedures are referred and controlled within the program. When a case is referred to a member of the National Taxpayer Advocate team, he or she will ensure that the problem is not lost or overlooked, and that it is resolved as promptly and efficiently as is possible. If a case cannot be resolved within five working days after receipt of the statement of the problem or complaint, the taxpayer is contacted by telephone, advised of the status of the case, and given the name and telephone number of the IRS employee who is responsible for the resolution of the problem. Typically, the Advocate system is used to resolve billing, procedural, computer-generated, and other problems that taxpayers cannot correct after one or more contacts with the IRS office that is handling the matter.

The National Taxpayer Advocate works through local team members who are responsible for the work that is conducted within his or her jurisdiction. Local Advocates are independent from IRS examination, collection, and appeals functions. They are responsible only to the National Taxpayer Advocate.

TAXPAYER RIGHTS

Under three incarnations of the so-called *Taxpayer Bill of Rights*, taxpayers are guaranteed various rights to representation before the IRS, a recording of any proceedings, and an IRS explanation of its position relative to the pertinent disagreement. Specifically, the taxpayer has a right to know why the IRS is requesting information, exactly how the IRS will use the information it receives, and what might happen if the taxpayer does not submit the requested information. Accordingly, prior to an initial audit or collection interview, an IRS employee or officer must explain, orally or in written form, the pertinent aspects of the procedures to come.[7]

---

[6] §7811(a)(2).
[7] §7521(b)(1).

Exhibit 13-3: Application for Hardship Relief—Concluded

OMB No. 1545-1504

Department of the Treasury - Internal Revenue Service

Request for Taxpayer Advocate Service Assistance
(And Application for Taxpayer Assistance Order)

Form **911**
(Rev. 6-2007)

Section I – Taxpayer Information *(See Pages 3 and 4 for Form 911 Filing Requirements and Instructions for Completing this Form.)*

1a. Your name as shown on tax return	2a. Your Social Security Number
1b. Spouse's name as shown on tax return	2b. Spouse's Social Security Number

3a. Your current street address *(Number, Street, & Apt. Number)*

3b. City	3c. State *(or Foreign Country)*	3d. ZIP code

4. Fax number *(if applicable)*	5. E-mail address

6. Employer Identification Number *(EIN) (if applicable)*	7. Tax form(s)	8. Tax period(s)
9. Person to contact	10. Daytime phone number ☐ Check if Cell Phone	11. Best time to call

12. Indicate the special communication needs you require *(if applicable)*

☐ TTY/TDD Line   ☐ Interpreter - Specify language other than English *(including sign language)* _____

☐ Other *(please specify)*

13a. Please describe the tax problem you are experiencing *(If more space is needed, attach additional sheets.)*

13b. Please describe the relief/assistance you are requesting *(If more space is needed, attach additional sheets.)*

I understand that Taxpayer Advocate Service employees may contact third parties in order to respond to this request and I authorize such contacts to be made. Further, by authorizing the Taxpayer Advocate Service to contact third parties, I understand that I will not receive notice, pursuant to section 7602(c) of the Internal Revenue Code, of third parties contacted in connection with this request.

14a. Signature of Taxpayer or Corporate Officer, and title, if applicable	14b. Date signed
15a. Signature of spouse	15b. Date signed

Section II – Representative Information *(Attach Form 2848 if not already on file with the IRS.)*

1. Name of authorized representative	2. Centralized Authorization File (CAF) number
3. Current mailing address	4. Daytime phone number ☐ Check if Cell Phone
	5. Fax number
6. Signature of representative	7. Date signed

Section III – Initiating Employee Information

Taxpayer name			Taxpayer Identification Number *(TIN)*		
1. Name of employee	2. Phone number	3a. Function	3b. Operating division	4. Organization code no.	

5. How identified and received *(Check the appropriate box)*

IRS Function identified issue as meeting Taxpayer Advocate Service (TAS) criteria

☐ (r) Functional referral (Function identified taxpayer issue as meeting TAS criteria).

☐ (x) Congressional correspondence/inquiry not addressed to TAS but referred for TAS handling.
Name of Congressional Representative _____

Taxpayer or Representative requested TAS assistance

☐ (n) Taxpayer or representative called into a National Taxpayer Advocate (NTA) Toll-Free site.

☐ (s) Functional referral (taxpayer or representative specifically requested TAS assistance).

6. IRS received date

7. TAS criteria *(Check the appropriate box.* **NOTE:** *Checkbox 9 is for TAS Use Only)*

☐ (1) The taxpayer is experiencing economic harm or is about to suffer economic harm.
☐ (2) The taxpayer is facing an immediate threat of adverse action.
☐ (3) The taxpayer will incur significant costs if relief is not granted (including fees for professional representation).
☐ (4) The taxpayer will suffer irreparable injury or long-term adverse impact if relief is not granted.
☐ (5) The taxpayer has experienced a delay of more than 30 days to resolve a tax account problem.
☐ (6) The taxpayer did not receive a response or resolution to their problem or inquiry by the date promised.
☐ (7) A system or procedure has either failed to operate as intended, or failed to resolve the taxpayer's problem or dispute within the IRS.
☐ (8) The manner in which the tax laws are being administered raise considerations of equity, or have impaired or will impair the taxpayer's rights.
☐ (9) The NTA determines compelling public policy warrants assistance to an individual or group of taxpayers (**TAS Use Only**).

8. What action(s) did you take to help resolve the problem *(Must be completed by the initiating employee)*

9. State the reason(s) why the problem was not resolved *(Must be completed by the initiating employee)*

10. How did the taxpayer learn about the Taxpayer Advocate Service

A taxpayer may be represented by an attorney, CPA (certified public accountant), or other person who is permitted to represent a taxpayer before the IRS and who has obtained a properly executed power of attorney. Absent an administrative summons, a taxpayer cannot be required to accompany the representative to an interview.[8]

After meeting a ten-day notice requirement, the taxpayer is allowed to make a tape recording of the IRS interview, using the taxpayer's own equipment. Similarly, if the IRS intends to record an interview with a taxpayer or his or her representative, it must give a ten-day notice to the taxpayer. In addition, upon receiving a request from the taxpayer and a reimbursement for duplication costs, the IRS must make available to the taxpayer a transcript of the interview or a copy of its tape recording.[9]

To protect the rights of so-called innocent spouses on joint returns, the IRS must inform spouses of their joint and several liability for tax deficiencies, and both spouses must receive separately mailed notices as to audit, appeals, and Tax Court proceedings.[10] This may be especially important where the spouses have divorced or separated subsequent to filing the original joint return.

The Service must inform taxpayers of their rights to representation in carrying out a dispute with the agency. The taxpayer can suspend at any time an interview with IRS personnel so as to include a representative.[11]

With respect to noncriminal tax matters before the IRS or a federal court, the common law privilege of confidentiality exists between a taxpayer and his or her tax practitioner, that is, one who is authorized to practice before the IRS. The privilege exists with respect to tax advice the practitioner has rendered. These provisions extend existing privilege protection previously only applicable between a taxpayer and his or her attorney. The privilege does not exist with respect to dealings with tax shelters (see Chapter 5).

THE AUDIT PROCESS

The U.S. Federal income tax system is based primarily on an assumption of self-assessment. All persons with taxable incomes that exceed a specific amount are required to prepare an accurate statement of annual income (i.e., an income tax return) and to remit in a timely fashion any amount of tax that is due. In a somewhat paternalistic sense, the IRS uses the examination of returns as an enforcement device to promote such voluntary compliance with the internal revenue laws. In a manner that is somewhat similar to the treatment by a parent of a child who is considering some forbidden behavior, the threat of an IRS audit encourages many taxpayers to report accurately their taxable incomes and to pay any tax liability that remains outstanding.

Because only a small number of tax returns can be audited each year, the IRS attempts to select for examination only those returns that will generate additional revenues for the Treasury. It primarily relies on sophisticated statistical models and computer technology to identify those returns that possess the greatest revenue return for the agency's investment of audit resources. However, in addition to this scientific selection process, a number of returns are manually selected for examination at an examiner's discretion.

---

[8]§7521(c).
[9]§7521(a); Notice 89-51, 1989-1 CB 691.
[10]§6103(e)(1)(B).
[11]§7521(b)(2).

Preliminary Review of Returns

All business and individual tax returns are reviewed routinely by IRS personnel and computers for simple and obvious errors, such as the omission of required signatures and Social Security numbers. After this initial review, income tax returns are processed through the IRS Automatic Data Processing (ADP) program.

One of the most important functions performed by the ADP program is the matching of the information recorded on a return with corresponding data received from third parties, for example, from an employer on Form W-2. This procedure, which is referred to as the Information Document Matching Program (IDMP), has uncovered millions of cases of discrepancies between the amount, say, of income that recipients have reported on tax returns and corresponding deductions or other information that has been transmitted by payors. In addition, the IDMP provides the IRS with a means by which to detect taxpayers who fail to file any return at all. In the typical year, about two million taxpayers are sent such failure-to-file inquiries as a result of the matching program.

ADP also is used to conduct the Service's Mathematical/Clerical Error Program. This process is designed to uncover relatively simple and readily identifiable problems that can be resolved easily through the mail.

Mathematical/Clerical Error Program   The Mathematical/Clerical Error Program is one of a number of special programs that are conducted by IRS computers. This program checks every return for mathematical errors, recomputes the tax due after properly applying the numbers that are included in the return, and summarily assesses any additional tax that is due or allows refunds or credits based on (previously) miscomputed deductions or credits. A summary assessment may be made concerning any deficiency that results from a mathematical or clerical error.[12] Consequently, the IRS need not send the taxpayer a formal notice of deficiency (i.e., a ninety-day letter, as discussed subsequently in this chapter) before the additional tax is assessed.

Above 5 percent of all paper filed returns show an error of this type. When a mathematical or clerical error is identified by the service center, the IRS mails the taxpayer a corrected tax computation and requests that he or she pay the additional tax within ten days of the date of the notice, or twenty-one days if the tax underpayment is less than $100,000. If the deficiency is paid within this period, no interest is charged on the underpayment. However, if the deficiency is not paid in a timely fashion, interest is imposed on the unpaid amount for a period that begins on the date of the notice and demand and ends on the date of payment.

A taxpayer may not petition the U.S. Tax Court with respect to a deficiency that results from a mathematical or clerical error. However, other administrative procedures will allow the taxpayer to contest the summary assessment without first paying the tax.

The IRS must give an explanation of the asserted error to the taxpayer. After receiving this explanation, the taxpayer has sixty days within which to request that the additional tax be abated. If a request for abatement is made, the assessment will be canceled automatically. However, the return is then identified for further examination if the taxpayer cannot justify satisfactorily or substantiate the figures that were included on the original return.

When an error results in a taxpayer overpayment of the tax, the IRS usually sends a corrected computation of the tax, together with a brief explanation of the error and a refund of the excess amount that was paid.

---

[12] §6213(b)(1).

The IRS does not consider such a contact that it makes with the taxpayer to be an examination. Therefore, a taxpayer who is contacted under the Mathematical/Clerical Error Program is not entitled to the administrative remedies that are available to taxpayers who are involved in a formal examination.

In addition to this testing of mathematical computations, the ADP program is useful for verifying one's compliance with estimated tax payment requirements. As a result of utilizing this system, the IRS has discovered that thousands of taxpayers have not been complying with the statutory estimated tax requirements, and that others collectively have been claiming millions of dollars in payments that actually never were made.

Unallowable Items Program   The IRS conducts another program that is similar to the Mathematical/Clerical Error Program called the Unallowable Items Program. Under this program IRS personnel question items that have been included on individual income tax returns that appear to be unallowable by law. These items may be identified manually or on their face by computer, and include such return elements as an overstatement of the standard deduction, a deduction of Social Security taxes paid, the claiming of an incorrect filing status, the deduction of Federal income taxes, or the deduction of lost (but not stolen) assets as a casualty loss.

If a return is identified as including an unallowable item, the IRS computes the seemingly necessary adjustment in taxes, and the taxpayer is notified by mail. Again, the IRS does not consider the contact that it makes with a taxpayer under the Unallowable Items Program to be an examination.[13] Consequently, it treats an adjustment in this circumstance as a correction of a mathematical or clerical error, and the taxpayer is not sent a formal notice of deficiency.

If the taxpayer is able to explain the questioned item adequately, the assessment is abated. However, the case will be continued as a correspondence or office audit if the taxpayer's response is deemed unsatisfactory.

SPOTLIGHT ON TAXATION

The Future

A new processing system, replacing the antiquated ADP system, is being phased in by the agency. Because the IRS's appropriation for computer improvements is perpetually inadequate given the growth in the number of taxpayers and the sophistication of some of the transactions reported, though, most believe that this system will be obsolete before it is fully implemented.

Selection of Returns for Examination

Each year the IRS determines the approximate number and types of returns that it intends to audit. The national office then prepares an audit plan to allocate its personnel to achieve the desired audit coverage. The primary goal of the IRS in selecting a return for examination is to review only those returns that will result in a satisfactory increase in the tax liability.

Computer and manual methods are used to select returns for examination. Computer programs select certain returns for examination, based on the potential

---

[13]Rev. Proc. 94-68, 1994-2 CB 803.

that exists for changes in the tax treatment of certain items on the return. Generally, this is done through the use of mathematical models, including correlations and discriminant functions. IRS personnel also manually select returns that they believe warrant special attention. The Service describes in nontechnical terms its selection procedures in its annual Publication 1. Selection criteria for audits are not disclosed by the Treasury.[14]

Although most of the initial IRS screening of the returns for audit is performed by computers, a more detailed selection procedure then is employed manually in the Examination Division of the local IRS office, where the classification staff ultimately selects those specific cases that will be examined. The number of returns that finally is selected by the staff is based on the examination resource (and other) capabilities of the respective offices.

Discriminant Function System   Once a return has been processed through the Service's ADP program, each return is rated by computer for its audit potential by means of a mathematical model, the **discriminant function formula** (DIF). This formula assigns numeric weights to certain (undisclosed by the IRS) return items, generating a composite score for the return. In this regard, the higher the DIF score, the greater the potential for a favorable-to-the-Treasury change to the return upon audit. Statistics provided by the Commissioner show a high correlation between DIF scores and such tax modifications, but the specifics of the formula are not disclosed.[15]

When the computer selects a return that has a high probability for an adjustment, as indicated by a high DIF score, an employee at the service center manually inspects the return to confirm its audit potential. If an acceptable explanation for the DIF score cannot be found after this manual examination of the return and its attachments, including explanatory data that the computer did not consider, the return is forwarded to the Examination Division at the appropriate local IRS office.

National Research Program   The National Research Program (NRP) is an initiative that is designed to furnish the IRS with statistics concerning the type and number of errors that are made on a representative sample of individual income tax returns. These statistics are used to develop and update the DIF formulas. Under the annual NRP procedures, perhaps 15,000 individual income tax returns are selected randomly for an extremely thorough examination. These returns then are examined comprehensively to determine the degree of their accuracy as filed.

Unlike the treatment that is given returns that are selected for general audit, the NRP examiner may not exercise any judgment in dealing with an item on the return selected for review. All errors are noted and corrected, regardless of their amount. This procedure is necessary to a determination of the actual error patterns that individual income tax returns exhibit, so that the statistics that underlie the DIF procedure are free from any major bias.

NRP audits integrate IRS data files with some of those from the Social Security Administration and the Census Bureau. Some of the NRP audits are transparent to the taxpayer, that is, all of the work is done with computer models and IRS personnel, and the taxpayer does not even know that the audit is being conducted. Most of the rest of the procedures require correspondence by mail with the taxpayer, with no in-person contact required. Those whose returns are audited and

---

[14]§6103(b)(2); Long v. U.S., 742 F2d 1173 (CA-9, 1984).
[15]Feltz v. IRS, 79 AFTR2d 97-747 (DCWWis).

require such in-person contact, though, likely will need professional assistance to meet the IRS data and documentation demands.

Areas of specific concern in the latest rounds of the NRP audits are not publicly known, but the following tax issues likely receive special attention in constructing the DIF scores through this program.

- Determining the basis of capital assets sold, especially for closely held stock and mututal fund shares.

- Transactions involving cash exchanges.

- Taxpayers and their income that is not subject to withholding procedures.

- S corporations, partnerships, LLCs, LLPs, and their owners.

- Self-employed individuals.

Other Selection Methods   In addition to the previously discussed computerized methods for identification of returns for IRS examination, returns may be selected manually, for a variety of reasons. An examination may be initiated, for instance, because of information that is provided by an informant or because the selected return is linked to another return that is currently under examination, using the Coordinated Industry Case Program (e.g., a partner's return may be selected as a result of a partnership audit).

Moreover, some returns automatically are reviewed by IRS personnel because the reported taxable income, gross receipts, or total assets exceed a predetermined materiality amount. For instance, individual returns with total positive income of $50,000 or more, or partnership returns with gross receipts or gross income of $500,000 or more, can be selected in this manner. Finally, a return may be selected for examination because the taxpayer has filed a claim for refund or otherwise has indicated that an adjustment in the original amount of tax liability is necessary.

"Economic reality" factors can be considered by the IRS in selection of returns for audit, but only where the agency has some other evidence that the taxpayer has underreported taxable income for the year. For instance, manual selection of a return and an economic-reality review might occur when an IRS employee, reviewing data in three-filing-year periods, finds indications that income might be underreported or deductions might be overstated or misclassified. Some of the factors believed to be perused in an economic reality audit include the following.

- Significant increases in interest, dividend, and other investment income.

- Significant decreases in mortgage and other reportable interest paid.

- Significant variance in self-employment or farming income during the period, relative to industry norms.

- Business and other expenditures not seemingly justified by income levels.

Current IRS audit initiatives also include the following.

- Frivolous returns, usually involving tax protestors.

- Tax shelter investors and their advisers.

- Exempt organizations, looking for compliance with disclosure rules and for unrelated business taxable income.

- Large corporations.

- Executive compensation, including options and other noncash transfers.

- Offshore transactions.

- High-income individuals.

- Nonfilers.

- Specific issues related to market segments, often specialized in the local area; for example, software companies on the West Coast.

Chances of Audit   Taxpayers often want to know what their overall probability of selection for an audit might be for a given year. In general, the IRS selects about 1 percent of all returns for examination, outside of the mathematical error program. The chances for selection increase, though, if the taxpayer:

- claims tax shelter losses;

- operates a cash-oriented business, such as a restaurant (both as an owner, selling food and drink for cash, and as a waiter, collecting tips) or repair/construction trade;

- claims business deductions that are excessive for the income level;

- has had prior-year returns that were audited and found incorrect; or

- claims itemized deductions that are excessive for the income level.

The probabilities of selection for audit in a recent tax year were as shown in Exhibit 13-4.

EXAMINATIONS

After a return is selected for audit, an IRS agent schedules it for a review in either a correspondence, an office interview, or a field examination. The type of examination to which the taxpayer is subject generally is determined by the audit potential of the return, the nature of the asserted error, and the type of taxpayer.

Correspondence Examinations

Many times, IRS personnel question only one or two items on a selected return. In these cases, an examination is typically conducted by telephone or mail. The IRS examiner requests that the taxpayer verify the questioned item of income, deduction, or credit by mailing copies of receipts, canceled checks, or other documentation to the district office or service center. If the taxpayer requests an interview, the issues become too complex, or the taxpayer is unable to communicate effectively in writing, the case is referred to the appropriate district office for resolution as an office or field examination.

Local office personnel usually conduct **correspondence examinations**. However, service center staff often conduct such a review if the questioned item is an itemized deduction on an individual taxpayer's income tax return.

A taxpayer who is subject to a correspondence examination is entitled to the same administrative and judicial appeal rights that are allowed to persons who are involved in office or field audits.

Issues that typically are addressed in the correspondence audit setting include itemized deductions for interest, taxes, charitable contributions, medical expenses, and simple miscellaneous deductions such as union dues.

Exhibit 13-4: Various Audit Statistics

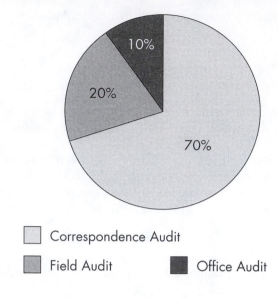

- ☐ Correspondence Audit
- ☐ Field Audit
- ■ Office Audit

Individuals' returns filed	135,000,000	
Individuals' returns audited	1,300,000	about 1% of filed returns
Correspondence audits	1,000,000	

Chances of Audit

Individual's Income ($000)	Nonbusiness Returns	With Schedule C
0–25	1.5%	3.8%
25–100	0.6	2.1
100+	1.3	3.9
C Corporation, assets		
$0–250K		0.7%
$250K–5M		1.0
$5–10M		3.4
$10M–250M		13.8
$250M+		35.2
S Corporation		0.4
Partnership		0.4
Gift Tax		0.8
Estate Tax, Gross Estate ($M)		
0–5		7.8
5+		23.4
Average proposed tax and penalty assessment, individuals' returns		
Correspondence audit		$7,800
Field audit		18,000
"No change" audit report		
Correspondence audit, individuals' return		17%
Field audit, individuals' return		14
C Corporation return		3

Office Examinations

When a return that has been selected for examination involves one or more issues that will require some analysis and the exercise of the IRS personnel's judgment, rather than a mere verification of record-keeping requirements, the audit usually is conducted at the pertinent IRS office. An office interview also will be scheduled if the examiner believes that an office examination is necessary to guarantee that the taxpayer's legal rights are respected.

If the IRS decides to conduct an office examination, the taxpayer is asked to come to the local IRS office for an interview and to bring any records and documents that support the questioned items. Generally, the auditor is given very little time in which to prepare for the session, and the scope of the examination is limited to the items that are listed in the audit notification letter.

Office audits usually are confined to individuals' income tax returns that include no business income. However, in recent years, the IRS has increased the scope of some office audits to include a limited number of small business returns. Issues that typically are examined in an office audit setting include dependency exemptions; income from tips, rents, and royalties; income from partnerships, estates, and trusts; deductions for travel and entertainment; deductions for bad debts; and casualty and theft losses.

A field examination may be conducted in lieu of an office audit if it is difficult for the taxpayer to bring the requested records to the district office or if the taxpayer for some other valid reason requests that the audit be conducted on his or her premises.

Field Examinations

Examinations that present complex issues that require more advanced knowledge of the internal revenue laws and accounting skills usually are conducted on the taxpayer's premises. A **field audit** is more comprehensive than a correspondence or office audit, and it usually is limited to an examination of corporation and individual business returns. In a field examination, the revenue agent reviews completely the entire financial operations of the taxpayer, including the business history of the taxpayer; the nature, amount, and location of taxpayer assets; the nature of the business operations; the extant accounting methods and system of internal control; and other financial attributes of the entity.

While an office audit ordinarily is limited to the items that are specified in the audit notification letter, a field examination may be open-ended. The agent is free to pursue any unusual items that are recorded in the tax return(s) or the records of the taxpayer (i.e., journals, ledgers, and worksheets) and to investigate other areas of which he or she may be suspicious.

The IRS prefers to conduct the field audit on the taxpayer's premises because the taxpayer's books and records may be more accessible and the agent is better able to observe the taxpayer's business facilities and the scope of its operations. However, it is sometimes possible to have the audit conducted at the office of the taxpayer's representative instead. Only one such inspection of taxpayer books and records may be made for a tax year.[16] The Code includes a broad set of restrictions as to access to the taxpayer's physical office by the IRS.[17] Taxpayers refusing to admit IRS personnel are subject to a $500-per-refusal fine.[18]

---

[16] §7605(b).
[17] §7606.
[18] §7342.

The IRS uses a team approach in its field audits, known as the Coordinated Examination Program, when it examines the returns of large corporate taxpayers. During this type of examination, a large group of IRS agents is used to investigate the operations of the taxpayer. Normally, such an investigation spans more than one IRS district as well.

Dealing with an Auditor

Most practitioners develop over time a list of "dos and don'ts" in negotiating with a government auditor. In the very best case, one will have dealt with the same auditor many times and will have become familiar with the nuances of that particular auditor's mode of operation. Whether this is the case or not, the following guidelines, dictated as much by common courtesy and decorum as by ethics and hard-core negotiating techniques, are likely to be useful.[19]

- Do conduct yourself courteously and professionally, showing that you have prepared yourself for the audit.

- Do review the strengths and weaknesses of your position before the agent arrives.

- Do cooperate with the auditor and promptly respond to all requests.

- Do establish internal timetables and responsibilities for completing the audit.

- Do provide the auditor with adequate work accommodations.

- Don't impede the audit process.

- Don't allow the auditor free access to and through the taxpayer's building.

- Don't let the agent browse through taxpayer information.

- Don't volunteer comments or information not requested by the agent.

- Don't attempt to bully or intimidate the auditor.

- Do assign one person to be the primary on-premises contact with the auditor— he or she cannot interview taxpayer employees on a random basis.

- Do verify the auditor's credentials before providing any information.

- Do request that all communications be in writing.

- Do keep track of time spent (by taxpayer, practitioner, and auditor) on the audit.

- Do meet at least daily with the auditor to review issues.

- Do agree to disagree on major irreconcilable issues.

- Do conduct a concluding conference to discuss audit recommendations.

- Do obtain copies of all government workpapers affecting the potential assessment.

- Do request clarification on the rest of the appeals process.

---

[19]Some of the material is adapted from a talk by Robert E. Dallman, Milwaukee WI, "The Audit Process."

Conclusion of Examination

Upon the conclusion of the examination, the IRS auditor or agent must explain to the taxpayer any proposed adjustments to the tax liability. A written **Revenue Agent's Report** (RAR) is prepared by the agent and is given to the taxpayer. The RAR contains a brief explanation of the proposed adjustments and lists the balance due or the overpayment.

The RAR also includes a waiver of the restrictions on assessment, which the taxpayer is asked to sign if he or she agrees with the proposed modifications. This waiver permits the IRS to assess any deficiency in tax immediately, without sending the taxpayer a formal notice of deficiency.

Even though the taxpayer may agree with the proposed adjustments to his or her return and sign the form, thereby indicating acceptance of the proposal, the case technically is not closed until the agent's report is reviewed and accepted by the district office review staff. Therefore, it is possible that an agreement that is worked out with the agent may not be accepted by the IRS.

After the taxpayer agrees to any increase in tax, he or she may either make an advance payment of the deficiency and accrued interest, to eliminate additional interest charges, or wait for a formal request for payment from the service center.

If the taxpayer disagrees with the agent's proposals, the IRS makes an immediate attempt to resolve the disagreement. The taxpayer normally is given an opportunity to discuss the proposed adjustments with the agent's group supervisor or with an appeals officer. If an immediate interview is not possible or if the issues remain unresolved after such an interview, the taxpayer receives a preliminary notice of deficiency, which is also referred to as a "thirty-day letter."

Thirty-Day Letter

When the taxpayer does not agree with the agent's proposed adjustments, a **thirty-day letter** is issued. This correspondence formally notifies the taxpayer of the examiner's findings, requests that the taxpayer agree to the proposed adjustments, and informs the taxpayer of his or her appeal rights. If the taxpayer does not respond to the notice within thirty days, he or she receives a statutory notice of deficiency, also known as a "ninety-day letter," discussed later in this chapter.

The taxpayer has thirty days from the date of the thirty-day letter to request a conference with an appeals officer. This request may be made orally with respect to an office examination or if the total proposed additional tax and penalties total $2,500 or less. The taxpayer's appeal must be in written form if the total proposed additional tax and penalties exceed $2,500,[20] and a formal protest, setting forth the specific facts and applicable law or other authority in support of the taxpayer's position, is required if the proposed tax and penalties exceed $10,000.[21]

[20]Reg. §§601.105(c)(2)(iii) and (d)(2)(iv).
[21]Reg. §§601.105(d)(2) and 601.106(a)(1)(ii).

File a Protest or Go Straight to Court?

In deciding whether to file a protest and request a hearing in the Appeals Office or to allow a ninety-day letter to be issued and skip directly to the courts for satisfaction, the taxpayer and his or her adviser must consider a number of factors.[22]

Factors in Favor of the Protest/Appeals Process

- An appeals officer can consider the hazards of litigation. This allows for the possibility of a settlement without the costs of litigation.

- The litigation path remains a possibility even if an appeal is pursued.

- The appeals process allows a further delay in the payment of the disputed tax. This can be an important criterion if (1) funds are not available with which to pay the tax, or (2) the taxpayer can earn more on the funds during the administrative period than is assessed in the form of interest.

- During the appeals process, the taxpayer will discover more of the elements of the government's position. In addition, the taxpayer gains additional time in which to formulate or polish his or her own position.

- Recovery of some court costs and attorney fees is available if the court finds that the government's case was largely unjustified and all administrative remedies were attempted. Thus, working through the appeals process is required if any costs are to be recovered.

Factors in Favor of Bypassing Appeals

- The likelihood of the government finding and raising new issues during the appeal is eliminated.

- The government receives a psychological message that the taxpayer is firmly convinced of his or her position, and negotiating advantages for the taxpayer may result.

- The conclusion of the dispute, whether for or against the taxpayer, is expedited.

THE APPEALS PROCESS

To minimize the costs of litigation in both time and money, the IRS encourages the resolution of tax disputes through an administrative appeals process. If a case cannot be resolved at the examination level, the taxpayer is allowed to appeal to a separate division of the IRS, known as the **Appeals Office**.

The Appeals Office has the exclusive and final authority to settle cases that originate in a district that is located within its jurisdiction. This division is under the supervision of the Commissioner of the IRS, with input from the Chief Counsel. The appeals function provides the taxpayer with a final opportunity to resolve tax disputes with the IRS without incurring litigation. Its objective is to resolve tax controversies without litigation on a basis that is fair and impartial to both the government and the taxpayer.

---

[22]Saltzman, IRS Practice and Procedure, Warren, Gorham & Lamont; ¶ 9.05(1).

Appeals Conference

The conference with the appeals officer is an informal proceeding. Although the appeals office may require allegations to be submitted in the form of affidavits or declarations under the penalty of perjury, testimony typically is not taken under oath.[23] The taxpayer, or his or her representative, meets with the appeals officer and discusses the dispute informally. According to the IRS's conference and practice rules, the appeals officer is to maintain a standard of strict impartiality toward the taxpayer and the government.

The appeals officer has the authority to settle all factual and legal questions that are raised in the examiner's report. He or she also can settle a tax dispute on the basis of the hazards of litigation. However, no settlement can be made that is based on the nuisance value of the case to the government.

The appeals officer may use a considerable amount of personal judgment in deciding how to handle the disputed issues of a case. He or she can split or trade issues where substantial uncertainties exist as to the law or the facts. On the other hand, the appeals officer may defer action on, or refuse to settle, a case or an issue to achieve greater uniformity concerning the application of the revenue laws and to improve the overall voluntary compliance with the tax laws.

Ninety-Day Letter

If the taxpayer and the IRS cannot agree on the proposed adjustments after an appeals conference, the regional director of appeals will issue a **statutory notice of deficiency**.[24] The statutory notice also is issued if the taxpayer does not request an appeals conference.

A statutory notice of deficiency, commonly referred to as a **ninety-day letter**, must be sent to the taxpayer's last known address by certified or registered mail before the IRS can assess the additional taxes that it believes are due.[25] Once a formal assessment has been made, the IRS is entitled to collect and retain the tax. However, a statutory notice is not required relative to deficiencies that result from mathematical errors or from the overstatement of taxes that were withheld or paid as estimated taxes.

After the statutory notice of deficiency is mailed, the taxpayer has 90 days (150 days if the letter is addressed to a taxpayer who is outside the United States) to file a petition with the U.S. Tax Court for a redetermination of the deficiency. If such a petition is not filed in a timely fashion, the deficiency is assessed and the taxpayer receives a notice and demand for payment of the tax.[26] Once this ninety-day period expires, the taxpayer cannot contest the assessment without first paying the tax, filing a claim for refund, and, if the claim is denied by the IRS, instituting a refund suit in a district court or the U.S. Court of Federal Claims.

Generally, no assessment or collection effort may be made during the ninety-day period, or, if a Tax Court petition is filed, until after the decision becomes final.

A mailing of the statutory notice to the taxpayer's last known address is sufficient to commence the running of the ninety-day period, unless the Commissioner has been notified formally of a change of address.[27] The statute does not require that the taxpayer receive actual notice; therefore, a notice that is sent by certified or

---

[23]Reg. §601.106(c).
[24]§7522.
[25]§§6212(a) and 6212(b)(1).
[26]§6213(c).
[27]§6212(b); McIntosh v. U.S., 85 AFTR2d 98-6501 (SDOh).

Exhibit 13-5: Income Tax Appeal Procedure

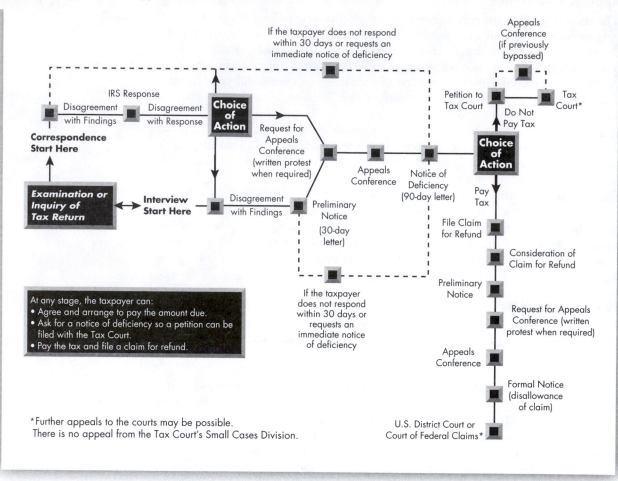

registered mail to the proper address is effective, even though it is never received by the taxpayer him- or herself.[28]

After a case has been scheduled (*docketed*) for review in the Tax Court, the taxpayer is invited to attend a pretrial settlement conference with an appeals officer and an IRS attorney. However, this conference typically is offered only if the case was not considered previously by the appeals office and if no related criminal prosecution is pending. If the taxpayer and the IRS agree to settle the dispute at this stage, they will enter into a written agreement stipulating the amount of any deficiency or overpayment. This stipulation is filed with the Tax Court, which will enter a decision in accordance with the agreement. The Tax Court can levy a penalty of up to $25,000 if it determines that the taxpayer did not pursue the available administrative remedies prior to approaching the court.[29]

Possibilities for appeal after completing the trial-level suit have been discussed in Chapters 2, 3, and 5. Exhibit 13-5 illustrates the appeals procedures, from the initial IRS examination to the hearing before the trial-level court. Exhibit 13-6 offers sample thirty- and ninety-day letters for the reader's perusal.

---

[28]§6212(a); *Lifter*, 59 T.C. 818 (1973), and *U.S. v. Ahrens*, 530 F.2d 781 (CA-8, 1976).
[29]§6673(a)(1)(c).

Exhibit 13-6: Sample Thirty- and Ninety-Day Letters

Notice of Adjustment—Thirty-Day Letter
Internal Revenue Service   Department of the Treasury
Date:
Social Security or Employee Identification Number:
Tax Year Ended:
Person to Contact:
Contact Telephone Number:
Contact Address:

Dear

Enclosed are two copies of our report explaining why we believe adjustments should be made in the amount of your tax. Please look this report over and let us know whether you agree with our findings.

If you accept our findings, please sign the consent to assessment and collection portion at the bottom of the report and mail one copy to this office within thirty days from the date of this letter. If additional tax is due, you may want to pay it now and limit the interest charge; otherwise, we will bill you. (See the enclosed Publication 5 for payment details.)

If you do not accept our findings, you have thirty days from the date of this letter to do one of the following:

1. Mail us any additional evidence or information you would like us to consider.

2. Request a discussion of our findings with the examiner who conducted the examination. At that time you may submit any additional evidence or information you would like us to consider. If you plan to come in for a discussion, please phone or write us in advance so that we can arrange a convenient time and place.

3. Discuss your position with the group manager or a senior examiner (designated by the group manager), if an examination has been held and you have been unable to reach an agreement with the examiner.

If you do not accept our findings and do not want to take any of the above actions, you may write us at the address shown above or call us at the telephone number shown above within thirty days from the date of this letter to request a conference with an Appeals Officer. You must provide all pertinent documentation and facts concerning disputed issues to the examiner before your case is forwarded to the Appeals Office. If your examination was conducted entirely by mail, we would appreciate your first discussing our findings with one of our examiners.

The Appeals Office is independent of the District Director. The Appeals Officer, who had not examined your return previously, will take a fresh look at your case. Most disputes considered by Appeals are resolved informally and promptly. By going to Appeals, you may avoid court costs (such as the U.S. Tax Court filing fee), clear up this matter sooner, and prevent interest from mounting. An Appeals Officer will promptly telephone you and, if necessary, arrange an appointment. If you decide to bypass Appeals and petition the Tax Court, your case will normally be assigned for settlement to an Appeals Office before the Tax Court hears the case.

Under Internal Revenue Code Section 6673, the Tax Court is authorized to award damages of up to $25,000 to the United States when a taxpayer unreasonably fails to pursue available administrative remedies. Damages could be awarded under this provision, for example, if the court concludes that it was unreasonable for a taxpayer to bypass Appeals and then file a

continued

Exhibit 13-6: (continued)

petition in the Tax Court. The Tax Court will make that determination based upon the facts and circumstances of each case. Generally, the Service will not ask the court to award damages under this provision if you make a good faith effort to meet with Appeals and to settle your case before petitioning the Tax Court.

The enclosed Publication 5 explains your appeal rights.

If we do not hear from you within thirty days, we will have to process your case on the basis of the adjustments shown in the examination report. If you write us about your case, please write to the person whose name and address are shown in the heading of this letter and refer to the symbols in the upper right corner of the enclosed report. An envelope is enclosed for your convenience. Please include your telephone number, area code, and the most convenient time for us to call, in case we find it necessary to contact you for further information.

If you prefer, you may call the person at the telephone number shown in the heading of this letter. This person will be able to answer any questions you may have. Thank you for your cooperation.

Sincerely yours,
IRS Examinations
Enclosures:
Examination Report (2)
Publication 5
Envelope

Notice of Deficiency—Ninety-Day Letter
Internal Revenue Service   Department of the Treasury
Date:
Social Security or Employer Identification Number:
Tax Year Ended and Deficiency:
Person to Contact:
Contact Telephone Number:

Dear

We have determined that there is a deficiency (increase) in your income tax as shown above. This letter is a NOTICE OF DEFICIENCY sent to you as required by law. The enclosed statement shows how we figured the deficiency.

If you want to contest this deficiency in court before making any payment, you have 90 days from the above mailing date of this letter (150 days if addressed to you outside of the United States) to file a petition with the U.S. Tax Court for a redetermination of the deficiency. To secure the petition form, write to U.S. Tax Court, 400 Second Street, NW, Washington, D.C. 20217. The completed petition form, together with a copy of this letter must be returned to the same address and received within 90 days from the above mailing date (150 days if addressed to you outside of the United States).

The time in which you must file a petition with the court (90 or 150 days as the case may be) is fixed by law and the court cannot consider your case if your petition is filed late. If this letter is addressed to both a husband and wife, and both want to petition the Tax Court, both must sign the petition or each must file a separate, signed petition.

If you dispute not more than $50,000 for any one tax year, a simplified procedure is provided by the Tax Court for small tax cases. You can get information about this procedure, as well as a petition form you can use, by writing to the Clerk of the Tax Court at 400 Second Street, NW, Washington, D.C. 20217. You should do this promptly if you intend to file a petition with the Tax Court.

You may represent yourself before the Tax Court, or you may be represented by anyone admitted to practice before the court. If you decide not to file a petition with the Tax Court, we would appreciate it if you would sign and return the enclosed waiver form. This will permit us to assess the deficiency quickly and will limit the accumulation of interest. The enclosed envelope is for your convenience. If you decide not to sign and return the statement and you do not timely petition the Tax Court, the law requires us to assess and bill you for the deficiency after 90 days from the above mailing date of this letter (150 days if this letter is addressed to you outside the United States).

If you have questions about this letter, please write to the person whose name and address are shown on this letter. If you write, please attach this letter to help identify your account. Keep the copy for your records. Also, please include your telephone number and the most convenient time for us to call, so we can contact you if we need additional information.

If you prefer, you may call the IRS contact person at the telephone number shown above. If this number is outside your local calling area, there will be a long distance charge to you.

You may call the IRS telephone number listed in your local directory. An IRS employee there may be able to help you, but the contact person at the address shown on this letter is most familiar with your case.

Thank you for your cooperation.

Sincerely yours,
Commissioner
By
Enclosures:
Copy of this letter
Statement
Envelope

Entering the Judicial System

If a taxpayer cannot resolve his or her dispute with the IRS administratively, he or she may seek judicial relief. As we have discussed throughout this text, the taxpayer can choose from among the U.S. Tax Court, the pertinent district court, and the U.S. Court of Federal Claims to initiate the lawsuit against the government.

The Tax Court will review the taxpayer's case, provided that he or she files a petition with the court within ninety days of the date of his or her statutory notice of deficiency. The district courts and the Court of Federal Claims cannot hear the taxpayer's case unless he or she is suing for a refund. Consequently, the taxpayer first must pay the disputed tax, and then file an (unsuccessful) claim for refund to obtain a judicial review in either of these latter two forums.

Deciding to Litigate

One should not consider tax litigation lightly. The additional costs to the taxpayer for attorney and accountant fees, in addition to filing and processing fees and the cost and time involved in gathering supporting documentation for the taxpayer's position, finding and coaching expert and other witnesses, and providing for one's own travel to the site of the hearing, make litigation a costly prospect. Given the right combination of facts and law, though, a suit might be the taxpayer's only chance to achieve an equitable solution.

Remember, nonetheless, that the IRS tends to litigate only cases that (1) it expects to win and (2) it expects will make good precedent to discourage other taxpayers. Moreover, because many taxpayers represent themselves before the Tax Court, procedural errors occur, usually to the detriment of the taxpayer. Thus, it is not surprising that the deck appears to be stacked against the taxpayer once he or she enters the judicial system, especially outside the Tax Court. The information in Exhibit 13-7 illustrates this situation.

Exhibit 13-7: Taxpayer and Government Victories in Tax Litigation

Forum	Percent of Partial Taxpayer Victories	Percent of Total Taxpayer Victories	Percent of Total Government Victories
U.S. Tax Court, Small Cases Division	49.0	5.0	46.0
U.S. Tax Court, all other	64.0	3.0	33.0
U.S. District Court	11.6	23.2	65.2
U.S. Court of Federal Claims	12.2	14.3	73.5

SUMMARY

In counseling clients, the tax professional must be aware of the organization and inner workings of the IRS. Strategic and tactical decisions as to how and when to appeal within the administrative system of the Service, assessing the strengths and weaknesses of the client's case, and determining available remedies can be made only with a thorough understanding of the agency and its operating style. Some of the most valuable advice that a client receives can be in the context of an audit selection letter or the handling of settlement alternatives thereafter.

TAX TUTOR

Reinforce the tax research information covered in this chapter by completing the online tutorials located at the *Federal Tax Research* web site: **http://academic.cengage.com/taxation/raabe**

KEY WORDS

By the time you complete this chapter, you should be comfortable discussing each of the following terms. If you need additional review of any of these items, return to the appropriate material in the chapter or consult the glossary to this text.

Appeals Office
Chief Counsel
Commissioner of Internal Revenue
Computing Centers
Correspondence examinations
Customer Service Sites
Discriminant function formula
Field audit
Internal Revenue Service
Internal Revenue Service Center

IRS Oversight Board
National Taxpayer Advocate
Ninety-day letter
Office audits
Processing Centers
Revenue Agent's Report
Statutory notice of deficiency
Taxpayer Assistance Order
Thirty-day letter
Treasury Department

DISCUSSION QUESTIONS

1. Why must the tax professional be cognizant of how tax law administration works?

2. What are the major functions of the national office of the IRS?

3. What are the chief responsibilities of
   a. The IRS Commissioner
   b. The IRS Chief Counsel
   c. The National Taxpayer Advocate
   d. Local Taxpayer Advocates

4. List three of the items included in one of the Taxpayer Bills of Rights.

5. Distinguish between the Math/Clerical Error program and the Unallowable Items program.

6. What are the chances of having a tax return audited this year?

7. What techniques other than the random selection of returns for audit does the IRS use in its enforcement function?

8. Why might it be desirable to settle with an agent, rather than to continue by appealing to a higher level within the IRS?

9. Relate some of the "audit etiquette" tactics that you have heard taxpayers or tax professionals discuss.

10. Which of the following methods is used to select tax returns for audit? More than one answer may be correct.
    a. DIF procedures
    b. Random samples
    c. Amount of gross income
    d. Type of income, for example, business or wages

11. Which type of audit is used most often to substantiate the reported items of income or deduction for individuals who have only wages?
    a. Field
    b. Office
    c. Correspondence
    d. Home

12. A revenue agent may do which of the following in an attempt to negotiate a settlement after the completion of an audit? More than one answer may be correct.
    a. Attempt to settle an unresolved issue based on the hazards of litigation.
    b. Settle a question of fact.
    c. Reach an agreement that will be accepted unconditionally by the IRS.
    d. Turn the case over to the Appeals Office.

13. When an agreement cannot be reached with a Revenue Agent, a letter is transmitted stating that the taxpayer has thirty days to do which of the following?
    a. File a suit in the U.S. Tax Court.
    b. Request an administrative appeal.
    c. Pay the tax.
    d. Find additional facts to support his or her position.

14. A statutory notice of deficiency gives the taxpayer ninety days to do which of the following?
    a. Pay the tax.
    b. Request an administrative appeal.
    c. File a suit in the U.S. Tax Court.
    d. File a protest.

15. Distinguish among the various means by which the IRS selects a tax return for examination. For this purpose, examine the criteria of:
    a. scope of review
    b. probability of selection
    c. preservation of taxpayer constitutional rights

16. Add two items to the "dos and don'ts" list included in the discussion of audit etiquette.

17. Suggest other information documents that the IRS computers could add to the IDMP.

18. Identify several items that you believe are included in the prevailing DIF model.

19. Carol takes some very aggressive positions on her tax return. She maintains, "With the downsizing of the government, my chances of getting caught are virtually zero." Is Carol's approach correct?

20. Should the IRS audit more or fewer returns every year? What issues would you consider in this regard if you were a politician? A wealthy individual?

21. What are the most important activities that the IRS currently is carrying out in its data collection and audit efforts?

EXERCISES

22. Make a chart that distinguishes among the various types of examinations that the IRS conducts relative to individual income tax returns, namely, office, correspondence, field, and NRP audits. For this purpose, examine the criteria of:
    a. scope of review
    b. type of documentation that typically is required of the taxpayer
    c. use of IRS personnel time and other resources
    d. opportunity for agent to use professional judgment in resolving issues

23. Respond to a client's comment: "We have a better than even chance of winning in the Tax Court, according to an article I read. Let's sue the government!"

24. With respect to the Small Cases Division of the U.S. Tax Court, which statement is true?
    a. The taxpayer (but not the IRS) can appeal a contrary judgment.
    b. The IRS (but not the taxpayer) can appeal a contrary judgment.
    c. Either the IRS or the taxpayer can appeal a contrary judgment.
    d. Neither the IRS nor the taxpayer can appeal a contrary judgment.

25. How should the tax professional advise a client whose charitable contributions are double that of the U.S. norm for his or her income level?

PROBLEMS

26. The President of the United States has hired you to assist in a trim-the-fat program with respect to the Federal government. The President has asked you to recommend specific steps to downsize the bureaucracy of the IRS, from the national office through the district headquarters, by 15 percent. Draft a memo to the President summarizing your recommendations. Augment your memo with diagrams supporting your proposals.

27. The IRS has issued a summons for the tax file held by CPA Ann Whitman for her clients the Harberts. The file consists of paper and electronic spreadsheets in which Whitman detailed some tax computations using assumptions that the IRS would find to be "too aggressive." In addition, the file includes notes from meetings with the Harberts, income and balance sheet data as to their personal assets, and other technical correspondence, including e-mail messages. In a memo to the tax research file, summarize the current status of the law as to whether the privilege of confidentiality protects these documents from the government.

RESEARCH CASES

28. Your supervisor says that the U.S. Constitution forces the IRS to reveal the make-up of the DIF formula that it uses to select tax returns for audit. Prepare a file memo assessing the supervisor's assertion.

29. Max and Annie are roommates sharing an apartment. Although they know each other well, they have respect for each other's privacy. Thus, when Max's 2003 Form 1040 was audited by the IRS, he made no mention of the audit to Annie. When Annie was clearing the answering machine that they shared, she heard the following message: "Max, this is Richard, the IRS auditor. My figures show that you owe the government $10,000 in taxes and another $4,500 in penalties and interest."

    When Annie brought up the message during dinner conversation that night, Max was furious. How could the IRS be so careless as to broadcast this news to a stranger? Didn't he have any privacy and confidentiality rights? Max calls you to determine whether he might have a case against the IRS or Richard, the agent. Prepare a file memo assessing Max's position.

30. You have just rendered service for a taxpayer as an expert witness in a case heard by the U.S. Tax Court. The taxpayer is requesting reimbursement for your fees and for those amounts paid to her attorney in presenting the case. Your billing rate for this type of engagement is $500 per hour, the market rate for such services in your city, plus out-of-pocket expenses (e.g., auto mileage, computer charges). How much of your fee will the taxpayer recover?

31. Examine some tax journal articles and treatises to put together a checklist, "How to Prepare for a Tax Audit."

32. Examine some tax journal articles and treatises to put together a checklist, "How to Prepare for an Appeals Conference."

33. Prepare a graph illustrating the trends in IRS audit activity over the past decade. First decide whether you are measuring audited returns, tax dollars recovered by audit, or budget resources dedicated to audit activities. Next decide which types of taxpayers and returns you will be graphing. Then find your data at **http://www.irs.gov**.

Tax Practice and Administration: Sanctions, Agreements, and Disclosures

Learning Objectives

- Identify various penalties that may be applied to tax practitioners who fail to perform as directed by the IRS, and related computations of interest charges.

- Identify various penalties that may be applied to taxpayers whose returns reflect improper amounts, and related computations of interest charges.

- Understand the application of the statutes of limitations, and taxpayer-government agreements that may be made with respect thereto.

Chapter Outline (continued)

THE ADVERSARIAL NATURE OF the Federal tax system has become apparent throughout this text, especially in Chapter 13. The revenue system is based on the notion of self-assessment, but the failure of the taxpayer to comply in detail with the requirements of the structure can lead to painful negotiations with the Internal Revenue Service (IRS) and prolonged litigation.

Yet, the Treasury need not wait for a resolution of the disputed tax issues alone to collect revenues. Penalties and interest play an ever-increasing role in the makeup of the Federal tax system—in many cases, the accumulated penalties and interest assessed by the IRS equal 50 percent of the disputed tax or more.

Interest charges are made by the Treasury so that the taxpayer gains no advantage or disadvantage with respect to the time value of money in deciding how to handle a tax dispute—to the extent that interest rates are developed to parallel those of the rest of the financial market, both parties are indifferent as to cash flow issues, and the negotiations can center on the tax issues alone. In Chapter 12, we discussed the role of present values in assisting taxpayers to make these decisions in an economically prudent manner.

Penalties have become more prominent in the Federal tax system for several reasons. The tax professional must incorporate into the research model the penalty-based "costs" of being too aggressive in taking a tax return or litigation position, and convey the computations of those costs to the client.

- In an environment where nominal tax increases are politically unpopular, penalty increases can supplement revenues in a manner that is acceptable to the public.

- Politics aside, penalties increase the tax cost of negotiating with the Treasury and may discourage challenges to tax precedents that are not founded in sound tax law.

- Penalties can bolster the self-assessment process by discouraging taxpayers from behaviors that the Treasury wishes to repress, such as working with tax shelters and ignoring filing deadlines and requirements.

- As professional tax preparers and advisers play a more important role in the development of tax return positions, the behavior of such third parties also must be controlled, both in keeping a free flow of information between the government and the taxpayer and in interpreting the tax law in an objective manner.

We conclude this chapter with a review of alternatives and strategies available to taxpayers in making various compromises and other agreements with the IRS as a result of the examination process. In today's tax practice, the professional must have a full working knowledge of the details of the tax administration process, so as best to serve clients and the fisc.

TAXPAYER PENALTIES

To promote and enforce taxpayer compliance with the U.S. voluntary self-assessment system of taxation, Congress has enacted a comprehensive array of penalties. Tax penalties may involve both criminal and civil offenses. Criminal tax penalties are imposed only after the usual criminal process of law is carried out, in which the taxpayer is entitled to the same constitutional guarantees that are given to nontax criminal defendants. Normally, a criminal penalty provides for imprisonment. Civil tax penalties are collected in the same manner as other taxes, and they usually provide only for monetary fines. Criminal and civil penalties are not mutually exclusive; therefore, a taxpayer may be liable under both types of sanctions.

Civil Penalties

The Code imposes two types of **civil penalties**. *Ad valorem penalties* are additions to tax that are based on a percentage of the delinquent tax. Unlike assessable penalties, ad valorem penalties are subject to the same deficiency procedures that apply to the underlying taxes. *Assessable penalties* typically are expressed as a flat dollar amount. Because of the lack of jurisdiction by the Tax Court or a specific statutory exemption, assessable penalties are not subject to review by the Tax Court. The Code characterizes tax penalties as additions to tax; thus, they cannot subsequently be deducted by the taxpayer.[1]

Civil penalties are imposed when the tax statutes are violated (1) without **reasonable cause**, (2) as the result of **negligence** or intentional disregard of pertinent rules, or (3) through a willful disobedience or outright **fraud**. The most important civil penalties include the following.

- Failure to file a tax return

- Failure to pay tax

- Failure to pay estimated income taxes

- Negligence, fraud, or substantial understatement of income tax

- Substantial understatement of the tax liability

- Failure to make deposits of taxes or overstatement of such deposits

- Giving false information with respect to withholding

- Filing a frivolous return

Failure to File a Tax Return   When a taxpayer fails to file a required tax return, a penalty is imposed unless it is shown that the failure is due to some reasonable cause and not to the taxpayer's willful neglect. The penalty is 5 percent of the amount of the tax, less any prior payments and credits, for each month (or fraction thereof) that the return is not filed. The maximum penalty that may be imposed is 25 percent (or five months' cumulative penalty). A fraudulent failure to file is subject to a 15 percent monthly penalty, to a 75 percent maximum.[2]

If the taxpayer's failure to file is due to willful neglect, there is a minimum penalty for a failure to file an income tax return within sixty days of the due date, including extensions. This minimum penalty is the lesser of $100 or the full amount of taxes that are required to be shown on the return. The penalty does not

---

[1]§6665(a)(1).
[2]§§6651(a)(1) and (f).

apply if the failure is due to reasonable cause.[3] This penalty is applied in lieu of, rather than in addition to, some other penalty.

No statutory or administrative definition exists for the term "reasonable cause." However, some courts define it to include such action as would prompt an ordinary, intelligent person to act in the same manner as did the taxpayer, under similar circumstances. One of the most commonly encountered examples of reasonable cause is the reliance on the advice of competent tax counsel.[4] Other examples of reasonable cause that the *Internal Revenue Manual* describes include the following.

- A timely mailed return that is returned for insufficient postage.

- Death or serious illness of the taxpayer or his or her immediate family.

- Destruction of the taxpayer's residence, place of business, or records by fire or other casualty.

- Proper forms that were not furnished by the IRS.

- Erroneous information obtained from IRS personnel.

- A timely mailed return sent to the wrong IRS address.

- An unavoidable absence by the taxpayer.

- An unavoidable inability to obtain records necessary to compute the tax.

- Some other inability to obtain assistance from IRS personnel.

However, the penalty will not be excused for any of the following reasons.

- The taxpayer lacks the necessary funds with which to pay the tax.[5]

- The taxpayer was hospitalized and suffered from an illness that was not incapacitating.[6]

- The taxpayer was incarcerated.[7]

- The taxpayer allegedly was ignorant of the laws.[8]

To avoid the penalty, the taxpayer must meet the burden of proof that the failure to file (or to pay) was due to reasonable cause. In these situations, the IRS's determination of the penalty is presumed to be correct.

SPOTLIGHT ON TAXATION

When Is a Return Filed?

To avoid the §6651 penalty, a return must be "filed." Some taxpayers think that sending in a blank form, or neglecting to sign the return, is enough to avoid this penalty, but the tax law says otherwise. The taxpayer

continued

---

[3]§6651(a)(3).
[4]See, for example, Chamberlin, TC Memo 2000-50.
[5]Langston, 36 T.C.M. 1703 (1977).
[6]Hernandez, 72 T.C. 1234 (1979).
[7]Jones, 55 T.C.M. 1556 (1988).
[8]*Lammerts Estate v. Comm.*, 456 F.2d 681 (CA-2, 1972).

---

continued

information must be included in a readable format, almost always on the correct IRS form, mailed by the due date, and signed by the appropriate parties. There must be enough information on the return so as to compute the correct amount of tax; thus, leaving lines or check-boxes empty will void the filing and the penalty will be assessed.

As electronic filing requirements are imposed on various taxpayers, both to speed up the system, and to eliminate the possibility of errors, IRS software will not accept an incomplete or frivolous return. This is also a way to verify tax identification numbers, so as immediately to identify those with other delinquent accounts, or with inadequate filing credentials.

Failure to Pay Tax If a taxpayer fails to pay either a tax that is shown on his or her return or an assessed deficiency within ten days of an IRS notice and demand, a penalty is imposed. The ten-day period becomes twenty-one days when the tax due is less than $100,000.[9] The penalty is 0.5 percent of the required liability, after adjusting for any prior payments and credits, for each month (or fraction thereof) that the tax is not paid—but it increases to 1 percent of the underpaid tax per month after notice and demand is issued by the IRS.[10] The maximum penalty that may be imposed is 25 percent of the outstanding tax. This penalty does not apply if the failure to pay is attributable to a reasonable cause, or to the failure to pay an estimated tax for which there is a different penalty.

For this purpose, reasonable cause is defined in a manner that is identical to that discussed in conjunction with the failure-to-file penalty, except that, if an individual is granted an automatic filing extension, reasonable cause is presumed to exist, provided that the balance due does not exceed 10 percent of the total tax.[11]

The failure-to-file penalty is reduced by the 0.5 percent failure-to-pay penalty for any month in which both apply. Thus, no more than a 5 percent total (non-fraud) penalty typically can be assessed against a taxpayer for any month. Nonetheless, after rendering sufficient notice to the taxpayer, the IRS can assess both the failure-to-pay and the failure-to-file penalties.

A taxpayer can avoid the failure-to-file penalty if an extension of the return's due date is granted by the IRS. However, with the two exceptions that we just discussed, the failure-to-pay penalty is imposed when the total amount of the tax is not paid by the unextended due date of the return.

> **Example 14-1** John Gray, a calendar-year taxpayer, filed his 2008 income tax return on October 20, 2009, paying an amount due of $1,000. On April 1, 2009, John had obtained a six-month extension of time in which to file his return. However, he could not assert a reasonable cause for failing to file the return by October 15, 2009 (the extended due date), nor did he show any reasonable cause for failing to pay the tax that was due on April 15, 2009. Gray's failure to file was not fraudulent. As a result, Gray is subject to a $35 failure-to-pay penalty and a $45 failure-to-file penalty, determined as follows.

---

[9]§6651(a)(3).

[10]§§6651(a)(2) and (d)(1). The monthly penalty rate is cut in half for taxpayers paying delinquent taxes under an installment agreement. §6651(h).

[11]§6654(d)(1)(B)(i).

Failure to pay

Underpayment	$1,000
Penalty percentage	× .005
Penalty per month outstanding	$ 5
Months (or fractions thereof) for which required payment was not made	× 7
Failure-to-pay penalty	$ 35

Failure to file

Underpayment	$1,000
Penalty percentage	× .05
Penalty per month outstanding (before reduction)	$ 50
Months (or fractions thereof) for which return was not filed	× 1
Unreduced penalty	$ 50
Less: concomitant failure-to-pay penalty (portion of October) [1 month × (.005 × $1,000)]	– 5
Failure-to-file penalty	$ 45

Accuracy-Related Penalty   Major penalties relating to the accuracy of the return data, including the existing negligence penalty and the penalty for substantial understatement of income tax liability, are combined in a single Code section. This consolidation of related penalties into a single levy eliminates the possibility of the stacking of multiple penalties when more than one type of penalty applies to a single understatement of tax.

The **accuracy-related penalty** amounts to 20 percent of the portion of the tax underpayment that is attributable to one or more of the following.

- Negligence or disregard of applicable Federal tax rules and Regulations

- Substantial understatement of income tax

- Substantial valuation overstatement

- Substantial overstatement of pension liabilities

- Substantial understatement of estate and gift tax valuation

The penalty applies only where the taxpayer fails to show either a reasonable cause for the underpayment or a good-faith effort to comply with the tax law.[12] When the accuracy-related penalty applies, interest on the penalty accrues from the due date of the return, rather than merely from the date on which the penalty was imposed.

Occasionally, a valuation overstatement penalty is encountered. This 20 percent penalty applies when an asset value has been overstated on a return, for example, to substantiate a charitable contribution deduction. It is assessed when the valuation used is 150 percent or more of the actual value, resulting in an underpayment of over $5,000 ($10,000 for C corporations).

Similarly, a 20 percent transfer tax valuation understatement penalty is assessed where the claimed value is 65 percent or less than the asset's actual value, resulting in an underpayment of over $5,000. The rate of both penalties is 40 percent

---

[12]§6662.

if a gross valuation misstatement is made, that is, the income tax valuation was at least 200 percent of actual value, or the transfer tax value was 40 percent or less of actual value.[13]

The practitioner is likely to encounter two of the elements of this penalty most frequently: (1) negligence or disregard of rules and (2) substantial understatement of tax. In the first penalty, "negligence" includes any failure to make a reasonable attempt to comply with the provisions of the Code.[14] This might occur when the taxpayer fails to report gross income, overstates deductions, or fails to keep adequate records with which to comply with the law. "Disregard" includes any careless, reckless, or intentional disregard of the elements of the tax law.

The negligence component of the penalty is waived where the taxpayer has made a good-faith attempt to comply with the law, as indicated by a full disclosure of the nonfrivolous position that may be contrary to that of the IRS. Such disclosure is made by completing Form 8275, reproduced as Exhibit 14-1, and attaching it to the return. If the return position is contrary to the language of a Regulation, Form 8275-R is used.

The second commonly encountered penalty, substantial understatement of income tax, occurs if the determined understatement exceeds the greater of (1) 10 percent of the proper tax liability or (2) $5,000. The understatement must exeed the lesser of the following for a corporation other than an S corporation or a personal holding company.[15]

▶ • 10 percent of the proper tax liability, or

  • $10,000, if greater

OR

▶ $10,000,000.

The amount that is subject to this penalty is reduced if the taxpayer either has substantial authority for the position that was taken in the return, or makes a full disclosure of a position taken in the return where there is a reasonable basis for the position, on Form 8275 or 8275-R.[16] More specifically, the taxpayer is not subject to this penalty where there is **substantial authority** for his or her position that supports a one-in-three likelihood of defeating contrary positions.[17]

For this purpose, "substantial authority" includes the Code, Regulations (proposed and temporary), court decisions, administrative pronouncements, tax treaties, IRS information and press releases, IRS Notices and Announcements, Letter Rulings, Technical Advice Memoranda, General Counsel Memoranda, Committee Reports, and "Blue Book" explanations of tax legislation.[18] Substantial authority does not include conclusions reached in tax treatises, legal periodicals, and opinions rendered by tax professionals.[19]

Clearly, greater weight is placed on the Code and temporary Regulations than will be assigned to Letter Rulings and IRS Notices, but the derivation of a weighted average among all of the competing positions with respect to a given tax question is not likely to be easily obtained.

---

[13]§6662 (e) through (h).
[14]§6662(c).
[15]§6662(d)(1).
[16]§6662(d)(2)(B). Tax shelters cannot use this provision.
[17]§6662(d)(2)(B).
[18]Reg. §1.6662-4(d)(iii).
[19]Notice 90-20, 1990-1 CB 328.

Exhibit 14-1: Disclosure Statement

Form **8275**	**Disclosure Statement**	OMB No. 1545-0889
(Rev. May 2001)	Do not use this form to disclose items or positions that are contrary to Treasury regulations. Instead, use Form 8275-R, Regulation Disclosure Statement. See separate instructions.	
Department of the Treasury Internal Revenue Service	▶ Attach to your tax return.	Attachment Sequence No. **92**

Name(s) shown on return	Identifying number shown on return

Part I   **General Information** (see instructions)

(a) Rev. Rul., Rev. Proc., etc.	(b) Item or Group of Items	(c) Detailed Description of Items	(d) Form or Schedule	(e) Line No.	(f) Amount
1					
2					
3					

Part II   **Detailed Explanation** (see instructions)

1

2

3

Part III   **Information About Pass-Through Entity.**   To be completed by partners, shareholders, beneficiaries, or residual interest holders.

Complete this part only if you are making adequate disclosure for a pass-through item.

Note: *A pass-through entity is a partnership, S corporation, estate, trust, regulated investment company (RIC), real estate investment trust (REIT), or real estate mortgage investment conduit (REMIC).*

1 Name, address, and ZIP code of pass-through entity	**2** Identifying number of pass-through entity
	3 Tax year of pass-through entity / / to / /
	4 Internal Revenue Service Center where the pass-through entity filed its return

For Paperwork Reduction Act Notice, see separate instructions.   Cat. No. 61935M   Form **8275** (Rev. 5-2001)

Civil Fraud If any part of an underpayment of tax is attributable to fraud, a substantial civil penalty is imposed. In addition, the taxpayer may be liable for a criminal penalty, which we will discuss later in this chapter. The civil fraud penalty is 75 percent of the underpayment that is attributable to the fraud.[20]

The burden of proof in a fraud case is on the IRS—it must show a fraudulent intent for the underpayment. This usually entails more than mere negligence, but a plan to defraud the government, often including a series of actions over time to evade the tax.

SPOTLIGHT ON TAXATION

Proving Fraud

The courts factor in the education and experience of the taxpayer in determining whether fraud has occurred. Is the taxpayer "smart" enough, say in terms of business and accounting training, to construct a plan to defraud, and then to carry it out? In cases of a complicated tax law or tax-reduction device, the taxpayer might successfully plead ignorance and avoid the fraud charge.

Under an all-or-nothing rule, if the IRS establishes that any portion of an underpayment is attributable to fraud, the entire underpayment is treated as attributable to fraud, and the penalty applies to the entire amount due. But if the taxpayer shows that any part of an underpayment is not attributable to fraud, the fraud penalty is not imposed with respect to that amount.[21] Neither the failure-to-file, nor the failure-to-pay penalty, nor the civil accuracy-related penalty, is assessed in these circumstances. However, the penalty for underpayment of estimated tax (discussed later) may still be assessed, and interest is assessed from the (extended) due date of the return.

Fraud is not defined in either the Code or the Regulations. One long-standing judicial definition of fraud describes it as "… actual, intentional wrongdoing … the intent required is the specific purpose to evade a tax believed to be owing."[22] This definition has been expanded to include acts that are done without a "bad or evil purpose." In *U.S. v. Pomponio*, the Supreme Court held that "willfulness," which is a crucial element of fraud, is present when the taxpayer's actions constitute "… a voluntary, intentional violation of a known legal duty."[23] Consequently, the taxpayer's deceptive or misleading conduct distinguishes fraud from mere negligence, or from other actions that are taken to avoid taxation, and not the presence of some (inherent or documented) evil purpose.

If a taxpayer is convicted of criminal fraud, he or she cannot contest a civil fraud determination. However, a charge that the taxpayer is guilty of criminal fraud may be contested when a civil fraud determination has been upheld. In a criminal fraud case, the IRS must prove "beyond a shadow of any reasonable doubt" that the taxpayer's actions were fraudulent. In a civil fraud case, there must be "clear and convincing evidence" that the taxpayer committed fraud.

---

[20]§§6663(a) and (b).
[21]§6663(b).
[22]*Mitchell v. Comm.*, 118 F.2d 308, 310 (CA-5, 1941).
[23]429 U.S. 10, 97 S.Ct. 22 (1976).

Ordinarily, the evidence that indicates that a taxpayer's conduct was fraudulent is circumstantial. Thus, the court must infer the taxpayer's state of mind from the evidence. Examples of fraud include the following.

- Keeping two sets of books, one in English and one in Japanese.[24]

- Making false accounting entries.[25]

- Destroying books or records.[26]

- Concealing assets or sources of income.[27]

- Consistently understating income or overstating deductions.[28]

- Purposely avoiding the making of business records and receipts.[29]

Failure to Make Estimated Payments   A penalty is imposed on both individuals and corporations who fail to pay quarterly estimated income taxes. This penalty is based on the amount and duration of the underpayment, and the rate of interest that currently is established by the Code. This rate, for instance, was 7 percent early in 2008. Unlike the similar interest computation, however, this penalty is computed without any daily compounding and is not deductible.

The penalty is calculated separately for each quarterly installment. Each penalty period begins on the date on which the installment was required, and it runs through the earlier of either the date that the amount is paid or the due date for filing the return. Any overpayment is first applied to prior underpayments and the excess is credited to later installments.[30] In this regard, the taxpayer must balance cash flow concerns with the payment requirements of the Code.

> **Example 14-2**   The taxpayer is required to have $100 paid in as estimates for the year. Payment schedule A would likely incur an underpayment penalty, while schedule B would not.
>
> | Quarter | Schedule A | Schedule B |
> |---------|-----------|-----------|
> | 1 | $ 10 | $ 40 |
> | 2 | 40 | 10 |
> | 3 | 10 | 40 |
> | 4 | 40 | 10 |
> | Total | $100 | $100 |

Individuals   An individual's underpayment of estimated tax is computed as the difference between the amounts that were paid by the quarterly due dates, and the least of the following.

- 90 percent of the tax that is shown on the current year's return;

- 100 percent of the prior year's tax, if a return was filed for that tax year of twelve months;

[24]*Noro v. U.S.*, 148 F.2d 696 (CA-5, 1945).

[25]*U.S. v. Lange*, 161 F.2d 699 (CA-7, 1947).

[26]*U.S. v. Ragen*, 314 U.S. 513, 62 S.Ct. 374 (1942).

[27]*Gendelman v. U.S.*, 191 F.2d 993 (CA-9, 1952).

[28]*Holland v. U.S.*, 348 U.S. 121, 75 S.Ct. 127 (1954) and Ragen, op.cit.

[29]*Garispy v. U.S.*, 220 F.2d 252 (CA-6, 1955).

[30]§§6654(b) and 6655(b).

- 90 percent of the tax that would be figured by annualizing the income that was earned during the year, up to the month in which the quarterly payment is due.[31]

For this purpose, unless the taxpayer can prove otherwise, taxes that are withheld are considered to have been remitted to the IRS in equal quarterly installments.[32]

The underpayment penalty will not apply if less than $1,000 in underwithheld tax is due. Thus, an individual can avoid the estimated tax underpayment penalty if (1) the preceding taxable year included twelve months, (2) the individual did not have any tax liability for the preceding year, and (3) he or she was a citizen or resident of the United States throughout the preceding taxable year.[33]

The IRS can waive the estimated tax underpayment penalty (but not the penalty that is based on the outstanding interest attributable thereto) (1) if the failure to make the payment was due to a casualty, disaster, or other unusual circumstance where it would be inequitable to impose the penalty, or (2) if the failure was due to reasonable cause rather than willful neglect during the first two years after the taxpayer retires after reaching age sixty-two, or becomes disabled.[34] The fourth installment penalty is waived if the corresponding tax return is filed with full tax payment by the end of the first month after the tax year-end (January 31 for calendar-year taxpayers).

Corporations An underpayment on the part of a corporation is defined as the difference between the amount of the installment that would be required to be paid if the estimated tax was equal to 100 percent of the tax that is shown on the return (or, if no return was filed, 100 percent of the actual tax that is due), and the amount that was actually paid on or before the prescribed payment date.[35]

The underpayment penalty will not apply if less than $500 in tax is due, or if the total payments that are made by the applicable installment date are equal to the least of the following.

1. 100 percent of the nonzero amount of tax that is shown on the corporation's tax return for the preceding year, provided that the preceding year contained twelve months;

2. 100 percent of the current-year tax liability; or

3. 100 percent of the tax that is due using a seasonal installment method, or annualizing the current year's income received for (1) the first two or three months, relative to the installment that is due in the fourth month of the tax year, (2) the first three, four, or five months, for the installment that is due in the sixth month, (3) the first six, seven, or eight months, for the installment that is due in the ninth month, or (4) the first nine, ten, or eleven months, for the installment that is due in the twelfth month as elected.[36]

Exception 1 does not apply to a "large corporation," that is, one that had a taxable income of $1 million or more in any of its three immediately preceding taxable years. To avoid an underpayment penalty, a large corporation must remit quarterly

---

[31]§6654(d). The rule is 110 percent of the prior-year tax if that year's AGI > $150,000.
[32]§6654(g).
[33]§§6654(e)(1) and (2).
[34]§6654(e)(3).
[35]§6655(b)(1).
[36]§§6655(d), (e), and (f).

estimated tax payments that are equal to its current year's tax liability, or it must meet Exception 3, as discussed.[37]

Failure to Make Deposits of Taxes or Overstatements of Deposits   The Code requires employers to collect and withhold income and Social Security taxes from their employees. Amounts that are withheld are considered to be held in a special trust fund for the United States, and they must be deposited in a government depository on or before certain dates prescribed by the statute and Regulations. An employer who does not have either the inclination or sufficient funds with which to meet its deposit obligations may be tempted to postpone the making of these deposits, that is, to "borrow" from the government the cash provided by employees. Consequently, the Code imposes heavy civil and criminal penalties on those who are responsible for the failure to make a timely deposit of the withheld funds.[38] A responsible party may be an officer or board member of a corporation rather than the corporation itself, even for charities and other exempt entities.

If an employer fails to deposit on a timely basis taxes that were withheld from employees, a penalty equal to a percentage of the underpayment is imposed. This rate varies from 2 to 15 percent, depending on when the failure is corrected.[39] The penalty may be avoided where the taxpayer can show that his or her actions were due to reasonable cause and not to willful neglect.

If any person who is required to collect, truthfully account for, and remit employment taxes willfully fails to do so, a penalty equal to 100 percent of the tax is imposed.[40] Therefore, when a corporate employer willfully does not pay to the government employment taxes that it withheld from an employee, the IRS effectively may collect the tax from those who are responsible for the corporate actions, such as the corporate directors, president, or treasurer.[41]

In addition to the civil penalties that have been discussed, criminal penalties may be imposed in an aggravated case of nonpayment.

Giving False Information with Respect to Withholding   All employees are required to give their employer a completed Form W-4, Employee Withholding Allowance Certificate. This form notifies the employer of the number of withholding exemptions that the employee is entitled to claim. The employer then calculates the amount of tax that must be withheld from each employee. A civil penalty of $500 is imposed on any person who gives to his or her employer false information with respect to withholding status or the number of exemptions to which he or she is entitled. This penalty is not imposed where there was a reasonable basis for the taxpayer's statement. Moreover, the IRS may waive all or part of the penalty if the actual income taxes that are imposed are not greater than the sum of the allowable credits and estimated tax payments.[42]

Employers who receive a Form W-4 from an employee, on which he or she claims more than ten exemptions, must submit a copy of the form to the IRS.[43]

---

[37]§§6654(d)(2) and (g)(2). The prior-year exception can be used in making the first-quarter installment, however. §6654(d)(2)(B).

[38]§6656.

[39]§6656(b)(1).

[40]§6672(a).

[41]§§6671(b), 7809(a).

[42]§6682.

[43]Reg. §31.3402(f)(2)-1(g).

Filing a Frivolous Return   A separate $5,000 civil penalty is assessed when the taxpayer is found to have filed a frivolous return.[44] Returns of this sort have been used to assert that the taxpayer's Fifth Amendment rights are violated by tax return disclosures,[45] that the taxpayer objects to the use of his or her tax receipts for defense or other uses,[46] that the government can collect taxes only in gold-based coins and certificates (which no longer circulate freely in the United States), or some other argument. Specifically, the penalty applies when the return

- does not contain information by which to judge the completeness of the taxpayer's self-assessment (e.g., if the return is blank);

- contains information or statements that on their face indicate that the self-assessment requirement has not been met (e.g., a "tax protestor" statement is attached); or

- otherwise takes positions that are frivolous or are meant to impede the administration of the tax law; for example, it takes a return position contrary to a decision of the U.S. Supreme Court, or it is not presented in a readable format.

SPOTLIGHT ON TAXATION

Frivolous Returns

The $5,000 penalty will not be assessed in the course of a typical dispute over the amount of tax due, for example, on an audit where both sides have defensible positions concerning the law. The penalty also is not applied in the case of a mathematical/clerical error. But the penalty relates to the original return as filed, that is, the penalty is not waived if the taxpayer "fixes" the problem by filing an amended return.

The frivolous return penalty applies even if the taxpayer legitimately owes a zero tax, and if the taxpayer was not required to file a return (e.g., due to low taxable income) but did so anyway.

Other Civil Penalties   A variety of other civil penalties may be imposed on taxpayers who fail to comply with the Code. Most of these penalties involve a specialized area of the tax law and ordinarily are not encountered by taxpayers. Consequently, one should be aware of the existence of such sanctions and refer to the Code and Regulations when working in such a specialized field to identify the events that might trigger such penalties.

Reliance on Written Advice of the IRS   The secretary of the Treasury must abate any civil penalty or addition to tax that is attributable to the taxpayer's reliance on erroneous written advice furnished by an IRS officer or employee. This abatement is available only with respect to advice given in response to a specific request by the taxpayer, and it is negated if the IRS error was made due to a lack of information provided by the taxpayer.[47]

---

[44]§6702.
[45]*Welch v. U.S.*, 750 F.2d 1101 (CA-1, 1985).
[46]*Fuller v. U.S.*, 786 F.2d 1437 (CA-9, 1986).
[47]§6404(f).

Criminal Penalties

In addition to the civil penalties that we have discussed so far, the Code prescribes a number of **criminal penalties** for certain acts of taxpayer noncompliance. The criminal penalties are intended "to prohibit and punish fraud occurring in the assessment and collection of taxes."[48] They are imposed only after the implementation of the constitutional criminal process, under which the taxpayer is entitled to the same rights and privileges as other criminal defendants.

SPOTLIGHT ON TAXATION

Tax Criminals

With Enron and other accounting scandals still destabilizing the economy, the question should be asked: What are the tax implications of these infractions? Are indictments of tax fraud and other tax-related criminal activities still to come?

Without knowing the workplan of the Treasury and Justice Departments, this question may not be answerable. But trends of the past decade or so would speak to a lack of interest by the Federal government in pursuing corporate tax crimes. Criminal tax investigations tend to involve both departments, mentioned above, of the President's cabinet, and they reflect the existence of convincing evidence of a serious tax infraction, not just a "fishing expedition." Civil penalties, audits, and appeals in the normal administration of the tax law are put on hold when a taxpayer is under a criminal tax investigation.

Are corporate taxpayers more compliant with the tax laws than they were in the past? Are the investigations less aggressive than they have been in the past? Why?

How else to explain the change in the work patterns of the criminal tax investigators? Today they tend to concentrate on smaller, mundane cases, not the high-profile violations of the Al Capones and Spiro Agnews of the past. And the investigations have declined in absolute terms as well, according to a think tank at Syracuse University. Estimates for the 2002 work year are for about 360 criminal tax prosecutions.

	2002	1992 or 1993
Criminal tax investigations initiated	2,500	4,000
Prosecutions for tax crimes	500	1,000
Corporate civil fraud penalties assessed	159	555
Corporate negligence penalties assessed	22	2,376

The IRS was not part of President George W. Bush's post-Enron Corporate Fraud Task Force, leading some to conclude that the government is not currently interested in pursuing tax criminals. And, even though there are 12 percent more corporate tax returns than there were a decade ago, the number of revenue agents employed by the agency to follow these returns has fallen by a quarter.

Previous comments by IRS personnel have admitted that the agency pursues only 20–30 percent of the known tax criminal cases, and that about $280 billion per year escapes collection because of this limited enforcement. Another report estimates that there are about 7,500 known "tax protestors" whom the government does not pursue.

---

[48]*U.S. v. White*, 417 F.2d 89, 93 (CA-2).

Prosecutions for tax crimes have brought down some highly visible individuals, including political and entertainment figures, but the penalties can be used against any taxpayer. Currently penalties are in public favor as part of "white collar" crime investigations. They can entail felony or misdemeanor infractions and are meant to punish the offender for evading the tax.

Nature of Criminal Penalties   Criminal and civil penalties are not mutually exclusive. Consequently, a taxpayer may be acquitted of a criminal tax offense, but still be liable for a corresponding civil tax penalty.

The IRS bears a greater burden of proof with respect to a criminal case. Moreover, the taxpayer holds the right to refuse to answer inquiries that are made by the IRS in a criminal setting if he or she would suffer a loss of some constitutional right by answering.

Ordinarily, criminal prosecutions are limited to flagrant offenses for which the IRS believes it is virtually certain to obtain a conviction. As a result, the IRS usually limits its charges to the civil penalty provisions. In the typical context, according to Section 100 of the *IRS Law Enforcement Manual IX*, criminal prosecutions are limited to cases in which (1) the additional tax that will be generated from a successful prosecution is substantial, (2) the crime appears to have been committed in three consecutive years, or (3) the taxpayer's flagrant or repetitive conduct was so egregious that the IRS believes that it is virtually certain to obtain a conviction. As a result, the IRS usually will not engage in a criminal prosecution when the taxpayer's noncompliance can be corrected by imposing civil penalties.

Criminal Tax Offenses   The principal criminal offenses that are addressed by the Code include the following.

- Willful attempt to evade or defeat a tax (i.e., tax evasion)—a felony offense that is punishable by a fine that is not to exceed $100,000 ($500,000 for corporations), reimbursement of the government's cost of prosecution, and/or imprisonment for a period that is not to exceed five years.[49]

- Willful failure to collect, account for, and remit any tax, by any person who is required to do so—a felony offense that is punishable by a fine that is not to exceed $10,000, reimbursement of the government's cost of prosecution, and/or imprisonment for a period that is not to exceed five years.[50]

- Willful failure to file a return, supply information, or pay tax or estimated tax—a misdemeanor offense that is punishable by a fine that is not to exceed $25,000 ($100,000 for corporations), reimbursement of the government's cost of prosecution, and/or imprisonment for a period that is not to exceed one year (five years and felony status for returns relative to money laundering rules, that is, large amounts of cash received by a business).[51]

- Willful making, subscribing, or aiding or assisting in the making of a return or other document that is verified by a declaration under the penalties of perjury, and that the person does not believe to be true and correct as to every material matter—a felony offense that is punishable by a fine not to exceed $100,000 ($500,000 for corporations), reimbursement of the government's cost of prosecution, and/or imprisonment for a period that is not to exceed three years.[52]

---

[49] §7201.
[50] §7202.
[51] §§7203 and 6050I.
[52] §7206.

- Willful filing of any known-to-be-false or fraudulent document—a misdemeanor offense that is punishable by a fine that is not to exceed $10,000 ($50,000 for corporations) and/or imprisonment for a period not to exceed one year.[53]

- Disclosure or use of any information that is furnished to a person who is engaged in the business of preparing tax returns, or providing services in connection with the preparation of tax returns, for purposes other than the preparation of the return—a misdemeanor offense that is punishable by a fine not to exceed $1,000 and/or imprisonment for a period not to exceed one year.[54]

In addition to the penalties just described, the Code prescribes a number of other criminal penalties that ordinarily are not encountered on a regular basis. Most of these penalties involve a specialized area of the tax law. Consequently, one should be aware of the existence of such sanctions and refer to the Code and Regulations when working in such a specialized field to identify them.

Defenses to Criminal Penalties The standard for conviction in a criminal case is establishment of guilt beyond a reasonable doubt. With respect to criminal tax cases, taxpayers have had some success in presenting one or more of the following defenses—that is, to establish some doubt in the minds of the court or the jury.

- Unreported income was offset fully by unreported deductions.[55]

- Unreported income was in reality a gift or some other excludible receipt.[56]

- The taxpayer was confused or ignorant as to the applicable law—one cannot intend to violate the tax law if he or she does not know what that law is.[57]

- The taxpayer relied on the erroneous advice of a competent tax adviser.[58]

- The taxpayer has a mental disease or defect, so could not have acted willfully to violate the tax law.[59]

- The statute of limitations (discussed later in this chapter) has expired.

- The taxpayer enters a plea bargain and accepts conviction on a lesser offense.

PENALTIES ON RETURN PREPARERS

Individuals who prepare income tax returns or refund claims for compensation are subject to a number of disclosure requirements and penalties for improper conduct in the preparation of those documents. These provisions were added to the Code after Congress found that about one-half of all taxpayers utilized some form of professional assistance in preparing their income tax returns. Moreover, a significant percentage of returns that were prepared by return preparers indicated some fraud potential.

---

[53] §7207.
[54] §7216.
[55] *Koontz v. U.S.*, 277 F.2d 53 (CA-5, 1960).
[56] *DiZenzo v. Comm.*, 348 F.2d 122 (CA-2, 1965).
[57] *U.S. v. Critzer*, 498 F.2d 1160 (CA-4, 1974). This is not a mere disagreement with the law, which is not an acceptable defense. *U.S. v. Schiff*, 801 F.2d 108 (CA-2, 1986), cert. den.
[58] *U.S. v. Phillips*, 217 F.2d 435 (CA-7, 1954).
[59] *U.S. v. Erickson*, 676 F.2d 408 (CA-10, 1982).

The return preparer penalties apply to all Federal tax returns. Most of them are mild, ranging from $50 for the failure to furnish an identification number to $1,000 for the aiding and abetting of an understatement of a tax liability. However, as these sanctions may be applied cumulatively, their magnitude can become more substantial. In addition, the criminal penalties that may be imposed on the return preparer provide for substantial monetary fines and jail terms.

We discussed some of these rules in Chapters 1 and 2. For both taxpayer and tax preparer, the penalty system "encourages" a lawful application of the tax rules by all, by raising the cost of the tax when specific requirements are violated.

Definition of Return Preparer

A **tax return preparer** (TRP) is any person who prepares for compensation, or employs one or more persons to prepare for compensation, all or a substantial portion of a tax return or claim for income tax refund.[60] A TRP can be an employer, employee, or a self-employed person. This distinction is important because certain penalties are imposed only on a selected type of preparer. For instance, only an employee preparer is subject to a negligence or fraud penalty, unless the employer participated in the wrongdoing. To determine whether the employer or employee return preparer (or both) is liable for a certain penalty, the Regulations that relate to that penalty must be consulted.

A person must prepare a tax return for compensation if he or she is to be subject to the return preparer sanctions. If a return is prepared gratuitously, the preparer is not a TRP. The preparer also must prepare all or a substantial portion of a return if the TRP sanctions are to apply. In determining whether the work that has been performed by the party is substantial, a comparison must be made between the length and complexity of the prepared schedule, entry, or other item and the total liability or refund claim.

The Regulations adopt two objective safe harbors in determining the Constitution of a substantial portion of a return or claim. If a schedule, entry, or other item involves amounts that are (1) less than $2,000 or (2) less than $100,000 and also less than 20 percent of the gross income (or adjusted gross income, where the taxpayer is an individual) that is shown on the return, then the item is not substantial.[61]

Definition of Return Preparation

In constructing a definition of the TRP, one first must define the domain of *return preparation*. Return preparation includes activities other than the mere physical completion of a return. The IRS asserts that tax advisers, planners, software designers, and consultants are all tax preparers, even though they may only review the return or give the taxpayer instructions on its completion. According to the Regulations, one who furnishes a taxpayer or other preparer with "sufficient information and advice so that completion of the return or claim for refund is largely a mechanical matter" is a TRP.[62] However, an adviser is not a TRP when the advice is given with respect to completed transactions or for other than tax return filing purposes.

---

[60]§7701(a)(36)(A).
[61]Reg. §301.7701-15(b)(2).
[62]Reg. §301.7701-15(a)(1).

A person is not a TRP merely because he or she:[63]

- furnishes typing, reproducing, or other clerical assistance;

- prepares a return or refund claim of his or her regular employer or of an officer or employee of the employer;

- prepares as a fiduciary a return or claim for refund;

- prepares a claim for refund during the course of an audit or appeal;

- provides general tax advice to a taxpayer;

- is an employee or official of the IRS, while performing job-related duties;

- prepares the return for no compensation; or

- works for IRS-sponsored programs such as Volunteer Income Tax Assistance, Tax Counseling for the Elderly, or a Low-Income Tax Clinic.

Being classified as a TRP is not directly based on the attainment of a certificate or degree, or the completion of continuing education requirements, but on the substantial completion of a tax return for compensation.

Preparer Disclosure Penalties

Five key **preparer penalties** may be imposed on those who do not comply with certain disclosure requirements.[64]

- A penalty of $50 for each return may be imposed on a TRP if the taxpayer is not given a complete copy of the return when it is presented to him or her for signature.

- A penalty of $50 for each return may be imposed on a TRP if he or she fails to sign the return.

- A penalty of $50 for each return is imposed on a TRP if the preparer's identification number or that of his or her employer, or both, is not listed on each completed return.

- A penalty of $50 for each failure is imposed on a TRP if he or she does not retain a copy of all returns that he or she prepared. Alternatively, he or she may retain a list of all of the taxpayers and their identification numbers for whom returns were prepared for the previous three years.

- A penalty of $50 for each failure to retain, and $50 for each item that is omitted, is imposed on a TRP who does not retain records that indicate the name, identification number, and place of work of each preparer who is employed during the twelve-month period that begins on July 1 of each year.

In each instance, the maximum penalty for any calendar year is $25,000.

Preparer Conduct Penalties

The Code contains a number of civil and criminal penalties that may be imposed on return preparers relative to their misconduct. The civil penalties were added to the Code because Congress found that a significant number of return preparers were engaging in improper practices, such as guaranteeing refunds or having tax-

---

[63] §7701(a)(36)(B) and Reg. §§301.7701-5(a)(2) through (7).
[64] §6695.

payers sign blank returns. However, except for the criminal penalty of aiding and assisting in the preparation of a false return, there were no lesser sanctions that could be applied to return preparers who were guilty of misconduct.

Civil penalties that may be imposed on preparers relate to:

- endorsing or negotiating a refund check;

- negligent understatement or intentional disregard of rules and Regulations;

- willful understatement of tax liability;

- failing to be diligent in applying eligibility rules for the earned income tax credit;

- organizing, or assisting in organizing, or promoting and making or furnishing statements with respect to an abusive tax shelter;

- aiding and abetting the understatement of a tax liability; and

- disclosure or use of return information for other than return preparation.

Return preparers always have been subject to criminal prosecution for willful misconduct. The two principal criminal preparer penalties involve those who:

- aid or assist in the preparation or presentation of a false return, affidavit, claim, or other document,[65] or

- disclose or use information for other than return preparation purposes.[66]

Endorsing or Negotiating a Refund Check A TRP may not endorse or otherwise negotiate an income tax refund check that is issued to another person. A preparer who violates this rule is subject to a $500 penalty.[67]

Understatements Due to Unreasonable Positions A tax preparer incurs a penalty for each occurrence of an understatement of tax due to the taking of an unreasonable position in the return. Where there is not a reasonable belief that the return position is more likely than not to be upheld on its merits upon a review, the penalty applies.[68] The penalty is waived if the return includes a disclosure of the preparer's nonfrivolous position, or if the preparer has acted in good faith in preparing the return.

The penalty applies to a tax return position that is taken on a Federal tax return or a claim for refund. The amount of the penalty does not relate to the amount of understated tax, the manner of computing most tax penalties. Rather, the unreasonable-position penalty is computed as the greater of $1,000 or one-half of the return preparer's fees derived from the engagement.[69]

The penalty is applied where the tax preparer knew or should have known of the disputed tax return position, and there was no **reasonable basis** for the position (likely a one-in-four chance that the position would be sustained on its merits), or a disclosure was not made on Form 8275 or 8275-R.

> **Example 14-3** Josie prepares a tax return that includes the claiming of a deduction that is contrary to an extant Revenue Ruling. Because of a new court decision in another circuit that is favorable to the deduction, Josie believes that

---

[65] §7206(2).
[66] §7213(a)(3).
[67] §6695(f).
[68] §6694(a)(2).
[69] §6694(a)(1).

there is a 70 percent chance that the position would be sustained in a suit relative to the deduction. No unreasonable-position penalty applies to Josie, whether the client wins or loses in court, and she need not disclose in any way her variance from the government position on her return.

Example 14-4 Continue with the facts of Example 14-3, except that Josie believes the following probabilities exist with respect to a court's treatment of her deduction, as supported by substantial authority.

Full support for her position	40%
Partial deduction allowed	35%
No deduction allowed	25%

No unreasonable-position penalty applies to Josie, whether the client wins or loses in court, and she need not disclose in any way her variance from the government position on her return. The return position is more likely than not to prevail.

Example 14-5 Return to the facts of Example 14-3, except that Josie believes that the position has a 30 percent probability of success in a court hearing. To avoid any unreasonable-position penalty, Josie must attach a Form 8275 to the return, revealing where and how she has deviated from the government's position relative to the deduction. There is a reasonable basis for the disclosed position.

Example 14-6 Return to the facts of Example 14-3, except that Josie believes that the deduction has a 5 percent probability of prevailing in court. Josie cannot take this filing position on any tax return. This is a frivolous position and would trigger an unreasonable-position penalty.

Willful Understatement A preparer is subject to a penalty if any part of an understatement of a taxpayer's liability is attributable to the preparer's willful attempt in any manner to understate the liability, or to the reckless or intentional disregard of IRS rules or Regulations.[70] A preparer is considered to have willfully attempted to understate the tax in this manner if he or she disregards information that has been supplied by the taxpayer, or by any other person, in an attempt wrongfully to reduce the taxpayer's levy.

The penalty is computed as the greater of $5,000 or one-half of the return preparer's related fees.

Organizing Abusive Tax Shelters A civil penalty may be imposed on any person who organizes or assists in organizing, or (even indirectly) participates in the sale of any interest in, a tax shelter, and who makes or furnishes a statement regarding an expected tax benefit that the person knows or has reason to know is either false or fraudulent, or contains a gross valuation understatement on a material matter.[71]

For this purpose, a gross valuation understatement is a statement of the value of any property or service that exceeds 200 percent of the amount that is determined to be its correct value, if the value of the property or service is directly

---

[70]§6694(b).
[71]§6700.

related to the amount of any allowable deduction or credit.[72] Accordingly, there does not need to be an understatement of tax before this penalty can be applied. The penalty, equal to one-half of the party's related fees from the engagement, can be triggered without an IRS audit, and it can be based only on the shelter's offering materials.

The amount of a valuation overstatement penalty is the lesser of $1,000 or 100 percent of the gross income that is derived from the activity, or is to be derived, by the taxpayer from the project. The IRS may waive all or a portion of the penalty that is attributable to a gross valuation understatement if there was a reasonable basis for the valuation, and it was made in good faith.[73]

Although the penalty is not aimed specifically at tax preparers, but rather at the tax shelter industry itself, professional tax advisers may be subject to the penalty because they often assist in organizing tax shelter projects.

Aiding and Abetting Understatement The Code imposes a civil penalty on any person who aids or assists, or procures or advises, in the preparation or presentation of any portion of a return or other tax-related document, if he or she knows or has reason to believe that the return or other document will be used in connection with any material tax matter, and that this use will result in the understatement of another person's tax liability.[74] This penalty may also be imposed on a person who acts in violation of the statute through a subordinate (e.g., an employee or agent) by either ordering or causing the subordinate to act, or knowing of and not attempting to prevent the subordinate from acting, wrongfully.[75]

The amount of the penalty is $1,000 ($10,000 for corporations) for each understating taxpayer. This penalty may be imposed only once per year for each understating taxpayer who is serviced by the TRP. However, it may be imposed in addition to other penalties. Thus, the preparer may also be prosecuted under the criminal statutes.[76]

Aiding or Assisting in the Preparation of a False Return A criminal penalty may be imposed on any person who willfully aids or assists in the preparation of a return or other document that is false as to any material matter. This penalty is the criminal equivalent to the civil penalty for aiding and abetting the understatement of any tax liability.

A person who is convicted of violating this statute is guilty of a felony and is subject to imprisonment for up to three years and/or may be fined an amount that cannot exceed $100,000 ($500,000 for corporations). This is one of the most severe tax preparer penalties under the Code.[77]

The persons who are prosecuted under this statute usually are accountants or other return preparers. However, a person who supplies false information that is used in the preparation of a return may also be subject to this penalty. The penalty can be assessed when it is merely a false tax-related document (like a Form 1099 or W-4), and not a tax return, that is prepared.

Disclosure or Use of Information by Return Preparers The Code imposes a civil penalty on any return preparer who discloses or uses any tax return information for other than the purpose of preparing a tax return. This penalty amounts to $250 per

---

[72]§6700(b)(1).
[73]§§6700(a)(2) and (b)(2).
[74]§6701(a).
[75]§6701(c).
[76]§6701(b).
[77]§7206(2).

improper use; a preparer's maximum penalty for any calendar year is $10,000. The Code also imposes a criminal penalty on any return preparer who knowingly or recklessly discloses or uses any tax return information for other than the specific purpose of preparing a tax return. One who is convicted of violating this statute is guilty of a misdemeanor and is subject to imprisonment for not more than one year and/or may be fined an amount that cannot exceed $1,000.[78]

The definition of a TRP for purposes of this criminal penalty is broader than that under the civil preparer statutes. For instance, a clerical assistant who types or otherwise works on returns that are completed by the preparer is a TRP for purposes of this provision; however, he or she would not be considered a TRP for purposes of the civil preparer penalty statutes.

Exhibit 14-2: Summary of Tax-Related Penalties

Criminal and civil penalties are not mutually exclusive, so a taxpayer or a preparer may be liable for both. Unlike civil penalties, which are collected in the same manner as would be true for the regular tax, criminal penalties are imposed only after the completion of the normal criminal process, in which the defendant is entitled to a number of constitutional guarantees and other rights, that is, he or she is deemed to be innocent until proven guilty.

IRC Section	Type of Infraction	Penalty
Civil Penalties		
6694(a)	Understatement due to unreasonable position	$1,000 or one-half of income derived, per return
6694(b)	Willful understatement of liability	$5,000 or one-half of income derived, per return
6695(a)	Failure to furnish copy to taxpayer	$50 per failure
6695(b)	Failure to inform taxpayer of certain record-keeping requirements or to sign return	$50 per failure
6695(c)	Failure to furnish identifying number	$50 per failure*
6695(d)	Failure to retain copy or list	$50 per failure*
6695(e)	Failure to file correct information return	$50 per failure to file; $50 per omitted item*
6695(f)	Negotiation or endorsement of refund checks	$500 per check
6695(g)	Failure to be diligent in applying eligibility rules for earned income tax credit	$100 per failure
6700	Organizing (or assisting in doing so) or promoting and making or furnishing statements with respect to abusive tax shelters	Greater of $1,000 or 100% of gross income derived by preparer from the project

---

[78] §§6713 and 7216(a).

IRC Section	Type of Infraction	Penalty
6701	Aiding and abetting an understatement of tax liability	$1,000 per return; $10,000 per return if taxpayer is a corporation
6713	Improper disclosure or use of return data	$250 per improper use; annual maximum $10,000
Criminal Penalties		
7201	Attempt to evade or defeat tax	Felony; fine of not more than $100,000 ($500,000 if a corporation) and/or imprisonment for not more than five years
7202	Willful failure to collect or pay over a tax	Felony; fine of not more than $10,000 and/or imprisonment for not more than five years, plus costs of prosecution
7203	Willful failure to file return, supply information, or pay tax	Misdemeanor; fine of not more than $25,000 ($100,000 if a corporation) and/or imprisonment for not more than one year (five years and felony relative to willful violation of cash receipts rules)
7204	Fraudulent statement or failure to make statement to employees	Fine of not more than $1,000 and/or imprisonment for not more than one year
7205	Fraudulent withholding exemption certificate or failure to supply information	Fine of not more than $1,000 and/or imprisonment for not more than one year
7206	Fraud and false statements; concealing or removing property	Felony; fine of not more than $100,000 ($500,000 if a corporation) and/or imprisonment for not more than three years
7206(2)	Aid or assistance in the preparation or presentation of a false return, claim, or other document	Felony; fine of not more than $100,000 ($500,000 if a corporation) and/or imprisonment for not more than three years
7207	Fraudulent returns, statements, or other documents	Fine of not more than $10,000 ($50,000 if a corporation) and/or imprisonment for not more than one year
7210	Failure to obey summons in tax matter	Fine of not more than $1,000 and/or imprisonment for not more than one year
7212	Attempts to interfere with administration of internal revenue laws, corruption, threats of force	Fine of not more than $5,000 and/or imprisonment for not more than three years
7216	Disclosure or use of information by preparer of return	Misdemeanor; fine of not more than $1,000 and/or imprisonment for not more than one year

*Annual maximum penalty = $25,000.

The preparer, as here defined, may disclose information that is obtained from the taxpayer without being subject to the civil or criminal penalty if such disclosure is pursuant to any other provisions of the Code, or to a court order.

See Exhibit 14-2 for a summary of the most important of the civil and criminal penalties that may apply to taxpayers, preparers, and shelter distributors.

INJUNCTIONS

The IRS is empowered to seek **injunctions** against two classes of persons of interest to our discussion: (1) TRPs and (2) promoters of abusive tax shelters. An injunction is a judicial order that prohibits the named person from engaging in certain specified activities. The courts have broad authority to structure any injunctive relief that is granted to fit the circumstances of the case as appropriate.

Action to Enjoin TRPs

The IRS may seek an injunction against a TRP who is guilty of certain misconduct to prohibit him or her from engaging in such misconduct or from practicing as a return preparer.

Before such an injunction can be issued, however, the preparer must have:

- violated a preparer penalty or a criminal provision of the Code,

- misrepresented his or her eligibility to practice before the IRS,

- guaranteed the payment of any tax refund or the allowance of a credit, or

- engaged in other fraudulent or deceptive conduct that substantially interferes with the administration of the tax laws.

In addition, it must be shown that the injunctive relief is appropriate to prevent the conduct from recurring. An injunction to prohibit the person from acting as a TRP may be obtained if the court finds that the preparer continually or repeatedly has engaged in misconduct, and that an injunction prohibiting such specific misconduct would be effective.[79]

Action to Enjoin Promoters of Abusive Tax Shelters

The IRS may obtain an injunction against a person who is guilty of promoting abusive tax shelters, or of aiding and abetting an understatement of the tax liability, to prohibit him or her from engaging in such conduct or activities. Before such an injunction is issued, a court must find that injunctive relief is appropriate to prevent this conduct from recurring.[80]

INTEREST

The Code provides for the payment of interest on underpayments and overpayments of tax, at an adjustable rate, compounded daily. The objective of these provisions is to compensate offended parties for the use of their funds. Moreover, the interest charge eliminates the benefits that taxpayers (or the government) could obtain by adopting aggressive positions in the creation or processing of tax returns in order to postpone or avoid the payment of their taxes.

Interest-Computation Conventions

Interest on underpayments is payable at a federally specified rate, from the last date that is prescribed for the payment of the tax to the date on which the tax is actually

---

[79]§7407.
[80]§7408.

paid. The last date that is prescribed for payment of the tax is usually the un-extended due date of the return that reports the amount of tax that is due.[81]

Interest is compounded on a daily basis.[82] Thus, given an interest rate that equals or exceeds about 15 percent, the obligation of the taxpayer or government could double in five years. The IRS has published interest-factor tables that auto-matically calculate the daily compounding for various rates of interest.[83]

The rate of interest that is used for underpayments and overpayments is ad-justed quarterly to reflect the Federal short-term interest rate for the first day of the quarter.[84] The new prevailing rate is published in a timely fashion, typically in a Revenue Ruling. Exhibit 14-3 documents the various IRS rates of interest that applied to over- and underpayments occurring through early 2008.

Where the taxpayer is subject to both underpayment and overpayment compu-tations for the same time period, whether the prior disputes involve income, trans-fer, or employment taxes, the amounts due and payable to the government are netted and a zero interest rate applies to those amounts.

> **Example 14-7** Mary Brown, a calendar-year taxpayer, filed her 2006 tax return and showed a balance due of $1,000. The return was filed on June 30, 2007, pursuant to a properly executed extension of time to file, and the tax was paid in full with the return. The prevailing IRS interest rate that applies to Brown's underpayment was 7 percent. She must pay about $15 of interest with her re-turn, determined as follows.
>
> | | |
> |---|---:|
> | Total tax outstanding | $ 1,000 |
> | Factor from Rev. Proc. 95-17, for 7 percent interest and seventy-six days' late payment | × .014680663 |
> | Interest assessed | $ 14.68 |
>
> If Brown does not remit the interest that she owes when she files the return, interest will continue to accrue, on both the tax and the $15 of interest itself, un-til the obligation is paid in full. If this amount is paid within ten days of the re-ceipt of an IRS notice and demand for payment, however, no further interest accrues.

Interest accrues on the full amount of the tax liability that is appropriate under the Code, regardless of the amount of tax that is entered on the return. Moreover, interest is imposed on an assessable penalty, additional amount, or addition to the tax if these amounts are not paid within twenty-one calender days of the date on which the IRS requests its payment. Interest on penalties generally is imposed only from the date of this IRS notice and demand, and not from the due date of the re-turn. However, the fraud, accuracy-related, and failure-to-file penalties run from the (extended) due date of the return.[85]

No interest is charged on criminal penalties or delinquent estimated tax pay-ments. However, recall that a nondeductible penalty is imposed in lieu of interest with respect to delinquent estimated tax payments. This penalty is computed in the same manner as would be the required interest, except that daily compounding of the penalty is not required.

---

[81]§§6601(a) and (b).
[82]§6622(a).
[83]Rev. Proc. 95-17, 1995-1 CB 556.
[84]§6621.
[85]§6601(e)(2). Interest begins to run after ten business days for amounts exceeding $100,000.

Exhibit 14-3: IRS Overpayment and Underpayment Interest Rates

Period	Rate
Prior to July 1975	6%
July 1, 1975–January 31, 1976	9
February 1, 1976–January 31, 1978	7
February 1, 1978–January 31, 1980	6
February 1, 1980–January 31, 1982	12
February 1, 1982–December 31, 1982	20
January 1, 1983–June 30, 1983	16*
July 1, 1983–December 31, 1984	11*
January 1, 1985–June 30, 1985	13*
July 1, 1985–December 31, 1985	11*
January 1, 1986–June 30, 1986	10*
July 1, 1986–December 31, 1986	9*

Period	Over-payment Rate*†	Under-payment Rate*†	Large Corporation Under-payment Rate*	Rate for Corporation Over-payments >$10,000*
January 1, 1987–September 30, 1987	8%	9%		
October 1, 1987–December 31, 1987	9	10		
January 1, 1988–March 31, 1988	10	11		
April 1, 1988–September 30, 1988	9	10		
October 1, 1988–March 31, 1989	10	11		
April 1, 1989–September 30, 1989	11	12		
October 1, 1989–March 31, 1991	10	11		
April 1, 1991–December 31, 1991	9	10	12%	
January 1, 1992–March 31, 1992	8	9	11	
April 1, 1992–September 30, 1992	7	8	10	
October 1, 1992–June 30, 1994	6	7	9	
July 1, 1994–September 30, 1994	7	8	10	
October 1, 1994–December 31, 1994	8	9	11	
January 1, 1995–March 31, 1995	8	9	11	6.5
April 1, 1995–June 30, 1995	9	10	12	7.5
July 1, 1995–March 31, 1996	8	9	11	6.5
April 1, 1996–June 30, 1996	7	8	10	5.5
July 1, 1996–April 15, 1998	8	9	11	6.5
April 16, 1998–December 31, 1998	7	8	10	5.5
January 1, 1999–April 15, 1999	6	7	9	4.5
April 16, 1999–April 15, 2000	7	8	10	5.5
April 16, 2000–April 15, 2001	8	9	11	6.5
April 16, 2001–June 30, 2001	7	8	10	5.5
July 1, 2001–December 31, 2001	6	7	9	4.5
January 1, 2002–December 31, 2002	5	6	8	3.5
January 1, 2003–September 30, 2003	4	5	7	2.5

Period	Over-payment Rate*	Under-payment Rate*†	Large Corporation Under-payment Rate*	Rate for Corporation Over-payments >$10,000*
October 1, 2003–March 31, 2004	3	4	6	1.5
April 1, 2004–June 30, 2004	4	5	7	2.5
July 1, 2004–September 30, 2004	3	4	6	1.5
October 1, 2004–March 31, 2005	4	5	7	2.5
April 1, 2005–September 30, 2005	5	6	8	3.5
October 1, 2005–June 30, 2006	6	7	9	4.5
July 1, 2006–December 31, 2007	7	8	10	5.5
January 1, 2008–March 31, 2008	6	7	9	4.5
July 1, 2006–December 31, 2007	7	8	10	5.5

*Daily compounding required.
†After 1998, noncorporate taxpayers use the second column for both under- and overpayments. Corporations still receive one percentage point less with respect to their smaller overpayments; that is, the first column applies.

In general, the IRS has no authority to forgive the payment of interest. Consequently, a taxpayer is required to pay the total amount of interest assessed on any underpayment, even though the delinquency was attributable to a reasonable cause, including an IRS loss of records and the illness, transfer, or leave of a pertinent IRS employee. However, the IRS can abate such interest where it is attributable to an unreasonable error or delay caused by an employee or officer of the IRS in response to the taxpayer's filing a claim on Form 843. Such a delay cannot be traceable to an interpretation of the tax law, but rather must relate to nondiscretionary, administrative, or managerial duties of procedure or return processing, including an IRS loss of records and the illness, transfer, or leave of a pertinent IRS employee.[86]

The government is required to pay interest at the applicable Federal rate to any taxpayer who has made an overpayment of tax. Interest on an overpayment runs from the date of the overpayment to the date on which the overpayment is credited against another tax liability, or, in the case of a refund, to a date that is not more than thirty days before the date of the refund check.

However, the IRS is allowed a specific period in which it may refund an overpayment without incurring interest. This interest-free period runs for forty-five days after the unextended due date of the return or, if the return is filed after its due date, for forty-five days after it is actually filed. If the refund is not made within this forty-five-day period, interest begins to accrue from the later of (1) the due date of the return or (2) the date on which the return was actually filed.[87]

> **Example 14-8** Joan Jeffries, a calendar-year taxpayer, filed her 2005 Federal income tax return on October 1, 2008. Her return showed an overpayment of $2,500, for which Jeffries requested a full refund. If the IRS refunds the $2,500 overpayment on or before November 14, 2008, no interest is due from the government. However, if the refund is paid after November 14, 2008, interest accrues from October 1, 2008, through a date that is not more than thirty days before the date of the refund check. (In any event, interest does not accrue as of April 16, 2008, for Joan.)

[86] §6404(e); *Dormer*, TC Memo 2004-167; TD 8789 (1998).
[87] §6611(e).

The date that is stated on the government's refund check determines whether the overpayment is refunded within the forty-five-day interest-free period. The date on which the refund is actually received does not control for this purpose. Thus, an interest-free refund may be paid, even though it is not received by the taxpayer until the forty-five-day period has expired.

SPOTLIGHT ON TAXATION

Prepaying Interest

If interest rates are relatively high, some taxpayers consider pre-paying the amount of tax in dispute, so as to stop the running of interest charges that will be due if the issue is found in favor of the government. A deposit of the tax (and perhaps of related penalty and interest charges) is set up with the Treasury. Such a prepayment might make sense because:

- The prepayment can trigger an immediate interest deduction.
- If the taxpayer prevails in the dispute, interest is payable back from the government on the full deposit amount.

Applicable Interest Rate

Different rates are used with respect to IRS overpayments and underpayments, as is evident in Exhibit 14-3. The overpayment rate (paid by the IRS) is two percentage points greater than the Federal short-term interest rate, compounded daily, and the underpayment rate (paid to the IRS) is three percentage points greater than the same Federal rate.

Large corporations pay interest at two percentage points higher than the usual underpayment rate. Corporations receive interest on overpayments at 1 1/2 percentage points lower than the usual overpayment rate, where the overpayment exceeds $10,000. Under- and overpayment rates are determined for the beginning of each calendar quarter, using the Federal rates in effect for the first month of that quarter.

STATUTES OF LIMITATIONS

The Code establishes a specific period of time, commonly referred to as a **statute of limitation**, within which all taxes must be assessed and collected, and all refund claims must be made. After the pertinent statute of limitations expires, certain actions may not be taken, because the expiration establishes an absolute defense for the party against whom legal action is brought. In other words, a taxpayer cannot be required to pay taxes that he or she rightfully owes if these taxes are not assessed and collected within the time periods that the Code has established.

Nature of Statutes of Limitations

Although the statute of limitations appears to be a legal loophole that rewards delinquent taxpayers who avoid detection, Congress believes that, at some point, the right to be free of stale claims must prevail over the government's right to pursue them. If the statutes permitted the lapse of an extended period of time between the initiation of a claim and its pursuit, the defense could be jeopardized because witnesses might have died or disappeared, memories might have faded, and records or other evidence might have been lost. Moreover, some statutes of limitations are designed solely to protect the government (e.g., the statute of limitations on credits or refunds). A number of such statutes limit the time period within which assessment, collection, and claim for refund or credit activities must be conducted.[88]

Assessment

Assessment of an internal revenue tax generally must be made within three years of the later of the date that the return was actually filed or the unextended due date of the return. A return that is filed prior to its due date, for this purpose, is deemed to be filed on its due date. The assessment period for a return that is filed after the due date starts on the day that follows the actual filing date, regardless of whether the return is delinquent or the due date was extended properly.

The period in which a tax may be assessed is extended to six years if the taxpayer omits from his or her reported gross income an amount that is greater than 25 percent of the reported gross income.[89] For this purpose, §61 gross income is used in the 25 percent computation, with two exceptions. First, the gross income of a business is *not* reduced by cost of sales. Second, income that is omitted from the return is ignored for purposes of constructing the base for the 25 percent test, if the omission is disclosed in the return or in an attached document.[90]

Although the limitations period is extended for a substantial omission of income, it (surprisingly) is not extended where the taxpayer has overstated the amount of his or her deductions, regardless of the amount of the overstatement.

Irregular Returns   A tax may be assessed at any time when a taxpayer files a false or fraudulent return with the intent to evade tax liability.[91] Once the fraudulent return is filed, the limitations period remains open indefinitely. A later filing of a nonfraudulent amended return will not start the running of the three- (or six-) year limitation period.[92]

When a taxpayer fails to file a return, the tax may be assessed at any time. For this purpose, one's failure to file need not be willful. A taxpayer who innocently or negligently fails to file still is subject to an unlimited period of assessment for the tax.[93]

Acceleration, Extension, and Carryback Effects   Generally, the filing of an amended return does not affect the length of the limitations period. However, the limitations period is extended by sixty days if the IRS receives, within sixty days of the expiration of the applicable statute of limitations, an amended return that shows the taxpayer owes an additional tax.[94] This provision was enacted to discourage taxpayers from waiting until the limitations period on an assessment was about to expire before submitting an erroneous amended return. Prior to the enactment of this provision, it was beneficial for the taxpayer to wait to file an amended return this way, because the IRS would not have enough time to assess more tax if an examination of the original return uncovered additional unreported errors or omissions.

---

[88] §6501.
[89] §6501(e)(1)(A).
[90] §§6501(e)(1)(A)(i) and (ii).
[91] §6501(c)(1).
[92] *Badaracco v. Comm.*, 464 U.S. 386, 104 S.Ct. 756 (1984).
[93] §6501(c)(3).
[94] §6501(c)(7).

The usual three-year assessment period can be reduced to eighteen months if a request for a prompt assessment is filed with the IRS.[95] This request usually is made for an income tax return of a decedent or an estate, or for a corporation that is in the midst of a dissolution. Generally, a prompt assessment is requested when all of the involved parties wish to accelerate the final determination of the tax liability.

A deficiency for a carryback year that is attributable to the carryback of a net operating loss, capital loss, or unused research or general business credit can be assessed at any time before the expiration of the limitations period for the year in which the loss occurred or the credit originated. This extension in the period of assessment for the carryback year is necessary to ensure that there is adequate time to process the refund claim and to allow the IRS to examine the return that gave rise to the carryback item.[96]

The period for assessment is not extended when a net operating loss, capital loss, or unused credit is carried forward.

IRS-Requested Extensions An extension of the period of limitations typically is requested by the IRS when an audit or an appellate review cannot be completed until after the statute of limitations expires. The taxpayer is not bound to agree with such a request, but such a refusal may prompt the IRS to stop negotiations prematurely and assess a deficiency against the taxpayer. Although the issuance of a statutory notice of deficiency does not preclude the taxpayer from obtaining a negotiated settlement with the IRS, he or she will be required to undertake a more costly procedure and file a petition with the U.S. Tax Court or pay the assessment and file a claim for refund. Consequently, a taxpayer normally should not refuse to sign a waiver of the statute of limitations, as requested by the IRS, unless the agent has completed the examination and there exist one or more unagreed-upon issues that the taxpayer is ready to litigate.

Collection

All taxes must be collected within ten years after a timely assessment has been made.[97] **Collection** can be made either by IRS levy or by the agency's commencement of an action in court. If the tax is not collected administratively by levy within the ten-year period, the IRS must commence an action in court to reduce the assessment to a judgment before the statute of limitation expires. Once a judgment for the assessed tax is awarded, the tax may be collected at any time after the normal period of collections has expired. Thus, collection is not barred after the ten-year period expires, provided that the IRS has obtained a timely judgment against the taxpayer.

The taxpayer and the IRS may agree to an extension of the normal collection period. The IRS will request such an extension whenever the taxpayer has agreed to extend the period of limitations for assessment of the tax. In addition, the taxpayer may request an extension to allow additional time in which to (raise and) submit any delinquent taxes. If the taxpayer agrees to extend the period of limitation on collections, the IRS may agree not to seize and sell the taxpayer's property to satisfy the tax liability.

The ten-year period of limitations begins only after an assessment is made. If an assessment can be made at any time, for example, because the taxpayer failed to

---

[95]§6501(d).
[96]§§6501(h) through (k).
[97]§6502(a)(1).

file a return or filed a fraudulent return, the tax may be collected within ten years of the date of assessment, regardless of when it eventually is made.

Claim for Refund or Credit

A taxpayer must file a timely and valid claim at the service center for the district in which the tax was paid to receive a refund or credit of an overpayment of tax. The claim should be made by individuals on Form 1040X, Individual Amended Income Tax Return, and by corporations on Form 1120X, Corporation Amended Income Tax Return.

Generally, an overpayment can be refunded or credited only to the person who was subject to the original tax. However, the IRS can apply overpayments to delinquent support obligations and certain certified nontax debts that are owed to the Federal government. Refunds in excess of $2,000,000 may not be made until they have been reviewed by the Joint Committee on Taxation.[98]

A taxpayer who reports a net operating loss, capital loss, or credit carryback can accelerate the processing of the refund by filing an Application for Tentative Carryback Adjustment on Form 1045 (for individuals) or Form 1139 (for corporations). The IRS has ninety days from the later of the date on which the application was filed or the last day of the month in which the return for the loss is due to examine the application and accept or deny the claim.[99] However, if the application is denied, the taxpayer cannot bring a suit for recovery of the overpayment, because the IRS's determination is only tentative. Instead, the taxpayer must file a refund claim on the appropriate form and wait for six months from the date on which the claim was filed, or until the IRS denies the refund claim, before legal action can be started.

Before a refund or credit can be issued, the IRS must review the taxpayer's claim. Even if the Commissioner agrees that the taxpayer has overpaid a tax, he or she has no authority to refund or credit the overpayment unless the taxpayer files the claim within the allowable period. Any refund of an overpayment that is made after the period for filing a timely claim is considered erroneous and a credit is considered void.

Limitations Period   A taxpayer who has filed a return must file a claim for credit or refund within three years of the date on which the return was filed or two years of the date on which the tax was paid, whichever is later. If the taxpayer did not file a return (e.g., because taxes were withheld from the taxpayer's wages, but the taxpayer did not file a return because his or her taxable income did not exceed the applicable exemptions and standard deduction), the claim for credit or refund must be made within two years of the date on which the tax was paid.[100]

The period within which a claim for credit or refund may be filed is extended when the taxpayer and the IRS agree to extend the statute of limitations on assessments. A claim can be filed within six months after the expiration of the extended assessment period.[101]

Other Extensions   The limitations period also can be extended where an overpayment results from a business bad debt or from a discovery of worthless securities.[102] A claim for refund or credit that is attributable to losses sustained from

---

[98]§6405(a).
[99]§6411(b) and Reg. §1.6411-1(b).
[100]§6511(a).
[101]§6511(c)(2).
[102]§6511(d).

worthless securities or business bad debts may be filed within seven years from the date that the return was due, without regard to any extension for filing the return. This period is extended further if the debt or loss increases a net operating loss carryback, since the taxpayer is entitled to three additional years for the filing of a claim that is based on the carryback.[103]

This provision was enacted because the determination of the date on which a debt or share of stock becomes worthless is a question of fact that may not be determined until after the year in which the loss actually occurred. If taxpayers were not allowed additional time in which to file refund claims for these items, they could incur substantial losses without the receipt of any tax benefits, because the deductions must be taken in the taxable year of the loss, not in a later year.

The period for filing a claim for refund is extended when the claimed overpayment results from the carryback of a net operating loss, capital loss, or certain credits. If a claim for credit or refund is attributable to the carryback of a net operating loss, net capital loss, or business credit, it can be filed within three years of the extended due date of the return for the year in which the losses occurred or the credits originated, rather than within three years of the due date of the return for the carryback year. Again, this provision was enacted because the existence and amount of these items might not be known until after the expiration of the usual three-year period for filing the claim.

Amount of the Credit or Refund If a claim for refund or credit is filed in a timely fashion, the amount of the taxpayer's refund or credit is limited to the portion of the tax that was paid during the three immediately preceding years, plus the period of any extension for filing the return.[104] The amount of tax that is subject to the claim may include amounts that were withheld and estimated payments that were made more than three years before the date on which the claim was filed, because these amounts are all deemed to have been paid on the due date of the return.

If a claim is filed after the three-year period, the amount of any refund or credit is limited to the portion of the tax that was paid during the two years that immediately precede the filing of the claim. This two-year period also is effective if a claim is filed for a year in which a return was not filed. Because this claim relates only to a two-year period, it may not protect payments that were made with the original return.

Suspension of Period of Assessment and Collection

Usually, a tax must be assessed within three years after the filing of a tax return, and it must be collected within six years of the assessment. However, under certain circumstances, the running of the statutes of limitations on assessment or collection is suspended.

When the IRS mails a statutory notice of deficiency (i.e., a ninety-day letter) to the taxpayer, the assessment and collection period is suspended for 150 days (210 days if the letter is addressed to a person who is outside the United States).[105] The statutes of limitations on assessment and collection also are suspended when a case is pending before the U.S. Tax Court. This suspension period begins when the taxpayer files a petition in the Tax Court contesting the deficiency, and it continues until sixty days after the decision of the Tax Court becomes final.

---

[103] §6511(d)(2)(A).
[104] §6511(b)(2)(A).
[105] §6503(a)(1).

When a taxpayer submits an offer in compromise for consideration by the IRS, the statute of limitations on assessment is suspended. This suspension period begins when the offer is submitted, and it continues until one year after the offer is terminated, withdrawn, or formally rejected.[106]

In addition to the circumstances just discussed, the statute of limitations also can be suspended when:[107]

- the taxpayer's assets are in the custody of the court;

- the taxpayer is outside the United States for six or more consecutive months;

- the taxpayer's assets are wrongfully seized;

- a fiduciary or receiver is appointed in a bankruptcy case;

- the IRS is prohibited under bankruptcy law from any assessment or collection of a tax; or

- the collection of excise or termination taxes on certain retirement plans or private foundations is suspended.

Mitigation of Statute of Limitations

Generally, the IRS cannot make an assessment and a taxpayer cannot obtain a refund after the statute of limitations has expired. However, §§1311 through 1314 of the Code include a complex set of rules designed to prevent the taxpayer or the IRS from taking advantage of an oncoming expiration of the period of limitations on assessment, collection, or refunds.

When an error has been made in the inclusion of an item of income, allowance, or disallowance of a deduction or other tax treatment of a transaction that affects the basis of property, the mitigation provisions will allow a submission of the error to be corrected, even though the normal period of limitations has expired for that year.

STATUTORY AGREEMENTS

The Code provides for two types of agreements that may be used to resolve tax disputes, namely, closing agreements and offers in compromise.

Closing Agreements

A **closing agreement** is a formal, written agreement that is made between a taxpayer and the IRS. It is the only agreement that the Code recognizes as being binding. Once it is approved, a closing agreement is final and conclusive on the part of both the government and the taxpayer, unless there is a showing of fraud, malfeasance, or a misrepresentation of a material fact, by either party.[108]

The purpose of a closing agreement is either (1) to enable the taxpayer and the IRS to resolve, finally and completely, a tax controversy for any period prior to the date of the agreement and to protect the taxpayer against the reopening of the matter at a later date; or (2) to determine a matter in a tax year that arises after the date of the agreement.

---

[106]Reg. §301.7122-1(f).
[107]§§6503(b) through (f). That section also contains other, less frequently encountered suspension possibilities.
[108]§7121(b).

The IRS is authorized to enter into a closing agreement in any case where there appears to be a benefit to the government in closing the case permanently and conclusively, or if the taxpayer demonstrates a need to close the case and the government's interests are not harmed. Typically, a closing agreement is used in cases where the IRS and the taxpayer have made mutual concessions relative to the case, and it is necessary or desirable to bar further actions by either party. Such an agreement also may be used when a corporation is winding up its business affairs or when a taxpayer needs some authentic evidence of his or her tax liability, say, to satisfy creditors.

As a matter of practice, the IRS discourages the use of closing agreements because of their finality. Moreover, the IRS would have a difficult time processing a large number of requests for these agreements. Consequently, it prefers to use a number of informal agreements that may not resolve conclusively the tax dispute that is under examination, or that may not provide for the same degree of finality as would a closing agreement.

Offers in Compromise

The Commissioner can make an **offer in compromise** for any civil or criminal case that does not involve sales of illegal drugs, prior to the time that the case is referred to the Justice Department for prosecution or defense. Once the case is referred to the Justice Department, however, the U.S. Attorney General has the final authority to compromise the case.[109] Compromise proposals entailing more than $50,000 in tax also must be supported by an opinion of the Chief Counsel.

In this context, the government will compromise a case only if there is doubt as to the liability or collectibility of the assessed tax. The IRS will not enter into a compromise with the taxpayer if the liability has been established by a valid judgment, and if there is no doubt as to the ability of the IRS to collect the amounts that are due.

A compromise agreement may cover the principal amount of tax, plus any corresponding interest or penalties. Ordinarily, the IRS will not compromise a criminal tax case unless it involves a violation of a regulatory provision of the Code or of a related statute that was not deliberately violated with an intent to defraud.

A compromise agreement relates to the entire liability of the taxpayer, and it conclusively settles all of the issues for which an agreement is to be made. It is a legally enforceable promise that cannot be rescinded unless there has been a misrepresentation of the assets of the taxpayer by falsification or concealment, or a mutual mistake relative to a material fact. Consequently, a taxpayer cannot decide later to bring a suit for refund with respect to any item that is so compromised. Moreover, if a taxpayer defaults on a compromise agreement, the IRS may collect the original tax liability, less any payments that were actually made, or sue to enforce the agreement.

An offer in compromise typically is made via Form 656, Offer in Compromise, and it must be accompanied by a comprehensive set of the taxpayer's financial statements. The offer may be revoked or withdrawn at any time prior to its acceptance. Form 656 is reproduced in Exhibit 14-4.

An offer in compromise is perhaps most appropriate in the following circumstances.

- There is doubt as to the taxpayer's liability for the tax (i.e., disputed issues still exist).

---

[109] §7122(a).

Exhibit 14-4: Offer in Compromise

Form **656** (February 2007)	Department of the Treasury — Internal Revenue Service ## Offer in Compromise	

Attach Application Fee and Payment *(check or money order)* here.	**IRS RECEIVED DATE**

Section I   **Taxpayer Contact Information**

Taxpayer's First Name and Middle Initial   Last Name

If a joint offer, spouse's First Name and Middle Initial   Last Name

Business Name

Taxpayer's Address *(Home or Business) (number, street, and room or suite no., city, state, ZIP code)*

Mailing Address *(if different from above) (number, street, and room or suite no., city, state, ZIP code)*

DATE RETURNED

Social Security Number (SSN)
(Primary)   *(Secondary)*

Employer Identification Number (EIN)
(EIN included in offer)   *(EIN **not** included in offer)*

Section II   **To: Commissioner of Internal Revenue Service**

I/We *(includes all types of taxpayers)* submit this offer to compromise the tax liabilities plus any interest, penalties, additions to tax, and additional amounts required by law *(tax liability)* for the tax type and period marked below: *(Please mark an "X" in the box for the correct description and fill-in the correct tax period(s), adding additional periods if needed).*

☐ 1040/1120 Income Tax — Year(s) _____

☐ 941 Employer's Quarterly Federal Tax Return — Quarterly period(s) _____

☐ 940 Employer's Annual Federal Unemployment (FUTA) Tax Return — Year(s) _____

☐ Trust Fund Recovery Penalty as a responsible person of *(enter corporation name)* _____ ,

for failure to pay withholding and Federal Insurance Contributions Act taxes (Social Security taxes), for period(s) ending _____ .

☐ Other Federal Tax(es) [specify type(s) and period(s)] _____

Note: If you need more space, use a separate sheet of paper and title it "Attachment to Form 656 Dated _____ ." Sign and date the attachment following the listing of the tax periods.

Section III   **Reason for Offer in Compromise**

I/We submit this offer for the reason(s) checked below:

☐ Doubt as to Collectibility — "I have insufficient assets and income to pay the full amount." You must include a complete Collection Information Statement, Form 433-A and/or Form 433-B.

☐ Effective Tax Administration — "I owe this amount and have sufficient assets to pay the full amount, but due to my exceptional circumstances, requiring full payment would cause an economic hardship or would be unfair and inequitable." You must include a complete Collection Information Statement, Form 433-A and/or Form 433-B and complete Section VI.

Section IV   **Offer in Compromise Terms**

I/We offer to pay $_____ *(must be more than zero)*. Complete Section VII to explain where you will obtain the funds to make this offer.

Check **only** one of the following:

☐ **Lump sum cash offer** – 20% of the amount of the offer $_____ must be sent with Form 656. Upon written acceptance of the offer, the balance must be paid in 5 or fewer installments.

$_____ payable within _____ months after acceptance
$_____ payable within _____ months after acceptance
$_____ payable within _____ months after acceptance
$_____ payable within _____ months after acceptance
$_____ payable within _____ months after acceptance

☐ **Short Term Periodic Payment Offer** – Offer amount is paid within 24 months from the date IRS received your offer. The first payment **must** be submitted with your Form 656. You **must** make regular payments during your offer investigation. Complete the following:

$_____ will be submitted with the Form 656. Beginning in the month after the offer is submitted *(insert month_____)*, on the _____ day of each month, $_____ will be sent in for a total of _____ months. *(Cannot extend more than 24 months from the date the offer was submitted.)*

- There is doubt as to the collectibility of the tax (i.e., the taxpayer's net worth and earnings capacity are low).

- Payment of the disputed amount would constitute an economic hardship for the taxpayer. For instance, the taxpayer is incapable of earning a living because of a long-term illness or disability, or liquidation of the taxpayer's assets to pay the amount due would leave the taxpayer unable to meet basic living expenses.

The IRS investigates the offer by evaluating the taxpayer's financial ability to pay the tax. In some instances, the compromise settlement includes an agreement for final settlement of the tax through payments of a specified percentage of the taxpayer's future earnings. This settlement procedure usually entails lengthy negotiations with the IRS, but the presumption is that the agency will find terms upon which to enter into a compromise with the taxpayer. The IRS is charged to use a "liberal acceptance policy" in compromising with taxpayers and to increase educational efforts so that taxpayer rights and obligations are better known.

The IRS has statutory authority to enter into a written agreement allowing taxes to be paid on an installment basis if that arrangement facilitates the tax collection.[110] The agency encourages its employees to use installment plans, and an individual is guaranteed the right to use an installment agreement when the amount in dispute does not exceed $10,000. The taxpayer uses Form 9465 to initiate the installment plan.

The IRS provides an annual statement accounting for the status of the agreement. The agreement may later be modified or terminated because of (1) inadequate information, (2) subsequent change in financial condition, or (3) failure to pay an installment when due or to provide requested information.

SUMMARY

In dealing with tax underpayments, the stakes include more than just the disputed tax. Interest charges accrue, and both the taxpayer and tax adviser can be subjected to significant amounts of civil and criminal penalties. Restrictions on the actions of the taxpayer and practitioner are expressed using such ambiguously defined terms as *reasonable cause* and *substantial authority*, such that the lay taxpayer is expected to project accurately the final holding of a judicial forum. Such is the condition of a tax system under which tax rates virtually cannot be raised, yet revenue needs continue to escalate. The tax professional must include these sanctions in the research process, communicating their effects to the client as needed.

TAX TUTOR

Reinforce the tax research information covered in this chapter by completing the online tutorials located at the *Federal Tax Research* web site: **http://academic.cengage.com/taxation/raabe**

---

[110]§6159.

KEY WORDS

By the time you complete this chapter, you should be comfortable discussing each of the following terms. If you need additional review of any of these items, return to the appropriate material in the chapter or consult the glossary to this text.

Accuracy-related penalty
Assessment
Civil penalties
Closing agreement
Collection
Criminal penalties
Fraud
Injunctions

Negligence
Offer in compromise
Preparer penalties
Reasonable basis
Reasonable cause
Return preparer
Statute of limitation
Substantial authority

DISCUSSION QUESTIONS

1. When should prevailing interest rates bear on tax decision making?
   a. The taxpayer is contemplating litigation in either the Tax Court or the Court of Federal Claims.
   b. An understatement of estimated tax payments is discovered late in the tax year.

2. What is the role of the statute of limitations in the Federal income tax system?

3. Indicate whether the following statements are true or false.
   a. The government never pays a taxpayer interest on an overpayment of tax.
   b. Penalties may be included as an itemized deduction on an individual's tax return.
   c. An extension of time for filing a return results in an automatic extension of the time in which the tax may be paid.
   d. The IRS can compromise on the amount of tax liability if there is doubt as to the taxpayer's ability to pay.
   e. The statute of limitations for assessment of taxes never extends beyond three years from the filing of a return.
   f. There is no statute of limitations relative to a taxpayer's claim for a refund.

4. Indicate whether, after both parties sign a closing agreement, the following result(s) occur. More than one answer may be correct.
   a. The taxpayer still may appeal to a higher level of the IRS.
   b. The interest on the assessment stops accruing immediately.
   c. The agreement is binding on both the taxpayer and the IRS.
   d. The tax must be paid, but a suit for refund can be filed in the District Court or U.S. Court of Federal Claims.

5. Ace filed her 2003 income tax return on January 25, 2004. There was no material understatement of income on her return, and the return was properly signed and filed. The statute of limitations for Ace's 2003 return expires on:
   a. January 25, 2007
   b. April 15, 2007

c. January 25, 2010

d. April 15, 2010

6. Blanche filed her 1998 income tax return on April 4, 2004. On December 14, 2004, she learned that 100 shares of stock that she owned had become worthless in 2003. Since she did not deduct this loss on the 2003 return, Blanche intends to file a claim for refund. This claim must be filed by no later than April 15,

a. 2005

b. 2008

c. 2010

d. 2011

e. There is no expiration date for the statute of limitations in this context.

7. Carl purposely omitted from his 2003 tax return $40,000 of the gross receipts that he collected as the owner of a saloon. His 2003 return indicated collective gross receipts of $25,000. The IRS no longer can pursue Carl with the threat of a collection of the related tax, interest, and penalties, as of April 15,

a. 2005

b. 2008

c. 2010

d. 2011

e. There is no expiration date for the statute of limitations in this context.

8. Diane accidentally omitted from her 2003 tax return $40,000 of the gross receipts that she collected as the owner of a saloon. Her 2003 return indicated collective gross receipts of $25,000. The IRS no longer can pursue Diane with the threat of a collection of the related tax, interest, and penalties, as of April 15,

a. 2005

b. 2008

c. 2010

d. 2011

e. There is no expiration date for the statute of limitations in this context.

9. Describe the civil fraud penalties, the definition of fraud, and the all or nothing rule for civil fraud. What are the differences in individual and corporate penalties for failure to make adequate estimated payments? What is a frivolous return?

10. Explain the imposition of criminal penalties. What is the relationship between criminal and civil penalties? What are the defenses against criminal penalties?

11. Discuss the penalties imposed on TRPs. Who is a preparer and what is defined as a tax return preparation and what is not preparation?

12. What is an injunction and when may the IRS seek an injunction?

13. What are the statutes of limitations for the IRS and taxpayers and why did Congress create them? When can they be shortened, extended, or suspended?

14. How has Congress used tax penalties to discourage the development of certain tax shelters?

15. Define and illustrate the following terms or concepts.
    a. Fraud
    b. Negligence
    c. Reasonable cause
    d. Lack of reasonable cause
    e. Civil penalty conviction
    f. Criminal penalty conviction

EXERCISES

16. Construct a scenario in which the tax adviser should recommend that the client terminate the challenge of the IRS with the following.
    a. Lawsuit
    b. Offer in compromise
    c. Closing agreement
    d. Appeals conference
    e. Office audit
    f. Correspondence audit

17. The client's return is found by the U.S. Tax Court to have included improper business deductions. The court agreed that the taxpayer's position had some statutory and judicial merit, but it held for the government nonetheless. Which of the following could the IRS charge with a preparer penalty?
    a. Taxpayer
    b. Partner of the accounting firm that prepared the return
    c. Employee of the client, who provided the accounting firm with the deduction data
    d. Staff member of the accounting firm, who used the deduction data to prepare the return
    e. Secretary of the accounting firm, who made copies of the return

18. Discuss which penalties, if any, the tax adviser might be charged with in each of the following independent circumstances. In this regard, assume that the tax adviser:
    a. provided information about the taxpayer's Federal income tax returns to the pertinent state income tax agency.
    b. provided information about the taxpayer's Federal income tax returns to the pertinent county's property tax agency.
    c. provided information about the taxpayer's Federal income tax returns to the FBI, which was interested in gathering evidence concerning the client's alleged drug dealing activities.
    d. suggested to the client various means by which to acquire excludible income.
    e. suggested to the client various means by which to conceal cash receipts from gross income.
    f. suggested to the client means by which to improve her cash flow by delaying for six months or more the deposit of the employees' share of Federal employment taxes.

g. suggested to the client means by which to improve her cash flow by delaying for six months or more the deposit of the employer's share of Federal employment taxes.

h. kept in his safe deposit box the concealed income of item (e).

19. Discuss which penalties, if any, the tax adviser might be charged with in each of the following independent circumstances. In this regard, assume that the tax adviser:

a. suggested that the client invest in a real estate tax shelter.

b. provided a statement of assurance as to the accuracy of the financial data that is included in the prospectus of a real estate tax shelter.

c. suggested to the promoters of a real estate tax shelter that a specific accounting technique, not recognized by generally accepted accounting principles, should be used to construct the prospectus.

d. failed, because of pressing time conflicts, to conduct the usual review of the client's tax return. The IRS discovered that the return included fraudulent data.

e. failed, because of pressing time conflicts, to conduct the usual review of the client's tax return. The IRS discovered a mathematical error in the computation of the taxpayer's standard deduction.

PROBLEMS

20. Lefty, a calendar-year taxpayer subject to a 34 percent marginal tax rate, claimed a charitable contribution deduction of $15,000 for a sculpture that the IRS later valued at $10,000. Compute the applicable overvaluation penalty.

21. Righty, a calendar-year taxpayer subject to a 34 percent marginal tax rate, claimed a charitable contribution deduction of $170,000 for a sculpture that the IRS later valued at $100,000. Compute the applicable overvaluation penalty.

22. Shorty, a calendar-year taxpayer subject to a 34 percent marginal tax rate, claimed a charitable contribution deduction of $400,000 for a sculpture that the IRS later valued at $150,000. Compute the applicable overvaluation penalty.

23. Baldy, a calendar-year taxpayer subject to a 34 percent marginal tax rate, claimed a charitable contribution deduction of $600,000 for a sculpture that the IRS later valued at $100,000. Compute the applicable overvaluation penalty.

24. Slim, who is subject to a 50 percent marginal gift tax rate, made a gift of a sculpture to Red, valuing the property at $7,000. The IRS later valued the gift at $15,000. Compute the applicable undervaluation penalty.

25. Tiny, who is subject to a 50 percent marginal gift tax rate, made a gift of a sculpture to Blondie, valuing the property at $80,000. The IRS later valued the gift at $150,000. Compute the applicable undervaluation penalty.

26. Fuzzy, who is subject to a 50 percent marginal gift tax rate, made a gift of a sculpture to Pinky, valuing the property at $100,000. The IRS later valued the gift at $250,000. Compute the applicable undervaluation penalty.

27. Jumbo, who is subject to a 50 percent marginal gift tax rate, made a gift of a sculpture to Curly, valuing the property at $100,000. The IRS later valued the gift at $500,000. Compute the applicable undervaluation penalty.

28. Compute the overvaluation penalty for each of the following independent cases involving the taxpayer's reporting of the fair market value of charitable contribution property. In each case, assume a marginal income tax rate of 35 percent.

	Taxpayer	Corrected IRS Value	Reported Valuation
a.	Individual	$ 30,000	$ 40,000
b.	C Corporation	30,000	50,000
c.	S Corporation	40,000	50,000
d.	Individual	150,000	210,000
e.	Individual	150,000	250,000
f.	C Corporation	150,000	900,000

29. Compute the undervaluation penalty for each of the following independent cases involving the executor's reporting of the value of a closely held business in the decedent's gross estate. In each case, assume a marginal estate tax rate of 50 percent.

	Reported Value	Corrected IRS Valuation
a.	$ 20,000	$ 25,000
b.	100,000	150,000
c.	150,000	250,000
d.	150,000	500,000

30. Kim underpaid her taxes by $15,000. Of this amount, $7,500 was due to negligence on her part because her record-keeping system is highly inadequate. Determine the amount of any negligence penalty.

31. Compute Dana's total penalties. She underpaid her tax by $50,000 due to negligence, and by $150,000 due to civil fraud.

32. Trudy's AGI last year was $200,000. Her Federal income tax came to $40,000, which she paid through a combination of withholding and estimated payments. This year, her AGI will be $300,000, with a projected tax liability of $60,000, all to be paid through estimates. Ignore the annualized income method. Compute Trudy's quarterly estimated payment schedule for the year, assuming that she wants to make the minimum necessary payments to avoid any underpayment penalties.

33. When Maggie accepted employment with Martin Corporation, she completed a Form W-4, listing fourteen exemptions. Since Maggie was single and had no exemptions, she misrepresented her tax situation in an attempt to increase her cash flow. To what penalties is Maggie exposed?

34. What is the applicable filing period under the statute of limitations in each of the following independent situations?

a. No return was filed by the taxpayer.

b. The taxpayer incurred a bad debt loss that she failed to claim.

c. A taxpayer inadvertently omitted a large amount of gross income.

d. Same as part c, except that the omission was deliberate.

e. A taxpayer inadvertently overstated her deductions by a large amount.

35. Kold Corporation estimates that its 2008 taxable income will be $900,000. Thus, it is subject to a flat 34 percent income tax rate and incurs a $306,000 liability. For each of the following independent cases, compute the minimum quarterly estimated tax payments that will be required from Kold to avoid an underpayment penalty.

a. Taxable income for 2007 was ($100,000). Kold carried back all of its loss to prior years and exhausted the entire net operating loss in creating a zero 2007 liability.

b. For 2007, taxable income was $200,000 and tax liability was $68,000.

c. For 2006, taxable income was $2 million and tax liability was $680,000. For 2007, taxable income was $200,000 and tax liability was $68,000.

36. Mimi had $40,000 in Federal income taxes withheld in 2008. Due to a sizable amount of itemized deductions, she figured that she had no further tax to pay for the year. For this reason and because of personal problems, and without securing an extension, she did not file her 2008 return until July 1, 2009. Actually, the return showed a refund of $2,400, which Mimi ultimately received. On May 10, 2012, Mimi filed a $16,000 claim for refund of her 2008 taxes.

a. How much of the $16,000 will Mimi rightfully recover?

b. How would your analysis differ if Mimi had secured from the IRS an automatic six-month extension of time for filing her 2008 return?

RESEARCH CASES

37. The Bird Estate committed tax fraud when it purposely understated the value of the business created and operated by the decedent, Beverly Bird. Executor Wilma Holmes admitted to the Tax Court that she had withheld several contracts and formulas that, had they been disclosed to the valuation experts used by the government and the estate, would have added $1 million in value to the business and over half that amount in Federal estate tax liabilities. Summary data include the following.

	Reported on Form 706	Other Amounts
Gross estate	$12 million	$1 million understatement
Deductions on original return	$ 2 million	
Interest on estate tax deficiency, professional fees incurred during administration period		$400,000

Holmes asks you for advice in computing the fraud penalty. Ignore interest amounts. She wonders whether to take the 75 percent civil penalty against the full $1 million understatement or against the $600,000 net amount that the taxable estate would have increased had the administrative expenses been incurred prior to the filing date of the Form 706. Write Holmes, an experienced

CPA (certified public accountant) with an extensive tax practice, a letter stating your opinion.

38. Blanche Creek has engaged your firm because she has been charged with failure to file her 2008 Federal Form 1040.

    Blanche maintains that the "reasonable cause" exception should apply. During the entire tax filing season in 2009, she was under a great deal of stress at work and in her personal life. As a result, Blanche developed a sleep disorder, which was treated through a combination of pills and counseling.

    Your firm ultimately prepared the 2008 tax return for Blanche, but it was filed far beyond the due date. Blanche is willing to pay the delinquent tax and related interest. However, she feels that the failure to pay penalty is unfair, as she was ill. Consequently, she could not be expected to keep to the usual deadlines for filing.

    Write a letter to Blanche concerning these matters.

39. The Church of Freedom encourages its members to file "tax protestor" returns with the IRS, objecting to both (1) the government's failure to use a gold standard in payment of tax liabilities, and (2) its sizable expenditures for social welfare programs. These returns routinely are overturned by the tax court as frivolous, with delinquent taxes, penalties, and interest due, and the church has engaged in a long-standing, sometimes ugly battle with the IRS over various constitutional rights. Meanwhile, church members continue to file returns in this manner.

    Ellen overheard church members talking about "roughing up" the IRS agents who were scheduled to conduct an audit of various members' returns. She went to the IRS and informed them of the danger that they might encounter. At the IRS's direction, Ellen then took a key clerical job at church headquarters. In this context, she had access to useful documentation and over a period of a few months gave to the IRS copies of church mailing lists and computer data. She also helped tape record key conversations among church leaders and search the church's trash for other documents. In other words, Ellen helped the IRS build a case of civil and criminal tax fraud against the church and various members.

    All of these materials were given voluntarily to Ellen by church leaders in her context as an employee. Church members never suspected that she was working with the IRS. After delivering the various materials to the IRS, Ellen quit her job with the church and severed all communications with the IRS.

    After the parties were charged with fraud, the government's case was found to be insufficiently supported by the evidence, and no penalties were assessed. Afterward, church leaders sued Ellen in her role as IRS informant, charging that she had violated their First Amendment rights of free association and their Fourth Amendment rights against illegal search and seizure. Government employees are immune from such charges, but Ellen was only an informant to the IRS and not its employee. Can the church collect damages from Ellen for informing on them?

40. Butcher attended meetings of tax protestors for many years in which the constitutionality of the Federal income tax and its means of collection were routinely challenged. Members of various protestor groups were provided with materials to assist them in preparing returns such that little or no tax would be due on the basis that, for instance, only gold- or silver-backed currency need

be submitted to pay the tax or that a tax bill had originated in the Senate rather than the House of Representatives. Some of the groups maintained that no returns need be filed by individuals at all on the grounds that the current law supporting a Federal income tax violates various elements of the U.S. Constitution.

The U.S. Tax Court routinely has overturned such means of avoiding the tax, charging that such protestor returns were frivolously filed and charging the protestors with delinquent taxes, interest, and a variety of negligence and other accuracy-related penalties, especially where taxpayers failed to file altogether. The results of these cases never were discussed in the meetings that Butcher attended, though. Thus, although he never joined any of the groups, Butcher felt comfortable with the arguments of the protestor groups and never filed a Federal income tax return for himself or his profitable sole-proprietorship carpentry business.

When the IRS discovered his failure to file and charged him with tax, interest, and penalties, Butcher went to the tax library and found that judicial precedent and administrative authority were stacked against him. He asked the court for relief from the civil fraud penalties related to his failure to file and failure to pay tax on the basis of his good-faith belief that the tax protestor information he had received was an acceptable interpretation of the law. Under this argument, a taxpayer cannot be found to willfully have failed to file and pay if he or she had a good-faith belief that no such requirement was supported by the Constitution. Should Butcher be required to pay civil fraud penalties?

41. Chang wants to claim a cost recovery deduction for the acquisition of master-work paintings to be hung in the reception area of her dental office. The paintings were specially chosen because of their tendency to relax the patients who would be viewing them, thereby facilitating the conduct of Chang's business. Chang lives and works in the Fifth Circuit. A recent Eleventh Circuit case seems to support such a deduction, in limited circumstances. Complete the following chart, indicating for each independent assumption the actions that Chang can take without incurring the civil penalty for substantial understatement of taxes, but still maximizing her legitimate deductions for the year.

Probability of Success in Court	Claim the Deduction?	File a Form 8275 Disclosure?
80%		
40		
20		
2		

42. Continue with the facts of Research Case 41. Now assume that you are Chang's tax adviser. You wish to eliminate any chance of incurring a preparer civil unreasonable position penalty. Indicate the actions that you would recommend that Chang take.

Probability of Success in Court	Claim the Deduction?	File a Form 8275 Disclosure?
80%		
40		
20		
2		

43. Your client, Lee Ann Harkness, has been accused of criminal tax fraud. A high school dropout, she received hundreds of thousands of dollars over the years

from Bentley, an elderly gentleman, in exchange for love and companionship. When Bentley died and Harkness was left out of the will, she sued the estate for compensatory payments earned throughout her years of attending to Bentley. The government now accuses Harkness of fraud in failing to file income and self-employment tax returns for the open tax years. Construct a defense on Harkness's behalf.

44. The Scooter Company, owned equally by Julie (chair of the board of directors) and Jeff (company president), is in very difficult financial straits. Last month, Jeff used the $100,000 withheld from employee paychecks for Federal payroll and income taxes to pay off a creditor who threatened to cut off all supplies. To keep the company afloat, Jeff used these government funds willfully for the operations of the business, but even that effort was not enough. The company missed the next two payrolls, and today other creditors took action to shut down Scooter altogether. From whom and for how much will the IRS assess in taxes and penalties in the matter?

45. For the completion and filing of his 2008 Federal income tax return, Ron retains the services of a tax preparer. Because of a particularly hectic tax preparation season, the preparer does not complete and file the return until June 2009. Is Ron excused from the failure to file and pay penalties under the reasonable cause exception?

Time Value of Money Tables

FUTURE VALUE OF $1

Periods	4%	6%	8%	10%	12%	14%	20%
1	1.040	1.060	1.080	1.100	1.120	1.140	1.200
2	1.082	1.124	1.166	1.210	1.254	1.300	1.440
3	1.125	1.191	1.260	1.331	1.405	1.482	1.728
4	1.170	1.263	1.361	1.464	1.574	1.689	2.074
5	1.217	1.338	1.469	1.611	1.762	1.925	2.488
6	1.265	1.419	1.587	1.772	1.974	2.195	2.986
7	1.316	1.504	1.714	1.949	2.211	2.502	3.583
8	1.369	1.594	1.851	2.144	2.476	2.853	4.300
9	1.423	1.690	1.999	2.359	2.773	3.252	5.160
10	1.480	1.791	2.159	2.594	3.106	3.707	6.192
11	1.540	1.898	2.332	2.853	3.479	4.226	7.430
12	1.601	2.012	2.518	3.139	3.896	4.818	8.916
13	1.665	2.133	2.720	3.452	4.364	5.492	10.699
14	1.732	2.261	2.937	3.798	4.887	6.261	12.839
15	1.801	2.397	3.172	4.177	5.474	7.138	15.407
20	2.191	3.207	4.661	6.728	9.646	13.743	38.338
30	3.243	5.744	10.063	17.450	29.960	50.950	237.380
40	4.801	10.286	21.725	45.260	93.051	188.880	1469.800

FUTURE VALUE OF AN ANNUITY OF $1 IN ARREARS

Periods	4%	6%	8%	10%	12%	14%	20%
1	1.000	1.000	1.000	1.000	1.000	1.000	1.000
2	2.040	2.060	2.080	2.100	2.120	2.140	2.220
3	3.122	3.184	3.246	3.310	3.374	3.440	3.640
4	4.247	4.375	4.506	4.641	4.779	4.921	5.368
5	5.416	5.637	5.867	6.105	6.353	6.610	7.442
6	6.633	6.975	7.336	7.716	8.115	8.536	9.930
7	7.898	8.394	8.923	9.487	10.089	10.730	12.916
8	9.214	9.898	10.637	11.436	12.300	13.233	16.499
9	10.583	11.491	12.488	13.580	14.776	16.085	20.799
10	12.006	13.181	14.487	15.938	17.549	19.337	25.959

FUTURE VALUE OF AN ANNUITY OF $1 IN ARREARS (CONTINUED)

Periods	4%	6%	8%	10%	12%	14%	20%
11	13.486	14.972	16.646	18.531	20.655	23.045	32.150
12	15.026	16.870	18.977	21.385	24.133	27.271	39.580
13	16.627	18.882	21.495	24.523	28.029	32.089	48.497
14	18.292	21.015	24.215	27.976	32.393	37.581	59.196
15	20.024	23.276	27.152	31.773	37.280	43.842	72.035
20	29.778	36.778	45.762	57.276	75.052	91.025	186.690
30	56.085	79.058	113.283	164.496	241.330	356.790	1181.900
40	95.026	154.762	259.057	442.597	767.090	1342.000	7343.900

PRESENT VALUE OF $1

Periods	4%	5%	6%	8%	10%	12%	14%	16%	18%	20%	22%	24%	26%	28%	30%	40%
1	0.962	0.952	0.943	0.926	0.909	0.893	0.877	0.862	0.847	0.833	0.820	0.806	0.794	0.781	0.769	0.714
2	0.925	0.907	0.890	0.857	0.826	0.797	0.769	0.743	0.718	0.694	0.672	0.650	0.630	0.610	0.592	0.510
3	0.889	0.864	0.840	0.794	0.751	0.712	0.675	0.641	0.609	0.579	0.551	0.524	0.500	0.477	0.455	0.364
4	0.855	0.823	0.792	0.735	0.683	0.636	0.592	0.552	0.516	0.482	0.451	0.423	0.397	0.373	0.350	0.260
5	0.822	0.784	0.747	0.681	0.621	0.567	0.519	0.476	0.436	0.402	0.370	0.341	0.315	0.291	0.269	0.186
6	0.790	0.746	0.705	0.630	0.564	0.507	0.456	0.410	0.370	0.335	0.303	0.275	0.250	0.227	0.207	0.133
7	0.760	0.711	0.665	0.583	0.513	0.452	0.400	0.354	0.314	0.279	0.249	0.222	0.198	0.178	0.159	0.095
8	0.731	0.677	0.627	0.540	0.467	0.404	0.351	0.305	0.266	0.233	0.204	0.179	0.157	0.139	0.123	0.068
9	0.703	0.645	0.592	0.500	0.424	0.361	0.308	0.263	0.225	0.194	0.167	0.144	0.125	0.108	0.094	0.048
10	0.676	0.614	0.558	0.463	0.386	0.322	0.270	0.227	0.191	0.162	0.137	0.116	0.099	0.085	0.073	0.035
11	0.650	0.585	0.527	0.429	0.350	0.287	0.237	0.195	0.162	0.135	0.112	0.094	0.079	0.066	0.056	0.025
12	0.625	0.557	0.497	0.397	0.319	0.257	0.208	0.168	0.137	0.112	0.092	0.076	0.062	0.052	0.043	0.018
13	0.601	0.530	0.469	0.368	0.290	0.229	0.182	0.145	0.116	0.093	0.075	0.061	0.050	0.040	0.033	0.013
14	0.577	0.505	0.442	0.340	0.263	0.205	0.160	0.125	0.099	0.078	0.062	0.049	0.039	0.032	0.025	0.009
15	0.555	0.481	0.417	0.315	0.239	0.183	0.140	0.108	0.084	0.065	0.051	0.040	0.031	0.025	0.020	0.006
16	0.534	0.458	0.394	0.292	0.218	0.163	0.123	0.093	0.071	0.054	0.042	0.032	0.025	0.019	0.015	0.005
17	0.513	0.436	0.371	0.270	0.198	0.146	0.108	0.080	0.060	0.045	0.034	0.026	0.020	0.015	0.012	0.003
18	0.494	0.416	0.350	0.250	0.180	0.130	0.095	0.069	0.051	0.038	0.028	0.021	0.016	0.012	0.009	0.002
19	0.475	0.396	0.331	0.232	0.164	0.116	0.083	0.060	0.043	0.031	0.023	0.017	0.012`	0.009	0.007	0.002
20	0.456	0.377	0.312	0.215	0.149	0.104	0.073	0.051	0.037	0.026	0.019	0.014	0.010	0.007	0.005	0.001
21	0.439	0.359	0.294	0.199	0.135	0.093	0.064	0.044	0.031	0.022	0.015	0.011	0.008	0.006	0.004	0.001
22	0.422	0.342	0.278	0.184	0.123	0.083	0.056	0.038	0.026	0.018	0.013	0.009	0.006	0.004	0.003	0.001
23	0.406	0.326	0.262	0.170	0.112	0.074	0.049	0.033	0.022	0.015	0.010	0.007	0.005	0.003	0.002	
24	0.390	0.310	0.247	0.158	0.102	0.066	0.043	0.028	0.019	0.013	0.008	0.006	0.004	0.003	0.002	
25	0.375	0.295	0.233	0.146	0.092	0.059	0.038	0.024	0.016	0.010	0.007	0.005	0.003	0.002	0.001	
26	0.361	0.281	0.220	0.135	0.084	0.053	0.033	0.021	0.014	0.009	0.006	0.004	0.002	0.002	0.001	
27	0.347	0.268	0.207	0.125	0.076	0.047	0.029	0.018	0.011	0.007	0.005	0.003	0.002	0.001	0.001	
28	0.333	0.255	0.196	0.116	0.069	0.042	0.026	0.016	0.010	0.006	0.004	0.002	0.002	0.001	0.001	
29	0.321	0.243	0.185	0.107	0.063	0.037	0.022	0.014	0.008	0.005	0.003	0.002	0.001	0.001	0.001	
30	0.308	0.231	0.174	0.099	0.057	0.033	0.020	0.012	0.007	0.004	0.003	0.002	0.001	0.001		
40	0.208	0.142	0.097	0.046	0.022	0.011	0.005	0.003	0.001	0.001						

PRESENT VALUE OF AN ANNUITY OF $1 IN ARREARS

Periods	4%	5%	6%	8%	10%	12%	14%	16%	18%	20%	22%	24%	26%	28%	30%	40%
1	0.962	0.952	0.943	0.926	0.909	0.893	0.877	0.862	0.847	0.833	0.820	0.806	0.794	0.781	0.769	0.714
2	1.886	1.859	1.833	1.783	1.736	1.690	1.647	1.605	1.566	1.528	1.492	1.457	1.424	1.392	1.361	1.224
3	2.775	2.723	2.673	2.577	2.487	2.402	2.322	2.246	2.174	2.106	2.042	1.981	1.923	1.868	1.816	1.589
4	3.630	3.546	3.465	3.312	3.170	3.037	2.914	2.798	2.690	2.589	2.494	2.404	2.320	2.241	2.166	1.879
5	4.452	4.330	4.212	3.993	3.791	3.605	3.433	3.274	3.127	2.991	2.864	2.745	2.635	2.532	2.436	2.035
6	5.242	5.076	4.917	4.623	4.355	4.111	3.889	3.685	3.498	3.326	3.167	3.020	2.885	2.759	2.643	2.168
7	6.002	5.786	5.582	5.206	4.868	4.564	4.288	4.039	3.812	3.605	3.416	3.242	3.083	2.937	2.802	2.263
8	6.733	6.463	6.210	5.747	5.335	4.968	4.639	4.344	4.078	3.837	3.619	3.421	3.241	3.076	2.925	2.331
9	7.435	7.108	6.802	6.247	5.759	5.328	4.946	4.607	4.303	4.031	3.786	3.566	3.366	3.184	3.019	2.379
10	8.111	7.722	7.360	6.710	6.145	5.650	5.216	4.833	4.494	4.192	3.923	3.682	3.465	3.269	3.092	2.414
11	8.760	8.306	7.887	7.139	6.495	5.988	5.453	5.029	4.656	4.327	4.035	3.776	3.544	3.335	3.147	2.438
12	9.385	8.863	8.384	7.536	6.814	6.194	5.660	5.197	4.793	4.439	4.127	3.851	3.606	3.387	3.190	2.456
13	9.986	9.394	8.853	7.904	7.103	6.424	5.842	5.342	4.910	4.533	4.203	3.912	3.656	3.427	3.223	2.468
14	10.563	9.899	9.295	8.244	7.367	6.628	6.002	5.468	5.008	4.611	4.265	3.962	3.695	3.459	3.249	2.477
15	11.118	10.380	9.712	8.559	7.606	6.811	6.142	5.575	5.092	4.675	4.315	4.001	3.726	3.483	3.268	2.484
16	11.652	10.838	10.106	8.851	7.824	6.974	6.265	5.669	5.162	4.730	4.357	4.033	3.751	3.503	3.283	2.489
17	12.166	11.274	10.477	9.122	8.022	7.120	6.373	5.749	5.222	4.775	4.391	4.059	3.771	3.518	3.295	2.492
18	12.659	11.690	10.828	9.372	8.201	7.250	6.467	5.818	5.273	4.812	4.419	4.080	3.786	3.529	3.304	2.494
19	13.134	12.085	11.158	9.604	8.365	7.366	6.550	5.877	5.316	4.844	4.442	4.097	3.799	3.539	3.311	2.496
20	13.590	12.462	11.470	9.818	8.514	7.469	6.623	5.929	5.353	4.870	4.460	4.110	3.808	3.546	3.316	2.497
21	14.029	12.821	11.764	10.017	8.649	7.562	6.687	5.973	5.384	4.891	4.476	4.121	3.816	3.551	3.320	2.498
22	14.451	13.163	12.042	10.201	8.772	7.645	6.743	6.011	5.410	4.909	4.488	4.130	3.822	3.556	3.323	2.498
23	14.857	13.489	12.303	10.371	8.883	7.718	6.792	6.044	5.432	4.925	4.499	4.137	3.827	3.559	3.325	2.499
24	15.247	13.799	12.550	10.529	8.985	7.784	6.835	6.073	5.451	4.937	4.507	4.143	3.831	3.562	3.327	2.499
25	15.622	14.094	12.783	10.675	9.077	7.843	6.873	6.097	5.467	4.948	4.514	4.147	3.834	3.564	3.329	2.499
26	15.983	14.375	13.003	10.810	9.161	7.896	6.906	6.118	5.480	4.956	4.520	4.151	3.837	3.566	3.330	2.500
27	16.330	14.643	13.211	10.935	9.237	7.943	6.935	6.136	5.492	4.964	4.525	4.154	3.839	3.567	3.331	2.500
28	16.663	14.898	13.406	11.051	9.307	7.984	6.961	6.152	5.502	4.970	4.528	4.157	3.840	3.568	3.331	2.500
29	16.984	15.141	13.591	11.158	9.370	8.022	6.983	6.166	5.510	4.975	4.531	4.159	3.841	3.569	3.332	2.500
30	17.292	15.373	13.765	11.258	9.427	8.055	7.003	6.177	5.517	4.979	4.534	4.160	3.842	3.569	3.332	2.500
40	19.793	17.159	15.046	11.925	9.779	8.244	7.105	6.234	5.548	4.997	4.544	4.166	3.846	3.571	3.333	2.500

Standard Tax Citations

Citations are presented for illustrative and prescriptive purposes. They do not necessarily track to actual documents.

Statutory

Constitution	U.S. Const. art. I, §8, cl. 2.
	U.S. Const. amend, XIV, §2.
Code	§101(b)(2)(B)(ii).
Public Laws	P.L. 109-123 Act §1563.

Administrative

Regulation	Reg. §1.162-5(a)(1).
Treasury Decision	T.D. 9643, 2009-1 C.B. 453.
Temporary Regulation	Reg. §1.469-4T(c)(2).
Proposed Regulation	Prop. Reg. §1.1176(b)(2).
Revenue Ruling	Rev. Rul. 2009-7, 2009-1 C.B. 712.
Revenue Ruling (temporary)	Rev. Rul. 2009-7, 2009-9 I.R.B. 712.
Revenue Procedure	Rev. Proc. 2009-21, 2009-1 C.B. 742.
Letter Ruling	Ltr. Rul. 200930042.
Technical Advice Memo	TAM 200905006.
Notice	Notice 2009-30, 2009-1 C.B. 989.
Notice (temporary)	Notice 2009-30, 2009-14 I.R.B. 989.
Announcement	Announcement 2009-11, 2009-4 I.R.B. 432.

Judicial

Board of Tax Appeals:	
GPO reporter	*Estate of D. R. Daly, 3 B.T.A. 1042 (1926).*
Tax Court Regular:	
(temporary citation)	*Mehan, Marty, 122 T.C. ___ , No. 5 (2009).*
Tax Court Regular:	
GPO reporter	*Mehan, Marty, 122 T.C. 396 (2009).*
Tax Court Memo:	
General (unpublished)	*Dixon, Michel, T.C. Memo. 2009-310.*
CCH reporter	*Dixon, Michel, 78 TCM 462 (2009).*
RIA reporter[1]	*Dixon, Michel, RIA T.C. Memo. ¶ 99,310 (2009).*

[1]Previously this reporter was published by Prentice-Hall (P-H).

Tax Court Small Cases Division:	*Brown, TC Summary Opinion 2009-109.*
District Court:	
West reporter	*Barber, Lori, 85 F.Supp. 2d. 967 (N.D.Ca., 2000).*
CCH reporter	*Barber, Lori, 2000-1 USTC ¶ 50,209 (N.D.Ca.).*
RIA reporter[1]	*Barber, Lori, 85 AFTR2d 2000-879 (N.D.Ca.).*
Court of Federal Claims:[2]	
West reporter	*Bennett, Courtney, 30 Fed. Cl. 396 (1994).*
CCH reporter	*Bennett, Courtney, 94-1 USTC ¶ 50,044 (Fed.Cl.).*
RIA reporter[1]	*Bennett, Courtney, 73 AFTR2d 94-534 (Fed.Cl.).*
Court of Appeal:	
West reporter	*Home of Faith, 39 F.3d. 263 (CA-10, 1994).*
CCH reporter	*Home of Faith, 94-2 USTC ¶ 50,570 (CA-10).*
RIA reporter[1]	*Home of Faith, 74 AFTR2d 94-5608 (CA-10).*
Supreme Court:	
GPO reporter	*Indianapolis Power & Light, 493 U.S. 203 (1990).*
West reporter	*Indianapolis Power & Light, 110 S.Ct. 589 (1990).*
CCH reporter	*Indianapolis Power & Light, 90-1 USTC ¶ 50,007 (USSC).*
RIA reporter	*Indianapolis Power & Light, 65 AFTR2d 90-394 (USSC).*

Books

Raabe, W., Whittenburg, G., and Sanders, D. 2009. *Federal Tax Research*, 8th ed. Mason, OH: South-Western.

Journals

Craig, C.K. and Toolson, R.B., A Tax-Efficient Dividend Strategy for Retirement. *Practical Tax Strategies* (March 2005).

Capitalization

Proper nouns and words derived from them are capitalized while common nouns are not. The names of specific persons, places, or things are proper nouns. All other nouns are common nouns. Examples of proper nouns include:

    the Congress

    the Code

    Section 172(a)

    the Regulations

    Regulations §1.102-1

    the President

    the Fifth Circuit

    the Tax Court

    a Revenue Ruling

    a Private Letter Ruling

[2]This court also has been known as the Claims Court and the Court of Claims.

Italics

In handwritten or typed papers underlining represents italics. The titles of books, magazines, newspapers, pamphlets, court cases, and tax services are shown in italics. Examples of items that are italicized include:

The Wealth of Nations

Journal of Taxation

New York Times

AICPA Code of Conduct

Circular 230

Statements on Responsibility in Tax Practice

Gregory v. Helvering

Cumulative Bulletin

Standard Federal Tax Reports

Federal Tax Coordinator 2d

Note: Do not italicize the titles of legal documents such as the U.S. Constitution and the U.S. Code.

Inline Lists

An inline list is an independent clause followed by a colon with each item in the list separated by a comma.

The College of Business Administration has five departments: Accounting, Finance, Information Systems, Management, and Marketing.

Displayed Lists

Displayed lists are used to make items easy to scan by the reader. Such lists should be introduced with an independent clause or by a complete sentence ending with a period. Examples of items that it would be appropriate to display in list form include:

- steps to solve a problem,

- rules,

- proposals to be discussed,

- checklists,

- recommendations, and

- procedures.

Periods are not used in lists unless the items in the list are complete sentences. The items in a list should be in the same form (i.e., nouns, phrases, clauses, or sentences). If the items in a list are to be numbered, use an arabic number followed by a period for each item. If the items are not numbered, say, because the list is not prioritized or sequential, consider using a bullet to draw the reader's attention to the items in the list (as shown above).

The punctuation mark preceding a list is a period or semicolon if the lead-in is a complete sentence. For instance

The stop light's colors were:

- Red,

- White, and

- Blue.

The stoplight had three colors.

- Red,
- White, and
- Blue.

Other Citation Systems

Many professions and academic disciplines have developed unique systems of citing published material. The more common style manuals include:

U.S. Government Printing Office *Style Manual*

The Chicago Manual of Style

MLA Handbook for Writers of Research Papers

The Bluebook, A Uniform System of (Legal) Citations

Publication Manual of the American Psychological Association

In addition to the manuals listed above, there are style manuals published for accounting, biology, chemistry, geology, linguistics, mathematics, medicine, and physics.

IRS Circular 230

Treasury Department Circular No. 230 Cat 16586R (Rev. 6-2005)

Regulations Governing the Practice of Attorneys, Certified Public Accountants, Enrolled Agents, Enrolled Actuaries, and Appraisers before the Internal Revenue Service

---

Department of the Treasury Internal Revenue Service

Title 31 Code of Federal Regulations, Subtitle A, Part 10, revised as of June 20, 2005

PART 10—PRACTICE BEFORE THE INTERNAL REVENUE SERVICE

Paragraph 1. The authority citation for subtitle A, part 10 is revised to read as follows:

Authority: Sec.3, 23 Stat. 258, secs. 2-12, 60 Stat. 237 et seq.; 5

U.S.C. 301, 500, 551-559; 31 U.S.C. 330; Reorg. Plan No. 26 of 1950, 15 FR 4935, 64 Stat. 1280, 3 CFR, 1949-1953 Comp., p. 1017.

§10.0 Scope of part

This part contains rules governing the recognition of attorneys, certified public accountants, enrolled agents, and other persons representing taxpayers before the Internal Revenue Service. Subpart A of this part sets forth rules relating to the authority to practice before the Internal Revenue Service; Subpart B of this part prescribes the duties and restrictions relating to such practice; Subpart C of this part prescribes the sanctions for violating the regulations; Subpart D of this part contains the rules applicable to disciplinary proceedings; and Subpart E of this part contains general provisions including provisions relating to the availability of official records.

Subpart A—Rules Governing Authority to Practice

§10.1 Director of Practice.

(a) *Establishment of office*. The Office of Director of Practice is established in the Office of the Secretary of the Treasury. The Director of Practice is appointed by the Secretary of the Treasury, or his or her designate.

(b) *Duties*. The Director of Practice acts on applications for enrollment to practice before the Internal Revenue Service; makes inquiries with respect to matters under his or her jurisdiction; institutes and provides for the conduct of disciplinary proceedings relating to attorneys, certified public accountants, enrolled agents, enrolled actuaries and appraisers; and performs other duties as are necessary or appropriate to carry out his or her functions under this part or as are prescribed by the Secretary of the Treasury, or his or her delegate.

(c) *Acting Director of Practice*. The Secretary of the Treasury, or his or her delegate, will designate an officer or employee of the Treasury Department to act as Director of Practice in the absence of the Director or a vacancy in that office.

§10.2 Definitions.

As used in this part, except where the text clearly provides otherwise:

(a) *Attorney* means any person who is a member in good standing of the bar of the highest court of any State, territory, or possession of the United States, including a Commonwealth, or the District of Columbia.

(b) *Certified public accountant* means any person who is duly qualified to practice as a certified public accountant in any State, territory, or possession of the United States, including a Commonwealth, or the District of Columbia.

(c) *Commissioner* refers to the Commissioner of Internal Revenue.

(d) *Practice before the Internal Revenue Service* comprehends all matters connected with a presentation to the Internal Revenue Service or any of its officers or employees relating to a taxpayer's rights, privileges, or liabilities under laws or regulations administered by the Internal Revenue Service. Such presentations include, but are not limited to, preparing and filing documents, corresponding and communicating with the Internal Revenue Service, and representing a client at conferences, hearings, and meetings.

(e) *Practitioner* means any individual described in paragraphs (a), (b), (c), or (d) of §10.3.

(f) *A tax return* includes an amended tax return and a claim for refund.

(g) *Service* means the Internal Revenue Service.

§10.3 Who may practice.

(a) *Attorney*. Any attorney who is not currently under suspension or disbarment from practice before the Internal Revenue Service may practice before the Internal Revenue Service by filing with the Internal Revenue Service a written declaration that he or she is currently qualified as an attorney and is authorized to represent the party or parties on whose behalf he or she acts.

(b) *Certified public accountants*. Any certified public accountant who is not currently under suspension or disbarment from practice before the Internal Revenue Service may practice before the Internal Revenue Service by filing with the Internal Revenue Service a written declaration that he or she is currently qualified as a certified public accountant and is authorized to represent the party or parties on whose behalf he or she acts.

(c) *Enrolled agents*. Any individual enrolled as an agent pursuant to this part who is not currently under suspension or disbarment from practice before the Internal Revenue Service may practice before the Internal Revenue Service.

(d) *Enrolled actuaries.*

(1) Any individual who is enrolled as an actuary by the Joint Board for the Enrollment of Actuaries pursuant to 29 U.S.C. 1242 who is not currently under suspension or disbarment from practice before the Internal Revenue Service may practice before the Internal Revenue Service by filing with the Internal Revenue Service a written declaration stating that he or she is currently qualified as an enrolled actuary and is authorized to represent the party or parties on whose behalf he or she acts.

(2) Practice as an enrolled actuary is limited to representation with respect to issues involving the following statutory provisions in title 26 of the United States Code: sections 401 (relating to qualification of employee plans), 403(a) (relating to whether an annuity plan meets the requirements of section 404(a) (2)), 404 (relating to deductibility of employer contributions), 405 (relating to qualification of bond purchase plans), 412 (relating to funding requirements for certain employee plans), 413 (relating to application of qualification requirements to collectively bargained plans and to plans maintained by more than one employer), 414 (relating to definitions and special rules with respect to the employee plan area), 419 (relating to treatment of funded welfare benefits), 419A (relating to qualified asset accounts), 420 (relating to transfers of excess pension assets to retiree health accounts), 4971 (relating to excise taxes payable as a result of an accumulated funding deficiency under section 412), 4972 (relating to tax on nondeductible contributions to qualified employer plans), 4976 (relating to taxes with respect to funded welfare benefit plans), 4980 (relating to tax on reversion of qualified plan assets to employer), 6057 (relating to annual registration of plans), 6058 (relating to information required in connection with certain plans of deferred compensation), 6059 (relating to periodic report of actuary), 6652(e) (relating to the failure to file annual registration and other notifications by pension plan), 6652(f) (relating to the failure to file information required in connection with certain plans of deferred compensation), 6692 (relating to the failure to file actuarial report), 7805(b) (relating to the extent to which an Internal Revenue Service ruling or determination letter coming under the statutory provisions listed here will be applied without retroactive effect); and

29 U.S.C. 1083 (relating to the waiver of funding for nonqualified plans).

(3) An individual who practices before the Internal Revenue Service pursuant to paragraph (d) (1) of this section is subject to the provisions of this part in the same manner as attorneys, certified public accountants and enrolled agents.

(e) *Others.* Any individual qualifying under paragraph (d) of §10.5 or §10.7 is eligible to practice before the Internal Revenue Service to the extent provided in those sections.

(f) *Government officers and employees, and others.* An individual, who is an officer or employee of the executive, legislative, or judicial branch of the United States Government; an officer or employee of the District of Columbia; a Member of Congress; or a Resident Commissioner may not practice before the Internal Revenue Service if such practice violates 18 U.S.C. 203 or 205.

(g) *State officers and employees.* No officer or employee of any State, or subdivision of any State, whose duties require him or her to pass upon, investigate, or deal with tax matters for such State or subdivision, may practice before the Internal Revenue Service, if such employment may disclose facts or information applicable to Federal tax matters.

§10.4 Eligibility for enrollment.

(a) *Enrollment upon examination.* The Director of Practice may grant enrollment to an applicant who demonstrates special competence in tax matters by written examination administered by, or administered under the oversight of, the Director of Practice and who has not engaged in any conduct that would justify the censure, suspension or disbarment of any practitioner under the provisions of this part.

(b) *Enrollment of former Internal Revenue Service employees.* The Director of Practice may grant enrollment to an applicant who, by virtue of his or her past service and technical experience in the Internal Revenue Service, has qualified for such enrollment and who has not engaged in any conduct that would justify the censure, suspension, or disbarment of any practitioner under the provisions of this part, under the following circumstances—

(1) The former employee applies for enrollment to the Director of Practice on a form supplied by the Director of Practice and supplies the information requested on the form and such other information regarding the experience and training of the applicant as may be relevant.

(2) An appropriate office of the Internal Revenue Service, at the request of the Director of Practice, will provide the Director of Practice with a detailed report of the nature and rating of the applicant's work while employed by the Internal Revenue Service and a recommendation whether such employment qualifies the applicant technically or otherwise for the desired authorization.

(3) Enrollment based on an applicant's former employment with the Internal Revenue Service may be of unlimited scope or it may be limited to permit the presentation of matters only of the particular class or only before the particular unit or division of the Internal Revenue Service for which the applicant's former employment has qualified the applicant.

(4) Application for enrollment based on an applicant's former employment with the Internal Revenue Service must be made within 3 years from the date of separation from such employment.

(5) An applicant for enrollment who is requesting such enrollment based on his or her former employment with the Internal Revenue Service must have had a minimum of 5 years continuous employment with the Internal Revenue Service during which he or she must have been regularly engaged in applying and interpreting the provisions of the Internal Revenue Code and the regulations thereunder relating to income, estate, gift, employment, or excise taxes.

(6) For the purposes of paragraph (b)(5) of this section, an aggregate of 10 or more years of employment in positions involving the application and interpretation of the provisions of the Internal Revenue Code, at least 3 of which occurred within the 5 years preceding the date of application, is the equivalent of 5 years continuous employment.

(c) *Natural persons.* Enrollment to practice may be granted only to natural persons.

§10.5 Application for enrollment.

(a) *Form; address.* An applicant for enrollment must file an application on Form 23, "Application for Enrollment to Practice Before the Internal Revenue Service," properly executed under oath or affirmation, with the Director of Practice. The address of the applicant entered on Form 23 will be the address under which a successful applicant is enrolled and is the address to which the Director of Practice will send correspondence concerning enrollment. An enrolled agent must send notification of any change to his or her enrollment address to the Director of Practice, Internal Revenue Service, 1111 Constitution Avenue, NW, Washington, DC 20224, or at such other address specified by the Director of Practice. This notification must include the enrolled agent's name, old address, new address, social security number or tax identification number, signature, and the date.

(b) *Fee.* The application for enrollment must be accompanied by a check or money order in the amount set forth on Form 23, payable to the Internal Revenue Service, which amount constitutes a fee charged to each applicant for enrollment. This fee will be retained by the United States whether or not the applicant is granted enrollment.

(c) *Additional information; examination.* The Director of Practice, as a condition to consideration of an application for enrollment, may require the applicant to file additional information and to submit to any written or oral examination under oath or otherwise. The Director of Practice will, on written request filed by an applicant, afford such applicant the opportunity to be heard with respect to his or her application for enrollment.

(d) *Temporary recognition.* On receipt of a properly executed application, the Director of Practice may grant the applicant temporary recognition to practice pending a determination as to whether enrollment to practice should be granted. Temporary recognition will be granted only in unusual circumstances and it will not be granted, in any circumstance, if the application is not regular on its face, if the information stated in the application, if true, is not sufficient to warrant enrollment to practice, or if there is any information before the Director of Practice indicating that the statements in the application are untrue or that the applicant would not otherwise qualify for enrollment. Issuance of temporary recognition does not constitute enrollment to practice or a finding of eligibility for enrollment, and the temporary recognition may be withdrawn at any time by the Director of Practice.

(e) *Appeal from denial of application.* The Director of Practice must inform the applicant as to the reason(s) for any denial of an application for enrollment. The applicant may, within 30 days after receipt of the notice of denial of enrollment, file a written appeal of the denial of enrollment with the Secretary of the Treasury or his or her delegate. A decision on the appeal will be rendered by the Secretary of the Treasury, or his or her delegate, as soon as practicable.

§10.6 Enrollment.

(a) *Roster.* The Director of Practice will maintain rosters of all individuals—

(1) Who have been granted active enrollment to practice before the Internal Revenue Service;

(2) Whose enrollment has been placed in inactive status for failure to meet the requirements for renewal of enrollment;

(3) Whose enrollment has been placed in inactive retirement status;

(4) Who have been censured, suspended, or disbarred from practice before the Internal Revenue Service;

(5) Whose offer of consent to resign from enrollment to practice before the Internal Revenue Service has been accepted by the Director of Practice under §10.61; and

(6) Whose application for enrollment has been denied.

(b) *Enrollment card.* The Director of Practice will issue an enrollment card to each individual whose application for enrollment to practice before the Internal Revenue Service is approved after July 26, 2002. Each enrollment card will be valid for the period stated on the enrollment card. An individual is not eligible to practice before the Internal Revenue Service if his or her enrollment card is not valid.

(c) *Term of enrollment.* Each individual enrolled to practice before the Internal Revenue Service will be accorded active enrollment status subject to his or her renewal of enrollment as provided in this part.

(d) *Renewal of enrollment.* To maintain active enrollment to practice before the Internal Revenue Service, each individual enrolled is required to have his or her enrollment renewed. Failure by an individual to receive notification from the Director of Practice of the renewal requirement will not be justification for the failure to satisfy this requirement.

(1) All individuals licensed to practice before the Internal Revenue Service who have a social security number or tax identification number that ends with the numbers 0, 1, 2, or 3, except for those individuals who received their initial enrollment after November 1, 2003, must apply for renewal between November 1, 2003, and January 31, 2004. The renewal will be effective April 1, 2004.

(2) All individuals licensed to practice before the Internal Revenue Service who have a social security number or tax identification number that ends with the numbers 4, 5, or 6, except for those individuals who received their initial enrollment after November 1, 2004, must apply for renewal between November 1, 2004, and January 31, 2005. The renewal will be effective April 1, 2005.

(3) All individuals licensed to practice before the Internal Revenue Service who have a social security number or tax identification number that ends with the numbers 7, 8, or 9, except for those individuals who received their initial enrollment after November 1, 2005, must apply for renewal between November 1, 2005, and January 31, 2006. The renewal will be effective April 1, 2006.

(4) Thereafter, applications for renewal will be required between November 1 and January 31 of every subsequent third year as specified in paragraphs (d)(1),(2) or (3) of this section according to the last number of the individual's social security number or tax identification number. Those individuals who receive initial enrollment after November 1 and before April 2 of the applicable renewal period will not be required to renew their enrollment before the first full renewal period following the receipt of their initial enrollment.

(5) The Director of Practice will notify the individual of his or her renewal of enrollment and will issue the individual a card evidencing enrollment.

(6) A reasonable nonrefundable fee may be charged for each application for renewal of enrollment filed with the Director of Practice.

(7) Forms required for renewal may be obtained from the Director of Practice, Internal Revenue Service, 1111 Constitution Avenue, NW., Washington, DC 20224.

(e) *Condition for renewal: Continuing professional education.* In order to qualify for renewal of enrollment, an individual enrolled to practice before the Internal Revenue Service must certify, on the application for renewal form prescribed by the Director of Practice, that he or she has satisfied the following continuing professional education requirements.

(1) *For renewed enrollment effective after March 31, 2004.* (i) A minimum of 16 hours of continuing education credit must be completed during each calendar year in the enrollment term.

(2) *For renewed enrollment effective after April 1, 2007.*

(i) A minimum of 72 hours of continuing education credit must be completed during each three year period described in paragraph (d)(4) of this section. Each such three year period is known as an enrollment cycle.

(ii) A minimum of 16 hours of continuing education credit, including 2 hours of ethics or professional conduct, must be completed in each year of an enrollment cycle.

(iii) An individual who receives initial enrollment during an enrollment cycle must complete two (2) hours of qualifying continuing education credit for each month enrolled during the enrollment cycle. Enrollment for any part of a month is considered enrollment for the entire month.

(f) *Qualifying continuing education-*

(1) *General.* To qualify for continuing education credit, a course of learning must—

(i) Be a qualifying program designed to enhance professional knowledge in Federal taxation or Federal tax related matters, i.e., programs comprised of current subject matter in Federal taxation or Federal tax related matters, including accounting, tax preparation software and taxation or ethics; and

(ii) Be conducted by a qualifying sponsor.

(2) *Qualifying programs—*

(i) *Formal programs.* A formal program qualifies as continuing education programs if it—

(A) Requires attendance. Additionally, the program sponsor must provide each attendee with a certificate of attendance; and

(B) Requires that the program be conducted by a qualified instructor, discussion leader, or speaker, i. e., a person whose background, training, education and experience is appropriate for instructing or leading a discussion on the subject matter of the particular program; and

(C) Provides or requires a written outline, textbook, or suitable electronic educational materials.

(ii) *Correspondence or individual study programs (including taped programs).* Qualifying continuing education programs include correspondence or individual study programs that are conducted by qualifying sponsors and completed on an individual basis by the enrolled individual. The allowable credit hours for such programs will be measured on a basis comparable to the measurement of a seminar or course for credit in an accredited educational institution. Such programs qualify as continuing education programs if they—

(A) Require registration of the participants by the sponsor;

(B) Provide a means for measuring completion by the participants (e.g., a written examination), including the issuance of a certificate of completion by the sponsor; and

(C) Provide a written outline, textbook, or suitable electronic educational materials.

(iii) *Serving as an instructor, discussion leader or speaker.*

(A) One hour of continuing education credit will be awarded for each contact hour completed as an instructor, discussion leader, or speaker at an educational program that meets the continuing education requirements of paragraph (f) of this section.

(B) Two hours of continuing education credit will be awarded for actual subject preparation time for each contact hour completed as an instructor, discussion leader, or speaker at such programs. It is the responsibility of the individual claiming such credit to maintain records to verify preparation time.

(C) The maximum credit for instruction and preparation may not exceed 50 percent of the continuing education requirement for an enrollment cycle.

(D) An instructor, discussion leader, or speaker who makes more than one presentation on the same subject matter during an enrollment cycle, will receive continuing education credit for only one such presentation for the enrollment cycle.

(iv) *Credit for published articles, books, etc.*

(A) Continuing education credit will be awarded for publications on Federal taxation or Federal tax related matters, including accounting, financial management, tax preparation software, and taxation, provided the content of such publications is current and designed for the enhancement of the professional knowledge of an individual enrolled to practice before the Internal Revenue Service.

(B) The credit allowed will be on the basis of one hour credit for each hour of preparation time for the material. It is the responsibility of the person claiming the credit to maintain records to verify preparation time.

(C) The maximum credit for publications may not exceed 25 percent of the continuing education requirement of any enrollment cycle.

(3) *Periodic examination.*

(i) Individuals may establish eligibility for renewal of enrollment for any enrollment cycle by—

(A) Achieving a passing score on each part of the Special Enrollment Examination administered under this part during the three year period prior to renewal; and

(B) Completing a minimum of 16 hours of qualifying continuing education during the last year of an enrollment cycle.

(ii) Courses designed to help an applicant prepare for the examination specified in paragraph (a) of §10.4 are considered basic in nature and are not qualifying continuing education.

(g) *Sponsors.*

(1) Sponsors are those responsible for presenting programs.

(2) To qualify as a sponsor, a program presenter must—

(i) Be an accredited educational institution;

(ii) Be recognized for continuing education purposes by the licensing body of any State, territory, or possession of the United States, including a Commonwealth, or the District of Columbia.

(iii) Be recognized by the Director of Practice as a professional organization or society whose programs include offering continuing professional education opportunities in subject matters within the scope of paragraph (f)(1)(i) of this section; or

(iv) File a sponsor agreement with the Director of Practice and obtain approval of the program as a qualified continuing education program.

(3) A qualifying sponsor must ensure the program complies with the following requirements—

(i) Programs must be developed by individual(s) qualified in the subject matter;

(ii) Program subject matter must be current;

(iii) Instructors, discussion leaders, and speakers must be qualified with respect to program content;

(iv) Programs must include some means for evaluation of technical content and presentation;

(v) Certificates of completion must be provided to the participants who successfully complete the program; and

(vi) Records must be maintained by the sponsor to verify the participants who attended and completed the program for a period of three years following completion of the program. In the case of continuous conferences, conventions, and the like, records must be maintained to verify completion of the program and attendance by each participant at each segment of the program.

(4) Professional organizations or societies wishing to be considered as qualified sponsors must request this status from the Director of Practice and furnish information in support of the request together with any further information deemed necessary by the Director of Practice.

(5) A professional organization or society recognized as a qualified sponsor by the Director of Practice will retain its status for one enrollment cycle. The Director of Practice will publish the names of such sponsors on a periodic basis.

(h) *Measurement of continuing education coursework.*

(1) All continuing education programs will be measured in terms of contact hours. The shortest recognized program will be one contact hour.

(2) A contact hour is 50 minutes of continuous participation in a program. Credit is granted only for a full contact hour, i.e., 50 minutes or multiples thereof. For example, a program lasting more than 50 minutes but less than 100 minutes will count as one contact hour.

(3) Individual segments at continuous conferences, conventions and the like will be considered one total program. For example, two 90-minute segments (180 minutes) at a continuous conference will count as three contact hours.

(4) For university or college courses, each semester hour credit will equal 15 contact hours and a quarter hour credit will equal 10 contact hours.

(i) *Recordkeeping requirements.*

(1) Each individual applying for renewal must retain for a period of three years following the date of renewal of enrollment the information required with regard to qualifying continuing professional education credit hours. Such information includes—

(i) The name of the sponsoring organization;

(ii) The location of the program;

(iii) The title of the program and description of its content;

(iv) Written outlines, course syllabi, textbook, and/or electronic materials provided or required for the course;

(v) The dates attended;

(vi) The credit hours claimed;

(vii) The name(s) of the instructor(s), discussion leader(s), or speaker(s), if appropriate; and

(viii) The certificate of completion and/or signed statement of the hours of attendance obtained from the sponsor.

(2) To receive continuing education credit for service completed as an instructor, discussion leader, or speaker, the following information must be maintained for a period of three years following the date of renewal of enrollment—

(i) The name of the sponsoring organization;

(ii) The location of the program;

(iii) The title of the program and description of its content;

(iv) The dates of the program; and

(v) The credit hours claimed.

(3) To receive continuing education credit for publications, the following information must be maintained for a period of three years following the date of renewal of enrollment—

(i) The publisher;

(ii) The title of the publication;

(iii) A copy of the publication;

(iv) The date of publication; and

(v) Records that substantiate the hours worked on the publication.

(j) *Waivers.*

(1) Waiver from the continuing education requirements for a given period may be granted by the Director of Practice for the following reasons—

(i) Health, which prevented compliance with the continuing education requirements;

(ii) Extended active military duty;

(iii) Absence from the United States for an extended period of time due to employment or other reasons, provided the individual does not practice before the Internal Revenue Service during such absence; and

(iv) Other compelling reasons, which will be considered on a case-by-case basis.

(2) A request for waiver must be accompanied by appropriate documentation. The individual is required to furnish any additional documentation or explanation deemed necessary by the Director of Practice. Examples of appropriate documentation could be a medical certificate or military orders.

(3) A request for waiver must be filed no later than the last day of the renewal application period.

(4) If a request for waiver is not approved, the individual will be placed in inactive status, so notified by the Director of Practice, and placed on a roster of inactive enrolled individuals.

(5) If a request for waiver is approved, the individual will be notified and issued a card evidencing renewal.

(6) Those who are granted waivers are required to file timely applications for renewal of enrollment.

(k) *Failure to comply.*

(1) Compliance by an individual with the requirements of this part is determined by the Director of Practice. An individual who fails to meet the requirements of eligibility for renewal of enrollment will be notified by the Director of Practice at his or her enrollment address by first class mail. The notice will state the basis for the determination of noncompliance and will provide the individual an opportunity to furnish information in writing relating to the matter within 60 days of the date of the notice. Such information will be considered by the Director of Practice in making a final determination as to eligibility for renewal of enrollment.

(2) The Director of Practice may require any individual, by notice sent by first class mail to his or her enrollment address, to provide copies of any records required to be maintained under this part. The Director of Practice may disallow any continuing professional education hours claimed if the individual fails to comply with this requirement.

(3) An individual who has not filed a timely application for renewal of enrollment, who has not made a timely response to the notice of noncompliance with the renewal requirements, or who has not satisfied the requirements of eligibility for renewal will be placed on a roster of inactive enrolled individuals. During this time, the individual will be ineligible to practice before the Internal Revenue Service.

(4) Individuals placed in inactive enrollment status and individuals ineligible to practice before the Internal Revenue Service may not state or imply that they are enrolled to practice before the Internal Revenue Service, or use the term enrolled agent, the designation "E. A." or other form of reference to eligibility to practice before the Internal Revenue Service.

(5) An individual placed in an inactive status may be reinstated to an active enrollment status by filing an application for renewal of enrollment and providing evidence of the completion of all required continuing professional education hours for the enrollment cycle. Continuing education credit under this paragraph (k)(5) may not be used to satisfy the requirements of the enrollment cycle in which the individual has been placed back on the active roster.

(6) An individual placed in an inactive status must file an application for renewal of enrollment and satisfy the requirements for renewal as set forth in this section within three years of being placed in an inactive status. The name of such individual otherwise will be removed from the inactive enrollment roster and his or her enrollment will terminate. Eligibility for enrollment must then be reestablished by the individual as provided in this section.

(7) Inactive enrollment status is not available to an individual who is the subject of a disciplinary matter in the Office of Director of Practice.

(l) *Inactive retirement status.* An individual who no longer practices before the Internal Revenue Service may request being placed in an inactive status at any time and such individual will be placed in an inactive retirement status. The individual will be ineligible to practice before the Internal Revenue Service. Such individual must file a timely application for renewal of enrollment at each applicable renewal or enrollment period as provided in this section. An individual who is placed in an inactive retirement status may be reinstated to an active enrollment status by filing an application for renewal of enrollment and providing evidence of the completion of the required continuing professional education hours for the enrollment cycle. Inactive retirement status is not available to an individual who is subject of a disciplinary matter in the Office of Director of Practice.

(m) *Renewal while under suspension or disbarment.* An individual who is ineligible to practice before the Internal Revenue Service by virtue of disciplinary action is required to be in conformance with the requirements for renewal of enrollment before his or her eligibility is restored.

(n) *Verification.* The Director of Practice may review the continuing education records of an enrolled individual and/or qualified sponsor in a manner deemed appropriate to determine compliance with the requirements and standards for renewal of enrollment as provided in paragraph (f) of this section.

(o) *Enrolled Actuaries.* The enrollment and the renewal of enrollment of actuaries authorized to practice under paragraph (d) of §10.3 are governed by the regulations of the Joint Board for the Enrollment of Actuaries at 20 CFR 901.1 through 901.71.

(Approved by the Office of Management and Budget under Control No. 15450946 and 1545-1726)

§10.7 Representing oneself; participating in rulemaking; limited practice; special appearances; and return preparation.

(a) *Representing oneself.* Individuals may appear on their own behalf before the Internal Revenue Service provided they present satisfactory identification.

(b) *Participating in rulemaking.* Individuals may participate in rulemaking as provided by the Administrative Procedure Act. See 5 U.S.C. 553.

(c) *Limited practice—*

(1) *In general.* Subject to the limitations in paragraph (c)(2) of this section, an individual who is not a practitioner may represent a taxpayer before the Internal Revenue Service in the circumstances described in this paragraph (c)(1), even if the taxpayer is not present, provided the individual presents satisfactory identification and proof of his or her authority to represent the taxpayer. The circumstances described in this paragraph (c)(1) are as follows:

(i) An individual may represent a member of his or her immediate family.

(ii) A regular full-time employee of an individual employer may represent the employer.

(iii) A general partner or a regular full-time employee of a partnership may represent the partnership.

(iv) A bona fide officer or a regular full-time employee of a corporation (including a parent, subsidiary, or other affiliated corporation), association, or organized group may represent the corporation, association, or organized group.

(v) A regular full-time employee of a trust, receivership, guardianship, or estate may represent the trust, receivership, guardianship, or estate.

(vi) An officer or a regular employee of a governmental unit, agency, or authority may represent the governmental unit, agency, or authority in the course of his or her official duties.

(vii) An individual may represent any individual or entity, who is outside the United States, before personnel of the Internal Revenue Service when such representation takes place outside the United States.

(viii) An individual who prepares and signs a taxpayer's tax return as the preparer, or who prepares a tax return but is not required (by the instructions to the tax return or regulations) to sign the tax return, may represent the taxpayer before revenue agents, customer service representatives or similar officers and employees of the Internal Revenue Service during an examination of the taxable year or period covered by that tax return, but, unless otherwise prescribed by regulation or notice, this right does not permit such individual to represent the taxpayer, regardless of the circumstances requiring representation, before appeals officers, revenue officers, Counsel or similar officers or employees of the Internal Revenue Service or the Department of Treasury.

(2) *Limitations.*

(i) An individual who is under suspension or disbarment from practice before the Internal Revenue Service may not engage in limited practice before the Internal Revenue Service under paragraph (c)(1) of this section.

(ii) The Director, after notice and opportunity for a conference, may deny eligibility to engage in limited practice before the Internal Revenue Service under paragraph (c)(1) of this section to any individual who has engaged in conduct that would justify censuring, suspending, or disbarring a practitioner from practice before the Internal Revenue Service.

(iii) An individual who represents a taxpayer under the authority of paragraph (c)(1) of this section is subject, to the extent of his or her authority, to such rules of general applicability regarding standards of conduct and other matters as the Director of Practice prescribes.

(d) *Special appearances.* The Director of Practice may, subject to such conditions as he or she deems appropriate, authorize an individual who is not otherwise eligible to practice before the Internal Revenue Service to represent another person in a particular matter.

(e) *Preparing tax returns and furnishing information.* Any individual may prepare a tax return, appear as a witness for the taxpayer before the Internal Revenue Service, or furnish information at the request of the Internal Revenue Service or any of its officers or employees.

(f) *Fiduciaries.* For purposes of this part, a fiduciary (i.e., a trustee, receiver, guardian, personal representative, administrator, or executor) is considered to be the taxpayer and not a representative of the taxpayer.

§10.8 Customhouse brokers.

Nothing contained in the regulations in this part will affect or limit the right of a customhouse broker, licensed as such by the Commissioner of Customs in accordance with the regulations prescribed therefore, in any customs district in which he or she is so licensed, at a relevant local office of the Internal Revenue Service or before the National Office of the Internal Revenue Service, to act as a representative in respect to any matters relating specifically to the importation or exportation of merchandise under the customs or internal revenue laws, for any person for whom he or she has acted as a customhouse broker.

- Par. 3. In part 10, subpart B is amended by revising §§10.20 through 10.32 and revising §10.34.

Subpart B—Duties and Restrictions Relating to Practice Before the Internal Revenue Service

§10.20 Information to be furnished

(a) *To the Internal Revenue Service*

(1) A practitioner must, on a proper and lawful request by a duly authorized officer or employee of the Internal Revenue Service, promptly submit records or information in any matter before the Internal Revenue Service unless the practitioner believes in good faith and on reasonable grounds that the records or information are privileged.

(2) Where the requested records or information are not in the possession of, or subject to the control of, the practitioner or the practitioner's client, the practitioner must promptly notify the requesting Internal Revenue Service officer or employee and the practitioner must provide any information that the practitioner has regarding the identity of any person who the practitioner believes may have possession or control of the requested records or information. The practitioner must make reasonable inquiry of his or her client regarding the identity of any person who may have possession or control of the requested records or information, but the practitioner is not required to make inquiry of any other person or independently verify any information provided by the practitioner's client regarding the identity of such persons.

(b) *To the Director of Practice.* When a proper and lawful request is made by the Director of Practice, a practitioner must provide the Director of Practice with any information the practitioner has concerning an inquiry by the Director of Practice into an alleged violation of the regulations in this part by any person, and to testify regarding this information in any proceeding instituted under this part, unless the practitioner believes in good faith and on reasonable grounds that the information is privileged.

(c) *Interference with a proper and lawful request for records or information.* A practitioner may not interfere, or attempt to interfere, with any proper and lawful effort by the Internal Revenue Service, its officers or employees, or the Director of Practice, or his or her employees, to obtain any record or information unless the practitioner believes in good faith and on reasonable grounds that the record or information is privileged.

§10.21 Knowledge of client's omission.

A practitioner who, having been retained by a client with respect to a matter administered by the Internal Revenue Service, knows that the client has not complied with the revenue laws of the United States or has made an error in or omission from any return, document, affidavit, or other paper which the client submitted or executed under the revenue laws of the United States, must advise the client promptly of the fact of such noncompliance, error, or omission.

The practitioner must advise the client of the consequences as provided under the Code and regulations of such noncompliance, error, or omission.

§10.22 Diligence as to accuracy.

(a) *In general.* A practitioner must exercise due diligence—

(1) In preparing or assisting in the preparation of, approving, and filing tax returns, documents, affidavits, and other papers relating to Internal Revenue Service matters;

(2) In determining the correctness of oral or written representations made by the practitioner to the Department of the Treasury; and

(3) In determining the correctness of oral or written representations made by the practitioner to clients with reference to any matter administered by the Internal Revenue Service.

(b) *Reliance on others.* Except as provided in §§10.33 and 10.34, a practitioner will be presumed to have exercised due diligence for purposes of this section if the practitioner relies on the work product of another person and the practitioner used reasonable care in engaging, supervising, training, and evaluating the person, taking proper account of the nature of the relationship between the practitioner and the person.

§10.23 Prompt disposition of pending matters.

A practitioner may not unreasonably delay the prompt disposition of any matter before the Internal Revenue Service.

§10.24 Assistance from or to disbarred or suspended persons and former Internal Revenue Service employees.

A practitioner may not, knowingly and directly or indirectly:

(a) Accept assistance from or assist any person who is under disbarment or suspension from practice before the Internal Revenue Service if the assistance relates to a matter or matters constituting practice before the Internal Revenue Service.

(b) Accept assistance from any former government employee where the provisions of §10.25 or any Federal law would be violated.

§10.25 Practice by former Government employees, their partners and their associates.

(a) *Definitions.* For purposes of this section—

(1) *Assist* means to act in such a way as to advise, furnish information to, or otherwise aid another person, directly or indirectly.

(2) *Government employee* is an officer or employee of the United States or any agency of the United States, including a *special government employee* as defined in 18 U.S.C. 202(a), or of the District of Columbia, or of any State, or a member of Congress or of any State legislature.

(3) *Member of a firm* is a sole practitioner or an employee or associate thereof, or a partner, stockholder, associate, affiliate or employee of a partnership, joint venture, corporation, professional association or other affiliation of two or more practitioners who represent nongovernmental parties.

(4) *Practitioner* includes any individual described in paragraph (f) of §

(5) *Official responsibility* means the direct administrative or operating authority, whether intermediate or final, and either exercisable alone or with others, and either personally or through subordinates, to approve, disapprove, or otherwise direct Government action, with or without knowledge of the action.

(6) *Participate or participation* means substantial involvement as a Government employee by making decisions, or preparing or reviewing documents with or without the right to exercise a judgment of approval or disapproval, or participating in conferences or investigations, or rendering advice of a substantial nature.

(7) *Rule* includes Treasury Regulations, whether issued or under preparation for issuance as Notices of Proposed Rule Making or as Treasury Decisions; revenue rulings; and revenue procedures published in the Internal Revenue Bulletin. Rule does not include a *transaction* as defined in paragraph (a)(8) of this section.

(8) *Transaction* means any decision, determination, finding, letter ruling, technical advice, Chief Counsel advice, or contract or the approval or disapproval thereof, relating to a particular factual situation or situations involving a specific party or parties whose rights, privileges, or liabilities under laws or regulations administered by the Internal Revenue Service, or other legal rights, are determined or immediately affected therein and to which the United States is a party or in which it has a direct and substantial interest, whether or not the same taxable periods are involved. *Transaction* does not include *rule* as defined in paragraph (a)(7) of this section.

(b) *General rules.*

(1) No former Government employee may, subsequent to his or her Government employment,

represent anyone in any matter administered by the Internal Revenue Service if the representation would violate 18 U.S.C. 207 or any other laws of the United States.

(2) No former Government employee who participated in a transaction may, subsequent to his or her Government employment, represent or knowingly assist, in that transaction, any person who is or was a specific party to that transaction.

(3) A former Government employee who within a period of one year prior to the termination of Government employment had official responsibility for a transaction may not, within two years after his or her Government employment is ended, represent or knowingly assist in that transaction any person who is or was a specific party to that transaction.

(4) No former Government employee may, within one year after his or her Government employment is ended, appear before any employee of the Treasury Department in connection with the publication, withdrawal, amendment, modification, or interpretation of a rule in the development of which the former Government employee participated or for which, within a period of one year prior to the termination of his or her Government employment, he or she had official responsibility. This paragraph (b)(4) does not, however, preclude such former employee from appearing on his or her own behalf or from representing a taxpayer before the Internal Revenue Service in connection with a transaction involving the application or interpretation of such a rule with respect to that transaction, provided that such former employee does not utilize or disclose any confidential information acquired by the former employee in the development of the rule.

(c) *Firm representation.*

(1) No member of a firm of which a former Government employee is a member may represent or knowingly assist a person who was or is a specific party in any transaction with respect to which the restrictions of paragraph (b)(2) or (3) of this section apply to the former Government employee, in that transaction, unless the firm isolates the former Government employee in such a way to ensure that the former Government employee cannot assist in the representation.

(2) When isolation of a former Government employee is required under paragraph (c)(1) of this section, a statement affirming the fact of such isolation must be executed under oath by the former Government employee and by another member of the firm acting on behalf of the firm. The statement must clearly identify the firm, the former Government employee, and the transaction(s) requiring isolation and it must be filed with the Director of Practice (and at such other place(s) directed by the Director of Practice) and in such other place and in the manner prescribed by rule or regulation.

(d) *Pending representation.* Practice by former Government employees, their partners and associates with respect to representation in specific matters where actual representation commenced before July 26, 2002, is governed by the regulations set forth at 31 CFR Part 10 revised as of July 1, 2002. The burden of showing that representation commenced before July 26, 2002, lies with the former Government employees, and their partners and associates.

§10.26 Notaries.

A practitioner may not take acknowledgments, administer oaths, certify papers, or perform any official act as a notary public with respect to any matter administered by the Internal Revenue Service and for which he or she is employed as counsel, attorney, or agent, or in which he or she may be in any way interested.

§10.27 Fees.

(a) *Generally.* A practitioner may not charge an unconscionable fee for representing a client in a matter before the Internal Revenue Service.

(b) *Contingent fees.*

(1) For purposes of this section, a contingent fee is any fee that is based, in whole or in part, on whether or not a position taken on a tax return or other filing avoids challenge by the Internal Revenue Service or is sustained either by the Internal Revenue Service or in litigation. A contingent fee includes any fee arrangement in which the practitioner will reimburse the client for all or a portion of the client's fee in the event that a position taken on a tax return or other filing is challenged by the Internal Revenue Service or is not sustained, whether pursuant to an indemnity agreement, a guarantee, rescission rights, or any other arrangement with a similar effect.

(2) A practitioner may not charge a contingent fee for preparing an original tax return or for any advice rendered in connection with a position taken or to be taken on an original tax return.

(3) A contingent fee may be charged for preparation of or advice in connection with an amended tax return or a claim for refund (other than a claim

for refund made on an original tax return), but only if the practitioner reasonably anticipates at the time the fee arrangement is entered into that the amended tax return or refund claim will receive substantive review by the Internal Revenue Service.

§10.28 Return of client's records.

(a) In general, a practitioner must, at the request of a client, promptly return any and all records of the client that are necessary for the client to comply with his or her Federal tax obligations. The practitioner may retain copies of the records returned to a client. The existence of a dispute over fees generally does not relieve the practitioner of his or her responsibility under this section. Nevertheless, if applicable state law allows or permits the retention of a client's records by a practitioner in the case of a dispute over fees for services rendered, the practitioner need only return those records that must be attached to the taxpayer's return. The practitioner, however, must provide the client with reasonable access to review and copy any additional records of the client retained by the practitioner under state law that are necessary for the client to comply with his or her Federal tax obligations.

(b) For purposes of this section-*Records of the client* include all documents or written or electronic materials provided to the practitioner, or obtained by the practitioner in the course of the practitioner's representation of the client, that preexisted the retention of the practitioner by the client. The term also includes materials that were prepared by the client or a third party (not including an employee or agent of the practitioner) at any time and provided to the practitioner with respect to the subject matter of the representation. The term also includes any return, claim for refund, schedule, affidavit, appraisal or any other document prepared by the practitioner, or his or her employee or agent, that was presented to the client with respect to a prior representation if such document is necessary for the taxpayer to comply with his or her current Federal tax obligations. The term does not include any return, claim for refund, schedule, affidavit, appraisal or any other document prepared by the practitioner or the practitioner's firm, employees or agents if the practitioner is withholding such document pending the client's performance of its contractual obligation to pay fees with respect to such document.

§10.29 Conflicting interests.

(a) Except as provided by paragraph (b) of this section, a practitioner shall not represent a client in his or her practice before the Internal Revenue Service if the representation involves a conflict of interest. A conflict of interest exists if:

(1) The representation of one client will be directly adverse to another client; or

(2) There is a significant risk that the representation of one or more clients will be materially limited by the practitioner's responsibilities to another client, a former client or a third person or by a personal interest of the practitioner.

(b) Notwithstanding the existence of a conflict of interest under paragraph (a) of this section, the practitioner may represent a client if:

(1) The practitioner reasonably believes that the practitioner will be able to provide competent and diligent representation to each affected client;

(2) The representation is not prohibited by law;

(3) Each affected client gives informed consent, confirmed in writing.

(c) Copies of the written consents must be retained by the practitioner for at least 36 months from the date of the conclusion of the representation of the affected clients and the written consents must be provided to any officer or employee of the Internal Revenue Service on request.
(Approved by the Office of Management and Budget under Control No. 15451726)

§10.30 Solicitation.

(a) *Advertising and solicitation restrictions.*

(1) A practitioner may not, with respect to any Internal Revenue Service matter, in any way use or participate in the use of any form of public communication or private solicitation containing a false, fraudulent, or coercive statement or claim; or a misleading or deceptive statement or claim. Enrolled agents, in describing their professional designation, may not utilize the term of art "certified" or imply an employer/employee relationship with the Internal Revenue Service. Examples of acceptable descriptions are "enrolled to represent taxpayers before the Internal Revenue Service," "enrolled to practice before the Internal Revenue Service," and "admitted to practice before the Internal Revenue Service."

(2) A practitioner may not make, directly or indirectly, an uninvited written or oral solicitation of employment in matters related to the Internal Revenue Service if the solicitation violates Federal or State law or other applicable rule, e.g., attorneys are precluded from making a solicitation that is prohibited by conduct rules applicable to all attorneys in their State(s) of licensure. Any lawful solicitation

made by or on behalf of a practitioner eligible to practice before the Internal Revenue Service must, nevertheless, clearly identify the solicitation as such and, if applicable, identify the source of the information used in choosing the recipient.

(b) *Fee information.*

(1)(i) A practitioner may publish the availability of a written schedule of fees and disseminate the following fee information—

(A) Fixed fees for specific routine services.

(B) Hourly rates.

(C) Range of fees for particular services.

(D) Fee charged for an initial consultation.

(ii) Any statement of fee information concerning matters in which costs may be incurred must include a statement disclosing whether clients will be responsible for such costs.

(2) A practitioner may charge no more than the rate(s) published under paragraph (b)(1) of this section for at least 30 calendar days after the last date on which the schedule of fees was published.

(c) *Communication of fee information.* Fee information may be communicated in professional lists, telephone directories, print media, mailings, and electronic mail, facsimile, hand delivered flyers, radio, television, and any other method. The method chosen, however, must not cause the communication to become untruthful, deceptive, or otherwise in violation of this part. A practitioner may not persist in attempting to contact a prospective client if the prospective client has made it known to the practitioner that he or she does not desire to be solicited. In the case of radio and television broadcasting, the broadcast must be recorded and the practitioner must retain a recording of the actual transmission. In the case of direct mail and e-commerce communications, the practitioner must retain a copy of the actual communication, along with a list or other description of persons to whom the communication was mailed or otherwise distributed. The copy must be retained by the practitioner for a period of at least 36 months from the date of the last transmission or use.

(d) *Improper associations.* A practitioner may not, in matters related to the Internal Revenue Service, assist, or accept assistance from, any person or entity who, to the knowledge of the practitioner, obtains clients or otherwise practices in a manner forbidden under this section.

(Approved by the Office of Management and Budget under Control No. 15451726)

§10.31 Negotiation of taxpayer checks.

A practitioner who prepares tax returns may not endorse or otherwise negotiate any check issued to a client by the government in respect of a Federal tax liability.

§10.32 Practice of law.

Nothing in the regulations in this part may be construed as authorizing persons not members of the bar to practice law.

-Par.2 Section 10.33 is revised to read as follows:

§10.33 Best practices for tax advisors.

(a) *Best practices.* Tax advisors should provide clients with the highest quality representation concerning Federal tax issues by adhering to best practices in providing advice and in preparing or assisting in the preparation of a submission to the Internal Revenue Service. In addition to compliance with the standards of practice provided elsewhere in this part, best practices include the following:

(1) Communicating clearly with the client regarding the terms of the engagement. For example, the advisor should determine the client's expected purpose for and use of the advice and should have a clear understanding with the client regarding the form and scope of the advice or assistance to be rendered.

(2) Establishing the facts, determining which facts are relevant, evaluating the reasonableness of any assumptions or representations, relating the applicable law (including potentially applicable judicial doctrines) to the relevant facts, and arriving at a conclusion supported by the law and the facts.

(3) Advising the client regarding the import of the conclusions reached, including, for example, whether a taxpayer may avoid accuracy-related penalties under the Internal Revenue Code if a taxpayer acts in reliance on the advice.

(4) Acting fairly and with integrity in practice before the Internal Revenue Service.

(b) *Procedures to ensure best practices for tax advisors.* Tax advisors with responsibility for overseeing a firm's practice of providing advice concerning Federal tax issues or of preparing or assisting in the preparation of submissions to the Internal Revenue Service should take reasonable steps to ensure that the firm's procedures for all members, associates, and employees are consistent with the best practices set forth in paragraph (a) of this section.

(c) *Applicability date.* This section is effective after June 20, 2005.

§10.34 Standards for advising with respect to tax return positions and for preparing or signing returns.

(a) *Realistic possibility standard*. A practitioner may not sign a tax return as a preparer if the practitioner determines that the tax return contains a position that does not have a realistic possibility of being sustained on its merits (the realistic possibility standard) unless the position is not frivolous and is adequately disclosed to the Internal Revenue Service. A practitioner may not advise a client to take a position on a tax return, or prepare the portion of a tax return on which a position is taken, unless—

(1) The practitioner determines that the position satisfies the realistic possibility standard; or

(2) The position is not frivolous and the practitioner advises the client of any opportunity to avoid the accuracy-related penalty in section 6662 of the Internal Revenue Code by adequately disclosing the position and of the requirements for adequate disclosure.

(b) *Advising clients on potential penalties*. A practitioner advising a client to take a position on a tax return, or preparing or signing a tax return as a preparer, must inform the client of the penalties reasonably likely to apply to the client with respect to the position advised, prepared, or reported. The practitioner also must inform the client of any opportunity to avoid any such penalty by disclosure, if relevant, and of the requirements for adequate disclosure. This paragraph (b) applies even if the practitioner is not subject to a penalty with respect to the position.

(c) *Relying on information furnished by clients*. A practitioner advising a client to take a position on a tax return, or preparing or signing a tax return as a preparer, generally may rely in good faith without verification upon information furnished by the client. The practitioner may not, however, ignore the implications of information furnished to, or actually known by, the practitioner, and must make reasonable inquiries if the information as furnished appears to be incorrect, inconsistent with an important fact or another factual assumption, or incomplete.

(d) *Definitions*. For purposes of this section—

(1) *Realistic possibility*. A position is considered to have a realistic possibility of being sustained on its merits if a reasonable and well informed analysis of the law and the facts by a person knowledgeable in the tax law would lead such a person to conclude that the position has approximately a one in three, or greater,

likelihood of being sustained on its merits. The authorities described in 26 CFR 1.6662-4(d)(3)(iii), or any successor provision, of the substantial understatement penalty regulations may be taken into account for purposes of this analysis. The possibility that a tax return will not be audited, that an issue will not be raised on audit, or that an issue will be settled may not be taken into account.

(2) *Frivolous*. A position is frivolous if it is patently improper.

- Par. 3. Sections 10.35, 10.36, 10.37 and 10.38 are added to subpart B to read as follows:

§10.35 Requirements for covered opinions.

(a) A practitioner who provides a covered opinion shall comply with the standards of practice in this section.

(b) *Definitions*. For purposes of this subpart-

(1) *A practitioner* includes any individual described in §10.2(e).

(2) *Covered opinion*—

(i) *In general.* A *covered opinion* is written advice (including electronic communications) by a practitioner concerning one or more Federal tax issues arising from—

(A) A transaction that is the same as or substantially similar to a transaction that, at the time the advice is rendered, the Internal Revenue Service has determined to be a tax avoidance transaction and identified by published guidance as a listed transaction under 26 CFR 1.6011-4(b)(2);

(B) Any partnership or other entity, any investment plan or arrangement, or any other plan or arrangement, the principal purpose of which is the avoidance or evasion of any tax imposed by the Internal Revenue Code; or

(C) Any partnership or other entity, any investment plan or arrangement, or any other plan or arrangement, a significant purpose of which is the avoidance or evasion of any tax imposed by the Internal Revenue Code if the written advice—

(1) Is a *reliance opinion;*

(2) Is a *marketed opinion;*

(3) Is subject to *conditions of confidentiality;* or

(4) Is subject to *contractual protection.*

(ii) *Excluded advice*. A *covered opinion* does not include—

(A) Written advice provided to a client during the course of an engagement if a practitioner is reasonably expected to provide subsequent written advice to the client that satisfies the requirements of this section;

(B) Written advice, other than advice described in paragraph (b) (2) (i) (A) of this section (concerning listed transactions) or paragraph (b) (2) (i) (B) of this section (concerning the principal purpose of avoidance or evasion) that—

(1) Concerns the qualification of a qualified plan;

(2) Is a *State or local bond opinion;* or

(3) Is included in documents required to be filed with the Securities and Exchange Commission.

(C) Written advice prepared for and provided to a taxpayer, solely for use by that taxpayer, after the taxpayer has filed a tax return with the Internal Revenue Service reflecting the tax benefits of the transaction. The preceding sentence does not apply if the practitioner knows or has reason to know that the written advice will be relied upon by the taxpayer to take a position on a tax return (including for these purposes an amended return that claims tax benefits not reported on a previously filed return) filed after the date on which the advice is provided to the taxpayer;

(D) Written advice provided to an employer by a practitioner in that practitioner's capacity as an employee of that employer solely for purposes of determining the tax liability of the employer; or

(E) Written advice that does not resolve a Federal tax issue in the taxpayer's favor, unless the advice reaches a conclusion favorable to the taxpayer at any confidence level (e.g., not frivolous, realistic possibility of success, reasonable basis or substantial authority) with respect to that issue. If written advice concerns more than one Federal tax issue, the advice must comply with the requirements of paragraph (c) of this section with respect to any Federal tax issue not described in the preceding sentence.

(3) *A Federal tax issue* is a question concerning the Federal tax treatment of an item of income, gain, loss, deduction, or credit, the existence or absence of a taxable transfer of property, or the value of property for Federal tax purposes. For purposes of this subpart, a *Federal tax issue* is significant if the Internal Revenue Service has a reasonable basis for a successful challenge and its resolution could have a significant impact, whether beneficial or adverse and under any reasonably foreseeable circumstance, on the overall Federal tax treatment of the transaction(s) or matter(s) addressed in the opinion.

(4) *Reliance opinion—*

(i) Written advice is a *reliance opinion* if the advice concludes at a confidence level of at least more

likely than not a greater than 50 percent likelihood) that one or more significant Federal tax issues would be resolved in the taxpayer's favor.

(ii) For purposes of this section, written advice, other than advice described in paragraph (b)(2)(i)(A) of this section (concerning listed transactions) or paragraph (b)(2)(i)(B) of this section (concerning the principal purpose of avoidance or evasion), is not treated as a *reliance opinion* if the practitioner prominently discloses in the written advice that it was not intended or written by the practitioner to be used, and that it cannot be used by the taxpayer, for the purpose of avoiding penalties that may be imposed on the taxpayer.

(5) *Marketed opinion—*

(i) Written advice is a *marketed opinion* if the practitioner knows or has reason to know that the written advice will be used or referred to by a person other than the practitioner (or a person who is a member of, associated with, or employed by the practitioner's firm) in promoting, marketing or recommending a partnership or other entity, investment plan or arrangement to one or more taxpayer(s).

(ii) For purposes of this section, written advice, other than advice described in paragraph (b)(2)(i)(A) of this section (concerning listed transactions) or paragraph (b)(2)(i)(B) of this section (concerning the principal purpose of avoidance or evasion), is not treated as a *marketed opinion* if the practitioner prominently discloses in the written advice that—

(A) The advice was not intended or written by the practitioner to be used, and that it cannot be used by any taxpayer, for the purpose of avoiding penalties that may be imposed on the taxpayer;

(B) The advice was written to support the promotion or marketing of the transaction(s) or matter(s) addressed by the written advice; and

(C) The taxpayer should seek advice based on the taxpayer's particular circumstances from an independent tax advisor.

(6) *Conditions of confidentiality.* Written advice is subject to *conditions of confidentiality* if the practitioner imposes on one or more recipients of the written advice a limitation on disclosure of the tax treatment or tax structure of the transaction and the limitation on disclosure protects the confidentiality of that practitioner's tax strategies, regardless of whether the limitation on disclosure is legally binding. A claim that a transaction is proprietary or exclusive is not a limitation on disclosure if the practitioner confirms to all recipients of the written advice that there is no

limitation on disclosure of the tax treatment or tax structure of the transaction that is the subject of the written advice.

(7) *Contractual protection.* Written advice is subject to *contractual protection* if the taxpayer has the right to a full or partial refund of fees paid to the practitioner (or a person who is a member of, associated with, or employed by the practitioner's firm) if all or a part of the intended tax consequences from the matters addressed in the written advice are not sustained, or if the fees paid to the practitioner (or a person who is a member of, associated with, or employed by the practitioner's firm) are contingent on the taxpayer's realization of tax benefits from the transaction. All the facts and circumstances relating to the matters addressed in the written advice will be considered when determining whether a fee is refundable or contingent, including the right to reimbursements of amounts that the parties to a transaction have not designated as fees or any agreement to provide services without reasonable compensation.

(8) *Prominently disclosed.* An item is *prominently disclosed* if it is readily apparent to a reader of the written advice. Whether an item is readily apparent will depend on the facts and circumstances surrounding the written advice including, but not limited to, the sophistication of the taxpayer and the length of the written advice. At a minimum, to be prominently disclosed an item must be set forth in a separate section (and not in a footnote) in a typeface that is the same size or larger than the typeface of any discussion of the facts or law in the written advice.

(9) *State or local bond opinion.* A *State or local bond opinion* is written advice with respect to a *Federal tax issue* included in any materials delivered to a purchaser of a State or local bond in connection with the issuance of the bond in a public or private offering, including an official statement (if one is prepared), that concerns only the excludability of interest on a State or local bond from gross income under section 103 of the Internal Revenue Code, the application of section 55 of the Internal Revenue Code to a State or local bond, the status of a State or local bond as a qualified tax-exempt obligation under section 265 (b)(3) of the Internal Revenue Code, the status of a State or local bond as a qualified zone academy bond under section 1397E of the Internal Revenue Code, or any combination of the above.

(10) *The principal purpose.* For purposes of this section, the principal purpose of a partnership or other entity, investment plan or arrangement, or other plan or arrangement is the avoidance or evasion of any tax imposed by the Internal Revenue Code if that purpose exceeds any other purpose. The principal purpose of a partnership or other entity, investment plan or arrangement, or other plan or arrangement is not to avoid or evade Federal tax if that partnership, entity, plan or arrangement has as its purpose the claiming of tax benefits in a manner consistent with the statute and Congressional purpose. A partnership, entity, plan or arrangement may have a significant purpose of avoidance or evasion even though it does not have the principal purpose of avoidance or evasion under this paragraph (b)(10).

(c) *Requirements for covered opinions.* A practitioner providing a *covered opinion* must comply with each of the following requirements.

(1) *Factual matters.*

(i) The practitioner must use reasonable efforts to identify and ascertain the facts, which may relate to future events if a transaction is prospective or proposed, and to determine which facts are relevant. The opinion must identify and consider all facts that the practitioner determines to be relevant.

(ii) The practitioner must not base the opinion on any unreasonable factual assumptions (including assumptions as to future events). An unreasonable factual assumption includes a factual assumption that the practitioner knows or should know is incorrect or incomplete. For example, it is unreasonable to assume that a transaction has a business purpose or that a transaction is potentially profitable apart from tax benefits. A factual assumption includes reliance on a projection, financial forecast or appraisal. It is unreasonable for a practitioner to rely on a projection, financial forecast or appraisal if the practitioner knows or should know that the projection, financial forecast or appraisal is incorrect or incomplete or was prepared by a person lacking the skills or qualifications necessary to prepare such projection, financial forecast or appraisal. The opinion must identify in a separate section all factual assumptions relied upon by the practitioner.

(iii) The practitioner must not base the opinion on any unreasonable factual representations, statements or findings of the taxpayer or any other person. An unreasonable factual representation includes a factual representation that the practitioner knows or should know is incorrect or incomplete. For example, a practitioner may not rely on a factual representation that a transaction has a business purpose if the representation does not include a specific description of the business purpose or the practitioner knows or should know that the representation is incorrect or incomplete. The opinion must identify in a separate section all factual representations, statements or finds of the taxpayer relied upon by the practitioner.

(2) *Relate law to facts.*

(i) The opinion must relate the applicable law (including potentially applicable judicial doctrines) to the relevant facts.

(ii) The practitioner must not assume the favorable resolution of any significant Federal tax issue except as provided in paragraphs (c)(3)(v) and (d) of this section, or otherwise base an opinion on any unreasonable legal assumptions, representations, or conclusions.

(iii) The opinion must not contain internally inconsistent legal analyses or conclusions.

(3) *Evaluation of significant Federal tax issues—*

(i) *In general.* The opinion must consider all significant Federal tax issues except as provided in paragraphs (c)(3)(v) and (d) of this section.

(ii) *Conclusion as to each significant Federal tax issues.* The opinion must provide the practitioner's conclusion as to the likelihood that the taxpayer will prevail on the merits with respect to each significant Federal tax issue considered in the opinion. If the practitioner is unable to reach a conclusion with respect to one or more of those issues, the opinion must state that the practitioner is unable to reach a conclusion with respect to those issues. The opinion must describe the reasons for the conclusions, including the facts and analysis supporting the conclusions, or describe the reasons that the practitioner is unable to reach a conclusion as to one or more issues. If the practitioner fails to reach a conclusion at the confidence level of at least more likely than not with respect to one or more significant Federal tax issues considered, the opinion must include the appropriate disclosure(s) required under paragraph (e) of this section.

(iii) *Evaluation based on chances of success on the merits.* In evaluating the significant Federal tax issues addressed in the opinion, the practitioner must not take into account the possibility that a tax return will not be audited, that an issue will not be raised on audit, or that an issue will be resolved through settlement if raised.

(iv) *Marketed opinions.* In the case of a *marketed opinion*, the opinion must provide the practitioner's conclusion that the taxpayer will prevail on the merits at a confidence level of at least more likely than not with respect to each significant Federal tax issue. If the practitioner is unable to reach a more likely than not conclusion with respect to each significant Federal tax issue, the practitioner must not provide the marketed opinion, but may provide written advice that satisfies the requirements in paragraph (b)(5)(ii) of this section.

(v) *Limited scope opinions.*

(A) The practitioner may provide an opinion that considers less than all of the significant Federal tax issues if—

(1) The practitioner and the taxpayer agree that the scope of the opinion and the taxpayer's potential reliance on the opinion for purposes of avoiding penalties that may be imposed on the taxpayer are limited to the Federal tax issue(s) addressed in the opinion;

(2) The opinion is not advice described in paragraph (b)(2)(i)(A) of this section (concerning listed transactions), paragraph (b)(2)(i)(B) of this section (concerning the principal purpose of avoidance or evasion) or paragraph (b)(5) of this section (a *marketed opinion*); and

(3) The opinion includes the appropriate disclosure(s) required under paragraph (e) of this section.

(B) A practitioner may make reasonable assumptions regarding the favorable resolution of a Federal tax issue (as assumed issue) for purposes of providing an opinion on less than all of the significant Federal tax issues as provided in this paragraph (c)(3)(v). The opinion must identify in a separate section all issues for which the practitioner assumed a favorable resolution.

(4) *Overall conclusion.*

(i) The opinion must provide the practitioner's overall conclusion as to the likelihood that the Federal tax treatment of the transaction or matter that is the subject of the opinion is the proper treatment and the reasons for that conclusion. If the practitioner is unable to reach an overall conclusion, the opinion must state that the practitioner is unable to reach and overall conclusion and describe the reasons for the practitioner's inability to reach a conclusion.

(ii) In the case of a *marketed opinion*, the opinion must provide the practitioner's overall conclusion that the Federal tax treatment of the transaction or matter that is the subject of the opinion is the proper treatment at a confidence level of at least more likely than not.

(d) *Competence to provide opinion; reliance on opinions of others.*

(1) The practitioner must be knowledgeable in all of the aspects of Federal tax law relevant to the

opinion being rendered, except that the practitioner may rely on the opinion of another practitioner with respect to one or more significant Federal tax issues, unless the practitioner knows or should know that the opinion of the other practitioner should not be relied on. If a practitioner relies on the opinion of another practitioner, the relying practitioner's opinion must identify the other opinion and set forth the conclusions reached in the other opinion.

(2) The practitioner must be satisfied that the combined analysis of the opinions, taken as a whole, and the overall conclusion, if any, satisfy the requirements of this section.

(e) *Required disclosures.* A covered opinion must contain all of the following disclosures that apply—

(1) *Relationship between promoter and practitioner.* An opinion must prominently disclose the existence of—

(i) Any compensation arrangement, such as a referral fee or a fee-sharing arrangement, between the practitioner (or the practitioner's firm or any person who is a member of, associated with, or employed by the practitioner's firm) and any person (other than the client for whom the opinion is prepared) with respect to promoting, marketing or recommending the entity, plan, or arrangement (or a substantially similar arrangement) that is the subject of the opinion; or

(ii) Any referral agreement between the practitioner (or the practitioner's firm or any person who is a member of, associated with, or employed by the practitioner's firm) and a person (other than the client for whom the opinion is prepared) engaged in promoting, marketing or recommending the entity, plan, or arrangement (or a substantially similar arrangement) that is the subject of the opinion.

(2) *Marketed opinions.* A *marketed opinion* must prominently disclose that—

(i) The opinion was written to support the promotion or marketing of the transaction(s) or matter(s) addressed in the opinion; and

(ii) The taxpayer should seek advice based on the taxpayer's particular circumstances from an independent tax advisor.

(3) *Limited scope opinions.* A limited scope opinion must prominently disclose that—

(i) The opinion is limited to the one or more Federal tax issues addressed in the opinion;

(ii) Additional issues may exist that could affect the Federal tax treatment of the transaction or matter that is the subject of the opinion and the opinion does not consider or provide a conclusion with respect to any additional issues; and

(iii) With respect to any significant Federal tax issues outside the limited scope of the opinion, the opinion was not written, and cannot be used by the taxpayer, for the purpose of avoiding penalties that may be imposed on the taxpayer.

(4) *Opinions that fail to reach a more likely than not conclusion.* An opinion that does not reach a conclusion at a confidence level of at least more likely than not with respect to a significant Federal tax issue must prominently disclose that—

(i) The opinion does not reach a conclusion at a confidence level of at least more likely than not with respect to one or more significant Federal tax issues addressed by the opinion; and

(ii) With respect to those significant Federal tax issues, the opinion was not written, and cannot be used by the taxpayer, for the purpose of avoiding penalties that may be imposed on the taxpayer.

(5) *Advice regarding required disclosures.* In the case of any disclosure required under this section, the practitioner may not provide advice to any person that is contrary to or inconsistent with the required disclosure.

(f) *Effect of opinion that meets these standards*—

(1) *In general.* An opinion that meets the requirements of this section satisfies the practitioner's responsibilities under this section, but the persuasiveness of the opinion with regard to the tax issues in question and the taxpayer's good faith reliance on the opinion will be determined separately under applicable provisions of the law and regulations.

(2) *Standards for other written advice.* A practitioner who provides written advice that is not a covered opinion for purposes of this section is subject to the requirements of §10.37.

(g) *Effective date.* This section applies to written advice that is rendered after June 20, 2005.

§10.36 Procedures to ensure compliance.

(a) *Requirements for covered opinions.* Any practitioner who has (or practitioners who have or share) principal authority and responsibility for overseeing a firm's practice of providing advice concerning Federal tax issues must take reasonable steps to ensure that the firm has adequate procedures in effect for all members, associates, and employees for purposes of complying with §10.35. Any such practitioner will be subject to discipline for failing to comply with the requirements of this paragraph if—

(1) The practitioner through willfulness, recklessness, or gross incompetence does not take reasonable steps to ensure that the firm has adequate procedures to comply with §10.35, and one or more individuals who are members of, associated with, or employed by, the firm are, or have engaged in a pattern or practice, in connection with their practice with the firm, of failing to comply with §10.35; or

(2) The practitioner knows or should know that one or more individuals who are members of, associated with, or employed by, the firm are, or have, engaged in a pattern or practice, in connection with their practice with the firm, that does not comply with §10.35 and the practitioner, through willfulness, recklessness, or gross incompetence, fails to take prompt action to correct the noncompliance.

(b) *Effective date*. This section is applicable after June 20, 2005.

§10.37 Requirements for other written advice.

(a) *Requirements*. A practitioner must not give written advice (including electronic communications) concerning one or more Federal tax issues if the practitioner bases the written advice on unreasonable factual or legal assumptions (including assumptions as to future events), unreasonably relies upon representations, statements, findings or agreements of the taxpayer or any other person, does not consider all relevant facts that the practitioner knows or should know, or, in evaluating a Federal tax issue, takes into account the possibility that a tax return will not be audited, that an issue will not be raised on audit, or that an issue will be resolved through settlement if raised. All facts and circumstances, including the scope of the engagement and the type and specificity of the advice sought by the client will be considered in determining whether a practitioner has failed to comply with this section. In the case of an opinion the practitioner knows or has reason to know will be used or referred to by a person other than the practitioner (or a person who is a member of, associated with, or employed by the practitioner's firm) in promoting, marketing or recommending to one or more taxpayers a partnership or other entity, investment plan or arrangement a significant purpose of which is the avoidance or evasion of any tax imposed by the Internal Revenue Code, the determination of whether a practitioner has failed to comply with this section will be made on the basis of a heightened standard of care because of the greater risk caused by the practitioner's lack of knowledge of the taxpayer's particular circumstances.

(b) *Effective date*. This section applies to written advice that is rendered after June 20, 2005.

§10.38 Establishment of advisory committees.

(a) *Advisory committees*. To promote and maintain the public's confidence in tax advisors, the Director of the Office of Professional Responsibility is authorized to establish one or more advisory committees composed of at least five individuals authorized to practice before the Internal Revenue Service. The Director should ensure that membership of an advisory committee is balanced among those who practice as attorneys, accountants, and enrolled agents. Under procedures prescribed by the Director, an advisory committee may review and make general recommendations regarding professional standards or best practices for tax advisors, including whether hypothetical conduct would give rise to a violation of §§10.35 or 10.36.

(b) *Effective date*. This section applies after December 20, 2004.

Subpart C—Sanctions for Violation of the Regulations

§10.50 Sanctions.

(a) *Authority to censure, suspend, or disbar*. The Secretary of the Treasury, or his or her delegate, after notice and an opportunity for a proceeding, may censure, suspend or disbar any practitioner from practice before the Internal Revenue Service if the practitioner is shown to be incompetent or disreputable, fails to comply with any regulation in this part, or with intent to defraud, willfully and knowingly misleads or threatens a client or prospective client. Censure is a public reprimand.

(b) *Authority to disqualify*. The Secretary of the Treasury, or his or her delegate, after due notice and opportunity for hearing, may disqualify any appraiser with respect to whom a penalty has been assessed under section 6701(a) of the Internal Revenue Code.

(1) If any appraiser is disqualified pursuant to this subpart C, such appraiser is barred from presenting evidence or testimony in any administrative proceeding before the Department of Treasury or the Internal Revenue Service, unless and until authorized to do so by the Director of Practice pursuant to §10.81, regardless of whether such evidence or

testimony would pertain to an appraisal made prior to or after such date.

(2) Any appraisal made by a disqualified appraiser after the effective date of disqualification will not have any probative effect in any administrative proceeding before the Department of the Treasury or the Internal Revenue Service. An appraisal otherwise barred from admission into evidence pursuant to this section may be admitted into evidence solely for the purpose of determining the taxpayer's reliance in good faith on such appraisal.

§10.51 Incompetence and disreputable conduct.

Incompetence and disreputable conduct for which a practitioner may be censured, suspended or disbarred from practice before the Internal Revenue Service includes, but is not limited to—

(a) Conviction of any criminal offense under the revenue laws of the United States;

(b) Conviction of any criminal offense involving dishonesty or breach of trust;

(c) Conviction of any felony under Federal or State law for which the conduct involved renders the practitioner unfit to practice before the Internal Revenue Service;

(d) Giving false or misleading information, or participating in any way in the giving of false or misleading information to the Department of the Treasury or any officer or employee thereof, or to any tribunal authorized to pass upon Federal tax matters, in connection with any matter pending or likely to be pending before them, knowing such information to be false or misleading. Facts or other matters contained in testimony, Federal tax returns, financial statements, applications for enrollment, affidavits, declarations, or any other document or statement, written or oral, are included in the term *information*.

(e) Solicitation of employment as prohibited under §10.30, the use of false or misleading representations with intent to deceive a client or prospective client in order to procure employment, or intimating that the practitioner is able improperly to obtain special consideration or action from the Internal Revenue Service or officer or employee thereof.

(f) Willfully failing to make a Federal tax return in violation of the revenue laws of the United States, willfully evading, attempting to evade, or participating in any way in evading or attempting to evade any assessment or payment of any Federal tax, or knowingly counseling or suggesting to a client or prospective client an illegal plan to evade Federal taxes or payment thereof.

(g) Misappropriation of, or failure properly and promptly to remit funds received from a client for the purpose of payment of taxes or other obligations due the United States.

(h) Directly or indirectly attempting to influence, or offering or agreeing to attempt to influence, the official action of any officer or employee of the Internal Revenue Service by the use of threats, false accusations, duress or coercion, by the offer of any special inducement or promise of advantage or by the bestowing of any gift, favor or thing of value.

(i) Disbarment or suspension from practice as an attorney, certified public accountant, public accountant, or actuary by any duly constituted authority of any State, territory, possession of the United States, including a Commonwealth, or the District of Columbia, any Federal court of record or any Federal agency, body or board.

(j) Knowingly aiding and abetting another person to practice before the Internal Revenue Service during a period of suspension, disbarment, or ineligibility of such other person.

(k) Contemptuous conduct in connection with practice before the Internal Revenue Service, including the use of abusive language, making false accusations and statements, knowing them to be false, or circulating or publishing malicious or libelous matter.

(l) Giving a false opinion, knowingly, recklessly, or through gross incompetence, including an opinion which is intentionally or recklessly misleading, or engaging in a pattern of providing incompetent opinions on questions arising under the Federal tax laws. False opinions described in this paragraph (l) include those which reflect or result from a knowing misstatement of fact or law, from an assertion of a position known to be unwarranted under existing law, from counseling or assisting in conduct known to be illegal or fraudulent, from concealing matters required by law to be revealed, or from consciously disregarding information indicating that material facts expressed in the tax opinion or offering material are false or misleading. For purposes of this paragraph (l), reckless conduct is a highly unreasonable omission or misrepresentation involving an extreme departure from the standards of ordinary care that a practitioner should observe under the circumstances. A pattern of conduct is a factor that will be taken into account in determining whether a practitioner acted knowingly, recklessly, or through gross incompetence. Gross incompetence includes conduct that reflects gross indifference, preparation which is grossly inadequate under the circumstances, and a consistent failure to perform obligations to the client.

-Par. 4 Section 10.52 is revised to read as follows:

§10.52 Violation of regulations.

(a) *Prohibited conduct*. A practitioner may be censured, suspended or disbarred from practice before the Internal Revenue Service for any of the following:

(1) Willfully violating any of the regulations (other than §10.33) contained in this part.

(2) Recklessly or through gross incompetence (within the meaning of §10.51(l)) violating §§10.34, 10.35, 10.36 or 10.37.

(b) *Effective date*. This section applies after June 20, 2005.

§10.53 Receipt of information concerning practitioner.

(a) *Officer or employee of the Internal Revenue Service*. If an officer or employee of the Internal Revenue Service has reason to believe that a practitioner has violated any provision of this part, the officer or employee will promptly make a written report to the Director of Practice of the suspected violation. The report will explain the facts and reasons upon which the officer's or employee's belief rests.

(b) *Other persons*. Any person other than an officer or employee of the Internal Revenue Service having information of a violation of any provision of this part may make an oral or written report of the alleged violation to the Director of Practice or any officer or employee of the Internal Revenue Service. If the report is made to an officer or employee of the Internal Revenue Service, the officer or employee will make a written report of the suspected violation to the Director of Practice.

(c) *Destruction of report*. No report made under paragraph (a) or (b) of this section shall be maintained by the Director of Practice unless retention of such record is permissible under the applicable records control schedule as approved by the National Archives and Records Administration and designated in the Internal Revenue Manual. The Director of Practice must destroy such reports as soon as permissible under the applicable records control schedule.

(d) *Effect on proceedings under subpart D*. The destruction of any report will not bar any proceeding under subpart D of this part, but precludes the Director of Practice's use of a copy of such report in a proceeding under subpart D of this part.

Subpart D—Rules Applicable to Disciplinary Proceedings

§10.60 Institution of proceeding.

(a) Whenever the Director of Practice determines that a practitioner violated any provision of the laws or regulations in this part, the Director of Practice may reprimand the practitioner or, in accordance with §10.62, institute a proceeding for censure, suspension, or disbarment of the practitioner. A proceeding for censure, suspension, or disbarment of a practitioner is instituted by the filing of a complaint, the contents of which are more fully described in §10.62.

(b) Whenever the Director of Practice is advised or becomes aware that a penalty has been assessed against an appraiser under section 6701(a) of the Internal Revenue Code, the Director of Practice may reprimand the appraiser or, in accordance with §10.62, institute a proceeding for disqualification of the appraiser. A proceeding for disqualification of an appraiser is instituted by the filing of a complaint, the contents of which are more fully described in §10.62.

(c) Except as provided in §10.82, a proceeding will not be instituted under this section unless the proposed respondent previously has been advised in writing of the law, facts and conduct warranting such action and has been accorded an opportunity to dispute facts, assert additional facts, and make arguments (including an explanation or description of mitigating circumstances).

§10.61 Conferences.

(a) *In general*. The Director of Practice may confer with a practitioner or an appraiser concerning allegations of misconduct irrespective of whether a proceeding for censure, suspension, disbarment, or disqualification has been instituted against the practitioner or appraiser. If the conference results in a stipulation in connection with an ongoing proceeding in which the practitioner or appraiser is the respondent, the stipulation may be entered in the record by either party to the proceeding.

(b) *Resignation or voluntary censure, suspension or disbarment*. In lieu of a proceeding being instituted or continued under paragraph (a) of §10.60, a practitioner may offer his or her consent to the issuance of a censure, suspension or disbarment, or, if the practitioner is an enrolled agent, may offer to resign. The Director of Practice may, in his or her discretion, accept or decline the offered censure, suspension, disbarment, or offer of resignation by an enrolled agent, in accordance with the consent offered. In any declination, the Director of Practice may state that he or she would accept an offer of censure, suspension, or disbarment, or, if the practitioner is an enrolled agent, offer of resignation, containing different terms; the Director of Practice may, in his or her discretion, accept or reject a revised offer of censure, suspension, disbarment, or offer of resignation by an enrolled agent, submitted in response to the declination or may counteroffer and act upon any accepted counteroffer.

(c) *Voluntary disqualification*. In lieu of a proceeding being instituted or continued under paragraph (b) of §10.60, an appraiser may offer his or her consent to disqualification. The Director of Practice may, in his or her discretion, accept or decline the offered disqualification, in accordance with the consent offered. In any declination, the Director of Practice may state that he or she would accept an offer of disqualification containing different terms; the Director of Practice may, in his or her discretion, accept or reject a revised offer of censure, suspension or disbarment submitted in response to the declination or may counteroffer and act upon any accepted counteroffer.

§10.62 Contents of complaint.

(a) *Charges*. A complaint must name the respondent, provide a clear and concise description of the facts and law that constitute the basis for the proceeding, and be signed by the Director of Practice or a person representing the Director of Practice under §10.69(a)(1). A complaint is sufficient if it fairly informs the respondent of the charges brought so that he or she is able to prepare a defense. In the case of a complaint filed against an appraiser, the complaint is sufficient if it refers to a penalty imposed previously on the respondent under section 6701(a) of the Internal Revenue Code.

(b) *Specification of sanction*. The complaint must specify the sanction sought by the Director of Practice against the practitioner or appraiser. If the sanction sought is a suspension, the duration of the suspension sought must be specified.

(c) *Demand for answer*. The Director of Practice must, in the complaint or in a separate paper attached to the complaint, notify the respondent of the time for answering the complaint, the time for which may not be less than15 days from the date of service of the complaint, the name and address of the Administrative Law Judge with whom the answer must be filed, the name and address of the person representing the Director of Practice to whom a copy of the answer must be served, and that a decision by default may be rendered against the respondent in the event an answer is not filed as required.

§10.63 Service of complaint; service and filing of other papers.

(a) *Service of complaint*.

(1) *In general*. The complaint or a copy of the complaint must be served on the respondent by any manner described in paragraphs (a) (2) or (3) of this section.

(2) *Service by certified or first class mail*.

(i) Service of the complaint may be made on the respondent by mailing the complaint by certified mail to the last known address (as determined under section 6212 of the Internal Revenue Code and the regulations thereunder) of the respondent. Where service is by certified mail, the returned post office receipt duly signed by the respondent will be proof of service.

(ii) If the certified mail is not claimed or accepted by the respondent, or is returned undelivered, service may be made on the respondent, by mailing the complaint to the respondent by first class mail. Service by this method will be considered complete upon mailing, provided the complaint is addressed to the respondent at the respondent's last known address as determined under section 6212 of the Internal Revenue Code and the regulations thereunder.

(3) *Service by other than certified or first class mail*.

(i) Service of the complaint may be made on the respondent by delivery by a private delivery service designated pursuant to section 7502(f) of the Internal Revenue Code to the last known address (as determined under section 6212 of the Internal Revenue Code and the regulations there under) of the respondent. Service by this method will be considered complete, provided the complaint is addressed to the respondent at the respondent's last known address as determined under section 6212 of the Internal Revenue Code and the regulations thereunder.

(ii) Service of the complaint may be made in person on, or by leaving the complaint at the office or place of business of, the respondent. Service by this method will be considered complete and proof of service will be a written statement, sworn or affirmed by the person who served the complaint, identifying the manner of service, including the recipient, relationship of recipient to respondent, place, date and time of service.

(iii) Service may be made by any other means agreed to by the respondent. Proof of service will be a written statement, sworn or affirmed by the person who served the complaint, identifying the manner of service, including the recipient, relationship of recipient to respondent, place, date and time of service.

(4) For purposes of this paragraph (a) "respondent" means the practitioner or appraiser named in the complaint or any other person having the authority to accept mail on behalf of the practitioner or appraiser.

(b) *Service of papers other than complaint.* Any paper other than the complaint may be served on the respondent, or his or her authorized representative under §10.69(a)(2) by:

(1) mailing the paper by first class mail to the last known address (as determined under section 6212 of the Internal Revenue Code and the regulations thereunder) of the respondent or the respondent's authorized representative,

(2) delivery by a private delivery service designated pursuant to section 7502(f) of the Internal Revenue Code to the last known address (as determined under section 6212 of the Internal Revenue Code and the regulations thereunder) of the respondent or the respondent's authorized representative, or

(3) as provided in paragraphs (a)(3)(ii) and (a)(3)(iii) of this section.

(c) *Service of papers on the Director of Practice.* Whenever a paper is required or permitted to be served on the Director of Practice in connection with a proceeding under this part, the paper will be served on the Director of Practice's authorized representative under §10.69(a)(1) at the address designated in the complaint, or at an address provided in a notice of appearance. If no address is designated in the complaint or provided in a notice of appearance, service will be made on the Director of Practice, Internal Revenue Service, 1111 Constitution Avenue, NW, Washington, DC 20224.

(d) *Filing of papers.* Whenever the filing of a paper is required or permitted in connection with a proceeding under this part, the original paper, plus one additional copy, must be filed with the Administrative Law Judge at the address specified in the complaint or at an address otherwise specified by the Administrative Law Judge. All papers filed in connection with a proceeding under this part must be served on the other party, unless the Administrative Law Judge directs otherwise. A certificate evidencing such must be attached to the original paper filed with the Administrative Law Judge.

§10.64 Answer; default.

(a) *Filing.* The respondent's answer must be filed with the Administrative Law Judge, and served on the Director of Practice, within the time specified in the complaint unless, on request or application of the respondent, the time is extended by the Administrative Law Judge.

(b) *Contents.* The answer must be written and contain a statement of facts that constitute the respondent's grounds of defense. General denials are not permitted. The respondent must specifically admit or deny each allegation set forth in the complaint, except that the respondent may state that the respondent is without sufficient information to admit or deny a specific allegation. The respondent, nevertheless, may not deny a material allegation in the complaint that the respondent knows to be true, or state that the respondent is without sufficient information to form a belief, when the respondent possesses the required information. The respondent also must state affirmatively any special matters of defense on which he or she relies.

(c) *Failure to deny or answer allegations in the complaint.* Every allegation in the complaint that is not denied in the answer is deemed admitted and will be considered proved; no further evidence in respect of such allegation need be adduced at a hearing.

(d) *Default.* Failure to file an answer within the time prescribed (or within the time for answer as extended by the Administrative Law Judge), constitutes an admission of the allegations of the complaint and a waiver of hearing, and the Administrative Law Judge may make the decision by default without a hearing or further procedure. A decision by default constitutes a decision under §10.76.

(e) *Signature.* The answer must be signed by the respondent or the respondent's authorized representative under §10.69(a)(2) and must include a statement directly above the signature acknowledging that the statements made in the answer are true and correct and that knowing and willful false statements may be punishable under 18 U.S.C. 1001.

§10.65 Supplemental charges.

If it appears that the respondent, in his or her answer, falsely and in bad faith, denies a material allegation of fact in the complaint or states that the respondent has insufficient knowledge to form a belief, when the respondent in fact possesses such information, or if it appears that the respondent has knowingly introduced false testimony during proceedings for his or her censure, suspension, disbarment, or disqualification, the Director of Practice may file supplemental charges against the respondent. The supplemental charges may be heard with other charges in the case, provided the respondent is given due notice of the charges and is afforded an opportunity to prepare a defense to such charges.

§10.66 Reply to answer.

The Director of Practice may file a reply to the respondent's answer, but unless otherwise ordered by the Administrative Law Judge, no reply to the respondent's answer is required. If a reply is not filed, new matter in the answer is deemed denied.

§10.67 Proof; variance; amendment of pleadings.

In the case of a variance between the allegations in pleadings and the evidence adduced in support of the pleadings, the Administrative Law Judge, at any time before decision, may order or authorize amendment of the pleadings to conform to the evidence. The party who would otherwise be prejudiced by the amendment must be given a reasonable opportunity to address the allegations of the pleadings as amended and the Administrative Law Judge must make findings on any issue presented by the pleadings as amended.

§10.68 Motions and requests.

(a) *Motions*. At any time after the filing of the complaint, any party may file a motion with the Administrative Law Judge. Unless otherwise ordered by the Administrative Law Judge, motions must be in writing and must be served on the opposing party as provided in §10.63(b). A motion must concisely specify its grounds and the relief sought, and, if appropriate, must contain a memorandum of facts and law in support. Before moving, a party must make a good faith effort to resolve with the other party any dispute that gives rise to, or is a concern of, the motion. The movant must certify such an attempt was made and state, if it is known, whether the opposing party opposes the motion.

(b) *Response*. Unless otherwise ordered by the Administrative Law Judge, the nonmoving party is not required to file a response to a motion. If the Administrative Law Judge does not order the nonmoving party to file a response, the nonmoving party is deemed to oppose the motion.

(c) *Oral motions and arguments*. The Administrative Law Judge may, for good cause and with notice to the parties, permit oral motions and oral opposition to motions. The Administrative Law Judge may, within his or her discretion, permit oral argument on any motion.

§10.69 Representation; ex parte communication.

(a) *Representation*.

(1) The Director of Practice may be represented in proceedings under this part by an attorney or other employee of the Internal Revenue Service. An attorney or an employee of the Internal Revenue Service representing the Director of Practice in a proceeding under this part may sign the complaint or any document required to be filed in the proceeding on behalf of the Director of Practice.

(2) A respondent may appear in person, be represented by a practitioner, or be represented by an attorney who has not filed a declaration with the Internal Revenue Service pursuant to §10.3. A practitioner or an attorney representing a respondent or proposed respondent may sign the answer or any document required to be filed in the proceeding on behalf of the respondent.

(b) *Ex parte communication*. The Director of Practice, the respondent, and any representatives of either party, may not attempt to initiate or participate in ex parte discussions concerning a proceeding or potential proceeding with the Administrative Law Judge (or any person who is likely to advise the Administrative Law Judge on a ruling or decision) in the proceeding before or during the pendency of the proceeding. Any memorandum, letter or other communication concerning the merits of the proceeding, addressed to the Administrative Law Judge, by or on behalf of any party shall be regarded as an argument in the proceeding and shall be served on the other party.

§10.70 Administrative Law Judge.

(a) *Appointment*. Proceedings on complaints for the censure, suspension or disbarment of a practitioner or the disqualification of an appraiser will be conducted by an Administrative Law Judge appointed as provided by 5 U.S.C. 3105.

(b) *Powers of the Administrative Law Judge.* The Administrative Law Judge, among other powers, has the authority, in connection with any proceeding under §10.60 assigned or referred to him or her, to do the following:

(1) Administer oaths and affirmations;

(2) Make rulings on motions and requests, which rulings may not be appealed prior to the close of a hearing except in extraordinary circumstances and at the discretion of the Administrative Law Judge;

(3) Determine the time and place of hearing and regulate its course and conduct;

(4) Adopt rules of procedure and modify the same from time to time as needed for the orderly disposition of proceedings;

(5) Rule on offers of proof, receive relevant evidence, and examine witnesses;

(6) Take or authorize the taking of depositions;

(7) Receive and consider oral or written argument on facts or law;

(8) Hold or provide for the holding of conferences for the settlement or simplification of the issues with the consent of the parties;

(9) Perform such acts and take such measures as are necessary or appropriate to the efficient conduct of any proceeding; and

(10) Make decisions.

§10.71 Hearings.

(a) *In general. An Administrative Law Judge will preside at the hearing on a complaint filed under paragraph (c) of §10.60 for the censure, suspension, or disbarment of a practitioner or disqualification of an appraiser. Hearings will be stenographically* recorded and transcribed and the testimony of witnesses will be taken under oath or affirmation. Hearings will be conducted pursuant to 5 U.S.C. 556. A hearing in a proceeding requested under paragraph (g) of §10.82 will be conducted *de novo.* An evidentiary hearing must be held in all proceedings prior to the issuance of a decision by the Administrative Law Judge unless: the Director of Practice withdraws the complaint; the practitioner consents to a sanction pursuant to §10.61(b); a decision is issued by default pursuant to §10.64(d), a decision is issued under §10.82(e); the respondent requests a decision on the record without a hearing; or the Administrative Law Judge issues a decision on a motion that disposes of the case prior to the hearing.

(b) *Publicity of Proceedings.* A request by a practitioner or appraiser that a hearing in a disciplinary proceeding concerning him or her be public, and that the record of such disciplinary proceeding be made available for inspection by interested persons may be granted by the Administrative Law Judge where the parties stipulate in advance to protect from disclosure confidential tax information in accordance with all applicable statutes and regulations.

(c) *Location.* The location of the hearing will be determined by the agreement of the parties with the approval of the Administrative Law Judge, but, in the absence of such agreement and approval, the hearing will be held in Washington, D.C.

(d) *Failure to appear.* If either party to the proceeding fails to appear at the hearing, after notice of the proceeding has been sent to him or her, the party will be deemed to have waived the right to a hearing and the Administrative Law Judge may make his or her decision against the absent party by default.

§10.72 Evidence.

(a) *In general.* The rules of evidence prevailing in courts of law and equity are not controlling in hearings or proceedings conducted under this part. The Administrative Law Judge may, however, exclude evidence that is irrelevant, immaterial, or unduly repetitious,

(b) *Depositions.* The deposition of any witness taken pursuant to §10.73 may be admitted into evidence in any proceeding instituted under §10.60.

(c) *Proof of documents.* Official documents, records, and papers of the Internal Revenue Service and the Office of Director of Practice are admissible in evidence without the production of an officer or employee to authenticate them. Any such documents, records, and papers may be evidenced by a copy attested or identified by an officer or employee of the Internal Revenue Service or the Treasury Department, as the case may be.

(d) *Withdrawal of exhibits.* If any document, record, or other paper is introduced in evidence as an exhibit, the Administrative Law Judge may authorize the withdrawal of the exhibit subject to any conditions that he or she deems proper.

(e) *Objections.* Objections to evidence are to be made in short form, stating the grounds for the objection. Except as ordered by the Administrative Law Judge, argument on objections will not be recorded or transcribed. Rulings on objections are to be a part of the record, but no exception to a ruling is necessary to preserve the rights of the parties.

§10.73 Depositions.

(a) Depositions for use at a hearing may be taken, with the written approval of the Administrative Law Judge, by either the Director of Practice or the respondent or their duly authorized representatives. Depositions may be taken before any officer duly authorized to administer an oath for general purposes or before an officer or employee of the Internal Revenue Service who is authorized to administer an oath in internal revenue matters.

(b) The party taking the deposition must provide the deponent and the other party with 10 days written notice of the deposition, unless the deponent and the parties agree otherwise. The notice must specify the name of the deponent, the time and place where the deposition is to be taken, and whether the deposition will be taken by oral or written interrogatories. When a deposition is taken by written interrogatories, any cross-examination also will be by written interrogatories. Copies of the written interrogatories must be served on the other party with the notice of deposition, and copies of any written cross-interrogation must be mailed or delivered to the opposing party at least 5 days before the date that the deposition will be taken, unless the parties mutually agree otherwise. A party on whose behalf a deposition is taken must file the responses to the written interrogatories or a transcript of the oral deposition with the Administrative Law Judge and serve copies on the opposing party and the deponent. Expenses in the reporting of depositions will be borne by the party that requested the deposition.

§10.74 Transcript.

In cases where the hearing is stenographically reported by a Government contract reporter, copies of the transcript may be obtained from the reporter at rates not to exceed the maximum rates fixed by contract between the Government and the reporter. Where the hearing is stenographically reported by a regular employee of the Internal Revenue Service, a copy will be supplied to the respondent either without charge or upon the payment of a reasonable fee. Copies of exhibits introduced at the hearing or at the taking of depositions will be supplied to the parties upon the payment of a reasonable fee (Sec. 501, Public Law 82-137)(65 Stat. 290)(31 U.S.C. 483a).

§10.75 Proposed findings and conclusions.

Except in cases where the respondent has failed to answer the complaint or where a party has failed to appear at the hearing, the parties must be afforded a reasonable opportunity to submit proposed findings and conclusions and their supporting reasons to the Administrative Law Judge.

§10.76 Decision of Administrative Law Judge.

(a) As soon as practicable after the conclusion of a hearing and the receipt of any proposed findings and conclusions timely submitted by the parties, the Administrative Law Judge will enter a decision in the case. The decision must include a statement of findings and conclusions, as well as the reasons or basis for making such findings and conclusions, and an order of censure, suspension, disbarment, disqualification, or dismissal of the complaint. If the sanction is censure or a suspension of less than six month duration, the Administrative Law Judge, in rendering findings and conclusions, will consider an allegation of fact to be proven if it is established by the party who is alleging the fact by a preponderance of evidence in the record. In the event that the sanction is disbarment or a suspension of a duration of six months or longer, an allegation of fact that is necessary for a finding against the practitioner must be proven by clear and convincing evidence in the record. An allegation of fact that is necessary for a finding of disqualification against an appraiser must be proven by clear and convincing evidence in the record. The Administrative Law Judge will provide the decision to the Director of Practice and a copy of the decision to the respondent or the respondent's authorized representative.

(b) In the absence of an appeal to the Secretary of the Treasury or his or her designee, or review of the decision on motion of the Secretary or his or her designee, the decision of the Administrative Law Judge will, without further proceedings, become the decision of the agency 30 days after the date of the Administrative Law Judge's decision.

§10.77 Appeal of decision of Administrative Law Judge.

Within 30 days from the date of the Administrative Law Judge's decision, either party may appeal to the Secretary of the Treasury, or his or her delegate. The respondent must file his or her appeal with the Director of Practice in duplicate and a notice of appeal must include exceptions to the decision of the Administrative Law Judge and supporting reasons for such exceptions. If the Director of Practice files an appeal, he or she must provide a copy to the respondent. Within 30 days after receipt of an appeal or copy thereof, the other party may file a reply brief in duplicate with the Director of Practice. If the reply brief is filed by the Director of Practice, he or she must provide a copy of it to the respondent. The Director of Practice must provide the entire record to the Secretary of the Treasury, or his or her delegate, after the appeal and any reply brief has been filed.

§10.78 Decision on appeal.

On appeal from or review of the decision of the Administrative Law Judge, the Secretary of the Treasury, or his or her delegate, will make the agency decision. The Secretary of the Treasury, or his or delegate, will provide a copy of the agency decision to the Director of Practice and the respondent or the respondent's authorized representative. The decision of the Administrative Law Judge will not be reversed unless the appellant establishes that the decision is clearly erroneous in light of the evidence in the record and applicable law. Issues that are exclusively matters of law will be reviewed de novo. In the event that the Secretary of the Treasury, or his or her delegate, determines that there are unresolved issues raised by the record, the case may be remanded to the Administrative Law Judge to elicit additional testimony or evidence. A copy of the agency decision or that of his or her delegate will be provided to the Director of Practice and the respondent contemporaneously.

§10.79 Effect of disbarment, suspension, or censure.

(a) *Disbarment*. When the final decision in a case is against the respondent (or the respondent has offered his or her consent and such consent has been accepted by the Director of Practice) and such decision is for disbarment, the respondent will not be permitted to practice before the Internal Revenue Service unless and until authorized to do so by the Director of Practice pursuant to §10.81.

(b) *Suspension*. When the final decision in a case is against the respondent (or the respondent has offered his or her consent and such consent has been accepted by the Director of Practice) and such decision is for suspension, the respondent will not be permitted to practice before the Internal Revenue Service during the period of suspension. For periods after the suspension, the practitioner's future representations may be subject to conditions as authorized by paragraph (d) of this section.

(c) *Censure*. When the final decision in the case is against the respondent (or the respondent has of-

fered his or her consent and such consent has been accepted by the Director of Practice) and such decision is for censure, the respondent will be permitted to practice before the Internal Revenue Service, but the respondent's future representations may be subject to conditions as authorized by paragraph (d) of this section.

(d) *Conditions*. After being subject to the sanction of either suspension or censure, the future representations of a practitioner so sanctioned shall be subject to conditions prescribed by the Director of Practice designed to promote high standards of conduct. These conditions can be imposed for a reasonable period in light of the gravity of the practitioner's violations. For example, where a practitioner is censured because he or she failed to advise his or her clients about a potential conflict of interest or failed to obtain the clients' written consents, the Director of Practice may require the practitioner to provide the Director of Practice or another Internal Revenue Service official with a copy of all consents obtained by the practitioner for an appropriate period following censure, whether or not such consents are specifically requested.

§10.80 Notice of disbarment, suspension, censure, or disqualification.

On the issuance of a final order censuring, suspending, or disbarring a practitioner or a final order disqualifying an appraiser, the Director of Practice may give notice of the censure, suspension, disbarment, or disqualification to appropriate officers and employees of the Internal Revenue Service and to interested departments and agencies of the Federal government. The Director of Practice may determine the manner of giving notice to the proper authorities of the State by which the censured, suspended, or disbarred person was licensed to practice.

§10.81 Petition for reinstatement.

The Director of Practice may entertain a petition for reinstatement from any person disbarred from practice before the Internal Revenue Service or any disqualified appraiser after the expiration of 5 years following such disbarment or disqualification. Reinstatement may not be granted unless the Director of Practice is satisfied that the petitioner, thereafter, is not likely to conduct himself contrary to the regulations in this part, and that granting such reinstatement would not be contrary to the public interest.

§10.82 Expedited suspension upon criminal conviction or loss of license for cause.

(a) *When applicable.* Whenever the Director of Practice determines that a practitioner is described in paragraph (b) of this section, the Director of Practice may institute a proceeding under this section to suspend the practitioner from practice before the Internal Revenue Service.

(b) *To whom applicable.* This section applies to any practitioner who, within 5 years of the date a complaint instituting a proceeding under this section is served:

(1) Has had his or her license to practice as an attorney, certified public accountant, or actuary suspended or revoked for cause (not including a failure to pay a professional licensing fee) by any authority or court, agency, body, or board described in §10.51(i); or

(2) Has, irrespective of whether an appeal has been taken, been convicted of any crime under title 26 of the United States Code, any crime involving dishonesty or breach of trust, or any felony for which the conduct involved renders the practitioner unfit to practice before the Internal Revenue Service.

(3) Has violated conditions designed to promote high standards of conduct established pursuant to §10.79(d).

(c) *Instituting a proceeding.* A proceeding under this section will be instituted by a complaint that names the respondent, is signed by the Director of Practice or a person representing the Director of Practice under §10.69(a)(1), is filed in the Director of Practice's office, and is served according to the rules set forth in paragraph (a) of §10.63. The complaint must give a plain and concise description of the allegations that constitute the basis for the proceeding. The complaint must notify the respondent—

(1) Of the place and due date for filing an answer;

(2) That a decision by default may be rendered if the respondent fails to file an answer as required;

(3) That the respondent may request a conference with the Director of Practice to address the merits of the complaint and that any such request must be made in the answer; and

(4) That the respondent may be suspended either immediately following the expiration of the period within which an answer must be filed or, if a conference is requested, immediately following the conference.

(d) *Answer.* The answer to a complaint described in this section must be filed no later than 30 calendar days following the date the complaint is served, unless the Director of Practice extends the time for filing. The answer must be filed in accordance with the rules set forth in §10.64, except as otherwise provided in this section. A respondent is entitled to a conference with the Director of Practice only if the conference is requested in a timely filed answer. If a request for a conference is not made in the answer or the answer is not timely filed, the respondent will be deemed to have waived his or her right to a conference and the Director of Practice may suspend such respondent at any time following the date on which the answer was due.

(e) *Conference.* The Director of Practice or his or her designee will preside at a conference described in this section. The conference will be held at a place and time selected by the Director of Practice, but no sooner than 14 calendar days after the date by which the answer must be filed with the Director of Practice, unless the respondent agrees to an earlier date. An authorized representative may represent the respondent at the conference. Following the conference, upon a finding that the respondent is described in paragraph (b) of this section, or upon the respondent's failure to appear at the conference either personally or through an authorized representative, the Director of Practice may immediately suspend the respondent from practice before the Internal Revenue Service.

(f) *Duration of suspension.* A suspension under this section will commence on the date that written notice of the suspension is issued. A practitioner's suspension will remain effective until the earlier of the following—

(1) The Director of Practice lifts the suspension after determining that the practitioner is no longer described in paragraph (b) of this section or for any other reason; or

(2) The suspension is lifted by an Administrative Law Judge or the Secretary of the Treasury in a proceeding referred to in paragraph (g) of this section and instituted under §10.60.

(g) *Proceeding instituted under §10.60.* If the Director of Practice suspends a practitioner under this section, the practitioner may ask the Director of Practice to issue a complaint under §10.60. The request must be made in writing within 2 years from the date on which the practitioner's suspension commences. The Director of Practice must issue a complaint requested under this paragraph within 30 calendar days of receiving the request.

Subpart E—General Provisions

§10.90 Records.

Availability. The Director of Practice will make available for public inspection at the Office of Director Practice the roster of all persons enrolled to practice, the roster of all persons censured, suspended, or disbarred from practice before the Internal Revenue Service, and the roster of all disqualified appraisers. Other records of the Director of Practice may be disclosed upon specific request, in accordance with the applicable disclosure rules of the Internal Revenue Service and the Treasury Department.

§10.91 Saving Clause.

Any proceeding instituted under regulations in effect prior to July 26, 2002, that is not final prior to July 26, 2002, will not be affected by this part and will apply the rules set forth at 31 CFR part 10 revised as of July 1, 2002. Any proceeding under this part based on conduct engaged in prior to July 26, 2002, which is instituted after that date, shall apply Subpart D and E of this part, but the conduct engaged in prior to July 26, 2002, shall be judged by the regulations in effect at the time the conduct occurred.

§10.92 Special Orders.

The Secretary of the Treasury reserves the power to issue such special orders as he or she deems proper in any cases within the purview of this part.

-Par 5. Section 10.93 is revised to read as follows:

§10.93 Effective date.

Except as otherwise provided in each section and Subject to §10.91, Part 10 is applicable on July 26, 2002.

Mark E. Matthews,

Deputy Commissioner for Services and Enforcement, Internal Revenue Service.

Approved: December 8, 2004. **Arnold I. Havens**, *General Counsel, Department of Treasury.* [FR Doc. 04-27678 Filed 12-17-04; 8:45 am]

BILLING CODE 4830-01-P

Addendum to Treasury Department Circular No. 230 (Rev. 7-2002)

Any proceeding under this part based on conduct engaged in prior to July 26, 2002, which is instituted after that date, shall apply Subparts D and E of this part, but the conduct engaged in prior to July 26, 2002, shall be judged by the regulations in effect at the time the conduct occurred. 31 CFR 10.91. In light of this, we are providing, as an addendum, the earlier version of Subparts B and C.

The following definitions pertain specifically to the manner in which the identified terms are used in a tax research context. Other uses for such terms are not examined.

A

ABA

The professional organization for practicing attorneys in the United States, namely, the American Bar Association.

Academic journals

Scholarly publications of law schools, business schools, and academic organizations. These publications are edited either by faculty members or by graduate students under the guidance of the school's faculty. The articles appearing in these publications are usually written by tax practitioners, academics, graduate students, or other noted commentators.

Accuracy-related penalty

Civil tax penalty assessed where the taxpayer has been negligent in completing the return or is found to have acted with a disregard of Internal Revenue Service rules and regulations, a substantial understatement of the income tax, a substantial valuation or pension liability overstatement, or a substantial transfer tax valuation understatement. A 20 percent penalty usually applies to the pertinent understatement, and related interest accrues from the due date of the return, rather than the date on which the penalty was assessed.

Acquiescence

A pronouncement by the Internal Revenue Service that it will follow the decision of a court case to the extent that it was held for the taxpayer. Announced in the Internal Revenue Bulletin. Modifies the citation for the identified case.

Action on Decision

A memorandum prepared when the Internal Revenue Service (IRS) loses a case in a court that recommends the action, if any, that the IRS should take in response to the adverse decision. See also acquiescence, nonacquiescence.

Administrative proceeding

A hearing between the taxpayer and an administrative agency of the government, typically the Internal Revenue Service, in an audit or appeal setting.

Administrative sources

Federal tax law that is created by the appropriate use of power that is granted to the Treasury Department by Congress. These sources of the law have a presumption of the authority of the statute, but they are subject to taxpayer challenge. Such sources include Regulations, rulings, revenue procedures, and other opinions that are used by the Treasury Department or the Internal Revenue Service.

AFTR

The citation abbreviation for the tax case reporter, American Federal Tax Reports. The first series of the reporter includes cases concerning pre-1954 Code litigation, and the second and third series include cases that address issues relative to the 1954 and 1986

Codes, respectively. Includes most tax case opinions issued by federal courts other than the Tax Court.

AICPA

The professional organization of practicing Certified Public Accountants (CPAs) in the United States, namely, the American Institute of CPAs.

All State Tax Guide

A concise state-by-state analysis of all major taxes, with citations to state materials, published by Research Institute of America.

Annotated tax service

A commercial tax research reference collection, that is, a secondary source of Federal tax law. Includes Code, Regulation and ruling analysis, judicial case notes, and other indexes and finding lists, organized by Code section number. The two most important annotated services are published by Commerce Clearing House and Research Institute of America.

Annotation

An entry in (especially) an annotated tax service, indicating a summary of a primary source of the Federal tax law that is pertinent to one's research, for example, a court case opinion digest or a reference to a controlling Regulation.

Announcements and Notices

The Internal Revenue Service issues Announcements and Notices concerning items of general importance to taxpayers.

Annual Proceedings

A collection of papers presented at a yearly meeting of tax professionals.

Appeals Office

The internal group of the Internal Revenue Service (IRS) that has the greatest authority to come to a compromise solution with a taxpayer concerning a disputed tax liability. Can consider the "hazards of litigation" in its deliberations. Failure to reach an agreement at this level of the IRS's organization means that the only subsequent appeal by either party to the dispute must be before a court of law.

Assessment

The process of the Internal Revenue Service (IRS) fixing the amount of one's tax liability. Although the U.S. tax system exhibits some degree of self-assessment, the IRS has the ultimate authority to assess the liability of every taxpayer.

Auto-Cite

A citator in Lexis, the primary objective of Auto-Cite is to provide accurate citations as soon as possible, within twenty-four hours of receipt of each case. Auto-Cite can also be used to determine whether cases, Revenue Rulings, and Revenue Procedures are still good law.

Average tax rate

The percentage of a taxpayer's income that is paid in taxes (i.e., computed by dividing the current-year tax liability by the taxpayer's income). The average tax rate is computed as a percentage of total taxable income (this generates the taxpayer's average nominal tax rate) or as a percentage of the taxpayer's total economic income (this generates the taxpayer's average effective tax rate).

B

Bittker & Lokken Federal Taxation of Income, Estates, and Gifts

A topical tax service published by Warren, Gorham & Lamont in five volumes, dedicated to Federal income and transfer taxation. Supplemented annually, the service includes a topical index and Code section, Regulation, case name, and Revenue Ruling finding lists.

Blended Model

A structure of international taxation under which the profits of a business are taxed partly under the full inclusion model, and partly under the territorial model. In the United States, for instance, U.S. taxpayers are subject to the full inclusion model, and non-U.S. taxpayers are subject to the territorial model.

BNA Daily Tax Report

A daily collection of the latest Regulations, rulings, case opinions, and other tax law revisions, as well as news reports, press releases, congressional studies and schedules, interviews, and other items of interest to the tax practitioner. Available through the mail and on various electronic tax services. One of the most important tax newsletters published because of its breadth of topics and its quality of analysis. In addition, the newsletter provides interviews with government officials, articles reviewing the day's events, and the full text of key documents discussed in the newsletter.

BNA Foreign Income Library

Approximately ninety Tax Management Portfolios written by experts in international taxation and business. The topics covered run the gamut from the foreign tax credit, to international aspects of social security taxes and foreign estates, to nontax issues such as the Regulation of foreign investments and currency exchange controls.

BNA International Service

A detailed analysis of worldwide taxation, and a source of international news updates, complementing the BNA Foreign Income Library.

BNA Tax Management Portfolios

A topical tax service published by the Bureau of National Affairs in a collection of more than 400 magazine-size portfolios, dedicated to U.S. income, foreign income, and estate and gift taxation. Prepared by an identified expert in the field, each portfolio includes a detailed analysis of the topic, working papers with which to implement planning suggestions, and a bibliography of related literature. Supplemented by a biweekly newsletter, the portfolio series includes a topical index and case name and Code section finding lists.

Board of Tax Appeals

An earlier name for the U.S. Tax Court, which did not have full judicial status. Opinions are recorded in the Board of Tax Appeals reporter, the citation abbreviation for which is BTA.

Boolean

A deductive logic search that allows for the intersection of terms by using connectors such as "or," "and," or "within # number of words."

Bureau of National Affairs (BNA)

A subsidiary of Tax Management. It offers a wide range of products covering all areas of Federal taxes. It is best known as the publisher of the BNA Tax Management Portfolios (BNA Portfolios). BNA Tax Management also offers electronic tax services, including the Tax Practice Library, and TaxCore.

C

Case brief

A concise summary of the facts, issues, holdings, and analyses of a court case. Used in a tax research context to allow subsequent review of the case by its author or another party. Includes complete citations of the briefed case, and other items addressed in the brief, to facilitate additional review when necessary.

CCH Citator

A citator published by Commerce Clearing House that is part of the Standard Federal Tax Reporter. The volumes of this loose-leaf service are labeled A to L and M to Z with a Finding List for Rulings in the back of the M to Z volume. This service covers the Federal income tax decisions that have been issued since 1913.

CCH Federal Tax Articles

A loose-leaf and bound index to Federal tax articles published by Commerce Clearing House. This index provides concise abstracts for each article cited in the index. The framework for organizing these abstracts is the Code section. More than 250 journals, law reviews, papers, and proceedings are included in the index.

CCH Federal Tax Service

The topical tax service of Commerce Clearing House. Explanatory text, called the analysis, is divided into sixteen major topic areas, designated A through P. The editors' comments and evaluations of the law are the basis of the main text, with footnotes used to direct researchers to primary sources.

CCH International Tax News

Created in conjunction with Horwath International, a newsletter included with subscriptions to any of the Commerce Clearing House international tax services.

CCH Standard Federal Tax Reporter

The annotated service of Commerce Clearing House dedicated to Federal income, estate, and gift taxation. Includes a weekly newsletter, topical index, tax calendar, rate tables and schedules, practitioner checklists, and case name, Code section, Regulation, and Revenue Ruling finding lists. In addition, it provides a two-volume Internal Revenue Code and a Citator.

CCH Tax Research Consultant

The topical service of Commerce Clearing House, similar to the Research Institute of America Federal Tax Coordinator.

CCH Tax Research NetWork

The Internet tax service provided by Commerce Clearing House (CCH). It can include all of the tax services available from CCH if the practitioner purchases these services.

CD-ROM system

West, Commerce Clearing House, Research Institute of America, and several other vendors have made available a collection of tax statutes, Regulations, rulings, cases, and other primary-source materials readable by a computer in a CD-ROM format. The related software allows the researcher to conduct an electronic search of the pertinent materials without incurring online charges. Subscribers receive a series of compact disks containing the source materials, and the software instructs the user that disks to insert into the CD-ROM reader at appropriate times.

Chief Counsel

The chief legal officer of the Internal Revenue Service. Responsible for making litigation and acquiesce/nonacquiesce decisions, and for developing interpretive material of the agency, including rulings and memoranda.

Circular 230

A tax Regulation detailing the requirements and responsibilities of those who prepare Federal tax returns for compensation. Includes educational, ethical, and procedural guidelines.

Citation

A means of conveying the location of a document. Appendix B of this text offers a standard format for citations used by tax researchers.

Citator

A research resource that presents the judicial history of a court case and traces the subsequent references to the case. When these references include the citing case's evaluations of the cited case's precedents, the research can obtain some measure of the efficacy and reliability of the original holding.

Citator 2nd Series

Published by Research Institute of America. The Citator 2nd Series is composed of three bound volumes plus paperback supplements, which cover from 1954 to the present. This citator series includes the history of cases that have been decided since 1954 and updates for cited cases appearing in the previous series. Within each volume, the cases are arranged in alphabetical order.

Cite

When one case refers to another case, it cites the latter case.

Cited case

With respect to a citator, the original case, whose facts or holding are referred to in the opinion of the citing case.

Citing case

With respect to a citator, the subsequent case, which includes a reference to the original (cited) case.

Citing Reference

In the Westlaw citator, a listing of all cases that refer to the cited case.

Civil penalty

In a tax practice context, a fine or other judgment that is brought against a taxpayer or preparer for a failure to comply with one or more of the elements of the Federal tax law. Examples include penalties for failure to file a return or pay a tax in a timely fashion.

Client letter

A primary means by which to communicate one's research results to the client. Includes, among other features, a summary of the controlling fact situation and attendant assumptions, a summary of the critical sources of the tax law that led to the researcher's conclusions, specific implications of the results of the project, and recommendations for client action.

Closed transaction

A tax research situation is closed when all of the pertinent transactions have been completed by the taxpayer and other parties, such that the research issues may be limited to the proper nature and amount of disclosure to the government on the tax return or other document, and to preparation activities relative to subsequent government review.

Closing agreement

A form with which the taxpayer and the Internal Revenue Service finalize their computations of a disputed tax liability.

Collateral estoppel

The legal principle that limits one's judicial exposure relative to a disputed item to one series of court hearings. In a tax environment, the principle can present hardships for the taxpayer who wishes to raise additional issues during the course of a judicial proceeding.

Collection

The process by which the Internal Revenue Service extracts an assessed tax liability from a taxpayer. Usually takes the form of the receipt of a check or other draft from the taxpayer, but can include liens or other garnishments of taxpayer assets.

Commerce Clause

The clause of the U.S. Constitution indicating that Congress has the power to regulate commerce with foreign nations, among states, and with Native American tribes. It grants powers to Congress and places constraints on the states' ability to tax interstate trade.

Commerce Clearing House (CCH)

A major commercial source of text and online information concerning domestic and international tax law.

Commissioner of Internal Revenue

The chief operating and chief executive officer of the Internal Revenue Service (IRS). Holds the ultimate responsibility for overall planning and for directing, coordinating, and controlling the policies and programs of the IRS.

Committee Report

A summary of the issues that were considered by the House Ways and Means Committee, Senate Finance Committee, or Joint Conference Committee, here relative to proposed or adopted changes in the language of the Internal Revenue Code. Useful in tax research as an aid to understanding unclear statutory language and legislative history or intent. Published in the Internal Revenue Bulletin.

Compilation

Broadly, a collection of primary sources, editorial comments, and annotations in a tax service (i.e., its collection of volumes).

Computing Centers

Internal Revenue Service service centers that manipulate data collected from tax returns.

Connectors

In using an online database or CD-ROM service, connectors are employed to link various parts of a search command using Boolean logic. For instance, "or," "and," and "within" are used as connectors in various research services.

Contingent fees

The practice under which a professional bases his or her fee for services upon the results thereof. The American Institute of Certified Public Accountants has held that the performance of services for a contingent fee can be unethical; one exception is available, though, where (as in tax practice) the results are subject to third-party actions (here the government, in an audit setting). Several states are relaxing this restriction, allowing certified public accountants to mix the form of their compensation between fixed and contingent fees.

Correspondence examination

An audit of one's tax return that is conducted largely by telephone or mail. Usually involves a request for substantiation or explanation of one or more items on a tax return, such as filing status, exemptions, and itemized deductions for medical expenses, interest, taxes paid, charitable contributions, or miscellaneous deductions.

Court of Appeals

A Federal appellate court that hears appeals from the Tax Court, Court of Federal Claims, or District Courts within its geographical boundaries. Organized into geographical circuits, although there are additional circuits for Washington, D.C., and for cases appealed from the Court of Federal Claims. Opinions are recorded in the Federal Reporter, various series, and in the American Federal Tax Reports and United States Tax Cases reporter series.

Court of Federal Claims

A trial-level court in which the taxpayer typically sues the government for a refund of overpaid tax liability. Hears nontax matters as well in Washington, D.C., or in other major cities. Opinions are reported in the Court of Federal Claims reporter and in the American Federal Tax Reports and United States Tax Cases case reporter series.

CPA Exam

A test by which the American Institute of Certified Public Accountants and the state boards of accountancy regulate admission to the Certified Public Accountants (CPA) profession and mainenance of CPA licenses. Part of the CPA exam requires that the candidate perform some tax research and writing tasks.

Criminal penalty

A severe infraction of the elements of the Federal tax law by a taxpayer or preparer. Felony or misdemeanor status for tax crimes can be accompanied by substantial fines or jail terms. Examples of tax crimes include tax evasion and other willful failures to comply with the Internal Revenue Code.

Cumulative Bulletin

An official publication of the Internal Revenue Service (IRS), consolidating the material that first was published in the Internal Revenue Bulletin in a (usually semiannual) hardbound volume. Publication alters the proper citation for the contents thereof.

Customer Service Sites

Internal Revenue Service service centers that deal with telephone and electronic contacts from taxpayers, in working with electronic filing of returns, and in answering telephone and online taxpayer inquiries.

D

Daily Tax Report

Available from Tax Analysts, a daily summary of tax developments, cases, rulings, and other information of interest to the tax professional.

Deduction Apportionment

In international taxation, deductions, expenses, and losses are assigned by allocation and apportionament to various income sources.

Determination Letter

An Internal Revenue Service (IRS) pronouncement issued by the local IRS office, relative to the agency's position concerning a straightforward issue of tax law in the context of a completed transaction.

Direct History

In the Westlaw citator, a listing of the citations to hearings of the cited case by lower level courts.

Discriminant function formula

A means by which, on the basis of probable return to the IRS in terms of collected delinquent tax liabilities, the Service selects tax returns for examination.

District Court

A trial-level court that hears tax and nontax cases. Organized according to geographical regions. Jury trials are available. Opinions are reported in the Federal Supplement Series and in the American Federal Tax Reports and United States Tax Cases reporter series.

Due Process Clause

Found in the Fourteenth Amendment to the U.S. Constitution, the clause (among other things) limits the territorial scope of a state's taxing authority, particularly in regard to interstate commerce.

E

Effective average tax rate

The proportion of a taxpayer's economic income that was paid to the government as a tax liability (i.e., it is computed by dividing the tax liability by the taxpayer's economic income for the year). Economic income includes nontaxable sources of income, such as gifts and inheritances, and tax-exempt interest.

En banc

When more than one Tax Court judge hears a case, the court is said to be sitting "en banc."

Enrolled agent

One who is qualified to practice before the Internal Revenue Service by means other than becoming an attorney or certified public accountant. Typically, one must pass a qualifying examination and meet other requirements to become an Enrolled Agent.

Equal Protection Clause

Found in the Fourteenth Amendment to the U.S. Constitution, the clause requires (among other things) that similarly situated persons or property be treated in a similar manner by the law. Although the Equal Protection clause does not reference taxation specifically, it has been relied upon to determine whether tax provisions treat different taxpayers equally.

Ethical standards

Boundaries of social or professional behavior, derived by the culture or its institutions. Tax ethics are described in various documents of governmental agencies or professional organizations.

F

Fact issue

A tax research issue in which the practitioner must determine whether a pertinent question of fact was satisfied by the taxpayer; for example, was an election filed with the government in a timely manner? What was the taxpayer's motivation underlying the redemption of some corporate stock?

Federal Research Library

The collection of primary and secondary tax source documents made available by Tax Analysts. Organized as a grouping of databases of documents.

Federal Tax Explanations

Analysis of tax laws covering individuals, businesses, trusts, and estates. Included in the Tax Analysts tax service.

Federal Tax Library

The searchable database of federal tax materials made available by Tax Analysts. Available in Basic and Complete versions.

Federal Taxation of Income, Estates, and Gifts

An authoritative tax treatise available on Westlaw and the Research Institute of America tax service, often cited as a leading secondary source of tax law.

Field audit

The review of a corporation or business tax return by an Internal Revenue Service agent. Typically involves more complex issues of law and/or fact than are the subject of a correspondence or office audit. Open ended in nature. The agent who conducts a field examination reviews all of the taxpayer's business and financial operations, accounting methods, and means of internal control.

File memorandum

A primary means by which to communicate the results of a research project to oneself, one's supervisor, and/or one's successor. Includes, among other features, a statement of the pertinent facts and assumptions, a detailed outline (and citations of) controlling tax law, a summary of the researcher's conclusions, and a listing of action recommendations for the client to consider.

Finding list

An index to primary tax law sources, such as court cases or Revenue Rulings, typically arranged alphabetically, and referring to paragraph or division citations in the tax service's compilations.

Fraud

In a tax practice context, a taxpayer action to evade the assessment of a tax. Criminal fraud requires a willful intent by the taxpayer. The Internal Revenue Service bears the burden of proof relative to fraud allegations.

Freedom of Information Act

Federal law that requires the Treasury (and other federal agencies) to release redacted documents to the public. In the tax research context, this allows for the publication of letter rulings and other Internal Revenue Service written determinations, and their use by the tax professional in the research process.

Full Inclusion Model

A structure of international taxation under which the profits of a business are taxed by the country in which the business is based, regardless of where the income is earned. A synonym is "worldwide taxation."

Full-Text Document

In the Westlaw citator, a tool that displays the full text and all versions of the citation for a case, a summary of the proceeding, headnotes, and key numbers.

Full-text search

A computerized version of a published index. A full-text search locates every occurrence of a word or phrase in every document available for the search.

G

General Counsel's Memorandum

A memoranda generated upon the request of the Internal Revenue Service, typically as a means to assist in the preparation of Revenue Rulings and Private Letter Rulings.

General Regulation

A Regulation issued under the general authority granted to the Internal Revenue Service to interpret the language of the Code, usually under a specific Code directive of Congress, and with specific congressional authority.

Golsen rule

Tax Court decisions are appealed to the Court of Appeals for the taxpayer's place of work or residence. The decisions of the Courts of Appeal are not always consistent. Thus, when a taxpayer whose circuit has ruled on a given issue brings a case that includes that issue before the Tax Court, the Tax Court follows the holding of the pertinent circuit, even if the Tax Court disagrees with the holding, or if another circuit has issued a contrary holding. This can lead to contradictory Tax Court rulings, based solely upon the state of the taxpayer's residence.

H

Headnote

Numbered paragraphs in which the editors of the court reporter summarize the court's holdings on each issue. These paragraphs appear in the court reporters before the text of the actual court case.

Hypertext (Hyperlinked)

A means of moving around within the documents of an electronic database by clicking on a mouse or keyboard where a special text color or character indicates that a related document is available. For instance, in reading a court case, the user might move to the opinion issued in another case cited in a footnote, or to a controlling Code section or Regulation that is cited in the document.

I

Independence

The American Institute of Certified Public Accountants requires the certified public accountant (CPA) who renders an opinion relative to a client's financial statements to be (and to appear to be) independent from the client. This principle entails restrictions as to the CPA's direct and indirect financial dealings with the client, and its simultaneous role as financial auditor.

Indirect History

In the Westlaw citator, a listing of the citations to those case opinions that refer to the cited case. The citator indicates whether the citing cases positively or negatively affect the precedential value of the cited case.

InfoTax

Provider of a CD-ROM tax research service, including Code and Regulations, court cases, and administrative pronouncements.

Injunction

The action by which the Internal Revenue Service or a court prevents (enjoins) a taxpayer, preparer, or tax shelter distributor from undertaking a specified action (e.g., preparing tax returns for compensation or offering a tax shelter for sale).

Internal Revenue Bulletin

An official weekly publication of the Internal Revenue Service that includes Announcements, Treasury Decisions, Revenue Rulings, Revenue Procedures, and other information of interest to the tax researcher.

Internal Revenue Code

The primary statutory source of the Federal tax law, a collection of laws that have been passed by Congress and incorporated in Title 26 of the U.S. Code. The Code was last reorganized in 1954. It presently is known as the Internal Revenue Code of 1986. The chief subdivision of the Code is the section.

Internal Revenue Service

A division of the Department of the Treasury, the Federal agency that is charged with the collection of Federal taxes and the implementation of other responsibilities that are conveyed by the Internal Revenue Code.

Internal Revenue Service Centers

Locations at which the Internal Revenue Service receives and processes tax returns, distributes tax forms, and performs other specified functional activities in the administration of the Federal tax laws.

Internet

A means by which millions of remote computer stations are connected and can be used by individuals at any such station. Search engines assist in finding pertinent materials, and download features allow users to view and obtain files from the remote locations. The Internet is organized chiefly using the World Wide Web, bulletin board and newsgroup systems, and file transfer protocols. The Internet is useful to the tax researcher as a means of finding primary and secondary source documents in a timely fashion, sharing tax newsletters and spreadsheets, and transferring data to and from taxing jurisdictions.

IRS Oversight Board

A group of at least nine individuals that acts as the board of directors of the Internal Revenue Service. Responsible for overseeing the agency's operational and internal control functions, approving mission plans and strategies, reviewing the agency's budget, and ensuring the proper treatment of taxpayers.

J

Joint Audit Program

Allows the Multistate Tax Commission to perform a comprehensive audit of a business's taxes simultaneously for several states.

Judicial sources

Certain federal court decisions that have the force of the statute in constructing the Federal tax law. The magnitude of this authority depends upon the level and location of the courts that issued the opinions.

K

KeyCite (KC)

A Westlaw citator that furnishes a comprehensive direct and indirect history for court cases. The indirect history includes secondary materials that have the cited case in their text. KeyCite allows the researcher to select a full history, negative history, or omit minor cases. This option is not available with the other citators.

KeySearch

A search aid employing the West numbering system of the key issues in court cases. When a researcher identifies the legal topic applicable to the search, this search aid formulates a query based on the underlying terms for the topic based on the key numbers system.

Kleinrock's TaxExpert

A CD-ROM and Internet tax research service provided by Kleinrock. It includes primary tax law sources plus an explanation of the law.

KWIC

Key word in context, a means by which to display electronic search results.

L

Law issue

A tax research question in which one must determine which provision of the Federal tax law applies to the client's fact situation. This entails the evaluation of various statutory, administrative, and judicial provisions with respect to the client's circumstances; for example, is the client's charitable contribution subject to the 30 percent of adjusted gross income limitation?

Law reviews

Scholarly publications of law schools. These publications are edited either by faculty members or by graduate students under the guidance of the school's faculty. Most law reviews also use an outside advisory board comprised of practicing attorneys and law professors at other universities to aid in selecting and reviewing articles. The articles appearing in these publications usually are written by tax practitioners, academics, graduate students, or other noted commentators.

Legislative Regulation

A Regulation by which the Internal Revenue Service is directed by Congress to fulfill a law-making function and to specify the substantive requirements of a tax provision.

LEXCITE

A citator service of Lexis. For the case citation entered, it ascertains parallel citations and then searches for all of the cites in the case law documents. It will find embedded references to a variety of documents such as cases, law reviews, journals, Federal Register, and Revenue Rulings.

Lexis

An Internet service for legal (tax) sources started in 1973 by LexisNexis.

LexisNexis

One of the largest legal and news services available on the Internet. An online database resource that allows the researcher to access a database consisting of the text of court cases, administrative rulings, and selected law review articles and to search these files for tax (and other) law sources that may be relevant to the research problem.

LexisNexis Academic

A version of the LEXIS and NEXIS database services designed for use at public libraries, universities, and law schools.

LexisNexis Tax Center

The home-base interface used by the researcher in the LexisNexis service.

Linking

A method of moving among the documents of an electronic database, as indicated by the controlling software. See hypertext.

Local citation

A citation that directs the researcher to the exact page where the cited case is mentioned in the citing case.

M

Marginal tax rate

The proportion of the next dollar of gross income (or other increase in the tax base) that the taxpayer must pay to the government as a tax. Thus, the marginal tax rate conveys the proportionate value of an additional deduction, or the cost of an increase to the tax base. Tax-effective decisions must take into account the marginal (and not the average or nominal) tax rate.

Memorandum decision

A decision of the Tax Court that, in the opinion of the chief judge, does not address any new issue of tax law. Accordingly, the government does not publish the opinion. Commerce Clearing House and Research Institute of America each publish annual collections of these Tax Court Memorandum decisions.

Mertens Law of Federal Income Taxation

A topical tax service designed chiefly by and for attorneys.

More Likely Than Not

The standard that a tax position must meet if a tax preparer penalty is to be avoided. An undisclosed tax position can be taken penalty-free if a tax professional believes that there is a greater than 50 percent chance that the position will be upheld by the highest court of review.

Multistate Alternative Dispute Resolution Program

Developed by the Multistate Tax Commission. It affords taxpayers the opportunity to resolve common tax issues with several states at once. The program also assists taxpayers in negotiating and drafting settlement agreements to be submitted to participating states.

Multistate Corporate Tax Guide

A two-volume treatise with responses by the states to questionnaires concerning income and sales/use tax issues.

Multistate Tax Commission (MTC)

Created in 1967 by the Multistate Tax Compact. The MTC adopted the Uniform Division of Income for Tax Purposes Act (UDITPA) as part of its Articles, issued Regulations interpreting the UDITPA and continues to issue apportionment rules. As of early 2008, there are forty-seven states participants in MTC.

Multistate Tax Compact

An organization of state governments that created the Multistate Tax Commission in 1967.

N

National Conference of Commissioners on Uniform State Laws

In 1957, it drafted the Uniform Division of Income for Tax Purposes Act to create a greater uniformity and consistency in the measurements of business income.

National Nexus Program

Developed by the Multistate Tax Commission. Its function is to facilitate information sharing among participating states.

National Research Program

A means by which the IRS develops its discriminant function formulae. The taxpayer's return is selected randomly for an extensive review, during which every item of income, credit, deduction, and exclusion is challenged by the government. The results of such reviews are used (other than to adjust the examined taxpayer's liability) to delineate criteria by which other taxpayers' returns are selected for examination.

National Taxpayer Advocate

Empowered to achieve a temporary delay in the normal enforcement procedures of the Internal Revenue Service, as specified in a Taxpayer Assistance Order.

Natural language

A search where a tax question is entered in standard English (natural language) words, phrases (entered within quotation marks), or sentences. The program determines the key terms for searching and relationships among the words (i.e., connectors to apply). This type of search is useful when the researcher is unsure as to which connectors and keywords would be the most effective.

Negligence

In a Federal tax context, a (nonwillful) failure to exercise one's duty with respect to the Internal Revenue Code or to use a reasonable degree of expected or professional care. Examples include the unacceptable failure to attempt to follow the IRS's rules and Regulations in the preparation of a tax return for compensation.

Nexis

An Internet service for news, financial, and business information, started in 1979 by LexisNexis.

Nexus

A sufficient business connection with a locality that gives taxing authority to the locality over the business.

Ninety-day letter

A statutory notice from the Internal Revenue Service (IRS) that the taxpayer has failed to pay an assessed tax. An issuance of such a letter usually indicates that the taxpayer has exhausted all of his or her appeal rights within the IRS and that the next forum for review will be a trial-level court. Strictly, the taxpayer has ninety days to petition the Tax Court to be relieved of the deficiency assessment. If no such petition is filed, the IRS is empowered to collect the assessed tax.

Nominal average tax rate

Determined by an inspection of the applicable rate schedule. The average nominal rate at which the taxpayer's total taxable income is taxed is computed by dividing the taxpayer's total tax liability by his or her taxable income. Tax-exempt income is not included in the denominator of this fraction.

Nonacquiescence

An announcement by the Internal Revenue Service (IRS) that it will not follow the decision of a court in a tax decision that was adverse to the agency. Notation is included in the proper citation of the disputed case. Announced in the Internal Revenue Bulletin.

O

Offer in compromise

The means by which the government offers to reduce the amount of an assessed tax, usually because of some doubt as to the "litigation-proof" magnitude or collectibility of the tax. A legally enforceable promise that cannot be rescinded, an offer in compromise relates to the entire liability of the taxpayer, and it conclusively settles all of the issues for which an agreement can be made.

Office audit

The audit of a nonbusiness tax return that is conducted at an Internal Revenue Service (IRS) district office. Usually requires some analysis and the exercise of the IRS personnel's judgment, rather than a mere inquiry or substantiation verification. Typically involves tip, rent, or royalty income, travel and entertainment deductions, and income from partnerships or other conduit entities.

OneDisc Premium

A Tax Analyst's single disc tax product, useful when the tax professional needs portability of documents. It contains an extensive list of primary sources and the commentary of Federal Tax Explanations.

Online system

In a tax research context, a collection of the text of court case opinions, statutes, administrative rulings, and selected law review articles. These text files can be searched by the practitioner using an Internet connection in an extremely fast and efficient manner, to assist him or her in locating tax law sources that may be relevant to the disputed tax issue.

Open transaction

A tax research issue is open when not all of the pertinent transactions have been completed by the taxpayer or other parties, such that the researcher can suggest to the client several alternative courses of action that generate differing tax consequences.

Oral presentation

A primary means of communicating the results of a research project to others by way of a telephone conversation or a more formal presentation system.

Organization for Economic Co-operation and Development (OECD)

An important international association of countries that believe in democratic governments and market economies. The goals of the OECD are to assist developing countries, support sustainable economic growth, boost employment, raise living standards, maintain financial stability, and generally contribute to world trade. Through its monitoring of world economics, the OECD has become known as one of the most reliable and prolific publishers of economic and social data and statistics.

P

Permanent citation

A Tax Court citation issued to a Tax Court decision containing the case name, volume number, reporter page number, and the year of the decision.

PH Citator

The first series of citators, formerly published by Prentice-Hall and now published by Research Institute of America. The first series consists of three bound volumes that cover all of the Federal tax cases dated between 1863 and 1953.

Practice before the IRS

The privilege to sign tax returns as preparer for compensation and to represent others before the Internal Revenue Service (IRS) or in court in an audit or appeal proceeding. This privilege is granted by the IRS and controlled under Circular 230.

Practitioner journal

Journals published by professional organizations and commercial companies. The objective of these journals is to keep tax practitioners abreast of the current changes and trends in the tax law.

Preparer penalties

A series of fines and other levies by which the Internal Revenue Service (IRS) encourages taxpayers and preparers to fulfill their responsibilities under the Internal Revenue Code. Examples include penalties for failure to sign returns, keep or furnish copies of returns, and provide required information to Federal agencies.

Primary authority

An element of the Federal tax law that was issued by Congress, the Treasury or Internal Revenue Service, or a Federal court, and thus carries greater precedential weight than elements of the tax law issued by other parties.

Private letter ruling

A written determination published by the Internal Revenue Service relative to its position concerning the tax treatment of a prospective transaction. Strictly, it cannot be applied to any taxpayer other than the one who requested the ruling. Text or summaries thereof are included in various commercial tax services.

Privileges and Immunities Clause

Grants citizens of each state all privileges and immunities of citizens in every other state. Note that the clause applies only to "citizens" of states. Since a corporation is considered a "person" but not a "citizen" under the law, corporations for the most part are not protected by the Privileges and Immunities clause.

Problem Resolution Program

An organizational means by which the Internal Revenue Service (IRS) attempts to satisfy taxpayer complaints, inquiries, and disagreements, short of the appeals process or litigation. The taxpayer can employ the Problem Resolution Program when the usual agency channels do not produce the desired results. Typically, the program is used to resolve billing, procedural, computer-generated, and other

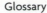

problems that the taxpayer has not resolved after one or more contacts with the appropriate IRS office.

Proceedings

The published versions of conference presentations. These proceeding are distributed to the participants at the conference and later to the general public in the form of a collection of articles.

Processing Centers

Internal Revenue Service centers that process Federal tax returns.

Professional journals

Synonym for practitioner journal.

Progressive tax rate

If the marginal rates of a tax rate schedule increase as the magnitude of the tax base increases, the schedule includes progressive tax rates.

Proportional tax rate

If the marginal rates of a tax rate schedule remain constant as the magnitude of the tax base increases, the schedule includes proportional tax rates.

Proposed Regulation

An interpretation or clarification of the provisions of a portion of the Internal Revenue Code, issued by the Treasury and available for comment (and possible revision) in a public hearing.

Public Purpose

Most state constitutions require that tax revenues be imposed only for public purposes. Public purpose rarely is defined in a constitution, however.

Q

Query

A means of searching an electronic database. Includes a definition of the scope of the search and a specification of the targeted terms in which the researcher is interested, often employing connectors in the grammar of the query.

R

Realistic possibility

The realistic possibility standard is met if analysis of the tax return position by a reasonable and well-informed person knowledgeable in the tax law(s) would lead such person to conclude that the position has approximately a one in three (or greater) likelihood of being sustained on its merits. Formerly the standard by which a tax preparer conduct penalty was applied.

Reasonable basis

The reasonable basis standard is met if analysis of the tax return position by a reasonable and well-informed person knowledgeable in the tax law(s) would lead such person to conclude that the position has approximately a one in four (or greater) likelihood of being sustained on its merits. A preparer penalty is avoided if there is a reasonable basis for a disputed tax position, and the position is disclosed on the return.

Reasonable cause

A means by which a taxpayer or preparer can be excused from an applicable penalty or other sanction. For instance, if the taxpayer failed to file a tax return on a timely basis because of illness or if the underlying records were destroyed by natural cause, the taxpayer likely would be excused from the penalty (but not from the tax or any related interest) because of this reasonable cause.

Regressive tax rate

If the marginal rates of a tax rate schedule decrease as the magnitude of the tax base increases, the schedule includes regressive tax rates.

Regular decision

A decision issued by the Tax Court that generally involves a new or unusual point of law, as determined by the Chief Judge of the court.

Regulation

An interpretation or clarification of the provisions of a portion of the Internal Revenue Code, issued by the Treasury under authority granted by Congress. Legislative Regulations directly create the details of a tax law. Both general and legislative Regulations carry the force of the statute, unless they are held to be invalid in a judicial hearing.

Research Institute of America (RIA)

A major commercial source of text and online information concerning domestic and international tax law.

Return preparer

Any person who prepares for compensation, or employs one or more persons to prepare for compensation, all or a substantial portion of a tax return or claim for income tax refund.

Revenue Agent's Report

Prepared upon the completion of the examination of a tax return to explain to the taxpayer the sources of any adjustments to the reported tax liability. If the taxpayer agrees to this recomputation, the associated tax, penalty, and interest become due. Lacking such agreement, other aspects of the appeals process are undertaken.

Revenue Procedure

A pronouncement of the Internal Revenue Service concerning the implementation details of a specific Code provision. Published in the Internal Revenue Bulletin.

Revenue Ruling

A pronouncement of the Internal Revenue Service concerning its interpretation of the application of the Code (typically) to a specific taxpayer-submitted fact situation. Published in the Internal Revenue Bulletin. Can be relied upon as precedent by other taxpayers who encounter similar fact patterns.

RIA Checkpoint

The Internet tax service provided by Research Institute of America. This is one of the most authoritative and well-known Internet tax services available. All services available from Research Institute of America may be accessed by subscription through Checkpoint.

RIA Checkpoint State & Local Tax (SALT)

Comprehensive tax service providing analysis of state and local taxes for all fifty states and the District of Columbia. All taxes imposed by states and most enacted by localities are covered by the service. Editorial explanations and annotations are included in the service.

RIA Citators

The citator service published by Research Institute of America. It includes two series of citators, the PH Citator and the Citator 2nd Series.

RIA Compare It

A feature of the state and local service, the user can compare the tax treatment of an item in one state to the treatment in another state or with the Federal treatment.

RIA Federal Tax Coordinator

Comprehensive topical tax service published by Research Institute of America. The editors' comments and evaluations of the law are the basis of the main text with footnotes used to direct researchers to primary sources. One of its strong points is its general background discussions summarizing the major issues.

RIA International Create-a-Chart

A feature offered by Research Institute of America with its international tax materials. It facilitates the creation of comparision charts for global tax laws. This feature enables the practitioner to summarize pertinent international tax information in a chart that can be exported to a word processing document.

RIA International Taxes Weekly

A weekly e-newsletter covering current developments and emerging issues related to international taxation.

RIA OnPoint

CD resource that allows the researcher to access a database consisting of the text of court cases, administrative rulings, and selected tax treatises and analytical articles and to search these files for tax law sources that may be relevant to the research problem.

RIA State and Local Create-a-Chart

A feature offered by Research Institute of America with its state and local tax service. It facilitates the creation of comparision charts from various state tax materials. This feature enables the practitioner to summarize pertinent multistate tax information in a chart that can be exported to a word processing document.

RIA Tax Advisors Planning System

A series of portfolios written by expert practitioners currently in practice. These portfolios, updated monthly, focus on specific issues relevant to taxpayers in the international economy, among other topical areas. Each portfolio includes commentary, advice supported by detailed explanations, integrated planning ideas, and current tax rules with citations to the controlling authorities.

RIA United States Tax Reporter

The annotated service of Research Institute of America dedicated to Federal income, estate, and gift taxation. Includes a weekly newsletter, topical index, tax calendar, rate tables and schedules, practitioner checklists, case name, Code section, Regulation, and Revenue Ruling finding lists. This tax service has a unique and functional paragraph numbering system. All paragraphs pertaining to a particular Code section incorporate that section number into the paragraph number. A single digit is added to the end of the Code section number, indicating the nature of the material contained in the paragraph.

S

Scholarly Review

Tax periodical that is directed at an academic audience, and wherein articles are written by those working at universities and law schools.

Seamless

Ability to perform a multi-step function with little or no effort. For example, the ability to retrieve references full-text through the computer by double clicking on the reference's title.

Secondary authority

An element of the Federal tax law that was issued by a scholarly or professional writer for example, in a textbook, journal article, or treatise, and thus carries less precedential weight than elements of the tax law issued by primary sources.

Shepardizing

Slang used in the legal profession used to describe the process of using a Shepard's citator.

Shepard's Citations

The full coverage of Shepard's citators available through Westlaw.

Shepard's Citator

The only major tax citator that is organized by case reporter series.

Shepard's Federal Tax Citator

A citator available through Westlaw and Lexis, organized by reference to the case reporter and volume number in which the case is found. Thus, to use the citator, the practitioner must know the court reporter citation for the case of interest.

Small Cases Division

The Tax Court allows taxpayers whose disputed tax liability does not exceed $50,000 to try the case before the court's Small Cases Division. Procedural rules of the division are somewhat relaxed, and taxpayers often represent themselves. The Small Cases Division decisions are not published, nor can either party appeal the holdings thereof.

Source Determination

In international tax law, different rules apply depending on where the income and deductions are "sourced."

State Research Library

The searchable database of state and local tax materials made available by Tax Analysts.

State Tax Reporters

A Commerce Clearing House state tax service that combines detailed explanations, primary source materials, and practical compliance guidance. All of the major taxes imposed by states and localities are covered by the service. Explanations are organized by tax type with links to related primary sources.

State Taxation

A treatise on state and local taxation, published by Warren, Gorham & Lamont.

StateNet

A Research Institute of America database consisting of all proposed and current enacted state legislation in full text. Proposed legislation's current status can be tracked on this database.

Statute of limitations

Provides the maximum amount of time within which one or both parties in the taxing process must perform an act, such as file a return, pay a tax, or examine a return. Various time limits apply relative to the Internal Revenue Code, although both parties can, by mutual agreement, extend one or more of these time limitations, if desired.

Statutory notice of deficiency

Synonym for a ninety-day letter.

Statutory sources

The Constitution, tax treaties, and the Internal Revenue Code are the statutory sources of the Federal tax law. They have the presumption of correctness, unless a court modifies or overturns a provision in response to a taxpayer challenge. In this regard, legislative intent and history can be important in supporting the taxpayer's case.

Substantial authority

A taxpayer penalty may be incurred if a tax return position is taken and not disclosed to the Internal Revenue Service where no substantial authority (generally, statute, Regulation, court decision, or written determination) supports the position.

Supremacy Clause

The clause in the U.S. Constitution that confers superiority to Federal laws over state laws. That is, Federal laws are "the supreme law of the land" and trump state laws. If a state law or constitutional provision is in conflict with a Federal law, the state provision is invalid.

Supreme Court

The highest Federal appellate court. Hears very few tax cases. Approves a writ of certiorari for the cases that it hears. Opinions are reported in the U.S. Supreme Court Reports (citation abbreviation, US); the Supreme Court Reporter (SCt); the United States Reports, Lawyer's Edition (LEd); the American Federal Tax Reports and United States Tax Cases reporter series; and various on-line services.

T

Table of Authorities

A service available through Westlaw and Lexis that lists cases that are cited within a case of interest.

Tax Analysts

A nonprofit entity organized to provide literary forums for the discussion of taxation. It disseminates timely and comprehensive state, Federal, and international tax information through their daily, weekly, and monthly print publications, scholarly books, and electronic database services.

Tax Analysts Worldwide Tax Daily

An international news daily with news updates from around the world, available on LexisNexis and elsewhere. It includes full-text PDF files of international tax documents and treaties discussed in its articles. The information is organized by countries and international organizations.

Tax Analysts Worldwide Tax Treaties

A tax service available on LexisNexis and elsewhere to compare income tax treaties. Side-by-side tables compare the tax rates on various types of income and withholding rates among over 170 worldwide taxing jurisdictions. Original, in-force, pending, terminated, and unperfected treaties can be viewed.

Tax and Accounting Sites Directory

Internet site linking to various government, publisher, and academic web pages of interest to the accounting or tax professional. Often called "Tax Sites."

Tax authority

Any source of the Federal tax law; in common usage, this term is used to refer to government agencies.

Tax avoidance

The legal structuring of one's financial affairs so as to optimize the related tax liability. Synonym for tax planning.

Tax awareness

The first requirement for effective tax planning on the part of decision makers. It requires decision makers to be alert for tax-optimizing alternatives.

Tax compliance

An element of modern tax practice in which a practitioner works with a client to file appropriate tax returns in a timely manner and represents the client in administrative proceedings.

Tax Court

A trial-level court that hears only cases involving tax issues. Issues regular and memorandum decisions. Meets in Washington, D.C., and in other major cities. Formerly called the Board of Tax Appeals. Regular opinions are reported in the U.S. Tax Court Reports. Memorandum opinions are published only by commercial tax services.

Tax ethics

The application of ethical standards to the tax practice.

Tax evasion

The reduction of one's tax liability by illegal means.

Tax Freedom Day

The Tax Foundation uses this device to measure the impact of tax liabilities on citizens' budgets. Expressed in terms of days of work, rather than percentages of a total income amount. The measure computes the day of the year when taxpayers have earned enough money to pay for all of their taxes.

Tax haven

A location that imposes one or more of its taxes at a lower rate than the jurisdiction to which it is being compared. These beneficial (or no) tax rate areas encourage wealthy individuals and businesses to establish residency or a presence within the tax haven's boundaries. Besides a low tax rate, tax havens generally are viewed as intentionally creating a tax structure that deliberately exploits the worldwide desire to engage in tax avoidance.

Tax journal

A periodic publication that addresses legal, factual, and procedural issues encountered in a modern tax practice. As a secondary source of Federal tax law, analyses in tax journals can be used in support of a taxpayer's case before a government agency or, especially, before a court.

Tax litigation

An element of modern tax practice in which a practitioner represents the client against the government in a judicial hearing.

Tax Management Portfolios

See BNA Tax Management Portfolios

Tax newsletter

A weekly, biweekly, or monthly publication or electronic document, often furnished as part of a subscription to a commercial tax service.

Typically provides digest-style summaries of current court case rulings, administrative pronouncements, and pending or approved tax legislation cross-referenced to the organization system of the tax service. Helps the practitioner to keep current relative to the breaking developments in the tax community.

Tax Notes

A weekly collection of the latest Regulations, written determinations, case opinions, congressional studies, policy analyses, and other items of interest to the tax practitioner. Available through the mail and on various electronic tax services.

Tax Notes Today

Version of the Tax Notes publication that discusses the latest developments in tax rulings, cases, transcripts, studies, and other documents of interest to the tax professional.

Tax planning

Synonym for tax avoidance.

Tax practice

Meeting the tax research, litigation, planning, and compliance needs of a client by a recognized tax professional.

Tax Practice Library

A basic electronic tax service of Bureau of National Affairs (BNA) furnishing access to primary sources, practice tools, and limited news sources. Rather than relying on the BNA Portfolio Series, Tax Practice Library has developed its own explanatory analysis. Other than offering fewer databases (no BNA Portfolio or journals), this service is almost identical to Portfolio Plus in its searching methods.

Tax research

An examination of pertinent sources of the state, local, and Federal tax law in light of all relevant circumstances relative to a client's tax problem. Entails the use of professional judgment to draw an appropriate conclusion and the communication of such conclusions or alternatives at a proper level to the client.

Tax service

A commercial tax reference including statutory, administrative, and judicial sources of Federal tax law. Structured to maximize the practitioner's ease of use via a variety of indexes and finding lists. Often includes the text of the pertinent tax authorities and relevant scholarly or professional commentary.

Tax treaty

An act of Congress that addresses the application of certain Internal Revenue Code provisions to a taxpayer whose tax base falls under the taxing statutes of more than one country. Published, among other places, in the Internal Revenue Bulletin. Generally, treaties are negotiated to prevent double taxation by providing reduced tax rates, or exempting certain types of income from taxation. The income receiving reduced rates, and tax holidays and exemptions, vary among countries.

TaxCore

BNA's web-based source of primary tax resources. Subscribers to several of Bureau of National Affairs' news services receive this service. It provides the hyperlinked primary sources and tax-related documents discussed and cited in the news reports.

Taxpayer Assistance Order

The taxpayer uses this request to engage an Internal Revenue Service Taxpayer Advocate to delay the implementation of an IRS action, such as a collection or seizure activity, where it appears that the taxpayer has received less than fair treatment through the administrative procedures of the agency.

Technical Advice Memorandum

A pronouncement of the National Office of the Internal Revenue Service stating the agency's position relative to the tax treatment of a taxpayer whose return is under audit. Text or discussion thereof may be included in the body of a commercial tax service.

Technical Memorandum

A document prepared in the production of a Proposed Regulation.

Temporary citation

A Tax Court citation issued to a Tax Court decision containing the case name, volume number, reporter, the case number, and the year of the decision. The page number is not included because the opinion has not yet been published.

Temporary Regulation

An administrative pronouncement of the Internal Revenue Service, typically concerning the application of a recently enacted or detailed provision of the tax law, especially where there is insufficient time to carry out the public-hearings process that usually accompanies the Regulations process. Temporary Regulations carry the force of law, although citations differ from those for permanent Regulations with regard to the prefix.

Terms and Connectors

The LexisNexis form of a Boolean search.

Territorial Model

A structure of international taxation under which the profits of a business are taxed by the country in which the business is earned.

Thirty-day letter

A notice from the Internal Revenue Service formally notifying the taxpayer of the results of an examination of the return and requesting that the taxpayer agree to the proposed modifications to the tax liability. A taxpayer's failure to respond to the letter triggers the statutory notice of a tax deficiency, that is, the ninety-day letter demanding the payment of the tax or a petition to the tax court.

Topical tax service

A professional tax research reference collection, that is, a secondary source of Federal tax law. Includes Code, Regulation, and ruling analysis; judicial case notes; and other indexes and finding lists organized by general topic. The most important topical tax services are published by the Research Institute of America and the Bureau of National Affairs.

Treasury Decision

A Regulation that has not yet been formally integrated into the published tax Regulation collection. Often issued in the Internal Revenue Bulletin.

Treasury Department

The cabinet-level government agency that is responsible for administering and enforcing laws that affect the currency. The Treasury has assigned its responsibilities relative to the Internal Revenue Code to the Internal Revenue Service.

U

Unauthorized practice of law

A prohibited aspect of modern tax practice by nonattorneys, entailing, for example, the issuance of a legal opinion or the drafting of a legal document for the client, for which the practitioner could be subject to legal or professional penalties.

Uniform Division of Income for Tax Purposes Act (UDITPA)

Drafted in 1957 by the National Conference of Commissioners on Uniform State Laws, to create a greater uniformity and consistency in the measurements of business income.

Uniformity Clause

Closely related to the Equal Protection concept. This clause, found in many state constitutions, requires (among other things) that similarly situated persons or property be treated in a similar manner, including the taxation of property or person.

Universal characters

Symbols that are holders for zero or more characters in searches. See Connectors.

U.S. Constitution

Ultimate source of the Federal tax law.

USTC

The citation abbreviation for the Commerce Clearing House reporter, United States Tax Cases. Includes most of the tax decisions of the Federal courts other than the Tax Court.

W

Warren, Gorham & Lamont's Index to Federal Tax Articles

An index to tax journal articles published by Warren, Gorham & Lamont. It provides citations and occasionally summaries for articles covering Federal income, gift, and estate taxation or tax policy that appear in over 350 periodicals. This index has permanent cumulative indexes provided in paper-bound volumes and is updated quarterly by paperback cumulative supplements. Both the topic and the author indexes contain full article citations.

Weekly Report

A tax newsletter published by BNA, expanding upon and summarizing materials that were included in the Daily Tax Report.

West Key Number System

A means used by the publisher to organize important topics in the tax law. Used as a reference by the tax services and citators published by West.

Westlaw

An online database resource provided by the West Group. Allows the researcher to access a database consisting of the text of court cases, administrative rulings, and selected law review articles and to search these files for tax (and other) law sources that may be relevant to the research problem.

Wildcard characters

See universal characters.

World Wide Web

A popular means by which to organize and present one's data to the Internet community. The IRS, various tax research services, and numerous law libraries offer home pages on the Web, such that tax professionals can search through the documents available on the computers of those hosting the Internet site.

Writ of certiorari

Document issued by the Supreme Court indicating the Court will hear the petitioned case. If the case will not be heard, certiorari is said to be denied.

Written determination

General description of Internal Revenue Service or Treasury pronouncements, including Revenue Rulings, Revenue Procedures, Private Letter Rulings, Technical Advice Memoranda, and Determination Letters.